AMERICAN POLICY AND THE CHINESE REVOLUTION
1925-1928

AMERICAN POLICY AND THE CHINESE REVOLUTION 1925-1928

by

DOROTHY BORG

Issued under the auspices of the
EAST ASIAN INSTITUTE,
COLUMBIA UNIVERSITY

1968
OCTAGON BOOKS, INC.
New York

Reprinted 1968
by special arrangement with Dorothy Borg

OCTAGON BOOKS, INC.
175 FIFTH AVENUE
NEW YORK, N. Y. 10010

LIBRARY OF CONGRESS CATALOG CARD NUMBER: 67-18753

Printed in U.S.A. by
NOBLE OFFSET PRINTERS, INC.
NEW YORK 3, N. Y.

INTRODUCTION TO THE OCTAGON EDITION

Many primary and secondary sources which have either a direct or an indirect bearing upon American policy and the Chinese revolution of 1925 to 1928 have become available to scholars since the original publication of this volume. Any comprehensive survey of so large a body of material would be a major undertaking, and no such task has been attempted in connection with the present publication. The following comments are limited to a few sources—books and collections of private papers—mostly of recent vintage, which form an indispensable part of the continuing effort to understand American-Chinese relations during the immensely complicated decade of the 1920s.

In general the histories of the United States in the interwar years emphasize the extent to which American diplomacy went through a transition period following World War I. Despite an apparent apathy toward foreign affairs, the American people were trying to determine the future course of their foreign policy. The choice seemed to lie between a retreat into the traditional isolationism of the United States or an advance into some form of internationalism as advocated during the Wilsonian era. While what Selig Adler has termed the "isolationist impulse" was strong, the challenge of the newer internationalist ideology could not easily be discounted. As a result, the trend was toward seeking some middle way that would enable the United States to avoid committing itself in either direction.

It is against this background that Donald R. McCoy discusses the foreign policy of Coolidge in his recent biography *Calvin Coolidge: The Quiet President* (Macmillan, 1967). The picture of the President that emerges from this volume is more balanced and therefore by and large more sympathetic than the almost uniformly critical one to which we are accustomed. In the conduct of foreign affairs Coolidge appears as a man whose attitude was more progressive than is commonly recognized but whose effectiveness was undermined by the quality that conditioned all his activities, his deep, inbred sense of caution. Partly because of his desire to avoid striking out on his own, Coolidge tended to subordinate his views to those of others. In particular, he allowed himself to be guided by what he regarded as the prevailing opinion in Congress and among the American people as a whole. The net result was a foreign policy that fluctuated in response to a variety of pressures but nevertheless managed to make some progress. McCoy, like most historians of the Coolidge period, emphasizes the Administration's Latin American policy, which, he feels, despite an unpromising start, ultimately developed into one of its few really fine achievements.

Sharply contrasting portraits of Frank B. Kellogg are sketched in the biographies of the Secretary that have been issued in recent years. In 1961 L. Ethan Ellis published a full-length biography, *Frank B. Kellogg and American Foreign Relations, 1925–1929* (Rutgers University Press) and a biographical essay that appeared in *An Uncertain Tradition: American Secretaries of State in the Twentieth Century,* edited by Norman A. Graebner (McGraw-Hill). Two years later Robert H. Ferrell wrote a relatively brief life of Kellogg that was published as part of Volume XI of the series entitled *The American Secretaries of State and Their Diplomacy* (Cooper Square Publishers).

Ellis' views of Secretary Kellogg are decidedly derogatory. He describes him as a "mediocrity" and a "run-of-the-mine" Secretary who was "well below the top level of Secretarial practitioners in the twentieth century." One of Ellis' main criticisms is that, lacking in self-confidence, Kellogg changed his mind frequently, especially in critical situations. In common with McCoy, Ellis believes that the Coolidge Administration's foreign policy suffered from hesitancy and vacillation yet succeeded ultimately in moving in the right direction. For the most part, however, Ellis does not attribute the progress that was achieved to the Secretary of State. When Kellogg veered on "new tacks," he says, it was usually as a result of outside pressures —most often the pressure of public opinion to which he reacted with such an inordinate sensitivity that "fear is hardly too strong a word" to describe it. As a case in point Ellis cites Kellogg's attitude toward Latin America, which he thinks gradually underwent a change, shifting from an "imperialistic" to a "more reasoned approach"; but the shift, he believes, occurred "as much from compulsion as from free choice."

Ferrell, on his part, maintains that historians have generally underestimated Kellogg's abilities. He regards the Secretary as a "fine diplomat," a "worthy successor" to Hughes, and in some ways "a more able individual than his well-known successor, Stimson." He ascribes the improvements in American foreign relations under the Coolidge Administration to Kellogg's exceptional common sense, his willingness to listen to advice, his "undoctrinaire" approach to problems. Kellog's policy toward Latin America was, in Ferrell's view, not the result of external influences but rather of the Secretary's own inner conviction that, irrespective of his personal predilections in the past, the time had come for a retreat from imperialism in that area.

In respect to China specifically, historians for the most part seem to agree that the Coolidge Administration followed a sound and forward-looking policy. Whether that policy deserves to be regarded as above the ordinary, however, is a complicated question about which there are all shades of opinion. Another moot point is whether too much credit for the Coolidge Administration's China policy has been given to Secretary Kellogg. One charge advanced by those who think the Secretary's role has been over-rated is that, while he was in part motivated by his own ideas about how to deal with the situation in China, he was almost equally motivated by his desire to satisfy public opinion. Another claim is that much of the credit accorded to Kellogg belongs to Nelson Johnson, who, it is said, as Chief of the State Department's Division of Far Eastern Affairs, initiated many of the ideas that formed the basis of our China policy during the period of the Nationalist Revolution. This claim has been elaborated in an article written by Russell D. Buhite, called "Nelson Johnson and American Policy Toward China, 1925–1928" (*Pacific Historical Review,* November 1966) .

The criticism concerning Kellogg's motives may well have much validity. It must also be said however that as a general rule it is extraordinarily diffi-cult to measure the influence of public opinion upon any official in the making of a particular policy and the case of the Secretary and the formu-lation of his China policy is no exception. Similarly, there may be good grounds for the view that historians have not done justice to Nelson Johnson. But Secretary Kellogg was an indefatigable worker, followed events in China very closely himself, and relied for advice on a variety of people, so that it is hard to evaluate the extent to which Johnson affected developments. Nevertheless, it is certainly true that the main ideas about the situation in China and American–Chinese relations that run through Johnson's personal papers for the 1920s parallel those that governed American policy.

Johnson's papers, which are now in the Library of Congress, were opened to scholars after his death in 1954. A brief autobiography covering the early part of his life, up to 1923, is also available in the Columbia University Oral History Collection. As this material shows, Johnson's boy-hood was spent in pioneer communities in the midwest, where his parents had settled, and in Washington, where he went to school. In his autobiog-raphy Johnson makes the characteristic comment that he liked to think that the qualities he had gained from his upbringing were, above all, a "tolerant view of people, . . . a quiet method of life." After school, Johnson went to college for a year, but, unable to afford any further formal education, left to enter the Foreign Service and was sent to China, where he became a student interpreter in 1907. For the next eighteen years he lived in various parts of China and travelled extensively throughout the country, especially from 1923 to 1925, when, having been appointed consul general-at-large, he was given the responsibility of inspecting the United States consulates throughout Eastern Asia.

By the time he became Chief of the Division of Far Eastern Affairs of the State Department, Johnson had therefore developed very definite ideas about the situation in China and how the United States should deal with it—ideas that underwent little change during the following years. Johnson's view of China, even before the Nationalist Revolution started, was that the Chinese were going through a major revolutionary crisis. He felt that they were waging a struggle to achieve two goals: on the one hand, to realize the promise of the 1911 revolution and, on the other, to westernize their country. He was convinced that they were involved in a gigantic undertaking which would not be finished within his lifetime. A refrain that recurs in many of his personal letters is that he had "no illusions" about the situation in China; or, as he himself phrased it, he was not one of the "enthusiasts" who built castles out of the "magnificent dreams" the Chinese had for their own future.

When the Chinese Nationalist Revolution started, Johnson saw it as a part of the prolonged conflict through which he thought the Chinese must inevitably pass. He seems to have known relatively little about contemporary developments in China, especially the conflicts within the Kuomintang, and to have formed his opinions largely on the basis of general impressions. He did not believe that the Nationalists had any strong Communist orientation. Nor did he expect them to follow the lead of the Soviet Union. Rather, he suspected that in the eyes of the Chinese, the Russians looked very much like other foreigners who, out of self-interest, were meddling in China's domestic affairs. He therefore regarded the ousting of the Borodin mission as no more than might have been expected and as evidence that the Chinese were determined to reject interference from any outside source.

As to the United States' relations with China, Johnson was convinced that the Chinese had a deep-rooted antagonism to all Westerners that would never change. In a report to the State Department on the alleged increase of antiforeign feeling in China in 1923, Johnson stated that in his opinion the situation was no different from usual. The Chinese, he said, would "never like us" or receive us on a "plane of equality." He ascribed their antipathy to several causes: the inherent differences between Eastern and Western peoples; the traditional Chinese attitude of exclusiveness; and the long record of foreigners in intervening, or at the least "meddling," in China's concerns. Under the circumstances, Johnson believed that as a matter of both expediency and morality Americans should follow a policy of leaving the Chinese to handle their own affairs.

Johnson's letters are full of instances where he advocated the application of such a policy. In 1923, for example, in a letter acknowledging a report on missionary activities in China, Johnson protested against what he regarded as the effort of American missionaries to make "war" on the Chinese Government's educational system by setting up competing institutions in which the teaching was based upon a foreign ideology. Missionaries, he declared, should limit themselves to the work they had been sent to China for: preaching the Christian gospel. In an entirely different situation, at the height of the Chinese Nationalist Revolution in February 1927, Johnson, writing to a colleague in the State Department, said that China was in a "state of flux" but "there was nothing to be done but to exercise the patience of the Gods and keep in the middle of the boat while it rocks." Similarly, at the time of his appointment as Minister to China in 1929, Johnson in numerous letters to friends asserted that, in his opinion, the greatest contribution the United States could make to the settlement of China's problems in the coming years was to leave the Chinese alone. China's problems must have a "Chinese solution." The most that the present generation of officials could hope to achieve was to avoid acts "calculated to leave regrets" in the minds of either the Chinese or the American people.

In sum, Johnson's ideas patently reflected the attitude of tolerance and accommodation that he ascribed to his upbringing. As indicated earlier, these ideas were in accord with official policy and undoubtedly exercised an influence on it, whether or not the influence is measurable.

With the exception of the Johnson papers, the collection of private documents that has the most direct bearing on American policy toward the Chinese Nationalist Revolution is that of John Van Antwerp MacMurray, which includes his correspondence from 1925 to 1929 when he was Minister at Peking. The collection, which is exceptionally large, is at Princeton, where it has been available for research since 1965. It also contains papers belonging to MacMurray's father, who after serving as a volunteer joined the United States Army to become a professional soldier.

It is evident from the biographical material prepared for the collection that, in comparison with Nelson Johnson, MacMurray enjoyed many privileges in his early years, including an education at Lawrenceville School and at Princeton University. He entered the Foreign Service in 1907, rose rapidly through the ranks, and served as Secretary of the Legation at Peking under Paul S. Reinsch during World War I. In 1919 he became Chief of the Division of Far Eastern Affairs and worked under Hughes during the Washington Conference.

MacMurray's papers do not substantially change the accounts of the role he played as Minister to China which appear in a number of books, including the present monograph, that deal with American Far Eastern policy in the

1920s. They do, however, supply a large amount of detail, some of which is significant and much of which is colorful.

The collection is rich in personal correspondence, especially in intimate letters from MacMurray to members of his family and close friends. These often contain his confidential opinions of developments and in particular reveal the intensity of his opposition to the Coolidge Administration's policy toward China. They consequently provide some interesting insights into the more personal aspects of his frequent bitter disputes with the State Department.

It is evident that as early as 1918 MacMurray hoped, with good reason, to be appointed Minister to China when Reinsch resigned. Instead, he was transferred to Washington as Chief of the Far Eastern Division. Despite this disappointment, the following period must have been one of the most satisfying of his career. He often worked in close association with Hughes who greatly valued his judgment and delegated a considerable amount of responsibility to him. As a result, MacMurray himself came to feel, as he frankly stated in later years, that in effect he was the "source of American Far Eastern policy" from 1919 to 1925.

While MacMurray's papers say nothing about his reaction to his appointment as Minister to China in early 1925, there can be little doubt that he expected on his arrival in Peking to put into effect the policies that he had been instrumental in formulating in Washington. Moreover, it is clear that he assumed that as Minister he would be given a very free hand in the conduct of the Administration's affairs in China. One of the many subjects on which MacMurray held decided views was the relationship that ought to exist between the Secretary of State and the Foreign Service Officer who was head of a mission abroad. The Foreign Service Officer, like the pilot of a ship, he often said, should be provided with a few over-all instructions but otherwise allowed to follow his own judgment with full assurance of his superiors' support. When, therefore, during his term as Minister, MacMurray gradually realized that the Department was not willing to implement his recommendations, he became increasingly bitter.

It is also apparent, however, that MacMurray's disappointment at having his advice rejected was not the only personal factor that contributed substantially to his clashes with the State Department and that he would under any circumstances have found it hard to accept Kellogg's policy toward China as it developed. MacMurray's writings as a whole reflect an extraordinary preoccupation with questions of discipline, perhaps, as some of his colleagues thought, because as the son of an army officer he had early been accustomed to a military point of view. Whatever the reason, his general attitude was that those who acted in disregard or defiance of existing law and order must be brought back into line by whatever means were necessary. He was, moreover, deeply imbued with the idea that any easing of authority under pressure would be construed as a sign of fear—a willingness to "curry favor," the disclosure of an attitude of "cringing" and "abjectness." The Administration's policy, which, in Kellogg's words, was based upon "patience" and "moderation" in dealing with the Chinese, therefore seemed to MacMurray profoundly "humiliating." In a letter written to one of his closest associates in Washington, in February 1927, he described the Department's response to the current crisis in China as one of studied self-effacement and expressed his overwhelming resentment of the instructions that he was exected to carry out. "I am ashamed," he said, "almost day by day ashamed of what I gather my government wants of me."

One of the best expressions of MacMurray's views of the course that the State Department should have adopted, during the period when he was Minister to China, is to be found in a fifty-six-page memorandum entitled "Developments Affecting American Policy in the Far East," written in November 1935. The memorandum, which was made available to scholars only a few years ago, can now be obtained both in the State Department archives and the MacMurray papers.

It is evident that MacMurray wrote the memorandum to prove a thesis. His argument is, in essence, that the major Powers (especially Great Britain, Japan, and the United States) that had participated in the Washington Conference had agreed to follow a cooperative policy in their future dealings with China; that contrary to his (MacMurray's) advice, the Coolidge Administration had acted independently rather than in collaboration with the other nations; and that, as a result, the United States must bear a substantial share of the blame for the breakdown of the cooperative policy, a breakdown that led to the rapid deterioration of the situation in the Far East, culminating in the conflict that developed between Japan and China in the early 1930s.

MacMurray's concept of the cooperative policy accepted by the Washington Conference Powers is explained in detail in his 1935 memorandum. It is, in effect, an elaboration of some of the ideas that dominated his dispatches to the State Department when he was Minister in Peking. Reduced to its simplest terms his theory was that at the Washington Conference the Powers had agreed to act jointly in their relations with China. Their ultimate purpose was to abolish the restrictions imposed on China by the so-called unequal treaties. In order to achieve this end, they were to adhere to the "hands-off-China policy" embodied in the Nine Power Treaty, so as to give the Chinese the opportunity to undertake the long-deferred task of improving the internal conditions of their country. In addition, it was understood, the Powers might actively aid China by providing it with joint loans, presumably through the Consortium, or with other kinds of concrete assistance. On the positive side, if China made advances in the betterment of its internal situation, the Powers were to respond by making commensurate concessions until the restraints imposed by the treaties had been entirely discarded. On the negative side, if the Chinese took matters into their own hands and violated or otherwise attempted to "tear up" the treaties, the Powers were to exercise whatever pressure was necessary to get them to act within legal bounds. As MacMurray's memorandum, as well as the record, shows, his emphasis after the outbreak of the Chinese Nationalist Revolution was mainly on the negative aspect of cooperation.

The difficulty with MacMurray's thesis is that his idea—that at the Washington Conference the Powers had agreed to an extensive system of cooperation—does not appear to have been supported by the views of his contemporaries in the United States Government, including those who were charged with the conduct of our Far Eastern policy. Because of the nature of the Chinese treaty system, ever since the nineteenth century the Powers with a similar treaty status had repeatedly acted in concert when their position in China was threatened. Consequently, when the antiforeign movement in China reached serious proportions in the 1925–1928 period, the question of whether the American Government should act alone or together with the other governments involved became a major issue in the United States. However, there is nothing to indicate that in trying to solve this issue Kellogg and Johnson or their successors in office, Stimson and Hornbeck, believed that the United States was in any way obligated to act in accordance with a cooperative policy such as MacMurray envisaged. They felt, as they frequently stated, that the Washington Conference was an extraordinary example of the value of cooperation under the right conditions, and they certainly shared ·the general fervent hope that such cooperation could be continued. But, in their opinion, whatever understanding as to future action had been reached by the Powers had been embodied in the treaties and agreements concluded at the Conference. They thought, therefore, that the Powers had largely undertaken to cooperate in the maintenance of the "hands-off-China policy" incorporated in the Nine Power Treaty and in the carrying out of certain relatively limited projects such as the convening of a conference on the Chinese tariff and the establishment of a commission on extra-territoriality. This kind of cooperation obviously fell far short of what MacMurray had in mind.

Perhaps the closest approach to MacMurray's idea that an extensive system of cooperation resulted from the Washington Conference is to be found in Akira Iriye's *After Imperialism: The Search For A New Order In*

The Far East 1921–1931 (Harvard University Press, 1965). However, Iriye's concept of the cooperative system that had been agreed upon at the Conference differs considerably from MacMurray's. According to his interpretation, at the instigation of the United States the Powers reached a tacit understanding that they would act collectively in regard to the important developments that occurred in China in the future. Iriye furthermore contends that, if they had adhered to this understanding, they might have engaged in joint efforts to bring about fundamental changes in the Far East. He suggests, for instance, that the Powers might have combined in an attempt to bolster some of the more promising regimes in control of Peking in the early and mid-1920s. In the short run, he maintains, this might have resulted in stabilizing the situation in China by putting an end to the conflicts between the warlords in the north and checking the growth of the radical movement in the south. In the long run, such joint undertakings might have served to assure permanent cooperation between the Washington Conference Powers and thus have averted the series of disasters that occurred in the 1930s and led to Pearl Harbor.

As far as the United States is concerned, it can only be repeated that the idea that anything analogous to a system of cooperation had been established at the Washington Conference does not conform to the view that prevailed in the State Department. Moreover, it is difficult to see how a system such as Iriye describes could have provided a solution to the problems of the Pacific area. Cooperation could hardly have been effective, if indeed it had been feasible, unless the ultimate objectives of the Powers were in accord. The real question is, therefore, what those objectives were, a question that may be unanswerable until our knowledge of the foreign policy of each of the countries involved is considerably greater than at present.

Iriye's book, however, goes beyond a consideration of the problem of cooperation. His account of Japan's activities in China from 1921 to 1931 is a valuable contribution to our understanding of the period. Moreover, he has used a methodology the importance of which should be recognized by all students interested in the study of foreign relations. Instead of exploring, for example, the policy of the United States toward China by limiting himself to a study of the relationship between the two countries, he has attempted to examine American policy in the context of the international relations of the Pacific area in their entirety. Thus the conduct of the United States as well as that of the other nations involved is seen as part of a complex process in which a group of nations are acting to a large extent in response to each other.

Finally, mention should be made of various publications that may provide a means of carrying the study of American public opinion toward the

Chinese Nationalist Revolution further than has been possible to date. These are publications that deal in whole or in part with the reaction of influential segments of the American public (including Congress) to the Russian revolution and the revolutions in Latin America during the 1920s. They include such volumes as, to mention only a few, Peter G. Filene's *Americans and The Soviet Experiment 1917–1933* (Harvard University Press, 1967); Christopher Lasch's *The American Liberals and The Russian Revolution* (Columbia University Press, 1962); Marian C. McKenna's *Borah* (University of Michigan Press, 1961); and the biographies of Coolidge and Kellogg already discussed.

The impression gained from such books is that the apparent opposition of the American people to any intervention in the Chinese Nationalist Revolution may not have stemmed, as is generally supposed, from their alleged pro-Chinese sympathies. For to all appearances they reacted to the revolutions in the Soviet Union and Latin America in much the same manner as to that in China. It may well be, therefore, that their attitude was determined by factors which, in the Wilsonian and post-Wilsonian era, governed their responses to revolutionary situations irrespective of where they occurred.

If this should prove to be the case it would lend support to a theory that the writer, for one, has gradually come to accept—namely, that the American people and the American Government tended, far more than has been recognized, to look upon developments in Eastern Asia not as separate from but as an integral part of global developments. The corollary to this theory is that, contrary to a widely held assumption, the motives underlying our policy in Eastern Asia may more often than not have been the same as those which formed the basis of our policies toward the rest of the world.

In closing I should like to draw the attention of the reader to the fact that this book is being reissued exactly as it was written over twenty years ago. Some of the comments will therefore sound strange coming, as they do, out of another era in history. But hopefully a book written closer to the event may also have some compensating features. For, as a result of the complete transformation that has taken place in our relations with China, it is becoming more and more difficult to recapture the atmosphere of the 1920s.

Dorothy Borg

November 1967

PREFACE

In the years 1925 to 1928 relations between China and the foreign Powers were strained. Because of this the period was marked by an unusual amount of diplomatic activity. Many foreigners, moreover, became deeply involved in China's struggle and expressed their opinions with far greater freedom than had been their custom in quieter times. As a result, the student of American policy during the Chinese Nationalist Revolution finds a wealth of first-hand material.

The chapters of this volume that deal with the activities of officials in the State Department are largely based on the 1925 to 1928 volumes of *Foreign Relations of the United States*. As far as the author is aware, no study of Sino-American relations during this period has been made since the release of the State Department papers. Records such as that which appears in the minutes of the *Special Conference on the Chinese Customs Tariff, October, 1925 — August, 1926,* unfortunately a rare item in the book collections of the United States, are exceptionally useful. Material indicating the trends of missionary opinion exists in abundance as missionary organizations have issued many periodicals, bulletins and reports. While less information is available concerning the views of American businessmen in China, publications such as those of the American Chamber of Commerce at Shanghai supply most of the essential data. The files of newspapers published in the United States from 1925 to 1928 are an indispensable guide to press opinion in this country.

The author did not, however, have to rely exclusively on printed documents but received invaluable assistance from many people who generously gave of their time and attention. It is in recognition of the service they rendered that this preface is written with deep appreciation.

The trying task of commenting in detail on so long a study was undertaken by several persons. Mr. Clarence E. Gauss, at the request of the American Institute of Pacific Relations, read the manuscript before publication and wrote a critical memorandum for which the author is especially grateful. Mr. John Van Antwerp MacMurray also read the entire manuscript and, although frankly disagreeing with the writer's views on a number of fundamental issues, made valuable suggestions that have substantially contributed to the text. Professor Nathaniel Peffer of Columbia University followed the manuscript through three separate drafts which he commented upon with patience and discernment. Similarly Professor Joseph P. Chamberlain, to whom the author has long owed a debt of gratitude, kindly gave advice and assistance.

Certain chapters were sent to people interested in particular aspects of the developments in China during the Nationalist Revolution. Despite the uncertainties of wartime conditions, Mr. Stanley F. Wright was good enough to carry on a correspondence across the Atlantic in which he commented upon an earlier draft of the chapter on the Special Tariff Conference. Judge Milton J. Helmick read the sections of the text that deal with technical legal problems. Mr. John B. Powell, who spent many hours discussing the developments of 1925 to 1928 with the author, went over the chapters that describe events with which he was closely associated. The material on missionary opinion was reviewed by a number of people especially qualified to speak on this subject: the Reverend Rowland M. Cross, Dr. Chester S. Miao, Dr. D. Willard Lyon, my friend Faith Williams Bisson, and Mr. Charles H. Fahs. The latter, and his colleague Miss Hollis W. Hering of the Missionary Research Library, also permitted the writer to draw persistently and unmercifully on their inexhaustible fund of knowledge.

Of the many who in conversation and correspondence provided assistance only a few can be named. Mr. Nelson T. Johnson, who played so important a role in the shaping of American policy throughout the period of the Chinese Nationalist Revolution, wrote a letter to the author, printed in the last chapter of this volume, which adds materially to an understanding of Secretary of State Kellogg's policy toward China. Moreover, Mr. Johnson managed to crowd into an hour's interview more information than could be discovered in a score of the most carefully chosen books. At the Mont Tremblant Conference of the Institute of Pacific Relations, and later in Washington, Dr. Stanley K. Hornbeck was kind enough to answer a list of miscellaneous questions. In addition, several years ago when this study was first undertaken, help was frequently secured from other members of the Far Eastern Division of the State Department, especially from Mr. Alger Hiss. Also at the Mont Tremblant Conference, Sir John T. Pratt generously devoted hours of his time to recalling, with exceptional vividness, the developments of 1925 to 1928, which he witnessed so fully from the British side, and later sent the writer several long memoranda. It is only to be regretted that it was not possible within the scope of this work to study British policy directly and that it has been necessary, for the most part, to limit the diplomatic material to the American *Foreign Relations* papers. Among others who assisted in various stages of this undertaking are Dr. M. Searle Bates, who gave helpful advice on an earlier draft of the chapter on missionary opinion; Dr. Tyler Dennett who, though skeptical of some of the author's ideas at the outset, offered constructive criticisms; and Mr. Ik Shuman, a friend and fellow-reporter on the old New York *World,* who supplied essential information concerning the American press. Needless to say none of the persons mentioned above are responsible for any part of this study and many of them may in fact disagree with the author's views.

To Mr. Edward C. Carter, Executive Vice-Chairman of the American Institute of Pacific Relations, under whose auspices this work is being published, the writer would like to express her profound gratitude, deepened by many years of association. Special thanks are also due other friends and colleagues of the Institute, particularly to William L. Holland and Marguerite Ann Stewart who, with the utmost consideration, have helped at every step of the way.

Finally, in writing this paragraph instead of a formal inscription, the author wishes to dedicate this book to a friend outside the field of political science — to Bertram D. Lewin, whose medical assistance in the years gone by brought this undertaking and a world of other matters into the realm of possibility.

DOROTHY BORG

September 1946

CONTENTS

xix

AMERICAN POLICY AND THE CHINESE REVOLUTION
1925-1928

CHAPTER I

BACKGROUND

The Chinese Revolution of 1925 to 1928 is essentially part of a far more extensive movement. As a vital factor in China's internal development, the Chinese Revolution started in the nineteenth century and is still a dominant force today. It is, moreover, by no means confined to political matters but flows like a broad and deep-channeled stream into every corner of Chinese life. In fundamental terms, the Chinese Revolution is the struggle of the Chinese people to make their own way of living conform more closely to modern concepts, whether on a level of national or individual existence. It constitutes the kind of transition period with which the West is thoroughly familiar, when the form and substance of political, economic, and social institutions must be reconsidered in order to meet the challenge of new demands and altered values.

The external part of the Chinese Revolution which deals with China's foreign relations entered an especially important phase in the spring of 1925. The treaty system which had been built by foreign Powers since the middle of the nineteenth century had imposed many restrictions on the sovereignty of China. Other countries held concessions, settlements, and leaseholds on Chinese territory; citizens of the Treaty Powers enjoyed the privileges of extraterritoriality; the most severe limitations were placed on the rates of the Chinese tariff; foreign troops had the right by legal arrangement to be stationed on Chinese soil.

During the many decades in which the treaty system developed, the Powers assumed that they could either obtain further privileges from China or preserve the *status quo* which was so generously working in their favor. But in 1925 this situation underwent a startling change. With unexpected violence and determination, the Chinese began to insist that foreign countries must relinquish the special position which they had acquired in China. The days when foreign governments could adopt an aggressive attitude toward the Chinese began to draw to a close, and the Treaty Powers suddenly found themselves in a defensive rather than an offensive position. The question was no longer what the Western nations and Japan would demand of China but what an intensely vocal and nationalistic China would demand of them.

1

Under these circumstances, the choice which confronted the Powers was limited to a few possibilities. They could attempt to maintain their privileges by the use of force, which was, however, likely to require the dispatch of a large military expedition to China. Short of this, it was possible to adopt a firm policy that might involve a threat of military action but also had the chance of obtaining compliance before it was essential to use coercive measures. On the other hand, the Powers could decide to abandon their special position in China and retreat before the increasingly aggressive nationalistic spirit of the Chinese. This could either be done with a feeling of resentment growing out of the belief that no other method was expedient or practicable, or with a more generous attitude derived from the conviction that the demands of the Chinese were, to a large extent, justified.

The first period, which constituted a direct introduction to the developments of the years 1925 to 1928 in China, was that of the Peace Conference at Versailles. Before this time, when the question of a modification of the Chinese treaty system had been raised, the Powers had in general taken the view that China could not expect any substantial change in the provisions of the treaties until she had "put her own house in order" (to use the customary phrase) and established her legal and other institutions on a sound basis that made it possible for foreigners to relinquish their special safeguards without fear of the consequences.[1] Chinese had, in fact, grown especially sensitive to the tendency on the part of foreign officials to make promises that were qualified by demanding as a prerequisite that China undertake a long and difficult program of reform.

During the First World War, China began to show signs of taking matters into her own hands.[2] In the minds of Chinese authorities and of certain sections of the public, the hope was entertained that entrance into the war might bring about some modification of the treaty system. This hope received some encouragement when, at the time that China declared war, the Allies made certain minor concessions. More important, however, was the fact that the Peking Government itself achieved substantial results by declaring that all treaties and agreements concluded with Germany and Austria-Hungary in the past were abrogated, by taking over the concessions of the Central Powers, and by placing their citizens under the jurisdiction of Chinese courts.

An even greater advance was made when the Peace Conference as-

[1] See terms of the 1902 and 1903 treaties, below, p. 49.
[2] For a good discussion of the periods of the World War and Versailles Treaty, see Robert T. Pollard, *China's Foreign Relations, 1917-1931*, New York, 1933, Chapters II and III.

sembled at Paris. The Chinese Delegation contained a number of Western-educated Chinese who had thoroughly learned the Wilsonian lesson of respect for the rights of weaker nations, and who were determined to obtain a proper hearing for the grievances of their own country. As a result they planned a diplomatic campaign which not only aimed at securing satisfaction for China in respect to the issues immediately connected with the treaties of peace, but also looked toward furthering the movement for a revision of the Chinese treaty system.

The Chinese Delegation at the Peace Conference had, in the main, three purposes: to fight Japan's claims to the German rights in Shantung and effect the abrogation of the agreements resulting from the Twenty-One Demands imposed by Japan in 1915; to present a well-considered and persuasive argument in support of a revision of the treaty system which might lead to further action on the part of the interested Powers; and to liquidate the interests which the conquered countries of Central Europe possessed in China before the war.

Although China, as is well known, suffered a bitter defeat in her struggle against Japan at the Versailles Conference, she also achieved certain gains that had important consequences in the period from 1925 to 1928. These will be discussed in some detail later, but in general they consisted of the formation of a vigorous and effective public opinion in China and an increased awareness in the United States of the intensity of the Chinese desire for independence from foreign control.

The argument of the Chinese Delegation for a modification of the treaty system was embodied in a memorandum entitled *Questions for Readjustment Submitted by China to the Peace Conference*.[3] In this it was asserted that China had, since the beginning of the twentieth century, made "remarkable progress" in the political, administrative, and economic fields, but that she had been "greatly retarded by a number of hindrances of [an] international nature." China wished, therefore, to submit to the Peace Conference certain questions which needed readjustment in order to remove all obstacles to the free development of her national life. While it was admitted that these questions were not directly connected with issues arising out of the World War, it was suggested that the object of the Conference was not only to conclude peace with the enemy but also to establish a new world based on the principles of justice and respect for the sovereignty of states embodied in President Wilson's Fourteen Points. It was argued that in recognition of this purpose, and in view of the fact that

[3] *Chinese Social and Political Science Review*, June, 1920, p. 135 *et seq.;* reprinted in *China Year Book*, 1921-22, pp. 719-741.

China's problems contained the seeds of a future conflict that might destroy the peace of the world, the questions submitted were deserving of further consideration by the Conference.

The memorandum discussed seven major restrictions on the sovereignty of China that were being imposed either by means of the provisions in the treaties or through the actions of individual foreign Powers. Detailed reasons were given for the removal of all these limitations. Among the most important proposals were those which suggested that each Power make an independent declaration that it did not possess any sphere of influence and that it was prepared to undertake a revision of previous agreements that conferred on it territorial advantages or preferential rights which created a sphere of interest; that all foreign troops and police agencies be withdrawn from China; that the Treaty Powers promise to relinquish their consular jurisdiction, upon the fulfillment of certain conditions on the part of the Chinese, by the end of 1924; that, also by the end of 1924, the foreign concessions and settlements be restored to China; that the Powers agree in principle that the existing tariff be superseded two years hence by the general tariff applied to the non-Treaty Powers and that complete tariff autonomy be declared at the end of a definite period to be fixed by mutual agreement.[4]

The Supreme Council at the Versailles Conference considered the memorandum of the Chinese Delegation but took the position that, as the purpose of the Conference was to formulate the treaties of peace with the conquered countries, it would be impossible to enter into a discussion of issues of a broader character. The suggestion was made, however, that the questions raised by the Chinese should be placed before the Council of the League of Nations when that body was established.

While the effort of the Chinese to have the subject of treaty revision become a matter of deliberation at the Conference failed, their attempt nevertheless attracted a significant amount of attention and constituted the first effective assault on the treaty system. Moreover, the request which the Chinese were making for the abolition of all exceptional foreign rights in China was actually fulfilled in respect to the defeated countries. The Treaties of Versailles, St. Germain, and Trianon formally acquiesced in the action taken by the Peking Government in 1917 in canceling China's agreements with Germany and Austria-Hungary.[5] This meant that an opening wedge had been driven into the treaty system and that, among

[4] For a more detailed description of the sections of the memorandum dealing with tariff and extraterritorial controls, see Chapter IV.

[5] See *Treaties and Agreements With and Concerning China, 1894-1919*, edited by John Van Antwerp MacMurray, New York, 1921, Vol. 2, pp. 1485-1494; Pollard, *op. cit.*, pp. 82-85.

other factors, citizens of the Central European countries would in future live and do business in China without the protection of special treaty provisions.

The breach in the wall of the treaty system was widened further when, in July, 1919, the Russian Government declared its willingness — in return for the recognition of the Soviet Government and the conclusion of a new agreement — to abandon all concessions and treaty rights in China including those of extraterritoriality. A little over a year later, the Chinese Government issued a mandate placing Russian subjects under Chinese jurisdiction instead of the jurisdiction of their own Consuls; in response, the Soviet Government declared that "Russian citizens in China remain henceforth deprived of any official Russian protection."[6]

Mention has been made of the development of a vocal public opinion at the time of the Versailles Conference — a development which foreshadowed the important rôle that the Chinese public played in the events of 1925. In particular the activities of the students in 1919 showed for the first time that the student movement was capable of influencing groups outside of its own ranks and of exercising an effective pressure on the Government.[7]

When news of the Shantung award reached China early in May, 1919, the students at Peking formed a gigantic parade and marched first on the Legation Quarter and then to the house of Tsao Ju-lin, the Minister of Communications, who was known as the leader of the pro-Japanese clique in the Peking Government. Mr. Tsao managed to escape, but his house was wrecked and one of his pro-Japanese colleagues who happened to be present was severely beaten. As a result a number of the students were arrested, but this only succeeded in intensifying the general feeling of rebellion. In Shanghai, a union of 20,000 students was formed at a mass meeting, and similar action was taken in large cities all over the country. Student strikes were declared and a boycott of Japanese goods was started with the result that the Government was finally forced to comply with the students' demands: the students that had been imprisoned after the attack on Tsao Ju-lin's house were liberated, and the leaders of the pro-Japanese group in the Government were dismissed from office. Moreover, the popular agitation strengthened the hand of the Chinese Delegates at the Peace Conference, who, at the end of June, refused to sign the Versailles

[6] *China Year Book*, 1921-22, pp. 625-626. For the formal relinquishment of all extra-territorial rights by the Soviet Government in 1924, see below, p. 51; see also G. W. Keeton, *The Development of Extraterritoriality in China*, New York, 1928, Vol. 1, p. 289.

[7] For an interesting discussion of the activities of the students at this time, see M. T. Z. Tyau, *China Awakened*, New York, 1922, Chapter IX.

Treaty on the ground that justice had been denied to China in the settle-ment of the Shantung question.

In addition, the intense patriotic fervor of the students stimulated business groups throughout the country to take action against the Japanese. The boycott which was initiated by student organizations was immediately endorsed by Chambers of Commerce and conducted with vigor, especially in Central and South China. Its declared purpose was to secure the with-drawal of the Japanese from Shantung, and it undoubtedly had an im-portant effect in keeping the attention of the public focused on the Shan-tung issue until that issue reached a solution at the time of the Washington Conference.[8]

Another significant element in the Versailles Treaty period was the sympathy of the United States for the Chinese position at the Peace Con-ference. The American Delegation at the Conference was generally re-garded as having extended its friendly protection to the Chinese. The Far Eastern experts on the Delegation worked in close association with their Chinese colleagues and appear to have served throughout in the capacity of informal advisers. Moreover, President Wilson did not approach the Shantung question as an isolated issue but made every attempt to relate it to the Chinese problem as a whole. The President repeatedly informed the British, French, and Japanese representatives that he wished not only to see the German rights in Shantung restored to China but believed that "all spheres of influence should be abrogated."[9] He had hoped, he said at a meeting of the Council of Four, that "by pooling their interest the several nations that had gained a foothold in China (a foothold that was to the detriment of China's position in the world) might forego the special position they had acquired and that China might be put on the same footing as other nations, as sooner or later, she must be." There was "a lot of combustible material in China and," he added prophetically, "if flames were put to it the fire could not be quenched, for China had a popu-lation of four hundred million people."[10] Nor did the President limit him-self to a discussion of spheres of influence but extended his remarks to include the need to set China free from all restrictions upon her sovereignty, especially those which were imposed by the extraterritorial system.[11]

Although the President lost his fight for China's case at the Peace Con-ference, he carried it to the American people. In speech after speech,

[8] C. F. Remer, *A Study of Chinese Boycotts*, Baltimore, 1933, Chapter VII.
[9] Ray Stannard Baker, *Woodrow Wilson and World Settlement*, New York, 1927, p. 247.
[10] *Ibid.*, p. 252.
[11] *Ibid.*, p. 253.

delivered while touring the country in defense of the Versailles Treaty, Mr. Wilson explained that, from the viewpoint of history, the situation was not merely one in which Germany had extracted certain rights from China in Shantung but that other nations had obtained similar concessions in many parts of China. "Everybody got in," he said, "except the United States. . . . No one of them was entitled to it; no one of them had any business in there. . . ."[12] Nor did he make any attempt to relieve the United States from blame: just so long as Americans could trade with the territories stolen by other countries, he declared, they were willing to have them stolen; Mr. Hay's policy of the open door was "not the open door to the rights of China but the open door to the goods of America."[13] The President sought, however, to turn the attention of the public away from the past toward the future. The exploitation of China was an old story, he said, and a new story was about to begin; with the establishment of the League of Nations it would be possible, through the pressure of public opinion, to obtain a fair hearing for China's case."[14]

It is of course impossible to gauge the impression which the President's addresses made upon the American public. Sentiment throughout the United States was generally regarded as strongly pro-Chinese, even before the Senate started its debate on the Shantung clauses of the Versailles Treaty. The fact that the Senators elected to fight the Treaty almost solely on the basis of their opposition to the Shantung provisions and to the Covenant of the League of Nations suggested that they believed that it would be easy to capitalize on the sympathy of the American people for China. That sympathy, no doubt, was considerably strengthened by the attitude of Congress and the President's speeches. It was to play an important part during the crisis of 1927 in China when members of Congress and leading newspapers throughout the United States expressed, with extraordinary vehemence, the ideas which President Wilson advocated during the controversy over the Versailles Treaty.

At the Washington Conference of 1920-1921, the Chinese faced a different situation from that which had arisen at Versailles. The peace-makers at the Versailles Conference had decided that there was no logical place on the agenda for a discussion of China's problems. The object of the Washington Conference, on the other hand, was to consider not only ways of restricting the naval armament race among the great Powers but also ways

---

[12] *The Hope of the World* (Messages and Addresses delivered by the President between July 10, 1919 and December 9, 1919), New York, 1920, p. 155.
[13] *The Public Papers of Woodrow Wilson, War and Peace*, edited by Ray Stannard Baker and William E. Dodd, New York, 1927, p. 316.
[14] *Ibid.*, p. 318.

of reducing the possible causes of war in the Pacific area. China was, there-fore, invited to the Conference specifically for the sake of participating in meetings which were to deal with Far Eastern questions.

While under these circumstances it was evident that the Chinese would have the opportunity to present at least part of their case, they nevertheless approached the Washington Conference with a feeling of deep apprehension. Conditions within China, which had been deteriorating for a long time, reached a state of political and financial disintegration before the Wash-ington Conference opened. In view of this fact, there was a possibility that the Powers might seize the opportunity to impose new controls on China which, even if they were undertaken as temporary measures to improve the existing situation, might eventually be transformed into permanent restric-tions on her sovereignty.[15]

When the Washington Conference convened, it devoted a large part of its time to a consideration of China's problems. The Chinese Delegates, at the outset, presented a program of ten principles which has frequently been called a "Bill of Rights."[16] By way of introduction, they explained that they wished to see these principles adopted by the Conference and later applied to specific questions. China desired to play a useful rôle in assisting the progress of the world, but in order to do so she must first meet the difficult issues that had developed out of the shift from an imperial to a republican form of government. China could solve her problems if given the oppor-tunity, but this meant not only freeing her from the threat of foreign aggression but also restoring to the Peking Government full control over its own internal affairs.

The program of ten points was obviously designed to further the ends which the Chinese Delegation had in mind. The Powers were asked to "engage to respect and observe the territorial integrity, and political and administrative independence of the Chinese Republic," and China, on her part, was prepared to pledge herself not to alienate or lease any portion of her territory. China was willing to apply "the principle of the so-called Open Door" in all parts of the country. She, furthermore, requested the Powers "to agree not to conclude between themselves any treaty or agree-ment directly affecting China or the general peace in these [the Pacific] regions without previously notifying China and giving to her an opportunity to participate."

[15] For a particularly valuable discussion of "China's Hopes" and "China's Fears" in approaching the Washington Conference, see W. W. Willoughby, *China at the Con-ference*, Baltimore, 1922, Chapter IV. Mr. Willoughby's book is a report of the Conference from the viewpoint of the Chinese Delegation.
[16] *Ibid.*, pp. 33-35; *China Year Book*, 1923, p. 1047.

While these principles looked toward the establishment of a world in which China would be protected from foreign aggression, most of the remaining points dealt with restrictions that had been imposed in the past. "All special rights, privileges, immunities or commitments, whatever their character or contractual basis, claimed by any of the Powers in or relating to China" were "to be examined with a view to determining their scope and validity, and, if valid, to harmonizing them with one another and with the principles declared by the Conference." Immediately, or as soon as circumstances would permit, the existing limitations on China's political, jurisdictional, and administrative freedom were to be removed; in addition, "reasonable, definite terms of duration" were to be attached to those commitments which were without time limits.

The character of the Conference was determined, as far as the Chinese were concerned, when the "Bill of Rights" was set aside and four resolutions proposed by Mr. Elihu Root were adopted in its place. The Root Resolutions[17] were subsequently incorporated with few alterations into the famous Nine Power Treaty:

It is the firm intention of the Powers attending this Conference:

(1) To respect the sovereignty, the independence, and the territorial and administrative integrity of China.

(2) To provide the fullest and most unembarrassed opportunity to China to develop and maintain for herself an effective and stable government, overcoming the difficulties incident to the change from the old and long-continued imperial form of government.

(3) To safeguard for the world, so far as it is within our power, the principle of equal opportunity for the commerce and industry of all nations throughout the territory of China.

(4) To refrain from taking advantage of the present conditions in order to seek special rights or privileges which would abridge the rights of the subjects or citizens of friendly states and from countenancing action inimical to the security of such states.

The difference between China's "Bill of Rights" and the principles formulated by Mr. Root was to represent China's gains and losses at the Washington Conference. The Root Resolutions relieved China of the fear that the Powers would use the Conference as a means of further restricting her independence. In addition, if carried out in good faith, they meant that China would be given a chance to develop her own national life without foreign interference. On the other hand, from the viewpoint of the Chinese, this was only half of the battle won. As the Chinese Delegates had clearly indicated, they did not merely want a guarantee of better conditions

[17] *China Year Book,* 1923, p. 1048.

in the future, they also wanted a modification of the controls on China's sovereignty which had long been hampering her freedom of action.

In accordance with this idea, the Chinese Delegation presented, one by one, the specific grievances which they wished to have considered at the Conference.[18] These fell into two categories: the infringements on China's sovereignty which had grown up by means of the treaty system and those which had developed in some other manner. The first, which consisted primarily of the fundamental problems of tariff autonomy and of extraterritorial rights, was to play a dominant part in China's relations with the Powers after the outbreak of the anti-foreign movement in 1925.

While the arguments presented by the Chinese at the Washington Conference in favor of the abolition of tariff and extraterritorial restrictions will be discussed in another chapter,[19] it is essential to note here that only minor concessions were made by the foreign Delegates at the Conference. The Chinese repeated the request which they had made at Versailles, that the Powers fix a definite date for the termination of tariff controls; they also asked for a limited change in the tariff rates which would give the Peking Government a larger revenue in the *interim* period before tariff autonomy was actually brought into effect. The foreign Delegations, however, turned a deaf ear to the plea for tariff autonomy and decided, instead, that a Special Conference should be held which would have the authority to grant a modest increase in the tariff schedules "as from such date, for such purposes, and subject to such conditions" as the members of the Conference should determine.

The principle of "administrative integrity" received equally rough treatment at the hands of the foreign Delegations when the Chinese attempted to apply it to the question of extraterritoriality. Again, as at the Paris Peace Conference, the Chinese asked for the abolition of the extraterritorial system at the end of a definite period and suggested that in the meantime plans be put into operation for the gradual relinquishment of extraterritorial rights. The foreign Delegations, however, took the position that nothing could be accomplished before an investigation had been conducted into the condition of the laws, the judicial system, and the administration of justice, in China. As a result they passed a resolution looking toward the establishment of a Commission which would survey the existing situation and recommend measures of reform that, if undertaken by the Chinese Government, would "warrant the several Powers in relinquishing, either progressively or otherwise, their respective rights of

[18] For a discussion of the points presented by the Chinese, see Pollard, *op. cit.*, Chapter VII; also Willoughby, *op. cit.*, *passim*.

[19] See Chapter IV.

extraterritoriality." That even these stipulations did not bind any of the foreign governments to take action was made clear since it was specifically stated that each of the Powers was "free to accept or reject all or any portion of the recommendation of the Commission."[20]

In respect to other problems discussed at the Conference, the Chinese achieved only a qualified success. Their gains in regard to the return of leased territories were limited to a promise from the British to hand back Weihaiwei, and an offer from the French to discuss the restoration of Kwangchow-wan at some future time.[21] Their request for the withdrawal of armed forces which were stationed on Chinese soil "without the authority of any treaty or agreement" met with the answer that such troops would be removed "whenever China shall assure the protection of the lives and property of foreigners in China." The demand for the abolition of foreign postal services was granted, excluding the leased territories, and subject to the conditions that China maintain an efficient postal service and give assurance that no change was contemplated in the postal administration so far as the status of the foreign Co-Director was concerned. The Chinese desire to have foreign radio stations, operating in China without official consent, brought under the control of the Chinese Government was granted only in part, since the leased territories and the South Manchuria Railway zone, where most of the Japanese stations were located, were excluded from the agreement.[22]

When, therefore, it came to specific questions, and especially to the major issues involved in a revision of the treaties, it was evident that the foreign Powers were determined not to ruffle the *status quo* to an extent that would seriously disturb their own interests. This did not prevent the Conference from entering into a further discussion of the principles which should govern the relations of the Treaty Powers and China in the future. Principles, supplementing those which had already been accepted in the Root Resolutions, were considered, and finally incorporated in the Nine Power Treaty.

The Nine Power Treaty designed a pattern of behavior which will be

[20] The advantage of this clause from the point of view of the Chinese was that it set aside the practice of insistence upon unanimity of action on the part of the Powers.

[21] In discussions conducted directly between China and Japan at the Washington Conference, the latter formally promised to return the Kiaochow leased territory. Among other important matters that were decided during these negotiations, which constituted a settlement of the Shantung question, were arrangements for the return of the Tsingtao-Tsinan railway to China, and for the withdrawal of all Japanese troops in the leased territory or along the railway.

[22] For the documents connected with the return of Weihaiwei, the withdrawal of troops, the abolition of postal services, and the operation of radio stations, see *Treaties and Agreements With and Concerning China, 1919-1929*, Washington, D. C., 1929, pp. 69, 71, 76.

referred to on a number of occasions throughout this study as the Washington formula. The Powers, on their part, promised to cease interfering with the internal development of the Chinese nation. They agreed not to encroach upon, or impair, the sovereignty, independence, and territorial and administrative integrity of China. In furtherance of this aim, they pledged themselves not to support any arrangements concluded by their nationals which were designed "to create spheres of influence or to provide for the enjoyment of mutually exclusive opportunities in designated parts of Chinese territory." The principles of the Open Door were broadly and clearly defined and the Powers agreed neither to act, nor to support their nationals in acting, in violation of those principles.[23]

While these provisions seemed to place all responsibility for good behavior at the doors of the foreign governments, this was not the whole story. According to the wording of the Nine Power Treaty, one of the primary aims of the signatories in protecting China from foreign interference was to give her the "fullest and most unembarrassed opportunity . . . to develop and maintain for herself an effective and stable government." Although it was not explicitly stated that China was assuming an obligation to put her house in order, such an obligation could be implied. Supplemented by the fact that the Powers refused to agree to any substantial revision of the treaty system, the Washington formula seemed to revert to the traditional idea that the Powers would not relinquish their treaty rights until China had developed the capacity to govern herself according to Western standards of efficiency. The new feature of the Washington formula was that the Powers were willing to leave China in peace while she undertook her job of house-cleaning.

The Nine Power Treaty and the Washington Conference, as a whole, produced two further results that had a marked influence on developments after 1925. The first of these was the strengthening of the so-called cooperative policy of the Powers in China, which received the blessing of the Washington Conference. The antagonism of the American public in particular to the view that the United States should act mainly in concert with other foreign nations in the Far East will be spoken of frequently later. The second consequence, which runs like a thread through American policy, was the conviction acquired by American officials that the United States assumed a moral leadership among the Powers at the Washington Conference which it was obliged to make every effort to maintain.

From the point of view of the Chinese people, the Conferences at Versailles and at Washington yielded little that was satisfying. Most of the

[23] Text of treaty, *ibid.*, p. 89.

limitations which had been imposed on China's independence remained intact. At the Paris Peace Conference the grievances of the Chinese had been listened to but not heard. At the Washington Conference constructive principles had been accepted but not applied to existing conditions. The idea that China should put her house in order was not one which could be expected to appeal even to the politically minded sections of the public, especially when the question of what constituted good house-keeping was to be decided by arbitrary standards imposed by foreigners whose own interests were at stake. While the disappointment of the Chinese over the failure of the Powers to rid China of the burden of the treaty system was temporarily kept under control, it added to what President Wilson termed "the combustible material in China"; when, in 1925, a match was struck, it did, in fact, start an unquenchable fire.

INTERNAL AFFAIRS

As the Washington Conference persistently emphasized, the Chinese were discovering through first-hand experience that the creation of a democracy is a challenging and difficult undertaking.[24] In the years following the Revolution of 1911, China found herself becoming not, as many had hoped, a representative republic but a rigid dictatorship that came close to reproducing pre-revolutionary conditions. Yuan Shih-k'ai, who had been made President of the new Republic, did not share the ideas of the reformers in the Kuomintang (the National People's Party) and their famous leader Dr. Sun Yat-sen and, moreover, showed no inclination to rule by means of parliamentary procedures. No sooner had President Yuan been firmly established in office than he ordered the dissolution of the Kuomintang and the expulsion of its members from Parliament. Parliament was left without a quorum by this action and it ceased to function; from 1913 until Yuan Shih-k'ai's death two and a half years later, China was ruled without any semblance of representative government.

Nor did matters show any signs of improvement with the death of Yuan Shih-k'ai, the "strong man" of China. Instead the nation embarked on a period of civil war which was to bring a decade of futile and purposeless misery. Yuan had not only left intact but had actually strengthened the system of provincial rule by Military Governors (later called *Tuchuns*) who commanded armies that were loyal to them rather than to the Central Government at Peking. During Yuan's lifetime, order had been preserved partly by the use of repressive measures and partly because the interests of

---

[24] A particularly interesting discussion of the period from 1911 to 1925 will be found in Harold M. Vinacke's, *A History of the Far East in Modern Times*, New York, 1933.

the militarists lay in supporting a dictatorial President in his struggle against the constitutionalists who wished to establish an effective civil government. After Yuan's death, there was no longer any central force to hold the *Tuchuns* together so that their personal rivalries and hungry ambitions became the dominating factor in Chinese political life.

In 1916, an abortive attempt was made to re-establish constitutional government. For a brief moment Li Yuan-hung, the new President of the Republic, seemed determined to strengthen the hand of Parliament, which had reassembled, against the hand of the militarists. While well-meaning, President Li proved too weak to put through his own good intentions, and finally, in June, 1917, under pressure from one of the worst of the military leaders, he issued an edict dismissing Parliament.

The dissolution of Parliament marked the decisive victory of military over civilian government in the North. For the next ten years, three different groups of militarists were to struggle for the control of Peking, which continued to represent the Central Government in theory but, in fact, was scarcely able to rule outside the walls of the capital. The three military cliques were the Anfu Club headed by Tuan Chi-jui, the Fengtien Party of the Manchurian warlord Chang Tso-lin, and the Chihli group led by Ts'ao K'un.

The continuous and interminable struggle between these factions is of importance in connection with later developments chiefly as an indication of the complete disintegration of political conditions in North China. From 1918 to 1920, Peking was controlled by the Anfu Club which, at the end of that time, was ousted by Chihli and Fengtien forces acting in a temporary alliance. During the next two years, Chang Tso-lin exercised the greatest influence at Peking, but in 1922 he was driven out in turn and retired to his base, the Manchurian provinces. A period of even greater confusion followed in which Wu Pei-fu, who had succeeded to power in Peking, attempted to reconcile North and South China by reconvening the old Parliament which had been dissolved in 1917, and recalling the former President, Li Yuan-hung. President Li was able to remain in office only one year before he was forced to flee by the head of the Chihli faction, Ts'ao K'un, who himself wished to become President. Although Ts'ao K'un managed to fulfill his ambitions through the simple expedient of bribing Parliament, his triumph, like that of his predecessors, was short-lived. Neither Chang Tso-lin and his followers nor the Anfu Club had any intention of remaining permanently in retirement while the spoils of politics fell to their rivals. They formed an alliance in the summer of 1924 and declared war on Peking. Events took a surprising turn, however, when in October Feng Yu-hsiang, China's "Christian General" who had formerly supported the Chihli group, deserted their cause and in a sudden and spectacular *coup* marched on Peking and seized the capital. General Feng further proceeded to co-operate with Chang Tso-lin and the leaders of the Anfu Club, and a Provisional Government was established at Peking with the experienced Anfuite, Tuan Chi-jui, as Chief Executive. Although this was not the end of China's civil war, the Provisional Government remained in power until the beginning of the revolutionary period in 1925, when China's internal and foreign affairs were again thrown into a state of tragic confusion by the senseless struggle of the northern military factions.

These events had an important effect on the outside world and, as will be seen later, contributed greatly to the difficulties that arose between China and the foreign Powers. The constant civil war in North China made it hard for many foreigners to see that the country was in the midst of a transition period, in which intense disorder might be accompanied by deep currents of constructive change acting underneath the surface. Moreover, the fact that many foreigners residing in China, as well as people abroad, focused their attention on conditions in the North led them to overlook developments at Canton which were producing very different results.

It will be remembered that in 1917 Parliament had been dismissed by President Li Yuan-hung under pressure from the militarists. The Kuomintang members, with their leader Sun Yat-sen, retired to Canton where they established a government which they wished to have recognized as the legal government of China. However, despite the fact that the Kuomintang cherished ideas of instituting a representative and republican form of administration, the Government at Canton seemed little better than its rival at Peking for the first five years of its existence. Dr. Sun Yat-sen was only able to maintain himself in power by the support of the Southern militarists, and on three separate occasions was forced to leave Canton for extended periods to seek security in the North.

On the last of these occasions, in 1922, Dr. Sun succeeded in effecting a drastic change in the fortunes of the Kuomintang — and, as it developed, in the fortunes of China. At Shanghai he held a series of conferences with the Russian envoy, Adolf Joffe, in which the groundwork was laid for a close understanding between the Kuomintang and the Soviet Union. A joint communiqué was issued, known as the Sun-Joffe Memorandum, in which Dr. Sun declared that in his opinion China was not yet ready for the introduction of communism or even of the Soviet system.[25] Mr. Joffe, on his part, agreed with this view and asserted that for the time being the

[25] Text of Sun-Joffe Memorandum in *China Year Book*, 1928, p. 318.

most important task of the Chinese was to establish internal unity and national independence. In the attainment of these aims, he said, the Chinese had the "warmest sympathy of the Russian people" and could count on the support of the Soviet Union.

Shortly thereafter, Dr. Sun's chief military opponent having been driven from Kwangtung, Dr. Sun was able to return to Canton. Having learned by this time that nothing could be accomplished unless a strong civil government was established in South China, he decided to reorganize the Kuomintang. One of his first moves was to invite a group of Russian advisers, expert in various fields, to assist him in the execution of his plans.[26]

The Russian mission arrived in Canton in September, 1923. Outstanding among its members was Michael Borodin, whose exceptional talents and remarkable grasp of the situation in China at once made him a central figure in the affairs of the Kuomintang. Borodin, whose immediate purpose came to be the creation of a Nationalist revolutionary movement, recognized that he was faced with an extremely difficult situation. The Kuomintang, far from being a party of radical or even liberal revolutionists, was a loosely-constructed coalition that relied for its support on the various groups that constituted the bourgeoisie (such as merchants, industrialists, landlords, intellectuals), and on the peasants and proletariat. While Borodin was determined to broaden the base of the Kuomintang by strengthening the Nationalist movement among the peasant and working classes, he was also convinced that a revolution would not be successful in China without the co-operation of all the groups in the Kuomintang.

At the outset, the primary aims of Borodin, and Sun Yat-sen and his followers, were to formulate a party program, to reconstruct the administrative machinery of the Kuomintang, to develop a highly-disciplined party organization, and to create the nucleus of a well-trained and powerful army. The latter object was accomplished through the establishment of a military academy at Whampoa under the direction of General Chiang Kai-shek, assisted by a group of Russian military advisers.

The drafting of a program that would not alienate any of the factions in the Kuomintang was obviously a difficult undertaking. After considerable deliberation this was accomplished, and a Manifesto was drawn up and adopted by the First National Congress of the Kuomintang in January, 1924."[27]

Although the Manifesto of the First Congress had an important bearing

[26] For a number of the outstanding books on the developments in Canton at this time, see the Bibliography.

[27] For Manifesto, see T. C. Woo, *The Kuomintang and the Future of the Chinese Revolution*, London, 1928, Appendix C.

on the domestic policies of the Kuomintang, it can only be considered here in its effect on the future of China's foreign relations. Approached from this point of view, the Manifesto was a significant document in that it gave the Chinese Nationalist movement an intensely anti-imperialist character. An anti-imperialist note was struck in the opening section, when, in re- viewing the modern history of China, it was stated — for the first time in any official pronouncement of the Kuomintang — that the Powers were to a large extent responsible for the progressive deterioration of conditions in China. "Since the occupation of China by the Manchus," it was said, "there reigned in the hearts of the Chinese race a feeling of injustice for a long time. After the country was thrown open to international commerce, foreign imperialism came like an angry tide. Armed plundering and eco- nomic pressure reduced the country to a semi-colonial status and caused her to lose her independence." The object of the Revolution of 1911, it was declared, had not been merely to rid the country of the Manchus but also to create a united nation, economically strong and democratically ruled, which could shake off the bonds of "semi-colonialism" and occupy a sovereign position in the world. The revolutionists had not achieved their goal, however; instead, under Yuan Shih-k'ai and later under the northern warlords, China had been reduced to a state of chaos. The foreign imperialists, taking advantage of the confused conditions throughout the country, had pursued their own selfish interests and attempted to strangle the political and economic life of the nation. Moreover, the arbitrary rule of the militarists and "the invasion of the imperialists" were growing worse every day, causing the nation "to sink deeper into the hell of a semi-colonial status."

The importance of the anti-imperialist aspect of the Manifesto could scarcely be over-estimated in terms of the future. The argument that China's difficulties were to a large extent due to the restrictions placed on her sovereignty by the foreign Powers was soon to be heard from all po- litically articulate classes of Chinese, not only in South China but in every part of the country. At the time of the meeting of the First National Congress, it was further strengthened by the platform on foreign policy adopted by the Congress. The key-note was the abolition of the "unequal" treaties, and it was declared that all agreements related to such matters as extraterritoriality, tariff controls, foreign concessions, and other special privileges of foreigners in China must be canceled. New treaties should be negotiated on the principle of equality and of respect for the sovereign rights of both parties. Foreign Powers that voluntarily abrogated the exist- ing agreements were to be regarded as "most-favored nations."

The First National Congress adopted other measures that went far to determine the course of future developments. Communists were admitted to membership in the Kuomintang on the understanding that they would adhere to the principles of the Party — principles which were carefully outlined and which represented to a large extent views that had long been advocated by Sun Yat-sen. The Congress also adopted a constitution which remodeled the entire structure of the Kuomintang along the lines of the Russian Communist Party. As a result the Kuomintang, which had heretofore been a weak and ineffective organization, became a powerful administrative body, able to undertake the functions of government and to provide the driving force of the Nationalist revolutionary movement.

The determination to direct the Nationalist Revolution into anti-imperialist channels which had been evident at the First National Congress was further carried out in the propaganda activities of the Kuomintang. Recognizing that Sun Yat-sen was the most valuable propaganda-agent that the Kuomintang possessed, Borodin urged him to seize every opportunity to spread his ideas through speeches and writing. Out of this grew the famous series of lectures known as the *San Min Chu I* (*The Three Principles of the People*) which Dr. Sun delivered at Canton from January to August, 1924.[28]

The three principles of Dr. Sun were, as is well known, the principles of nationalism, of democracy, and of livelihood. Of these the first was the only one which dealt in detail with China's international status. Dr. Sun argued that basically China resembled a "sheet of loose sand" because her people were not united by a genuinely patriotic feeling: they had developed a loyalty to family and clan but not to the nation as a whole. As a result China was unable to withstand the disasters that threatened her from without. Oppression by the foreign Powers had reduced her to a "semi-colonial" state — a state lower than that of the average colony which was at least able to claim some degree of protection from a mother-country. "Whose semi-colony is China?" Dr. Sun asked. "China is the colony of every nation that has made treaties with her, and the treaty-making nations are her masters. China is not the colony of one nation but of all, and we are not the slaves of one country but of all." The only reason that China had survived with any degree of independence was that the Powers wanted to avoid war in the Far East and, therefore, checkmated one another by establishing a balance of power. However, it was still the intention of the major Treaty Powers to "crush China," and this aim could be attained by diplomacy as well as by military force. "The concentrated thinking of the Powers will

---

[28] *San Min Chu I*, edited by L. T. Chen, (translated by Frank W. Price), Shanghai, 1927.

certainly evolve some consummate method for overthrowing China. . . .
Just a paper and pen and a mutually satisfactory agreement will spell our
ruin. It is only necessary that the diplomats of the different countries meet
in one place and make their signatures; in one day the signing of a document, in one day united political action can wipe out China." And, if by
"some good luck" China should escape military control and diplomatic
oppression, she would still be destroyed by the economic tyranny of other
nations "which is day by day pressing in upon us and sucking our very
life blood."

Dr. Sun did not survive long after the delivery of the *San Min Chu I.*
At the end of 1924 he traveled north with the intention of co-operating
with the Tuan Chi-jui Administration at Peking in an attempt to establish
a government under which China could be united. On his arrival at the
capital in December he found that the northern leaders were not willing
to consider any basis of agreement which was acceptable to him. Already
an incurably sick man, he died at Peking in March, 1925.

Dr. Sun left a Will which, like the legend built around his memory,
became one of the most valuable and effective political instruments of the
Kuomintang.[29] In it he stated that he had devoted forty years of his life
to an attempt "to elevate China to a state of freedom and independence"
and declared that his followers must do their utmost to realize the ideas
embodied in his writings, in the *San Min Chu I,* and in the Manifesto of
the First National Congress of the Kuomintang. In a final appeal to his
countrymen he urged them to fight on "with renewed vigor . . . for the
solution of our national problems and to abolish the unequal treaties with
foreign nations." "These things," he said, "must be done in the shortest
possible time."

Little more than two months after Sun Yat-sen's death, developments
took an unexpected turn when foreigners at Shanghai, entirely by accident,
set into motion a train of events which showed the amount of anti-foreign
hostility that was latent throughout the length and breadth of China.
While the anti-foreign demonstrations that followed the May 30th Incident
made a profound impression on foreigners, they continued to think of
"China" in terms of conditions in the North and in the Yangtze Valley and
remained relatively unaware of the developments within the Kuomintang.
Nevertheless with the May 30th Incident, the anti-foreign aspect of the
Chinese Nationalist Revolution got underway and until the summer of 1928
when the Nationalist Government (formed after the so-called split in the
Kuomintang) took Peking, the Revolution was to run an intensely complex
and dramatic course.

[29] Text of Will in *China Year Book,* 1928, p. 1323.

CHAPTER II

MAY 30, 1925

THE SHANGHAI INCIDENT

The Shanghai Incident of May 30, 1925, was the beginning of a new phase in China's relations with the Powers. Just as a relatively minor cause may stir an individual to profound anger, so the Incident of May 30th touched off the hostility to foreigners which the Chinese had been holding under tight control. The bitter disappointment which the Chinese people had experienced over the decisions of the Versailles and Washington Conferences, and their intense resentment of the superior position of foreigners in China, rose to the surface in a sudden furious expression of feeling. That this feeling had been given direction by the propaganda activities of the Kuomintang, made it more purposeful and dangerous. While in the past the Chinese people had only engaged in sporadic demonstrations such as that of the student movement and boycott of 1919, they were to exercise a determining influence on their country's policy in the future. After the May 30th Incident, the fact was established that China would act in vigorous defense of her own demands.

During the winter of 1924-1925, foreigners in China seem to have been unaware of any drastic increase in anti-foreign feeling throughout the country. In January, 1925, the American Minister, Jacob Gould Schurman, hearing reports of a growing anti-foreign movement, asked the Consul General at Shanghai to sound out the opinion of missionaries and business men on this subject. The business men stated that their representatives in the interior had not observed any such developments, while the missionaries declared that they were not aware of any change in the Chinese attitude toward foreigners in general but that there was a certain amount of agitation directed purely against Christian educational institutions.[1]

The immediate cause of the events of May 30th centered in laboi disputes in the Japanese mills at Shanghai.[2] Since December, 1924, there

---

[1] *Papers Relating to the Foreign Relations of the United States* (1925), p. 722. These papers, published by the Department of State, will be referred to hereinafter as *Foreign Relations*. Page references are to the China sections of the volumes of *Foreign Relations* (1925, Vol. 1; 1926, Vol. 1; 1927, Vol. 2; 1928, Vol. 2; 1929, Vol. 2). Where direct quotations have been used from cables that have been paraphrased, the words "cable paraphrased" appear in the footnotes.

[2] The following account of the May 30th Incident is taken largely from *Report of the Proceedings of the International Commission of Judges* and *Trial of Rioters at the Mixed Court*, Shanghai, 1925.

had been strikes in the Japanese mills which, accompanied by considerable violence, resulted in one instance in the death of a Japanese employer. On May 15th, a riot in the Nagai Wata Mill ended in the police firing on the strikers, seriously wounding several, one of whom, Ku Chung-hung, died of his wounds two days later.

The students and laborers in Shanghai held a memorial service for Ku Chung-hung on May 30th. Following the service, they entered the Louza district of the International Settlement where they conducted anti-foreign demonstrations. The students carried banners bearing such slogans as: "The Japanese have killed some of our Chinese and let us rally to the assistance of our brethren," "Abolish Extraterritoriality," "Cancel All Unequal Treaties."

Hearing of these activities, several police officers arrived on the scene from the Louza district which was in charge of Inspector Everson. Some of the agitators were arrested and taken to the police station, where they were followed by a group of their comrades. Gradually the charge room of the station filled with students and a general melée ensued before the police succeeded in ousting the intruders.

Outside the building there was a large gathering, consisting primarily of afternoon shoppers and casual passers-by. The police attempted to push back the crowd, the group of students ejected from the charge room now being in the forefront. At first the police had no difficulty, but when the crowd reached the Town Hall, some 300 feet from the police station, it began to offer resistance. Just why the temper of the crowd changed is not clear. Some eye-witnesses felt that it was due to the attempt of student agitators in the front ranks to stimulate a riot. Others believed that a "rougher" element joined the group, which was increasing rapidly, and that it was this influence which caused the disturbance.

In any case, the crowd suddenly turned back and moved toward the police station. By this time there were approximately 2,000 persons facing a force of some twenty to thirty policemen. Inspector Everson, believing that the building was about to be seized, determined to take drastic action. He ran toward the crowd, yelling in English, "Stop or I will shoot," and in Chinese, "Stop or I will kill." As the crowd kept moving forward he gave orders to fire which were not heard above the general din. A ragged volley followed from the police. Twelve Chinese were killed and seventeen wounded.

As soon as the events of May 30th became known, Chinese throughout the country united in their condemnation of the action of the Shanghai police.[3] Again there was set in motion a wave of articulate public opinion which, while similar to the movement of 1919, hurled itself forward with far more momentum. The extraordinary feature of this popular expression was that it emanated from people in all parts of the country and from an extensive cross-section of Chinese society. From May 30th on, demonstrations, strikes, and boycotts were conducted in areas widely scattered over North, Central, and South China. While the movement was directed against foreigners in general, Japan and Great Britain were made to bear the brunt of the attack at the outset. Ostensibly this was due to the fact that the Shanghai disorders had started in Japanese mills and that the police of the International Settlement were under the command of a British officer. Within a few weeks, however, a remarkable change occurred; Chinese hostility shifted away from the Japanese and concentrated its full force upon the British. A number of reasons for this development were given at the time.[4] It was argued that Great Britain's large financial and commercial interests in the Yangtze Valley and the Hongkong area made her a natural target of attack in these regions where most of the anti-foreign disturbances were taking place. There were also many who believed that the anti-foreign movement was being organized and sustained by the Communist Party, and that the Communists were singling out Great Britain as, in their view, the foremost representative of imperialism, and, therefore, the arch-enemy of the Chinese. In addition, because Japan was generally suspected, at this time, of trying to further her own ends through playing a conciliatory rôle toward China, many felt that the Japanese were, by various devices, aiding in the deflection of the anti-foreign movement against the British.

Throughout most of the month of June the entire city of Shanghai was in a state of acute tension. There were further shootings, one of which — called the Battle of Thibet Road — resulted in the death of several Chinese and the wounding of a number of Chinese and foreigners.[5] On the evening of May 31st a mass meeting was held by Chinese student and labor organizations. It was decided to call a general strike to take effect on the following day. Among those endorsing the strike resolution was Mr. Fong Chu-pah, Acting Chairman of the Chinese General Chamber of Commerce.[6] At the same time, a protest was made public by the Shanghai

[3] For a more detailed account of the anti-foreign movement throughout China, see Chapter III.

[4] For discussions of this point see, for example, Remer, *A Study of Chinese Boycotts*, pp. 92, 127; *Foreign Relations* (1925), p. 664; *China Weekly Review*, Aug. 29, 1925, p. 263.

[5] *North China Herald*, June 6, 1925, p. 412.

[6] For an account of the meeting, see *ibid.*, p. 424. There has been considerable discussion as to whether or not Mr. Fong acted under duress. See, for example, *China Year Book*, 1926-27, p. 922.

Bankers' Association and the Shanghai Native Bankers' Association, condemning the "indiscriminate rifle-shooting" of the police and placing the responsibility for the May 30th Affair on the shoulders of the Municipal authorities.[7]

In response to the strike order, Chinese banks, business houses, and shops throughout the International Settlement closed on June 1st.[8] This was the first phase of the strike and it lasted until June 26th. The second and more serious phase involved the Chinese employees in foreign enterprises. Chinese workers left public services such as the Municipal Electricity Department, the Shanghai Mutual Telephone Company, the Shanghai Tramway Company, and the Waterworks Company. The strike was especially severe throughout the Japanese and British mills, in the printing departments of the leading foreign newspapers, and among seamen. All in all it was estimated about 85,000 workers were involved in the movement by the end of June.[9] According to newspaper accounts, funds for the support of the strikers were sent in from northern cities and from all parts of the Yangtze, involving contributions from the Peking Government, leaders of all political factions, the Chinese Bankers' Association and Chinese Chambers of Commerce.[10]

Faced with what was obviously a situation of the utmost gravity, the Shanghai Municipal Council declared a state of emergency. Residents were forbidden to collect in crowds, hold meetings, deliver speeches, or act in any way that might "incite to a breach of the peace." Strikers were warned that strong measures would be taken to put down any attempts at violence.[11] Marines of five different nationalities were landed to do police duty and take over the work of the strikers in the public utilities.[12] The Shanghai Volunteer Corps was mobilized.[13] The Controller of Food Supplies was authorized to requisition supplies of food and distribute them in any way he deemed necessary.[14]

ATTITUDES AMONG FOREIGNERS IN CHINA

Among those who were least prepared for the events of May 30th, and the anti-foreign movement which followed, were the foreigners residing in China. As already indicated, they had not, in the preceding months, sensed

[7] *North China Herald,* June 6, 1925, p. 419.

[8] There are of course innumerable accounts of the strike. The following facts are taken largely from contemporary issues of the *North China Herald.*

[9] The figure of 85,000 is taken from *China Year Book,* 1926-27, p. 924. Very much larger figures are frequently given.

[10] *North China Herald,* June 13, 1925, pp. 444-445; June 20, 1925, p. 463; July 4, 1925, p. 502.

[11] Proclamation of the Municipal Council in *ibid.,* June 6, 1925, p. 412.

[12] *China Weekly Review,* June 13, 1925, p. 39.

[13] *North China Herald,* June 16, 1925, p. 419.   [14] *Ibid.*

any change in the feelings of Chinese toward them. After May 30th, however, the intense hostility exhibited by the Chinese forced foreigners to re-examine their own attitudes toward the people among whom they were living. The first object of concern was the incident at the Louza Police Station. Many foreigners at once censured the Chinese, while others placed the blame on the Shanghai police. Most vocal among those holding the Chinese responsible was the *North China Daily News,* (of which the weekly edition was called the *North China Herald*), the outstanding British publication in Shanghai, which was known for the strong influence it exerted on many foreigners in China.[15] In an editorial entitled "Unconditional Surrender," the editors stated:

> Our Peking correspondent tells us that the Wai Chiao Pu[16] is preparing to make representations to the Powers. As regards this, if there are any representations to make they should be from the Powers to the Wai Chiao Pu — representations on the outrageous behaviour of the students who assailed the police, are doing their utmost to foment public riot, and have published both locally and to all China a black lie of Saturday's encounter, saying that the police came upon them when they were holding a peaceful meeting and shot them down in cold blood. If there is to be any interference at this juncture by the Wai Chiao Pu, it should be directed towards the students . . . ordering them to go back to their classrooms and attend to things which properly belong to their callow youth. . . . There is only one way in which peace can be brought back and that is by the unconditional surrender of the students and other agitators.[17]

Similarly, the Shanghai Municipal Council issued a Manifesto announcing that the police had been compelled to fire into the crowd on May 30th, because the students and other "disaffected persons" had made inflammatory speeches, attacked and molested the police, and attempted to force an entrance into the Louza Police Station.[18] At the trial of the students arrested on May 30th, which was held in the Shanghai Mixed Court from June 2nd to June 11th, the prosecution blamed the students in the following terms:

> I am going to prove that the students — we call them students though a better word would be schoolboys — that the students or schoolboys who started this trouble all came from a Bolshevik University — the Shanghai University of Seymour Road. . . . I think the Court will agree that you can

---

[15] The writer wishes to emphasize here that the *North China Daily News and Herald* were British publications but have been cited frequently throughout this study because they both influenced and represented the views of many Americans.

[16] The Wai Chiao Pu is the Chinese Foreign Office.

[17] *North China Herald,* June 6, 1925, p. 423.

[18] *British Chamber of Commerce Journal,* June-August, 1925, p. 173.

get no better material than ignorant schoolboys, such as these people are, to run wild; no better material to use as tools for Bolshevism. They are ignorant and conceited. They think they are big men and there is no better material than that for the cunning Bolsheviks to use to create discord in this unfortunate country.[19]

On the other hand, the *China Weekly Review* and the *Peking Leader* — both American publications — felt that the blame for the shooting on May 30th ought in justice to be shared by all the parties involved. J. B. Powell, editor of the *China Weekly Review,* while demanding the suppression of the "forces of anarchy and disorder," insisted that the May 30th Incident was fundamentally an expression of the pent-up wrath and racial antagonism fostered by half a century of contact between East and West. Believing that one of the main causes of friction was the old, imperialistic attitude maintained by many foreigners in China, he specifically accused "the small-minded men in high positions" in the Shanghai International Settlement of being "imbued not only with racial antagonisms but also with the public — in this case the Chinese — be damned attitude."[20] The *Peking Leader* affirmed that it was "easy to imagine what a furore" would have been aroused if policemen in New York or Chicago had fired on an unarmed crowd of students similar to that which collected in front of the Louza Police Station.[21]

An especially sharp conflict of opinion was apparent between missionaries and business men who, along with diplomatic officials, formed the three outstanding groups of Americans in China. While many missionaries hesitated to express their views and, in any case, by no means all shared the same attitude, those who did issue official statements after the May 30th Affair put themselves on record as sympathizing with the Chinese. Among the mission and education groups whose statements received extensive publicity were the National Christian Council (representative of Protestant organizations in China), the faculty of Yenching American Christian University, the Peking Station of the American Board of Commissioners for Foreign Missions (Congregational), the staff of the Young Men's Christian Association, the Board of Directors of the Young Women's Christian Association, and an assembly of thirteen Chinese and foreign Christian schools in Peking.[22] The general trend of the announcements was to censure the

---

[19] *Report of the Trial of the Chinese Arrested During the Riot of May 30, 1925*, Shanghai, 1925, p. 4.

[20] *China Weekly Review,* July 4, 1925, p. 85.

[21] *Peking Leader,* June 5, 1925, p. 4.

[22] All these statements, including the ones quoted here, appear in the *Peking Leader,* Special Supplement, June 14, 1925.

police for the shooting at the Louza Station, to demand an investigation of the incident by a Sino-foreign commission, and to assert that the disturbances at Shanghai were only symptoms of a far more fundamental conflict. The Yenching faculty spoke of the "grave, underlying estrangement and misunderstanding" between Chinese and foreigners, and the staff of the Y.M.C.A. described the May 30th Affair as "an expression of a serious underlying condition of unrest and distrust." Most of the statements closed by declaring, in a carefully considered but vigorous manner, that the only way in which the tension between Chinese and foreigners could be resolved was by a revision of the "unequal" treaties.

In many foreign quarters, these declarations of missionaries and educators were received either with apprehension or with outright disapproval. Ferdinand L. Mayer, the American chargé in Peking, cabled to Washington that "in informal conversations with representative American missionaries, Legation has indicated grave inexpediency of such pronouncements at this stage."[23] The China Press and the North China Herald maintained views similar to those of the Legation, the Herald expressing itself in the following terms:

> While on the subject of "poisoning sound judgment" may we address a word to certain foreign educationalists, who, without having been anywhere near Nanking Road on May 30, or having the slightest right to pass judgment, have rushed in to offer advice. . . . Many of their letters have come our way. They all open with a great pretense of detachment and impartiality but a very few sentences show clearly enough that all they have listened to is the student version. We can make much allowance for the excitement of Chinese but for some of their foreign advisers it is less easy.[24]

The China Weekly Review felt also that the actions of certain missionaries had been based on insufficient evidence and, in the editor's opinion, were probably soon regretted by many who endorsed them.[25]

While the foreign business groups in China made relatively few official announcements at this time, their point of view is generally regarded as having approached that of the North China Herald. One example of this is found in the fracas which developed between the American Chamber of Commerce in Hankow and Senator William E. Borah in Washington. On June 17th, Senator Borah made public a statement which declared that:

> The United States has done nothing to result in its being drawn into conflict with China. The United States has not evinced any imperialistic designs in China and I venture to believe the American public as a whole

[23] Foreign Relations (1925), p. 652.
[24] North China Herald, June 13, 1925, p. 450.
[25] China Weekly Review, July 18, 1925, p. 129.

would like to see the national rights and interests of China fully respected. Personally I would favor the withdrawal of extraterritorial rights in China as speedily as practicable and a policy adopted by all which would respect the territorial integrity and national rights of a great people.[26]

In response, the Hankow Chamber cabled the Department of State, deprecating Mr. Borah's declaration as likely to stimulate disruptive elements "at a time when the Moscow Third International is admittedly concentrating in the East with a view to creating chaos."[27] This stimulated Senator Borah, in turn, to make some strongly-worded remarks in regard to the Chamber:

The American Chamber of Commerce in China is a part of the imperialistic combine which would oppress and exploit the Chinese people. . . . They care very little if it drags the American people into war and sacrifices thousands of our people. . . . Anyone who is at all familiar with what has been going on in China for the last ten years, and the manner in which foreigners have disregarded and bruited the Chinese interests, will have no doubt as to what is the real cause of the trouble in China at the present time. So far as I am concerned they are not going to hide the cause of the trouble. These interests including the American Chamber of Commerce are the real cause of this trouble. . . . In my former statement, I expressed my personal views, but I am prepared with facts to disclose a condition of affairs which would be exceedingly distasteful, in my opinion, to the American Chamber of Commerce.[28]

While these controversies were taking place in public, official opinion was expressing itself, behind the scenes, through the usual guarded channels of diplomacy. At the time of the May 30th Incident, and throughout June, Ferdinand L. Mayer remained in charge of the American Legation at Peking, pending the arrival from the United States of John Van Antwerp MacMurray, the recently appointed Minister to China. In a cable to the State Department, sent on June 19th, Mr. Mayer gave his views of the Chinese

[26] *Ibid.*, August 8, 1925, p. 179. Two groups of Americans, consisting in all of 320 persons—mostly missionaries and educators—signed a cable and a letter endorsing Mr. Borah's position. (*Peking Leader*, July 5, 1925, p. 2; July 7, 1925, p. 1; July 15, 1925, p. 1; below, pp. 87-88).

[27] *New York Times*, June 16, 1925, p. 4. In August 1925, Senator Borah sent a letter to the Baltimore *Sun* stating that he was not in favor of the abolition of extraterritorial privileges overnight, but that he did believe that the Powers should immediately aid in creating a condition that would enable abolition to be accomplished without further delay. The Powers, he declared, were "plainly not working sincerely" toward such an end so that a situation remained where foreign interests were exploiting life in China "beyond the power of human language to portray." "Is it not sheer pretense," he asked, "under such conditions to taunt China with a challenge to put her house in order?" (*Peking Leader*, August 20, 1925, p. 1.)

[28] *China Weekly Review*, August 8, 1925, p. 179.

situation. Conditions, he said, were "extremely critical," weighted with alarming potentialities for the future. He regarded the disturbances as more nationalist than anti-foreign but nevertheless believed that the anti-foreign movement was profoundly serious and might well develop beyond control. The two causes which he singled out as contributing to the crisis were the Shanghai Incident and Soviet activities. In regard to the former he said: "In my opinion the widespread agitation centers psychologically in the Shanghai Incident; that therefore we should settle this as satisfactorily as possible at once, when it is hoped the agitation throughout the country will subside temporarily at least."

In respect to the Communists, Mr. Mayer declared that the situation was being "exploited in every manner possible by the Soviets," though "just how much they had to do with the actual initiation of the Shanghai Incident is at present impossible to say."[29]

One of the most interesting and vivid statements, not only of American official opinion, but also of conditions in China at this time, was written by Mr. MacMurray shortly after his arrival in Peking, early in July. The American Minister described the Chinese people as "aroused to an emotional fervor" that exceeded anything his long years of observation of the growth of nationalism in China had led him to expect. "The Shanghai Incident," he wrote, "seems to have awakened instincts and passions hitherto dormant, and given an element of fanaticism to what were behind the somewhat unsympathetic [unsystematized?] and desultory aspirations of the small articulate portion of the Chinese people."

To obtain an accurate picture of the situation, Mr. MacMurray stated, it was necessary to realize that mixed with the genuine aspirations of the movement for Chinese independence were unreal elements springing from emotions and phantasies that could not be treated on a logical basis or even on the level of political concepts. This idea he expressed in his statement a number of times, writing, for example, that "it is so much a matter of psychological rather than material considerations that I feel that any attempt to evaluate the situation must take account of imponderable emotional elements far more than of any concrete claims or grievances." One fundamental factor, Mr. MacMurray declared, was that the Chinese, particularly since the war, had — in common with other Asiatic peoples — grown more self-conscious, quicker to assert themselves, less in awe of the West, and more resentful of the "assumed superiority of the white races." Mr. MacMurray continued:

[29] *Foreign Relations* (1925), p. 667.

That tendency has been vastly complicated, however, by more subtle elements of feeling latent in the minds of the Chinese and now brought to the surface by an emotional upheaval. Chinese who were heretofore most friendly and congenial with foreigners are now stirred to intoler- ance and pour out of their memories long stored-up recollections of abuses and indignities on the part of foreigners toward their people — instances of jostling off the sidewalks, of the kicking of rickshaw coolies, and the like. Even though it expresses itself in political terms, the present crisis of feeling, it seems to me, is to be construed as a revulsion against what the individual Chinese feels to be the offense to his personal dignity and self-esteem, implicit in the overbearing attitude of the white man towards the Chinese. It is an inferiority complex which under the stress of an almost nation-wide excitement prompts him to a hysterical self- assertion that is subjective rather than objective and that involves anti- foreign feeling only indirectly and as an assertion of self.

This feeling has been further complicated by the fact that thinking Chinese are aware of the failure they are making in the organization of their national life and morbidly conscious of the poor showing that they have made in the eyes of foreign nations. It is especially true of Chinese human nature that it flinches from recognition of its own deficiencies and by an instinctive subconscious process seeks excuses in the action of others. It is natural and easy for the Chinese to gloss over the miserable political conditions which they realize and resent, by reference to such catchwords as *unequal treaties* or *foreign imperialism*.[30]

NEGOTIATIONS AND SETTLEMENT

On June 6th, the Diplomatic Body at Peking appointed a committee to investigate the circumstances surrounding the May 30th Incident. Arriving at Shanghai a few days later, the committee conducted extensive inquiries and interviewed many officials, including Stirling Fessenden, an American who was Chairman of the Shanghai Municipal Council, and Kenneth John McEuen, Commissioner of Police.[31] The latter had become a figure of particular significance, having been singled out by the Chinese as a special target for attack. In his position as Police Commissioner he was regarded as primarily responsible for the May 30th Affair, and it was generally felt that he had neglected his duties both in respect to taking precautionary measures and in his handling of the incident at the Louza Station.

While carrying on its investigation the committee representing the Diplomatic Body came into contact with a similar delegation appointed by the Chinese Government. The two groups decided to enter into negotia- tions but this was made difficult, if not impossible, by the fact that the foreign representatives had been given entirely different instructions from

[30] *Ibid.*, p. 799.
[31] *Ibid.*, p. 664.

those accorded the Chinese. The interested Legations had limited their delegates to a consideration of issues directly connected with the events of May 30th, such as the suspension of certain police officials, the return of the strikers to work, and the demobilization of the International Settlement.[32] The Chinese, on the other hand, wished to discuss a list of thirteen demands which went far beyond the immediate situation.[33]

The thirteen demands of the Chinese carried great weight as they expressed the will of important sections of Chinese public opinion. They were first drawn up on June 7th, at a meeting of the Shanghai Commercial and Labor Association, the Shanghai Street Unions, the National Chinese Students' Federation, and the Shanghai Chinese Students' Union.[34] A week later they were revised by the Chinese General Chamber of Commerce, in a manner that deleted some of the more radical demands, and were endorsed by forty organizations including many merchants' and bankers' associations.[35] With few amendments they were then accepted by the Chinese Government at Peking as a basis for negotiation with the foreign Powers.

Since the thirteen demands incorporated some of the basic issues between Chinese and foreigners and formed an important part of the history of this period they are given here in full:

1. Abolition of all extraordinary military measures.
2. Release of all Chinese who have been arrested in connection with this affair and reopening of all schools closed or occupied in the International Settlement.
3. Punishment of those to blame, who, pending their trial (on very grave charges), should be immediately suspended from their duties.
4. Indemnity to the victims (dead and wounded) and to the laborers, merchants, and students who have suffered loss as a result of this affair.
5. Formal apologies.
6. Restitution of the Mixed Court to the Chinese Government.
7. The Chinese employed in the factories and homes of foreigners, seamen, and workers, who have struck because of the agitation produced by the incident, shall be reinstated without reduction of pay for the period of the strike.
8. Liberal treatment for laborers, i.e., no punishment shall be inflicted if they wish to abstain from work.
9. Regarding the status of the International Settlement:
    (a) The Chinese shall participate in the Municipal Council and ratepayers' meetings. The ratepayers will choose their representatives in

[32] *Ibid.*, p. 667.
[33] *Ibid.*
[34] Text of demands in *China Year Book,* 1926-27, p. 928; account of meeting in *North China Herald,* June 13, 1925, p. 443.
[35] Text of Chamber's demands in *China Year Book,* 1926-27, p. 929. The demands of the students and labor unions included, for example: "Extraterritoriality must be abolished forthwith."

proportion to the amount of the taxes paid by them. In voting they will have the same rights and privileges as the foreign voters.

(b) In determining the right to vote, examination shall be made to see whether properties actually belong to the titleholder, or whether he is simply an agent or representative. Only the actual owner will have the right to vote and if the property is held by an agent it is the real owner who will vote.

10. The Municipality shall not construct roads outside of the International Settlement; those which are already constructed shall be ceded back unconditionally to the Chinese Government, which will have control of them.

11. The regulations concerning the press, the rights of wharfage, and the stock exchanges should be repealed.

12. Chinese in the International Settlement shall have freedom of speech, of assembly, and of the press.

13. The Secretary of the Municipal Council, Benbow-Rowe, shall be dismissed.[36]

As a result of the differences between the instructions given the delegation of the Chinese Government and that of the Diplomatic Body, negotiations broke down almost immediately and, on June 18th, the interested Heads of Legation recalled their representatives to Peking.[37] At the same time, the Ministers issued a communiqué, explaining the reason for terminating the negotiations and expressing their willingness to request authority from their home governments to consider those Chinese proposals which dealt with a reorganization of the International Settlement and of the administration of justice in the Settlement.[38]

The failure of the delegations to conduct any satisfactory discussions was followed, on the part of the Chinese Government, by two notes addressed to the foreign Powers. One of these reiterated the thirteen demands;[39] the other was an urgent request for a readjustment of China's treaty status.[40] The latter became the basis of negotiations carried on between the Powers during the summer of 1925, and led to the convening of the Tariff Conference and the Commission on Extraterritoriality.[41]

In the immediate situation, the Diplomatic Body at Peking, while not accepting the thirteen demands *per se,* continued to work for a quick settlement of the May 30th Incident. With this in mind, they wrote a report based on the investigation conducted by their commissioners at Shanghai.

[36] *Foreign Relations* (1925), p. 671.
[37] *Ibid.,* pp. 667-668.
[38] *Ibid.*
[39] *Ibid.,* p. 676.
[40] *Ibid.,* p. 763.
[41] See Chapter IV.

The conclusions which they reached were surprisingly severe in their censure of the Shanghai Administration.[42] In respect to Mr. Fessenden they said:

It is to be regretted that the Chairman of the Municipal Council, although aware of the situation and of the developments likely to ensue, did not cause all adequate precautionary measures to be taken especially in regard to the police.

Consequently the heads of missions feel compelled to express the opinion that his conduct is not devoid of blame.

Concerning the role which Colonel McEuen had played in the events of May 30th they were even more critical:

Colonel McEuen, Commissioner of Police, after being informed of the events which were impending, nevertheless considered himself justified in leaving his post, indeed more than an hour and a quarter elapsed between the moment when the demonstrators entered the International Settlement and that when the shots were fired, but during all this time Colonel McEuen was not at his post. Finally, it does not appear that he made the necessary arrangements to disperse the demonstrators and obtain control of the demonstration. He thus showed negligence, lack of judgment, and lack of professional ability. His is the responsibility therefore primarily involved.

The diplomatic representatives concerned consider that he should be replaced.

The report of the Diplomatic Body went on to say that Inspector Everson, being a subordinate official, could only act to carry out the orders of his superiors and therefore could at most be criticized for lack of judgment in refusing to obtain re-enforcements. Further, they stated, the police regulations of the International Settlement were, in their opinion, defective, and furnished one of the causes of the May 30th Incident; in the case of disturbance and riots, it was indispensable that any recourse to arms by the police should be preceded by a warning, such as the sounding of a bugle, "comprehensible to all and capable of being heard at a distance."

In concluding the report, the Diplomatic Body expressed the conviction that the arrangements for the students' demonstrations of May 30th had been made on Chinese soil and that the Chinese Government ought, on its part, to inflict punishment on the responsible officials.

On July 1st, the Heads of Legation forwarded their findings to the Shanghai Municipal Council and declared their intention of making the report public.[43] By this means they hoped to weaken the force of the anti-foreign movement which was gathering strength throughout the country.[44] The situation in Shanghai itself, though generally regarded as less explosive

[42] Text of report printed in *Foreign Relations* (1925), p. 675.
[43] *Ibid.*, p. 674.
[44] See Chapter III.

than in the days immediately following the May 30th Affair, was considered more fundamentally serious.[45] Even the reopening of the Shanghai shops and business houses at the end of June was undertaken primarily for the sake of conducting a boycott in place of the strike—which under any circumstances was regarded as having only the value of a demonstration as far as commercial enterprises were concerned.[46]

Unfortunately, instead of stabilizing the situation, the Diplomatic Body's report proved a fresh source of conflict, giving rise to a sharp controversy between the Ministers at Peking and members of the Shanghai Municipal Council. The controversy was actually part of a long struggle that dated back to the establishment of the Land Regulations of 1869, which formed the only legal constitution of the Settlement.[47] Neither in the Land Regulations, nor in any other official document, had the powers of the Municipal Council or its relation to the Diplomatic Body and the Consular Body at Shanghai been defined. In sending its report on the May 30th Incident to the Municipal Council, the Ministers recommended the immediate dismissal of Mr. McEuen, and the immediate alteration of the police regulations in accordance with their suggestions.[48] But the Council replied with an "absolute refusal" to accept the Diplomatic Body's recommendations and, in addition, claimed that it was "primarily responsible only to the electorate of the International Settlement at Shanghai."[49] In taking this position it appears to have been supported by the British Consul General at Shanghai and, in the opinion of British officials in Peking, by the British community in the Settlement and mercantile interests both in China and in Great Britain.[50] There were also indications that the United States and Japanese Consuls General in Shanghai shared the attitude of their British colleague.[51]

Most of the Heads of Legation, however, adopted the view that their recommendations must be made effective, no matter what position the Shanghai Municipal Council might see fit to adopt. Mr. Mayer cabled to Washington that he regarded the decisions of the Diplomatic Body "wise from the point of view of general political expediency" and necessary in order to place the Powers "on solid ground vis-à-vis Chinese public opinion" in case the negotiations for the settlement of the May 30th Incident were

[45] *China Weekly Review*, July 18, 1925, p. 125.
[46] *China Press*, June 25, 1925, p. 1.
[47] See Chapter X for a discussion of the Shanghai Municipal Council.
[48] *Foreign Relations* (1925), p. 674.
[49] *Ibid.*, p. 682. Quoted from a report of the Ministers at Peking which does not contain the text of the Shanghai Municipal Council's reply to the Ministers.
[50] *Ibid.*, pp. 678, 680.
[51] *Ibid.*, pp. 676, 678.

long delayed.[52] The Diplomatic Body as a whole wired the Consular Body that they hoped the Municipal Council would not resign but that "even if" it did so this "must not impede execution of instructions of Heads of Legation."[53]

The attitude of the interested Ministers in Peking was that the Shanghai Municipal Council was taking advantage of the current crisis in the belief that it offered an auspicious occasion "to force the long-standing issue" of its claim to practical autonomy.[54] Thus presented, the problem was whether or not the Diplomatic Body had the power to control the Municipal Council and, if necessary, to dismiss it and substitute an administration of the Settlement by the Consuls.[55] As the Ministers did not themselves know the answer to this question, they agreed upon an identic telegram, based on a text drafted by Mr. MacMurray, to be sent to their respective governments, which stated that the Heads of Legation found themselves under the necessity of asking for authorization to reconsider — "if need be in consultation with the Chinese authorities"— the existing Land Regulations with a view to establishing the Settlement on a basis which would eliminate "any possibility of a doubt" that members of the Diplomatic Body had "an authority commensurate with their international responsibilities."[56] Mr. Kellogg responded by immediately granting the authority which they requested to the American officials at Peking.

At this point, however, the discussions started on a new phase which centered in London. Sir Austen Chamberlain, then British Secretary for Foreign Affairs, stated that, apart from the attitude of the Shanghai Municipal Council, he would prefer to hold a judicial investigation of the May 30th Incident rather than to proceed any further on the basis of the decisions reached by the Diplomatic Body.[57] As a result the report of the Diplomatic

---

[52] *Ibid.*, p. 676.

[53] *Ibid.*

[54] *Ibid.*, p. 682.

[55] *Ibid.*, p. 680. According to an account of a meeting of the interested Heads of Legation written by Mr. Mayer, Mr. MacMurray "expressed considerable doubt" whether the Heads of Legation were legally competent to dismiss the Council.

[56] *Ibid.*

[57] *Ibid.*, p. 685. For a general statement of Sir Austen Chamberlain's views on the May 30th Affair, see House of Commons Debates, Vol. 185, p. 906 *et seq.* In a debate on June 18, 1925, he said in part: "These conditions [i.e. poor factory conditions] do not justify the advance of a murderous mob crying 'Kill the foreigner' upon the police station in which there were a large stock of arms. It was not until, according to information I have at present, the police station was in danger, with all the arms it contained, that the order was given to fire. If that be the case then I say that the order given to fire saved bloodshed instead of causing it." (p. 922.) As far as the powers of the Shanghai Municipal Council were concerned, the British Secretary for Foreign Affairs observed to the American Ambassador in London that it was absurd for the Council to regard itself as solely

Body was suppressed, an action which led to most unfortunate consequences.[58] The document became shrouded in mystery and the Chinese were convinced that it had been withheld because of findings in their favor. In addition, the clamor against the delay in settling the May 30th Incident was greatly increased, adding substantially to the already existing tension.

Sir Austen Chamberlain seems to have feared that the dismissal of Police Commissioner McEuen without a formal trial would incur the censure of Parliament.[59] He suggested that Mr. McEuen be suspended from office "without prejudice" during the investigation and urged the appointment of a Commission of Inquiry to consist of four judges, representing Great Britain, the United States, France, and Japan.[60] He specifically stated that he saw no reason to include a Chinese on the Commission as China had no part in the administration of the International Settlement, and the Chinese Government, he said, had "shown a persistent desire to use the Shanghai Incident as an argument in a different and larger issue instead of judging it strictly on its own merits."[61]

Sir Austen's views were strongly opposed, on two counts, by United States Minister MacMurray. In respect to the treatment of Mr. McEuen, Mr. MacMurray wired to Washington:

> If, as indicated . . . the British Government may be expected to persist to the end in this shortsighted view, it seems necessary to accept that fact. . . .
> Under these circumstances it seems to me wiser to yield to the extent of contenting ourselves for the time being with his suspension. . . .
> I remain however convinced that Shanghai affair can never be really settled and the intense and widespread bitterness of the Chinese be allayed so long as McEuen is retained in his post.
> Unless therefore it can be arranged that McEuen if acquitted will nevertheless retire from post in which his presence is a challenge and an incitement to anti-foreign feeling, we owe it to ourselves to dissociate ourselves so far as possible from the policy of obstinately ignoring Chinese sensibilities which has already proved the chief [omission] in the present crisis in China.
> Concretely I recommend that we should inform British Foreign Office that for sake of avoiding indefinite delay in settlement of the Shanghai Affair we will not insist upon McEuen's resignation before the inquiry; but that we feel so strongly that his retention in his post would perpetuate the Chinese rancour against the position of foreigners throughout China and render abortive any negotiations for the settlement of the Shanghai Incident,

---

responsible to its electors and at the same time claim protection from the foreign Powers. (*Foreign Relations*, 1925, p. 685.)

[58] The suppression of the Diplomatic Body's report has at times led historians into making the mistake of confusing it with the report drawn up by the Commission of the Diplomatic Body which had been sent to Shanghai; the two were very different in content.

[59] *Foreign Relations* (1925), p. 700.

[60] *Ibid.*, p. 686.

[61] *Ibid.*

that we would prefer to hold aloof from any such negotiations unless assured that he will ask to be retired in the event of his vindication by the inquiry.[62]

Such spectacular action was, however, not necessary as the British assented to the American proposal and Mr. McEuen was in fact retired after the investigation.[63]

The second issue on which Mr. MacMurray disagreed with Sir Austen Chamberlain concerned the appointment of a Chinese jurist to the Commission of Inquiry. The American Minister felt that, if the Chinese were represented, it would have a good effect on public opinion, while lack of representation might readily produce harmful results.[64] After further discussion the Foreign Office in London agreed, and an official invitation to appoint a Chinese Commissioner was extended to the Peking Administration on September 15th.[65] Unfortunately this action, instead of being accepted as a conciliatory gesture, led to the creation of still more antagonism. The Wai Chiao Pu replied that a judicial inquiry would, in its opinion, "only serve the purpose of further complicating the issue" as the lapse of time and changed circumstances had resulted in most of the requisite evidence disappearing and that the investigation already held by the committees of the Diplomatic Body and of the Chinese Government made "re-investigation . . . unnecessary" and only "a waste of time."[66] As a result of the attitude of the Chinese Government, the Commission of Inquiry was boycotted by the Chinese and no Chinese witnesses appeared during the trial.[67]

The so-called International Commission of Judges met in October, 1925, and conducted, in all, thirteen sessions.[68] The members of the Commission were E. Finley Johnson (American), Chief Justice of the Philippines; Henry C. Gollan (British), Chief Justice of Hongkong; Kitsuburo Suga (Japanese), Judge of the Hiroshima Appellate Court.

The decisions of the Commissioners were not made known until December, when separate summaries of the three reports were published. It was then found that the British and Japanese Opinions differed radically from that of the American Judge. Justices Gollan and Suga exonerated

[62] *Ibid.*, pp. 700-701.
[63] *Ibid.*, pp. 703, 706.
[64] *Ibid.*, p. 688.
[65] *Ibid.*, p. 707.
[66] *Ibid.*, pp. 708-709.
[67] *China Year Book*, 1926-27, p. 944.
[68] The proceedings of the trial were published in a volume entitled *Report of the Proceedings of the International Commission of Judges*. This does not, however, include the Opinions of the Judges, which were not published in full. Summaries were issued by the various governments concerned and have been reprinted in many places; the following account is taken from the *China Year Book*, 1926-27, p. 951 *et seq.*, except where otherwise indicated.

the police and the officials of the International Settlement from all blame in connection with the May 30th Incident; Justice Johnson, on the contrary, asserted that adequate precautions had not been taken to prevent the shooting at the Louza Station and severely censured Mr. McEuen, recommending that he be replaced in office by someone "whose performance of duty" would be "more nearly commensurate with his very high responsibilities."

Far more startling, however, than the differences between the conclusions of the Commissioners concerning the circumstances involved in the May 30th Incident, was the wide variation in the scope of the subject matter dealt with in the Opinions. The British and Japanese jurists limited themselves strictly to matters directly connected with the May 30th Incident. Judge Johnson, on the other hand, not only dealt with the happenings on and immediately preceding May 30th, but also analyzed what he regarded as the proximate and long-standing causes of the Shanghai disturbances. He gave the reasons for his action in the following terms:

After hearing the witnesses and examining the exhibits and records, I am fully persuaded that the anti-foreign feeling existing in China today was no more occasioned by the disturbances which took place on the 30th day of May, 1925, at Shanghai, than the killing of the Archduke Francis Ferdinand, heir of the Hapsburg throne, at Serajevo on June 28th, 1914, had to do with bringing on the great World War. Those disturbances were no more the real cause of the present anti-foreign agitation in China than the firing upon Fort Sumter on the 19th day of April, 1861, had to do with the Civil War in America.[69]

Following this, Judge Johnson set forth conclusions, which covered seventeen points in all, including:

That the question of extraterritoriality . . . should speedily and without delay be mutually discussed and settled. There exists a basis of settlement which would be fair and reasonable to all parties.

That the grievance of the Chinese people concerning unjust treaties negotiated with selfish and perhaps dishonest officials is another question which should be carefully considered, mutually discussed and justly settled by all of the friendly nations. . . .

That the question of participation on the part of the Chinese people in the actual government of the city of Shanghai, so far as treaty relations will permit, should be taken up, mutually discussed, and settled. The present situation, from the standpoint of many, is intolerable and until settled will continue to be a source of serious grievances.

That those in authority with power to act in order to lessen the complaint of the Chinese people should as speedily as possible bring to a close the negotiations which have been pending for some years relating to the status of and character of the Mixed Court.

[69] *Chinese Student Monthly*, May, 1926, p. 13. This section of Judge Johnson's report is omitted from most published versions.

That the foreigners in China have failed to take into account the principles of liberty and independence which they themselves have by precept and example spread abroad throughout China, concerning which the young and rising generation have been apt students.[70]

When news of the character of Judge Johnson's report first reached the United States Government, some consternation was felt that it exceeded the terms of reference given the Commission and included what were regarded as "embarrassing and unnecessary dicta."[71] The State Department, nevertheless, decided to publish a summary of Judge Johnson's opinion that would include, in undiluted form, all the criticisms that he had presented. In fact, when it was rumored that the British and Japanese might favor the suppression of the Commissioners' statements, the United States Government declared that it would, if necessary, publish the American report independently.[72]

That the action of Judge Johnson would meet both with praise and with censure was a foregone conclusion. One need only place side by side the comments of the *China Weekly Review* and the *North China Herald* to recognize the wide range of feeling stimulated by the American Commissioner's decision. The *China Weekly Review* described the tone of the conclusions as "admirably judicial and restrained."[73] The *North China Herald* declared that Judge Johnson's remarks included "so many rumours and hearsays and biases that one wonders that a man of his judicial reputation and ability could stoop to such generalities."[74]

Before long, however, the waters closed over the controversy surrounding Judge Johnson's dicta. If opinions such as those voiced by Judge Johnson had been expressed before the May 30th Incident, they would have caused a far greater disturbance, especially among foreigners in China. But seven months passed between the May 30th Incident and its final settlement, and during this time the situation in China underwent a radical change. Foreigners, who in the past had taken their privileged position for granted, looked to the future with a feeling of grave uncertainty. The patience of the Chinese, which had been accepted as acquiescence, was at an end, and underneath was revealed an amount of hostility that astonished even the most experienced observers.

[70] *Foreign Relations* (1925), p. 713.
[71] *Ibid.*, pp. 713, 715, 717. The situation was rendered particularly embarrassing as the United States Government had insisted, contrary to the advice of the British Foreign Office, on limiting the judicial inquiry to facts directly connected with the May 30th Incident. (See *ibid.*, pp. 694-715.)
[72] *Ibid.*, p. 719.
[73] *China Weekly Review*, January 23, 1926, p. 206.
[74] *North China Herald*, January 9, 1926, p. 49.

Chapter III

SPREAD OF THE ANTI-FOREIGN MOVEMENT

The anti-foreign movement which spread across China in the summer of 1925 was a direct reaction to the May 30th Incident. At first, demonstrations took place — large parades, mass meetings, street lectures, the posting of handbills, the shouting of demands before the homes of prominent officials, and similar activities indicative of widespread agitation. "Shoot to kill," a phrase contained in the official instructions of the Shanghai police, became part of the anti-foreign propaganda and extensive use was made of posters depicting Chinese students being murdered by foreign policemen. Cries such as "Kill the British and Japanese" and "Down with Imperialism" were heard from crowds in many cities. Lists of proposals were circulated that ranged from demands for an apology from the Powers to insistence on an economic boycott and abolition of the privileges granted by the "unequal" treaties. While many demonstrations occurred without friction, others led to attacks on individuals and property, to rioting, and to clashes with armed forces that produced grave — and in some cases fatal — results.[1]

One of the first expressions of sympathy for the victims of the May 30th Incident occurred on June 3rd at Peking when some 15,000 students paraded the streets and attempted to enter the Legation Quarter. Agitation of this kind continued in the capital for several weeks and, although limited to students at the beginning, soon spread to commercial and labor groups. Formal protests from the Diplomatic Body finally led to additional Chinese troops being stationed around the Legation Quarter.[2]

The reaction of Peking was speedily followed by more serious developments in other cities. At Chingkiang, on June 5th, a crowd forced its way into the British Concession where it wrecked the Municipal Building, set fire to a number of houses, and assaulted the British Consul, beating him severely.[3] Order was finally restored and maintained by Chinese soldiers and police. In Chungking, a mob surrounded a compound in which British citizens had taken refuge. A naval party was landed from a British gunboat to protect the compound and disperse the crowd, but in doing so it wounded four Chinese.[4] Riots outside a British factory at Nanking resulted in the

---

[1] The best accounts of the events which occurred at this time are to be found in the contemporary press.

[2] *Foreign Relations* (1925), p. 652; *North China Herald*, June 6, 1925, p. 417.

[3] *North China Herald*, June 6, 1925, p. 449.

[4] *China Year Book*, 1926-27, p. 962.

wounding of several workmen by the Chinese police.[5] At Kiukiang, on June 13th, students and laborers rushed into the British Concession, attacked the British and Japanese consulates, looted several buildings, and completely gutted the local branch of the Bank of Taiwan.[6]

Of all the "incidents" along the Yangtze, however, the most serious took place at Hankow. Here a mob broke into the British Concession on June 11th and assaulted the police and members of the Municipal Council. Sailors were landed from H.M.S. *Bee* but, in the meantime, the crowd began to loot Japanese shops and beat some of the shopkeepers, one of whom died of his injuries. The mob then attempted to re-enter the British Concession but was held back by water from a fire hose until the sailors — believing they had lost control of the situation — fired, killing four Chinese and wounding six.[7]

While these were the most conspicuous of the events precipitated by the May 30th Incident, there were many similar happenings in other Chinese cities during the summer of 1925. These occurrences were followed by a boycott which was carried on in all sections of the country although it varied greatly in intensity from one area to another.[8] The boycott was relatively mild in North China where it was maintained for only a brief period of time.[9] In the Yangtze Valley, on the contrary, the movement was vigorous and continued, although with fluctuations, until the end of 1926. In this region, the boycott derived considerable strength from the support given by the Chambers of Commerce of Hankow, Hanyang, and Wuchang, which formed an association for the severance of economic relations with Great Britain and sent delegates throughout the Yangtze area to enlist as large a following as possible.[10]

It was in South China, however, that the boycott reached its full proportions. It had, in fact, been evident from the outset that the situation in South China would differ from that in other parts of the country as any anti-foreign activities taking place in the vicinity of Canton could not fail to fall under the influence of the Kuomintang. As that organization had

[5] *Ibid.*, p. 963.
[6] *North China Herald*, June 20, 1925, p. 463.
[7] *China Year Book*, 1926-27, p. 961.
[8] Professor C. F. Remer in *A Study of Chinese Boycotts* shows that the 1925-1926 movement had certain interesting and distinctive features among which were: (1) Before 1919, Chinese boycotts were largely conducted by merchants; the activities of 1919-1921 and 1923 brought the students into prominence; the disturbances of 1925-1926 for the first time enlisted the support of the laborers. (2) The experiences of 1925 and 1926 led to the improvement of the boycott technique in China, a matter which became evident in its use against the Japanese in 1928 and 1931.
[9] *Ibid.*, pp. 95-98.
[10] *Ibid.*, pp. 98-102.

already developed an efficiency, skilled leadership, and driving power that was without parallel in the rest of China, it was bound to produce very different results. Actually within a short time, the Kuomintang took hold of the boycott movement and forged it into a powerful weapon with which it proceeded to conduct an economic war that was one of the longest and most severe in history.

In carrying on the boycott, the Kuomintang centered its efforts on Hongkong. Here, on June 20th, a general strike was declared which was to start at the same time as a similar strike in Canton called in response to the May 30th Incident. Within a few days, thousands of workers left Hongkong for Canton and shipping was stopped between the two ports. The strike then spread to the British and French concessions on the island of Shameen (at Canton) where there was a general exodus of all Chinese employees excepting those in the postal, police, and telegraph services.

While these events were developing, it became known that a large parade was scheduled to pass along the river opposite Shameen on June 23rd. On June 22nd, Sir J. Jamieson, the British Consul-General at Canton, sent a letter to the local government stating that he had heard of plans for a patriotic demonstration in which the students intended "to make martyrs of themselves by attacking the bridges leading on to Shameen." He had even been told, he said, that they were drawing lots to see which association should have the honor of sacrificing itself for its country's cause. While this story might well, he believed, be the "figment of a fertile imagination," he nevertheless felt that, in case it had any solid foundation, he was bound to warn the Kwangtung Government that any attempt to penetrate the British concession would be resisted by "force of arms." Due precautions were being taken, he declared, to guard against acts of mob violence such as had taken place at Chinkiang, Kiukiang, and Hankow. Should they occur at Canton, he asserted, "the blood of those who call upon crowd psychology to commit deeds of violence would be on their own heads. I write in this strain so that it may not be said hereafter that brutal Imperialist rifles wantonly massacred unoffending Chinese youth."[11]

Owing to the bitterness and recrimination that have persistently surrounded the Shameen Incident, it is virtually impossible to find an account that would not be challenged by many for its accuracy. The following sent to the State Department at Washington by Douglas Jenkins, the American Consul-General at Canton who was an eyewitness, is a relatively objective version. Describing the measures adopted before June 23rd in preparation for the scheduled parade, Mr. Jenkins said that "barricades were constructed

[11] China No. 1 (1926) Cmd. 2636, p. 3.

on the back bund (at Shameen) facing the native city and machine guns were placed at strategic points"; the volunteer corps was also called "to stand by."

Concerning the events of June 23rd, he wrote:

The procession appeared about 2:30 P.M. It was orderly and at first consisted only of students, Boy Scouts, laborers, etc. For about half an hour it continued to pass Shameen and as there was no sign of trouble, onlookers began to breathe with more ease, feeling that the danger of an outbreak was over.

It was then observed, however, that soldiers were bringing up the rear of the procession and that they were armed. These troops consisted of Whampoa Cadets and ordinary Cantonese contingents. No actual count could be made but it is estimated there were more than a thousand men in line.

Just as the first of the troops reached a point in front of the Victoria Hotel near the British bridge the procession stopped, probably because of some congestion ahead. The troops began to show signs of nervousness and the students and civilians nearby seemed to increase their yelling and waving. Suddenly the soldiers were seen to break their formation and a shot rang out. This was followed by several more in rapid succession and then a perfect din of rifles and machine guns began.

It is impossible to say from which side the first shot was fired. The British and other foreigners are practically unanimous in declaring that a Chinese fired first, but the Chinese assert that the shot came from Shameen. At any rate the firing spread rapidly along the bund and the French were hotly engaged almost immediately after the British. Heavy firing lasted about fifteen minutes, bullets smashing into houses facing the canal and striking the trees and roofs of buildings all over the two concessions. The mystery is that more Europeans were not killed or wounded.[12]

The Shameen Incident was immediately followed by the Hongkong boycott, undertaken as a retaliatory gesture against the British, and, as stated before, maintained with exceptional vigor by the Kuomintang. The boycott was unlike any of the other anti-foreign demonstrations occurring in China at the time — and, in fact, unlike any previous experience of the Chinese — in that it was the product of a labor movement, so well-organized that it could be compared with similar developments in highly industrialized countries.

At the outset of the boycott, every fifty strikers nominated a representative to a Strikers' Delegates' Conference. This conference appointed in turn an executive committee of thirteen men which became known as the Canton Strike Committee and which was placed in control of the situation at

[12] *Foreign Relations* (1925), p. 752. In respect to the killed and wounded, one Frenchman was killed and four British wounded on Shameen; on the Canton side of the river, fifty Chinese were killed and a hundred wounded. (*China Year Book*, 1926-27, p. 988.)

Canton.[13] A court was established that tried violators of the strike regulations and other persons who were accused of disturbing the peace.[14] The Strike Committee appointed approximately three thousand pickets who were either stationed in ports throughout Kwangtung where they subjected seagoing cargoes to careful scrutiny, or were placed on the Kwangtung highways to examine freight and search foreign and Chinese travelers.[15] Regulations were passed which stated in part that no imports to, or exports from, Kwangtung belonging to any nation whatsoever would be allowed to go via Hongkong or Macao, and that no vessel passing through Hongkong or Macao would be permitted to discharge cargo in inland Kwangtung.[16] While British merchandise and ships were barred in any case, non-British freight and boats which had not touched at Hongkong and Macao were given freedom of trade. Goods which sought to infringe these rules were confiscated and sold at auction by special committees.[17] Other committees were set up to handle funds. Money to support the strike and boycott was obtained from many sources. The Central Kuomintang Bank, which suddenly found itself prosperous as a result of the shift of trade from Hongkong to Canton, contributed to the maintenance of the pickets. Even wealthy Chinese are said to have assisted in financing the strikers. Large sums were also furnished by the overseas Chinese who had long played an important rôle in furthering the revolutionary movements at home. That these funds were necessary for the continuation of the strike and boycott becomes apparent when it is considered that Canton's labor population had been increased by the immigration of some 200,000 workers from Hongkong, most, if not all, of whom were in need of financial support. It was estimated that T. V. Soong, then Kwangtung Minister of Finance, paid out Ch.$15,000 daily for this purpose alone.[18]

Travelers who visited Canton at this time testified to the strict discipline with which the boycott was carried out. The picket barrier was said to be "tight as a drum," with the pickets acting as though they were soldiers in a war against Hongkong and Great Britain. The boycott was described as "complete." The rule that no British goods could enter Kwangtung was made effective in every way. Canton experienced a shipping boom and all ships were forced to agree that they would not stop at Hongkong and Macao.[19]

[13] Harold Isaacs, *The Tragedy of the Chinese Revolution,* London, 1938, p. 76.

[14] *Ibid.*

[15] Remer, *op. cit.,* p. 104.

[16] *Ibid.,* p. 103.

[17] Isaacs, *op. cit.,* p. 67.

[18] Louis Fischer, *The Soviets in World Affairs,* London, 1930, Vol. 2, p. 644.

[19] Above taken from George Sokolsky's account of his visit to Canton in *China Year Book,* 1926-27, p. 972 *et seq.*

Similarly, those who visited Hongkong during this period gave evidence of the critical state to which the island was being reduced. Lewis S. Gannett, editor of the *Nation* magazine in New York, who made a trip to China during the winter of 1925, gave an account of conditions in the Colony:

> Canton has been pecking at the British Empire for nearly seven months. Gradually the British Empire has become aware that what seemed a mosquito has poison in its bite. . . . In 1924 Hongkong's harbor averaged 210 vessels a day. When Canton began to strike against Hongkong, and the Hongkong Chinese joined, Hongkong's shipping dropped to 34 vessels a day. Real-estate values shrank and they have been cut in half. Hundreds of little firms failed. The share values of the great British banks, the strongest financial institutions in the East, like the Hongkong and Shanghai Banking Corporation and the Chartered Bank of India, Australia, and China, dropped more than a hundred points. In six months British shipping at Canton fell from nearly three million tons in 1924, to a third of a million in 1925. To save Hongkong, the British Government at London voted a loan of three million pounds sterling. That may not be enough; the strike is still on.[20]

As the boycott progressed, conditions became even worse.

"Certainly," one student of the boycott wrote several years later, "in October, 1926, even after the boycott had ended, Hongkong had all the appearance of a deserted village. Business was dead. Buildings were empty, offices were closed and there was little activity of any kind."[21]

From 1924 to 1926, the percentage of all of China's imports coming from Hongkong decreased from 24 percent to 11 percent; the percentage of exports going to the Colony, from 22 percent to 10 percent.[22] Exports from the British homeland to Hongkong fell to approximately two-thirds of their normal value.[23] British exports to China as a whole declined relatively nine times as much as exports from the United States to China during the same period, a fact which has been largely ascribed to the Hongkong boycott.[24]

The boycott lasted from June, 1925, to October, 1926, an extraordinary length of time for such an undertaking. Many attempts to reach a settlement were made during these months.[25] One of the stumbling blocks was that the Canton administration, which consisted of members of the Kuomintang,

---

[20] Lewis S. Gannett, article in *The Nation*, March 31, 1926, p. 336.

[21] Dorothy Orchard, "China's Use of the Boycott as a Political Weapon," *Annals of the American Academy of Political and Social Science*, November, 1930, p. 260.

[22] Remer, *op. cit.*, p. 111. The official statistics for the trade of Hongkong which are normally published annually were not issued for 1925 and 1926.

[23] Orchard, *loc. cit.*

[24] *Ibid.*

[25] A detailed account of the negotiations can be found in *China Year Book*, 1926-27, p. 979 *et seq.*

insisted that all negotiations must be carried on directly with the Strike Committee, a condition which the Hongkong Government refused to accept, declaring that it would deal only with the Government of Canton.[26] The bitterness of feeling in Canton was, moreover, considerably increased by the action both of certain officials and of the British community in the Colony. Sir Cecil Clementi, then Governor of Hongkong, issued public statements denouncing the Strike Committee. He accused the Committee of exercising a "tyranny" over the Cantonese people and asserted that it was "only the unlawful activities of the Canton Strike Committee instigated by Bolshevik intrigue" which prevented the resumption of normal relations between Canton and Hongkong "on the old familiar footing."[27] A mass meeting was held in the Colony where the inaction of the British Government was condemned as weakness. According to a Reuter's dispatch, the audience argued that no help could be expected from the "anti-Red" groups in Canton until the British Government had assisted in expelling the clique which was "usurping" authority and which was "backed by Bolshevik commanders, advisers, machine guns and money." It was asserted that just as Hongkong had contributed generously when Great Britain went to the defense of Belgium in 1914, the British Government should support its colony in the present crisis.[28] A resolution was passed asking the British Government to intervene, by force if necessary, to end the strike and boycott. Intervention, it was said, would not involve hostilities elsewhere in China as the Cantonese authorities were not recognized by the Administration at Peking and all that was necessary was for the British Foreign Office to inform the Wai Chiao Pu in advance that the operations in Kwangtung were purely local.[29]

The Hongkong boycott ended officially on October 10, 1926. It had an important influence on the Chinese Revolution of 1925-1928, both in respect to its effect on developments within the Kuomintang, and in terms of China's relations with other nations. It is impossible within the framework of this study to present in any detail the complex history of the Kuomintang throughout these years. Nevertheless, for the sake of an understanding of later events, it is well to bear in mind that during the period of the Hongkong boycott, the Kuomintang was still operating as a coalition made up of many diverse political factions, and that the success of the boycott — because it had been achieved by labor groups — essentially increased the power of the left wing of the Party. This very fact, however, made the conservative members of the Kuomintang even more suspicious of the liberals

[26] *Ibid.*
[27] *Ibid.*, p. 982.
[28] *China Year Book*, 1926-27, p. 974.
[29] *Remer,* op. cit., p. 105.

and the radicals who were their working partners within the coalition, and even more fearful of the outcome of the Revolution.

While this affected the Powers eventually, people outside of China, and even foreigners within the country, continued to know little about the Kuomintang at this time. Until the summer of 1926, the Kuomintang governed only a small corner of China; and the Central Government of Peking, plus the warlords who were fighting over a vast area of the country, were still the main concern of other nations. Moreover, from the point of view of the interests of the Powers, the May 30th Incident, the anti-foreign agitation in cities throughout China, the Shameen Affair, and the Hong-kong boycott were all part of the same story which had only one meaning: however bitterly the Chinese might oppose each other on internal issues, they were united in their determination to have China achieve international independence, free from the restrictions imposed by the "unequal" treaties.

CHAPTER IV

STEPS TOWARD TREATY REVISION

Following the May 30th Incident in Shanghai, the State Department in Washington was deluged with messages from its officials in China. The need for furnishing the United States Government with a full and accurate picture of developments was obviously present. Questions of policy arose which included both immediate problems, such as the protection of American nationals, and long-term issues, such as the various phases of treaty revision which had been given a new and different aspect by the outbreak of the anti-foreign movement.

The urgency of the Chinese situation was further impressed. upon officials in the State Department through the unusual measures adopted by the American press. Contrary to a custom which has long been honored in its observance, news about China was lifted from the inside spaces of our papers and accorded the status of front-page "copy." The immediate reaction of most American editors to the May 30th Incident was one of confusion. The *Literary Digest* remarked that the dispatches in the American papers saw the "sudden blaze of anti-foreign hatred in China" as wholly different from previous manifestations of enmity against foreigners.[1] Such well-known publications as the Washington *Star*,[2] the Washington *Post*,[3] and the *New York Times*[4] stressed the great potential danger in the Chinese crisis. The conservative Detroit *Free Press* stated at once that the United States and Great Britain must co-operate and save China from the "Reds" and the "warlords,"[5] while the New York *Herald Tribune*[6] and the New York *Evening Post*[7] declared that the "red hand of Bolshevism" — as it was repeatedly called — was the instigator of the trouble in China. War between the Soviet Union and Japan — or the aggrandizement of Russia or Japan at the expense of China — was freely predicted as a result of the critical conditions reported to be developing in China.[8] On the other hand, as more

[1] *Literary Digest*, June 20, 1925, p. 12.
[2] *Ibid.*, p. 14.
[3] *Ibid.*, p. 12.
[4] Article by Thomas F. Millard in the *New York Times*, June 5, 1925, p. 1.
[5] *Literary Digest*, June 27, 1925, p. 13.
[6] *Ibid.*, June 20, 1925, p. 12.
[7] *Ibid.*, p. 12.
[8] See article in the *Literary Digest*, January 9, 1926, p. 8, "Critical Hours in China," which deals entirely with this subject.

news reached this country concerning the demands of the Chinese for a revision of the treaties, sympathy was shown for the Chinese claims by such influential publications as the New York *World*,[9] the New York *Evening World*,[10] the *New York Times*,[11] the Washington *Star*,[12] the Washington *Post*,[13] the Washington *News* (a Scripps-Howard paper),[14] the Baltimore *Sun*,[15] and the Philadelphia *Public Ledger*.[16] The New York *World*, for example, supported a stand in favor of the withdrawal of extraterritorial rights and declared that when other nations pulled their hands "out of Chinese pockets and away from Chinese throats," and accorded China the sovereign rights that were due every nation, the anti-foreign "crusade" would cease — "and not before."[17] The New York *Evening World* indicated its views briefly in the succint question: "Why should every nation in China have rights but China?"[18] The *New York Times* expressed itself with greater editorial caution, but urged a policy whereby the Powers would set a time limit that would allow for the gradual relinquishment of their treaty privileges in China.[19]

Although the interest of the American press settled down after a few months into a sporadic concern with the affairs of China, it is mentioned here to show the seriousness with which the May 30th Incident and the outbreak of the anti-foreign movement were treated in this country. While people in the United States were certainly not fully aware of the apprehension with which Americans in China regarded the situation, they nevertheless recognized the existence of a genuine crisis. The State Department, on its part, was subjected to the pressure arising both from the attitude of the public in the United States and of our nationals in China who were emphatically voicing their contradictory opinions.

In addition, it must be remembered that the State Department was being influenced by more than the events which developed in the year 1925. One important factor in the State Department's thinking was the recognition that a difficult situation had been created by the failure of the Powers to fulfill the commitments to China which had been made at the Washington Conference. As the treaty revision movement was in the forefront of

[9] *Literary Digest*, July 25, 1925, p. 8.
[10] *Ibid.*
[11] *Ibid.*
[12] *Ibid*, pp. 8-9.
[13] *Ibid*, October 10, 1925, p. 14.
[14] *Ibid*, September 12, 1925, p. 14.
[15] *Ibid.*, October 10, 1925, p. 14.
[16] *Ibid.*, July 25, 1925, p. 9.
[17] Quoted in *Peking Leader*, July 24, 1925, from editorial of June 18, 1925.
[18] *Literary Digest*, July 25, 1925, p. 8.
[19] *New York Times*, July 3, 1925.

people's minds during the period of the Chinese Revolution, it may be well to consider more fully certain aspects of that movement touched upon earlier.

Briefly stated, of all the demands made by the Chinese in respect to treaty revision, the most important were those concerned with extraterritorial and tariff controls. In 1902 and 1903, Great Britain, the United States, and Japan had concluded commercial treaties with China which dealt with both of these issues. In respect to extraterritoriality, a clause was inserted in all the treaties which was identic except for minor changes in wording; the clause in the American treaty read: "The Government of China having expressed a strong desire to reform its judicial system and to bring it into accord with that of Western nations, the United States agrees to give every assistance to such reform and will also be prepared to relinquish extraterritorial rights when satisfied that the state of the Chinese laws, the arrangements for their administration, and other considerations warrant it in so doing."[20]

In respect to the tariff, the treaties of 1902 and 1903 seemed to offer some hope to China of changing the tariff rate which had been imposed by agreements made in the middle of the nineteenth century and maintained ever since.[21] The 1902-03 treaties contemplated the levy of a surtax which would have raised the import duty to $12\frac{1}{2}$ percent, but this increase was made contingent upon the abolition by the Chinese of a system of taxation known as *likin*.[22] A further difficulty was also involved in that the consent of all the Treaty Powers had to be obtained before any modification of the tariff rates could be undertaken.[23]

Because of the provisos inserted in the terms of the 1902-03 agreements, no revision of the earlier agreements was made by the Treaty Powers at this time as far as the extraterritorial system was concerned and only slight modifications of the customs duties were effected.[24] Nevertheless the

[20] MacMurray, *Treaties and Agreements With and Concerning China*, 1894-1919, Vol. 1, p. 425, Article 4; see the Treaty with Great Britain, p. 347, Article 8, Section 2, and the Treaty with Japan, p. 411, Article 1.
[21] George H. Blakeslee, *The Pacific Area*, Boston, 1929, p. 6.
[22] Article IV of the American treaty. Mr. Stanley K. Hornbeck has defined *likin* in the following terms: "*Likin* was, in its original and strict meaning, a charge levied on goods in transit, calculated on the value of the goods, at the rate of one or more thousandths. But in a broad sense and in popular usage the term *likin* is *now* employed to designate collectively a broad category of taxes levied in various amounts and under a variety of names upon internal trade." (Harold S. Quigley and George H. Blakeslee, *The Far East*, Boston, 1928, p. 124, footnote; requoted from Mr. Hornbeck's *China Today: Political*.)
[23] George Nye Steiger, *China and the Occident*, Boston, 1944, p. 28.
[24] In 1902, 1918, and 1922, the Powers agreed, because of the general rise in prices, to allow increases in the specific customs duties in order to give China an effective 5 percent *ad valorem*. (Blakeslee, *op. cit.*, p. 6.)

Chinese regarded the provisions cited above as being in the nature of a pledge — however vague — which the Powers ought to redeem at some future time. This was brought out clearly in the memorandum, mentioned in the first chapter of this book, which the Chinese Delegation presented to the Versailles Conference in 1919. Recalling the clauses of the commercial treaties which dealt with the question of extraterritoriality, the memorandum stated that the issue to be decided was whether or not the "state of Chinese laws and the arrangements for their administration" had now reached "a point to satisfy the treaty Powers."[25] "While we do not claim," it was said, "that the Chinese laws and their administration have now reached such a state as has been attained by the most advanced nations, we do feel confident to assert that China has made very considerable progress in the administration of justice and in all matters pertaining thereto. . . ."[26] In view of the advance made, the Chinese asserted that the reasons for the introduction of consular jurisdiction into China had ceased to exist and that little more was necessary for a fulfillment of the conditions set forth in the treaties of 1902-03.[27] In order to meet these conditions fully, they were willing, they declared, (1) to promulgate five new codes of law (a Criminal, a Civil, and a Commercial Code, a Code of Civil Procedure and a Code of Criminal Procedure), and (2) to establish modern courts in all localities where foreigners resided.[28] China, they concluded, would complete these undertakings by the end of 1924 but, in return, she requested the treaty Powers "to give their promise" that upon the fulfillment of the above-mentioned conditions they would "at once relinquish their consular jurisdiction and the jurisdiction of their special courts . . . in China."[29]

In the same memorandum, the Chinese bitterly criticized the restrictions imposed by the treaty system on the Chinese tariff, stating that they were "unfair, unscientific, out of date" and not designed to "meet China's economic needs."[30] The fact that the customs duty could not be altered without the consent of all the Treaty Powers had, it was said, made it impossible to obtain any proper adjustment of the treaty rate for more than half a century.[31] The memorandum asked the Treaty Powers, represented at the Versailles Conference, to issue a declaration proclaiming that, at the end of a definite period to be fixed by mutual agreement, China should be

[25] "Questions for Readjustment Submitted by China to the Peace Conference," in *Chinese Social and Political Science Review*, 1919-1920, p. 135.
[26] *Ibid.*
[27] *Ibid.*, p. 136.
[28] *Ibid.*, p. 138. See also Chapter VIII, below.
[29] *Ibid.*, pp. 138-139.
[30] *Ibid.*, p. 153.
[31] *Ibid.*, p. 156.

"free to regulate, of her own accord, her customs tariff"; further, it requested that during this period the Powers negotiate with China tariff conventions which would be reciprocal in treatment, differentiate luxuries from neces- saries and have as the basis of the new rate on necessaries an import duty of not less than $12\frac{1}{2}$ percent.[32]

While, as we have already seen, the attempt of the Chinese to obtain a reconsideration of the treaty system at the Versailles Conference failed, certain substantial gains were made, from the Chinese viewpoint, during and after the first World War, in respect to the extraterritorial issue. When China declared war against Germany and Austria-Hungary in 1917, she abrogated the agreements and conventions existing between herself and those countries. This abrogation was formally acknowledged in the Treaties of Versailles, St. Germain, and Trianon. While no explicit reference was made to extraterritorial matters, the effect of the abrogation of the earlier agreements was to bring to an end the extraterritorial privileges of Ger- many, Austria, and Hungary. Moreover, Germany in 1921, and Austria in 1925, concluded new treaties with China specifically stating that their citizens were under the jurisdiction of Chinese courts.[33]

In addition, Russia was deprived of her extraterritorial rights in China by a decree of the Chinese Government issued in 1920. Four years later, on May 31, 1924, an agreement was signed between China and the Soviet Union in which it was declared that "The Government of the Union of Soviet Socialist Republics agrees to relinquish the rights of extraterri- toriality and consular jurisdiction"; Russian nationals were to be regarded, henceforth, as "entirely amenable to Chinese jurisdiction."[34]

As far as the other Treaty Powers were concerned, China, it will be recalled, renewed her assault on the treaty system at the Washington Con- ference. In a statement of Chinese demands presented by Dr. Sao-ke Alfred Sze, the Chinese Delegation requested that "immediately," or as soon as circumstances would permit, the "existing limitations upon China's political jurisdictional and administrative freedom of action" be removed.[35] Dr. Wang Chung-hui, one of China's foremost jurists, speaking on the extra- territorial issue, referred to the clauses concerning this subject inserted into the commercial treaties of 1902 and 1903 and said that while it was a matter of opinion as to whether or not the state of China's laws had attained the standard to which she was expected to conform, no one would deny that

[32] *Ibid.*, p. 161.
[33] W. W. Willoughby, *Foreign Rights and Interests in China*, Baltimore, 1927, Vol. 2, pp. 577-579; Blakeslee, *op. cit.*, p. 27.
[34] Willoughby, *op. cit.*, pp. 579-586.
[35] *Conference on the Limitation of Armaments* (United States Government document, proceedings of the Conference), Washington, D. C., 1925, p. 868.

she had made great progress. China did not, he told the Conference, desire the "immediate and complete abolition of extraterritoriality" but wished rather to invite the Powers to co-operate "in taking the initial steps toward improving and eventually abolishing the existing system." In the name of the Chinese Delegates, he asked that the Powers agree to relinquish their extraterritorial rights at the end of a definite period, and that they negotiate with China for the adoption of a plan "for progressive modification and ultimate abolition of the system of extraterritoriality in China," to be carried out within the period that had been agreed upon.[36]

In responding to Dr. Wang, the American Secretary of State, Mr. Charles Evans Hughes, said that he believed that the principles which the United States, Great Britain, and Japan wished to follow had been laid down in the commercial agreements of 1902 and 1903, so that the remaining issues were primarily questions of fact. "What," he asked, "is the state of the administration of justice in China? What are the laws? And how are they administered?" Whatever steps were taken in the future, Mr. Hughes declared, they should in his opinion be preceded by an inquiry into existing conditions for the purpose of obtaining "a very definite notion" of the administration of justice in China.[37]

On Mr. Hughes' recommendation, a sub-committee was appointed which drafted a resolution on extraterritoriality that was subsequently accepted by the Conference.[38] The resolution declared that the Powers would establish a Commission "to inquire into the present practice of extraterritorial jurisdiction in China, and into the laws and the judicial system and the methods of judicial administration of China," with a view to reporting to the governments of the Powers concerned their "findings of fact" and "their recommendations" as to such means as they found suitable to improve the existing conditions of justice in China, and to further the efforts of the Chinese Government to effect legislation and reforms that would warrant the Powers "in relinquishing, either progressively or otherwise, their respective rights of extraterritoriality." Each of the Powers was, however, to be left "free to accept or to reject all or any portion of the recommendations of the Commission." The Commission was to be constituted within three months after the adjournment of the Washington Conference and to complete a report within a year of its first meeting.

From the point of view of Sino-foreign relations, the most important effect of this resolution was that it disappointed the hope of the Chinese that a definite date would be fixed for the relinquishment of extraterri-

---

[36] Dr. Wang's speech quoted, *ibid.*, pp. 934-936.
[37] Mr. Hughes' speech quoted, *ibid.*, p. 936.
[38] *Ibid.*, p. 938. For text of resolution, see *ibid.*, p. 1644.

torial rights, and that it substituted, in the place of a definite program looking to the abolition of extraterritoriality, a commission of inquiry which had only the power to make a general survey of conditions and offer recommendations which the foreign governments might accept or reject as they saw fit.

The attitude adopted at the Washington Conference toward the extraterritorial issue was paralleled by the attitude taken toward the restoration of tariff autonomy to China. In one of the early sessions of the Conference, Dr. Wellington Koo, speaking for the Chinese Delegation, asked for the release of China from tariff control.[39] He supplemented this request with the statement that, as it would take some time to establish the new régime, certain *interim* measures should be considered that would increase the customs duty first to $12\frac{1}{2}$ percent and then to a higher rate.[40]

The tariff issue was referred to a sub-Committee which entered into a prolonged debate on the subject that lasted many weeks.[41] The resolution that was finally framed omitted any reference to tariff autonomy.[42] Instead it recommended that immediate steps be taken to hold a Special Conference representing China and the Powers, which should prepare the way for the speedy abolition of *likin,* with a view to increasing the Chinese import tariff to the $12\frac{1}{2}$ percent mentioned in the 1902-03 commercial treaties. As an *interim* measure, the Conference was to authorize the levy of a surtax of not more than 5 percent *ad valorem* on luxuries and $2\frac{1}{2}$ percent on other imports, "as from such date, for such purposes, and subject to such conditions as it might determine." The terms of the resolution were to be incorporated in a tariff treaty and the Conference was to be convened within three months after the treaty came into force.

Upon the presentation of this resolution to the Committee as a whole, Dr. Koo expressed the keen disappointment of the Chinese Delegation that their demand for tariff autonomy had been set aside. "The Chinese Delegation," he said, "cannot but wish that a different view had prevailed. Tariff autonomy is a sovereign right enjoyed by all independent states. Its free exercise is essential to the well-being of a State." Furthermore, he added, the restoration of tariff autonomy to China meant merely the recognition of a right which was hers and which she had relinquished against her will.[43]

These remarks Dr. Koo supplemented with a statement that had an important bearing on the future:

[39] *Ibid.,* p. 920.
[40] *Ibid.,* p. 924.
[41] See Willoughby, *China at the Conference,* Chapter VII, *passim.*
[42] *Conference on the Limitation of Armaments,* text of the resolution, pp. 1630-1638.
[43] *Ibid.,* pp. 308, 1176.

In view of the inherent difficulty and injustice of the present regime and of the wholesome and desirable effect which restoration of tariff autonomy is sure to have upon the trade and economic development of China, as well as upon the evolution of her fiscal system, the Chinese Delegation feels in duty bound to declare that though this Committee does not see its way to consider China's claim for the restoration of her tariff autonomy, it is not their desire in assenting to the agreement now before you, to relinquish their claim; *on the contrary, it is their intention to bring the request up again for consideration on all appropriate occasions in the future.*[44]

The tariff resolution was incorporated into a Tariff Treaty and accepted by the Conference Delegates for reference to their various governments. The American Senator, Oscar W. Underwood, who had been Chairman of the sub-Committee which drafted the resolution, went out of his way to explain the attitude of the members of the sub-Committee.[45] According to his analysis, they had been convinced that, because of the unsettled conditions existing in China, tariff autonomy "would probably work in the end" to the "injury" both of China and of the world. If he was a judge of the situation, he said, or of the temper of conditions throughout the world, when "China established a parliamentary government of all the provinces of China and dispensed with the military control that now existed in many of the provinces . . . so that the outside Powers might feel that they were dealing with a Government that had entire and absolute and free control of the situation, China could expect to realize the great ideals of sovereignty" that she had asked for at the conference table.

By the close of the Washington Conference, the Treaty Powers had, therefore, expressed the intention of constituting a Commission on Extraterritoriality within three months following the adjournment of the Conference, and of convening a Special Conference on the Chinese Customs Tariff within three months after the effective date of the Tariff Treaty. But the road to the realization of these plans was to present many unexpected obstacles. The Commission on Extraterritoriality was, according to the terms of the resolution, to meet by May 6, 1922.[46] As it appeared advisable to make certain preparations (such as the translation of Chinese law codes) in advance, the Chinese and foreign governments agreed to postpone the meeting of the Commission until the fall of 1923.[47] In the meantime, however, further and more serious trouble arose through the constant deterioration of the political conditions in China, culminating in the ousting of Li Yuan-hung, President of the Chinese Republic, in June, 1923, which

[44] *Ibid.,* pp. 312, 1180. Italics not in original.
[45] *Ibid.* Senator Underwood's statement is quoted on p. 1182.
[46] Pollard, *China's Foreign Relations, 1917-1931,* p. 256.
[47] *Ibid.*

was followed by a period when there was no organized authority at Peking.[48] These circumstances led a number of the Treaty Powers to feel that it would be impossible to achieve constructive results from any discussion conducted at this time on the abolition of extraterritoriality.[49] Nevertheless, when the government of Marshal Ts'ao K'un was established in October, 1923, the United States, prompted by the Chinese Minister at Washington, proposed that the Commission on Extraterritoriality should start its work in November, 1924.[50] Unfortunately this suggestion encountered new difficulties in the form of objections raised by the French Government which had entered into a controversy with the Chinese Foreign Office that is generally known as the "gold-franc dispute."[51]

The point at issue between the Chinese and the French was the manner in which China should pay the remaining installments of the Boxer Indemnity.[52] The Chinese Government wished to discharge its obligations in francs, while the French insisted on receiving "gold" francs at the rate of exchange which had prevailed before the World War. The matter could only be settled by an agreement on the legal interpretation of the documents governing the Boxer settlement. Although it was evident that it would take some time to reach a solution of the problem, the French took the position that they would not co-operate in the next steps of the program adopted at the Washington Conference until the gold-franc dispute had been adjusted. This applied not only to the investigation to be made by the Extraterritorial Commission but also to the ratification of the Tariff Treaty.

Early in 1925, however, the situation assumed a more promising aspect and, in April of that year, the Chinese and French Governments reached an agreement through compromise.[53] Three months later the French Government ratified the Washington Treaty on the Chinese Customs Tariff, which consequently came into force on August 5, 1925.[54]

When, therefore, in their demonstrations against foreigners in 1925, the Chinese denounced the policy of the Treaty Powers, the United States Government, together with most of the other governments involved, felt that it had been placed in an unfortunate position by the failure to meet the obligations assumed at the Washington Conference. The tendency of

[48] *Ibid.*, p. 258.
[49] *Ibid.*
[50] *Ibid.*, p. 259.
[51] *Ibid.*
[52] The facts concerning the gold-franc dispute related here are taken from *ibid.*, pp. 260-266.
[53] *Ibid.*, p. 266.
[54] *Foreign Relations* (1925), p. 761.

the Powers, as will be seen, was to regard the Washington Conference program as a fixed base, representative of the kind of commitments that they had been willing to make up to this time, and from which they might move forward at whatever pace they believed was justified by conditions in China. A major part of the demands being made by the Chinese, on the other hand, went far beyond anything that had been agreed upon at Washington.

It was not long before the impact of the anti-foreign movement upon the spiritless government at Peking forced the latter into action. On June 24, 1925, the Chinese Foreign Office delivered two notes to the Powers. In the first, it said that although the Chinese Government had repeatedly approached the foreign Powers for a readjustment of its treaty relations — notably at the Versailles and Washington Conferences — "very little" had been accomplished in substantial results.[55] At the time that China joined the Allied and Associated Powers in the World War, the note continued, she was encouraged to hope for a definite improvement in her international status:

> Great therefore must be [the] disappointment to her people when after the Great War had been won and the common cause achieved, her own international status should remain unimproved and is in some respects even inferior to that of the defeated nations for in [none] of them do we find the existence of extraterritorial courts, foreign concessions, leased territories and an externally imposed conventional tariff.

Written in moderate terms, the note asked for a readjustment of China's treaty relations so that they would conform with the "legitimate national aspirations" of the Chinese people. It asserted that the "inequalities" of the treaty system and the extraordinary privileges granted to foreigners would always prove a source of friction between China and the Powers and must inevitably result in further catastrophes such as the incident at Shanghai on May 30th. It declared that the treaties had been designed in the first instance largely to meet the exigencies of a particular time and that, the situation having greatly changed, the special privileges conferred on foreigners were no longer warranted by circumstances. In closing, the hope was expressed that the foreign governments would "fully appreciate the mutual advantages" to be derived from a proper revision of the treaties and would therefore give "an encouraging response" to the proposal of the Chinese Government.

The second communication sent to the Powers by the Chinese Government, on June 24, was the note already quoted which contained thirteen

[55] Text of note, *ibid.*, p. 763.

specific demands that were presented as "part of the questions" to be settled in connection with the May 30th Incident, the remainder being covered by an over-all request for the revision of the treaties.[56]

On the receipt of these messages from the Chinese Foreign Office, Secretary of State Kellogg sent a cable to Ferdinand L. Mayer, then in charge of the American Legation at Peking, that constituted a significant expression of the attitude with which the State Department in Washington approached the situation in China:

> Department feels that the Chinese proposal should be made the occasion of evidencing to the Chinese our willingness to consider sympathetically and helpfully the modification of existing treaties in measure as the Chinese authorities demonstrate their willingness and ability to fulfill their obligations and to assume the protection of the foreign rights and interests now safeguarded by the exceptional provisions of existing treaties.
>
> In discussing with your colleagues the text of the reply which each will make to the identic notes of the Chinese Foreign Office of June 24 you will take occasion to impress upon them this Government's desire that the Powers concerned expedite preparations for the holding of the Special Conference regarding Chinese customs tariff stating that this Government believes that that Conference should be requested, after accomplishing the work required by the treaty, to make concrete recommendations upon which a program for granting complete tariff autonomy to China may be worked out. You will also make clear to your colleagues this Government's desire that the preparations for the despatch of the Commission to investigate the question of extraterritoriality be proceeded with without delay and state that this Government feels that this Commission should be requested to include in its report recommendations upon which a program for the gradual relinquishment of extraterritorial rights may be based which may be carried out *pari passu* with steps to be taken by the Chinese Government looking to the adoption of laws and the establishment of legal institutions capable of giving legitimate foreign interests the protection now given under the treaties.[57]

The most significant elements in Mr. Kellogg's reaction to the Chinese request for a thorough revision of the treaties were his attitude of sympathy and his willingness to proceed beyond the precise commitments made at

[56] *Ibid.*, p. 670. See above, pp. 30-31.

[57] *Ibid.*, p. 767. The suggestion that the United States should adopt a policy that would exceed the letter of the Washington resolutions, in order to consider plans for the gradual abolition of extraterritoriality and of tariff controls, appears to have been made originally by Nelson T. Johnson, then Chief of the Division of Far Eastern Affairs in the State Department. Mr. Johnson made this suggestion at an interview between the Chinese Minister and the Secretary of State, held in Washington on June 30, 1925, which Mr. Johnson attended. (For details, see *Foreign Relations*, 1925, p. 769.) The instructions to the American Legation at Peking quoted above were sent July 1, 1925.

the Washington Conference. It soon became apparent, however, that to the British Foreign Office the views of the Secretary seemed in some respects more generous than the situation warranted.

The difference between the British and American Governments lay not so much in the actual measures they were willing to adopt as in the manner in which they were disposed to execute them. While the State Department was anxious to approach the situation in a decidedly conciliatory spirit, the Foreign Office believed that conditions called for the assumption of a severe, if not a threatening, tone. The British position was clearly indicated in the draft of a statement, intended for use as an identic reply by the Powers to the Chinese note of June 24th, and sent to Washington by the Foreign Office on July 7th. The first part of the text contained views corresponding to those set forth by Mr. Kellogg in his instructions to the United States Legation at Peking.[58] It urged the speedy convocation of the Tariff Conference; asserted that the agreement to be made in respect to the Chinese tariff ought to be "of a more far-reaching and comprehensive nature" than that contemplated in the Washington Customs Treaty; and expressed the hope that the Tariff Conference would be "but the first step in a comprehensive revision of the treaties.[59] But these assertions were qualified by the following statements concerning the attitude the Powers might adopt if they were compelled to relinquish their treaty position through force rather than given the opportunity to alter it through negotiations:

The agitation now proceeding, unless the Powers have misjudged it, is pregnant with graver responsibilities than the mere disintegration of responsible authority. It seems to be taking the form of an organized movement designed to extort forcibly from the Powers the unconditional abandonment of their rights and obligations conferred upon them by the present treaties. The Powers hope that they are mistaken in this estimation, but they feel it their duty solemnly to warn the Chinese Government that should these apprehensions be justified, an entirely new situation will be created in which not only will the hope of the Powers for constructive cooperation with China be frustrated but they will be obliged to consult together as to the immediate measures necessary to protect their interests until the realization of these hopes shall again become possible.[60]

A communication sent to the State Department in conjunction with the draft reply explained the omission of any direct reference to the question of extraterritorial rights. His Majesty's Government declared that they were in full accord with Washington's views regarding the relinquishment

[58] *Ibid.*, p. 775. The British Foreign Office had been informed of the content of the instructions sent by the State Department to the American Legation.
[59] *Ibid.*, p. 776.
[60] *Ibid.*, p. 777.

of extraterritoriality (as set forth in the instructions to the American Legation), but that they felt that any indication at this time that the Powers were willing to go to such lengths in meeting the Chinese demands in this respect was "fraught with danger and liable to be regarded as a capitulation."[61]

The State Department viewed the British dispatches in a spirit of frank criticism. In a note to the British Government, Secretary Kellogg took the position that this was not the proper time to issue a public statement on the conditions developing in China.[62] Moreover, he asserted that

This Government feels very definitely . . . that the growing spirit of national unrest in China, which, in this present situation, is being encouraged by radical statements and ideas emanating from those holding revolutionary theories regarding Government and the relations of states, must be met by something more concrete than mere promises of action such as were written into the new commercial treaties which followed the settlement of the Boxer uprisings in 1900. It feels, furthermore, very strongly that this condition in China can best be met by consistent and scrupulous observance by the Powers of the obligations already undertaken by them at the Washington Conference for the alleviation of what the Chinese regard as anomalous inequalities imposed upon them by former treaties. While it might with truth be urged that government in China today is ineffective, it may also be said that little opportunity is given to any section of the Chinese people to make their government effective because of a continued scarcity of funds necessary to the maintenance of good and effective government. In so far as an import tariff can serve to furnish funds for government purposes the Treaty Powers cannot escape a certain direct responsibility due to the positive control that they exercise over Chinese customs receipts . . . and the least that these Powers can do is to agree to an early calling of the Conference on Chinese Tariff provided for in the Treaty of February 6, 1922. Public opinion in the United States definitely favors some such course.

In the same note, Mr. Kellogg made the following observations concerning the British Government's views on the immediate treatment of the extraterritorial issue:

You state in your Note of July 3, 1925, that the British Government is somewhat apprehensive lest the Chinese Government interpret a promise to expedite the meeting of the Commission on Extraterritoriality as a sign of weakness on the part of the Powers. This Government does not share in that apprehension. It, as well as other Governments which participated in the Washington Conference in the autumn of 1921, affixed its signature in good faith to the Resolution regarding extraterritoriality in China. . . . The conditions which now prevail in China differ only in degree from those

[61] Ibid.
[62] Text of note, ibid., pp. 780-783.

which prevailed while the Resolution was being adopted and since its adoption. This Government cannot recognize that any such condition prevails which would invalidate its undertakings embodied in the Resolution. This Government cannot believe that a policy which consists in carrying out agreements undertaken in good faith and already overdue can be interpreted as a sign of weakness.

In respect to his statement to the American Legation at Peking, that the United States Government desired to have the Commission on Extraterritoriality make recommendations which might furnish a basis for a program aiming at the gradual relinquishment of extraterritorial rights, Mr. Kellogg explained in his note to the British that he deemed it wise "to go beyond the mere letter" of the Washington resolution in order to have "some feasible plan of action for the future."

Setting aside the British draft reply to the Chinese note, the Department of State formulated its own response which it communicated for consideration to the other interested foreign Powers on July 23, 1925.[63] This document proved to be an important and comprehensive statement of American policy.[64] That it was designed to express the friendliest feelings toward the Chinese was evident in the opening sentences:

Careful consideration has been given to the important questions raised in the Note of the Chinese Government by the Government of the United States which has for some time been aware of the growing feeling in China in favor of a readjustment of the Chinese treaty relations with the foreign Powers, and has watched the growth of that sentiment with a constant and sympathetic interest. It is believed that the Chinese Government does not require to be reminded of the concrete evidence of this interest which has been made manifest on each occasion when a question of treaty revision has occupied the attention of the two countries. The United States is now prepared to consider sympathetically and helpfully the Chinese Government's proposal for the modification of existing treaties in measure as the Chinese authorities demonstrate their willingness and ability to fulfill their obligations. . . .

The draft note then proceeded to review the situation in respect to the customs tariff, stating that the United States sympathized with the feeling of the Chinese that the existing tariff schedules constituted a severe handicap on China's ability to adjust her duties to her economic needs. With respect to the reform of the Chinese judicial system, it expressed the American Government's gratification at the progress made during the last quarter century, but pointed out that in recent years the lack of a stable

[63] *Ibid.*, p. 793.
[64] Text, *ibid.*, pp. 795-797.

government in China had made it difficult for courts and judiciary to exercise their functions in a normal manner.

The most important sections of the declaration dealt with the immediate measures the United States was willing to take. First, it laid down as a general principle the necessity of maintaining a "constant and scrupulous observance" of the obligations entered into at the Washington Conference. Next, the United States Government declared its readiness to appoint delegates to the Tariff Conference and expressed its willingness "to accept any reasonable proposal for extending the scope of that Conference to enable it to deal fully and completely with all matters related to its purpose." To this it added the statement that it was prepared "either at the Tariff Conference or at a subsequent time, to take up the subject of a comprehensive revision of the treaties, looking toward ultimate tariff autonomy." Lastly, the desire was expressed to send a commission to China to examine the whole question of extraterritoriality "in the expectation that the investigation . . . will help to guide the Treaty Powers as to what, if any, steps should be taken as regards the relinquishment by gradual means, or otherwise, of extraterritorial rights at this time."

When the American draft was communicated to the representatives of the other Powers at Peking with the suggestion that it might form the text of an identic reply to the Chinese note, it met with considerable opposition. The British Foreign Office complained to the State Department that the tone of the text was too "encouraging." Moreover, they felt that the reference to the ultimate grant of tariff autonomy was "both gratuitous and likely to encourage Chinese pretensions unnecessarily," and that the request for recommendations concerning the steps that might be taken leading to the abolition of extraterritoriality was ill-advised as the Commissioners should be left free to make any recommendations they desired without "a lead from the Powers."[65] While willing to make concessions on the first points to the extent of deleting some of the more sympathetic phrases of the original text[66] and of omitting any specific mention of tariff autonomy, Secretary Kellogg stood his ground on the third issue, insisting that the draft left the Extraterritorial Commission entirely free to exercise its own judgment.[67] The British thereupon accepted the State Department's views and adopted the American draft on August 11th; in doing so they frankly

[65] *Ibid.*, p. 805.
[66] A number of phrases were deleted, such as that the United States had felt a *constant and sympathetic interest* toward the movement for treaty revision, and that it was prepared to consider *sympathetically and helpfully* the Chinese proposal for a readjustment of treaty relations.
[67] *Ibid.*, p. 815.

admitted, however, that they were to a large extent motivated by their desire to maintain a solid front among the Treaty Powers.[68]

While this exchange of opinion was being carried on between Washington and London, the Japanese were crystallizing their ideas. In general, they regarded the British attitude as "too stiff" and the American attitude as too liberal. On the whole, they were more receptive to the Chinese demand for the abolition of the extraterritorial system than to the request for tariff autonomy.[69] In respect to the latter, they voiced decided objections to entering into any discussion that went beyond the terms specified in the Washington Customs Tariff Treaty. Furthermore, they were opposed to the idea of a "comprehensive revision of the treaties," as advanced by both the Americans and the British, and maintained that the magnitude of Japanese interests in China would render any such procedure "extremely difficult."[70] On the positive side, the Japanese expressed their earnest desire for a compromise, declaring that they desired "above all things" to maintain joint action with the United States and Great Britain.[71]

The Japanese attitude made it difficult to find a solution acceptable to all the nations concerned, and for a while it looked as though no agreement would be reached on the text of an identic note. In the meantime the governments of the other Powers were gradually shaping their views. The Italians and Dutch indicated that they were in favor of the draft submitted by the United States Government.[72] The French criticized the British text as "too sharp" and the American as "too mild and liberal" but, beyond that, reserved judgment for the time being.[73]

Criticism of the American draft reply to the Chinese note was not, however, made solely by the officials of foreign governments. After a discussion with the Japanese Minister in Peking, who explained the unwillingness of his Government to subscribe to the American draft in so far as it conveyed a formal promise to consider tariff autonomy at the Special Tariff Conference, Mr. MacMurray cabled to Washington:

I have . . . ventured to tell my Japanese colleague that I would be willing to convey to you . . . an explanation of my personal view that it would not be tacitly [tactically?] sound to announce publicly at this time that we are prepared to go beyond the terms of the Washington Conference provisions lest we should thus prejudice the possibility of our restraining the importunities of artificially formed unions of coolies and schoolboys who are organizing to uphold diplomatic relations of the Government.

[68] *Ibid.*
[69] *Ibid.*, pp. 806, 808, 812, 818.
[70] *Ibid.*, p. 818.
[71] *Ibid.*, p. 812.
[72] *Ibid.*, p. 816.
[73] *Ibid.*

... Seeking, however, to detach myself from my preconceptions that antedated a first-hand experience of the abnormal Chinese reaction to the Shanghai Incident of May 30th, I cannot but acknowledge (if the Department desires my frank opinion) that it would be wiser to adhere literally to the provisions of the Washington Conference and let any developments therefrom be recommended by the Special Conference, rather than anticipate them at this time when even the most reasonable concession is liable to be interpreted as an abdication on principle of rights which we possess and ought not to surrender except upon adequate assurances of at least an honest effort to extend to our interests the treatment that one civilized government accords to the citizens of another. That is not now the case and I foresee no possibility of its being the case so long as China continues to be a congeries of competing military factions. We are in fact dealing not with a government but a simulacrum which there are certain obvious political conveniences in recognizing. To go beyond the letter and beyond the spirit of our Washington Treaty obligations in recognizing the hypothetical sovereignty of that government is not only to exceed what I recall as the purposes of the Washington Conference but also to encourage a spirit of irresponsibility with which even the soberest Chinese have recently been infected through various Bolshevik and juvenile nationalistic influences.[74]

In the midst of these complications, created by the diversity of opinion among officials representing the foreign Powers, the Chinese Government, on August 19th, issued an invitation to the Treaty Powers to attend the Special Conference on the Chinese Customs Tariff which was to be convened at Peking on October 26th, 1925. The actual content of the Chinese note was extremely significant as it indicated that the Chinese Government intended to introduce the issue of tariff autonomy at the earliest possible moment:

... it may be recalled that on January 5, 1922, at the Washington Conference, the Chinese Delegation ... declared that it was their intention to bring up again the question of the restoration to China of her tariff autonomy for consideration on all appropriate occasions in the future. In pursuance of the above declaration the Chinese Government proposes that the said question be also brought up at the forthcoming conference and expects some arrangement will be made to remove the tariff restrictions hitherto imposed on China.[75]

On the day following the issuance of the Chinese invitation to the Tariff Conference, the Japanese Government announced its willingness to accept the American draft reply with certain amendments. There was to be no reference to any extension of the scope of the Tariff Conference or to

[74] *Ibid.*, p. 809.
[75] *Ibid.*, p. 839.

ultimate tariff autonomy, and the phrase, "comprehensive revision of the Treaties," was to be omitted.[76]

With this the controversy concerning the policies of the various Powers prior to the meeting of the Special Conference on the Chinese Customs Tariff and the Commission on Extraterritoriality drew to a close. Secretary Kellogg accepted the Japanese proposals in respect to the American text and, by September 1st, the representatives of all the Treaty Powers had endorsed the amended version of the draft. On September 4th, identic notes were dispatched to the Chinese Government.[77]

On September 2nd — before the reply of the Powers reached the Peking authorities — Secretary of State Kellogg delivered an address on American policy in respect to Chinese affairs at a meeting of the American Bar Association in Detroit.[78] He declared that the essentials of United States policy were ". . . to respect the sovereignty and territorial integrity of China, to encourage the development of an effective stable government, to maintain the 'open door' or equal opportunity for the trade of nationals of all countries, to carry out scrupulously the obligations and promises made to China at the Washington Conference, and to require China to perform the obligations of a sovereign state in the protection of foreign citizens and their property."

Reviewing China's treaty relations with the Powers, Mr. Kellogg emphasized the increasing strength of the movement for treaty revision, which he ascribed to "an advance in education and a growing feeling of nationalism among the Chinese." In dealing with the forthcoming Tariff Conference and the appointment of the Commission on Extraterritoriality, the Secretary repeated many of the ideas, and even much of the phraseology, which had been agreed upon by the Powers for the text of the identic note to be delivered to the Peking Government. At the same time, however, he used the occasion to express the views which had been deleted from the note in deference to the wishes of the British and Japanese. Thus, in discussing the Tariff Conference he stated that it was his belief that the Powers had "all come to the conclusion" that the Conference would have to be "broadened beyond the strict letter of the Washington Treaty." For its own part, the United States was willing, he declared, either at the Tariff Conference or at some subsequent time to consider "a comprehensive revision of the treaties dealing with the entire subject of the tariff."[79] Similarly, he reverted to the tone of sympathy which he had employed at the beginning of the negotia-

[76] *Ibid.*, p. 821.
[77] Text of American note, *ibid.*, p. 831.
[78] Text in *ibid.*, pp. 823-830.
[79] *Ibid.*, p. 828.

tions for the identic note and which had been criticized by the representatives of other governments as too encouraging to Chinese "pretensions." Referring, for example, to the desire of the Chinese to be relieved of extraterritorial restrictions, he said that the American people sympathized with these aspirations and that the United States Government would be willing to give up extraterritorial rights as soon as China demonstrated that her laws and judicial system were adequate for the protection of foreigners.[80] In an equally conciliatory vein, he asserted that while the "riots and anti-foreign demonstrations" in China were making a readjustment of treaty relations difficult, they did not constitute a "reason why the United States and other Powers should not scrupulously adhere to the pledges they made to China in the Washington Conference to meet her in the spirit of helpfulness with the hope that she may realize her ambitions."[81] Through his concluding remarks, he assured the Chinese that the people of the United States did not "wish to control, by treaty or otherwise, the internal policies of China, to fix its tariffs, or establish and administer courts" but that, on the contrary, they looked forward to the day when this would not be necessary.[82]

In addition to announcing that the Special Conference on the Chinese Customs Tariff would convene at Peking in October, 1925, the Secretary of State declared that the United States had appointed as its representatives to the Conference, the American Minister, Mr. MacMurray, and Silas H. Strawn, a lawyer from Chicago.[83] In his instructions to the American Delegation written in September and early October of 1925, Mr. Kellogg amplified the views set forth in his public statements, defining his attitude in unmistakable terms:

It has been my idea from the beginning that within the near future we would have to release China from its conventional tariffs and give up extraterritoriality. That is the trend of modern events in relationship to all self-governing countries where extraterritorial privileges have existed. It is reasonable to suppose that a great nation like China will not long permit foreign control of its domestic affairs. It was with a view to meeting what I believe to be a growing demand in China that I shaped the policy outlined in the note of the Nine Powers and in my speech at Detroit. I believed then and I believe now that such action will go further toward alleviating the anti-foreign sentiment in China than anything else. It is my desire, therefore, if we can work out a plan whereby tariff autonomy will now or eventually be given to China and extraterritoriality given up, that this be done and that you bear this in mind in your negotiations. I believe also that this meets the approval of the great body of American sentiment and will be approved by

---

[80] *Ibid.*, p. 829.
[81] *Ibid.*, p. 830.
[82] *Ibid.*
[83] *Ibid.*, p. 829.

the Senate and the Congress. . . . A middle ground might be found . . .
whereby the Powers renounce in principle conventional tariffs and China
levies certain rates for a term of years which would insure protection of
foreign interests. This might satisfy the Chinese sentiment and the public
sentiment of this country and assure that definite steps had been taken for
the renunciation of tariff control. I am not, of course, prepared to say that
it is wise for us to declare for unconditional surrender of conventional
tariffs and extraterritoriality at once. We may be driven to this position
if the Powers are not willing to make reasonable concessions.[84]

In another set of instructions, the Secretary explained that he desired
to work out a program which would take into account both the aspirations
of the Chinese and the problems confronting foreigners as a result of the
critical situation existing in China:

Until the last few months, it had been the belief of this Government,
and presumably that of the other foreign Governments concerned, that the
provisions of the [Washington] Customs Treaty would suffice for the present
to meet the Chinese desires on the subject of tariff revision. The events of
the last few months have, however, made it evident that these provisions
will not satisfy those desires as a step in progress toward ultimate tariff
autonomy. Chinese aspirations toward freedom from what they consider
to be oppressive restrictions imposed upon them by the Powers are not confined to customs matters alone, but embrace other subjects upon which they
are equally insistent that radical changes be made. I am sympathetic with
the aims of the Chinese, and desire to bring about such modifications in our
treaties with China as may be just and practicable; but I do not desire to
apply abstract principles in disregard of actual conditions in China and of
such practical courses of action as may be recommended by a careful consideration of these conditions. I am of the opinion, however, that, with
respect to the Tariff, the Special Conference ought to go beyond the strict
scope of its activities as defined in the Customs Treaty and enter into a discussion of the entire subject of the conventional tariff, even including proposals looking toward ultimate tariff autonomy. I am also of the opinion
that other subjects dealt with in our treaties with China deserve reconsideration at an early date and that the Special Conference may well serve as the
first step toward a consideration of these matters.[85]

In respect to the attitude with which the American Delegation should
approach the work of the Tariff Conference, Mr. Kellogg made the following statements during the course of his instructions:

I am of the opinion that the ultimate interests of the United States will
best be served by your work being approached in the broadest spirit and
with the purpose of rendering the utmost possible contribution to the improvement of trade and of the general welfare in China. . . .[86]

[84] *Ibid.*, p. 849.
[85] *Ibid.*, p. 842.
[86] *Ibid.*, p. 843.

We are going into the forthcoming Conference seriously to co-operate with China in arriving at some workable solution of the question of the Chinese tariff, which will go so far as it is fair to go in satisfying the nationalistic aspirations of the Chinese and yet insure American trade freedom from unequal or discriminatory treatment. If we cannot do this in co-operation with the other Powers at this Conference we must then negotiate separately. . . .[87]

I feel that much can be accomplished . . . if emphasis is laid upon our sincere desire to co-operate rather than dictate to the Chinese in these matters.[88]

In respect to the specific provisions of a treaty which would be acceptable to the United States, Mr. Kellogg suggested: (a) the recognition in principle of tariff autonomy for China; (b) a guarantee of most-favored-nation treatment for American commerce; (c) the acceptance of a Chinese general tariff to be applied for a specific period; (d) a decision at the end of this period as to whether to continue (or revise) the general tariff, or to restore complete tariff autonomy to China.[89]

Almost two months after the Special Tariff Conference had held its opening session at Peking, Mr. Kellogg, on December 14, 1925, delivered an address before the Council on Foreign Relations in New York, in which he further expressed his views to the public in a statement that marked the end of the first phase of American policy during his administration:

I have every hope that the aspirations of China to regain the control over her tariffs and to establish the jurisdiction of her courts over foreigners living within her borders will be worked out by the Conference [on the Chinese Customs Tariff] with the assistance of the Commission on Extraterritoriality.

It must not be forgotten, however, that the tariff conventions and extraterritorial rights were not forced upon China for the purpose of extending foreign influence but were made by mutual agreement for the purposes of aiding commerce, protecting foreign citizens, and settling long-standing, difficult questions between China and the other nations. I believe the time has passed when nations capable of maintaining self-government can be expected to permit foreign control and domination. Nevertheless one of the difficulties with which foreign countries have to deal in the case of China is the instability of its government and the constant warfare between various contending factions. China is a great nation; it has made wonderful progress and is now struggling to maintain a republic. In this she has the sympathy and the good will of the American people and everything that we can legitimately do to aid her, will be done.[90]

[87] *Ibid.*, p. 855.
[88] *Ibid.*, p. 858.
[89] *Ibid.*
[90] *Foreign Affairs*, Special Supplement, Vol. 4, No. 2.

Chapter V

MISSIONARY OPINION

MISSIONARY OPINION IN THE UNITED STATES

While the United States was groping for a policy that would meet the threatening tide of anti-foreign feeling in China, one section of the American public was expressing its views with little hesitation. This section consisted of the Protestant missionary societies within the United States which, shortly after it became known that Mr. Kellogg was in favor of convening the Special Tariff Conference and the Commission on Extraterritoriality, issued official statements setting forth their convictions.[1]

The proportion of the total interests of the United States in China that was directly or indirectly related to the work of missionaries was very great indeed. Between four and five thousand American Protestant missionaries[2] were living in China in 1925, out of a total American community of approximately 9,800.[3] The annual expenditure in China of American mission societies was in the neighborhood of $10,000,000[4] and while estimates concerning their property holdings varied, the lowest estimate valued them at $43,000,000.[5]

[1] The American Catholic missionary movement in China was in its infancy at this time, and there is no indication that American Catholic missionaries took an official stand on Chinese political issues. Nor has the writer been able to find any significant material on the attitude of the Catholic Church toward the Chinese demands for treaty revision. As will be seen later, however, the Pope granted recognition to the Chiang Kai-shek Government soon after the Nationalist troops captured Peking in the summer of 1928.

[2] World Missionary Atlas, p. 82.

[3] China Year Book, 1928, p. 4.

[4] "The Missionaries' Opportunity in China," by Julean Arnold, in Chinese Recorder, October, 1925, p. 639.

[5] Professor C. F. Remer gives the following interesting table of estimates made concerning the American holdings in China, in Foreign Investments in China, p. 308:

Recent Estimates of American Holdings in China
(In millions of U.S. $)

Author	Business Investments	Securities and Obligations of the Chinese Government	Property of Missions and Philanthropic Societies
Warnshuis 1924 (?)			80.0
Lee 1924	30.0	39.3	
State Department 1928.....	95.4		52.1
Dickens 1929	113.8		
Remer 1930	155.1	41.7	43.0

It was evident, therefore, when the Chinese raised the issue of treaty revision so forcefully in 1925, that among the American interests most closely involved were those of the mission groups active in China. While the treaties, taken in general, applied to American missionaries in the same way as they applied to all American citizens living or traveling in China, there were two aspects of the treaties which the missionaries themselves regarded as having a special influence on their work. The first consisted of those provisions which granted extraterritorial rights to the nationals of the Treaty Powers; the second involved the so-called "toleration clauses," which affected only missionaries and Chinese Christians.

Stated briefly, the main purpose of the "toleration clauses" was to give to Christians freedom of worship and freedom to teach the Christian religion; and to allow missionaries the right to travel and to rent land and buildings in the interior of China for the sake of carrying on their work.[6] In the Sino-American Treaty of 1858, a clause was inserted which declared that hereafter those who quietly professed or taught Christian doctrines should not be harassed or persecuted on account of their faith, and that "any persons, whether citizens of the United States or Chinese converts," who taught or practiced the principles of Christianity should "in no case be interfered with or molested."[7] This article was repeated in the Sino-American Treaty of 1903.[8] It should be observed, however, that neither in this clause, nor in any of the other provisions of the treaties, were extraterritorial privileges granted to Chinese converts to Christianity; they were merely accorded immunity from discrimination and oppression because of their religion.[9] Much confusion arose over this point and missionaries were frequently accused of seeking to assist Chinese converts who were in legal difficulty, by sheltering them under the cloak of their own privileged status.

The issue of the right of missionaries to live and rent land in the interior had a more elaborate legal history than the recognition of religious freedom. The treaties of 1842 and 1844 had given to missionaries, in common with other nations of the Treaty Powers, the right to reside in the Treaty Ports, but missionaries were prohibited from entering the interior of China for purposes of religious propaganda.[10] Nevertheless, as time went by, Christian missionaries of all nationalities established themselves in many places throughout the interior of China and were permitted by the Chinese authorities to acquire land and construct buildings for use as residences,

[6] A. L. Warnshuis, *National Christian Council Bulletin*, November, 1925, p. 9.

[7] Willoughby, *Foreign Rights and Interests in China*, Vol. 2, p. 704.

[8] See MacMurray, *Treaties and Agreements With and Concerning China, 1894-1919*, Vol. 1, p. 430.

[9] Willoughby, *op. cit.*, p. 714.

[10] *Ibid.*, pp. 702-703.

hospitals, schools, churches, etc.[11] It was not until the conclusion of the Sino-American Treaty of 1903, however, that an express treaty right was granted to "missionary societies" to rent and to lease in perpetuity "buildings or lands in all parts of the Empire for missionary purposes."[12] While this right was not extended to individual missionaries, it was the view of the State Department at Washington that "inasmuch as China, through her officials, has in numerous instances permitted the subjects of other nationalities to purchase lands in certain localities in the interior, this Government may, with good reason, consider such purchases as precedents establishing the right of Americans, whether members or non-members of a missionary body, to make similar purchases."[13]

In the summer of 1925, the missionary societies in the United States lost little time in taking action concerning the general question of treaty revision and the particular provisions of the treaties which involved extraterritorial privileges for missionaries. When, on July 2nd, an announcement appeared in the American press that the United States Government was prepared to meet in conference with the other interested Powers in accordance with the agreements reached at the Washington Conference, Mr. Fennell P. Turner, Secretary of the Foreign Missions Conference of North America, an organization representative of ninety-eight Protestant agencies in the United States,[14] sent a letter to Secretary of State Kellogg:

This announcement is received with profound satisfaction by the large body of citizens of the United States who are supporters of the Mission Boards of the Churches of the United States which carry on a very extensive philanthropic, educational and religious work in China. We are gratified that our own Government has taken the lead among the Powers in expressing its willingness to meet with the representatives of other Powers in conference to frame a new policy towards China, as suggested in the Nine Power Treaty and accompanying resolutions adopted at the Washington Conference.

We desire to convey to you, Mr. Secretary, our congratulations that it was possible for you to make the announcement with regard to the proposed Conference at this critical moment.[15]

Five days later, the Secretaries of Boards with missions in China and the Chairman and Secretaries of the Committee of Reference and Counsel

[11] *Ibid.*, p. 709.

[12] MacMurray, *op. cit.*, pp. 430-431.

[13] Instructions sent by the State Department to the Legation at Peking, quoted in Willoughby, *op. cit.*, p. 712.

[14] According to information furnished by the Foreign Missions Conference of North America, that organization had in 1925 a total membership of Boards and Societies of 104, 98 of which were in the United States.

[15] *33rd Foreign Missions Conference of North America*, 1926, p. 74.

(of the Foreign Missions Conference of North America) signed and made public a statement which was also forwarded to the Secretary of State. After expressing their appreciation of the action of the State Department in respect to the early assembling of the Tariff Conference and the Commission on Extraterritoriality, they said:

At this distance from China we are not competent to form an opinion as to the responsibility of those involved in the reported local disturbances, but we record our conviction that a permanent settlement of the difficulties existing in China will be effected not by the use of (or, by the show of) force, but by friendly conference between those concerned.

While believing that China's greatest and most difficult problems are within herself and that their solution involves the establishment of stable and just government, the realization of national unity, and the adoption and enforcement of enlightened laws, we believe justice to China demands the readjustment of the treaty relations between China and other nations as suggested at the Washington Conference; and that, until these treaties are readjusted, there will inevitably continue to be misunderstandings between China and other nations. We identify ourselves with those who are endeavoring to secure justice for China in all her relations with the other nations because it is the simple and inalienable right of China.[16]

This statement carried the signatures of fifty-seven men and women, many of whom occupied positions of great influence in the missionary field.[17] Its publication was followed by a telegram sent to President Coolidge by Dr. Robert E. Speer, then Chairman of the Foreign Missions Conference of North America, and Mr. Turner, reaffirming the opinions set forth in the messages addressed to the Secretary of State.[18]

While the missionary organizations were thus beginning to mobilize in support of a so-called "pro-Chinese" policy, the *Christian Century*, one of the leading religious journals in the United States, commenced to express its views. In an analysis of the causes underlying the May 30th Incident, the editors wrote:

It is absurd to see in such an outburst as this only another evidence of the machinations of Moscow. We do not doubt but that Russia is able to contemplate with some complacency the sight of Chinese rising against the political and economic pretensions of other nations. It is probable that certain Russian agents have helped matters to a crisis. But all the Russian agents in the Far East could have done nothing had not the other foreign nations given them plenty of grievances on which to play. The Shanghai explosion comes as a result of a mounting exasperation, particularly on the part of the young Chinese, as they have seen their country exploited both

[16] *Ibid.*, p. 75.
[17] *Ibid.*
[18] *Ibid.*

politically and economically by other states. And the most significant feature of this exploitation is the unanimity with which Chinese of all groups have sided with the students. . . . The firing on students of Shanghai by the foreign police has served to fuse all Chinese partisans into a single body of protest.

Later in the same article, the writer declared:

This is a cloud much larger than a man's hand. It may mean that the failure of the west to deal generously and sympathetically with the east will force the anti-occidental feeling into a specific movement within the next few months. The grave nature of such a development needs no explanation.

The seriousness of the situation which thus confronts Christian missionaries in China can hardly be exaggerated. For months the anti-Christian agitation among students has been insisting that Christianity is nothing more than a religious mask for the economic and political imperialism of the west. With China in the desperate mood suggested by the Shanghai riots, it is clear that Christianity must divorce itself from any suspicion of such a relationship if it is to have any part at all in the further forming of the new China. . . . Certainly if there is any hesitation to make the break clean between the commercial and political aims of the west and the aims of our religious enterprise, there is no chance to win back the confidence of the already suspicious Chinese. It remains to be seen whether even this break — if the missionaries have daring enough to make it — can undo the damage which this firing in China's streets has already done. And, despite all the explaining that will now be done, the students are sure to remember one fact — it was the foreigner who opened fire.[19]

In August, 1925, the *Christian Century* discussed the policy of the United States towards China in a long editorial, the gist of which was as follows: Most western diplomats maintain that whatever the blunders committed in the past, China is now suffering from the mismanagement of her own affairs. The attitude of such officials is often expressed by saying, "Let China put her own house in order and then we shall be ready to discuss her grievances with other nations." This is the view of the professional diplomat and the professional diplomat, especially in relation to the Far East, occupies a position of immense importance. In the United States, a vast public ignorance and a lack of interest has left the control of our Chinese policy in the hands of a "little coterie of professional Far Eastern 'experts' " in the State Department. These men have done well on the whole, but they have shown again and again that the pattern of their thinking is rigid — and rigidity is no asset in trying to come to terms with a revolution. China is in revolution, not only politically but to the most profound depths of her social order. Fortunately, President Coolidge, Senator Borah, and others, are not blindly following the path of the professional

[19] *Christian Century*, June 18, 1925, pp. 788-789.

diplomats. To say that the disorder in China is wholly Chinese in origin, and that nothing can be done until China has effected internal reforms, is childish. Even if it were true that the foreign nations have arrived at their present position in China with clean hands — an assumption which is fantastic — it would still be evident that the present temper of China will not allow the maintenance of a privileged status for foreigners. What the policy of the United States ought to be is clear: the line indicated by Senator Borah is the only possible line of wisdom. The United States Government must cut through whatever jungle of diplomatic red tape may hinder quick and decisive action and convince the Chinese that it seeks no unjust favors for its nationals and that the first interest of our mutual relations is the welfare of China's own people. The crux of the matter lies in the words *quick* and *decisive*. There is a way of going about the negotiation of international affairs which will defeat the object sought, no matter what the legal outcome. The United States showed an ability to use direct and rapid methods at the Washington Conference; it must show the same ability now. The anti-foreign tide is running so strongly in China that to delay is to accept defeat. All the future depends on our acting swiftly and generously to meet the "honorable aspirations" of the new China.[20]

In September, in an editorial entitled "Set the Missionaries Free!" the *Christian Century* began a series of articles in which it insisted that the mission Boards in the United States should take action that would free the missionaries from the obstacles created by the extraterritorial system. Extraterritoriality, the *Christian Century* declared, "is the perfect fruit of western imperialism in China"; it came at the mouth of the cannon, has been maintained by gunboats and marines and permits foreigners to play the rôle of the demi-god.

> . . . the missionary body must be ready to trust itself to the same conditions of life and work which obtain for the Chinese. Either that, or it might as well quit. We believe in the insight of the missionaries. We believe they are ready to see the last of extraterritoriality.

> The next move is up to the missionary societies. The governments are working with excessive caution toward a review of the Chinese situation. It is even possible that they may adopt a plan whereby extraterritoriality will eventually be done away. But the mission cause cannot afford to wait for the governments. The mission cause is in sight of defeat at this moment because, in the eyes of the Chinese, it is inextricably bound up with the economic imperialism of western nations. Individual missionaries can only make individual protests. It is time for the missionary organizations to make it clear to the world that the Christian cause as a whole is done with

[20] *Ibid.*, August 20, 1925, pp. 1041-1043. For similar views see the issue of October 8, 1925, p. 1232.

gunboats. The missionaries deserve this much support from their home base. Without it, support of any other kind will be useless.

Long before the governments feel their way toward action, the mission Boards should send instructions to their missionaries cutting them loose from the incubus of extraterritoriality. No missionary, no mission institution, should be permitted to take further advantage of a status which is unjust and which is part of a system which Christianity is set to destroy. Any missionary who is not willing to work under such a policy should be provided with passage home. And the mission Boards should announce to the world what they are doing, so that none of their workers may, even by mistake, be implicated longer with participation in this international outrage.[21]

Throughout the next months, the *Christian Century* continued to challenge the mission Boards to go on record against the maintenance of the extraterritorial system. The editors set forth a program which advocated: (1) that mission Boards instruct their workers not to take advantage of extraterritorial privileges and provide for the recall of those who were not prepared to work in China under such circumstances; (2) that a public announcement be made of the complete abandonment by the missionary body of all appeals for protection or calls for indemnity due to the endangering of lives or property; (3) that "immediate and concerted pressure" be brought on the western governments by the mission societies to ensure the cancellation of the "toleration clauses" when the treaties were revised. Concerning this last point on its program, the *Christian Century* stated forcefully that there should be "no hesitancy, no uncertainty, in taking action."[22]

Views quite similar to the editorial opinions of the *Christian Century* were expressed by many missionary leaders at this time. From the 17th to the 20th of September, 1925, a conference was held at Johns Hopkins University which received wide publicity. It was an unofficial gathering of persons interested in China who hoped, through informal discussion, to clarify their ideas concerning the developments that had taken place since the May 30th Incident.[23] Many missionaries were present, and one of the most significant addresses made at the Conference was that of the Reverend John Leighton Stuart, President of Yenching University, who had only recently come from China.[24] In his analysis of the disturbances in China, Dr. Stuart said that there was one dominating and all-important fact, namely, that the real government of China was public opinion. "Never

[21] *Ibid.*, September 10, 1925, p. 114.
[22] *Ibid.*, October 8, 1926, pp. 1234-1236.
[23] *American Relations with China: A Report of the Conference Held at Johns Hopkins September 17-20, 1925*, Baltimore, 1925, p. 7.
[24] *Ibid.*, pp. 36-40.

before in their long history," he assured his audience, "have the Chinese people been so nearly unanimous, so well informed, and so deeply stirred as they are now over this issue of their sovereign rights in relation to other countries."[25]

"The Chinese people," he continued, "without exception, so far as I have observed, are at one in this sentiment. The students held largely responsible are only the most highly sensitized part of the population. This nationalistic self-consciousness has been slowly forming for many years, more recently with amazing celerity; but it formed into a ferment of vivid and violent energy immediately on hearing of the shooting affray in Shanghai on May 30th. It has become highly organized and is quite articulate."[26]

Dr. Stuart argued that a recognition of the dominant influence of public opinion in China at this time must lead the Conference members to certain fundamental conclusions. One was that to attempt to protect American interests or enforce American policies by military or naval force would merely further inflame the "already excited national mind" of the Chinese.[27] Another conclusion was that in the forthcoming conferences the Western Powers would be judged by the Chinese people more for the manner in which they conducted the negotiations than for their actual outcome. It was essential, in Dr. Stuart's view, that the Chinese people should be convinced that the Powers were willing to treat them racially and politically as equals and that the foreign governments were not making diplomatic concessions in a spirit of condescension or with a feeling of compulsion.[28] If, Dr. Stuart observed, his ideas seemed merely "visionary pro-Chinese sentimentalism" to some of his listeners, they would do well to consider the consequences of having the vast population of China become — as it might easily — anti-American.[29]

Speaking further of the attitude of the Chinese toward the United States, Dr. Stuart said that the Chinese were waiting "with a certain eager, frightened expectancy" for the American Government to act; will the American nation, they wondered, maintain a "position of amiable inactivity," making compromises with the other Powers so as to have a united policy in China, or, will it lead in an "act of aggressive good," even if it costs something?[30]

Our response to their desire seems to me to be the supreme question in what may otherwise become an impending cataclysm. The situation is

[25] *Ibid.*, p. 36.
[26] *Ibid.*
[27] *Ibid.*, p. 37.
[28] *Ibid.*, p. 39.
[29] *Ibid.*
[30] *Ibid.*

undeniably full of menace but the menace will be in our failure to take the initiative. A reform of international relations with China can be effectively mediated only through the United States. Great Britain has lost the chance to do generously and graciously what will ultimately be forced upon her. This is our superlative opportunity. Not only so, but I for one am convinced that once the Chinese demands have been properly understood and safeguarded, as the Chinese people would be foremost in insisting should be done in actually putting them into effect, American opinion will agree that those demands are reasonable and righteous. Even though we should have to stand some loss of property or even of life it would be a small price to pay for the infinitely larger gains. . . .[31]

The best way to help China put her own house in order is for us first to remove the humiliations and the handicaps in her foreign relations. . . .[32]

The missionary situation in China was discussed with frankness at the Johns Hopkins Conference. A preliminary study had been prepared by Dr. A. L. Warnshuis, Secretary of the International Missionary Council, whose work on the "toleration clauses" has been widely quoted.[33] Dr. Warnshuis enumerated the advantages and disadvantages of the "toleration clauses," and in considering the former pointed out that these provisions had made possible most of the mission activity carried on in China since the middle of the nineteenth century. On the negative side, he emphasized that while the treaties only allowed a foreign Power to intervene as a protector of the faith of a Chinese Christian, the result had been in practice to separate the Chinese Christians from the mass of their fellow countrymen. "So much was this the case," he said, "that until comparatively recent years the Chinese authorities unwisely but persistently made a sharp distinction in the terms used to describe Christian and other Chinese subjects." In Dr. Warnshuis' view, the situation created by the "toleration clauses" constituted a serious blow to the sovereignty of the Chinese state by virtually removing Chinese Christians from its jurisdiction. Moreover, he believed that in the eyes of the Chinese the missionaries had, because of their special privileges, become part of the "aggressive west" which sought security in agreements forced from the Chinese Government through war. Like the *Christian Century*, Dr. Warnshuis urged the mission Boards in the United States, Great Britain, and other countries to inform their governments at once that they wished to see the "toleration clauses" brought to an end.[34]

In respect to the general situation in China, Dr. Warnshuis took the position that interference by foreign nations was out of the question and

[31] *Ibid.*
[32] *Ibid.*, p. 40.
[33] *Ibid.*, p. 108; see also *Chinese Recorder*, November, 1925, pp. 704-725; the *National Christian Council Bulletin*, November, 1925, pp. 7-12; Willoughby, *op. cit.*, p. 719.
[34] *American Relations with China, cit.*, pp. 111-112.

that the best the Powers could do was to settle those matters with which they were concerned, leaving the Chinese people free to give their undivided attention to the development of stability within their own country.[35] Dr. Warnshuis also predicted that opinions would differ concerning whether or not missionaries had a right to participate in the controversy over the revision of the treaties because of the fact that the problems involved were political rather than religious. He frankly stated that he favored missionaries entering into this dispute on the grounds, first, that as citizens they shared in the responsibility for their government's policy, and, second, that as it was impossible for missionaries to renounce the protection and obligations conferred by the treaties, the only way of improving the situation was to alter the provisions of the treaties. He urged missionaries to use whatever knowledge and influence they possessed to see that the treaties were changed in a manner that conformed more closely with the principles that ought to prevail in international relations.[36]

In the general round table discussion dealing with the missionary situation in China which took place at the Johns Hopkins Conference, Dr. R. E. Diffendorfer, Secretary of the Board of Foreign Missions of the Methodist Episcopal Church, declared that he was prepared to recommend to his Board that they advocate a policy whereby the United States Government would assume the leadership in the movement for the abolition of extraterritoriality.[37] Moreover, he said, he would suggest that an announcement be made that missionaries who did not wish to live among the Chinese people without the protection of extraterritoriality should return to the United States.[38] Dr. Diffendorfer explained the firm stand which he adopted against the maintenance of extraterritorial privileges as follows:

The reason I feel this so keenly is because I think the time has come when the so-called Treaty Powers need to divest themselves of the traditional handling of this question and with a bit of imagination see that there is a new day upon us and a new attitude that must be met. I hope that I personally and all the missionaries of the Methodist Episcopal Church, both here and in China, as well as the rest of us, will see to it that the point of view that has crept into our thinking about China in recent years, that it is in our power and right to deliver to the Chinese just as much as we want to deliver to them, is a point of view that should be abandoned forever.[39]

Other mission leaders participating in the round table at the Johns

[35] *Chinese Recorder*, November, 1925, p. 705.
[36] *Ibid.*, p. 715.
[37] *National Christian Council Bulletin*, December, 1925, p. 9.
[38] *Ibid.*
[39] *American Relations with China*, p. 114.

Hopkins Conference also expressed their views on the subject of treaty revision. Dr. James H. Franklin of the American Baptist Foreign Missionary Society stated that his organization had already told the United States Government that it was in favor of a "new deal for China" and had urged the State Department to "press for action in which all of China's righteous aspirations" would be met.[40] Dr. William E. Strong, representing the American Board of Commissioners for Foreign Missions (Congregational), said that he thought his Board would be willing to go on record against the continuance of the "toleration clauses." He added that missionaries in China felt they were being misunderstood by those Chinese who in denouncing extraterritorial rights were counting the missionaries among the "defenders of imperialism, capitalism, militarism, and any other *isms*," with the result that missionaries were increasingly eager to relinquish their special privileges.

It is evident, however, that no expression of opinion by individual missionaries, no matter how far their voices might carry, could exercise the same influence as official action by the mission Boards. As already noted, statements had been issued in July on the initiative of the Foreign Missions Conference of North America which were in the nature of temporary measures adopted in response to the critical emergency that had arisen in China. On the whole, these declarations went no further than to urge the United States Government to fulfill the obligations it had undertaken at the Washington Conference. As the weeks went by, it became apparent that, after further consideration, the mission Boards were determined to take a more clear-cut and positive stand.

On the 2nd and 3rd of October, 1925, an unofficial meeting of American mission administrators was convened in New York by a committee of the Foreign Missions Conference. Eighty-five representatives of thirty-two different organizations attended, and resolutions were adopted which had a far-reaching effect.[41] The resolutions were forwarded to the United States Government and were, at the same time, submitted to the various missionary Boards in the United States with the suggestion that they should take any action that they regarded as wise.[42]

The preamble of the resolutions stated that the signatories heartily sympathized with China "in her aspirations for just, equal, and fraternal relations with other nations and in her sense of the present injustice of the existing treaties." The first resolution urged an early revision of the treaties, to be effected in a way that would realize the principles of the

[40] *Ibid.,* p. 115.
[41] *33rd Foreign Missions Conference of North America,* 1926, p. 77.
[42] *Ibid.*

Nine Power Treaty signed at the Washington Conference. Further resolutions declared that the members of the Conference agreed:

With reference to extraterritorial jurisdiction:

a. That we express ourselves in favor of the abolition of extraterritoriality in China at an early date,

b. That we further express the opinion that the determination of that date and of the provisions that may be considered mutually desirable should be undertaken cooperatively on terms of equality by China and the other Powers.

With reference to the treaty provisions according special privileges to missions and missionaries:

a. That, when our respective governments negotiate the new treaties which are so urgently needed, we wish it to be understood that we do not desire any distinctive privileges for missions and missionaries imposed by treaty upon the Chinese Government and people.

b. That, correlatively, we consider it desirable that the Chinese Government by such legislation as may be deemed necessary define the rights and privileges of missionaries in particular to acquire and hold property and to carry forward their work in China.

c. We also express our desire and judgment that the principle of religious liberty should be reciprocally recognized in all future relationships between China and other nations.[43]

From October, 1925, to the end of the year, most of the large mission Boards in the United States endorsed the above resolutions and many issued supplementary statements which, in the aggregate, formed an impressive record of missionary opinion. The American Board of Commissioners for Foreign Missions published a number of statements in which they urged the American Delegates to the Special Tariff Conference to stand for an adjustment of treaty relations that would recognize the absolute sovereignty of China; recommended the abolition of extraterritoriality at an early date, to be undertaken, if necessary, without the co-operation of the other foreign Powers; and disclaimed all special privileges accorded to their missionaries by the existing treaties.[44]

In messages addressed to President Coolidge and Secretary of State Kellogg, the American Baptist Foreign Mission Society and the Woman's American Baptist Foreign Mission Society went on record as opposing any display of force to meet the situation in China. "We feel deeply the gravity of the present moment," they said, "and believe our Government will take the largest and most sympathetic view of the aspirations of the Chinese people." They also expressed their sympathy with the desire of the Chinese

[43] Ibid., pp. 78-79.
[44] National Christian Council Bulletin, March, 1926, p. 15.

to abolish the extraterritorial system, adding that while they recognized that time would be required to effect the necessary judicial reforms in China they, nevertheless, hoped that "immediate and definite steps" would be taken to place on the Government of China, "as soon as practicable, complete responsibility for the protection of the lives and property of American citizens residing or traveling there."[45]

Among the other large missionary societies which endorsed the resolutions passed at the October 2nd and 3rd meeting of the American mission administrators, and which additionally published separate pronouncements, were the Boards of Foreign Missions of the Presbyterian Church in the U. S. A. and of the Methodist Episcopal Church. Both of these organizations officially approved the "progressive" position taken by the United States Government in setting into motion the work of the Special Tariff Conference and the Commission on Extraterritoriality.[46]

In all, twenty-one missionary organizations adopted the October resolutions of the American mission administrators and their action was acknowledged and made public at the annual meeting of the Foreign Missions Conference in January, 1926.[47] On the same occasion, the Foreign Missions Conference seized the opportunity to reaffirm the text of the October resolutions and to re-emphasize its deep sympathy with "the patriotic aspirations of China for just, equal, and fraternal relations with other nations."[48]

At the same time as the mission Boards were adopting these measures, other influential religious organizations were engaging in similar activities. In October, 1925, the Federal Council of Churches of Christ in America, representing more than twenty million members,[49] appointed a committee under the chairmanship of Dr. S. Parkes Cadman to present a statement to Secretary of State Kellogg.[50] The statement asserted at the outset that the desire of the Chinese people to attain national freedom must awaken the sympathy of men and women everywhere, and continued:

The Shanghai Incident of May 30th, which was the immediate occasion of the nation-wide spirit of protest against the present status of China in her relation to other nations, is only symptomatic of deep-rooted trouble. The central demand of the Chinese is for a fundamental revision of the "unequal treaties" under which for many decades foreigners in China have had certain privileges and rights which infringe on her independence and sovereignty. In particular, the Chinese are protesting against a further

[45] *Ibid.*, pp. 15-16.
[46] *China Christian Year Book*, 1926, pp. 504, 505, 507.
[47] *National Christian Council Bulletin*, March, 1926, p. 14.
[48] *33rd Foreign Missions Conference of North America*, 1926, p. 77.
[49] *Year Book of the Churches, 1924-25*, p. 254.
[50] *National Christian Council Bulletin*, December, 1925, p. 8.

continuance of extraterritoriality and of foreign control of customs duties. Whatever may have been the justification in the past, it seems clear that the time has now come when changed conditions require all who accept the principle of the Golden Rule to sympathize keenly with these desires of the Chinese people.[51]

The statement of the Federal Council went on to express its appreciation of the State Department's policy as shown in the calling of the Special Tariff Conference and the convening of the Commission on Extraterritoriality, and to urge the United States Government to demonstrate in its dealings with China a "thorough respect for the Chinese people, free from any taint of condescension or racial pride." In its conclusion it took a firm stand concerning the maintenance of tariff controls and extraterritorial privileges:

The Federal Council of the Churches of Christ in America . . . urges all Christian people to join in creating a public opinion which will stand unequivocally for the abolition of extraterritoriality, will favor the restoration of tariff autonomy to China, and will invite the Chinese Government and people to co-operate in working out as promptly as possible, practicable programs for securing these and other needed changes.

We believe that our Government should act in concert with other nations, and use its full influence to that end; if, however, international agreement should prove impossible, we urge our Government to act independently in securing full justice between the United States and China.[52]

The position taken by the Federal Council and the mission Boards was supported by the Protestant Episcopal Church which, at its general convention, authorized its National Council to co-operate with the missionary organizations and with the Federal Council of the Churches of Christ in America, in securing action by the United States Government that would "lead to the revision of our treaty relations with China in the interest of attaining complete reciprocity between our two nations."[53] With a similar purpose in mind but expressing themselves even more directly, the Disciples of Christ — who exercised considerable influence through the numerous periodicals which they published in various parts of the United States — passed a resolution requesting the Government in Washington to "do all in its power to secure for China tariff autonomy and the abolition of extraterritoriality."[54]

From the foregoing it is evident that the official opinion of the missionary group within the United States not only approved the action of the State Department in calling together the Special Tariff Conference and

[51] *Ibid.*, pp. 8-9.
[52] *Ibid.*, p. 8.
[53] *Ibid.*, March, 1926, p. 17.
[54] *World Call*, November, 1925, p. 53.

the Commission on Extraterritoriality, but was prepared to support a funda-mental revision of the treaties. Although there was a certain amount of variation between the emphasis placed upon one issue or another by different missionary organizations, the mission body as a whole moved toward the same goals in harmony. This was clearly indicated in a study, made by the National Christian Council in China, of the actions taken by the missionary societies in the United States and Great Britain during 1925 and 1926:

> The action of the missionary societies, both individually and through their respective conferences, was so general that there can be no doubt that the great majority of them hold:
> (a) that these international issues concern them and that they have a duty in expressing an opinion in regard thereto
> (b) that the missionary societies welcome the announcements of their respective governments that the latter are ready to take steps toward a com prehensive revision of the existing treaties
> (c) that in the revision of the treaties:
> (1) the missionary societies desire no special privilege for mis-sionaries or mission work and that,
> (2) they would welcome the abolition of the present articles of the treaties relating to extraterritoriality.

As far as the United States was concerned, the study reached the conclu-sion that it was apparent, from the action of the Federal Council of the Churches of Christ in America, that the position taken by the missionary societies was in accord with the general attitude of their constituencies.[55]

AMERICAN MISSIONARIES IN CHINA

While many of the mission Boards in the United States were thus willing to urge our Government to undertake an extensive revision of its treaties with China, American missionaries in China were finding it more difficult to achieve group action.[56] This was owing to numerous causes, of which

[55] *National Christian Council Annual Report*, 1925-26, p. 127.

[56] It has been pointed out to the writer that a serious obstacle to group discussion by American missionaries in China lay in the structure of missionary organizations in the field which tends "to retard the process, among missionaries working for the same society, of reaching group opinions at all times and in times of crisis . . . to inhibit effective expressions of group judgment." The smallest grouping of any one society's missionaries is usually called a station; several mutually accessible stations form a mission; all the missions in a much larger area, sometimes covering all of China, are united in a confer-ence or council. The mission and the conference, or council, are likely to meet only once a year. Each group in succession forwards its common opinions to the next higher group which, finally, forwards them to the missionary society in America. Normally, expressions of opinion are not regarded as effectively valid until they have been passed by the largest group—quite possibly a year after they were first considered by the smaller, local body. (Based on a memorandum to the writer from Dr. D. Willard Lyon.)

some of the most urgent had little or nothing to do with political considerations. There were, for example, serious differences in the religious views of the so-called Modernists and Fundamentalists which tended to carry over into many aspects of missionary thinking.[57] Also, the growth of an "indigenous" Christian Church in China was creating increasingly important problems, among which was the question of the kind of relationship the foreign missionary body should have to an "indigenous" Church which sought eventually to be largely Chinese in direction, control, and personnel.[58] Moreover, the various denominations of the Protestant Church that had grown up in the West proved "puzzling to most Chinese" and, in 1922, steps had been taken toward the formation of the Church of Christ in China whose object was, in part, to include different denominations.[59] A further complication facing the missionaries was the movement against the Christian schools in China which attracted considerable attention when, in 1924, a number of Chinese educational organizations showed decided opposition to Christian education, demanding, particularly, that the government should insist on the registration of foreign schools and colleges, and that such registration be granted only on condition that religious instruction be barred from the curriculum.[60]

[57] In respect to the conflict between the Fundamentalists and the Modernists, Dr. Kenneth S. Latourette in his *A History of Christian Missions in China*, New York, 1929, states: "We have already noted the rift which 'fundamentalism' and 'modernism' were bringing in in Protestantism in Great Britain and America. The conflict was early carried to China and there became even more divisive than in the Occident. The reasons for this intensification of the struggle are not far to seek. Here were strongly represented the denominations in which the controversy was most acute. Here, too, Christian colleges were prominent and growing rapidly, and in them . . . liberalism was often strong. . . . In China, on the other hand, conservatives were especially numerous. In addition to large denominations noted for adhering to the historic statements of the Faith was the great China Inland Mission which drew its missionaries from the conservative wings of most of the Evangelical bodies. Nearly all the smaller missions, too, of which China counted scores, were earnest supporters of the older Evangelical position. The stage was set for sharp conflict." (pp. 794-795.)

[58] The growth of an "indigenous" Chinese Church had long been one of the foremost subjects of discussion among missionaries. See Latourette, *op. cit.*, p. 672 *et seq.;* p. 801 *et seq.*

[59] See *An Adventure in Church Union* (pamphlet published by the Church of Christ in China).

[60] Report of the Executive Committee to the General Board, China Christian Education Association, in *Educational Review*, July, 1925, p. 277. In November, 1926, the Peking Ministry of Education did in fact pass regulations for the registration of mission schools. The requirements included: the Board of Control must have a Chinese majority and a Chinese Chairman; the purpose of the school must not include the propagation of religion; religious instruction and services must not be required; the curriculum must conform to government regulation. (*China Christian Year Book*, 1928, p. 176) From November, 1926, on, regulations were also passed by the Kuomintang Government.

It was against this background of issues, compelling consideration, that the missionaries found themselves confronted with the 1925 crisis. We have already seen that, after the May 30th Incident, a number of mission groups in China issued statements asserting that the disturbances in Shanghai were primarily a symptom of profound misunderstanding between Chinese and foreigners which could only be eliminated by a reconsideration of the existing treaties.[61] In a letter addressed to the Shanghai Municipal Council on June 8, 1925, the National Christian Council (generally known as the N.C.C.) asked for an investigation of the shooting at the Louza Police station and also urged that Chinese representatives be included on the Shanghai Municipal Council in order to remove one of the sources of friction. The importance of the N.C.C.'s statement derived from the fact that the N.C.C. was the official over-all body organized to serve as a link between the many Protestant missionary, church, and other organizations working in China, and to furnish a means by which the Christian forces of China could express themselves unitedly on significant issues.[62] Following the publication of the N.C.C.'s communication to the Municipal Council, the British newspaper, the *North China Herald,* denounced the actions of the N.C.C. as a piece of "meddlesome interference" and accused it of further stimulating the animosity of the Chinese toward foreigners.[63] Moreover, the *North China Herald* indicated that the claim of the N.C.C. to speak as a council genuinely representative of the Christians in China was open to question; "there is more than a little suggestion," the editors remarked, "that its members are self-appointed and imaginary."[64]

The attack of the *North China Herald* on the N.C.C. at this early date was only the first broadside in a conflict carried on with exceptional vigor and harshness throughout the next four years. One of the most significant aspects of this dispute was that it demonstrated, with unusual clarity, the irreconcilable differences of opinion that existed among the foreign community in China at this time. On July 16, 1926, the Executive Committee

[61] See above, pp. 25-26.

[62] *North China Herald,* August 1, 1925, p. 93; *National Christian Council Annual Report,* 1925-1926, p. 221. It should be remembered throughout that the N. C. C. was an international organization (inclusive of Chinese) and not primarily American.

[63] See above, p. 26.

[64] *North China Herald,* June 27, 1925, p. 491. In response to the above quotation, Dr. E. C. Lobenstine, Secretary of the N. C. C., wrote to the editor of the *North China Herald:* "Perhaps you were out of China in May, 1922, when for ten days the most representative Christian gathering of Protestant Christians that has ever met in China was in session in the Town Hall. The 1,200 delegates to that conference devoted a considerable amount of time and attention to organizing the National Christian Council. The Council, elected at that time, is composed of approximately 100 members. . . . The National Christian Council is, therefore, as official and representative as the bodies concerned knew how to make it. . . ." (*North China Herald,* August 1, 1925, p. 93.)

of the N.C.C. issued a message to the Christians in China which, while partly religious in character, also dealt with political developments. Reviewing the N.C.C.'s activities in relation to the May 30th Incident, the Executive Committee said that it had delegated several of its members to visit the editors of foreign and Chinese newspapers in Shanghai in order to urge them to present the facts concerning the disturbances at the Louza Police station with the utmost care and not to pass judgment until the full story was known.[65] The message of the N.C.C. also sought to analyze the causes of the crisis in China. Under *internal causes* it listed such matters as militarism, civil war, political corruption, and banditry; under *external causes*, it enumerated "foreign aggression and domination; unequal treaties; racial pride; smuggling of opium, other narcotics and firearms; lack of understanding of the Chinese temperament and aspirations, etc." Furthermore, the authors of the message asked whether Christians should not take "prompt steps" to alter these conditions in order "to promote a better understanding between, and appreciation of, China and the foreign Powers."[66]

These portions of the N.C.C.'s statement evoked further caustic criticism from the *North China Herald,* which asserted that in so far as the N.C.C. advised on religious topics it was within its rights, but that where it dealt with other matters it was "guilty of unwarrantable impertinence." The best way, the editors declared, that the N.C.C. could take " 'prompt steps' " to improve relations between China and the Powers was to abstain from tampering with political affairs and to concentrate on religious subjects which were "indeed its only concern."[67]

In October and November, 1925, Dr. E. C. Lobenstine, an American, then Secretary of the N.C.C., sent two official letters to the Bishops, Superintendents, and Secretaries of missions in China. These were reprinted in the *North China Herald* with italics inserted by the editors (as reproduced below) which were intended to draw the readers' attention to phrases and sentences that the *North China Herald* regarded as especially objectionable. In the first communication,[68] Dr. Lobenstine explained that at a meeting of the Executive Committee of the N.C.C. held in the middle of October, the Committee had discussed a request submitted by a group of missionaries in China who urged the N.C.C. to "approach the responsible representatives of foreign governments" with the aim of furthering a policy that would look toward the abolition of all unequal treaties.

[65] *Chinese Recorder,* August, 1925, p. 521.
[66] *Ibid.,* p. 522.
[67] *North China Herald,* July 25, 1925, p. 45.
[68] *Ibid.,* November 28, 1925, p. 275.

"The Council," wrote Dr. Lobenstine, "did not feel itself in a position thus directly to approach the foreign governments. While it was aware that some mission and church bodies, and some groups of individuals, desired it to do so, it was aware also that there were others, probably a majority, who would desire to have these questions considered first by their own administrative bodies before anything were to go forth from the Council in the name of its constituency."

Inasmuch, Dr. Lobenstine continued, as these matters affected mainly the missions, it was decided *"to request them to give these important questions their prompt and earnest attention with a view to such action as to them seems wise."* In order that the decisions should have the largest influence, the missions were *"urged to take action before the convening of the conference on extraterritoriality"* and were asked *"to report their decision to the Legations of their respective nations."* After discussing the possibility of the missions' waiving the special privileges granted by the "toleration clauses," Dr. Lobenstine wrote that the Executive Committee did not, however, wish to suggest that the deliberations of the mission groups be limited to these clauses, but thought rather that the whole question of extraterritoriality should be carefully studied.

In his second communication,[69] Dr. Lobenstine forwarded the resolutions which had been passed at the unofficial meeting of mission Administrators held in New York in October, and drew attention to the fact that these resolutions had been sent to the United States Government. "It would appear," he said, "from this statement and from the resolution adopted by the Johns Hopkins Conference that the *missions are likely to have the full backing of their home Boards in any action* regarding the 'toleration clauses' and extraterritoriality that *they may deem it right to make. . . . It seems to us desirable,"* he added, *"that such actions as may be taken by the missions should be reported to your respective governmental officials in China* in addition to such other publicity as you may desire to give to them."

One of the results of Dr. Lobenstine's letters was to swell the tide of abuse against the N.C.C. — and many of the mission leaders and organizations connected with it — that was already angrily filling the correspondence columns of the *North China Herald*.[70] An anonymous author signing himself "A Missionary Correspondent" wrote, in part, that

The Reverend E. C. Lobenstine, Secretary of the National Christian Council, stated in a recent meeting . . . that he had sent letters to the secretaries of various missions throughout China, giving them advice as to

[69] *Ibid.*
[70] See, for example, issues of November 21 and 28, 1925.

what their missions should do in regard to political matters, especially the waiving of their rights or privileges under extraterritoriality. He also indicated that he had reason to believe that many of the missions would act upon his advice. This is only a straw showing which way the wind is blowing or an evidence that the N.C.C. regards it as within its province to advise or dictate to all missionaries in regard to political policies as well as religious work. The pressing of buttons by the N.C.C. out here which results in the passing of political resolutions by the Mission Boards in the United States and England, and the forwarding of same to the State Department in Washington, D. C., and their widespread publication is well-known.[71]

The *North China Herald* endorsed the views of its anonymous contributor and in an editorial written in response to objections presented by Dr. Lobenstine[72] declared that

Dr. Lobenstine objects to the phrase about the N.C.C. "pressing buttons" and he says that the action of the Mission Boards in Great Britain and America were taken on their own initiative and without the previous knowledge or upon recommendation of the N.C.C. . . . The fact that the N.C.C. as such made no recommendation to the home Boards, does not exclude the possibility of something having been done by its officers individually which such a phrase as "pressing buttons" would describe with sufficient accuracy. . . . In the case of treaty revision it is indeed inconceivable that the American and Canadian Boards took the line they did without having received advices from China which may not have been official but would be none the less officious. . . .[73]

We do not think it is too much to say that the National Christian Council, for all the lofty name it bears and the high claims it makes for the furtherance of religion, peace and goodwill upon earth, stands revealed as a political despotism, unscrupulous in its ways and disastrous in its ends. It has begun, with or without meaning to do so, by stirring up Chinese Christians to political agitation; and the end of its activities will be to imperil the whole missionary cause in China.[74]

While the N.C.C. was thus seeking to mobilize the opinion of missionaries in China and was being accused, directly and indirectly, of attempting to influence official policy in the United States and Great Britain, various mission groups were slowly taking action. In Tientsin, at a meeting of business men, a resolution was passed strongly criticizing a local American publication for printing a United Press dispatch which stated that Senator Borah had declared himself in favor of the abolition of extraterritoriality as soon as possible.[75] Immediately following this development, messages were

[71] *Ibid.*, November 21, 1925, p. 363.
[72] For Dr. Lobenstine's letter, see *ibid.*, November 28, 1925, p. 397.
[73] *Ibid.*, p. 377.
[74] *Ibid.*
[75] *China Weekly Review*, July 25, 1925, p. 129.

sent to Senator Borah by two groups consisting in all of over three hundred persons, largely missionaries and educators, expressing their enthusiastic approval of the stand the Senator had taken. One of these messages characterized the rebellious agitation among the Chinese as a healthy sign of growing patriotism and a justifiable protest against the existing treaties which, they said, were essentially unacceptable to any self-respecting nation. As far as missionary enterprise in China was concerned, it would, the signatories affirmed, be rendered useless if the foreign Powers engaged in any extensive military intervention in order to deal with the Chinese crisis.[76]

The most important of the missionary associations in China to adopt an official position concerning the Chinese demands for a revision of the treaties was the Peking Missionary Association which, in November, 1925, passed resolutions that were forwarded to the respective governments of its members. The resolutions declared that the "toleration clauses" of the treaties ought to be cancelled when new treaties were negotiated between the foreign Powers and the Chinese Government. In respect to the issue of extraterritoriality the Peking missionaries asserted that, as missionaries, they desired to see the end of the extraterritorial system but that they fully recognized the complexity of the problems at stake and that many persons other than missionaries were involved; nevertheless, they expressed the hope that extraterritorial rights would be abrogated as soon as possible.[77]

A considerable number of individual missions, as well as unofficial groups of missionaries, also took action between the early summer of 1925 and the close of the year; the American societies and American nationals among them belonged for the most part to the Methodist Episcopal (North and South), the Congregational, the Baptist (North), and the Presbyterian (North) Churches of the United States.[78] Virtually every statement objected to the maintenance of a privileged position for missionaries through the retention of the "toleration clauses"; many requested the early abolition of extraterritoriality and of tariff controls; a number emphatically opposed the use of force in coping with any disturbances that might occur in China. It was stipulated in most of the resolutions that copies should be sent to Secretary of State Kellogg or to the American Legation at Peking and, in certain instances, it was stated that the signatories intended to use what influence they possessed with the United States Government to secure the

---

[76] *The Present Situation in China and Its Significance for Christian Missions,* Committee of Reference and Counsel, New York, 1925, p. 31.

[77] *China Christian Year Book,* 1926, pp. 511-512.

[78] See statements reprinted in *China Christian Year Book,* 1925, pp. 514-530; *National Christian Council Bulletin,* December, 1925, pp. 5-16.

adoption of measures that would lead to the re-establishment of full tariff autonomy and the withdrawal of extraterritorial privileges.

The most significant and outspoken expression of opinion issued by any missionary group in China at this time was that of a conference held in Shanghai in January, 1926, under the auspices of the N.C.C., for Dr. John R. Mott, Chairman of the International Missionary Council, who was on a visit to China from the United States.[79] Sixty-four workers were present representing twenty-four organizations, not more than half of which were members of the N.C.C.[80] After a discussion of the subject of treaty revision, a short resolution was framed and adopted, the most important section of which read: "Extraterritoriality and the 'tolerance clauses' are in many important ways now prejudicial to the progress of the Christian movement in China. The Delegates to the Conference are unanimous in their conviction that both should be removed."[81]

Commenting on this resolution the *Chinese Recorder,* a long-established and well-known missionary magazine published at Shanghai, characterized it as "historic."[82]

In 1926, in a survey of the actions taken by missionaries in China in respect to the political situation, the N.C.C. declared that it was impossible to estimate with any degree of accuracy what proportion of the missionary body was in sympathy with the position that had been adopted by their home Boards. More specifically, it stated that:

The number of missions that have expressed themselves officially along the lines adopted in the resolution of the missionary Boards appears to be much greater than the number of missions which have adopted a position differing from their home Boards. The Council knows of very few, if any, missions which have taken definite action opposing that adopted by their own Boards. . . . There is a considerable number of missions, the members of which have not . . . expressed themselves on this question. In the case of a few it is clear that this is due to their taking the position that churches and missions should not express themselves in matters of this kind; others who are in sympathy with the general position taken by the conference of missionary societies in Great Britain and America, doubt the wisdom of any change at the present time and some would appear to desire a continuance for the present of the *status quo.* The impression gained however . . . is that in the main the missionary body accepts the general position adopted by the missionary Boards, and that in case a vote

[79] For proceedings, see *Report of Conference on Church in China Today,* China Press, Shanghai, 1926.
[80] *National Christian Council Bulletin,* March, 1926, p. 5; *Chinese Recorder,* February, 1926, p. 77.
[81] *National Christian Council Bulletin,* March, 1926, p. 8.
[82] *Chinese Recorder,* February, 1926, p. 80.

were called for by their societies, the great majority would sustain the position of their Boards.[83]

To some mission leaders the lack of any widespread, forceful support of a policy of treaty revision on the part of the missionary groups in China came as a disappointment.

"Bishop Roots," the *Chinese Recorder* observed editorially in December, 1925, "said in the New York Conference that dilatoriness in working out a clear cut policy for clearing up China's grievances makes her suspicious of the good faith of America. This state of hesitancy he called 'stagnation'. To some who have talked with us the general silence of missionaries as to China's appeal for 'fairness and justice' and their 'special privileges' appears as a state of stagnation."[84]

On the other hand, those who disapproved of the stand taken by the missionaries who openly declared themselves in favor of a drastic revision of the treaties increased their efforts as time went by to counteract what they regarded as the excessive influence of the missionary world on the policy of the United States Government and the views of the American public.[85] In 1926, for example, the *Far Eastern Review*, an American business magazine published in Shanghai, began to hammer away at the thesis that American policy in China was dedicated solely to religious, educational, and charitable enterprise at the expense of commercial interests. The most spectacular article on this theme which appeared in the *Far Eastern Review* was written by its editor, George Bronson Rea, and published in June, 1926. Mr. Rea claimed that over a period of twenty-five years, the "once intelligent trade doctrine" of the United States had been replaced by a policy which relegated to the background the trader and the financier, and expressed itself only in terms of missionary endeavor. In fact, Mr. Rea declared, "the selection of our Minister to Peking is determined by qualifications that meet the endorsement of missionary Boards." In order to prove this contention, Mr. Rea quoted a passage from the autobiography of Henry Morgenthau, and another from the diary of Colonel House. The first quotation indicated that President Wilson had refused to appoint Mr. Morgenthau as Minister to China on the ground that he was a Jew; the second went a step further and asserted that no one but an "orthodox Christian" would be considered as Minister to China.[86] "These disclosures tell us in so many words," Mr. Rea remarked, "that Jews, Catholics, Unitarians, Mormons, and other good

---

[83] *National Christian Council Annual Report*, 1925-1926, p. 128.

[84] December, 1925, p. 775.

[85] For later developments along these lines, especially after the Nanking Incident, see below, Chapter XVI.

[86] *Far Eastern Review*, June, 1926, p. 242.

Americans who profess creeds at variance with the religious principles of our major Protestant missionary Boards can never be appointed to the post of American Minister to China."[87] Later in the same article Mr. Rea wrote:

It has been brought forcibly to the attention of the American commercial bodies in China that, no matter how able their Minister may be or how sincerely desirous he is to protect and advance their interests, his hands are tied at all critical junctures by instructions from Washington bearing the earmarks of having been inspired by the element controlling our major national enterprises in China. With the vast political power of the churches behind it, this element exerts, perhaps unconsciously, an influence at Washington, that no President, statesman, or politician, would dare to antagonize. The successful development of their plans can be attained only by maintaining a sympathetic atmosphere in America towards China, for should popular opinion change and become hostile, it would automatically shut off the stream of voluntary contributions upon whose continuous and increasing flow depends the very existence of the movement. Adequate protection of American trade rights that might involve the use of force or severe diplomatic pressure and so create an anti-American sentiment in China or an anti-Chinese opinion in the United States, must necessarily be highly prejudicial to the success of such a movement, and while we do not insinuate that actual pressure is brought to bear in order to shape our government's policy, yet we do insist that the subconscious reaction of Washington to the desire of our uplift organizations is one of deference and subservience, if not of actual fear. The effect on a trade programme that calls for firm diplomacy is such that every American diplomat appointed to the Peking post sooner or later loses the confidence of his nationals engaged in advancing our material interests in the country.

The effect of this policy on the general international programme which looks to America for leadership is seen in the present tendency to placate the Chinese by surrendering extraterritoriality and those other safeguards deemed essential for the protection of foreign lives and properties in the treaty ports and in the interior. It is not going too far to assert that the present unrest and anti-foreign agitation have their origins in the movement for elevating the cultural status of the Chinese. In fact, every close student of Chinese affairs traces the present outburst of anti-foreign sentiment to the emotional hysteria set in movement by overzealous missionary and educational uplifters.[88]

While the *Far Eastern Review* continued to maintain an editorial policy along these lines, Rodney Gilbert, an American, well known for his work on the staff of the British *North China Daily News and Herald,* wrote articles condemning the alleged influence of missionaries on public and governmental opinion in the United States. In June, 1926, Mr. Gilbert predicted that the assault on certain missions which had occurred in South China,

[87] *Ibid.,* pp. 242-243.
[88] *Ibid.,* p. 243.

in areas under the control of the Kuomintang, would result in turning into an attitude of hostility the sympathy that missionaries had been showing toward the Nationalist movement. "The few noisy opportunists in every missionary body," Mr. Gilbert wrote, "who saw in the blatant clamour of the Chinese radicals for their sovereign rights and their legitimate aspirations an opportunity to curry favor with the Chinese and protect missionary interests, have been discreetly silent for some time."[89] Any such shift in the attitude of missionaries would, he felt, alter the policy of the United States Government towards China:

> If no other country is affected by this change in missionary sentiment, America will be. What the missionaries find it politic to think about China is reflected by the whole church-going population of the country and is impressed most emphatically upon the representatives in Congress in ninety out of every hundred congressional districts. If the missionaries want to be patient and conciliatory with a view to earning the good will of an anti-foreign rabble, America is flooded from end to end with sentimental slush about this country and if the Legation Quarter were invaded and the American Minister were ejected so that some colonel . . . could occupy his quarters, American action would probably be confined to pompous protest.
> If the missionary cause is seriously threatened, however, matters go differently, for missionary opinion can move American gunboats and bring them into lively action when no other force can make them shift their moorings. A change in missionary attitude therefore, means, in the first place, that the tide of unspeakable drool which has been going home for a year about China's rights and aspirations will be abruptly stemmed in both America and England. . . .[90]

"Those who say," Mr. Gilbert asserted later in the same article, "that America could never be brought to endorse intervention in this country know nothing of the American people's penchant for hysterically sentimental crusading nor the power of the medium through which the missionaries work in shaping public opinion."[91]

Later in the year 1926, Mr. Gilbert began to insist that the idea that missionaries should waive their rights and privileges was one which few missionaries outside the Treaty Ports would endorse and was, in fact, only the view of small groups in Peking, Shanghai, and Canton, who were willing to compromise "with the forces of demoralization, brutality and atheism" among the Chinese. Mr. Gilbert's point was that the missionaries who favored treaty revision were expressing their opinion while their opponents remained silent, with the result that the foreign governments did not have

[89] *North China Herald,* July 10, 1926, p. 90.
[90] *Ibid.,* p. 91.
[91] *Ibid.*

access to any views except those of "propagandists — bent upon surrendering everything to the Reds and their 'nationalistic' hirelings on the off chance of winning what they call 'China's good will'."[92]

In response to Mr. Gilbert's charges, Dr. Rawlinson wrote in a long letter to the *North China Herald* that the facts were entirely contrary to Mr. Gilbert's representations. While on the whole the mission body in China had been inarticulate, Dr. Rawlinson said, twenty-three groups of Christians — groups that were mostly large and influential — had supported the policy of their home Boards in respect to treaty revision, while only seven — all comparatively small in number — had passed neutral resolutions, and none had taken a negative stand. When opposition was voiced, he asserted, it came, with only one or two exceptions, from single individuals who had published letters in the press. Moreover, Dr. Rawlinson claimed that the newspapermen who were attacking the N.C.C. and many representatives of the mission group in China had at no time taken the trouble to ascertain any facts concerning missionary opinion.[93]

Fuel was added to the flames of this stubborn and intense controversy by the dispute over the resignation of the China Inland Mission from the N.C.C. in March, 1926. This argument derived its significance from the fact that the China Inland Mission was one of the foremost missionary organizations in China, representative, however, of the so-called "conservative wing" of missionary opinion.[94] At the time of its resignation, the China Inland Mission gave no reasons for its action and, when asked for a statement by the N.C.C., sent a formal reply asserting that it had "consistently abstained" from making any detailed explanation of its withdrawal and still felt that this was "the wise course to pursue." The *North China Herald* declared that "although doctrine was certainly involved" in the resignation of the China Inland Mission, "politics were an equal stumbling block." The N.C.C. responded that the *North China Herald* had no right to draw any such conclusion since the China Inland Mission had made no mention of politics in the pronouncements which had been issued.[95]

The activity of missionaries in respect to the movement for treaty revision was a striking feature of American-Chinese relations in 1925 and

[92] *Ibid.*, November 6, 1926, p. 282.
[93] *Ibid.*, October 30, 1926, p. 213.
[94] See above, p. 83, footnote.
[95] For statements of the China Inland Mission and the N. C. C., see the latter's *Bulletin*, June, 1926, and *The National Christian Council: A Five Years' Review, 1922-1927*, pp. 35-36. For the views of the *North China Herald*, see the issue of April 16, 1927, p. 105. The China Inland Mission was an international mission with about 1,300 members, of which, roughly speaking, more than one-third was British, one-third from the European continent, and less than one-third United States citizens. (Memorandum furnished by China Inland Mission.)

1926. By the end of 1925 virtually every large mission organization in the United States had issued an official statement of its views and an attempt had been made to ascertain the opinions of American missionaries in China. In thus plunging into the midst of the controversy over a revision of the Chinese treaty system immediately after the May 30th Incident, the behaviour of missionaries differed greatly from that of other American groups. American business men and newspapermen in China, members of Congress and the press in the United States, did not for the most part seek to exercise whatever influence they possessed until the Nationalist revolutionary movement reached its most critical stage in 1927. It was precisely at this time, however, that the mission body — whether in terms of organizations, groups, or individual leaders — was least prepared to take part in political matters.[96]

[96] See Chapter XVI.

CHAPTER VI

THE SPECIAL TARIFF CONFERENCE

As the opening of the Special Conference on the Chinese Customs Tariff approached in the autumn of 1925, political conditions inside China grew rapidly worse. This situation persisted throughout the period of the nine long months that the Special Conference was in session and produced difficulties that were virtually insurmountable. While all political groups among the Chinese continued to agree on an anti-foreign policy in regard to their country's external relations, they remained as far apart as ever in respect to domestic concerns.

The appearance of the anti-foreign movement in different parts of China during the summer of 1925 had given a semblance of unity to the country as a whole. This was entirely misleading, however, as in reality China remained divided into different areas that were either under the control of rival warlords or, in the case of the Canton region, under the jurisdiction of the Kuomintang. Tuan Chi-jui was still head of the Provisional Government at Peking but his position was precarious and could be maintained only as long as he was able to enlist the support of one or more of the warlords.[1] While Feng Yu-hsiang and Chang Tso-lin had originally co-operated in the establishment of the Tuan régime, by the summer of 1925 they were again opposed to each other and engaged in preparations for a fresh civil war. Marshal Feng had control over Northwest China and Marshal Chang over the provinces of Manchuria. In addition there were numerous other warlords, most of whom were ready to compete for power in order to enlarge their spheres of influence. Outstanding among these was Wu Pei-fu, who had long been an important figure in the Chinese political scene, and Sun Ch'uan-fang, who had recently risen to prominence as a military leader in the Shanghai area.

It was this division of China into different rival factions that created problems for the Tariff Conference which could not be resolved either by diplomatic skill or by fundamental concepts of policy. In the negotiations conducted during the summer of 1925, the Powers had promised to fulfill the terms of the Washington Customs Treaty. According to the provisions of the Treaty, they were pledged to raise the duty on China's imports by a surtax not exceeding 5% *ad valorem* on luxuries and 2½% on other

---

[1] For a convenient account of the political developments in North China at this time, see Harley Farnsworth MacNair, *China in Revolution*, Chicago, 1931, p. 59 *et seq.*

articles. The Treaty also contemplated a further increase in the tariff to a 12½% rate on condition that the Chinese abolished the system of *likin*.[2] Mr. Kellogg had proceeded even further, first, by indicating that he was willing to accept a plan that would increase the duty on certain classes of commodities beyond the 12½% level[3] and, secondly, by demanding a frank consideration of the question of tariff autonomy.[4]

In practical terms, however, a rise in the tariff meant filling the empty coffers of Tuan Chi-jui and his associates in the Provisional Government at Peking. As the Tuan régime was no more than one of many contending cliques in China, it was evident that — unless provisions were made that would effectively guard against such a contingency — any funds which resulted from an increase in the tariff would be used, not for the benefit of the Chinese people, but for the maintenance of Tuan in power. Under these circumstances, there was little chance that Chang Tso-lin, Wu Pei-fu, and the other warlords of China would sit passively by while the Delegations at the Special Conference entered into negotiations which could only have the immediate effect of strengthening the position of a rival faction. All signs pointed to the renewal of civil war which actually broke out in the middle of October before the opening of the Tariff Conference.[5]

The civil war, which lasted throughout the winter of 1925-1926, had many aspects. The most important from the point of view of the Powers was that Chang Tso-lin and Wu Pei-fu formed an alliance against Feng Yu-hsiang who was supporting the Tuan régime. They laid siege to Peking, where the Special Tariff Conference was in session, and defeated Marshal Feng's troops in April, 1926. Tuan Chi-jui and many of his officials fled and the Provisional Government was declared at an end.

With the overthrow of the Tuan Administration, the Powers determined to abandon the pretense that there existed a central authority in China. Marshals Wu and Chang established a Regency Cabinet but this was regarded as merely an official façade and was never recognized by foreign nations. The situation resolved itself into a division of power between various warlords in the North and the Kuomintang in the South, which continued to give evidence of a constant increase in strength. The

[2] *Conference on the Limitation of Armaments* (United States Government document; proceedings of the Conference), p. 1635.

[3] On October 23, 1925, Mr. Kellogg cabled to Mr. MacMurray: "Our Government would not object in principle if higher rates were placed on American luxuries. . . ." See *Foreign Relations* (1925), p. 859.

[4] See above, Chapter IV.

[5] This aspect of the political situation in China was constantly discussed in the press, and civil war was freely predicted for some time before it commenced; see contemporary issues of the *North China Herald*, for example.

confused conditions, together with the non-existence of any recognized Chinese Government, meant that no Chinese Delegation could be accredited to the Special Conference. The formal sessions, therefore, terminated in April — at the time of the fall of the Tuan régime — and while informal meetings were held until July, they were conducted solely by the foreign Delegations without any Chinese representatives present.

Nevertheless, despite all the genuine difficulties which confronted the Delegates, the Special Conference moved ahead with considerable vigor in its early stages until the political situation in China became virtually hopeless. This was true notwithstanding the fact that before the opening of the Conference opposition was expressed by representatives of most of the political factions in China. In the summer and early autumn of 1925, statements attacking the Conference were issued by Dr. C. T. Wang and Admiral Tsai,[6] both Delegates to the Conference, Mr. Tang Shao-yi,[7] one of China's elder statesmen, Feng Yu-hsiang,[8] Wu Pei-fu,[9] Sun Ch'uan-fang,[10] and various leaders of the Kuomintang.[11] The main difference of opinion indicated by these statements was that some objected to the holding of the Special Conference under any circumstances, while others thought that, if properly handled, it might be made to serve a useful purpose. The former believed that to enter into negotiations on the basis of the old system of "unequal" treaties amounted to a tacit acceptance of China's status as a semi-colonial country. They argued that China should compel — not request — the foreign Powers to fulfill the demands of the Nationalist program and that, if the Chinese people were not as yet strong enough to impose their will on others, they should wait until the time was ripe.[12] On the other hand, there were those who felt that the Special Conference ought to be made a means of achieving a drastic revision of the treaties and, in their view, the first essential was to obtain a pledge from the foreign Delegations that tariff autonomy would be restored to China. Dr. C. T. Wang, in a statement issued in the middle of October, declared that tariff autonomy would be the first

[6] *China Weekly Review*, August 8, 1925, p. 182.

[7] *North China Herald*, October 16, 1925, p. 58; October 24, 1925, p. 140.

[8] *China Weekly Review*, August 8, 1925, p. 182.

[9] *Ibid.*, October 31, 1925, p. 224.

[10] *Ibid.*, October 24, 1925, p. 183.

[11] *Ibid.*, August 8, 1925, p. 182.

[12] Mr. Tang Shao-yi's views as expressed in an exchange of messages with the Peking Government were especially widely quoted. Mr. Tang asserted that China could only acquire strength as an international Power by first putting her own house in order through the establishment of a sound, democratic government. (See *North China Herald*, October 16, 1925, p. 58; October 24, 1925, p. 140.) After this was accomplished he thought China should force the Powers to accept her whole program for Treaty revision. (*China Weekly Review*, October 17, 1925, p. 156.)

item on the Conference agenda and that, if the foreign Delegations refused to concede tariff autonomy, the Conference would be ended as far as the Chinese were concerned. "If the Powers," he said, "will not in an amicable manner consent to China's control of the customs, then we will be obliged to decline to recognize their control and take it over ourselves, despite their objections."[13]

The Special Conference on the Chinese Customs Tariff opened on October 26, 1925.[14] Tuan Chi-jui, as Chief Executive of the Republic of China, made a welcoming speech which said in part:

We wish to avail ourselves of this occasion to renew our claim for tariff autonomy. The idea of tariff autonomy is not a new one. It is an inherent right of a sovereign nation. We, therefore, trust that the friendly nations, actuated by a spirit of equality and mutuality, will appreciate our position. . . . Furthermore, the general feeling of unrest and dissatisfaction, either within a nation or between nations, may be traced to economic inequality. The establishment of a tariff régime in China on a basis of equality is the means toward stabilizing the economic relations between China and the world, and forms the foundation of international remarks.[15]

Following Marshal Tuan's speech, Dr. C. T. Wang presented the program of the Chinese Delegation, which contained five proposals:

1. The participating Powers formally declare to the Government of the Republic of China, their respect for its tariff autonomy and agree to the removal of all the tariff restrictions contained in existing treaties.
2. The Government of the Republic of China agrees to the abolition of *likin* simultaneously with the enforcement of the Chinese National Tariff Law which shall take effect not later than the first day of January in the 18th year of the Republic of China (1929).
3. Previous to the enforcement of the Chinese National Tariff Law, an *interim* surtax of 5% on ordinary goods, 30% on "A" grade luxuries (namely, Wine and Tobacco) and 20% on "B" grade luxuries shall be levied in addition to the present customs tariff of 5% *ad valorem*.
4. The collection of the above-mentioned *interim* surtaxes shall begin three months from the date of signature of the agreement.
5. The decisions relative to the four articles shall be carried into effect from the date of signature of the agreement.[16]

[13] *China Weekly Review*, October 17, 1925, p. 155.

[14] Dr. M. T. Z. Tyau. *The Special Conference on the Chinese Customs Tariff, October, 1925-April, 1926.* Peking, 1928, contains the minutes of the formal sessions of the Conference. Unless otherwise specified, references throughout the remainder of this chapter are to the above publication.

[15] Pp. 36-37.

[16] P. 40.

While many other issues were introduced at the beginning of the Conference, the questions of the restoration of tariff autonomy and the abolition of *likin,* as presented in the Chinese program, dominated the first phase of the negotiations. It was evident from the outset that the Chinese Delegates felt the pressure of the anti-foreign movement and were influenced more by political than economic considerations.[17] At the same time they were, of necessity, fully aware of the suspicions entertained by most people — and essentially shared by the foreign Delegations — that the Tuan Government intended to use any increase in revenue purely for its own advantage.

Dr. C. T. Wang, speaking in support of the Chinese proposal for the return of tariff autonomy, asserted that while it was often said that the right of tariff autonomy had been denied to China because of the lack of unification of the country, this argument revolved in a vicious circle: no government could function without the freedom to obtain funds and the Chinese Government had been "bound hand and foot" by its treaties with the Powers. Another argument, he continued, used against the grant of tariff autonomy, was the fear in some quarters that any increase in revenue would be squandered. His reply to this was that the funds would be devoted to the abolition of *likin,* the payment of debts, and the development of railways and other constructive enterprises.[18]

The Japanese, reversing the position they had taken in the negotiations leading up to the Conference (namely, that they did not wish to go beyond the terms of the Washington Customs Treaty), declared that they were willing to consider the return of tariff autonomy to China on the understanding that this would be brought about in "successive stages." They presented a plan that provided for the conclusion of treaties between China and each of the foreign Powers which would determine the taxes on specified articles.[19] This scheme was predicated upon the fact that the Japanese were fearful of a drastic and indiscriminate change in the Chinese tariff rates because their exports were of cheaper quality than those of other nations, and more likely to be affected both by higher duties and by the competition Chinese manufactures might offer if adequately protected by a tariff wall.

Mr. MacMurray, at an early session of the Conference, submitted a detailed program drafted by the American Delegation.[20] The plan endorsed

[17] See article by C. T. Wang in the *Special Tariff Conference Issue* published as a supplement to the *China Weekly Review* of November 1, 1925, p. 9.

[18] P. 70.

[19] P. 45 *et seq.;* p. 115; also proceedings of the first and second meetings of the Committee on Tariff Autonomy, *passim.*

[20] In a letter to the author, Mr. MacMurray states that these proposals had been worked out in consultation with Dr. Wang on the eve of the opening session of the Tariff Conference; and that he had declared them entirely satisfactory and had undertaken on

the Chinese proposal that tariff autonomy should be re-established on January 1, 1929, but set forth a number of *provisos*. Outstanding among these were clauses providing for the abolition of *likin* as a prerequisite to the recognition of tariff autonomy and for the application of the customs revenue (to be derived from surtaxes levied prior to 1929) to certain specified purposes.[21]

---

behalf of the Chinese Delegation to accept and support them when presented. Whatever the reason, it is clear that the Chinese did not pursue any such course.

[21] The American plan read as follows:

I. That the Powers, other than China, authorize the levying of a surtax of $2\frac{1}{2}\%$ on all goods to be effective on February 1, 1926, and that there be prepared immediately a schedule of luxuries upon which a rate of 5% shall be authorized to be effective not later than July 1, 1926. The increased revenues thus derived shall be held by the Customs Administration subject to such disposition as may be agreed upon by this Conference.

II. That provision shall be made for the levying of the full amount of these surtaxes at the land frontiers.

III. That a new treaty be made which shall provide:

1. three months after the treaty here concluded shall come into force, the Chinese shall be at liberty, as an *interim* measure, and until tariff autonomy shall become effective, to impose a new and uniformly enforced schedule of duties at rates from 5% (the present rate) to $12\frac{1}{2}\%$ on imports, and from 5% (the present rate) to $7\frac{1}{2}\%$ on exports;

2. that from the same date, the rates of duties levied at all land frontiers shall be the same as those levied at the maritime frontiers;

3. that the increase of the Customs revenues derived from putting into effect these provisions shall be accumulated by the Customs Administration and applied for the purposes hereinafter specified;

4. that *likin* and related internal taxes which may be agreed upon shall be abolished;

5. that for the purpose of abolishing *likin*, funds from the customs revenues shall be apportioned among the Provinces in lieu of *likin;*

6. that if *likin* be collected anywhere in violation of agreements entered into for its abolition, the taxpayer shall be entitled to a refund from the Customs Administration of the full amount which he paid as *likin;*

7. that the increase in the Customs revenue derived from the increase in rates of duty shall be devoted to the following purposes:

a) compensation to the Provinces in lieu of *likin,*

b) payment of rebate charges,

c) refunding of the unsecured debt,

d) administrative expenses of the Central Government;

8. that subject to the fulfillment of the provision of Articles 4, 5, 6 and 7 above, the present treaty restrictions on the Chinese tariff shall cease to be effective and the Chinese National Tariff Law shall come into force January 1, 1929, as suggested by the Chinese Delegation;

9. that an effort be made to devise a plan whereby it may be expected that the treaty will go into force at an early date after signature;

10. that if requested by a majority of the Contracting Powers before January 1, 1928, China shall convene on May 1, 1928, a Conference of representatives of the Contracting Powers, for the purpose of declaring whether *likin* has been abolished and of negotiating any further agreements that may need to be arrived at with regard to the subject matter of this treaty. (See p. 94. For table showing a comparison of the Japanese, Chinese, and American plans, see pp. 145-150.)

Just as the American draft differed in these important respects from that presented by the Chinese at the opening session, so the views of the foreign Delegates as a whole differed from those of their Chinese colleagues. The foreign representatives insisted repeatedly that the return of tariff autonomy could not be discussed as an isolated issue since it was closely related to other matters, especially to the question of the abolition of *likin*.[22] The Chinese, on the other hand, took the position that they were unwilling to proceed with the Conference until the principle of tariff autonomy had been formally endorsed by the foreign Delegations. Dr. Wang stated, specifically, that the Chinese Government set great store on receiving from the Powers a declaration of their respect for China's tariff autonomy.[23] Furthermore, the Chinese made it evident that they were definitely opposed to regarding the enjoyment of tariff autonomy as dependent upon the abolition of *likin*. The Chinese Government sent a formal statement to the Conference declaring that *likin* would be abolished by January 1, 1929,[24] and the Chinese Delegation described in detail the methods by which it was proposed to reach this goal.[25] When, however, the foreign representatives attempted to bring the question of *likin* into the discussions at the Conference, the Chinese refused on the basis that *likin* was a system of domestic taxes and as such should not be made the subject of negotiations with outside Powers. "The view of the Chinese Delegation," they said in a memorandum submitted to the Conference, "is that the abolition of *likin* is a measure which China voluntarily declares she is prepared to do. We have already put before you the measures whereby we can abolish *likin* within three years, i.e., not later than January 1, 1929. We believe the Foreign Delegations are ready to admit that such a reform is after all an internal problem. . . ."[26]

Criticism of the Chinese method of procedure was voiced with particular emphasis by Silas H. Strawn, who played an active role in conducting

[22] See second meeting of Committee on Provisional Measures, p. 145 *et seq.*

[23] P. 81.

[24] P. 82.

[25] P. 82.

[26] P. 157. It was doubtful whether *likin* could be abolished in view of the fact that it was a local tax, and that different areas of China were under the control of various leaders hostile to the Central Government. On October 31, 1925, Mr. Kellogg cabled to the American Delegation:

". . . the Department is skeptical of the final success of negotiations which involve an undertaking for the abolition of *likin* on the part of the present Chinese Administration or of any government which is likely to succeed it. Since, however, the Chinese Delegation has made a proposal which includes a plan for the abolition of these provincial taxes and, as this certainly is to the advantage of foreign trade, the Department considers it is best to encourage the Chinese to put this proposal into effect." (*Foreign Relations, 1925,* p. 875.)

the discussions for the United States. *Likin,* he protested, must be eliminated before the Chinese Tariff Law came into operation; any other course meant merely adding *likin* to whatever increase was made in the customs duties.[27] Moreover, he said, as he interpreted the Washington Customs Treaty, it contemplated that the various foreign Delegations should collaborate with China in finding a way to abolish *likin.*[28] Mr. Strawn indicated that, in his opinion, the Chinese were adopting an arbitrary attitude; a conference, he observed, was a place where people "sit around and confer," but it was not expected that they should lay down ultimata.[29]

Despite Mr. Strawn's objections and those of his foreign colleagues, the wishes of the Chinese Delegation prevailed. A statement was drafted which was the same in substance as the first two proposals presented by the Chinese on the opening day of the Conference. In it, the Powers affirmed that they recognized China's right to enjoy tariff autonomy and agreed to the going into effect of the Chinese National Tariff Law on January 1, 1929; the Chinese Government, on its part, announced that the abolition of *likin* would be carried out before that date.[30]

This statement was unanimously accepted by the members of the Conference on November 19, 1925, although in the case of most of the countries involved, it was subject to ratification by their respective governments.[31] Dr. Wang congratulated the Conference on its accomplishments, saying that it had "set a milestone for fair play and just dealings between China and the friendly Powers."[32] Dr. W. W. Yen, also representing China, assured the other Delegations that when the results of their deliberations were announced to the Chinese nation "there would be intense gratification, which would certainly lead to a much better understanding between the Chinese people and the rest of the world."[33]

After the resolutions concerning tariff autonomy and the abolition of *likin* had been issued to the public, the Conference settled down to the less spectacular aspects of its work which were conducted behind closed doors. From the outset of the Conference, the foreign Delegations emphasized two points which essentially influenced all the negotiations, namely, that they had the power to fulfill the terms of the Washington Customs

[27] P. 184. According to Mr. Kellogg's own statement he did not give the American Delegation any instructions as to whether the grant of tariff autonomy to China should be made dependent upon the abolition of *likin.* (*Foreign Relations,* 1925, p. 883.)
[28] P. 180.
[29] P. 184.
[30] P. 249.
[31] P. 197.
[32] P. 198.
[33] P. 199.

Treaty and therefore regarded this as their primary responsibility; and that they did not have the authority to go beyond the provisions of the Washington Treaty so far as concluding any final arrangements were concerned. In other words, the foreign Delegations had the right, given them by the Washington Treaty, to authorize the levy of $2\frac{1}{2}\%$ and 5% surtaxes and to decide under what conditions and for what purposes the revenue derived from these surtaxes was to be applied.[34] But if the Special Conference reached an agreement on matters which exceeded or fell outside of the provisions of the Washington Treaty, this would of necessity have to be embodied in the draft of a new treaty which the Delegations would be obliged to submit to their respective governments to go through the regular constitutional processes involved in the ratification of a treaty.

The difficulty lay in the fact that the so-called Washington surtaxes of $2\frac{1}{2}\%$ and 5% could not yield a sum which would meet the requirements of the Chinese Government but that, on the other hand, the negotiation and ratification of a new treaty would obviously entail a long delay. To meet this situation, the plans presented by both the Chinese and American Delegations at the outset of the Conference included recommendations for the levy of *interim* surtaxes that were to be higher than those specified in the Washington Treaty. Mr. MacMurray in submitting the American proposals stated that the United States Delegation was prepared to authorize the levy of the Washington surtaxes at once and to proceed with the negotiation of a new treaty which would provide *interim* surtaxes at a higher rate.[35] Mr. Strawn, commenting on the American proposals, explained the situation as follows: The Chinese Government was in need of funds and the foreign Powers wished to provide as much relief as possible. Legally all that the American Delegation could do without further delay was to implement the Washington surtaxes and to recommend a new treaty for ratification to their government. The experts agreed that the revenue to be derived from $2\frac{1}{2}\%$ and 5% surtaxes would not exceed $30,000,000 and that the abolition of *likin* required $70,000,000. For this reason, the American Delegation was proposing the draft of a new treaty which would authorize the levy of *interim* surtaxes ranging from 5% to $12\frac{1}{2}\%$. Mr. Strawn added — with an eye to the political situation in China — that the American Delegates placed particular emphasis upon the collection, custody, and distribution of the surtax

[34] See text of Washington Treaty on the Chinese Customs Tariff, *Conference on the Limitation of Armaments* (United States Government document; proceedings of the Conference), p. 1635.

This statement is not meant to suggest that the Delegations could act purely on the basis of their own judgment; in most instances their decisions had to receive the approval of the Foreign Offices of their respective governments.

[35] P. 94.

revenue by the Customs Administration which they felt would safeguard the funds from seizure by any local factions.[36]

The views of the foreign Delegates in general were the same as those expressed by Mr. Strawn. The first step to be undertaken, they felt, was the authorization of the Washington surtaxes. With this in mind, they repeatedly urged upon their Chinese colleagues the advisability of bringing the Washington Treaty into force.[37] As time went by it became evident, however, that the Chinese representatives did not wish to follow this procedure.[38] While no direct statement was made on the subject by the Chinese Delegates throughout the first four months of the Conference, it was apparent to all that they were seeking to avoid entering into any discussion of the imposition of the Washington surtaxes.

Following the acceptance of the resolutions on the restoration of tariff autonomy and the abolition of *likin*, a Committee of the Conference began to debate the purposes for which the funds derived from an increase in the tariff rates might be used. The Chinese Delegation adopted the attitude which they had already shown in the negotiations dealing with the question of the abolition of *likin*, and which they were to maintain in respect to many of the important issues raised at the Conference, namely, that certain matters pertained primarily to the internal conditions of China and could not reasonably be regarded as subjects for deliberation at an international conference. Dr. Yen declared at length and with emphasis that any attempt by the foreign Delegates to examine the financial condition of the Chinese Government would be regarded as an interference in the domestic concerns of China. One of the objects of the Washington Treaty, he stated, was to determine the purposes to which the surtax revenue was to be devoted; but, he claimed, the foreign Delegations seemed prepared to go beyond the terms of the Washington Treaty and to "investigate into how China was going to carry out those purposes." The matter of procedure, he asserted, was "not to be made the subject of decision, or, to use a fairly strong word, imposition on the part of the Powers."[39]

[36] P. 118 *et seq.* The point in respect to the Chinese Maritime Customs Administration was that it enjoyed the confidence of the Powers. While the Customs Service was a Chinese Government organization, it had, for over half a century, been headed by a British subject whose authority was extensive; moreover, although in the 1920's a large proportion of the Customs employees were Chinese, the highest posts were held by foreigners. In general, the Customs Administration was noted for its efficiency and integrity. (Blakeslee, *The Pacific Area*, pp. 17-19. For criticisms of the Chinese Maritime Customs Administration, see Willoughby, *Foreign Rights and Interests in China*, Vol. 2, p. 768. For Mr. Strawn's views on the Customs Service, see below, p. 186.)

[37] See, for example, p. 190.

[38] *Ibid.*

[39] For Dr. Yen's statement, see p. 253.

It was generally recognized by the Conference that the proceeds of the increased tariff were to be devoted to three purposes: (1) the administrative expenses of the Central Government at Peking, (2) the funding of the unsecured debt, and (3) the abolition of *likin*.[40] As these issues raised many difficult problems in turn, committees and sub-committees were appointed to deal with them. The Committee on *Likin* attempted to define *likin* in order to arrive at an agreement concerning the kinds of taxes to be classified under this term.[41] The Chinese Delegates affirmed that they had always understood *likin* to be a tax on goods in transit.[42] Mr. Strawn, on the other hand, argued that any such definition was too vague and stated that in his opinion *likin* should be regarded as embracing destination taxes, consumption taxes, excise or license duties, examination or protection fees, and taxes of "whatever nature, levied directly or indirectly upon the conveyance or handling" of foreign duty-paid imports.[43] The British representatives' supported Mr. Strawn's view in general and suggested that *likin* be defined as "all taxes on goods from the point of import or production up to the point of consumption in the shop."[44] They also maintained that the consumption taxes should be "moderate" and should be levied without discrimination between foreign and domestic commodities.[45] No solution was reached as the Chinese Delegates reiterated that they had always defined *likin* as a tax on goods in transit and that any new definition would require careful thought.[46]

In the deliberations on the question of China's debts, the Chinese again adopted the position that the question of debt consolidation was a domestic issue which could not properly be regarded as part of the business of the Special Conference; the Chinese Government, they explained, intended to appoint a commission to deal with the problem.[47] This matter was also set aside for the time being and most of the work on debt consolidation was undertaken later at informal meetings of Conference members.[48]

[40] The Chinese also suggested that funds be earmarked for the development of railways and other constructive enterprises. The American plan had added to the three purposes noted above a fourth: the payment of rebate charges if *likin* were illegally exacted.

[41] Pp. 266-277.

[42] P. 271.

[43] P. 267.

[44] P. 274.

[45] P. 274.

[46] P. 271.

[47] P. 302.

[48] P. 304. In the meetings dealing with the consolidation of debts, various Delegations submitted plans, but there was a sharp division of opinion over the questions involved and no solution was reached. The conversations concerning the debt were—according to the report of the American Delegation—broken off by the British on May 3, 1926. For details of this phase of the negotiations, see below, p. 111. (The section of the American

Another problem which came under discussion at this time was the rate of the *interim* surtaxes to be imposed before January 1, 1929, the date on which tariff autonomy was to be re-established. It will be recalled that the Chinese plan, presented at the outset of the Conference, had proposed an *interim* surtax of 5% on ordinary goods, 20% on so-called grade "B" luxuries, and 30% on grade "A" luxuries (such as wine and tobacco), while the American and Japanese programs had recommended a schedule of rates which would not have exceeded 12½% on imports.

The main difficulty in respect to this matter was not so much the question of the tariff rates as it was that the entire issue reverted back to the problem of the purposes for which funds to be derived from the increased tariff were to be employed. The foreign Delegates — especially the American — insisted that it was impossible to determine the rates of the surtaxes before the Chinese Government had provided definite information as to the amount of money needed to carry out such purposes as the Conference had in mind.[49] This posed once more the difficult problem of whether or not the Tuan régime, or any other faction that seized power in Peking, would use the funds obtained from the surtaxes for the purposes suggested by the Conference or for the furtherance of its own political ambitions.

In December, the Conference took a two months' recess during which an attempt was made to untangle some of its knottier problems through informal discussions.[50]

When the Conference reconvened on February 18, 1926, the negotiations entered a new stage. The Chinese Delegation immediately submitted two resolutions. The first declared that the Powers resolved and agreed that the annual revenue to be derived from the *interim* surtaxes would amount to between $90,000,000 and $100,000,000, a sum which the Chinese had already, on a number of occasions, indicated was essential for the fulfillment of the purposes to which the Conference agreed the proceeds of the surtaxes should be devoted.[51] The second resolution stipulated that a 2½% surtax on ordinary dutiable articles should be made effective as of April 1, 1926, and a 5% surtax on luxuries, not later than June 1, 1926.[52]

Delegates' report on the Special Conference which deals with debt consolidation will be found in *Foreign Relations*, 1926, pp. 829-833. For some of the plans submitted by the various Delegations, see Stanley F. Wright, *China's Struggle for Tariff Autonomy*, Shanghai, 1938, pp. 525-536.) The issue of the consolidation of debts was a particularly unpopular one among the Chinese people and charges were frequently made that the foreign Delegations were merely assuming the functions of debt-collecting agencies. Also, a considerable proportion of the foreign debt consisted of the so-called "Nishihara loans" which were bitterly resented by the Chinese and which many thought should be repudiated.

[49] Pp. 310-315.
[50] For negotiations conducted during recess, see Wright, *op. cit.*, pp. 524-537.
[51] P. 224.
[52] P. 224.

In the course of the deliberations on the second resolution, the Chinese finally disclosed the motives which had led them to skirt the issue of the Washington surtaxes up to this point. Mr. Strawn recalled that at the beginning of the Conference, the American Delegation had offered to implement the 2½% and 5% surtaxes immediately. At that time, he said, he had not heard any dissenting voice except that of China, who was unwilling to accept the proposition "for some reason of her own which he did not know." He had been prepared to renew the offer at any time, he declared, and "if China was being deprived of the 2½%, it certainly was not the fault of the foreigners."[53]

In answer to this, the Chinese Delegates explained that if the Chinese Government had accepted a 2½% and 5% surtax at the outset of the Conference, it would have exposed itself to the charge of obtaining what it could for government expenses and letting the rest go. There had been a general outcry, they declared, against convening the Conference because of the fear that it would do nothing more than execute the terms of the Washington Treaty. However, they said, the sympathetic attitude of the foreign Delegates had won over the Chinese people, so that there was now no opposition to the work of the Conference and it was, therefore, possible to support the Washington surtaxes.[54]

The negotiations conducted throughout the next months centered to a considerable extent on the Chinese insistence that the resolution on *interim* surtaxes, being considered by the Conference, should state specifically that the annual revenue to be obtained from such surtaxes would amount to $90,000,000. This matter became the subject of seemingly endless discussion, conducted, at times, in a decidedly acrimonious fashion. In its essence, it boiled down to the all-too familiar issue that the Powers feared that the Tuan Government — either through its own volition or under pressure from others — would misuse the money to be derived from the surtaxes (or that the funds would be seized and misused by some rival faction). In order not to offend the feelings of the Chinese, the foreign Delegates made few references to the political conditions in China throughout the earlier sessions of the Conference, but as the situation went from bad to worse more pointed remarks were made. Count de Martel, the French Minister, on one occasion, inquired whether the Peking Government was not attempting to obtain full liberty to spend the funds from the surtaxes in its own way;[55] on another occasion, he asked bluntly whether the Chinese Government intended to float a loan, using the $90,000,000 that they hoped to receive

[53] P. 230.
[54] Pp. 230, 238.
[55] P. 483.

from the surtaxes as security.[56] Several Delegates stated that they understood that the income from the Washington surtaxes had already been pledged by the Tuan Administration.[57] Allusions were made to occurrences outside the Conference which the foreign Delegates said made them want to proceed with caution.[58] Colonel Peel of the British Delegation remarked at one of the later sessions that he wished to raise a point, although he did so with diffidence: as the principal sources of revenue were in the hands of "certain people" who were not entirely in accord with the Central Government at Peking, no one could tell what would meet with the approval of the Chinese nation as a whole; it was therefore, he said, difficult to predict the attitude of the British Government toward any arrangement that might be made at the Conference.[59]

The American Delegation attempted to meet the problem of safeguarding the funds against misuse by one or another of the political groups in China through a resolution which they submitted to the other members of the Conference. The resolution stated in part that the surtax revenue should be held by the Customs Administration to be disposed of according to plans to be agreed on at the Conference, and that "pending such disposition the said revenue, or any part thereof, shall not be in any way, directly or indirectly, pledged or hypothecated to secure any indebtedness heretofore or hereafter incurred or created by the Chinese Government or any department, bureau or agency thereof."[60] In explanation of this statement, Mr. Strawn said that it was in no way intended as a "reflection on the gentlemen" who were conducting the negotiations, but "as a protection to the Chinese Delegates in anticipation of the importunities of *tuchuns* and warlords, by putting it beyond the powers of anybody to raise any money on anticipated revenue."[61]

The American resolution called forth a sharp rebuke from Dr. Yen who said that the "Chinese Delegation could not consider, much less consent to, the imposing of such humiliating conditions;" no Delegation, he asserted, could accept such wording in a formal document.[62] Mr. Strawn answered that the terms were not "humiliating" but "protective" in view of the disturbed political situation existing in China.[63] The representatives of the Powers did not want to wake up some day, he said, to the realization that the

[56] P. 388.
[57] P. 434.
[58] P. 492.
[59] P. 493.
[60] P. 395.
[61] P. 395.
[62] Pp. 396, 401.
[63] P. 396.

militarists had forced the Peking Administration to borrow money on funds which were not, as yet, at its disposition.[64] In line with this general argument, a number of the other foreign Delegates insisted that the revenue should be held by the Customs Administration to insure its not being seized by one or the other of China's warring political leaders.[65] After further debate, the Chinese agreed that the draft resolution should provide for the funds being placed in the custody of the Customs Administration, to be used for such purposes as the Conference might later determine.[66]

In March — when it looked as though the Conference might reach an agreement on many of the more significant issues — the Japanese added a new complication by submitting a *proviso* which stated that in case the purposes and conditions related to the expenditure of the Washington surtax revenue should not have been agreed upon before May 31, 1926, the surtaxes should not take effect until fifteen days after such an agreement had been reached.[67] This meant that the imposition of the surtaxes, instead of being fixed for a definite date, such as June 15th, would be made contingent on a settlement concerning the purposes and conditions involved in their use. The Japanese explained that this was a technicality but that any other method of procedure would not be in accord with the provisions of the Washington Treaty and might therefore meet with opposition from the Tokyo Foreign Office.[68] The Chinese, however, were not willing to accept the Japanese *proviso*.[69]

The meeting discussing the Japanese *proviso* was the last to be held during the formal session of the Special Conference, with the exception of the meetings of one of the technical committees. Actually one of the most valuable and permanent contributions of the Conference was the technical work done by the foreign experts, primarily the British, American, and Japanese.[70] Based on detailed schedules of proposed surtaxes submitted by the Chinese, the American Delegates suggested that, in dealing with the *interim* surtaxes, the tariff should be graded in six to eight classes ranging from $7\frac{1}{2}\%$ to 25% (a significant increase over the maximum of $7\frac{1}{2}\%$ originally recommended by the United States Delegation).[71] After considerable discussion, a schedule of rates and classifications, following the general lines

[64] P. 403.
[65] Pp. 395-404.
[66] P. 462.
[67] P. 476.
[68] Pp. 477-481.
[69] P. 503.
[70] *Foreign Relations* (1926), pp. 826-828. The American Technical advisers were Stanley K. Hornbeck and Mahlon F. Perkins.
[71] *Ibid.*, p. 828.

of the American proposals, was agreed upon by the technical advisers and submitted on March 25, 1926, by the American, British, and Japanese Delegations.[72] This list eventually formed the basis of China's National Tariff Law in 1929. It meant that the Chinese had profited by the work of the foreign experts who possessed an intimate knowledge of the issues at stake.[73]

As stated earlier, the Tuan Administration was overthrown in April, 1926, and a Committee of Public Safety ruled for a few weeks, which was in turn followed by a Regency Cabinet established on May 13th. With the exception of Dr. W. W. Yen and Admiral Tsai, all of the Chinese Delegates to the Special Conference fled from Peking. The Powers, it will be recalled, did not recognize the Regency Cabinet and the Chinese ceased, from this time on, to co-operate in the work of the Conference. The chaotic situation in North China was further complicated by the growth of power of the Kuomintang in the South which was preparing for the famous Northern Expedition that was launched in the early summer of 1926.

As the foreign Delegates were anxious to continue the work of the Conference, despite the extreme confusion presented by the political developments in China, they proceeded to meet informally. The British suggested that the Powers make a public declaration which would in effect have amounted to an appeal to the Chinese people to sink their internal differences and establish a stable government so that the tariff negotiations could be carried to a quick and satisfactory conclusion.[74] The United States Delegation opposed this scheme, believing that it indicated a desire on the part of the British representatives to adjourn the Conference indefinitely and return home.[75] The Americans were convinced that such a move would be likely to precipitate a new wave of anti-foreign outbreaks in China and felt that "no opening should be left for the Chinese to say that the foreign Delegations were not seriously attempting to help China and that they were not acting in good faith."[76] As a practical form of procedure, the American representatives recommended that the foreign Delegations try to reach an agreement on a concrete program which would form the basis of a new treaty; having reached such an agreement, if there was no Chinese Government competent to sign a treaty, the foreign Powers could "conscientiously lay this program on the table to be taken up at the appropriate moment."[77]

Secretary of State Kellogg agreed with the views of the United States

[72] Wright, op. cit., p. 600.
[73] Ibid.
[74] Foreign Relations (1926), pp. 745-746.
[75] Ibid., p. 746.
[76] Ibid., p. 832.
[77] Ibid.

Delegation and, accordingly, sent instructions to the American Ambassador at London, Alanson B. Houghton, which stated that

> ... the American Delegation will, with the approval of the Department, take the position that it is prepared to go on with the Conference as far as political conditions will permit, no matter what other nationalities may refuse to go along with them. You may bring the above informally to the attention of the British Foreign Office and explain orally that this Government is of the opinion that the gravity of the situation in China respecting foreign rights and interests demands that the interested Powers who have been participating in the Tariff Conference should exhaust every effort to fulfill the undertaking entered into at the Washington Conference and the promises made to the Chinese Government last fall. You will express to the British Foreign Office, this Government's sincere hope that the British Government may find itself able to continue to co-operate with us and the other interested Powers in bringing to a conclusion the task which was begun last October and upon which it would appear much progress has been made.[78]

Actually the British Government seems to have had no intention of withdrawing from the Special Conference.[79] Instead they agreed with the other governments concerned that no stone should be left unturned in the effort to reach an agreement among the foreign Delegations that would at least implement the Washington Customs Treaty. In May, 1926, therefore, the British, American, and Japanese advisers co-operated in revising the draft resolution authorizing the Washington surtaxes which had been under discussion during the formal sessions of the Conference while the Chinese were still participating in the negotiations.[80]

The revised text when completed by the technical advisers differed in two important respects from the original draft. First, it specified the manner in which the surtax revenue should be used: (1) $9,000,000 annually for the abolition of *likin;* (2) $750,000 monthly for the administrative expenses of the government; (3) the remainder for the liquidation of the unsecured and inadequately secured debt. Secondly, while the original resolution contemplated impounding all of the surtax revenue, the revised draft provided for the distribution of one-half the money, stipulating that only the funds to be used for the liquidation of the debts should be held by the Maritime Customs Administration.[81]

The draft of the resolution as revised by the British, American, and Japanese representatives was presented to the other foreign Delegations on

[78] *Ibid.*, p. 748.
[79] *Ibid.*, pp. 749, 755.
[80] *Ibid.*, p. 750.
[81] *Ibid.*, pp. 750, 834.

May 15th and was unanimously adopted with the understanding that the Delegates would refer it to their respective Governments for approval.[82] Secretary of State Kellogg immediately gave his assent,[83] but further issues were raised by the British and Japanese Governments.

The views of the British at this stage of the negotiations centered to a certain extent on the question of debt consolidation, but expanded from there to include a consideration of the principles that should determine the policy of the Treaty Powers. On the 28th of May, the British Foreign Office sent a memorandum to the State Department in Washington which became one of the cornerstones of British policy for this period.[84] It showed how profoundly the ideas of the British Government had altered from the "severe" attitude adopted during the negotiations conducted in the summer of 1925 when they recommended sending a note "to warn the Chinese Government" that, if the anti-foreign movement in China continued, the Powers would be "obliged to consult together as to the immediate measures necessary to protect their interests."[85]

Because of the importance of the British memorandum of May 28th, it is quoted here at some length:

> The United States Government will no doubt recollect that His Majesty's Government were from the first averse to the imposition on the Chinese Government of any scheme of consolidation of the unsecured debt as part of the work of the Tariff Conference and that they only agreed later and with great reluctance to the discussion of any such scheme at the Conference. If the schemes of the foreign Delegations for the consolidation of the unsecured debt should postulate too strict a control over China's customs revenues (shortly to be increased by tariff autonomy) His Majesty's Government are afraid that a dangerous deadlock may arise, for the discussions on this subject show that the Chinese, though willing to bind themselves to devote a proportion of their revenues to the unsecured debt, have declined to allow the details of debt consolidation to be dealt with by the Tariff Conference, and will refuse to submit to any extension of foreign control — for that of any other purpose — over China's customs revenues.
>
> His Majesty's Government, after full consideration and prolonged consultation with their Delegation in Peking, have come to the conclusion that, while they are ready to agree to any reasonable scheme for dealing with the unsecured debt put forward by the Chinese and agreed to by the other Powers, it would not be right to associate themselves with any attempt to force upon the Chinese a greater degree of foreign control over the revenues required for that purpose than they are prepared voluntarily to concede. A policy involving increase of foreign control, and capable of being regarded as an encroachment on that sovereignty and independence

---

[82] *Ibid.*, pp. 753, 833.
[83] *Ibid.*, p. 754.
[84] Text of memorandum, *ibid.*, pp. 755-757.
[85] See above, p. 58.

of China which the Powers agreed at Washington to respect, is so funda-
mentally opposed to the traditional policy of the United States towards
China that His Majesty's Government are disposed to believe that the
State Department will share their anxiety on this subject.

It is true that His Majesty's Government originally desired to exact
proper guarantees from China in regard to the abolition of *likin* as a
condition precedent to the grant of the Washington surtaxes, but they
have come to the conclusion that, in the altered circumstances and
changed asmosphere of today, any attempt to insist upon guarantees
against the will of the Chinese Government would only result in post-
poning indefinitely the liquidation of the Washington promises. They
are as anxious as the United States Government fully to implement these
promises at the earliest possible moment, and believe that it would be
contrary to the intentions of both governments, both at and subsequent
to the Washington Conference, to subordinate the fulfillment of these
promises to the imposition upon China of a scheme for the consolidation
of her unsecured debt and extension of foreign control over her customs
revenues. Any failure to implement the Washington Treaty might create
a very dangerous situation, and His Majesty's Government, now, therefore,
hold the view that if any reasonably satisfactory assurances are given by the
Chinese Government as to the use which it proposes to make of the new
revenues the Powers should accept such assurances, abstain from any attempt to impose control or exact guarantees, and forthwith authorize the
levy of the surtaxes. They feel confident that a policy, so closely in accord
with the friendship and generosity always displayed by the United States
of America towards the people of China, will receive the full and cordial
support of the United States Government.

In general, therefore, the British felt that the Powers should avoid
adopting a policy which involved an increase of foreign control over the
functions of the Chinese Government, and which could be regarded as a
further curtailment of the independence of China as a nation. Applying
this principle to the specific problems on hand, the British Government
objected to any agreement which would provide that a certain portion of
the revenue, obtained from the Washington surtaxes, should be held in
custody by the Maritime Customs Administration for the sake of the consolidation of the unsecured debt. In addition, the British suggested that
the Powers should authorize the levy of the Washington surtaxes immediately, asking only that the Chinese Government give "reasonably satisfactory assurances" as to the use it intended to make of the funds.

In transmitting the British memorandum to the State Department,
Mr. Houghton observed that, in his opinion, the British were anxious to
have the Conference make some gesture that would serve to quiet anti-
foreign — and especially anti-British — feeling in China. This, he thought,
was the reason for their desire to grant the Washington surtaxes immedi-

ately and for their opposition to foreign control of the customs revenue for debt consolidation.[86]

The reaction of the American Delegation at the Special Tariff Conference to the British memorandum was expressed in a cable to the State Department in Washington, which said in part:

The British cable evidences misconception of the underlying purpose of debt consolidation which is not so much one for the satisfaction of China's foreign creditors as it is for the re-establishment of China's credit, which is necessary precedent to continuation of China's foreign trade and her development.

Rebellious and impatient attitude of China's foreign creditors is caused not so much by their failure to receive payment of their debts as by the persistent ignoring and violation by the Chinese Government of its contracts with foreign creditors and the superimposing of domestic loans ahead of the foreign debts, the proceeds of which loans have been devoted to carrying on of useless wars.

The British cable evidences solicitude that if the Powers are too insistent upon an orderly consolidation of China's debts it will prejudice British trade. On the contrary we believe that the leading Chinese merchants and bankers will agree with foreign traders and creditors that the re-establishment of China's credit is her most vital problem. The thoughtful Chinese welcome an equitable debt consolidation to that end.

We would be doing a great injustice to the Chinese people as well as to foreign trade if we agreed upon treaty largely increasing China's revenue without consolidating her debts and attempting to re-establish her credit. Unrestrained by such obligation the Chinese Government would continue in the future as it has in the past to dissipate all the revenue in the perpetuation of useless wars.[87]

[86] *Foreign Relations* (1926), p. 755.

On May 6, 1926, Ambassador Houghton had cabled to the State Department a report of a conversation with Victor Wellesley, British Deputy Under Secretary of State for Foreign Affairs:

"He [Wellesley] pointed out that the Chinese did not favor debt consolidation. Since more debt consolidation looked toward giving security to the many, and in some instances very questionable, loans made by the Northern Government, which proceeds had in part been used to fight against the South, he indicated that he was fearful about what attitude might be taken by Canton in regard to such debt consolidation, in view particularly of British interests in South China."

[87] *Foreign Relations* (1926), pp. 758-759. The question of debt consolidation remained a moot point between the British and American Delegations. On May 3, 1926, Mr. Stewart of the British Delegation had announced, at a meeting of the Conference, that he was under instructions to discontinue taking part in the informal conversations being conducted on the subject of the debts. Later, the British indicated that the debt issue was the primary reason for the failure of the Conference to reach a definite agreement. In response to a statement of the British views to this effect, Mr. MacMurray cabled the State Department in December, 1926: "If debt consolidation was the fundamental cause of the unwillingness of the British Delegation to proceed with the work of the Conference, then Wellesley's [British Deputy Under Secretary of State for Foreign Affairs] statement that this question wrecked the Conference would appear to be explicable only on the

The British, however, continued to work on the basis of the ideas embodied in their memorandum. They realized that the policy which they advocated rested on the hypothesis that there existed in Peking, a government which could, with justification, be called *the* Government of China and which would spend the new funds at its command wisely, in the service of the Chinese people. But this was obviously not the case. The administration of Chang Tso-lin and Wu Pei-fu had not been recognized by the Powers, and the importance of other political groups in China could scarcely be overlooked in any realistic estimate of the situation. To meet this fundamental difficulty, the British Delegation at the Special Conference suggested that the following procedure be adopted in respect to the Washington surtax agreement which had been accepted by the foreign members of the Conference and referred to their respective governments: When the protocol was endorsed by the various governments, they should determine whether there was a Chinese Government to treat with, in which case the protocol should be submitted as a basis for negotiation, accompanied by a note stating that, if any of the provinces opposed the agreement, the collection of the surtaxes should be postponed until such opposition had been removed.[88] The British proposal was informally approved by the other foreign Delegations.[89]

By the middle of June, all the foreign governments, with the exception of the Japanese, were ready to accept the Washington surtax protocol as a basis for negotiation with the Chinese.[90] In private meetings with the American and British Delegations, the Japanese stated that their Government did not wish to implement the Washington surtaxes independently of the larger treaty which would provide for the *interim* surtaxes that the Special Conference had had under consideration from the outset. To this they added, however, that if all the other Powers were prepared to authorize the Washington surtaxes at once, the Japanese Government would agree to the protocol as drafted if the sections granting funds for the abolition of *likin* were deleted.[91] This meant that all of the revenue from the surtaxes, except the $750,000 to be devoted monthly to the administrative expenses of the Government, would be impounded to await further disposition by the

---

theory that the British Government preferred to see the Conference wrecked rather than meet in a spirit of compromise the views of the other Delegations, or that on or about May 3rd the British Government reversed itself as to its willingness to discuss any plan of debt consolidation whatsoever." (*Ibid.*, p. 862; see also, pp. 831, 749, 752, 759.)

[88] *Ibid.*, p. 758.
[89] *Ibid.*
[90] *Ibid.*, p. 760.
[91] *Ibid.*, p. 761.

Conference. Any such policy was, of course, contrary to the views expressed in the British memorandum which urged the Powers to refrain from any action that would involve an increase of control over the Chinese customs.

In notifying the State Department, on June 28th, of the stand taken by the Japanese, the American Delegation commented as follows:

> The Japanese attitude during the past six weeks has been very disappointing to the American Delegation especially in view of the very cordial spirit of co-operation which had existed between the two Delegations throughout the Conference. . . . The new attitude of the Japanese, indicative of a desire to dictate terms, or, in the alternative, of a readiness to take independent action, has been a surprise. The situation is probably to be explained by reason of a difference of opinion between the Japanese Foreign Office and the Japanese Delegation. . . . Whatever the cause, the effect has not been the less annoying with respect to proceeding with the work of the Conference.
>
> While it is, of course, impossible to ascertain the exact purpose of the Japanese proposals, one cannot avoid the impression that the Tokyo Foreign Office does not desire, at the present juncture, to make any commitments, preferring to watch the development and outcome of the present political situation in Peking.[92]

At the same time, the American Delegation stated that the Japanese were apparently launching a newspaper campaign designed to place the blame for a delay in the work of the Conference — or for its eventual failure — on the American Delegation. As one of the points emphasized in the newspaper articles was Mr. Strawn's coming departure for the United States, which was presented in a manner to suggest that the American Delegates no longer wished to co-operate in the proceedings of the Conference, Mr. Strawn himself issued a statement clarifying his position to the local press.[93]

While the foreign Powers were thus struggling with a continuous series of problems, the internal situation in China was becoming constantly more involved. On June 30th, the American Delegation cabled Secretary of State Kellogg that Chang Tso-lin and Wu Pei-fu would probably form a cabinet in the expectation that the Washington surtax protocol would be negotiated, thus enabling them to borrow money to continue the war against Feng Yu-hsiang.[94] The Powers, the American Delegation observed, were facing two horns of a dilemma. If they implemented the Washington surtaxes, the Kuomintang and Feng Yu-hsiang and his supporters would say that the Special Conference was running counter to the aims of the

[92] *Ibid.*, p. 762.
[93] *Ibid.*, pp. 762-763.
[94] June 30th cable; in *ibid.*, p. 763-766.

Washington Customs Treaty which certainly did not intend to have one party in China use an increase in the tariff revenue for the sake of waging a civil war against opposing groups; on the other hand, if the Powers failed to implement the surtaxes, Marshals Chang and Wu and their followers would charge the Powers with bad faith.

In the same cable, the American Delegates stated that according to present indications they would shortly have to choose between one of three plans of action: (a) refuse to negotiate the protocol with the Chang-Wu cabinet on the ground that the United States had not recognized it as a central government; (b) follow the Japanese scheme and recognize the cabinet, giving it unconditionally $750,000 monthly for administrative expenses, and impounding the remainder of the revenue; (c) accompany the protocol with a note such as that suggested by the British, which would in effect state that all opposition by the provinces would have to be removed before the surtaxes would be authorized. In their opinion, the American Delegation continued, the State Department should adopt plan (b), unless it was prepared to withhold recognition until China evolved a stable government, "which course might ultimately be best for the Chinese people," but which the Americans believed the other Powers, especially the British and Japanese, would not consent to at this time.

The Secretary of State responded to the telegram of the United States Delegates by saying that in his view the whole protocol should go into effect; if, however, the British and Japanese would not accept the protocol as drafted, plan (b) was the next best scheme. In regard to sending the note proposed by the British, Mr. Kellogg felt that the United States should probably not join in any such action as it would mean that the protocol would not be put into force and the charge might be made that the Powers were unwilling to fulfill the Washington agreements. Instead he suggested that the American Delegation should proceed to implement the surtaxes provided for in the Washington Treaty "on the assumption that the only Chinese Government we can deal with is the central government." In contemplating this line of action, the Secretary declared that "undoubtedly we are running some risk. However, heretofore our policy in regard to carrying out the Washington treaties has been to go as far as it was possible to go."[95]

On July 3rd, the foreign Delegates at the Special Conference held a meeting in which they made a final attempt to reach an agreement on the Washington surtax protocol.[96] The Japanese representatives reiterated

[95] *Ibid.*, p. 766 (cable paraphrased).
[96] *Ibid.*, pp. 837-840.

the point of view of their Government.[97] The British Minister, Sir Ronald Macleay, stated that the British Government regretted that it had been impossible to agree on a plan which would furnish a basis for negotiations with the Chinese. "In these circumstances," he continued, "His Majesty's Government is of the opinion that no useful purpose will be served by the foreign Delegations continuing these informal negotiations ... and that it would be preferable to await the resumption of the Conference and the formulation of the Chinese proposals." He added that the British Government wished it clearly understood that they desired to implement the Washington Treaty as soon as possible and that they had no intention, after an agreement on that issue had been reached, "to suspend the proceedings of the Conference or to break off negotiations for the conclusion of a Tariff Treaty."[98]

In a long report to the State Department, the American Delegation summarized Mr. MacMurray's remarks which followed those of Sir Ronald Macleay:

Mr. MacMurray, at the conclusion of the British statement, said that, in view of the attitude taken by the Japanese and British Delegations, it appeared that a deadlock had been reached and that further progress at that time was impossible. Mr. MacMurray said that the situation was most disappointing to the American Delegation who had hoped that the draft protocol of May 15 might be adopted as the first step toward tariff autonomy. He voiced the opinion that under present circumstances no further progress could be made until a new Chinese Government should come into being and he particularly warned the Delegates that if a discontinuance should lend itself to further nationalistic and bolshevist propaganda in China serious consequences would ensue.[99]

In spite of further deliberations, it became evident that the foreign representatives would be unable to reach an agreement that would bring the Washington surtaxes into effect. The report of the American Delegation described the close of the meeting in the following terms:

It being evident at this point that unanimity could not be had with respect to further action at the present time, the question arose whether the foreign Delegates should undertake to agree among themselves upon a recess or permit the Conference to remain *in statu quo* pending further developments. After considerable discussion it was deemed advisable to take no action which might be construed as indicating a desire on the part of the foreign Delegates to bring about any definite adjournment of the Conference. The following statement was ultimately agreed upon and given to the press: "The Delegates of the Foreign Powers to the Chinese

[97] *Ibid.,* p. 837.
[98] *Ibid.,* p. 838.
[99] *Ibid.*

Customs Tariff Conference met at the Netherlands Legation this morning. They expressed the unanimous and earnest desire to proceed with the work of the Conference at the earliest possible moment when the Delegates of the Chinese Government are in a position to resume discussion with the foreign Delegates of the problems before the Conference."[100]

In commenting on the complicated situation brought about by the suspension of the Conference and the improbability of its being resumed at least for several months, the American Delegation wrote that

The confused state of this question, in so far as the foreign Powers were concerned, was brought about by the action of the Japanese in insisting on the elimination of two of the most important sections of the agreement and in otherwise employing tactics which prevented further action being taken. The British also had a large part in the steps which caused the prolonged consideration of this question and its postponement to an indefinite date.[101]

Actually even the hope of the Delegates that the Conference would reconvene in a few months was not fulfilled. The Special Conference on the Chinese Customs Tariff never reopened and only one other informal session was held. In July, Mr. MacMurray reported that a cabinet was being organized on the insistence of Wu Pei-fu that steps be taken to compel the Powers to continue the Conference.[102] On July 23rd, a meeting was called by Admiral Tsai, who proposed a resolution that the Conference should resume its work on or about September 1, 1926. The foreign Delegates opposed this, however, adhering to the view adopted at the July 3rd meeting that they would be glad to reconvene the Conference when there was a Chinese Government in a position to participate in the negotiations; looking into the future, they said, it was impossible to foresee a fixed date when such a condition would exist and they were, therefore, unable to commit themselves to any definite schedule.[103] The truth of the matter was that the foreign representatives did not like to meet with Admiral Tsai even in informal discussions as they were afraid this might be used by Marshals Wu and Chang as evidence of foreign recognition of their régime.[104] Justification for their fears appeared to be provided, when a new Chinese Delegation was appointed by presidential mandate at the end of July, to represent the Peking Government at the Special Conference.[105]

[100] *Ibid.*, p. 839.
[101] *Ibid.*
[102] *Ibid.*, p. 847.
[103] *Ibid.*, p. 846.
[104] *Ibid.*, p. 848.
[105] *Ibid.*, p. 853.

It is frequently said that the Special Tariff Conference was entirely futile. In considering its influence on the tariff problem — as distinguished from political matters — many factors point to such a conclusion. The Delegates did not succeed in carrying out the task with which they were specifically charged, namely, the realization of the Washington Customs Treaty, and they were even less able to conclude a new treaty with more far-reaching aims. In spite of these failures the Conference achieved some important results. Outstanding among these was the passage of the resolution providing for the return of tariff autonomy by January 1, 1929, and divorcing the issue of tariff autonomy from that of the abolition of *likin*. Although the resolution was never ratified by the Powers (owing to the inability of the Delegates to agree on the draft of a general treaty of which the resolution was to form a part), January 1, 1929 was kept as the goal for the re-establishment of tariff autonomy, and virtual tariff autonomy was achieved by that date. Also the abolition of *likin* continued to be treated as a separate problem. Further the Chinese National Tariff Law, which came into effect in 1929, was based on schedules drawn up by the technical experts at the Special Conference.

An estimate of the political aspects of the Conference leads to very different conclusions. If the Conference had been held before the May 30th Incident, the Powers probably would have refused to discuss a program that exceeded the requirements laid down in the Washington Customs Treaty. That they were willing to enter into negotiations that went far beyond the obligations undertaken at the Washington Conference, furnished impressive evidence of the effectiveness of the anti-foreign movement.

On the other side of the balance, the Special Conference demonstrated that a revision of the Sino-foreign treaties involved more than political and economic problems. The basic tendency throughout the negotiations was for the foreign spokesmen to offer the Chinese a substantial increase in revenue but to hedge the offer with numerous restrictions and qualifications. Moreover they persisted in inquiring into conditions which the Chinese regarded as questions of internal administration that were not the concern of foreigners. Thus the attitude of the foreign representatives seemed often to reflect a habit of mind inherited from the long years in which the Treaty Powers were accustomed to exercise special privileges in China. The value of the British memorandum of May 28th lay in its attempt to break through traditional ways of thinking and place the negotiations on a level more in keeping with ideas of international equality.

The program which the American Delegation submitted to the Special Tariff Conference undoubtedly followed the suggestions made by Secretary of State Kellogg before the Conference convened. It sought to fulfill the terms of the Washington Customs Treaty, attempted to conclude a new treaty with rates higher than those of the Washington surtaxes, and agreed to a fixed date for the return of tariff autonomy. Whether the American Delegation conducted the negotiations in the broad and flexible spirit that Mr. Kellogg had emphasized, is more open to question.

In any case, it is impossible to judge the work of the Conference without recognizing that the political situation in China virtually ruled out any satisfactory settlement. The wisdom of the Treaty Powers' granting an increase in revenue to the Tuan Government, or to the later Administration of Wu Pei-fu and Chang Tso-lin, was, to say the least, doubtful. It was also difficult to devise a plan whereby the funds collected from the surtaxes could be equitably distributed among the various factions in control of different parts of China. However, the political situation was soon to undergo a radical change. When the Special Conference closed, the Northern Expedition of the Kuomintang was already underway. With the spectacular success of the Nationalist armies, conditions altered so that it was possible within a few months to consider a different kind of solution to the tariff problem.

CHAPTER VII

THE EVOLUTION OF A POLICY

Mr. Kellogg in the summer of 1925 had outlined a program which rested upon the convening of the Special Conference on the Chinese Customs Tariff and the constitution of the Commission on Extraterritoriality. It had evidently been his intention to work out through these two agencies a policy by which the United States could deal with the revolutionary situation in China. At the close of the Special Tariff Conference, however, American policy did not seem to possess any more definite shape or substance than it had shown when Mr. Kellogg concluded the negotiations that brought the Conference into existence. The Commission on Extraterritoriality, which had begun its meetings in China in January, 1926, was in the midst of carrying on its investigations — which it conducted entirely in secret — and did not complete its report until the autumn of that year. In the meantime, events in China were developing rapidly, requiring of the United States and the other Treaty Powers a further evolution of policy which was achieved on a move-by-move basis, as in a game where the action is too swift and unexpected to allow for the execution of any preconceived plan.

When the Special Tariff Conference closed, the Powers were still primarily concerned with the problem of how to deal with a China divided into different and opposing factions that were lacking in any cohesive force. The efforts of the régime supported by Wu Pei-fu and Chang Tso-lin at Peking, to achieve recognition by reopening the Tariff Conference and appointing an ostensibly official Chinese Delegation to conduct negotiations, led the Kuomintang to lodge strong protests with the Treaty Powers. Eugene Chen, who had been given the post of Acting Minister of Foreign Affairs at Canton, addressed a message to the American Government which was written in the stinging and vigorous style that characterized many of his diplomatic communications. Mr. Chen said that his Government opposed the reconvening of the Special Customs Conference because it involved the consideration of issues which only a central government, that was truly representative of the Chinese nation, would have the right to discuss. "None is so blind as to fail to see," he wrote, "that the present phantom government in Peking is a creation of a brace of medieval militarists and a bunch of Mandarin statesboys and statescoolies whose obvious purpose is to grab the proceeds of whatever doles and loans that America and the other Powers may be willing

122

to grant in order to maintain the *status quo* that conflicts with every vital interest of Nationalist China."[1]

On receipt of Mr. Chen's note, Mr. MacMurray decided to avail himself of the opportunity to issue a public statement which would make it entirely clear that the United States Government was not supporting the claims of the Wu-Chang régime to be the central government of China as against the claim of any other faction, and was not, in fact, committed to any political group in China.[2] Douglas Jenkins, the Consul-General at Canton, was therefore instructed to send an answer to Mr. Chen which declared that the American Minister found in Mr. Chen's protest, and in similar protests presented by the representatives of other factions, evidence of a disheartening lack of unanimity among the Chinese people concerning the efforts that were being made by the Powers to revise the treaties — a lack of unanimity that was of serious concern at a moment when there existed "no central government supported by all sections of China and recognized by the interested Powers." The American Minister, the note added, believed it scarcely necessary to observe that in any readjustment of treaty relations with China, his Government had in view "the benefit of China as a whole and not of any individual military or political faction."[3]

In order to assure this communication's receiving as wide an audience as possible, it was immediately given to the press by the American Legation at Peking.[4] Privately, Mr. MacMurray sent word to Mr. Chen that he believed the note might serve a useful function if the Kuomintang did not attempt to capitalize on it for propaganda purposes.[5] On being told this, Mr. Chen remarked with frankness that the American Minister's message "furnished too good an opportunity to be missed"[6] and he replied, within a few days, with a caustic criticism of United States policy: American policy was wrong because the United States Government failed to see that the situation in China was revolutionary and not evolutionary, and could, therefore, only be met by a fundamental revision of the treaties — not by a series of piecemeal readjustments executed on the installment plan; this meant that there should be substituted, for the old "unequal" treaties, new agreements consistent with the sovereignty and independence of China.[7]

Shortly after this interchange of notes, Mr. MacMurray sent to the Department of State in Washington a long statement of his view of the kind

[1] *Foreign Relations* (1926), p. 844.
[2] *Ibid.*, pp. 848-849.
[3] *Ibid.*, p. 846.
[4] *Ibid.*
[5] *Ibid.*, p. 847.
[6] *Ibid.*, p. 849.
[7] *Ibid.*, p. 851.

of diplomatic relations the United States should maintain in China, at least temporarily, to meet the existing difficulties. The gist of the most significant parts of his message[8] was: There has been no régime at Peking since 1918 which could assert even a plausible claim to being a legitimately constituted government. Each has in turn exercised diminishing power. Nevertheless the Treaty Powers found it advantageous to grant at least *de facto* recognition to each group in control of the Chinese capital so long as it acted as a conservative force, employing what influence it possessed to safeguard legitimate foreign interests. The developments of the last year have, however, made it futile to expect a conservative or even friendly influence to characterize any new régime at Peking. The Peking Administration has become increasingly an agent of one military faction or another and exercises control over only a limited area around the capital. It is distinguished from the other political factions in China only by obtaining the recognition of the Powers, but, in turn, curries favor with its own people by pursuing an antiforeign policy. Under these circumstances, there is no hope of its making any attempt to meet its international obligations and the practical reason for a continuation of the diplomatic fiction of a central government has, therefore, come to an end. "It is as though we had taken to the Central Government as a life raft in the political shipwreck of the Chinese Republic; and that raft, its buoyancy lost now, is no longer keeping us afloat. To keep it afloat we are swimming, but despite this, it must soon drag us down."

The decline of the central government, Mr. MacMurray continued, accords with an unmistakable trend toward political decentralization among the Chinese. "As I foresee the development through which China is destined to pass before it will be able to evolve a reasonably coherent organization of government, it must experience first a resolution into a loose confederation, with autonomous component regions, held together by bonds of sentiment rather than of law, merely tolerating in degrees both various and fluctuating the continuance of essential national services such as the railways and telegraph, customs, salt, posts, and perhaps the judicial system."

As there is nothing the United States can do to check the tendency toward decentralization, Mr. MacMurray added, the time has come when it should face conditions as they exist and accommodate itself to them. A start has already been made in this direction as, for example, in cases involving the protection of nationals which are more and more frequently being handled through local authorities rather than through the Peking Foreign Office. In fact, support of the régime at Peking makes it more difficult to secure protection and fair treatment for our citizens as the Peking Ad-

[8] *Ibid.*, pp. 671-680 (cable paraphrased).

ministration offers no help and the regional authorities, resentful of our support of a rival faction, are likely to withhold the assistance that they might give if approached directly. "If our supreme duty in China is, as I conceive it to be, to do everything we can do legitimately and honorably to maintain the interests of Americans here and at home, we must to that end adopt methods conforming to actual conditions. We do not need to temporize, nor need we alter in its essentials our policy towards China as a whole, but even though we look forward still hopefully and with a desire to be helpful to eventual re-establishment here of an actual central government, we should face the fact that no longer in China's political turmoil is the Peking régime more than an unrepresentative unit.

"We do not recognize today the existence in Peking of a government. We ought to withhold such recognition in my opinion, not only until a substantial government has come into being, but we should declare our intention publicly and unequivocally to that effect."

Mr. MacMurray stated additionally that the proposal to discard, openly and officially, the fiction that there existed a central government in Peking had been maturing slowly in his mind, but that he did not feel warranted in committing himself to it "up to the time when the possibilities of carrying out the Washington Customs Treaty provisions were exhausted by the American Delegation to the Tariff Conference." If, he said, it had been possible to obtain the consent of the other Powers for the immediate negotiation of an agreement on the Washington surtaxes, he would have regarded it as "a defensible sequel and probably a wise one" to the long negotiations conducted at the Conference. At the time of writing however — August, 1926 — he felt that it was impossible to implement the Washington Customs Treaty without being conscious that what was being professedly done for the whole of China would, in reality, do no more than furnish funds for one faction to conduct civil war. "Except for the somewhat remote possibility of the establishment of a real Government here," he wrote, "working out of an arrangement for accomplishing this purpose [the realization of the Washington Treaty] might prove feasible by means of a separate arrangement, either severally or collectively, with the various regional administrations."[9]

In pursuance of the scheme which he was suggesting, Mr. MacMurray drafted a statement which he recommended for issuance by the State Department within the immediate future. One of the reasons which led him to feel that the matter was urgent was that he believed that Feng Yu-hsiang and his party — the Kuominchun — would soon re-establish themselves in

[9] *Ibid.*

power in Peking. Marshal Feng had just returned from Moscow where, in Mr. MacMurray's words, he had been "freshly schooled ... in revolutionary methods as contrasted with evolutionary methods and in the doctrines of repudiation." As Mr. MacMurray saw the situation, Marshal Feng was likely to cancel all the existing treaties, in which instance the United States would be in a far better position if it had already announced a policy based on the thesis that there was in existence no government representative of the Chinese nation.[10] In the statement which Mr. MacMurray drafted for publication by the State Department, he reviewed past developments, stressing the diminishing power of the successive régimes that had controlled Peking, and concluded with the assertion that the United States Government felt it would no longer serve a useful purpose to recognize as the central government of China any administration which was "not in fact generally representative of the Chinese people and competent to exercise the ordinary functions of government."[11] In respect to the manner in which the announcement should be issued, Mr. MacMurray raised the question whether the State Department should seek the co-operation of the British and Japanese Governments. "While I think that co-operation with them," he wrote, "would be preferable ... I am doubtful, because of our experiences with the indecisiveness and vacillation characterizing British opinion regarding China at present, and with Japanese meticulousness in insisting that their own views should prevail...." The American Minister suggested that, rather than attempt to achieve parallel action, he might limit himself to a discussion of the intentions of the United States Government with his British and Japanese colleagues in Peking.[12]

Secretary of State Kellogg, after careful consideration, responded by opposing Mr. MacMurray's scheme for issuing an official announcement concerning the relations of the United States with the régime at Peking. Fundamentally, Mr. Kellogg's position appears to have been that, as the United States Government had to a large extent assumed the leadership in trying to effect a revision of the treaties with China, it would be a mistake to take the initiative in issuing a statement declaring that there existed no responsible government at Peking — a statement which he felt would amount to saying that there was no government qualified to enter into and enforce new treaty arrangements, including any agreements that might be made in connection with the Special Tariff Conference. "I cannot believe that it is wise," he said, "for the United States to take the lead in abandoning the Conference and in giving public notification to China

[10] Ibid., pp. 679-680.
[11] Ibid., p. 681 (cable paraphrased).
[12] Ibid., pp. 680-681 (cable paraphrased).

that she has no government. . . . It would bring the hostility of the Chinese people upon us and give to other nations an opportunity to lay the blame upon us for the failure of the Conference and furnish them at the same time with a sought-for excuse for abandoning the Conference. . . . The action you suggest, I feel certain, would fail to be understood in the United States and would meet quite likely with disfavor."[13]

While Mr. MacMurray and the Secretary of State were exchanging views as to what, if any, modification of the policy of the United States was best suited to the problems presented by the political situation in China, the situation itself was undergoing a profound and rapid change. Throughout the time that the Special Tariff Conference had been in session, the attention of outsiders, as already indicated, was for the most part directed toward the conflict between the warlords in the northern and central areas of China. During this period, the Kuomintang was engaged in making preparations for the so-called Northern Expedition, which was to be a military campaign that had as its aim the conquest of China; these preparations were finally completed in May, 1926, and the Northern Expedition was formally started.

There are few chapters in modern history more significant or more bewilderingly complex than that which deals with the Northern Expedition and the inner development of the Chinese Revolution of which it formed such a vital part. At this time, however, only a few of its aspects affected China's relations with the United States to any far-reaching extent. Foremost among these was the unexpected and sudden military success of the Kuomintang armies which, consisting of about 100,000 men placed under the command of General Chiang Kai-shek, waged a campaign against Marshal Wu Pei-fu in the summer of 1926.[14] In June they proceeded northward, advancing only gradually, but by the 12th of July they had managed to capture Changsha. From Changsha the Nationalist troops, fighting their way toward the Yangtze, progressed rapidly and in September attacked the important commercial center formed by the triple cities of Hankow, Hanyang, and Wuchang. Hankow and Hanyang were taken early in September and Wuchang fell, after a five-weeks' siege, on October 11th. The surrender of Wuchang marked the defeat of Wu Pei-fu, who was thereby virtually obliterated as a force in current Chinese politics. Thus, within a few months, the Kuomintang had succeeded in conquering a vast section of Chinese territory and in eliminating one of its most powerful enemies.

Even before the final defeat of Wu Pei-fu, the balance of power had

---

[13] *Ibid.*, p. 682 (cable paraphrased).

[14] For the military events of the Northern Expedition, see MacNair, *China in Revolution*, p. 108 *et seq*, and Arnold Toynbee (ed.), *Survey of International Affairs*, 1926, p. 295 *et seq*.

been radically altered by Feng Yu-hsiang's entering into a formal alliance with the Kuomintang so that his troops were fighting in co-operation with the Nationalist armies. In the fall of 1926, the revolutionary forces marched east to attack General Sun Ch'uan-fang, one of China's numerous warlords who controlled the area around Shanghai; by December they had taken Kiangsi and Fukien and were preparing for a continued drive northward that had the conquest of Shanghai itself as one of its primary objectives.

But the military success of the Kuomintang was only one aspect of the Northern Expedition which altered the situation in China. While the Nationalist armies conquered territory, the political workers of the Kuomintang sought to spread the revolutionary movement among the mass of the people in the newly conquered areas so that the Party, which had heretofore been narrowly confined to the region around Canton, would rest, in future, upon a broad and firm foundation. Propaganda techniques of all kinds were used to explain the objectives of the revolution and to give information concerning the domestic and foreign problems of the Chinese nation.[15] Branches of the Kuomintang were established throughout the territory won by the Nationalist troops, and peasants and laborers were organized into local unions headed by an All-China Peasant Union and an All-China Federation of Labor. While no reliable statistics are available to show the growth of the peasant and labor movement during this period,[16] there is little doubt that the activities of the Kuomintang achieved an extraordinary success.

Toward the close of the year 1926, the government of the Kuomintang moved from Canton to Hankow where it hoped to gain the co-operation of the industrial proletariat. But this measure, as well as the organizing work carried on among the peasants and laborers in general, inevitably increased the friction that had existed from the outset between the radicals, conservatives, and liberals, who made up the Kuomintang, and between the factions-within-factions existing in these groups. While the non-Chinese world was little aware of the developments within the Kuomintang, there were definite indications at this time that the coalition which made up the Nationalist movement would not be able to hold together much longer.

The extension of Kuomintang influence on so large a scale naturally created new problems for the governments of the foreign Powers. The first question was how to deal with the Kuomintang or Nationalist Government

[15] Of the many accounts of the techniques used during the political campaign that went hand-in-hand with the military campaign of the Northern Expedition, the writer has found especially helpful: Woo, *The Kuomintang and the Future of the Chinese Revolution,* Chapters VII and VIII, and H. Owen Chapman, *The Chinese Revolution, 1926-1927,* London, 1928, Chapter II.

[16] Woo, *op. cit.,* p. 209.

and what kind of recognition, if any, to grant it for the sake of carrying on diplomatic intercourse. While in the statement of policy which Mr. Mac-Murray had sent to the Department in Washington at the end of July, he had not placed any emphasis upon the expansion of the Kuomintang's power (although the Nationalist troops had already passed Changsha), he had maintained that the realities of the situation made it essential to treat with the various Chinese factions on a regional basis. After the revolutionary armies reached the Yangtze in September, 1926, the British who, due in part to the serious situation created by the Hongkong boycott, had long realized the potential strength of the Kuomintang, raised the issue of what policy to adopt toward the Nationalist régime.[17] In a note to the Department of State in Washington, they inquired as to the views of the United States Government concerning the position of the Nationalist Administration; the relation of that Administration to the authorities at Peking; and the prospects, in the light of the new conditions caused by the increase in power of the Kuomintang, of resuming the work of the Special Tariff Conference.[18] To this the State Department answered with a brief statement that laid down certain principles to which the authorities in Washington were adhering at this time with marked tenacity:

The Government of the United States has followed with close attention the recent developments in China. It is of the opinion, however, that the situation has not so far altered as to necessitate any change in the policy which it has adopted in the past, namely, *to hold itself in readiness to enter into relations and to negotiate with any Government representing China*

[17] As early as February, 1926, Mr. MacMurray had cabled to the Secretary of State:
"The opinion held by the British Foreign Office, he [the Chinese Secretary to the British Legation] stated, is gravitating in the direction of early recognition of the Canton Government, and if independence was the desire of the people of South China and if capacity for the maintenance of a comparatively satisfactory separate administration was shown thereafter by them, to continue to withhold recognition would not be right.
". . . I cannot but feel that the motive which impels the British Government to make a decision so momentous is the hope that by placating the Canton régime, the strike and boycott can be terminated. . . . I myself am unable to perceive in regard to Canton and other regions of South China that any basis exists for viewing them as a political entity which is separate from the remainder of China. While it is true that they have for several years maintained an autonomous administration of their own with some degree of success, all along their so-called independence has been a political fiction rather than a reality. A faction which has been ousted from power has in a particular section of China maintained its organization without considering itself actually separate, in fact, from China as a whole. For example, in representing China at Paris it participated with the Peking Government. . . . In its territories it permits the Central Government to function with regard to customs, wine and tobacco, salt, telegraphic and postal services. . . ." (*Foreign Relations*, 1926, p. 655, cable paraphrased.)
[18] *Ibid.*, p. 854.

which appears to be capable of fulfilling the obligations which it may undertake. On the other hand this Government is not prepared to enter into negotiations with a view to concluding a general tariff agreement with individual provinces or groups of provinces.[19]

In the meantime, the Kuomintang Government, keenly aware of its new growth in strength, was proceeding to adjust the existing conditions to suit its own needs. Toward the end of September, it became generally known that the Cantonese Administration was considering the levy of surtaxes of $2\frac{1}{2}\%$ on ordinary goods and 5% on luxuries.[20] While such duties were no more than the equivalent of the Washington surtaxes, the scheme, as rumored, planned to impose the surtaxes without subjecting them to any of the conditions that had been discussed by the Special Tariff Conference. Far more important than this, however, was the principle involved, as the action contemplated by the Nationalist Government amounted to a unilateral repudiation of the tariff sections of the treaties existing between China and the Powers, and could, therefore, be regarded as a defiance of the whole treaty system.

Mr. MacMurray, in South China at the time that this situation arose, expressed his views in a series of cables to the Legation at Peking. He said that in his opinion the imposition of the surtaxes by the Cantonese would result in similar surtaxes being put into force in all sections of China in disregard of the conditions contemplated by the Washington Customs Treaty. Once a break had been made away from treaty obligations by any Chinese group, he believed that "nothing would be left to prevent the forces in control of any given region from making at will an indefinite increase of such taxes. Thus there would be a new situation in which in effect both the previous treaty provisions as to customs and the Washington Customs Treaty itself would be repudiated."[21]

Concerning the policy which the United States should pursue if the Nationalist Government put into effect its plan for the levy of the surtaxes,

[19] *Ibid.*, p. 855. (Italics not in original.) The Secretary of State reiterated this view in a conversation with the Italian Ambassador at Washington in November, 1926:

"The Secretary informed the Ambassador that the policy of this Government was to enter into friendly relations with any government representing China, capable of negotiating for China and committing China; that the question of extending recognition to the régime at Canton had not been considered by this Government; that we were not prepared to enter into relations of a formal nature with any part of China; that doubtless the question of extending recognition would have to be considered if and when that régime obtained control over the greater part of China." (Memorandum by Nelson T. Johnson, Chief of the Division of Far Eastern Affairs, *Foreign Relations, 1926*, p. 684.)

[20] *Ibid.*, p. 863.

[21] *Ibid.*, p. 868 (cable paraphrased).

Mr. MacMurray made the following recommendation: "I believe that resolute action by the Powers chiefly interested should be taken against this method of indirect repudiation of treaties, even so far as to give naval protection to the Canton customs and to take any action which may prove to be feasible in preventing the levy of the proposed taxes by Cantonese authorities."[22]

"To me it seems," he added later, "that if we are not to stand by and see the Treaties torn up, we must make a determined resistance to the proposed taxes."[23]

Mr. MacMurray explained further that, as he judged the situation, the policy which he advocated would not result in its being necessary to take any drastic action, as he believed that the Nationalist Government would abandon its plan if it realized that "the Powers were in earnest." He based this view on conversations which he had recently held with Eugene Chen and T. V. Soong, and which had left with him "an extremely strong impression" that the Kuomintang officials had a real desire to adopt a conciliatory attitude toward the Powers, mainly because they dreaded any complication that might embarrass them in their military and political undertakings. In fact, Mr. MacMurray thought it might be worthwhile — "and politic even if it were unsuccessful" — to attempt to persuade the Cantonese, together with other factions in China, to set aside their differences to the extent of appointing representatives to discuss a tariff agreement with the foreign governments.[24]

Ferdinand L. Mayer, in charge of the Legation during Mr. MacMurray's absence in South China, forwarded the above message to the State Department in Washington, and added his own views:

> Before I received the Minister's telegram of September 30, I had reached exactly the conclusion at which he arrived. To me this appears as a final test whether we shall stand by while treaties and all obligations and rights due to the American Government and American citizens, if not in fact their personal safety and their commercial interests, are disregarded and jeopardized . . . or whether we shall take action preventing this, producing a change in the atmosphere and ceasing to be longer in the defensive position into which the Chinese have cleverly manoeuvred us. . . .
>
> In view of the facts, I cannot recommend too strongly that everything possible be done by the Department to gain an agreement between the United States and Great Britain and Japan to prevent, even by means of a naval blockade or of some feasible measure of force similar to that, the imposition of the new taxes.

[22] Ibid.
[23] Ibid.
[24] Ibid.

In conclusion Mr. Mayer declared that if the Japanese refused to proceed "in accord with this plan for forcible, if necessary, prevention of the taxes," he would "strongly advocate" that the United States should undertake action with the British alone; the French and Italians he thought might be willing to take part.[25]

When the dispatches of Mr. MacMurray and Mr. Mayer, urging the United States Government to adopt a vigorous policy supported by the threat of punitive action, reached the State Department in Washington, it soon became evident that the Secretary of State and his advisers in the Division of Far Eastern Affairs were neither sympathetic to these recommendations nor inclined to alter their own estimate of the situation. Mr. Kellogg cabled a brief statement to Mr. Mayer at the Legation in which he declared:

Department does not perceive the urgency of initiating discussions with Great Britain and Japan looking to naval demonstrations or other means of preventing collection of taxes which have not yet been put into effect. . . . When and if the new taxes are imposed on American trade, Jenkins should protest to the Canton authorities in accordance with the procedure which has been followed in the past in connection with other taxes which have been imposed from time to time in different parts of the country contrary to American treaties with China. A similar protest should of course be made by you at Peking.[26]

On October 6th, Mr. Chen finally announced that the new taxes of 2½% and 5% were actually to be put into effect and that their collection would commence five days later; at the same time he intimated that friction might be avoided if the collection were undertaken by the Chinese Maritime Customs Administration.[27]

Immediately following the issuance of this announcement, a meeting was held by the Diplomatic Body at Peking. According to the report sent to the Department of State by Mr. Mayer, the new taxes were unanimously opposed by all the foreign representatives, with the exception of the British.

[25] *Ibid.*, pp. 869-870 (cable paraphrased). Douglas Jenkins, American Consul General at Canton, also urged the State Department to take a firm stand. In a letter to the Legation, subsequently forwarded to Secretary Kellogg, he wrote:

"It would be a fatal mistake in the opinion of the writer merely to protest against the institution of the taxes and then permit the Canton régime to proceed as though the Powers took no further interest in the matter. The so-called Nationalist Government is now far stronger than it has ever been in the past and the Powers must find some means either to prevent its growing interference in our trade rights or to control and regularize its activities in the interests of all concerned." (*Foreign Relations,* 1926, p. 865.)

[26] *Ibid.*, p. 871.
[27] *Ibid.*, p. 874.

The interested Heads of Legation agreed to inform their respective governments, he said, that it was their unanimous opinion that the Powers had arrived at the "parting of the ways" and that the levy of the Canton taxes would mean the beginning of the end of foreign treaty rights in China. Mr. Mayer continued to describe the meeting as follows:

> We all believed that we could not warn our governments too solemnly in this regard and that we should earnestly solicit them to decide upon a means of preventing the success of the effort of the Canton authorities to tear up the treaties with the alternative that foreign persons and interests in China would be increasingly and inevitably imperilled. It was further the consensus of opinion among all the diplomatic representatives, except for the Japanese Chargé d'Affaires, that the only practical method of procedure in the above respect was to bring the Canton régime up sharply with a determined protest to be backed by force if necessary; that once the Cantonese realized the Powers were in earnest there would be the very least likelihood of the necessity of a resort to force.[28]

Mr. Mayer also forwarded a statement drafted by the Diplomatic Body which the Ministers believed might properly serve as an identic note to be presented by the Powers to the Nationalist Government. The text of the statement declared that the Powers could not recognize the legality of the new taxes which were being imposed in "direct violation of the treaties" and against which they wished to protest "most emphatically."[29]

The draft of the note was immediately approved by Secretary of State Kellogg since it was in complete accord with the policy which he had already outlined of limiting the action of the United States to the filing of a formal protest.[30] Proceedings were retarded by the British, however, who took the position that, as it would in any case be impossible to prevent the levy of the new taxes, the Powers should center their efforts on an attempt to obtain assurances from the Cantonese that the taxes would be collected by the Maritime Customs Administration, thereby making certain that the functions of that organization would remain unimpaired and would not be encroached upon by the establishment of some new, rival body.[31] At a meeting of the Diplomatic Body, the British Minister therefore suggested rewording the note to be presented to the Nationalist Government so that it would convey a hint that, if the collection of the taxes were entrusted to the Customs Administration and guarantees were given that there would be no further increase of illegal taxation, the Powers would be willing to accept

[28] *Ibid.*, p. 876.
[29] *Ibid.*
[30] *Ibid.*, p. 879.
[31] *Ibid.*, p. 883.

the situation.[32] After considerable discussion, the foreign Ministers adopted the proposal of their British colleague but, according to an account forwarded to the State Department by Mr. Mayer, did so with an obvious lack of enthusiasm. "Recognition was given to the fact," Mr. Mayer wrote, "that at this time whatever we could do would be only a device for 'saving face', inasmuch as the Powers concerned were unwilling to undertake the adoption of a resolute policy: the only practical means to check treaty violation."[33] Concerning the policy which the United States should adopt toward the scheme presented by the British, Mr. Mayer added:

As to whether it is advisable for us to agree to the British proposal, I frankly believe that it makes no particular difference what action we take regarding the new taxation, or in China in general, by way of trying to safeguard our citizens' rights under the treaties, unless a realization is brought home to the Chinese that there is a purpose to employ force to protect these rights if necessary. I consider that without this any regional or other arrangements we may make, or any protest we may present, will only be respected so far as is desired by the Chinese who are the particular authorities at the time.[34]

The British proposal was, nevertheless, not put into execution as the Department of State in Washington refused to give its consent. Mr. Kellogg was opposed to the idea of the Maritime Customs Administration becoming involved in the question of collecting the new taxes and he did not wish to enter into any arrangements with the various political factions occupying different areas of China.[35] He therefore instructed Mr. Mayer to proceed along the lines the Department had indicated at the outset and file a protest against the imposition of the taxes, irrespective of the action the other Treaty Powers might adopt.[36]

"Filing such a protest," Mr. Kellogg cabled, "does not necessarily carry an implication that it is the intention of the Government of the United States to seek by means of force to obtain its treaty rights. The feeling of the Department is that it is necessary that the record of this Government should be clear on this question when the time arrives to negotiate with the Government of China for revision of its treaty provisions relating to the tariffs."[37]

Finally, on October 29th, the Treaty Powers, through the Diplomatic Body, all agreed on the draft of a note which made no reference to the col-

[32] *Ibid.*, pp. 883-884.
[33] *Ibid.*, p. 884.
[34] *Ibid.*, p. 884 (cable paraphrased).
[35] *Ibid.*, p. 885 (cable paraphrased).
[36] *Ibid.*
[37] *Ibid.*

lection of the new taxes by the Maritime Customs Administration but merely asserted that the levy of the taxes was illegal and in direct violation of the treaties.[38] The note was sent to Eugene Chen on behalf of the Diplomatic Body.[39] Mr. Chen promptly returned it, affirming that the relations of the Powers with the Nationalist Government had not as yet been placed upon a basis that entitled the foreign Ministers to raise any question concerning an infraction of the treaties; he would be ready, he said, to discuss this or any similar matter when the Powers had arrived at a point where they were willing to recognize that national authority had long since ceased to be exercised by the régime at Peking and was now vested in the Nationalist Government at Canton.[40]

At the time that Mr. Chen's communication reached the Diplomatic Body, attention shifted from Canton to Peking where the Administration made a move which constituted a far more profound and arresting challenge to the treaty system than anything that had as yet been undertaken by the Kuomintang. The general background of the matter, stated briefly, was that most of the treaties between China and the Powers contained a clause which provided that after a certain period of time — usually ten years — either one party or both might demand a revision of certain sections of the agreement.[41] The ten-year clause of the Sino-Japanese Treaty of 1896 fell due in October, 1926, and according to the terms of the treaty any modification had to be effected within six months.[42] On October 20th, the Peking régime notified the Japanese that it wished to negotiate an extensive revision of the agreement and, furthermore, implied that if the negotiations were not completed within six months it would denounce the treaty in its entirety.[43]

This was only the prelude, however, to the adoption of a more spectacular and defiant measure on the part of the Government at Peking. The treaty which had been concluded between China and Belgium in 1865 also allowed for the modification of its terms at ten-year intervals, one of which was to expire on October 27, 1926.[44] In April of 1926, the Wai Chiao Pu announced that it desired a revision of the agreement and that it intended to regard the old treaty as no longer in force when the ten-year period

[38] *Ibid.*, p. 896.
[39] *Ibid.*, p. 900.
[40] *Ibid.*, pp. 900-901.
[41] Pollard, *China's Foreign Relations, 1917-1931*, p. 312.
[42] MacMurray, *Treaties and Agreements With and Concerning China, 1894-1919*, Vol. 1, p. 73.
[43] *China Year Book*, 1928, pp. 786-787.
[44] For an account of the dispute over the Sino-Belgian treaty, see Pollard, *op. cit.*, pp. 312-321.

reached an end.[45] The Belgian authorities contended that only the Belgian Government — and not the Chinese — had a right, according to the provisions of the treaty, to demand any alteration of its terms and that the act contemplated by the Chinese was, therefore, illegal.[46] As this was a matter which concerned the legal interpretation of the treaty exclusively, the Belgian Government suggested referring the issue to the Permanent Court of International Justice.[47] But the Chinese refused to co-operate in any such move on the ground that the fundamental question involved was not one of legal technicalities but rather of "the application of the principle of equality of treatment in the relations between China and Belgium."[48] The Belgians, having adopted a conciliatory attitude from the outset, indicated that they were willing to enter into negotiations for a new treaty and an attempt was made to frame a *modus vivendi* that would operate in the *interim* period between the termination of the old treaty and the beginning of the new.[49] In the end, it proved impossible to find a common ground of agreement to form the basis of the *modus vivendi* and, on November 6, 1926, the Government at Peking announced that the Sino-Belgian treaty was abrogated.[50] The Belgian Government, on its part, proceeded to bring the case before the Court of International Justice, under Article XXXVI of the Court's Statute, acting alone as the Chinese Government had rejected this proposal. In January, 1927, the President of the Court made an order continuing in force provisionally, pending a decision of the case, certain sections of the Sino-Belgian Treaty of 1865. Almost immediately thereafter, however, the Belgian Government decided to attempt once more to settle the issue by diplomatic rather than judicial means, and virtually asked the Court to suspend proceedings while negotiations were conducted between Chinese and Belgian officials.

The importance of this matter to the United States and the other Treaty Powers did not need underscoring. While the Sino-American Commercial Treaty of 1903 was not due to be revised until 1934, it was clear

[45] *China Year Book,* 1928, pp. 770-771.

[46] Article 46 of the Sino-Belgian Treaty of 1865 read in part: "If the Government of His Majesty the King of the Belgians should hereafter consider it necessary to introduce changes in any clauses of the present Treaty, he shall have full liberty in this respect to open negotiations after an interval of ten years has elapsed from the day of the exchange of ratifications. . . ." (*China Year Book,* 1928, pp. 771-772.)

[47] *Ibid.,* p. 773.

[48] *Ibid.,* p. 784. The Chinese Government contended that the termination of the Belgian Treaty was in accord with Article 19 of the Covenant of the League of Nations, based on the principle of *rebus sic stantibus,* and that, therefore, if an appeal were made to any international tribunal they would prefer the Assembly of the League (the appeal to be made under Article 11 of the Covenant). See discussion of this in Pollard, *op. cit.,* p. 318.

[49] *China Year Book,* 1928, p. 782.

[50] Pollard, *op. cit.,* pp. 315-316.

that if the Chinese Government once embarked on a unilateral denunciation of the treaties it was likely to maintain this course and that a policy used against one nation today could readily be applied to another tomorrow. With these ideas in mind, Mr. MacMurray sent to the State Department a number of important cables in which he not only expressed his views of the immediate situation but also discussed the significance of the actions of the Chinese as measured against a longer sweep of history.

In respect to the immediate issue, Mr. MacMurray felt that the denunciation of the Belgian Treaty was a direct result of the attitude the Powers had adopted toward the levy of the new taxes by the Nationalist Government at Canton. He termed the denunciation of the treaty "a deliberate attempt to find out to what extent the Treaty Powers were complaisant towards a repudiation of treaty obligations by China." A division of opinion as to how to handle the matter had existed among Chinese officials he said, and the victory went to those who made it clear that, "in consequence of the inertia shown by the Powers in the making of their dilatory and patently platonic statement concerning the violation of treaty rights brought about by the illegal taxes imposed at Canton," the régime at Peking might safely go the Cantonese one better and actually begin to tear up the treaties.[51]

The significance of the action taken is emphasized further by the following fact: In the exceedingly disingenuous statement which the Foreign Office issued is an assertion that national aspirations are hardly fit matters to submit to adjudication.[52] If in its context this has any meaning beyond impertinence or bombast, it constitutes a warning that the intention of the Peking Administration is to take the position that abrogation of the so-called unequal treaties has become such a necessity for the nation as to give justification for treating the obligations of China as scraps of paper. Until 1934 our own treaty of 1903 is not due to be revised. But my belief, which I confidently venture to express, is that even though in the meanwhile we should make concessions beyond what the Washington Conference contemplated, by way of bowing to the storm, some specious occasion will have been made by the Chinese before that date to declare our treaty terminated. That is, unless in the meantime our intention not to tolerate such treatment of our rights has been made very clear.

In order to forestall the grave difficulties which he felt lay ahead, Mr. MacMurray urged the Department of State to take action, at least to the extent of informally protesting to the Chinese:

I feel most strongly that we should take occasion informally to intimate

[51] *Foreign Relations* (1926), p. 996 (cable paraphrased).

[52] The Chinese Government had stated that the real question at issue was "political in character" and that "no nation could consent to the basic principle of equality between states being made the subject of a judicial inquiry." (*China Year Book*, 1928, p. 784.)

that the United States Government does not have any sympathy with the Chinese in the doctrine of international irresponsibility which has stood in the way of our recognition of the Russian régime. I beg to suggest respectfully that if the Secretary were in person to make an informal intimation to that effect, it would be greatly influential in acting upon the Chinese as a deterrent from pursuing the course of action which would, I gravely apprehend, lay the foundation for a new war in a not very distant future in the Far East.[53]

To Mr. MacMurray's suggestion, the Secretary of State responded briefly by saying that the Department would prefer to have the Chinese raise the question of a revision of the Sino-American treaty in its own way, leaving the United States "free to accept or reject the proposal" as the occasion might require. He observed, further, that he did not understand Mr. MacMurray's reference to Russia and that it seemed to indicate a danger of confusing the United States Government's policy vis-à-vis China with the policy which it had pursued vis-à-vis the Soviet régime.[54]

In his reply to these remarks of the Secretary's, Mr. MacMurray wrote the best exposition of his view — matured through many years of experience — of the essentials of American policy toward China in this moment of history that has appeared in any public document. His way of reasoning, as seen in the substance of his statement, was:

There exist in China two rival schools of thought in regard to a revision of the treaties — one evolutionary, the other revolutionary. The former believe that the adjustment of China's treaty relations should be carried out by the mutual consent of China and the Powers and they are eager to see the people of China earn their own salvation by making themselves sovereign in their own land and proving themselves capable of bearing the responsibilities of a sovereign nation. "It was this theory which the Washington Conference proceeded upon and which was the basis of the treaties and resolutions that resulted. It was also the inspiration of the Special Conference on the Tariff and of the Commission on Extraterritoriality which were held under its terms. *The Washington Conference resulted in our leadership of a co-operative activity among the Powers most interested in a policy of self-abnegation and of co-operation with China to enable her by evolutionary processes to achieve her own political destiny.*"[55] The failure of China to use her opportunities effectively, together with the Powers' failure to put into effect the Washington Treaty, opened the way for the Soviet through "disruptive influences" to arouse an anti-foreign feeling in the so-called semi-colonial nations of the East, particularly China, and

[53] *Foreign Relations* (1926), pp. 996-997 (cable paraphrased).
[54] *Ibid.,* p. 998.
[55] Italics not in original.

to persuade them that the way of gaining freedom from foreign oppression was to do as Russia has done: declare a debt to be an injustice that need not be paid and declare a treaty obligation to be a curtailment of sovereignty that ought to be repudiated by a self-respecting people. China has arrived at the crossroads between these two doctrines — the evolutionary and the revolutionary; she has already gone a step upon the road of repudiation. "Before China makes her choice irrevocably, it is my feeling that we are obliged both to China and ourselves to speak some friendly words of warning."[56]

Three days before Mr. MacMurray wrote this statement, he had cabled to Washington a report of his impressions of the Nationalist Government, derived from his recently completed tour of South China, which supplemented the views given above. He described the Cantonese group of officials as men "experimenting quite intelligently but unscrupulously" to determine how far the foreigners in China — and especially the Americans — could be driven by their anxiety about current conditions to disregard the greater possible dangers that lay in the future; in line with this policy, he said, the Cantonese were devoting their ingenuity to creating situations which played upon the tendency of the foreign Powers to yield a principle rather than to risk an incident.

Mr. MacMurray asserted further:

In case one power yields, the same will have to be done by the others, and in time an end will come to those rights making commerce with China possible. The Cantonese do not see that when once back to conditions prevalent a century past, and complicated and worsened by China's present internal strife, there will come again a time when Western pressure will force new conflicts and once more begin the old cycle: hostilities over a long period, subjugation, and special conditions for intercourse imposed. The United States may not become in our day — and may not at all, though it is more likely now than in the century past — the active agent to counteract the attitude of exclusiveness and arrogance towards the West which today the Chinese are reviving (dating from the taking of the [factories?] at Canton). But I for one feel we have a responsibility for effort directed toward saving the Chinese from their own folly. Their folly is of a historically characteristic form, whose results [threaten?] more or less directly to involve us in the disaster of indefinitely retarding in China the development of a rational, ordered political and economic entity and of relationships between the Western Powers and China that are normal.[57]

The political concepts held by Mr. MacMurray, and the attitude of officials in Washington as shown in the cables of the State Department, were

[56] *Foreign Relations* (1926), p. 1000 (cable paraphrased).
[57] *Ibid.*, p. 899 (cable paraphrased).

applied throughout the autumn and winter of 1926 to incidents that developed in connection with the revolutionary activities taking place in Kuomintang territory.[58] One issue that arose concerned the policy adopted by the British who, as a consequence of what they regarded as "serious piratical outrages" committed in Canton harbor by strike pickets in the course of carrying out the Hongkong boycott, ordered their naval forces to seize and disable all boats employed by the strike pickets. The British Ambassador inquired of the Department of State whether, in view of the recent seizure and imprisonment of an American citizen at Canton, the United States wished to associate itself with the action of the British.[59] On being asked for his advice, Mr. MacMurray cabled to Washington that he was convinced the United States should adopt a "firm attitude" and inform the administration at Canton that if it could not protect American citizens, the United States Government would "be compelled with regret to take on its own account measures necessary to that end." He urged that instructions be given to the American naval commander in South China to seize and

[58] Even earlier than this an incident had arisen in the North, which foreshadowed, clearly, the attitude that Secretary of State Kellogg was to take toward the enforcement of treaty rights in China. In March, 1926, the forces of Marshals Chang and Wu, which controlled the Taku Forts that guarded the entrance to Tientsin from the sea, laid mines and fired on foreign ships, including two Japanese destroyers, thereby preventing navigation in and out of Tientsin. Because free access to Peking from the sea had been guaranteed by the so-called Protocol of 1901, the Ministers of the Protocol Powers, which included the United States, decided to deliver what was virtually an ultimatum to the Tuan Government demanding, among other matters, a cessation of hostilities in the Channel from Taku Bar to Tientsin, the removal of all mines and other obstructions, and abstention from interference with foreign shipping. A crisis was averted by the immediate compliance of the Peking Government with the demands of the ultimatum. The Incident had, however, grave repercussions among the Chinese public. In Peking, several thousand students held demonstrations demanding a severance of relations with the Protocol Powers. During the demonstrations the police fired on the crowd killing forty and wounding eighty persons.

The Taku Incident was, to a large extent, handled for the United States by Mr. MacMurray. In general the American Minister took the position that—to quote his own words—"a display of international naval force for the purpose of enforcing the protocol" was "practicable and necessary." Mr. MacMurray believed that this would not only serve to protect American life and property against the dangers of mine fields and bombardment but would also help to maintain the position of the foreign Powers in the "rear-guard action" which they were "being forced to conduct in China." (*Foreign Relations*, 1926, pp. 595-596.)

Secretary Kellogg on his part sent the following significant cable to the American Legation, after the crisis over the Taku Incident had been resolved:

"I learn with much gratification that forceful action has not been necessary to settle questions of maintaining protocol status of Tientsin. I think that in general it should be our policy not to use force of arms to enforce treaty rights unless such action is necessary in order to protect American lives." (*Foreign Relations*, 1926, pp. 603-604. For documents on the Taku Incident, see *ibid.*, pp. 592-604.)

[59] *Ibid.*, p. 723.

disable any strike boat that attacked a United States citizen but recommended at the same time that action should be limited to the protection of American nationals, making it less drastic than the policy recommended by the British.[60] Even a policy of more limited action did not, however, coincide with the State Department's wishes when finally crystallized, and in the end the Secretary cabled to the British Government that the United States did not care to associate itself with the plan suggested by the British, believing that the standing instructions issued to the American naval forces offered sufficient protection to the lives and property of American citizens.[61]

An incident, which similarly illustrated the attitude both of Mr. Mac-Murray and of the authorities in Washington, occurred at Hankow in November, 1926, when a strike of the customs employees seemed imminent and the question arose whether the Powers should attempt to protect the customhouse by naval landing parties. The Ministers at Peking wired to their respective governments for instruction. Mr. MacMurray, in presenting his estimate of the situation to the Secretary of State, declared that, in his opinion, "this attempt of destructive elements to paralyze" the workings of the Customs Administration should be "averted by the landing, if necessary, of naval forces sufficient to forestall acts of violence by the strikers against those seeking to do business with the Customs and against loyal staff members."[62] To do this the Secretary replied in words that revealed a great deal concerning his approach to the problems with which he was confronted in China:

> The Chinese Maritime Customs was brought into existence by the Government of China. It is a Chinese national service; it functions under the orders and protection of the Government of China, and the foreigners employed in it are servants of that Government. If that Government should desire the destruction of the Customs Administration, or if the desire of the Chinese people is to destroy the Government of China and the Customs Administration it has created, the basis of right upon which this Government may intervene in order to prevent either purpose from being accomplished is difficult to see. In consequence I am unable to see my way clear, in regard to preventing the operation of the customhouse at Hankow from being paralyzed, to authorize landing an armed naval force in co-operation with other Powers.[63]

At the time this controversy over the protection of the customhouse was taking place, the question of the resumption of the work of the Special Conference on the Chinese Customs Tariff arose once again. In considera-

[60] *Ibid.*, p. 725 (cable paraphrased).
[61] *Ibid.*, pp. 726-727.
[62] *Ibid.*, p. 964.
[63] *Ibid.*, p. 966 (cable paraphrased).

tion of the very real possibility that Chang Tso-lin and his associates in the Peking régime might ask for a reopening of the Conference, Mr. MacMurray and Secretary Kellogg entered into an exchange of ideas concerning the best policy to adopt in the face of such a contingency.[64] After considerable deliberation they agreed that of all the courses that might be followed, the wisest was to have each country impose the Washington surtaxes on its own nationals, but, in doing so, waive all the conditions contemplated by the Special Tariff Conference.[65] In discussing other plans that might be adopted the American Minister and the Secretary made several observations worth noting. Mr. MacMurray stated that of all the schemes that presented themselves, he would prefer one which attempted to bring about negotiations between the Treaty Powers and a Chinese delegation that represented the Chinese people as a whole, but that he feared neither the Peking régime nor the Kuomintang would be willing to co-operate in such a program.[66] Mr. MacMurray also remarked that the idea of conceding unanimous tariff autonomy immediately, with the sole condition that most-favored-nation treatment be granted, had certain "theoretical attractions" but, in view of the temper of the Chinese people, it would not be likely to alleviate their sense of grievance against the Treaty Powers — "especially," he said, "since it would follow the success of the Canton régime in ignoring treaties by imposing illegal surtaxes and the riposte of Peking in tearing up the Belgian Treaty, I am afraid that it would only intoxicate the Chinese further with a sense of triumph, with the result that their zeal for the ousting of foreigners out of China altogether would be diverted merely to other questions."[67] Secretary Kellogg, on his part, declared that if control of most of China were secured by the Nationalists, the United States might have to give consideration to entering into a treaty for the relinquishment of tariff control as long as it provided for most-favored-nation treatment.[68] Concerning the resumption of the Special Tariff Conference, the Secretary observed that the Department was of the opinion that the Peking régime would not have the power to bind any substantial part of China and that the Canton Administration would probably repudiate the Conference. Nevertheless, the door should be left open to the possibility of reconvening the Conference, as it had been "the attitude of the United States to do everything it can do to make clear that it is willing to meet the aspirations of China in regard to the tariff question."[69]

[64] *Ibid.*, pp. 855-860.
[65] *Ibid.*, pp. 857-859.
[66] *Ibid.*, p. 857.
[67] *Ibid.*, pp. 857-858.
[68] *Ibid.*, p. 859.
[69] *Ibid.*

No sooner had Mr. MacMurray and Secretary Kellogg reached these tentative conclusions concerning the policy the United States should adopt toward the tariff issue than, swept along by the current of the Revolution, the circumstances surrounding that issue underwent a further change. On December 2nd (1926), Owen O'Malley, the British Chargé d'Affaires at Peking, informed Mr. MacMurray that the Nationalists were intending to levy the same $2\frac{1}{2}\%$ and 5% taxes at Hankow that they had imposed at Canton. According to reports, if the Powers consented to the levy of the duties, the Nationalists would agree to their collection by the Maritime Customs Administration, but if the Powers refused their consent, a separate collecting agency would be established.[70]

Reviewing these developments, Mr. O'Malley explained the point of view of his government: the British Foreign Office was determined not to repeat the mistake made at Canton of simply lodging a protest for the sake of the record because they regarded any such action as "clearly futile and merely irritating." The chief issue still being the preservation of the Maritime Customs Administration, the first essential was to prevent the establishment of a rival organization. The Foreign Office intended, therefore, to agree to the levy of the new taxes and make some arrangement for their collection by the Customs Administration. If the other Treaty Powers objected to co-operating in this matter, the British would probably act independently.[71]

Mr. MacMurray's reaction to the developments at Hankow was in keeping with the theories he had already defined:

"Realizing," he cabled to Washington, "we are not prepared to insist that our treaty rights be respected, the Nationalists have manoeuvered us around to where talk about the Washington Treaty obligations being mutual is academic. We have a choice only of allowing the Nationalists to destroy the Customs organization and the treaty system of trade, or of giving the benefits of the Washington surtaxes to the Chinese without conditions."[72]

There was only one way, in Mr. MacMurray's view, of making a "substantial salvage of the wreck" presented by the conditions into which matters had deteriorated: instead of agreeing to the imposition of the new taxes by the Nationalist Government — as recommended by the British — the Treaty Powers should themselves take immediate steps to put into force the Washington surtaxes. "Our taking the position of carrying out our Washington obligations," the American Minister asserted," is vastly different from yield-

[70] *Ibid.*, p. 902.
[71] *Ibid.*, pp. 902-904 (cable paraphrased). This account of Mr. O'Malley's statements is based on a report of Mr. MacMurray's.
[72] *Ibid.*, p. 905 (cable paraphrased).

ing to a violation of our treaty rights and afterward referring to the treaty by way of excusing our weakness."[73] Mr. MacMurray also emphasized his conviction that the taking of a strong stand was an urgent necessity:

"Unless we are prepared to undertake a last-ditch stand to prevent our being bullied into unconditionally surrendering vastly more than we took upon ourselves to give up under reasonable safeguards, the Washington Customs Treaty and the Special Conference would seem to be dead historical topics."[74]

Moreover, he thought determined action might have its effect, as — "despite our having shown that we did not actually mean the protests we made at Canton and Hankow" — the Nationalists might still believe that, if backed up against the wall, the Treaty Powers might make good their protests.[75]

In order to be in a position to bring into effect the policy which he was proposing, the American Minister asked for instructions from Washington. Replying with a confused and discursive statement, the Secretary, on the one hand, declared that Mr. MacMurray had already been given the authority to implement the Washington surtaxes, and, on the other, asserted that the Department believed the only method to follow was that which had been used in respect to the levy of the new taxes at Canton, namely, to file a protest for the sake of keeping the record clear and to postpone the final settlement of the tariff issue until the time when there would appear a government in China able to exercise control over a substantial part of the nation. Moreover, Mr. Kellogg said, the Department still objected to the Customs Administration collecting the surtaxes on the ground that this would involve the Customs authorities in the question of the disposition of the surtax revenue, thereby tying up the entire organization with the "varying fortune of the factions" in China.[76]

As the Secretary's message was too contradictory to furnish a basis for further action, Mr. MacMurray sent another cable: "Shall or shall I not go on in the hope of reaching an agreement . . .?" he asked. "I am led to doubt whether I have made sufficiently clear in my telegrams that our treaty position is nearly at the point of collapse and that to forestall the catastrophe the time element is vital."[77] On this occasion Mr. Kellogg responded by definitely granting the American Minister the authority to go ahead and enter into arrangements with the other Treaty Powers for implementing the

[73] *Ibid.*
[74] *Ibid.*, p. 903 (cable paraphrased).
[75] *Ibid.*
[76] *Ibid.*, pp. 908-910.
[77] *Ibid.*, p. 911 (cable paraphrased).

Washington surtaxes. At the same time he stated that the United States Government preferred not to become involved in the matter of giving directions to the Customs authorities as to which of the parties at each port in China the surtax revenue should be distributed; the entire settlement of this question should, the Department felt, be left to the Customs Administration.[78]

The principle underlying the State Department's attitude was that the United States ought to deal solely with a central government in China and that, if for a temporary period such a government was not in existence, the United States should nevertheless refrain from entering into diplomatic relations with various regional groups and factions. The reasons for the maintenance of this attitude were explained in a cable to Mr. MacMurray that consisted of the report of a conversation, between Mr. Kellogg and the Japanese Ambassador at Washington, concerning the levy of the new taxes at Hankow:

I [the Secretary] stated ... that this Government believed that on a question of this kind, to enter into arrangements with one or another Chinese faction was unwise because of the danger that a policy such as that would result merely in dividing China more or less permanently into separate parts; and that this Government, rather than to pursue that policy, had been in favor of giving you, its Minister in China, authorization to consider with your colleagues a proposal by which the Chinese Government would be authorized to make a levy, uniformly upon foreign trade throughout China, of the surtaxes provided by the treaty of Washington, the only reservation to be that the Chinese Maritime Customs should collect the taxes. I said that we wished to avoid being involved in any questions as to disposing of the funds so derived among the warring factions.[79]

In the meantime, Mr. MacMurray and Mr. O'Malley were seeking to enlist the co-operation of the other Ministers at Peking. It soon became evident that the Japanese were opposed to the plan of immediately sanctioning the levy of the Washington surtaxes which the British and American Governments were proposing.[80] Mr. MacMurray and the British Chargé thereupon decided that the only means of getting the Japanese to reconsider their position was to obtain the unanimous consent of the remaining Treaty Powers and then bring matters into the open by demanding a show of hands at a meeting of the Diplomatic Body.[81] They proceeded to set this

[78] *Ibid.*, p. 912. Mr. Kellogg added that although this was the preference of the Department, they were willing to leave the final decision of the question to Mr. MacMurray in view of his more intimate knowledge of the situation.

[79] *Ibid.*, p. 914 (cable paraphrased).

[80] *Ibid.*, pp. 913-914; see *ibid.*, pp. 377-379 for objections raised by Japanese Ambassador in Washington in talks with Mr. Kellogg.

[81] *Ibid.*, pp. 915-916.

scheme into motion, but Mr. MacMurray was suddenly prevented from taking further action by a new set of instructions from Washington.[82] The attitude of the State Department appears to have been that it was not prepared to insist upon the immediate implementation of the Washington surtaxes if all the Treaty Powers were not in agreement, and that it preferred to drop the issue rather than oppose the wishes of the Japanese.[83] Faced with the State Department's decision, Mr. MacMurray informed Washington, with some bitterness, that as the British still intended to press for a show of hands on this issue, the United States was likely to find itself the only nation prepared to side with the Japanese.[84] The Secretary of State replied by asserting that the Department continued to maintain the point of view that action should be deferred until complete unanimity had been attained; but, he added, if matters came to a "showdown" while there was still disagreement among the Powers, the American Minister should vote with his British colleague.[85]

On the day that Washington's message reached Peking — December 18, 1926 — a meeting of the Diplomatic Body was held at the instigation of the British. Here, Mr. O'Malley presented his colleagues with a formal statement of British policy which has since become known as the December memorandum or the Christmas memorandum.[86] This document, which was of historic importance, will be dealt with in detail later, but it is essential to note at this time that the memorandum sought especially to find a solution to the immediate problem of the imposition of the new taxes by the Nationalists. Tracing the development of its own attitude and actions throughout the course of recent events, the British Government stated:

> The Cantonese did, in fact, seize the Washington surtaxes by levying, in defiance of the treaties, certain additional taxes on the foreign trade of that port. His Majesty's Government have with much reluctance joined in the protest against the new taxes for the sake of maintaining solidarity with the Powers but they are not satisfied that this is the right policy for the present situation. They regret that they did not more insistently press their views at an earlier stage ... but they think it is still not too late, despite the protest already made, to return to the alternative course proposed in the memorandum of 28th May.[87] His Majesty's Government therefore strongly

[82] *Ibid.*, p. 917.
[83] *Ibid.*, pp. 913-914, 918.
[84] *Ibid.*, p. 917.
[85] *Ibid.*, p. 918.
[86] *Ibid.* Text of memorandum, *ibid.*, pp. 923-929.
[87] Earlier in the memorandum it had been stated that in the memorandum of May 28th, which the British had sent to the United States Government (see above, p. 112) they had urged that: "The Powers should abstain from any attempt to exact guarantees on conditions, but should forthwith authorize the levy of the Washington surtaxes." (*Ibid.*, p. 927.)

urge that the Powers should now authorize the immediate levy of the Washington surtaxes unconditionally throughout China. They hope that this may provide a basis for regularizing the position at Canton.[88]

Despite this definite expression of the British attitude and the vaguer indications of American policy, the Treaty Powers — owing largely to the continued opposition of the Japanese — were not able to agree on a joint declaration sanctioning the levy of the Washington surtaxes.[89] The Nationalists proceeded, therefore, to impose the taxes illegally in the territory under their control, although they did not use the services of the Maritime Customs Administration for the collection of the revenue.

The action of the Cantonese in relation to the taxes led the Peking régime to adopt similar measures which created additional problems that led to further friction. At the beginning of January, 1927, the Peking Administration passed a mandate authorizing the imposition of the Washington surtaxes and entrusting their collection to the Maritime Customs Administration.[90] Sir Francis Aglen, Inspector General of Customs, immediately expressed his disapproval of involving the Administration in the collection of the revenue, explaining that in view of the opposition of the Japanese to the levy of the taxes, the mandate could not be fulfilled.[91] Moreover, he asserted that the Nationalists had threatened to regard the collection of the surtaxes by the Customs Administration as an " 'act of war' " and had stated that they would, if an attempt were made to carry out the orders of the Peking régime, " 'smash' " the Customs organization in the ports under their control.[92] As a result of the position adopted by Sir Francis Aglen, the Peking Government issued another mandate on January 31st dismissing him from the office of Inspector General.[93]

The Diplomatic Body, agreeing with Sir Francis Aglen's estimate of the situation, felt that the actions of the Peking officials constituted a serious danger to the continued existence of the Customs Administration. They therefore drafted a memorandum to be delivered to Dr. Wellington Koo, then Foreign Minister at Peking, setting forth their objections and attempting to persuade the Peking régime to rescind its orders both in regard to the collection of the taxes by the Customs Administration and to the dismissal of the Inspector General.[94] Upon the receipt of an account of these develop-

[88] *Ibid.*, p. 928.
[89] *Ibid.*, p. 936; *ibid.* (1927), pp. 375-376, 377-379.
[90] *Ibid.* (1927), p. 372.
[91] *Ibid.*, p. 458.
[92] *Ibid.*
[93] *Ibid.*, p. 457.
[94] *Ibid.*, pp. 459-460.

ments, Secretary Kellogg cabled at once that he did not wish the American Minister to participate in the delivery of the memorandum to the Peking Government, but his instructions arrived too late as Mr. MacMurray, together with four other Ministers of the Treaty Powers, had already had an interview with Dr. Koo.[95] The main result of the Department's attitude was that the United States held aloof from the subsequent negotiations. These negotiations ended with the Peking authorities giving assurances that they would not enforce the order requiring the Customs Administration to collect the surtaxes and that arrangements would be made whereby Sir Francis Aglen would be allowed to continue nominally in the post of Inspector General, although he was to go on home leave.[96] To Mr. MacMurray the successful efforts made to maintain the Customs service amounted to a preservation of the "last financial, and indeed governmental, link bebetween the Chinese people as a whole and the Foreign Powers."[97]

The settlement of the issue of the Customs Administration could not, however, meet all of the problems raised by the illegal imposition of the Washington surtaxes by the Peking Administration. The question still remained as to whether or not the Treaty Powers desired to adopt some joint measure which would regularize the taxes. The Diplomatic Body deliberated this issue once more but, as on all previous occasions, found it impossible to reach an agreement.[98] Mr. MacMurray, on his part, was no longer inclined to push the matter vigorously; his attitude had altered since the beginning of the negotiations on the surtaxes, and he now felt that the tide of developments in China could no longer be stemmed, and that the best the Powers could do was make an effort to swim in the strongly-defined current. He wrote to Mr. Kellogg:

I must very regretfully report that with the recent offer of the British Government to subject its nationals to the Chinese régime in all matters of taxation,[99] with the Peking Government's imposition of surtaxes, and with the attack upon the integrity of the Maritime Customs Service inaugurated by its brusque dismissal of Aglen . . . we have arrived at a point where we are helpless in all matters relative to the taxation of foreign trade. Both North and South have definitely broken away not only from the 'old' treaties but from the Washington Customs Treaty as well. Protests against treaty violations are bound to be fruitless; and foreign commerce will henceforth have no safeguards against the arbitrary exactions of the local authorities along the line from point of landing to destination.[100]

[95] *Ibid.*, pp. 460-461.
[96] *Ibid.*, pp. 462, 464-465.
[97] *Ibid.*, p. 465.
[98] *Ibid.*, pp. 375-380.
[99] Refers to British memorandum of January 27, 1927; see below, pp. 286-287.
[100] *Foreign Relations* (1927), pp. 380-381.

Mr. MacMurray then described numerous new taxes which were being collected in different parts of China and drew the following conclusions:

The old Canton system of monopolies and special privileges and of artificial restrictions upon foreign trade is rapidly building itself up again now that safeguards of the treaties have been overridden. I fear the time for protests and the time for action have gone by and that there is nothing for it but to let the Chinese — at the cost of great loss to their interests and to our own — learn by experience that that system is economically unsound and unworkable in the modern organization of the world.

In the absence of something [some?] concrete and positive means of meeting this situation I see no alternative at the present time but to bow to the storm and accept with what grace we may the fact that our trade is now absolutely without such treaty protection in China as it has in most other countries despite the fact that it is here subject to an infinity of restrictions and exactions which, so far as I am aware, are known in no other country. . . .[101]

Mr. MacMurray's discouraged view of the state of America's relations with China received the thoughtful consideration of officials in Washington, and the Secretary of State sent the following reply, the significance of which must at once have been apparent to the Legation at Peking:

For some time Department has realized the increasing difficulty of obtaining complete recognition of the rights of United States nationals in China conferred by the existing treaties between the United States and China.

It is not possible to use military and naval forces of the United States to enforce the rights guaranteed under the existing treaties; therefore, until the present treaties can be replaced by new and effective treaty relations, Department is of the opinion that a policy of patience and watchfulness is the only path that can be followed.[102]

The above statement, which was written in February, 1927, defines with exceptional clarity the policy that had been developed by officials in Washington during the difficult and challenging months that opened with the first successes of the Nationalist troops as they marched toward the Yangtze. As a result of the advance of the revolutionary armies and the consequent strengthening of the anti-foreign movement in China, not only the Kuomintang administration but also the Peking régime had been led to violate different parts of the treaty system in a way that threatened the treaty system as a whole. In addition, a series of incidents had taken place which in some cases disregarded the rights of foreigners based on the general principles of international law, and in others disregarded privileges that had been exercised by foreigners in China for many decades.

[101] *Ibid.*, p. 381.
[102] *Ibid.*, p. 382.

The Department of State appears at the outset to have met the infringements of the rights and privileges of its nationals by treating each episode as it arose as though it were an isolated matter to be judged solely on its own merits. As one emergency followed another, however, it became evident that officials in Washington continued to be governed by the same fundamental attitudes and the same basic convictions. Even the most cursory view of the State Department's actions shows the unbroken consistency of its behavior. In respect to the illegal collection of the Washington surtaxes, for example, the Department took the position that it was not prepared to adopt a so-called "strong policy" to prevent the Chinese from levying the taxes. It refused to exercise force or even threaten forceful action, preferring rather to accept the situation and postpone any further consideration of the important issues involved until conditions made it possible to undertake negotiations for a thorough revision of the treaties. In connection with the denunciation of the Sino-Belgian Treaty, the State Department's policy followed the same principles: Secretary Kellogg rejected the idea of taking a positive stand for the purpose of dissuading the Chinese from embarking on a course of treaty repudiation, because he believed that the United States should remain free to enter into negotiations for a new agreement to replace the Sino-American Treaty of 1903 if it so desired. Similarly, when cases arose involving questions of property rights and of the alleged arbitrary imprisonment of American citizens, the State Department refused to use military pressure against the Chinese and limited itself to registering diplomatic protests and to reliance on other customary procedures employed for the defense of its citizens' rights under peacetime conditions. In regard to issues involving the Maritime Customs Administration, which touched closely upon the financial and trading interests of foreigners in China, the State Department again refused to adopt any aggressive measures, this time on the ground that the Administration was a Chinese institution with which foreign governments had no right to interfere.

The State Department does not appear to have defined its own policy until a substantial body of turbulent and angry water had already flowed over the diplomatic dam. Possibly the officials in Washington were not themselves aware, until they viewed events in retrospect, of the consistency of their own conduct. In any case, the instructions to Mr. MacMurray, quoted above, accurately described the policy which the United States had been pursuing as "a policy of patience and watchfulness," to be maintained until the time should arrive when new treaties could be negotiated between the United States and China to replace the provisions of the old.

The attitude taken by the State Department essentially raised the question, however, of what conditions had to be fulfilled by the Chinese before the United States Government was prepared to undertake the negotiation of new agreements. On this matter the State Department appears to have followed a few broad and general principles. It would only enter into negotiations, it said, with a Chinese Government which represented the Chinese people as a whole and was capable of carrying out its commitments. On numerous occasions Mr. Kellogg made it plain that he was not willing to establish diplomatic relations with any group in China until, in his view, it had obtained the support of the greater part of the nation. He even refused to make regional arrangements with one or more individual factions when the issues involved were strictly circumscribed in character. To deal with separate factions in China, he argued, ran the risk of dividing the country "more or less permanently" into several parts. Throughout the year 1926, he applied these principles to the different political parties in North and South China with what appears to have been genuine impartiality. The consequence of this important aspect of American policy was that it committed the United States, temporarily at least, to playing an inactive rôle in respect to developments in China. The attitude of the State Department, which said to the Chinese that the United States was unwilling to take further action until a stable, strong, and representative government was established in China, meant that little could be done until the situation had undergone a drastic transformation. Whether such a transformation could take place within the near future seemed at the time decidedly open to question.

To understand the marked difference between the views of the State Department at Washington and the American Minister at Peking, it is essential to consider the angle from which Mr. MacMurray approached the Chinese situation. Mr. MacMurray had attended the Washington Conference in 1921 when he was Chief of the Division of Far Eastern Affairs in the State Department. He had devoted himself, with an energy that stemmed from his sincere and strong convictions, to the work undertaken by the Conference. He believed that the Conference had in the end produced a formula which ought to guide the relations of China and the Treaty Powers for some time to come and which, if adhered to, would benefit Chinese and foreigners alike. The Washington formula (discussed at the outset of this study)[103] was accepted by Mr. MacMurray as meaning that China should be given the opportunity to develop into a well-organized and efficiently administered state while the Treaty Powers pursued a "policy of self-abnegation" on condition that China attain its aims through orderly and legal processes.

[103] See Chapter I.

When therefore the Nationalist movement increased in China after 1925 and was accompanied by a strong upsurge of anti-foreign feeling, which virtually forced Chinese officials of all shades of political opinion to take an aggressive attitude toward the Treaty Powers and to violate the terms of the treaties, it seemed to Mr. MacMurray that the Chinese were no longer adhering to their part of the bargain that had been incorporated in the Washington formula. He believed that the Chinese nation, instead of maintaining the position it had assumed at the Washington Conference as a member of the community of nations bound (in theory at least) to follow the acknowledged practices of international law, was by the use of illegal and revolutionary methods again placing itself outside the circle of Powers which were regarded as responsible and law-abiding. Mr. MacMurray thought that the Chinese would suffer seriously from the consequences of their own actions. While discussing the infractions of treaty rights by the Nationalists in Canton, he stated his views clearly in words that have already been quoted:

The Cantonese do not see that when once back to conditions prevalent a century past and complicated and worsened by China's present internal strife, there will come again a time when Western pressure will force new conflicts and once more begin the old cycle: hostilities over a long period, subjugation, and special conditions for intercourse imposed.... Their folly is of a historically characteristic form, whose results [threaten?] more or less directly to involve us in the disaster of indefinitely retarding in China the development of a rational, ordered, political and economic entity and of relationships between the Western Powers and China that are normal.

In addition, from the point of view of the United States, Mr. MacMurray undoubtedly believed that to protect the trade and other interests of Americans in China, the State Department should actively defend the rights and the privileges of its citizens. He did not therefore advocate a "policy of patience and watchfulness" but on the contrary was in favor of a strong and vigorous policy. He consistently recommended the taking of a firm stand, which would at times have involved the use of military pressure, in dealing with the incidents that arose and threatened the treaty sytem and the position of American nationals in China. In pursuing this course, Mr. MacMurray found himself engaged in a constant discussion with the State Department in Washington — a discussion which was to increase rather than diminish in gravity as time wore on because of the simple fact that the American Minister and the Secretary of State approached the situation in China with a different set of ideas and were each bound by the vigor and genuineness of their own convictions.

On the whole, the developments in China during the year 1926 may be said to have presented many problems to officials in the United States Government which had to be met as emergencies that called for quick decisions and for quick action. Nevertheless, in the end, it was apparent that American policy had developed into something more tangible and solid and that its evolution was well under way. One other important event related to the government's activities still remains to be considered, however, namely, the work of the Commission on Extraterritoriality which conducted its investigations in China throughout the better part of the year.

CHAPTER VIII

THE COMMISSION ON EXTRATERRITORIALITY

Throughout 1926, the results of the work of the Commission on Extra-territoriality in China were awaited on all sides with impatience and anxiety. It was generally recognized that the findings of the Commission were bound to have a strong influence on the attitude of the Powers toward the abolition of the extraterritorial system and there was widespread speculation concerning the conclusions the Commission would reach: would they hasten or retard the revision of the extraterritorial terms of the treaties? The Kuomintang Government at Canton took the position that it would not co-operate with the Commission in any of its activities on the ground that extraterritoriality should be abandoned at once and that further investigation and discussion was therefore beside the point.[1] The public in general complained because the work of the Commission was carried on behind an unyielding wall of secrecy and nothing was known of its progress from the time the Commissioners met in January, 1926, until their Report was issued twelve months later.

The Commission consisted of the representatives of twelve Treaty Powers[2] and of China. The day originally set for the meeting of the Commissioners was December 18, 1925, but owing to the civil war in North China, transportation was interrupted and some of the Commissioners were unable to reach Peking on time.[3] The opening session was therefore not held until January 12th[4] when Silas H. Strawn, the American Commissioner, who was at the same time taking part in the Special Tariff Conference, was elected chairman of the Commission.[5]

The task of the Commission, as defined at the Washington Conference, was to gather together a body of facts concerning the structure and operation of the judicial system in China (including the practice of extraterritoriality), and to make recommendations both for the improvement of existing conditions and for assisting the Chinese Government to effect such reforms as "would warrant the several Powers in relinquishing either progressively

[1]*Report of the Commission on Extraterritoriality in China*, Washington, D.C., 1926, p. 6.
[2] America, Belgium, the British Empire, Denmark, France, Italy, Japan, the Netherlands, Norway, Portugal, Spain, Sweden.
[3] *Report of the Commission on Extraterritoriality in China*, p. 4.
[4] *Ibid.*
[5] *Ibid.*

154

or otherwise their respective rights of extraterritoriality."[6] The Commission held twenty-two sessions in all, which were devoted to an examination of the Chinese codes and laws; to a consideration of the various problems arising out of the exercise of extraterritorial jurisdiction in China; and, finally, to the framing of a joint Report.[7] A traveling committee, given the responsibility of conducting investigations in the field, made a five-weeks' tour of courts, prisons, detention-houses, etc., in various provinces. Their ability to collect information was limited, however, first, by the fact that the Nationalists refused to allow the committee to survey conditions in the territory under Kuomintang control and, secondly, by the continued dislocation of the transportation system which made travel in many areas impossible.[8]

Soon after the Commissioners began their work in China, the Chinese Commissioner, Dr. Wang Chung-hui, informed Mr. MacMurray that, although the resolution of the Washington Conference establishing the Commission had provided only for a report that would supply factual data and make recommendations, the Chinese Government felt that the powers of the Commissioners should be enlarged so that they could enter into some definite agreement about the procedure to be followed regarding the abolition of extraterritoriality.[9] Commenting on this proposal to Washington, Mr. MacMurray cabled:

> Strawn and I recommend strongly that the powers of the Commission be not enlarged.... It is our belief that there is unanimous sentiment against modification of the treaties at present in view of the revolutionary conditions obtaining here and the absence of a government which is capable of enforcing law. The Chinese demand is preposterous. The Commission's Report will present facts for Governments to consider seriously before they should take any action.[10]

Approached directly by the Chinese Government on this same issue, Secretary of State Kellogg responded that before empowering someone to enter into negotiations for a revision of the treaties he wished to have on hand the Report and the recommendations of the Commission and therefore regarded it as essential for the Commission to be allowed to complete its investigations.[11]

During the months when the Commission was engaged in its work, there appears to have been little interchange of opinion between the State

[6] See above, p. 52.
[7] *Report of the Commission on Extraterritoriality in China*, p. 5.
[8] *Ibid.*, pp. 5-6. The Commission obtained a great deal of information from consular reports received from all parts of China. (*Foreign Relations*, 1926, p. 972.)
[9] *Foreign Relations* (1926), p. 968.
[10] *Ibid.* (cable paraphrased).
[11] *Ibid.*, p. 969.

Department in Washington and Mr. Strawn.[12] In April, Mr. Strawn forwarded what he termed a "forecast of the general purport" of the Commissioners' Report, which he based on informal conversations with some of the Commissioners:

The following admitted facts preclude the possibility of the surrender by the several Powers of their extraterritorial rights guaranteed them by their several treaties with China:

1. The absence of a Central Government in China, recognized as such by the several Powers;

2. Complete and arbitrary control of every department of governmental activity by the militarists who are constantly warring among themselves;

3. Absence of laws enacted by a duly constituted authority subject to repeal only by that authority;

4. Absence of competent and trained judges, free from all outside influences, political and military;

5. Chaotic condition of the finances of China with no provision for the payment of adequate compensation to the judiciary.

In view of these fundamental facts, the surrender by the several Powers of their extraterritorial rights at this time not only would put in jeopardy the lives and property of their nationals residing in China, but also would be prejudicial to the Chinese themselves and would postpone the time when the Chinese people may realize their ambition to have complete autonomy in judicial matters.[13]

Nevertheless, Mr. Strawn continued, although the Report would probably oppose the relinquishment of extraterritorial rights under the existing circumstances, it would also make certain recommendations looking toward the eventual abolition of extraterritoriality. He proceeded to sketch these recommendations which fell into two categories: those the Powers might accept in order to modify the existing practice of extraterritoriality, and those the Chinese might adopt by way of remedying certain defects in their judicial system.[14]

Mr. Kellogg's answer to Mr. Strawn outlined clearly the attitude of the Department toward the work of the Commission and contained some very significant statements:

---

[12] *Ibid.*, pp. 966-984.

[13] *Ibid.*, p. 973.

[14] *Ibid.* In concluding his forecast of the content of the report, Mr. Strawn said: "The foregoing is a brief outline of what seems to us might be the basis of a report. We have not submitted our suggestions to any of the other Commissioners. They may not agree with us." (*Ibid.*, p. 975.)

It is clear that the outline of the final report, its character, and many of its most important features, were in accord with the suggestions presented above by Mr. Strawn.

Regarding the tentative recommendations you have made, my feeling is that you ought to be permitted to use your personal judgment unhampered with respect to details by instructions from the Department, the reason being that the Department should remain free as to the making of any treaty regarding extraterritoriality after your report is received. Since I am unfamiliar with the local conditions in China I can give you on this subject only the most general instructions. It has been my desire to renounce extraterritoriality in regard to China, and everywhere else, as soon as such action is compatible with the requirements of protecting American lives and interests. Therefore I should wish that you make your report without being confined by definite instructions on detail and make it without considering the desires of other countries except for those of their suggestions which commend themselves to your judgment. I do not desire that you should recommend as a prerequisite to extraterritoriality being relinquished, any requirements from China which you do not believe are absolutely necessary to protect American interests before extraterritoriality is relinquished. Ideal conditions are not expected by us, but we must have assurance of course that American citizens will be fairly protected by the Government. It has been my hope that we could give up extraterritoriality in China within a reasonable time. Possibly we may be forced into such a position that we will feel compelled to do it without delay, but I wish first to have your honest judgment on the situation.[15]

These remarks of the Secretary, made in June, 1926, do not appear to have been followed by any further advice or instruction from the Department.[16] Mr. Strawn was presumably given a free hand and the contents of the Commission's Report were not forwarded to Washington until after the Report was completed and signed by the Commissioners in the middle of September.[17]

The *Report of the Commission on Extraterritoriality in China,* as it was called, was a document of exceptional importance. Since it set forth a mass of detailed information concerning the practice of extraterritoriality in China and the structure and operation of the Chinese judicial system, little more can be done here than to present a skeleton outline, limited to some of the outstanding points which the Commissioners themselves emphasized.

The Report was divided into four sections in the following manner: Part I, Present Practice of Extraterritoriality; Part II, Laws and Judicial System of China; Part III, Administration of Justice in China; Part IV, Recommendations.

[15] *Ibid.,* pp. 978-979.
[16] *Foreign Relations* (1926) contains no cables on this subject between June 11, 1926, and September 17, 1926.
[17] See *Foreign Relations* (1926), p. 979.

Part I. Present Practice of Extraterritoriality[18]

I. Foreign Courts[19]

The Commissioners emphasized at the beginning that some of the Treaty Powers had developed far more extensive systems of extraterritoriality in China than others. Great Britain and the United States were, for example, the only two nations which had established special courts and a professional staff; France and Italy had special judges; and Japan and Norway, a few specially trained consular judges. With these exceptions, the extraterritorial system functioned through consular courts presided over by a consular officer acting alone, or, in some instances, assisted by assessors. Great Britain was the only nation which had provided for trial by jury.

In respect to the functioning of the extraterritorial courts in China, the Commissioners gave the following general picture:

The foreign courts possessed civil and criminal jurisdiction in three clearly defined types of cases:

(a) Cases in which the parties on both sides were of the same nationality as the court.

(b) Cases in which the plaintiff or complainant was a foreigner not of the same nationality as that of the court.

(c) Cases in which the plaintiff or complainant was Chinese.

In general, therefore, the foreign courts exercised jurisdiction over their nationals in China when they were defendants in civil cases and the accused in criminal cases. All civil cases fell within their competency as courts of first instance, but in criminal cases certain more serious crimes might be tried in a foreign court beyond the territorial limits of China. The procedure in respect to the appeal of cases varied according to the nationality involved: in some instances, the appeal was to an extraterritorial court established in China, in others to a court in a neighboring region (such as, for example, the Netherlands courts at Batavia), and in still others to courts in the European homeland. No matter which of the Powers was concerned, however, the final appeals lay at all times to the highest competent tribunals residing in the respective capitals of the nations involved. In regard to the law to be applied, the foreign courts in China applied the same systems of law as were in force within the boundaries of their own countries — sometimes with, and sometimes without, modification. When prisoners were sentenced, they might be sent to foreign prisons in China or to prisons beyond

[18] Unless otherwise stated, all references throughout the rest of the chapter are to the *Report of the Commission on Extraterritoriality.*
[19] Pp. 11-13.

the territorial limits of China, depending largely upon the length of the sentence.

II. Chinese Courts[20]

In addition to presenting information concerning the operation of foreign courts in China as they dealt with cases in which foreigners were the accused or defendants, the Commissioners reviewed the situation in respect to the treatment of those cases in which Chinese were the accused or defendants and foreigners the complainants or plaintiffs. According to the arrangements made in the extraterritorial provisions of the treaties, these cases, whether civil or criminal, were tried in Chinese courts, with the extraterritorial Powers possessing the right to send a representative — usually known as an assessor — to watch the proceedings; the assessor might, if he so desired, protest in detail against the proceedings and he could present, examine, and cross-examine witnesses. Originally, when the extraterritorial treaties were first concluded, the complete administration of justice in China was in the hands of the district magistrates, so that all claims and complaints of foreigners against Chinese were essentially tried in the magistrates' courts with the assessors taking part in the manner stipulated by the terms of the treaties. Over the years, special practices had grown up at Shanghai,[21] Amoy, and to a certain extent at Hankow, which increased the powers of the assessors. Also, an unexpected development occurred when, after 1904, the Chinese began the reorganization of their judicial system and established a number of modern courts which took the place of the old magistrates' courts functioning in the same area, and in which the presence of an assessor was not permitted. As the Powers were not willing to relinquish their treaty right to send an assessor, the district magistrate continued to exercise jurisdiction in so-called "mixed cases" where Chinese were the defendants or accused, and foreigners the plaintiffs or complainants. Foreigners were, therefore, given the option of appearing before the district magistrate or waiving the right to have an assessor and taking their cases to modern courts. Furthermore, appeals from the orders and decisions of the courts of the district magistrates hearing mixed cases lay to a court composed of the Chinese Commissioner for Foreign Affairs and the foreign consul concerned sitting with the Commissioner to watch the proceedings. Beyond this there was no appeal, strictly speaking, but if the decision of the Commissioner was still disputed by the assessor, the matter might be taken to Peking for negotiation between the Ministry of Foreign Affairs and the

[20] Pp. 13-19.
[21] See Chapter X.

interested Legation. The laws, which were applied by all the courts and tribunals exercising jurisdiction over cases brought by foreigners against Chinese, were the Chinese laws, ordinances, rules and regulations in force in Chinese courts, subject, in certain special instances, to modifications such as the enforcement of the by-laws of the settlements and concessions.

III. Observations of the Commissioners[22]

The part of the Report dealing with the practice of extraterritoriality in China concluded with a section devoted to observations made by the Commissioners:

(1) Limitations on China's jurisidictional freedom: The system of extraterritoriality was established in China as a *modus vivendi* necessary for harmonious relations between China and the Powers until the evolution of the laws and legal conceptions of China should render it unnecessary. Although, in the course of history, extraterritoriality in its relation to the sovereign rights of a country was regarded in a quite different light, it had come to be considered as a limitation upon the rights of the state which granted it. It was on this aspect of the question that China had in recent years laid great stress. This was no doubt largely due to the growth of nationalistic feeling in China, along with the rapid expansion of foreign interests which had resulted in bringing into greater prominence the anomalies of the present system.

(2) Multiplicity of courts and diversity of laws: It was obvious that with so many foreign courts existing in China, each administering the laws of its own country, anomalies must arise from time to time. Some examples of these anomalies were: the court in which a trial took place had no jurisdiction over an alien plaintiff or witness; a defendant who desired to bring a counterclaim against an alien plaintiff was unable to do so except under special circumstances; where several persons had jointly committed a crime it was necessary to have as many trials in different national courts as there were accused of different nationalities.

(3) Inaccessibility of the courts: When a serious crime was committed by a foreigner in China he could only be prosecuted (unless he was a British or American citizen) outside the territorial limits of China and, in many instances, only in Europe. Even in cases where a foreigner could be prosecuted before a consular court in China, such a court might be established at a very long distance from the place where the offense was committed, and it was often difficult to secure the attendance of the necessary witnesses or to produce other essential evidence.

[22] Pp. 19-25.

(4) Procedure in appeals: Similarly, under most of the extraterritorial systems operating in China, appeals from the judgment of the foreign courts had to be taken to courts beyond the territorial limits of China. This was obviously unfair for Chinese litigants and sometimes inconvenient for foreigners.

(5) Immunity of foreigners from the operation of Chinese regulations: Courts of the Treaty Powers in China applied the same laws as were in force within the territorial limits of their home countries, with or without modifications. The power to make such modifications without specific legislative authority in each case was of course limited and did not as a rule extend to the enforcement of Chinese subsidiary legislation, such as regulations relating to taxation, to the press, to traffic, etc. From the immunity of foreigners in this respect, there arose an anomalous situation which caused friction between foreign nationals and the Chinese authorities.

(6) Irregular protection of Chinese: Some extraterritorial Powers extended protection too readily to Chinese in China by allowing Chinese citizens as well as their firms and property to be registered by their consulates. By so doing they removed those persons, their property, and their business interests from the jurisdiction of Chinese laws and Chinese courts. No justification existed for such protection and a number of the Powers, realizing this, had taken steps to control and remedy the situation.

Difficulties arose also when persons of Chinese origin who had acquired foreign citizenship, either by birth or naturalization, came or returned to places in China where the treaties did not permit foreigners to reside, to own property, or to trade, and by holding themselves out to be Chinese were able to set aside these restrictions of the treaties. In case of trouble, such persons claimed the protection of their consuls and thus sought to avoid the obligations which they had contracted under the guise of being Chinese citizens. The fact that some Powers did not require compulsory registration of their nationals in China made it more difficult to keep track of such offenders.

(7) Inviolability of foreign premises: According to the treaties, foreign premises were not subject to search or entry by Chinese judicial or other authorities, therefore, Chinese criminals who fled to such premises could not be arrested without due requisition by Chinese authorities addressed to the consular authorities. The result was that, at times, extraterritorial nationals gave, or seemed to give, protection to Chinese citizens. When the premises were located in the interior, distant from a consulate, the rôle of protector by the foreigner concerned became especially apparent. A similar situation arose when a foreign court had occasion to arrest or serve a process upon

a person under its jurisdiction who rented or had taken refuge on premises belonging to China or persons of another extraterritorial nationality.

(8) Mutual assistance between courts: The foreign courts in China, both among themselves and in relation to the Chinese and mixed courts, practiced to a certain extent co-operation with respect to the mutual summoning and examination of witnesses, arrest of offenders, etc. This mutual assistance was, however, voluntary and did not have sufficient basis in treaties or other formal agreements.

(9) Lawyers: As a rule, when a lawyer was admitted to practice before his own national courts in China, he was as a matter of courtesy admitted to practice in the other foreign courts in China if the courtesy was reciprocated. Foreign lawyers were also permitted to plead in the mixed courts of Shanghai. With regard to the appearance of lawyers in the other Chinese courts hearing mixed cases, this right was denied to the foreign plaintiffs except that such plaintiffs as took their cases before the modern courts were entitled to engage a Chinese lawyer to represent them.

Part II. Laws and Judicial System of China

I. Work of Codification[23]

The Report reviewed briefly the reform movement which had sprung up in China for the revision of the existing legal and judicial systems. The immediate cause of this movement was the promise made by Great Britain and the United States in the commercial treaties of 1902 and 1903, to surrender their extraterritorial rights when the state of the Chinese laws, the arrangements for their administration, and other considerations warranted them in so doing. As a result, the Imperial Law Codification Commission, which prepared the drafts of various codes of law, was instituted. The new criminal code prepared by the Commission was promulgated in 1909 and a new system of courts was established under the laws passed in 1907 and 1909.

After the Revolution of 1911 and the establishment of the Republic, the name of the Commission was changed to the Revised Law Codification Commission and it continued the work which had been started under the Imperial Government. As the task was very extensive in scope, involving the complex problem of reconciling Chinese customs which had existed for centuries with the principles of foreign law, it had been carried on continuously since 1914. All of the codes and some of the laws, ordinances, and regulations in force in the Chinese Courts in 1926 were the work of the Codification Commission.

[23] P. 29.

II. The Constitution[24]

The main point made in the Report concerning the constitution was that under the republican form of government adopted by China in 1912, the laws should derive their validity from the constitution. The Commissioners declared, however, that the state of affairs in respect to a constitution in China was "vague and unsatisfactory" as three different constitutions had been passed since 1912 and each had been set aside in turn. There had been fundamental agreement in all the three constitutions that Parliament was the sole law-making body in China and that the President was limited to the promulgation and execution of the laws. But few of the laws applied in the Chinese courts had, in fact, ever been enacted or confirmed by Parliament; they were based, instead, on mandates of the President or orders of the Minister of Justice, neither of whom had, strictly speaking, any legal or constitutional authority to make laws. From the juridical point of view the laws were therefore regarded by the Commission as regulations applied with the force of law by the court, but subject to change or rescission at any time by their creators, namely, the President and the Ministry of Justice.

III. Laws

(A) Laws and Regulations Relating to Criminal Matters[25]

In respect to the Provisional Criminal Code, the Commissioners found that a new draft which had been completed, although not yet promulgated, corrected various defects of the original code instituted in 1909, and amended five years later.

The Commission, however, pointed to weaknesses in some of the other laws and regulations governing criminal matters: The police offenses law, it was asserted, conferred too much power upon the police, especially in connection with the detention both of persons already convicted of having violated police regulations and, under certain circumstances, of those who had been accused but not as yet tried. The significance of the latter provision was said to lie in the fact that it touched "the daily life of every resident," exposing him to detention for police offenses which were "generally of a trifling nature." The law relating to the suppression of robbery, insurgency, and brigandage, was criticized as "too drastic." Objections were raised to the Criminal Procedure Regulations on the ground that they denied appeal in minor cases and that the provisions for arrest and bail

[24] Pp. 30-32.
[25] Pp. 32-39.

needed to be liberalized and made more precise. The same regulations were also found at fault in that they left such matters as the relevancy, admissibility, and materiality of evidence to the discretion of the judge who lacked any satisfactory guide as judicial precedents in China had not yet developed to an extent where they could furnish the needed assistance. The Army and Navy Regulations were criticized on several counts, and it was pointed out that they acquired unusual significance, first, because the military and naval courts played a highly influential rôle in China owing to the "continual and widespread civil warfare"; secondly, because these courts exercised extensive power, having jurisdiction over all persons in the armed services who committed offenses against military or non-military laws and over civilians who violated military and naval codes. The rules governing the trial proceedings in the courts of the district magistrates were also singled out for their exceptional importance, owing to the fact that most of the litigation in China was in the hands of the magistrates' courts; emphasis was placed upon such aspects of the regulations as the denial to litigants of the right of legal counsel (although lawyers were allowed to submit briefs) and the exemption of magistrates from the delivery of written judgments.

(B) Laws and Regulations Relating to Civil Matters[26]

Until recently, the Report said, Chinese lawmakers had not found it necessary to differentiate between criminal and civil law, and both had been dealt with in one code, the *Ta Ching Lu Li*. Although about fifteen years had elapsed since the institution of the new Chinese legal system, no statutory provision had as yet been made for a civil code and definite legislation had been provided only in respect to a few civil matters. In view of this situation the sources relied upon in civil cases were: certain provisions of the *Ta Ching Lu Li;* decisions of the Supreme Court (which were based on the *Ta Ching Lu Li,* general legal principles, and customs); specific laws promulgated since the Revolution of 1911.

The Commissioners found that in practice this procedure offered substantial difficulties. The courts tended to look for guidance in the use of legal principles to the provisions of the draft codes, but, as these by no means covered the essential ground, there were wide gaps which could be filled in a variety of ways; thus, the public had no means of knowing, in advance of litigation, which legal principles might be applied. As far as the Supreme Court decisions were concerned, the Report said that, although they were undoubtedly "a very useful source of civil law," it was difficult

[26] Pp. 39-45.

to state with accuracy the extent to which they corrected the deficiency arising from the absence of a civil code and other statutory civil laws; moreover, a definite provision was needed to ensure the general recognition of all the decisions of the Supreme Court by the lower courts.

Concerning the civil procedure regulations, the Report placed considerable emphasis upon the fact that the detention of civil defendants was still possible in China and that, although there were certain reasons for the existence of such a situation, nevertheless the safeguards against bad faith on the part of the plaintiff were not sufficient. It was also shown that, up to the year 1925, civil judgment debtors could be detained for as long as three years, a period which was then reduced to three months. The regulations governing civil proceedings in the courts of the district magistrates, being in many respects similar to those governing criminal proceedings in the same courts, were criticized on much the same basis except that there was no revision of civil judgments by the high court, contrary to the practice in criminal cases.

The Commissioners made various important comments concerning the laws and rulings which had been passed by the Chinese Government — in 1919 and 1920 — in respect to foreigners who were the nationals of Powers that did not possess extraterritorial rights. Cases of this kind, it was decreed, should be tried in modern courts and should be transferred to such courts even if they arose in districts where no modern court existed; exception was made, however, for cases in the remote interior when transference might prove too difficult, and it was stipulated that special arrangements for the trial should be made by the Ministry of Justice. Moreover, the trial of cases involving non-extraterritorial foreigners was to be conducted before specially trained judges and procurators (except in cases falling within the original jurisdiction of the high court). Detention and imprisonment of non-extraterritorial nationals was to be effected in modern prisons and detention-houses or — in regions where these did not exist — in a proper building provided for this purpose.

Rules concerning the application of foreign laws had been put into force in 1918. They provided for the application of foreign laws in the Chinese courts in certain cases involving foreigners and were in the nature of private international law. Commenting upon these the Commissioners declared that since these rules prescribed that "the capacity of a foreigner in China is defined by national law" they were of the greatest importance to foreigners, particularly in respect to matters relating to personal status, such as marriage, divorce, family relations, succession, etc., upon which subjects Chinese law and customs were in many instances "fundamentally different from those of foreign countries."

(C) Laws and Regulations Relating to Commercial Matters[27]

Many difficulties connected with the trial of civil cases, the Commissioners said, were also found in the handling of commercial matters. There were few commercial laws and rules in force and deficiencies had to be met through the same means that were employed in civil practice. Reference was made, however, to certain laws and regulations which had been promulgated, such as those concerned with commercial associations, chambers of commerce, trade-marks, copyrights, stock exchanges, etc.

(D) Miscellaneous[28]

The most important comments made in respect to various miscellaneous laws described in the Report were those dealing with the martial law of China. Martial law could be proclaimed by the President, or in time of war or emergency by the commanding officer in the particular area affected, although in the latter instance a report had to be sent to the President; upon the declaration of martial law, the jurisdiction of the administrative and judicial authorities was either wholly or partially transferred to the military authorities. This situation assumed a special significance in the eyes of the Commissioners because events in China had brought about a condition where martial law — "or declarations purporting to be 'martial law' " — was declared with such frequency that normal legal procedures were hampered and the security which, under other circumstances, would be accorded civilians through the functioning of civil courts was endangered. This practice, it was said, constituted "a grave menace to the proper administration of civil law in China."

(E) General Observations on Laws[29]

The Commissioners expressed their appreciation of the efforts made in recent years to reorganize the legal and judicial systems of China. These efforts had resulted in the formation of a system of modern courts, with regulations governing civil and criminal procedure, and in the creation of a body of substantive law. With the general principles of the new laws the Commissioners declared themselves to be "satisfied," but in respect to the situation in general they made a number of observations:

(1) Absence of fundamental legal provisions: The Chinese constitutions had aimed at the establishment of a Republic on a legal basis. The

[27] Pp. 45-47.
[28] Pp. 48-51.
[29] Pp. 51-55.

framers of the Constitution sought to define the fundamental rights and duties of Chinese citizens; to provide an authoritative method of enacting, promulgating, and rescinding laws; and to separate the administrative, legislative, and judicial functions of government. In the early years of the Republic considerable progress was made toward the fulfillment of these aims, but further advance was impeded by the civil conflict which had been carried on intermittently since the establishment of the Republic and had resulted in discarding the constitutions and in weakening the authority of the Central Government.

Thus the rights and duties of the individual Chinese, the powers of legislative, administrative, and judicial officers, and the separation of these powers, no longer rested upon any firm constitutional basis. It had therefore been possible for administrative officials — who were constantly changing and in many instances were nominees of military leaders — to encroach upon the functions of the legislature and judiciary. Moreover, as the influence of these officials increased, fewer and fewer attempts were made to give popular sanction to the Chinese laws and their administration; instead, civil laws and civil courts were replaced by military law and military courts whose procedures and penalties were far more drastic.

(2) Anomalies of legislation: Not only did the fundamental law of China rest upon an uncertain constitutional basis, but a similar condition existed in respect to the supplementary legislation which was declared to be in force by ministries and other authorities such as the civil governors, the magistrates, and the police. In addition, a practice existed of promulgating laws which could not be put into execution until further and more detailed regulations for their enforcement had been passed, and these regulations in many cases were either long delayed or never came into being. Similarly numerous laws had been promulgated, containing provisions that referred by anticipation to other laws which did not exist.

Furthermore, in consequence of the fact that so little time had elapsed since the new legal system had been brought into effect, the assimilation of modern principles of law had not kept pace with the actual legislation. This had in turn produced two anomalies in the existing situation: Some of the ancient laws and legal principles which dated from former times remained in force and were applied side-by-side with the new legislation, tending to nullify, in part at least, the benefits to be derived from the reorganization of the legal system; the application of a number of the new laws was restricted both in respect to their provisions and to the places where they were enforced. The Civil and Criminal Procedure Regulations, for example, were only applied *in toto* in the few modern courts that had been established, and even in these courts some of the subsidiary legislation was out of harmony with the more up-to-date principles of the procedural regulations.

(3) Matters unprovided for by law: Although much progress had been made in the revision and codification of Chinese law along Western lines, there still remained a number of important matters that were not covered by any legislation. Among these were:

a) Matters usually dealt with in civil code, such as general principles, obligations, things, family and inheritance.
b) Matters usually dealt with in a commercial code, such as negotiable instruments, banking, maritime matters and insurance.
c) Bankruptcy.
d) Patents.
e) Practice of pharmacy and medicine.
f) Registration of vital statistics.
g) Lunacy.
h) Cadastral registration of land.
i) Notaries public.
j) Expropriation of land.

While draft codes had been prepared in relation to some of these matters (such as a Civil Code and parts of a Commercial Code), they had not as yet been promulgated. Moreover other subjects, such as those specified under (d) and (h) above, had not even been provided for in draft form.

IV. The Judicial System

(A) The Modern Courts[30]

The system of modern courts, instituted after 1907, contemplated the organization of a completely new judicial system similar to that of Japan and of continental European countries. Although about seventeen years had elapsed, the Commissioners observed, since the inauguration of the new system, it had not been possible to establish and maintain more than 136 courts. The original plan had provided for a Supreme Court at Peking; at least one high court in each province with branch courts wherever necessary; district courts in each district with branch district courts wherever necessary; and, finally, local courts. Procuratorates were to be attached to all of the modern courts. By 1926, there had been brought into existence: the Supreme Court, twenty-three high courts, twenty-six branch high courts,

[30] Pp. 58-66.

sixty-six district courts, and twenty-three branch divisions of district courts; all of these had corresponding procuratorates.

Where district courts or branch divisions of district courts had been instituted, they took over the judicial functions formerly exercised by the district magistrates and by any local courts existing within the district. The high courts were usually located in provincial capitals and the branch high courts in other parts of the province. The Supreme Court was at Peking and was the highest court of justice in China. Regulations had been put into effect governing the organization and functioning of these courts and their procuratorates.

(B) Transition Courts[31]

The object in establishing courts classified as transition courts was to attempt to bring the old magistrates' courts more into harmony with the modern courts. Because of this, it was stated in the Report, the organization and rules of these courts were a mixture of old and modern procedures. Regulations passed in 1917 and 1923 had contemplated, as part of the transition court system, the temporary creation of judicial offices in every district where no modern court was as yet established. Each office was to have attached to it one or two well-trained judges who were to take over the judicial functions of the magistrate in that district. Only forty-six judicial offices had, however, been instituted by 1926.

(C) Magistrates' Courts[32]

Magistrates' courts, the Commissioners said, had existed in China for centuries and until the establishment of the modern courts they were practically the only judicial forms throughout the whole country. In 1926, there were still about 1800 magistrates' courts as against 150 modern courts of first instance. Various regulations, including those establishing judicial offices, had been passed from time to time in an attempt to limit and prescribe the jurisdiction of the magistrates' courts in order that the interests of justice might be "better served."

(D) Military Courts[33]

The Report divided military and naval courts into two classes: the permanent and the provisional. In times of peace, it declared, the jurisdic-

[31] Pp. 66-68.
[32] Pp. 68-69.
[33] Pp. 71-72.

tion of the military courts was largely confined to persons in the armed services, but in times of war or when martial law had been proclaimed the jurisdiction of these courts was greatly enhanced.

(E) Police Tribunals[34]

Offenses committed against the police offenses law and against regulations promulgated by the police were tried in police tribunals at the police stations. Under the Chinese judicial system, however, the acts of the police officials were regarded as administrative and not as judicial. This was a point upon which the Commissioners placed considerable emphasis, stating that the police in China had "rather extraordinary powers" since they might sentence a person to thirty days detention (sixty days in the metropolitan area) and no appeal was possible on the facts of the case.

(F) General Observations on the Judicial System[35]

As a preface to their observations concerning the structure of the Chinese judicial system, the Commissioners emphasized that the plan for reorganization, as in the case of China's new legal system, had been modeled on European and Japanese lines and was "in its conception quite satisfactory." Since the institution of the system, however, a number of changes had been made which tended to obliterate the well-defined lines of demarcation between administrative and judicial functions and between the jurisdiction of the courts of first instance and appellate courts. Specifically, the Commissioners made the following observations:

(1) Control of the judiciary and discharge of judicial functions by administrative officials: Any system such as that in use in China, whereby the Minister of Justice could delegate a considerable part of his supervisory powers over the provincial judicial organizations to the provincial civil governors, instead of to the highest judicial authorities in the provinces, tended to obliterate the lines which divided judicial from administrative functions. Thus the civil governor of a province, who was an administrative official, had control over the judiciary in his province, a control which "should alone be exercised by the Ministry of Justice or by the highest judicial authority of the province." This situation gained additional significance from the fact that the civil governor was a legislative authority issuing regulations which carried penal provisions ranging from fines to six months' imprisonment.

(2) Magistrates' Courts: The magistrates' courts were "admittedly

[34] Pp. 73-74.
[35] Pp. 79-83.

unsatisfactory," since the magistrate discharged judicial functions which should on no account be performed by an administrative official, while the trial officer[36] attached to the magistrates' courts had neither the same training or standing as judges in the modern courts. These conditions made the services of a lawyer especially necessary, but it was precisely in the magistrates' courts that the right to legal counsel was denied. Detention in civil cases was permitted and the magistrates were exempt from delivering a written judgment in local court cases although such cases might involve imprisonment up to five years. Although remedial measures existed in the form of provisions for appeal and review (in criminal cases only), they were inadequate to guard against injustice. In addition, the magistrate in his administrative capacity could inflict fines up to $60 and pass sentence of detention up to thirty days, against which there was no appeal except to a superior administrative authority and to the administrative court at Peking. As by far the larger portion of litigation in China fell within the jurisdiction of the magistrates' courts, the situation was regarded as being "in need of reform."

(3) Transition Courts and Judicial Offices: The transition courts and the judicial offices attached to magistrates' courts were of temporary character and could naturally "not be regarded as satisfactory."

(4) Military Courts: The military and naval courts in China exercised jurisdiction in all cases of military and non-military offenses when committed by persons in the military service; this meant that civilians had to bring their complaints against such persons before military or naval courts. These courts also possessed jurisdiction over civilians in times of emergency. Such conditions tended to strengthen the power of the military over the civilian part of the population. Moreover, the procedure in the military and naval courts had certain special features: trials were conducted *in camera;* legal counsel was denied; appeal was not allowed; corporal punishment up to 600 blows of the bamboo was permitted.

(5) Police Tribunals: The police in China occupied a "peculiar position" which gave them far greater authority than that exercised by the police of other countries. As all their acts were regarded as administrative, except where they were functioning as judicial police, there was no appeal against an act of a police officer except to a superior administrative authority. In addition, the police in China had certain powers which extended into

[36] Trial officers were persons with some legal training who, when the reorganization of the judicial system was started, were attached to the magistrates' courts to replace somewhat similar officials known under the old régime as the magistrates' judicial secretaries (p. 68). The actual trial of cases took place before the trial officer, while the magistrate assumed the rôle of procurator.

legislative and judicial spheres. Thus the police could make regulations and punish offenders against such regulations (up to thirty days' detention) without the accused being able to appeal to a court of law. Infractions of the police offenses law were tried in police tribunals, also without the right of appeal to a court of law.

These powers of the police were still further enlarged when the police functioned as judicial police and acted in a procuratorial capacity in the investigation of crimes. They could in such a capacity arrest persons and conduct examinations without any reference to the law courts. This was "also a situation . . . in need of remedy."

V. The Prison System[37]

During the latter part of the Ching Dynasty, China had begun to develop a prison system of the modern type; after the 1911 Revolution, attempts were made to continue this process. Nevertheless, by 1926, only sixty-three modern prisons had been brought into existence and 1,600 of the old type prisons were still in operation.

The organization of the new modern prisons, the method of examining and selecting prison personnel, and the rules relating to the treatment of prisoners were regarded by the Commissioners as, in the main, "satisfactory." The difficulty lay rather in the fact that modern prisons still constituted such a small percentage of the prisons in China.

Part III. Administration of Justice in China[38]

The question of the way in which the Chinese laws were applied and the actual functioning of the judicial system were discussed in Part III of the Report. A general picture of the political background and its influence on the administration of justice, as it appeared to the Commissioners, was given in a few preliminary remarks. When the Republic was established, it was said, the modern legal and judicial systems of China were in their infancy, having been instituted a few years before by a group of public-spirited Chinese whose work continued under the republican regime. During the first years of the Republic the governmental organization was fairly stable but, in the period that followed, disorder set in and increased, bringing about a lessening of the authority of the Central Government and an assumption of power by various provincial groups. From the autumn of 1924 until the spring of 1926, the administration at Peking was under the control of a Provisional Government supported by the militarist leaders.

[37] Pp. 83-86.
[38] Pp. 89-90.

Since 1917, the provinces of Kwangtung and Kwangsi had refused to recognize the authority of the Central Government and other provinces had at various times taken the same attitude. In addition, almost continuous civil war had been carried on in various parts of China over a period of years, and, growing out of this confused state of affairs, brigandage had become widespread, constituting a further menace to the lives and property of the civilian population.

Under the republican form of government, the matter of legislation had been left to Parliament, but each Parliament had in turn proved ephemeral in nature and had contributed little of a permanent character to the legislation of China. The responsibility for bringing laws into force had therefore, of necessity, fallen upon the President, the Minister of Justice, and other ministers. Yet, the instability of the tenure of ministerial office had made it difficult to maintain any sort of continuity in legislative policy.

Among the many serious consequences stemming from this disorganization, there were four which had a particular bearing upon the conduct of judicial administration: First, the reins of government had fallen into the hands of military leaders who, by virtue of their powerful position, could assume at will administrative, legislative, and judicial functions, thus tending to eradicate the line which should be drawn between these three different aspects of government. Secondly, the government treasury had been depleted to such an extent that funds were lacking at times with which to pay the judicial and police officials. In the third place, the uniformity of the legal and judicial systems had been impaired because of the independent laws and courts created in areas which regarded themselves as autonomous and refused to recognize the authority of the Central Government. Lastly, the disturbed conditions existing throughout China retarded the development and perfection of the new legal and judicial systems which the Chinese were attempting to put into practice.

I. Interference by the military authorities[39]

Few sections of the Commission's Report were written in as outspoken a manner, or were designed to create as striking an impression, as the section dealing with the interference by the military authorities in the administration of justice in China. For this reason it is quoted verbatim:

One of the chief factors which militates against the normal administration of justice in China to-day is the interference with the departments of civil government by the military leaders. These leaders, possessing, as they do, their own armies engaged in constant warfare, exercise almost unre-

[39] Pp. 90-97. For emphasis placed on these sections by Mr. Strawn, see below, p. 187.

strained authority over the lives, liberty, and property of the people in the areas which happen for the time being to be within their control. This authority includes the power to control, directly or indirectly, if they so desire, official appointments in the civil administration both of the national and provincial governments with the exception of certain services such as the Customs Administration in which there is a large measure of foreign direction. The exodus to places of safety of civil officials appointed by one military party from an area, the capital included, which has just been taken over by their opponents is a matter of common occurrence.

The military interference with the civil administration extends to the judiciary so that the independence of this branch of the government is endangered. Irregularities in this respect usually occur under the guise of the application of martial law which, however, is declared without regard to the legal provisions on the subject. In other instances, there is simply an open assumption of authority. Another important factor is the control by the military of the finances of the Government, so that the courts are dependent upon the military for their financial support.

By virtue of Chinese law itself, the legal position of the military renders them immune from the jurisdiction of the ordinary courts, while their power in fact often renders them immune from all courts. This immunity is liable to be extended to the friends of the military and to the commercial firms and organizations in which they are interested. Ample evidence of the foregoing is brought out by the fact that the military are constantly committing crimes which go unpunished, for it is generally difficult for aggrieved civilians to obtain any redress from military authorities commanding their own armies when such redress must be sought in military courts controlled by these authorities.

The assumption of jurisdiction by the military and police officials over cases that should be disposed of by the ordinary law courts has formed the subject of comment and instruction by the President of China. In this mandate the President points out that the legislative, executive, and judicial powers should be separated; that, nevertheless, cases of assumption of jurisdiction by military or police departments over civil and criminal cases have recently been brought to his notice, and that in future there should be no repetition of such irregularities.

The callous attitude of the military with respect to the situation above described is emphasized by the fact that since the Extraterritoriality Commission has been sitting in Peking, or shortly prior thereto, there have been notable instances of executions and other acts perpetrated by them both in the city of Peking itself and in the provinces in complete disregard of the principles of justice. . . .[40]

In support of the last statement the Commissioners presented abstracts of eleven cases which had occurred at Peking in 1926. They declared that it was of particular importance to note that these cases took place during the very time when the Commission was making its investigations and in

[40] Pp. 90-92.

the very city where it was holding its sessions. Moreover, the cases were "matters of common knowledge" in which the substantial facts were "admitted and beyond dispute." The following one of the group of eleven cases is cited here as a typical example:

The Case of Shao Piao Ping

On April 26, 1926, Shao Piao Ping, editor of a Chinese newspaper known as the *Ching Pao,* was shot by order of the military authorities. He had been arrested on the preceding day by the metropolitan [Peking] police and handed over by them to the military. It is commonly understood that Shao was executed because of his editorial writings, alleged to be propaganda against the military party which had captured Peking in the early part of that month. So far as the Commission is informed, the judicial authorities made no investigation and took no action of any kind with respect to this execution.[41]

After relating the facts in the eleven cases and as a final conclusion, drawn from their survey of conditions connected with the interference by the military in the administration of justice in China, the Commissioners expressed their views in a strong statement:

"The Commission believes it well within the range of moderation to state that in China at the present time there is no effective security against arbitrary action by the military authorities with respect to life, liberty, or property, in so far as such security can be afforded by an effective functioning of the Chinese civil and judicial authorities."

II. Other Instances of Interference[42]

In respect to interference in the judicial system by other than military authorities, the Commissioners charged that civil and administrative officials frequently issued instructions to magistrates who were trying mixed cases in which foreigners were plaintiffs. From the standpoint of the foreign Powers, they said, this practice constituted an interference with the judicial functions of the magistrates, although in the Chinese view it was justified on the ground that the procedure for the trial of mixed cases as provided for in the treaty was only of a quasi-judicial nature.

III. The Laws and Their Application[43]

Although the laws studied by the Commission had been promulgated by the Government at Peking, they were not universally applied in all parts

[41] P. 93.
[42] P. 97.
[43] Pp. 97-99.

of China. This state of affairs, the Commissioners asserted, arose from two causes, namely, the open refusal of certain parts of China to recognize the Central Government and the enforcement of subsidiary legislation by provincial and other powerful officials who were without constitutional authority.

Furthermore, certain laws were applied in a manner that ran counter to their purpose. With respect to the granting of bail, for example, the provisions of the Chinese laws were in the main "acceptable" but judicial officials, in applying these provisions, showed an "attitude of illiberality and a disposition to withhold bail rather than to grant it." Similarly, the laws relating to criminal offenses provided penalties for "any act of violence or cruelty against the defendant, or accused, or any person implicated in or connected with a case"; nevertheless, "cases of torture for the purpose of extracting confessions of guilt and for the punishment of certain offenses, as well as cases of ill treatment of prisoners," still occurred in China, although largely in the interior and more remote parts of the country.

IV. The Judicial System and Its Application[44]

The Commissioners made the following comments concerning the judicial system and its application:

(1) The traveling committee appointed by the Commission visited twenty-three modern courts and reported that "the machinery for administering the law appeared to be satisfactory." However, the modern courts were insufficient in number, being at a ratio of one modern court of first instance to every 4,400,000 of the population.

(2) Trained judges and procurators were also limited to a very small number, amounting to only 1,293.

(3) The salaries of judicial officials — although a difficult question to gauge — appeared to compare unfavorably with those of other professions of similar standing.

(4) It is a matter of common knowledge that the Central Government was finding it increasingly difficult to pay any of its employees. While the Commission was sitting at Peking there had been trouble in respect to paying judicial officials, a situation which culminated in a strike. The traveling committee had found in the provinces that the financial support of the courts was obtained almost entirely from court fees and grants from the provincial authorities. Thus the Central Government was losing its financial control over the judiciary. Moreover, uncertainty in the payment of salaries must essentially have an unfortunate effect upon the men in the service and deter others from entering it. It was therefore necessary to make some pro-

[44] Pp. 99-103.

vision for the Ministry of Justice to receive an adequate sum annually so that the financial side of the judicial and prison systems could be "centralized in that ministry to the exclusion of the provincial and other authorities" who were "diverting public revenues from their normal channels."

(5) In view of the laws related to the magistrates' courts, the administration of justice in these courts could not be expected to be satisfactory. On the other side of the balance, however, was the fact that the Chinese Government was constantly devoting its attention to the improvement of conditions in the magistrates' courts.

(6) Both the police tribunals and the military tribunals were also to be classified as unsatisfactory for the reasons that had already been indicated.

(7) The traveling committee visited fourteen modern prisons and fifteen modern detention-houses and had few criticisms to make in respect to them, although it found some instances of overcrowding and objected in general to the low level of the salaries and the lack of sound financial support. While the committee did not visit any of the old-style prisons and detention-houses, there were indications of unhygienic and unhealthful conditions, lack of food, and malpractices; but the Chinese Government appeared to be well aware of these problems and was making efforts to effect remedies.

(8) Various complaints had been brought to the attention of the Commission concerning alleged abuses of their powers by the police. The fact that the police could arrest persons for the slightest infractions combined with the fact that, after arrest, they could, through the exercise of their judicial or procuratorial functions, detain them for long periods at their discretion, appeared to lend credence to these complaints.

Part IV. Recommendations[45]

Having made their findings of fact in parts I, II, and III, the Commissioners proceeded to made recommendations based upon the results of their investigations. In introducing these recommendations they made the following important statement:

"The Commissioners are of the opinion that, when these recommendations shall have been reasonably complied with, the several Powers would be warranted in relinquishing their respective rights of extraterritoriality."[46]

The recommendations themselves were divided into four brief sections, of which the first three read:

I

The administration of justice with respect to the civilian population in China must be entrusted to a judiciary which shall be effectively pro-

[45] Pp. 108-109.
[46] P. 107.

tected against any unwarranted interference by the executive or other branches of the Government, whether civil or military.

II

The Chinese Government should adopt the following program for the improvement of the existing legal, judicial and prison systems of China:

1. It should consider Parts II and III of this Report relating to the laws and to the judicial, police, and prison systems, with a view to making such amendments and taking such action as may be necessary to meet the observations there made.

2. It should complete and put into force the following laws:
    (1) Civil code.
    (2) Commercial code (including negotiable instruments law, maritime law and insurance law).
    (3) Revised criminal code.
    (4) Banking law.
    (5) Bankruptcy law.
    (6) Patent law.
    (7) Land expropriation law.
    (8) Law concerning notaries public.

3. It should establish and maintain a uniform system for the regular enactment, promulgation, and rescission of laws, so that there may be no uncertainty as to the laws of China.

4. It should extend the system of modern courts, modern prisons, and modern detention-houses with a view to the elimination of the magistrates' courts and of the old-style prisons and detention-houses.

5. It should make adequate financial provisions for the maintenance of courts, detention-houses and prisons and their personnel.

III

It is suggested that, prior to the reasonable compliance with the recommendations above mentioned but after the principal items thereof have been carried out, the Powers concerned, if so desired by the Chinese Government, might consider the abolition of extraterritoriality according to such progressive scheme (whether geographical, partial, or otherwise) as may be agreed upon.[47]

The fourth section of the recommendations dealt with means for correcting the existing systems and practice of extraterritoriality in China.[48]

[47] Pp. 107-108.
[48] Pp. 108-109. It is important to note that in making recommendations for the improvement of the extraterritorial system, the Commission went beyond the requirements of the Washington Conference resolution which stated that the Commission should "inquire into" the practice of extraterritoriality but did not contemplate the framing of recommendations for the alteration of the systems in use. It is also significant that the Commission took into consideration many aspects of the extraterritoriality question and did not limit itself purely to the issue of consular jurisdiction. This was the result of prolonged discussion between Dr. Wang Chung-hui and the foreign Commissioners (See *Foreign Relations*, 1926, pp. 970, 971, 977, and Pollard, *China's Foreign Relations 1917-1931*, pp. 282-284.)

First, it was suggested that the Treaty Powers should, so far as practicable, administer in their extraterritorial or consular courts such laws and regulations of China as they thought it "proper to adopt." Secondly, several recommendations were made in regard to mixed cases and mixed courts. As a general rule, it was said, mixed cases, in which nationals of the Powers were plaintiffs and Chinese were defendants, should be tried before the modern Chinese courts without the presence of an assessor to enter into the proceedings in any way. Also the existing mixed courts, their organization and procedure, should be brought more into accord with the organization and procedure of the modern Chinese judicial system. In the third instance, the Commissioners emphasized that the extraterritorial Powers should correct abuses which had arisen through the extension of foreign protection to Chinese, and to business and shipping interests the actual ownership of which was wholly or mainly Chinese. Along the same lines, they also recommended that all the Treaty Powers should insist upon compulsory periodical registration of their nationals in China. The fourth proposal made by the Commissioners was that the necessary arrangements should be made in respect to judicial assistance between the Chinese authorities and the authorities of the extraterritorial Powers and between the officials of the extraterritorial Powers themselves. Among the specific matters which they stressed were those connected with the prompt execution of judgments, summonses, and warrants of arrest or search, concerning persons under either Chinese or foreign jurisdiction. The final recommendation of the Commissioners dealt with the important question of taxation as it affected extraterritorial nationals. "Pending the abolition of extraterritoriality," they said, "the nationals of the Powers concerned should be required to pay such taxes as may be prescribed in laws and regulations duly promulgated by the competent authorities of the Chinese Government and recognized by the Powers concerned as applicable to their nationals."

The report was signed by all thirteen Commissioners on September 16, 1926. Dr. Wang Chung-hui, however, wrote after his signature that he did not wish it to be inferred that he was willing to approve "all the statements contained in Parts I, II, and III." By this act, he endorsed the recommendations made by the Commissioners but stated that he was not in full agreement with the Commissioners' views concerning the existing state of the Chinese legal and judicial systems, the administration of justice in China, and the current practice of extraterritoriality.

With the conclusion of the Report, the Commissioners forwarded it to their respective governments privately, stating that the Commission was of the opinion that it did not possess the authority to make any of the contents public.[49] As no information was released by the various governments involved, the public continued to await further developments with impatience. On November 22nd, an article appeared in an American newspaper which was obviously based upon a knowledge of the content of the Report.[50] Secretary of State Kellogg cabled to Mr. MacMurray at once that, because of the pressure being exercised in the United States and "in order to avoid speculative comment," the State Department proposed to give the Report to the press within a week and had notified the governments of the other Treaty Powers of its intention.[51] The Chinese Foreign Office adopted the position that in view of the reservations made by Dr. Wang Chung-hui in respect to Parts I, II, and III of the Report, the publication of these sections might give rise to misapprehensions and should be withheld; they were prepared, however, to make public the recommendations contained in Part IV.[52] Despite this, the State Department in Washington persisted in its original plan and issued the Report in its entirety on November 29, 1926.[53] On the same day the Chinese Government released Part IV, together with Dr. Wang's statement concerning the other three sections.[54]

During the time when the Commission on Extraterritoriality was engaged in its study and investigations, Secretary Kellogg set aside any further consideration of the extraterritorial issue. He hoped the Report of the Commission would serve as a guide for the future development of American policy. "I have expected," he cabled Mr. Strawn in March, 1926, "that the Commission would find it possible to make recommendations of a constructive nature upon which some definite policy regarding this Government's attitude on the subject of the extraterritorial provisions of its treaties might be laid."[55]

Mr. Kellogg did not define the steps of a program that he would have regarded as "constructive" in character. But it is apparent from his instructions to Mr. Strawn that his views had not changed since the summer of 1925. In the instructions, quoted earlier in this chapter, he indicated his intention of negotiating a treaty on the subject of extraterritoriality and declared again that he wished to renounce the extraterritorial privileges of the United States "within a reasonable time" and as soon as conditions would permit. Moreover, he added the significant statement that he did not expect conditions in China to be ideal but was prepared to ask only the fulfillment

[49] Foreign Relations (1926), p. 982.
[50] Ibid.
[51] Ibid., pp. 982-983.
[52] Ibid., p. 983.
[53] Ibid., pp. 983-984.
[54] Ibid., p. 983, footnote 68.
[55] Ibid., p. 969.

of such requirements as were "absolutely necessary to protect American interests."

If the Secretary was hoping for encouragement to effect a radical change in the extraterritorial provisions of the treaties within the near future, the Report of the Commission dealt rather roughly with his expectations. The Commissioners laid down a scheme for the reform of existing conditions which, if undertaken by the Chinese Government, would, they said, warrant the Treaty Powers considering the abolition of the extraterritorial system. But the program of reform which they outlined was so vast in scope that it not only demanded an extensive development of the Chinese legal and judicial systems but also required fundamental changes in the political life of the nation. Even the Commissioners' suggestion that the Treaty Powers might consider a plan for the progressive withdrawal of extraterritorial rights before all of the recommendations of the Report had been met, "but after the principal items thereof had been carried out," indicated a method of advance that was, to say the least, slow and difficult.

Furthermore, one of the outstanding features of the Report presented an unfortunate obstacle to the use of the recommendations of the Commission as a basis for the creation of a future policy. Among the points most strongly emphasized by the Commission were the chaotic conditions in China. The Commissioners discussed these conditions as though they amounted to little more than a relatively superficial struggle between warlords who, because of their conflicts, made it impossible to establish a government at Peking with the capacity to maintain order. But any such estimate of the situation overlooked the strength of the revolutionary movement that was affecting every aspect of Chinese life. One example of the Commissioners' seeming lack of awareness of the profound nature of the forces at work lay in the reference in the Report to the consequences of the anti-foreign movement that had developed since the May 30th Incident. Classifying this matter under the heading of "interference" with the administration of justice, the Commissioners said:

"In the case of the recent [1925-1926] troubles in Canton and vicinity, strikers, in defiance of the regularly constituted courts, set up courts of their own for the trial of strike-breakers. During the summer of 1925 also there were in the Yangtze Valley serious manifestations of anti-foreign feeling, leading to riots and attacks upon both the persons and property of foreigners, yet the judicial authorities either did not or could not take any effective action with respect to these matters."[56]

[56] P. 97.

In other words, the Commissioners viewed the disturbances which occurred in China in 1925 and 1926 as isolated incidents that might have been handled in law courts functioning in accordance with normal peacetime procedures, rather than as manifestations of a great national upheaval. In thus failing to take account of the significance which lay behind the disordered conditions in China, the Report of the Commission on Extraterritoriality also failed to furnish a guide to those statesmen who were aware of the fact that they were dealing with a political, economic, and social revolution.

CHAPTER IX

FURTHER DEVELOPMENTS OF 1926 – I

MR. STRAWN AND SENATOR BORAH

Mr. Strawn on his return to the United States delivered numerous speeches on the situation in China. As the most active spokesman for the American Government at the Special Tariff Conference, and as Chairman of the Commission on Extraterritoriality, his speeches naturally attracted the attention of many people and were widely quoted in the United States and in China; in fact, where verbal battles were to occur in the future over questions of treaty revision, Mr. Strawn's words were frequently to be cited as proving or disproving one point or another.

One of Mr. Strawn's first addresses, and one which was characteristic of many of the statements that he made concerning China during the following years, was given before a meeting of the Industrial and Commercial Clubs of Chicago in October, 1926.[1] The most important part of the speech was a long passage which sought to give a thumb-nail sketch of conditions in China. Mr. Strawn's point in presenting such a survey was that in order to help the Chinese people it was essential for foreigners to face the situation in China in realistic terms. "He does the Chinese people a great injustice," Mr. Strawn said, "who bases his judgment of conditions obtaining in China on propaganda which has been spread throughout the world for a number of years or upon such information as he may be able to get by a short visit to China as a tourist."[2]

In reviewing some of the basic facts concerning China, Mr. Strawn emphasized such matters as illiteracy, the lack of industrial development, and, especially, the inadequacy of the transportation system. China had no highways, only about 8,000 automobiles as compared to 20 million in the United States, and 7,000 miles of railway as against 265,000 in the United States. While the operating ratio of the railroads in China was in relation to their earnings less than that of any other country, this had little effect

[1] For full text, see *Far Eastern Review*, January, 1927, pp. 12-15. Mr. Strawn made many speeches and wrote numerous articles on China during the next years. For examples, see *China Weekly Review* of February 6 and December 4, 1926; *Far Eastern Review*, September, 1927; *Chinese Students' Monthly*, March, 1927.

[2] In a letter quoted in the *North China Herald* Mr. Strawn wrote: "By telling the truth about the situation I may be able to help the Chinese people. . . . No one can help China unless he starts with a knowledge of the facts." (*China in Chaos*, a special issue of the *North China Daily News and Herald*, April 1, 1927, p. 4.)

as the earnings were confiscated in their entirety by the warlords. Every railroad in China was controlled by the military; when the equipment was not being used for the movement of troops, its use was sold by the warlords to the "unfortunate shippers" at "outrageous rates," the usual "squeeze" for the use of a freight car being $5 per ton in addition to the freight rate. No attention was paid to the maintenance of equipment so that it was rapidly becoming useless and the railways would soon cease to operate, compelling the "unfortunate people" of China to turn again to the barrow, or pack their freight upon their backs — most of the camels, donkeys, and cattle of the farmers having already been taken over by the soldiers.

In describing the government of China, Mr. Strawn explained that there had been a revolution in 1911 which overthrew the Manchu Dynasty and aimed to set up a Republic. Many patriotic, well-educated and intelligent Chinese had been doing their best to establish a republic with a stable government but had met with little success in the face of the continuing wars carried on by warlords who were "actuated by but two motives — greed and aggrandizement."

"It would be unreasonable," he said, "to expect any people much less those of a country so vast in area, so numerous in population, so without means of communication, and so illiterate as the Chinese, to evolve a republic along occidental lines within the short space of fourteen years. Today we cannot regard China as a republic in anything more than name."

As indicative of the instability of the Chinese Government, Mr. Strawn observed that since the 1911 Revolution, China had had eight Presidents, or Chief Executives, 42 Cabinets with a continuously changing membership, and 25 Ministers of Justice. The last President, Ts'ao K'un, was locked up at Peking from December, 1924, to April, 1925, because it was said he bought his office; yet no formal charges were ever made against him and he was never brought to trial. On April 10, 1926, the Chief Executive Tuan Chi-jui fled to the foreign Legation Quarter at Peking and from there to the foreign concession in Tientsin where he remained. Two other Presidents of the Chinese Republic had preceded him to that asylum, as well as 26 former Governors of the several provinces and a large number of other high officials who had either incurred the anger of their political opponents or were charged with "having too generously helped themselves from the public treasury."

Mr. Strawn said further that:

Since April 10, 1926, there has been no government in China. The authority of the Central Government is gone. No regard is paid to the orders or wishes of the so-called 'Regency Cabinet'. . . . The entire country is overrun by soldiers and bandits. Foreign Legations are unable to secure any redress for the wrongs done to their nationals in any part of China. Provincial officials hold the Central Government and its orders in contempt. Long past due obligations, foreign and domestic, for money borrowed and for materials furnished to operate the railroads and public utilities give the Central Government little or no concern. The officials, who are the mere puppets of the warlords, are interested solely in devising ways and means of increasing the loans and raising funds to meet the requirements of their masters.

Outrageous internal taxes of every conceivable kind are levied upon merchants and tradesmen, the revenue from which does not go to the support or maintenance of the civil functions of the Government but to the military. The officials remain unpaid.

The only departments of the Government that are capably and economically administered in an orderly and businesslike manner are the post office, the Maritime Customs and the Salt Administration which are under the control of foreign employees.

No Chinese citizen dares protest or attempt to do anything to bring order out of the chaos that obtains. Every newspaper article which escapes the censor and which may be regarded as a criticism of the dominant warlord or his underlings, subjects the editor to the peril of summary execution without even the pretense of a trial.

I have stated a few of these facts that you may have some idea of the difficulties confronting the foreign Powers in their efforts to do something for the patient, industrious and long-suffering Chinese people.

In China we hear much of the sovereign rights of the Chinese *Republic*. The Chinese politicians do not seem to be interested in the rights of the *people*.

Besides discussing general conditions in China, Mr. Strawn spoke of the work of the Special Tariff Conference and the Commission on Extraterritoriality. He emphasized especially the chaotic state of Chinese political affairs during the time that the Special Tariff Conference was in session. At the beginning of the Conference, the American Delegation, followed by the Delegations of other nations, proposed the immediate implementation of the Washington surtaxes. The Chinese Delegates refused because, their Chairman said, if they accepted the proposition the foreign Delegates would "run out" on them and would not give them tariffs to yield a total revenue of $100,000,000 which the Chinese insisted that they needed. The Powers, therefore, on the initiative of the American Delegation, offered not only to give the Chinese the Washington surtaxes but also to begin immediately the negotiation of a new treaty which would grant China all the additional revenue the traffic could bear. Despite the fact that Peking continued to be the vortex of military activity and that the Chinese Delegates disappeared, the foreign Delegations persisted in their efforts to frame a tariff schedule; in fact, their technical advisers practically reached an agreement with the

Chinese technical advisers upon this matter. The work could not be completed, however, because there was no Chinese Government with which to negotiate. "Humorous as it may seem, instead of the foreign Delegates 'running out' on the Chinese, the Chinese Delegates including the distinguished Chairman 'ran out' on us;" "... it is no fault of the Powers," Mr. Strawn declared, "that the Conference was not concluded and China did not realize her desires."

Concerning the work of the Commission on Extraterritoriality, Mr. Strawn explained that the Report of the Commission was about to be issued and declared that he hoped it would tend to correct "much misinformation" that had been published in the United States concerning the question of extraterritorial jurisdiction in China. Moreover, he denied that China had been forced in the past into making extraterritorial treaties by the Powers:

> For many years the Chinese have insisted that the exercise of extraterritorial rights in their country impinged on their sovereign dignity, that those rights should be surrendered, and that China was coerced into the making of extraterritorial treaties by the foreign Powers. The absurdity of this charge will appear when we reflect upon the strength of the Swiss navy — Switzerland's treaty ... was concluded in 1918.

In addition to objecting to the extraterritorial system, Mr. Strawn said, the Chinese had other complaints against foreigners. Chinese politicians desired to have the concessions restored to China, but the foreigners and thoughtful Chinese would vigorously oppose retrocession because they knew that if the concessions and settlements were returned they would rapidly disintegrate and be destroyed; foreigners would lose their property and the Chinese who were living in the settlements would be subjected to the levy of outrageous taxes which they were now in a position to escape.

Chinese agitators, Mr. Strawn continued, also complained because the administration of the Chinese Maritime Customs was under a foreign Inspector-General and they clamored for his dismissal, insisting that the revenue was seized and subverted to the uses of the foreign imperialistic Powers. To this Mr. Strawn answered that, "Everyone who has made even a casual study of China's financial situation knows that the foreign Inspector-General of Customs is the only anchor between order and absolute chaos in China. There is no Chinese or group of Chinese, however strong and well-intentioned they might be, who could withstand the importunities of their friends, or resist the bayonet of warlords, if the Customs funds were taken from the control of the foreign Inspector-General and placed in the hands of Chinese officials."

Mr. Strawn closed his speech with the following observations:

One of the big world problems is — what can the other nations do to help rescue the Chinese people from the enslavement of the warlords and bring order out of the existing chaos? As I stated on a previous occasion, he who could prescribe a cure for all the ills of China would be the greatest pathologist the world has seen. In solution of this problem, as in that of any other difficult question, we must commence with a knowledge of *facts* and not rely upon false premises if we hope to arrive at an accurate solution.

During my eleven months' residence in Peking I came to have an affectionate regard for many of those who were trying to carry on a Government in the face of insuperable difficulties. I have a most sympathetic consideration for the great mass of the Chinese people who are impoverished and enslaved by the warlords. . . .

The attitude of the United States toward China has always been helpful and sympathetic. Conditions in China change so rapidly it would seem impossible for our Government to announce in advance any definite policy which could meet the changing conditions.

The United States and the other Powers have done everything that could be done to carry out the letter and the spirit of the Washington Treaty respecting the tariff and the Resolution respecting extraterritoriality. The work of the Extraterritoriality Commission is completed, that of the Tariff Conference is unfinished, not because of any failure on the part of the foreign Powers but because of the conditions in China which I have attempted to describe.

The President and the Secretary of State are entirely sympathetic with our creditors in their efforts to collect the long past due debts from the Chinese Government and also with the interests of our merchants and manufacturers who are desirous of promoting trade with the Chinese. The responsibility of our relations with China rests primarily upon the President and the Secretary of State. I have an abiding confidence in their ability and willingness to discharge that duty wisely and well.

In an article written in December, 1926, after the publication of the Report of the Commission on Extraterritoriality, Mr. Strawn discussed the content of the Report, emphasizing by a verbatim quotation those sections which dealt with the disturbed conditions in China.[3] Furthermore he made it plain that in his opinion the situation had not changed since the time when the Report was concluded:

Indicative of the fact that there has been no change since I left China with respect to the absolute domination of every activity by the military, may I quote from a letter which I have just received from Peking as to a recent occurrence there:

"Some soldiers were trying to get into a theater without paying and the doorkeeper remonstrated. As a tumult was proceeding a general who was

[3] Article published in *Chinese Students' Monthly*, March, 1927, pp. 14-20. (It is stated in *China in Chaos*, p. 4, that this article was written in December.) For passages quoted from the *Report of the Commission on Extraterritoriality*, see above, pp. 173-174.

driving past in a car stopped to find out what was the matter. When informed that soldiers were trying to get into the theater without paying, he hopped out of the car and had the trouble makers presented to him. He then ordered that they be shot forthwith. They were and their heads were at once hacked off and put on each side of the theater door. When the people came out they had something to look at and regretted that they missed a real melodrama by being inside."

In the same article Mr. Strawn dealt with the nationalist issue:

I take it that a national spirit of patriotism is the honest conviction of a people of a country that each individual has a direct interest in, responsibility for, and duty toward, his country as a whole as distinct from a selfish, individual, family, local, or provincial interest. In a country where for centuries the vital interests of the people have not extended beyond the family circle and where family considerations dominate all others, the evolution of a new nationalism or patriotism as the western people understand it must necessarily be slow.... Personally I do not believe that patriotism and nationalism can be founded upon hatred of other nations or other people.... The Chinese people must come to believe that all non-Chinese are not anti-Chinese. Racial prejudice does not evidence a great people.[4]

From the tenor of Mr. Strawn's speeches and writings it was at once evident that they were bound to evoke a vigorous response. The United

[4] In a speech delivered in Manchester, England, of which an account was given (presumably a reprint from a British newspaper) in the *Far Eastern Review* of September, 1927, Mr. Strawn spoke of the Nationalist movement in China. The account in the *Review* reads in part:

"Alluding to what was called the Nationalist movement in China, Mr. Strawn said the difficulty was that those who belonged to this movement did not understand nationalism as we understood it. They did not understand it in the sense that sent thousands of young fellows to France to die. By them nationalism was interpreted to mean that a man's first duty was to his family. The family unit system was the basic difficulty in dealing with China. Whenever a Chinaman got into office he thought it his first duty to rob the Government to benefit his family. [Laughter] For a time the Cantonese movement did well, but then the people in the movement began to quarrel among themselves. Whenever you got the Chinese up to a culminating point at which you conceived it possible to do something and make an agreement the Chinese must have a row among themselves because of a fear that one or another would get hold of the National treasury. [Laughter]"

Later in the same account, it is said that Mr. Strawn discussed the question of intervention in China:

"The natural tendency was to go in and spank the Chinese but that would be like spanking a featherbed. [Laughter] It would have no effect because there were too many of them. It would cost a great deal more than there was to be got out of it. If the Powers went in together the result would be to solidify the Chinese and that would mean interminable guerilla warfare. In no way as he saw the situation could they go into China by force. But they could not permit irresponsible soldiers and warlords to destroy the lives and property of their citizens in the treaty ports where most of those citizens and most of the property was situated." (p. 394.)

States Government issued an announcement declaring that Mr. Strawn's statements reflected only his own views and not those of the Government at Washington.[5] However the most formidable voice to be raised in opposition to Mr. Strawn was that of Senator Borah, Chairman of the Senate Foreign Relations Committee, who had already made himself known for championing what was generally regarded in the United States as the "Chinese cause."

In a speech filled with somewhat old-fashioned eloquence, delivered at Washington, in November, 1926, Mr. Borah outlined his own views in a way that was evidently intended to refute some of Mr. Strawn's basic arguments.[6] With an irony that must have been consciously designed, Senator Borah stated that it was the purpose of his speech to present the *facts* concerning the Chinese situation realistically. He referred to Mr. Strawn directly at the outset: "The Honorable Silas H. Strawn ... has said in a public address ... that there is no Government in China, that there is little hope for China, unless, as I infer from his remarks, she finds a dictator of the type of Mussolini." He further quoted an important passage from one of Mr. Strawn's speeches in which it was stated that China was not suffering from imperialism, unequal treaties, extraterritoriality, or the lack of tariff autonomy, but from the greed and ambition of her warlords.

The difficulty, Senator Borah continued, was that people in discussing China were likely to think only in terms of the facts which formed part of the present and not in terms of those facts which, existing in the past, had contributed to the creation of current conditions. The first great fact was that China was dominated, in all matters that were essential to a nation's growth and prosperity, by foreign Powers: forty of her cities were under foreign control; her natural resources were being divided among outside nations; her tariff duties were fixed by thirteen different countries; foreigners

---

[5] *Congressional Record*, 69th Congress, 2nd Session, Vol. 68, Part I, p. 878.

[6] Text of speech, *United States Daily*, November 17, 1926, pp. 1, 15, 16.

Mr. Claudius O. Johnson in his book, *Borah of Idaho*, states: "Borah came out in 1925 for the abolition of extraterritorial rights in China. According to Raymond Clapper he was the only Senator who favored such a move at the time. His correspondence files of this period are full of letters on the subject of extraterritoriality from professors, newspaper men, ministers and the public generally. . . . The Senator himself wrote a great many letters on the subject."

Mr. Johnson quotes one of these letters of the Senator's written to a Congressman who was evidently concerned over the "red scare" in China:

" 'It seems to me that we are overworking these days the "red" proposition. Whenever a people becomes dissatisfied with oppressive measures and rebel they are called "reds". . . . I haven't any doubt at all but that Russia is playing as strong a hand as she can in China. So are Great Britain and Japan and so are other nations.

" 'The "reds" are not the authors of the child labor rules of China. The "reds" are not in control of forty of her different cities and ports; and the "reds" are not maintaining the unjust and unfair customs laws.' " (p. 349.)

were exempt from Chinese law; foreign warships patrolled her coasts and foreign gunboats policed her rivers; Chinese children worked in foreign factories under conditions that were governed by rules as "merciless as death."

The second important fact was that the spirit of nationalism was fast laying hold upon the hearts and the minds of four hundred million people. This was nationalism of the same kind that the Western nations practised and taught. Yet the foreign Powers were reluctant to admit and unwilling to accept its existence in China. In this connection Senator Borah spoke with strong feeling of the principle of self-determination and the "right of all people to have their own form of government and live their own lives" which the Allied and Associated Powers had sought to bring into effect after the World War:

> This spirit of nationalism was augmented and stressed by the World War and it is today the most tremendous fact in the life of the Chinese people. . . . China is asking for the right to self-determination and they believe that the great obstacle to that realization is these encroachments upon their territory of which I have spoken, this attack upon her sovereignty which is now a matter of history.
>
> Disturbances and conflicts and strife among themselves, of course, there are, and that is important. It will take some time for these things to run their course. But the Chinese problem at bottom is nationalism coming into the presence of imperialism.

The remainder of his speech Senator Borah devoted to inveighing against a policy of intervention in China: "The time has gone by in China when you can shoot down men as they did last July a year ago and see a nation bow like whipped slaves." The policy of the United States had, he declared, been characterized "by a fine consideration for the rights and aspirations of the Chinese people."

> We are told that our policy means failure, that force must be accepted as the basic principle of a successful Oriental policy — that force is the only thing they understand and therefore the only thing they respect.
>
> This is the old cruel, brutal, imperialistic policy, the revolting creed which not only made possible but certain the World War.
>
> Let us not make any mistake, my friends, the national feeling in China will compel respect. Four hundred million people imbued with the spirit of independence and of national integrity are in the end invincible. There is no power which can master them or hold them in subjection. Warships and gatling guns and dead students may mislead some but the forces which determine the actions of empires and great nations lie deeper.

OPINIONS IN CHINA

The speeches of Mr. Strawn and of Senator Borah were naturally matters of special concern to the American community in China. The American

Chamber of Commerce at Shanghai sent a cable to its Washington office stating that "The American Chamber of Commerce heartily endorses statements and speeches made by Mr. Silas Strawn in regard to the political situation in China."[7] Mr. J. J. Underwood, the Washington representative of the Chamber, was instructed to give to the cable the widest possible distribution. This was made known in the Chamber's *Bulletin* printed in Shanghai, in which it was stated that the Board of Directors had gone on record as endorsing all that Mr. Strawn had said in the United States concerning the situation in China. "We feel," the *Bulletin* asserted, "that the entire membership of the American community here will agree that this is the first time the real conditions have been presented to the American public in no uncertain terms."[8]

The *Far Eastern Review*, which in its advertisements proclaimed that it had an editorial policy "not controlled by but in harmony with the policies of the American Chamber of Commerce,"[9] published an article in December, 1926 under the eloquent title: "Our Hat is Off to Silas Strawn!":[10]

Mr. Strawn has been making speeches in the United States in which he described conditions in China exactly as they are. He did not make such speeches in China when he was here and therefore he was rather severely criticized by many who wished him well but who were amazed that he should have fallen for the fairy tales of Peking. Apparently they were wrong — Mr. Strawn appeared to fall but it was only a stumble. He straightened up and told the story tellers that he was a man of facts and could only deal with facts. His speeches have exacted from the American government officials a left-handed *démenti* which is all froth because if the Government sent Mr. Strawn to investigate and he reported, they must either stand by his report or admit that, in so serious a matter, they selected the wrong individual. Furthermore, if Mr. Strawn's report is untrue, what is the truth? If his facts are straight, what interest has the government in suppressing them? Let there be an end to this miserable game of deceit and conceit, this make-believe politics in which nobody dares offend anyone else particularly when the second party in the offense happens to be a vacuum!

The fact that they admired "Mr. Strawn's bigness and courage in telling the truth about China" did not, the *Far Eastern Review* explained, mean that the editors wished to join forces with "those hard-boiled foreigners" who wanted to return to a policy of several generations ago "when the foreigners unloaded a cargo of gunboats in the Yangtze and West Rivers and told China to swallow her gorge or be damned." But, they asked, what was

[7] American Chamber of Commerce of Shanghai *Bulletin*, December, 1926, p. 3.
[8] *Ibid.*
[9] See, for example, *ibid.*, October 9, 1927, advertisement on p. 9.
[10] *Far Eastern Review*, December, 1926.

the hurry in altering the unilateral treaties in the face of the civil war and chaotic conditions in China? "China has waited 84 years for change. Suppose, it has to wait a full 90."

The *North China Herald*, which, while it was a British publication, undoubtedly (as has been said earlier) both represented and influenced the ideas of many Americans in China, also fully supported the views which Mr. Strawn had presented in his speeches. On the back cover of a special issue entitled *China in Chaos*,[11] quotations from Mr. Strawn's speeches were printed in a fashion so prominent as to indicate that they expressed some of the editors' most fundamental convictions:

It is a primal instinct of human nature to attempt to blame someone else for one's misfortunes or shortcomings. I submit that any student of conditions in China today must conclude that the present troubles of the Chinese people are internal and not external, and that the anti-foreign and anti-Christian feeling now obtaining in some parts of China is the result of persistent agitation and propaganda intended to excite the Chinese people into a state of frenzy and unrest.

Anyone who has investigated conditions in China today must conclude that extraterritoriality, unequal treaties, imperialism and other slogans to which I have referred have nothing to do with China's troubles. These catchwords are being overworked by the agitators many of whom are bolshevists, the politicians, and the militarists, to conceal from the long-suffering, patient and industrious people of China the pathetic fact that they are being impoverished and enslaved to the ambition of the warlords for greed and aggrandizement.

Its own object, the *North China Herald* said, was the same as that of Mr. Strawn, namely, to tell the truth concerning China which was the only means of helping the Chinese people; one need only read the Report of the Commission on Extraterritoriality to be convinced "of the almost criminal character of the propaganda" which served to befog the whole Chinese issue abroad.[12]

[11] For further discussion of *China in Chaos,* see Chapter XVI.
[12] *China in Chaos,* p. 3.
The *North China Herald* had long opposed any drastic alteration in the extraterritorial system:
"Just as there should be no Tariff Conference going on in Peking now, so there should be no Commission to sit upon extraterritoriality. China should be told firmly and frankly that the evidence against her fitness to govern her own people and administer justice to them is so overwhelming that it is an insult to the intelligence of the Occidental people to ask them to 'investigate' her fitness to assume jurisdiction over outsiders." (Rodney Gilbert, *North China Herald*, November 7, 1925, p. 271.)
"In spite of a determination on the part of the Powers to give China's aspirations for the abolition of extraterritoriality the most lenient and indulgent consideration possible, officials and people have made such an amazing show of their incapacity to give themselves peace, comfort, or justice during the past six months, that no Power could even consider an amendment to the present extraterritorial system unless it

On the other hand, part of the American press in China found fault with Mr. Strawn's views. The *North China Star* referred bluntly to the "botch of things" made by Mr. Strawn and the other American negotiators who came to China and said that the United States and China could easily settle their difficulties if given half a chance in the appointment of the men who were to represent them.[13] The editor, Charles James Fox, asserted that the American public believed that "China belongs to the Chinese" and that the public would dictate American policy and "no amount of Strawns or other public investigators or spokesmen of 'American interests' in China" would make the slightest difference.[14] At the same time, The *North China Star* supported Senator Borah's views, applauding him "as one of the greatest men in the world" who, fortunately for the Chinese people, was defending the cause of China.[15]

The *China Weekly Review* on its part took the position that the weaknesses in the Report of the Commission on Extraterritoriality and in Mr. Strawn's speeches were one and the same, namely, the failure to recognize the "obvious fact" that conditions in China were entirely due to a revolutionary situation which had been in progress for a long time. Mr. Strawn encountered innumerable difficulties while he was in China and as a result he saw "dirt and filth and corruption, inefficiency and dishonesty, and intrigue galore;" these he put down in his Report and his speeches. Had he had the opportunity "to get out into the 'real China'" he would have gained a sense of the situation as it actually existed; the fault was not Mr. Strawn's, but having analyzed the bad in China he should return again to analyze the good.[16]

The *Peking Leader*, which printed relatively few editorials of its own, quoted editorials from the Baltimore *Sun* and the Philadelphia *Public*

---

were prepared at the same time to order its nationals to leave the country." (Rodney Gilbert, *North China Herald*, July 10, 1926, pp. 90-91.)

When a copy of the Report of the Commission on Extraterritoriality reached China, the editors of the *North China Herald* stated that they were impressed by the fair-mindedness of the Commissioners:

"There is no road to real reform except by showing up the misdeeds of her [China's] oppressors and this report by a Commission, which included representatives of twelve foreign countries, accorded an unequalled opportunity for tearing away the veil of shams and hypocrisy which have done the Chinese people such infinite harm in the last few years. Furthermore, it is grossly unfair to the foreign community of China that the truth should not be known as widely as possible." (*North China Herald*, December 18, 1926, p. 530.)

[13] *North China Star*, January 9, 1927. Where page numbers are not indicated in dealing with newspapers the reference is to an editorial.

[14] *Ibid.*, January 26, 1927.

[15] *Ibid.*, December 8, 1926.

[16] *China Weekly Review*, February 12, 1927, p. 276.

Ledger. The first praised Senator Borah's speech with unqualified enthusiasm saying that it combined "the strains of high idealism and hard practical sense" that characterized the Senator at his best; moreover, it declared, the Senator did well to urge Americans to look "beneath the surface gloom and irritating provocation" in the Chinese situation before deciding whether they were prepared to support or oppose "the aspirations of modern China."[17] The editorial in the *Ledger* expressed particular approval of Mr. Borah for "recognizing the claims of nationalism" in China and for condemning any policy of force or "violent attempts" to maintain foreign control.[18]

The attitudes thus expressed by various American groups and publications in China were naturally in keeping with their views on other important topics of the times. During 1926 the issues which proved most controversial were primarily related to the problems involved in the movement for treaty revision, the possibility of foreign intervention in China, and the sudden growth in importance of the Kuomintang.

We have already seen that the American missionaries in China, as well as in the United States, began to play a rôle in the movement for the abolition of extraterritoriality almost as soon as the United States Government announced its intention of urging the other foreign Powers to join in convening the Special Tariff Conference and the Commission on Extraterritoriality. As stated earlier, the American business organizations in China did not take nearly as active a part as the missionaries in the controversy over a revision of the treaties until the spring of 1927, after the Nanking Incident had occurred with its grave implications for the safety of all foreigners in China. One of the few official statements issued by American business organizations in China, in the period before 1927, was that of the American Chamber of Commerce at Tientsin which published a pamphlet for the expressed purpose of submitting its views on the extraterritorial issue to Mr. Strawn before the Commission on Extraterritoriality began its work. The general conclusions reached by the Chamber in respect to the abolition of extraterritoriality were:

> ... until such time as China's control of all China is absolute, until such time as its judicial system is capable of free and independent action and its orders and judgments operative and effective within the area of its jurisdiction and over military and administrative officials, any question of relinquishing extraterritoriality or even of fixing a definite time in the future when such relinquishment should take place is entirely premature irrespective of the Chinese law or the manner in which it is administered.

> It is the opinion of the American Chamber of Commerce of Tientsin that even if the above described conditions ceased to exist, yet even then the

[17] *Peking Leader,* December 25, 1926.
[18] *Ibid.*

methods of judicial administration are such as to preclude the relinquishment of extraterritoriality.[19]

Of the American publications in China, the *China Weekly Review* expressed its editorial opinion with the greatest vigor and the most frequency. In doing so it came into conflict with the *North China Herald*, a conflict which became acute when the situation in China grew more threatening after the Nanking Incident and when the *Review* itself adopted a more determined and uncompromising policy. There were, however, serious points of difference earlier, one of which centered on the numerous articles printed by the *North China Herald* in 1926 advocating intervention — or what was sometimes called "benevolent intervention" — by the Powers in China.

The main argument in favor of intervention presented by the *North China Herald* was that the civil war in China would never cease or the generally chaotic conditions be resolved into a state of peace and relative prosperity unless pressure was brought from the outside by the foreign Governments in order to achieve this end. "It is sheer hypocritical nonsense," the *North China Herald* asserted, "to talk of China 'working out her own salvation.' Nothing but resolute treatment from outside will deliver her from the malady that is destroying her and others."[20] In another editorial it declared: "We have said and we say again plainly that without assistance from abroad we very much doubt China's ability to recover these blessings [restoration of peace, ordered government, etc.] at least within any measurable number of years ... it is living in a fool's paradise to shut one's eyes to the conditions prevailing from one end of China to the other and pretend that the terrible mess in which she finds herself is going to be put right by the pretty-pretty talk of idealists safely housed in foreign concessions."[21] Intervention, it was further stated, should not be "a punitive nor a debt collecting enterprise" but should be designed to restore peace and order, financial stability, the proper functioning of the railroads, etc., and should afford an adequate opportunity for the development of trade and industry.[22] The masses of the Chinese had never resisted intervention in the past and would never resist in the future. Resistance might come from Russian-inspired agitators, from militarists and their political "jackals," but the Chinese people as a whole possessed too large a degree of common sense not to see that intervention would work to their benefit.[23] While the *North China*

[19] *Memorandum of the American Chamber of Commerce of Tientsin Relative to Extraterritoriality in China*, 1925, p. 7.
[20] *North China-Herald*, November 13, 1926, p. 298.
[21] *Ibid.*, November 20, 1926, p. 343.
[22] *Ibid.*, September 11, 1926, p. 500.
[23] *Ibid.*

Herald seemed to vary as to what it meant by the term "intervention," it stated at one point that the editors had in mind not an aggressive policy but a policy to be carried out along the lines of the assistance given to Austria by the League of Nations through the medium of loans, help in the administration of finances, and similar activities.[24] At other times, however, the editors appear to have contemplated an international military expedition.[25]

The *China Weekly Review* took the position that intervention in China on the part of the powers was not possible. In an article written in 1925, the editor, J. B. Powell, asserted that to intervene in China would need a force of some 200,000 men and that there was not a "legislature in the world" that would vote appropriations for the purpose of sending troops to China.[26] Returning to this theme repeatedly throughout the next year, Mr. Powell maintained that the deciding factor in any form of intervention would be the United States and that it would be an absolute impossibility to induce the American Government to vote funds for a military expedition to China.[27] The American people had been brought up for too many generations on missionary propaganda to change their minds suddenly and want to give China "a licking;" there was even a feeling among American businessmen that a "strong and independent China" would make the best customer for American products.[28] Moreover there was no sound reason for sending an army to uphold "treaties negotiated a half century ago" which had been outdated and were no longer in accord with modern sentiment in China or elsewhere.[29] The spirit of nationalism in China was "virulent" and, as Judge Johnson had said during the conduct of his inquiry into the May 30th Incident, " 'You can't shoot it down and you can't lock it up in prison.' "[30] In the face of this fact and in view of the unwillingness and inability of the Treaty Powers to intervene in China, what was the best way out of the situation? The use of conciliation instead of force.[31]

"Assuredly," Mr. Powell wrote in direct response to the editorial policy being pursued by the *North China Herald*, "there can be no armed intervention for the purpose of 'helping' China any more than there can be armed intervention for the purpose of 'coercing China.' ... The Powers can do nothing except maintain a benevolent neutrality while China is working out her experiment."[32]

[24] *Ibid.*, December 4, 1926, p. 441.
[25] *Ibid.*, September 11, 1926, p. 500; *China in Chaos*, p. 1.
[26] *China Weekly Review*, August 15, 1925, p. 207; December 19, 1926, p. 63.
[27] *Ibid.*, August 7, 1926, p. 232.
[28] *Ibid.*, November 20, 1926, p. 315.
[29] *Ibid.*, December 19, 1925, p. 64.
[30] *Ibid.*, p. 63.
[31] *Ibid.*, p. 64.
[32] *Ibid.*, October 9, 1926, p. 145.

At another time he stated in less moderate language that nothing could keep China from obtaining a revision of the treaties except intervention, "an obvious impossibility except for those who are too blind or ignorant to sense the changed international situation."[33]

In general the *China Weekly Review's* policy was to adopt what it termed a "middle-of-the-road course" in respect to the question of treaty revision.[34] Mr. Powell objected on the one hand, with the full force of his active pen, to those foreigners in China who were loosely classified under the term of "diehards" and who, he declared, refused to recognize the vast changes taking place in the development of the Chinese nation. He repeatedly criticized such people for refusing to see the storm signals ahead and acting like villagers on the side of a volcano who insisted that as there had been no volcanic eruption in their lifetime there was nothing to fear.[35] On the other hand, he also opposed those who advocated an immediate abandonment of all the special privileges permitted foreigners in China by means of the treaty system:

It was lack of protection of foreigners in China by the government of China in the nineteenth century and the lack of treaty guarantees for their existence and protection in this country which proved an important contributing factor to the wars fought between China and certain Powers. . . . A sudden abrogation of the treaties without adequate guarantees for the safety of foreign persons and property in China by the central government could scarcely fail to bring more war with concomitant weakening of this land and its people. But because we do not advocate abrogation of the treaties does not mean that either missionaries or businessmen should pursue the policy of the ostrich of burrowing under cover and refusing to consider any change at all.[36]

In respect to the specific issue of extraterritoriality, Mr. Powell wrote during the time that the Commission on Extraterritoriality was undertaking its work:

Briefly it is to be hoped that the result of the present investigation of extraterritoriality will be a change from the past negative policy of the Powers to a future definite and positive policy that will help China organize her courts and modernize her administration of justice. . . . In the past, the Powers have stood by their treaties and in effect they have said, "Nothing doing, until you have brought your courts up to our standards" forgetting that it has required the West many centuries to develop its system of courts and that they are not perfect yet. . . . It is to be hoped that the future policy may be expressed in the words "We are going to give you an opportunity to

[33] *Ibid.*, November 13, 1926, p. 286.
[34] *Ibid.*, August 15, 1925, p. 207.
[35] *Ibid.*, July 18, 1925, p. 109.
[36] *Ibid.*, December 12, 1925, p. 34.

develop your courts and the administration of justice over our nationals and their interests in China and we are going to help you in this work, but at the same time we are going to demand a square deal just as we grant a square deal to Chinese nationals residing in our territories."[37]

In general Mr. Powell supported vigorously what he believed to be the policy of the Administration in Washington — a policy which he regarded as one of "peaceful readjustment" surrendering neither to the more radical claims for an immediate and complete revision of the treaties nor to the demands for intervention.[38] The United States was, in his opinion, in a difficult position, feeling the pressure on the one hand of the Chinese insistence that the State Department should take a more positive stand, and, on the other, of the attitude of the foreign Powers that the United States went too far in its sympathy for China.[39] But there were occasional moments — as in November, 1926 — when Mr. Powell joined in expressing some of the criticisms of American policy that were heard most frequently:

As a matter of fact American policy toward China is purely negative, based apparently on Mr. Kellogg's fear of hurting anybody's feelings. The Washington correspondent of one of the leading American newspapers who recently was in China stated that before the State Department could make up its mind on Chinese policy it first had to determine whether British or Japanese feelings would be wounded. The result naturally is that nothing is done, which is of course the best thing in the lack of an intelligent positive policy. America is losing the opportunity of a lifetime for cultivating good-will in China at this juncture. . . . So America does nothing and by doing nothing unconsciously helps China by preventing anybody else from doing anything drastic.[40]

The editorial comment of the *China Weekly Review* coincided in many important respects with that of the *North China Star* and the *Peking Leader*. Like Mr. Powell, Charles James Fox of the *North China Star* was strongly opposed to a policy of intervention. He criticized the " 'diehards' " in sharp language as people who "foolishly" believed that "trade or other privileges can be maintained, or obtained, by the use of gunboats and bayonets. . . . They forget that 1926 is not 1900 nor is it 1914." Moreover, he said, the " 'diehards' " had shouted so long and so loudly in condemnation of the chaotic conditions in China that their "stock of superlative terms of abuse" was running low. They would not bring about intervention, he predicted;

[37] *Ibid.*, Special Supplement on Extraterritoriality, June 19, 1926, p. 11.
[38] *Ibid.*, October 2, 1926, p. 116.
[39] *Ibid.*, p. 115.
[40] *Ibid.*, November 20, 1926, p. 315.

the United States Senate and public opinion would not allow itself to be drawn into any such scheme.[41]

As in the *China Weekly Review*, there ran throughout the editorials of the *North China Star* a strong consciousness of the fundamental changes that were taking place in the national life of China. A " 'New China' " was pictured as emerging from a "long and costly struggle" with the old forces that had for so long dominated the Chinese scene.[42] "The present struggle of the Chinese Nationalists," it was said, "is being watched with most sympathetic interest by the liberal and progressive elements in all countries throughout the world. . . . China's nationalism today is receiving international support."[43] For the foreign governments this meant primarily that a "new policy" was needed to meet the changes that had occurred in China. The Powers should abandon the old diplomatic policy of acting in concert with each other, since they had never been able to unite in support of any definite program, and should individually enter into negotiations with China for a revision of their treaties.[44] Given evidence of good faith the Chinese would be reasonable in their demands, according proper consideration to the foreign interests which had been built up on the basis of the extraterritorial system and of the Settlements and Concessions. Good will and good faith were the prime requisites for the governments concerned and an appreciation of each others' points of view.[45] "Show good will. Act in good faith. These are platitudes but at the present time they are true policies."[46]

Mr. Fox also criticized American policy on much the same basis as the *China Weekly Review:*

A definite and independent plan in China is really an important factor in American foreign policy. . . . Except for a rather marked tendency to tag along after the British, nobody seems able to guess with any degree of certainty what America's policy in China really is, and this uncertainty is as pronounced in the Legation itself, and even in the State Department as it is among those Americans here or at home who take a real interest in Sino-American relations.[47]

The editorial policy of the *Peking Leader,* like that of the *China Weekly Review,* developed gradually during the period of the Chinese Revolution, becoming more vigorous in 1927 when Grover Clark made a series of speeches during a trip to the United States, in which he took a very definite stand

[41] *North China Star*, December 8, 1926.
[42] *Ibid.*, December 22, 1926.
[43] *Ibid.*, December 4, 1926.
[44] *Ibid.*, January 9 and 12, 1927.
[45] *Ibid.*, January 12, 1927.
[46] *Ibid.*, January 13, 1927.
[47] *Peking Leader,* January 5, 1927.

concerning the question of treaty revision and the rôle the State Department should play in the establishment of a new and different relationship between China and the rest of the world. After the May 30th Incident, however, and throughout 1925 and 1926, Mr. Clark placed most of his emphasis upon the disordered condition of China and the need for the Chinese to recognize that their problems were internal and not external in origin: ". . . the fundamental cause for the present status of China among the nations of the world is the condition of China herself."[48] ". . . just as soon as the Chinese people work out for themselves a Government which can speak and act for the whole nation, which the people of the whole nation will obey, which will be in a position to keep its international pledges . . . and fulfill its international obligations, which can give to foreigners in this country something of the same security they have at home and that foreigners in other leading nations enjoy, as soon as this is done China will secure full equality of treatment."[49] ". . . if those [Chinese] . . . really want to serve their country they can do so much more effectively by directing their energies toward the cleaning up of China's domestic affairs than by agitating against foreigners. If China were united and orderly with a national Government that really controlled the whole country, the problems of Sino-foreign relations would vanish like the morning mists before the morning sun."[50]

In dealing with the attitude of the foreign governments toward treaty revision, the *Peking Leader,* like the *North China Star* and the *China Weekly Review,* advocated following a middle-of-the-road course. Mr. Clark believed that an immediate abrogation of the treaties — and especially of the extraterritorial clauses — would lead to trouble that might readily cause serious international complications.[51] On the other hand, he felt that it was easy to understand the Chinese desire to be rid of the treaties and he regarded the treaties as "temporary expedients" which had to be maintained under current conditions but should not be used as a permanent basis for action on the part of other nations.[52] He blamed foreign diplomats for attempting to hold China "to a strict conformity to technical phrases written down in black and white" instead of recognizing "the intangible emotional factors" in the situation; to discuss technical rights and wrongs with the Chinese at this time was, he said, "not only hopeless but unwise . . . one might as well and as reasonably attempt to reason with a man in a high fever."[53]

"In the face of this condition the foreign diplomats will gain nothing

[48] *Ibid.,* July 4, 1925.
[49] *Ibid.,* July 3, 1925.
[50] *Ibid.,* February 26, 1926.
[51] *Ibid.,* April 24, 1926.
[52] *Ibid.,* May 30, 1926.
[53] *Ibid.,* November 25, 1926.

by an insistence upon their paper rights. There seems to be no vision, no realization of the fact that an unprecedented situation must be dealt with under a new formula and that the old formulas are worse than useless."[54]

As the year 1926 progressed, the most spectacular feature of the Chinese situation, as we have already seen, was the success of the Northern Expedition undertaken by the Nationalist forces. Among foreigners in China there was naturally an intense and widespread interest in the developments effected by the Kuomintang. In November, 1926, the *North China Herald* stated:

> Moscow's agents have done their work well and even yet we see only the beginning of its effects. . . . We do not for a moment dispute the growth of genuine nationalism and all that it implies in respect to treaty revision and the like. But this for a moment has become a side issue. A new power has come into existence, ruthless and immoral beyond the worst excesses of the Boxers, with a menace not only for foreigners but for the whole life of China. . . .
>
> A power within a power has been allowed, even encouraged, to come into being. The passions of the dregs of the population have been sedulously inflamed by outrageous propaganda; and by several symptoms it becomes apparent that the mob is getting out of control of those who criminally set it on.[55]

In an editorial published on Christmas of the same year, the *North China Herald* said that only hope could be the basis of its Christmas wishes:

> In 99 cases out of a 100 not the system of government is at fault but those who administer it; and countries are miserable, not because their political constitution is bad but because they are governed by bad men. Here is the true hopefulness for China's outlook. The new forces recently let loose, like all such forces in their first manifestation, are wild, ill-controlled, extravagant, and unreasonable. We will not speak of those others, transient we trust, which decent men hold in contempt. But at the core of all there lies a genuine ideal, a sincere wish to make China a better place.[56]

On the other hand, almost as soon as the Nationalist troops had reached the Yangtze, the *China Weekly Review* began to view the situation with optimism:

> Despite the alleged Bolshevik affiliations of the Kuomintang Party which have created apprehension in many influential quarters, there is beginning to develop a feeling among both foreigners and the commercial-financial classes of the Chinese that the recent developments in Central China which have brought a considerable section of the Yangtze under the sway of Canton

[54] *Ibid.*
[55] *North China Herald*, November 20, 1926, p. 343.
[56] *Ibid.*, December 31, 1926, p. 620.

may be the beginning of the turn toward improved conditions in the Chinese political situation.

The basis of the optimism expressed by the *Review* was that the situation in North China had deteriorated into continuous personal "squabbles" between political leaders who had long since ceased to consider the welfare of the Chinese people or of the nation as a whole, while the Kuomintang had a genuine program:

> . . . there is hope for ultimately better conditions in consequence of the Cantonese victories simply because the Cantonese Party stands for something. There may not be agreement with the principles for which the Cantonese stand but there must be an admission that they do have a program and are rapidly getting into a position to put it into effect. . . .

Thus the development of the Cantonese situation and extension of the influence of the Kuomintang is the most promising element in the present situation because it is something definite and tangible and has a program.[57]

While Mr. Powell continued to maintain this attitude editorially, considerable space was given in the *China Weekly Review* to articles by Chinese and foreigners who sought to explain the background, the aims, and the political complexion of the Kuomintang concerning which foreigners had relatively little information at this time. Enthusiasm and confidence were expressed in regard to the Kuomintang as a whole: "Canton is the new hope of China," it was said in one article;[58] and in another: "As a revolutionary force in China it [the Kuomintang] has no rival today. . . . Whatever may happen to the Party itself no doubt exists that its program may ever fail to exert its full influence in the building up of a strong, unified China."[59] Generally an effort was made to show that the Nationalist movement was not communistic: "Why is the Kuomintang, in the eyes of foreigners, so closely identified with communism?" Dr. C. C. Wu wrote. "This is due to misunderstanding or ignorance!" There was no division between the Left and Right factions in the Kuomintang, he said, because there was "no schism in the party doctrines."[60] "It is not purely a political group of extremists as many people imagine," C. T. Liang asserted, "for it has a very constructive program."[61] In an article entitled "What If Canton Should Win Out?" Randall Gould of the United Press stated that the " 'Canton idea' " was a "conservative idea, a bourgeois idea, an idea designed to carry Canton in the footsteps of the great material Powers of the world." In spite of all the

[57] *China Weekly Review*, September 18, 1926, p. 60.
[58] *Ibid.*, October 9, 1926, p. 148.
[59] *Ibid.*, October 2, 1926, p. 124.
[60] *Ibid.*, September 25, 1926, p. 90.
[61] *Ibid.*, October 2, 1926, p. 124.

Canton talk about co-operation with Soviet Russia in the great work of the world revolution, Mr. Gould said, it was "rather more than a safe bet" that if the United States and the other leading Powers showed the slightest desire to give a helping hand to a victorious Canton, the gesture would be accepted along with a recognition that it implied respect for the maintenance of foreign treaties.[62]

The attitude of the *North China Star* toward the successes of the Chinese Nationalists was one of strong and outspoken sympathy. The Cantonese were regarded as representative of the new forces in China, and the Peking régime as representative of the old.[63] In an article already quoted, Mr. Fox stated that the Nationalist movement was receiving the support of liberals and progressives throughout the world. Mr. Fox, however, counseled against the radical elements in the Kuomintang:

> The radical group in the nationalist movement must be kept within bounds as has always been the case with the more radical members of any group political or otherwise. Because the nationalist movement has a small anti-foreign wing, this is no reason for the whole movement being denounced as such, especially when such general denunciation has a marked tendency to encourage the very situation the critics are warning against.[64]

The *Peking Leader,* which published few editorials during the time that the Northern Expedition achieved its most significant results, was primarily interested in encouraging a policy of moderation. It was afraid that the Cantonese were deliberately attempting to provoke armed intervention on the part of the Powers in order to stimulate a violent anti-foreign outbreak and that they were the more likely to achieve this end because certain groups of foreigners were also advocating intervention in order to bring about "the subjugation of China by foreign force":

> The chief burden of responsibility rests on the more reasonable ones on both sides. They are in the majority and if they choose they can keep control. But to do so they must be active, not passive. If they remain silent and inactive, the extremists will have their way and the long end will be disaster vastly worse than anything at present whatever the immediate results may be.[65]

As time went by and foreigners obtained more information about the struggle within the Kuomintang and as that conflict entered its final critical phase, the editors of the *China Weekly Review,* the *North China Star* and

---

[62] *Ibid.,* October 9, 1926, p. 149.
[63] *North China Star,* December 22, 1926.
[64] *Ibid.,* December 11, 1926.
[65] *Peking Leader,* September 16, 1926.

the *Peking* Leader supported the so-called "rightwing" of the Party. In the earlier stages, however, they endorsed the Nationalist movement as a whole. They regarded it as part of the deep revolutionary current that was transforming much of China. In it they saw a concrete hope for the future. American policy, they felt, should seek to keep pace with China's gradual evolution into a modern state.

Chapter X

FURTHER DEVELOPMENTS OF 1926 — II

SHANGHAI PROBLEMS

In 1926, two issues arose in Shanghai which were closely associated with the movement for a revision of the treaties. One concerned the question of Chinese representation on the Shanghai Municipal Council and the other the rendition of the Shanghai Mixed Court to the Chinese. While neither issue was, strictly speaking, related to the Sino-foreign treaties, nevertheless the demands for the restoration of the Court and for the inclusion of Chinese members on the Shanghai Municipal Council had long been an outstanding part of the Chinese program for a readjustment of China's relations with the Powers. Moreover, as Shanghai was the center of much of the financial, commercial, and trade life of the Chinese nation, and as the foreign community in the settlement was by far the largest in China, the affairs of Shanghai essentially assumed an aspect of international importance.

When the anti-foreign movement broke out in Shanghai, following the May 30th Incident, one of the demands most frequently heard from the Chinese was for a drastic revision of the status of the International Settlement and for the restitution of the Mixed Court to the Chinese Government. These points were incorporated in the thirteen demands which were drawn up by the Chinese General Chamber of Commerce and endorsed by forty organizations in Shanghai, and which were later adopted by the Chinese Government as a basis for negotiation with the foreign Powers. At that time the Diplomatic Body stated that it wished to treat as separate matters the controversy over the shooting at the Louza Police Station and the more far-reaching questions involved in a reorganization of the Settlement and of the Mixed Court.[1] Nevertheless, the foreign Ministers took great pains to make clear, both to the Chinese Government and to the public, that they were asking their home governments for the authority to discuss the rendition of the Court and the possibility of including Chinese members on the Shanghai Municipal Council as soon as the negotiations concerning the May 30th Incident had been concluded.[2] Although Mr. Mayer, then in charge of the American Legation at Peking, cabled for the necessary authority to the Department in Washington, the issue appears to have been lost

[1] See above, p. 33 *et seq.*
[2] *Foreign Relations* (1925), pp. 668-683.

sight of for the time being.[3] Some months later, however, negotiations over the Mixed Court, which had been in progress before the May 30th Incident, were resumed by the Diplomatic Body and the Chinese Government at Peking. The issue of Chinese representation on the Municipal Council, on the other hand, did not become the object of definite diplomatic negotiations during the 1925-1928 period, although the American Government offered to open negotiations in February, 1927. Attempts were made, however, by the Shanghai Municipal Council and the foreign electorate in the International Settlement to resolve the problem locally.

The question of Chinese representation on the Shanghai Municipal Council was indeed a worn and battered political football with which Chinese and foreigners had long since become familiar. The controversy over the administration of Shanghai had started as early as 1869 when the Land Regulations were drawn up which formed the basis of government in the International Settlement.[4] These regulations had decreed that the electorate of the Settlement should be made up only of foreigners who were landowners or householders — "ratepayers" — with certain property qualifications that were specified. The electorate was given many responsibilities, among which was the election of the members of the Municipal Council. It was further laid down in the regulations that the Council should consist of not more than nine, nor less than five, members all of whom were to be foreigners. The Council and the electorate together were granted an exceptional amount of power which was increased by the fact that the Council was in no way made subject to the control of any Chinese authority and that even its relationship to the Consular Body at Shanghai and to the Diplomatic Body at Peking was only vaguely defined.[5]

As the Land Regulations could only be amended through an elaborate diplomatic process, they had remained virtually unaltered throughout the years. This presented an especially complicated problem as, in the decades following 1869, the International Settlement had grown beyond recognition. From 1869 to 1925, the foreign population had increased from some 1,600 persons to over 29,000, and the Chinese population from 75,000 to more than 810,000.[6] But the electorate numbered only 622 voters in 1925 since it was still governed by the Land Regulations, which meant that only foreigners possessing the necessary property qualifications were allowed to vote.[7]

[3] *Ibid.*

[4] Richard Feetham, *Report to the Shanghai Municipal Council,* Shanghai, 1931 (referred to hereafter as *Report*). Contains text of Land Regulations of 1869, Vol. 1, pp. 68-83.

[5] William C. Johnstone, *The Shanghai Problem,* London, 1927, pp. 27, 68.

[6] For earlier figures, see Feetham, *Report,* Vol. 1, p. 62; for later figures, see *Annual Report of the Shanghai Municipal Council,* 1926, pp. 106, 173.

[7] Figure taken from *Shanghai Municipal Gazette,* April 16, 1925, p. 169.

The discussion concerning the right of the Chinese to vote in the Settlement and to be represented on the Municipal Council was as old as the Land Regulations themselves. Those who drafted the Land Regulations had first intended to give the Chinese an active share in the municipal government, but for various reasons this scheme was finally set aside.[8] When the issue was again raised in 1906, the entire conception of Chinese participation in the municipal system had been watered down to the idea of admitting the Chinese in an advisory capacity. By an arrangement made between the Municipal Council and a group of Chinese, it was decided that the Chinese should organize a consultative committee which would meet regularly with members of the Council.[9] A committee was thereupon elected by forty representatives of local Chinese guilds.[10] The Ratepayers objected to this plan, however, and in order to quash it a resolution was introduced at the Annual Meeting of Ratepayers stating that the Land Regulations did not authorize the Council to recognize any such body as the consultative committee which had been proposed.[11] The resolution was carried by an overwhelming majority, about ten votes being cast in opposition.[12]

The next attempt to establish some formal method of consultation between members of the Shanghai Municipal Council and an advisory board of Chinese was made in 1915 and was again unsuccessful, this time because it was linked with other issues affecting the Settlement.[13] One important feature of this episode was that it showed that the Chinese had increased their demands: while they were willing to accept a purely advisory position in the government of the Settlement, they stated clearly that they regarded this as a temporary measure which would have to be replaced by Chinese representation on the Municipal Council.

It was only four years later that the Chinese Delegates at the Versailles Conference asked directly for the right of Chinese to vote in the International Settlement and to become members of the Municipal Council. Again, however, the Chinese broadened the scope of their proposals by declaring that they would no longer be satisfied with the fulfillment of their earlier demands but regarded even representation on the Municipal Council as merely a preparatory step that must lead to the complete restoration of the Settlement to the Chinese Government.[14]

[8] Feetham, *Report*, Vol. 1, pp. 95, 113-117; Johnstone, *op. cit.*, p. 228; A. M. Kotenev, *Shanghai, Its Mixed Court and Council*, Shanghai, 1925, p. 15; *Problems of the Pacific*, Institute of Pacific Relations, New York, 1929, p. 356.

[9] Feetham, *Report*, pp. 116-118.

[10] *Ibid.*, p. 118.

[11] *Ibid.*, pp. 119-122.

[12] *Ibid.*, p. 122.

[13] *Ibid.*, p. 124.

[14] Kotenev, *op. cit.*, p. 40.

The action of the Chinese Delegation at the Versailles Conference had strong repercussions in Shanghai where an extensive campaign was conducted by the Chinese for the revision of the Land Regulations and the election of Chinese members to the Municipal Council[15] As a result the Municipal Council held a meeting to discuss the question of Chinese participation in the government of the Settlement. The Councilors voted unanimously against Chinese representation on the Council "on any consideration" but at the same time approved a plan for the creation of an advisory board of Chinese. The board was to consist of five members to be nominated by the Chinese, the nominations to be subject to the vote of the Consular Body at Shanghai; the nominees were, moreover, to have certain property qualifications and they were not to hold any official position under the Chinese Government.[16]

The plan for the advisory board was presented at the Annual Meeting of Ratepayers in 1920 and was unanimously adopted by the voters.[17] Another resolution was also introduced, requesting an amendment of the Land Regulations that would give the Chinese three seats on the Municipal Council; it was accompanied by a petition for its endorsement signed by 8,000 Chinese in the Settlement.[18] This resolution was rejected at the Ratepayers' Meeting by a majority of about three to one.[19]

After some delay, the advisory board authorized by the voters was brought into being. It did not, however, play an effective rôle in the life of the Settlement as it met only at long intervals and rarely deliberated on matters of genuine importance.[20] After the May 30th Incident, the advisory

[15] Ibid., p. 40; Johnstone, op. cit., p. 237; Feetham, Report, p. 124.

[16] Account of the Meeting, in Feetham, Report, p. 125. Mr. Edward C. Pearce, Chairman of the Shanghai Municipal Council at this time, described the Council's action in vetoing the proposal for Chinese Councilors, in the following terms:

"In reaching this vote, the meeting was unable to dissociate the demand for Chinese representation on the Council from the efforts of the past few years, and particularly since the signing of the Armistice, to secure the abolition of extraterritoriality, Settlements, Concessions, and Spheres of Influence, and general expression was given to the view that these efforts must be met and resisted until, by good government, and by the adoption of a policy of progression and development in accord with the standards common to every enlightened nation, China has shown that she is fitted to receive full retrocession of those rights which she contends have been wrongfully wrested from her, but which in fact the foreigner has vested in him by treaty or has been forced to assume and exercise from motives of self-preservation and protection, or because of the hopeless inability of China to exercise them herself for the benefit of her own people and of those who seek a domicile in her lands." Extract from open letter of Mr. Pearce to the Senior Consul at Shanghai. (Feetham, Report, p. 125.)

[17] Ibid., p. 126.

[18] Ibid., p. 127.

[19] Ibid.

[20] Johnstone, op. cit., p. 239.

board resigned in a body, declaring that it had been led to take this action by "the absence of any desire on the part of the Council to punish those who participated in the shooting affray of May 30 and to do justice to the Chinese."[21]

Such, in the briefest terms, was the background which led the Chinese after the May 30th Incident to insist upon the reorganization of the municipal government in the Settlement. Whether because the strength and intensity of the anti-foreign movement gave them confidence, or for some other reason, the Chinese again presented proposals that went beyond any concrete terms they had suggested previously. In the thirteen demands supported by a large section of the Chinese community in Shanghai and by the Chinese Government at Peking, it was stated that: "The Chinese shall participate in the Municipal Council and Ratepayers' Meetings. The Ratepayers will choose their representatives in proportion to the amount of the taxes paid by them. In voting they will have the same rights and privileges as the foreign voters."[22] In effect this meant that the Chinese were asking for a majority of members on the Shanghai Municipal Council, a request which far exceeded the plan for three Chinese members which had been submitted at the Annual Ratepayers' Meeting of 1920 and roundly rejected.

On the foreign side, the general issue of a reorganization of the municipal government was taken up immediately after the May 30th Incident. The National Christian Council, in an open letter to the Municipal Council already referred to, recommended that "full consideration" be given at an early date to the inclusion of Chinese members; such direct representation, it was said, would do much to improve the relations between Chinese and foreigners.[23] In his judicial report on the May 30th Incident, Justice Johnson declared that the situation in respect to Chinese participation in the government of the International Settlement seemed to many persons "intolerable" and that it would remain "a source of serious grievance" until the time when a solution was found.[24] At the end of August, 1925, the British Chamber of Commerce at Shanghai and the Shanghai Branch of the China Association (also a British commercial group) passed a resolution in which they expressed their sympathy with China's "national aspirations" and stated that they wished to give public expression to their support of the principle of direct Chinese representation on the Municipal Council.[25] Moreover, when the *North China Herald* criticized the British Minister, Sir

[21] Feetham, *Report*, p. 125.
[22] For additional demands concerning the status of the International Settlement see above, pp. 30-31.
[23] See above, p. 84.
[24] See above, pp. 37-38.
[25] *British Chamber of Commerce Journal*, September, 1925, p. 223.

Ronald Macleay, for declaring in a public address that he regarded the refusal to grant the Chinese a significant rôle in the administration of the Settlement as a "mistake,"[26] the British Chamber and the Shanghai Branch of the China Association issued a letter saying that they wished "completely to dissociate themselves" from the opinion expressed by the editors. "We are whole-heartedly in agreement," they wrote to the editors, "with the view that Chinese should be given representation on the Municipal Council in the International Settlement. We intend to give our full support to their claim to representation and we disagree entirely both with the substance and the form of your comments."[27]

In March, 1926, a dinner was given by the members of the Shanghai Municipal Council to a group of Chinese who were regarded as leaders of the Chinese community in Shanghai. According to newspaper accounts it was the first time that any such gathering had ever been held.[28] Mr. Stirling Fessenden, as chairman of the Municipal Council, gave a long speech which was characterized by frankness and sincerity.[29] He reviewed the developments that had taken place in Shanghai after the May 30th Incident, stating that among the most important issues under discussion were those of Chinese representation on the Council and the rendition of the Mixed Court. He referred to the resolution passed by the British Chamber of Commerce and the China Association in favor of both these measures and declared that the Council would present a special resolution at the forthcoming Annual Ratepayers' Meeting, stating that it would "welcome" Chinese representation on the Council. "We shall emphasize," he assured his audience, "the desirability of the Chinese participating in the government of the Settlement; and we intend, moreover, if the resolution is passed by the Ratepayers, to do what we can to make such representation effective at the earliest possible date."

The rest of Mr. Fessenden's speech dealt with the general political atmosphere in Shanghai. The prospect in Shanghai, he said, was "none too bright"; it was quite possible that an incident such as that which had taken place at the Louza Station might recur in the immediate future with more serious consequences. All the elements to cause trouble were present. The working classes were being exploited by third parties for their own ends. One party professed to have in view what it vaguely termed "social revolution"; another wished to further what it believed to be its own national and political aims in China.

---

[26] North China Herald, September 12, 1925, p. 337.
[27] Ibid., September 19, 1925, p. 389.
[28] China Weekly Review, March 27, 1926, p. 81.
[29] The North China Herald, March 26, 1926, p. 522, contains the text of Mr. Fessenden's speech. The quotations which follow are taken from this source.

"I assure you most earnestly," Mr. Fessenden said, "that we see the possibility of grave trouble ahead. I assure you that in the face of it we will be forbearing and conciliatory to the utmost degree.

"But equally I must make it clear once more that there is a degree of forbearance beyond which in the community's interest it is not safe to go: that a time may come when we may have to meet force with force in the maintenance of public safety."

Mr. Fessenden asked for the co-operation of the Chinese present to avoid the development of a situation in which conflict would be inevitable and he suggested that, as outstanding and responsible representatives of the Chinese community, they should attempt to assume the leadership of the Chinese working classes in the Settlement in order to counter the influences to which the laborer had been subjected "by others of a very different nature."

A month after this speech of Mr. Fessenden's had been delivered, the Annual Meeting of Ratepayers was held on April 15, 1926; a total of 377 voters were present.[30] Mr. Fessenden, in his opening address, again reviewed the crisis that had followed the May 30th Incident. This time, however, he asserted that a charge had been made by many — particularly in "missionary and educational circles" — that the attempts to settle the May 30th Incident had not been handled in a way to accord justice to the Chinese because foreigners in Shanghai were blinded by their own "attitude of superiority" and their insistence that "the white man was infallible." Mr. Fessenden stated that these accusations were "untrue and misleading" and that they did not apply "either directly or by implication" to the Shanghai Municipal Council. After referring to the great amount of attention which had been given to the subject of Chinese representation on the Council since the May 30th Incident, Mr. Fessenden said that he wished to propose a resolution of great moment in the history of the Settlement:

"Resolution VI: That in the opinion of this meeting the participation of the Chinese residents in the government of the Settlement is desirable; and that the Council be hereby authorized and instructed to make forthwith representations to the Powers concerned with a view to securing the addition of three Chinese members at an early date."

As to who the Chinese Councilors should be, Mr. Fessenden said, he had little to suggest except that the Council should obtain their names through the Commissioner for Foreign Affairs of the Chinese Government. "The great difficulties of securing them by election are manifest to both Chinese and foreigners," he declared.

[30] The following account of the Ratepayers' Meeting is based on a verbatim report printed in the *Shanghai Municipal Gazette*, April 15, 1926, p. 121 *et seq.*

In support of the Resolution, Mr. Fessenden asserted that there were two decisive points which made the endorsement of the resolution essential: the fact that the Chinese paid a large proportion of the taxes in the Settlement, and the recognition that the future prosperity and development of Shanghai depended "entirely and absolutely" upon the existence and maintenance of mutual good will and co-operation between the Chinese and foreign communities. Recalling the various stages of the long controversy which had been waged over Chinese representation in the government of the Settlement, he concluded by saying:

"The Council of 1920 was unanimously opposed to Chinese representation and the resolution was rejected by an overwhelming vote of the Ratepayers.

"Foreign public opinion, I believe, has changed to a great extent in recent years. The Council of 1926 is in favor of this resolution and I venture to hope that it will be adopted, if not unanimously, at least by as great a majority as its predecessor of 1920 was rejected."

Following Mr. Fessenden's address an amendment to Resolution VI was proposed by one of the Ratepayers, Lawrence K. Kentwell. The amendment sought to authorize the Council to make representations to the Powers "with a view to hastening the election to the Council of Chinese members *with due regard to the taxes paid by the Chinese Ratepayers.*"[31] Mr. Kentwell explained that, in his opinion, to allot three seats to the Chinese would defeat the purpose of the Resolution which was to improve the relations between Chinese and foreigners and, above all, to obliterate signs of racial differences. Any decision, he said, which overlooked the two main considerations of the immensity of the Chinese population in the Settlement and of the bulk of the municipal rates paid by them, could not escape being denounced as "arbitrary." There were some people, he observed, who did not see "clearly or close enough the signs of the times" and who were therefore afraid that the proposed amendment would give the Chinese an undue influence in the affairs of the Settlement. But the Chinese, he affirmed, did not want "to put the foreigners out of business" and would surely be glad to accept any practical scheme whereby Chinese and foreigners would share in the government of the Settlement on an equal basis with neither seeking to dominate the other.

Mr. O. M. Green, editor of the *North China Daily News and Herald*, rose in response to Mr. Kentwell's remarks and urged the meeting to vote "emphatically" for the original resolution and "not to listen" to the proposed amendment which was "impractical" and not only destined for failure

[31] Italics not in original.

but in failing was bound to furnish "fuel to the agitators in the Chinese community." Mr. Green supported the idea of according the Chinese three seats on the Council and declared that, conditions having changed, he felt sure the Ratepayers desired to show that they recognized the spirit of the times and were prepared to co-operate with the Chinese. Nevertheless, he thought it should be made clear that the Chinese had "no claim of any kind whatever" to a change in the constitution of the Settlement. The Settlement had not been extorted from China but was originally given to foreigners for the sake of "getting them out of the way," in much the same spirit as a bad bone might be thrown to a dog that was in ill favor; it was only by means of the energy exhibited by foreigners that Shanghai had been transformed from little more than a swamp into a great city.

Mr. Fessenden also opposed the amendment that had been introduced by Mr. Kentwell and explained why the members of the Shanghai Municipal Council had drafted Resolution VI in the form presented to the meeting:

You will realize that the Resolution itself constitutes what is probably the greatest departure from governmental procedure ever made by this community. . . .
We do not fail to appreciate the fact that the day will come when all Chinese territory will be under Chinese control — when Shanghai will be a great cosmopolitan city, the nerve center of China's foreign trade. But we believe that our Chinese fellow citizens are no less anxious than we ourselves that that end should be attained by evolutionary rather than revolutionary means. We know also that many of them desire that the existing form of Municipal Administration, under which the Settlement has reached its present postion, should be maintained. It is for that reason that we have preferred to adopt a method by which they may gradually be initiated into the principles and practices of the municipal government of this city. We believe that they have a great contribution to make to the future development of the local administration; and we have endeavored to ensure that this contribution shall be made to the best advantage of both parties concerned.
For these reasons, ladies and gentlemen, we are not prepared to go further than we have gone. . . .

Both Resolution VI and the amendment proposed by Mr. Kentwell were voted upon at the Ratepayers' Meeting. The Resolution was passed with the almost unanimous approval of the Ratepayers, only one vote being registered in opposition. Mr. Kentwell's amendment, on the other hand, received only six votes in its support.

In adopting Resolution VI and offering the Chinese three seats on the Shanghai Municipal Council, the Ratepayers were of course falling far short of the demands for representation in the municipal system of the Settlement which the Chinese had been making since the May 30th Incident. This fact was emphasized by the Chinese on the day the Annual Meeting of Ratepayers was held. In the morning, the Chinese General Chamber of Commerce published a Manifesto declaring that: "Chinese representation on the Council should be made proportionate to the amount of taxes they actually pay." This statement, according to the Manifesto, originated in the conviction maintained by the Chinese community in the Settlement that racial equality was "absolutely essential to the success of co-operation between foreigners and Chinese in Shanghai."[32]

After the decisions reached at the Annual Meeting became known, the Chairman of the Chinese General Chamber of Commerce, Mr. Yu Yah-ching, held a press interview in which he declared that he was opposed to the action taken by the Ratepayers as it was contrary to the thirteen demands originally formulated by the Chinese Chamber and officially accepted by the Government at Peking. These demands, he pointed out, had expressly stated that Chinese representation on the Council should be "in proportion to the amount of the rate payable and paid to the Municipal revenue" and that Chinese should participate both in the Municipal Council and in the Rate-payers' Meetings.[33]

The views expressed by the Chinese General Chamber of Commerce were further supported by the Chinese Ratepayers' Association. The Association passed a resolution in which it declared its disapproval of the action taken at the Annual Meeting of Ratepayers and reiterated the demand of the Chinese Chamber that representation on the Council should be based on the number of Ratepayers in the Settlement.[34]

As the result of the attitude of the Chinese, nothing was done at this time toward the appointment of three Chinese members to the Shanghai Municipal Council. In accordance with the terms of Resolution VI, however, the Council notified the Chinese and foreign authorities in Peking

[32] *China Weekly Review,* April 24, 1926, p. 190.
[33] *North China Herald,* April 17, 1926, p. 113.
[34] *Ibid.*

In February, 1927, the Chinese Ratepayers' Association elected a provisional committee of nine Chinese to co-operate with the foreign members of the Shanghai Municipal Council and "to assume an equal share of the responsibility in the administration of municipal affairs." It was explained by Dr. C. T. Wang as chairman that it had been decided to elect the provisional committee in lieu of appointing three Chinese members to the Shanghai Municipal Council. Three Councilors, Dr. Wang said, would be "quite insufficient" and the Chinese Ratepayers would, therefore, continue to demand an equal share in the administration of municipal affairs. Dr. Wang's statement was more or less predicated on the assumption that the Settlement would be returned to the Chinese within a brief period and that the appointment of a provisional committee was an *interim* measure. (*North China Herald,* February 19, 1927, p. 277.)

of the measure adopted at the Annual Ratepayers' Meeting. The proposal for the appointment of three Chinese Councilors was thereupon endorsed by the Chinese Government, by the Diplomatic Body, and, locally, by the Kiangsu Provincial Government.[35]

The actions of the members of the Municipal Council and of the electorate were approved by both the *North China Herald* and the *China Weekly Review*. Following Mr. Fessenden's announcement that the Council intended to ask the Ratepayers to support a resolution for Chinese representation on the Council, the *North China Herald* expressed its point of view editorially:

> The Council, representing the whole foreign community, acknowledges that the time has arrived when in the growth of this city, in its progress and development, its Chinese residents shall have a definite share in the operation of the policy of the municipal government and shall partake of the responsibilities of maintaining peace and order. Even in the mere fact of this recognition lies Chinese representation on the Council, for henceforth the Council cannot and will not function without Chinese advice and assistance.[36]

After the Annual Meeting of Ratepayers, the *China Weekly Review* applauded the action taken by the voters and severely criticized the recommendations which had been proposed by Mr. Kentwell. Of the latter it said that "suddenly . . . and without careful study of the issues involved to pass resolutions which would in effect turn over the government and administration of Shanghai to the Chinese would be nothing short of madness."[37] In any case, the *Review* maintained, three Chinese Councilors would be fully able to present the attitude of the Chinese community.[38]

Actually the three Chinese Councilors voted for by the Ratepayers were not to take their seats on the Shanghai Municipal Council until two years later.[39] Nevertheless the action taken by the Administration and by the voters in the Settlement in the spring of 1926 showed that the temper of the foreign community at Shanghai had undergone a substantial change within a few years. The idea of Chinese representation on the Municipal

[35] *Annual Report of the Shanghai Municipal Council*, 1927, p. 80.
[36] *North China Herald*, March 20, 1926, p. 513.
[37] *China Weekly Review*, April 14, 1926, p. 190.
[38] *Ibid.*, May 15, 1926, p. 282.
[39] In 1928, in addition to the three Chinese Councilors, an arrangement was made whereby six more Chinese were allowed to serve on committees of the Council, having charge of the various administrative departments of the municipality. At a special Ratepayers' Meeting of 1930, the electorate voted to increase the number of Chinese members on the Shanghai Municipal Council to five. On this basis, the Council consisted of nine foreigners and five Chinese. (Pollard, *China's Foreign Relations, 1917-1931*, p. 385; Johnstone, *op. cit.*, p. 240.)

Council, which was so firmly rejected in 1920, was no longer questioned in 1926 except by the few foreigners who believed that the offer of three seats on the Council was not sufficiently liberal. The May 30th Incident, and the events which followed it, had so altered conditions in China that even those who were most readily classified as "Shanghai diehards" felt that they wished to make some concessions to the Chinese. Times were changing, it was said at the Annual Meeting of 1926, and the foreign population of the International Settlement must adjust itself to the new situation created in China.

On the other hand, both the officials of the Settlement and the electorate at the Ratepayers' Meeting made it clear that they did not wish to go beyond the offer of three seats on the Municipal Council to the Chinese. Such a gesture was regarded as adequate and generous by the foreign residents of the Settlement and no serious consideration was given to any more radical proposals. This fact should be borne in mind as there are indications, which will be noted later, that Secretary of State Kellogg and the Administration in Washington would not have been averse to making far more extensive changes in the status of the International Settlement than anything contemplated by the foreign community at Shanghai, either in 1926 or for a long time to come.

SHANGHAI MIXED COURT

The question of the rendition of the Shanghai Mixed Court, like that of representation on the Shanghai Municipal Council, was an old and familiar story in the history of the relationship between Chinese and foreigners.

In the thirteen demands presented by the Foreign Office at Peking to the Heads of Legation, the Chinese asked for the restitution of the Mixed Court to the Chinese Government. The term "restitution" applied to the fact that the Court had been taken over by the Consular Body in Shanghai in 1911. The Court had originally come into existence in 1864 and had received its constitution in 1869, the year in which the Land Regulations were drafted.[40] The Mixed Court was instituted as a Chinese Court and placed under the authority of a Chinese magistrate. It was to have jurisdiction (a) in commercial, civil, and criminal cases which involved either solely Chinese litigants, or foreigners without extraterritorial rights, and (b) in suits where Chinese and non-extraterritorial foreigners were defendants. In all such cases, it was specifically stated, the magistrate was to conduct the trial and reach decisions without interference from the foreign consuls. The powers of the Chinese magistrates were limited, however, as it was stipulated

[40] A copy of the rules of 1869 can conveniently be found in Keeton, *The Development of Extraterritoriality in China*, Vol. 1, p. 351.

that they could only impose minor means of punishment and that more serious cases would have to be referred to the district magistrate in the Chinese City of Shanghai. Suits between Chinese and foreigners were to be conducted in accordance with the treaties — that is to say that where such foreigners acted as plaintiffs, a Consul or his deputy might sit at the trial alongside the Chinese Magistrate. No provision was made for a Court of Appeals and appeals were to be sent to the *Taotai* who was to adjudicate with the assistance of the Consul involved in the case. Warrants for arrest in the Settlement were to be countersigned by the Senior Consul and, where a foreigner was involved, by his own Consul.

Friction over the Shanghai Mixed Court developed early and continued throughout the many years that the Court remained in existence.[41] A ceaseless conflict was carried on between the Chinese magistrates and the foreign assessors. In this struggle the assessors gradually gained ground until in cases where foreigners were concerned, they came virtually to occupy the position of co-judges.[42] Furthermore, by the end of the nineteenth century, the assessors participated in all cases except in purely Chinese civil suits where the magistrate continued to sit alone.[43] In criminal cases, even those involving only Chinese litigants, the assessors took part on the ground that they affected the law and order of the Settlement and were therefore of concern to the Shanghai Municipal Council and the government of the International Settlement in general, for which the assessors regarded themselves as trustees.[44] Also, as some of the punishments required by the existing Chinese Criminal Code seemed "barbarous" to many foreigners, the assessors tried to soften the execution of justice by the application of Western standards.[45]

Denunciations of the conduct of the Court were constantly heard from both Chinese and foreigners. Foreigners charged that the magistrates were subject to every kind of political influence and that they functioned primarily as the servants of their political superiors.[46] The claim was also made that the magistrates were, on the whole, men of inferior capabilities, who were of too low rank and received too little pay for the position which they occupied.[47] Serious trouble was caused by the lack of any proper provision for the appeal of cases and there were constant demands for the establishment

---

[41] Manley O. Hudson, "The Rendition of the International Court at Shanghai," in the *American Journal of International Law*, Vol. 21, 1927, p. 456.

[42] Data paper by a member of the British Group, Institute of Pacific Relations, in *Problems of the Pacific* (1929), p. 361; quoted in Feetham, *Report*, p. 171.

[43] *Ibid.*

[44] Keeton, *op. cit.*, p. 360.

[45] *Ibid.*, pp. 360-363.

[46] Kotenev, *op. cit.*, p. 73.

[47] *Ibid.*

of a Court of Appeals.[48] Objections were raised to the limitations put upon the Court's power in criminal cases which necessitated the transference of persons guilty of serious crimes to the jurisdiction of the district magistrate who, it was said, frequently decreed only a nominal punishment.[49] The question of the Senior Consul or his deputy countersigning all of the summonses, warrants, and court orders issued by the Chinese Magistrate created an unfortunate amount of ill-feeling.[50] In addition, there were innumerable other sources of friction involving such matters as the law to be applied in the Court, the authority of the Shanghai Municipal Police, the administration of prisons, the rendition of Chinese fugitives from justice who had escaped to the Settlement, etc.

The situation was further complicated with the outbreak of the Revolution of 1911. At the end of that year, Shanghai went over to the revolutionaries and two of the Mixed Court magistrates fled, taking with them the funds which the litigants had deposited with the Court.[51] As a result the Mixed Court was left in a state of extreme confusion which required immediate action. The Consular Body, taking the situation in hand, announced that it would assume control of the Court, a measure which was, however, to be regarded as purely temporary. The Consuls asked the Shanghai Municipal Council to pay all the expenses of the Court, even including the salaries of the magistrates, and to receive all fines and appoint a separate financial officer to be entrusted with the deposits.[52] A month later the Consular Body took a further important step by asserting that foreign assessors should attend the trial of all cases, even of civil suits which involved only Chinese litigants.[53]

The taking over of the Court by the Consular Body proved not to be temporary. From 1911 on, the Court functioned as a foreign institution under the control of foreign Consuls, divorced from the rest of the Chinese judicial system. Operating in this fashion, it had no legal basis in any of the treaties between China and the Powers. Nor was it recognized by other Chinese courts, the Supreme Court at Peking declaring specifically that the Shanghai Mixed Court could not be regarded as a "judicial tribunal."[54]

After 1911, the Chinese persistently asked for a rendition of the Mixed Court, just as they demanded representation in the municipal system of the International Settlement. Diplomatic negotiations were carried on in 1914

[48] Johnstone, op. cit., p. 153.
[49] Keeton, op. cit., p. 353.
[50] Johnstone, op. cit., p. 149.
[51] Kotenev, op. cit., p. 169.
[52] Ibid., p. 173.
[53] Ibid., pp. 173-174.
[54] Ibid., p. 175.

and almost reached a successful conclusion, but it proved impossible to agree on some of the terms, which included such demands by the interested Heads of Legation as that the Chinese magistrates even if appointed by the Chinese Government should be subject to the endorsement of the Consular Body at Shanghai and that foreign assessors should be present at the trial of purely Chinese civil cases.[55] At the Versailles Conference, the Chinese Delegation asked for alterations in the status of the Court which would have prevented foreign assessors from taking part in the trial or decision of any cases involving only Chinese litigants and would have permitted warrants which were issued by a Chinese court outside of the Settlement to be executed within the Settlement boundaries without revision by foreign officials.[56] In 1922, the negotiations for the rendition of the Court were resumed and failed again because of the difficulty of reaching an agreement on the important issue of foreign participation in the trial of cases which, although they involved only Chinese, affected the maintenance of law and order in the Settlement.[57] Two years later, the Chinese Government submitted a new set of proposals for the consideration of the Diplomatic Body which included recommendations that would have permitted foreign assessors to sit in all cases affecting foreigners (a condition which was open to wide interpretation) and in cases where Chinese had violated the municipal regulations.[58]

The proposals submitted by the Chinese Government in 1924 were made the basis of negotiations with the foreign Powers. Before the negotiations were entered into, however, objections were raised by the State Department in Washington on the grounds that the rendition of the Shanghai Mixed Court to the Chinese might be regarded as "resulting from weakness or as indicating, or being preliminary to, a surrender of extraterritorial rights in the near future."[59] A cable to this effect was sent to the American Minister, Mr. Jacob Gould Schurman, at Peking, and it was further stated that the Department's doubts were increased by the wide disregard of treaty rights being shown by the provincial officials in China; moreover, it was said, the question of changing the status of the Mixed Court had best be left to the Commission on Extraterritoriality provided for at the Washington Conference.[60] Mr. Schurman, however, held very different views and cabled in response:

[55] Willoughby, *Foreign Rights and Interests in China,* Vol. 1, p. 6.
[56] Kotenev, *op. cit.,* p. 274.
[57] Hudson, *op. cit.,* p. 460.
[58] Keeton, *op. cit.,* p. 388.
[59] Mr. Charles Evans Hughes was then Secretary of State and Mr. MacMurray was Chief of the Far Eastern Division of the State Department.
[60] *Foreign Relations* (1925), p. 525.

"Court belongs to Chinese. We foreigners found it a derelict in 1911 and took possession of it. Chinese have never been reconciled to the seizure and the court's decisions are not recognized anywhere in China. If we returned the Court the regard shown for China's rights would strengthen not weaken us in the assertion of our own treaty rights."[61]

Furthermore, Mr. Schurman said, the issue of the rendition of the Mixed Court formed a basic cause of the resentment of Chinese against foreigners and until this cause was removed it would be impossible to secure any public improvements in Shanghai with the co-operation of the Chinese. He also expressed the opinion that as the other Powers were prepared to proceed with the negotiations, opposition from the United States would be "fatal" to American interests and policy; nor did he believe that the issue would be used as an opening wedge for the surrender of extraterritorial rights as, in his estimation, the two issues of the rendition of the Court and the abolition of extraterritoriality existed as separate entities which were not likely to be confused in the Chinese mind.[62] On Mr. Schurman's insistence, the State Department authorized him to proceed with the negotiations, declaring that they did not wish to adopt an isolated position in opposing rendition "even for a temporary period," and that they were prepared to rely on the American Minister's statement that restitution of the Court to the Chinese was not associated in the public mind with the surrender of extraterritoriality.[63] In the end, however, the negotiations undertaken in 1924 were interrupted by political disturbances in China.[64]

After the May 30th Incident, the outcry among the Chinese for representation in the municipal government of the International Settlement was coupled with the demand for the return of the Shanghai Mixed Court to Chinese control. In November, 1925, the Chinese Foreign Office submitted to the Diplomatic Body a draft formula which contemplated various radical changes in the constitution of the Court.[65] A few weeks later negotiations were started through commissions set up informally by the interested foreign Ministers and the Wai Chiao Pu, but after several months of effort it became evident that the negotiations had reached a deadlock.[66] Mr. MacMurray sent a cable to the State Department in May, 1926, describing the situation:

The inability of the foreign and Chinese delegates to agree upon terms of rendition arises from the insistence of the Chinese representatives that

[61] *Ibid.*, p. 526.
[62] *Ibid.*
[63] *Ibid.*, p. 527.
[64] Keeton, *op. cit.*, Vol. 1, p. 388.
[65] *Foreign Relations* (1926), p. 1029.
[66] *Ibid.*, pp. 1030-1031.

the reconstituted court shall consist partly of a purely Chinese court organized and conducted practically as would be the case if it were functioning in an area under Chinese control. The foreign representatives have done their best to satisfy this desire to the utmost practical limit, but they have, of course, been obliged to stop short of undertaking to alter the mode of administration of the International Settlement. They have kept in mind that the court that functions in the International Settlement must be in such relations with the Municipal Council and the foreign Consuls concerned that it shall serve as an efficient instrument in the control of the International Settlement and in the maintenance of its peace and neutrality. One means essential to the attainment of this end is the functioning of foreign Assessors in all police and criminal cases arising in the Settlement, and to this the Chinese representatives have interposed, up to the present moment, an absolute veto.[67]

Mr. MacMurray emphasized several times the disappointment of the members of the Diplomatic Body that the difficulties which had been encountered in the negotiations would make it impossible to reach an agreement before the first anniversary of the May 30th Incident when it was feared that a new wave of anti-foreign feeling might sweep over the International Settlement at Shanghai. The Ministers, the Consular Body at Shanghai, and the members of the Municipal Council were making every effort, he said, to settle outstanding questions "with the special hope of ameliorating Sino-foreign tension before May 30th."[68]

As far as the Mixed Court issue was concerned, Mr. MacMurray felt that one of the greatest difficulties lay in the attitude of the Chinese commission which was conducting the negotiations. He thought that the members were not disposed to grant an "even open-minded" hearing to the foreign point of view.[69] In his opinion, this was due to the fact that the authority and power of the Peking Government had dwindled to such an extent that its officials had little sense of responsibility and were primarily bent on insuring their tenure of office by piling up "a record of patriotic zeal in opposing foreigners."[70] Therefore, after it became apparent that the discussions had reached a deadlock, Mr. MacMurray suggested that the negotiations should be transferred to the Consuls and the local Chinese authorities at Shanghai, an idea which was accepted by the other foreign Ministers.[71]

Mr. MacMurray said in recounting the subsequent developments:

The interested Ministers resolved at that point upon the experiment of transferring the negotiation of a preliminary agreement along the lines

[67] *Ibid.*, p. 1029.
[68] *Ibid.*, p. 1030; see, also, *ibid.*, p. 1029.
[69] *Ibid.*, p. 673 (cable paraphrased).
[70] *Ibid.*
[71] *Ibid.*, p. 1031.

they had tried in vain to get the Foreign Office to consider, to the Consular Body at Shanghai. An offer of a more satisfactory agreement from the viewpoint of foreign interests than the compromise proposed by the Ministers to the Foreign Office was made within a few days to the consuls by Sun Ch'uan-fang. Presumably this was not because he is better than other Chinese militarists, but because in fact he does control the Shanghai area, is involved in its prosperity himself, and, therefore, is interested parties [party?] in assuming responsibility for seeking a settlement which might contribute to produce conditions of order in his bailiwick favorable to trade.[72]

After eight conferences, an agreement for the return of the Mixed Court to the Chinese was concluded at Shanghai. It was signed in September, 1926, by the interested foreign Ministers at Peking and by the Chinese Government.[73]

The agreement provided for the establishment by the Kiangsu Provincial Government of the Shanghai Provisional Court in place of the Mixed Court.[74] Concerning the conduct of criminal cases affecting peace and order in the Settlement — including a breach of the Land Regulations and the By-Laws — it was stated that the Senior Consul should appoint a deputy "to sit with the Judge to watch proceedings," but that the concurrence of the deputy was not to be necessary for the validity of the judgment and that he was not to have the right to question prisoners or witnesses without the consent of the Judge, although he might record his objections. This clause applied also to all criminal cases in which the accused was in the employ of a foreigner having extraterritorial rights.

All laws (including laws of procedure) and ordinances applicable in other Chinese courts were to be applied in the Provisional Court. In civil or criminal cases where an extraterritorial foreigner was plaintiff or complainant, it was asserted that "the Consul of the nationality concerned or the Senior Consul may send an official to sit jointly with the Judge in accordance with the provisions of the treaties." A Court of Appeal was to be established to deal with criminal cases directly affecting the peace and order of the Settlement and with mixed criminal cases. The President of the Provisional Court was to act concurrently as President of the Court of Appeal; where the Senior Consul's deputy or a consular official sat in the original hearing a different deputy was to sit in the appeal. Judges of the Provisional Court and the Court of Appeal were to be appointed by the Kiangsu Provincial Government.

Other clauses of the 1926 rendition agreement (together with an ex-

[72] *Ibid.*, p. 673 (cable paraphrased).
[73] Hudson, *op. cit.*, p. 460.
[74] Text of the agreement in Keeton, *op. cit.*, p. 393.

change of notes which supplemented the agreement) covered a wide variety of issues. Among the most important provisions were two which stated: that all summonses, warrants, and orders of the Court were valid when signed by the Judge, although those executed on premises occupied by extraterritorial foreigners had still to be countersigned by a Consul; and that only in cases involving ten years' imprisonment or more, did the Court have to report to the Kiangsu Provincial Government for approval, the arrangement being that if approval were refused the case was to be reheard.

The settlement affecting the rendition of the Court was to remain in force for three years, at the end of which time any modifications could be proposed. It was expressly stated, however, that the agreement in no way bound the Chinese Government in any discussion with the Powers concerning the abolition of extraterritoriality.[75]

The provisions of the Mixed Court agreement received the full support of the United States Government. Mr. MacMurray informed Washington in July that he considered the draft agreement "a very acceptable solution" of the Mixed Court problem. "Rendition of the Court," he cabled further, "should have a very salutary effect on Chinese public sentiment."[76] The Secretary of State responded immediately by approving the terms of the agreement.[77] Moreover, when obstacles arose which might have prevented the agreement from going into effect, Mr. MacMurray showed a vigorous and determined desire to push matters through to their ultimate conclusion. On one occasion when it looked as though some of the foreign Powers might seek to block the negotiations, he suggested to the State Department that the United States should announce "very bluntly" that it would if necessary make a public statement of its attitude.[78] In the end, however, no drastic action was necessary as full agreement was reached by all the parties concerned.[79]

While the matter of the rendition of the Court was made the subject of formal negotiations between representatives of the Chinese and foreign governments, it nevertheless paralleled the action taken in respect to the inclusion of Chinese in the Shanghai Municipal Council by illustrating clearly the temper of the foreign community in Shanghai at this time. In general, the foreigners who were in favor of Chinese representation on the Municipal Council were also ready to support the proposal for the return of the Mixed Court to the Chinese. Mr. Fessenden in speaking at the Annual

[75] For statement of the Commission on Extraterritoriality on Mixed Courts in China, see above, p. 179.
[76] *Foreign Relations* (1926), p. 1032.
[77] *Ibid.*, p. 1033.
[78] *Ibid.*, p. 1034; see also *ibid.*, p. 1033.
[79] *Ibid.*, p. 1040.

Meeting of Ratepayers in 1926 stated that the members of the Shanghai
Municipal Council regarded an early and satisfactory adjustment of the
Mixed Court issue as a matter of "special importance to the community at
this time"; "I can assure both you and our Chinese friends," he said, "that
we intend to do all we can towards this end."[80] The *China Weekly Review*
emphasized repeatedly its desire to see the Mixed Court restored to the
control of the Chinese and declared that most foreign residents of Shanghai
realized that some definite move had to be made in this direction.[81] In
July, 1926, the *North China Herald* stated editorially:

> One point must be clearly borne in mind. There is no question but the
> Mixed Court must be handed back. When the Manchus fell in 1911, the
> Consular Body were justified in taking over the control of it in view of the
> general state of flux and uncertainty. But their right to have retained it is
> another matter. . . . Long before the events of May 30th, rendition was being
> negotiated in Peking. The question was first taken up more than ten years
> ago and discussions, though unavoidably interrupted from time to time,
> have always been continuous.[82]

The editors of the *North China Herald* made it clear that they were
in no way arguing for the abolition of extraterritorial rights; but, they said, the
scare raised by certain portions of the foreign community in the International Settlement that rendition of the Mixed Court would threaten the
entire extraterritorial system was unfounded.[83]

This statement of the *North China Herald's* was presumably a reference
to activities of the American lawyers in Shanghai who were strongly opposed to the rendition agreement. In July, the Far Eastern American Bar
Association published a letter attacking an article which had appeared in the
local press, containing what purported to be the next of the agreement under
negotiation and which was, in fact, in all essential points similar to the
provisions of the final settlement.[84] The American lawyers charged that the
extraterritorial rights of all foreigners in Shanghai were being threatened.
They explained that the general proposal for the return of the Court met
with their approval but that it must be effected on terms that would make
it an "ideal court," not on terms that would re-establish the conditions that
had existed before 1911 and would subject the Court to the "caprices and
whims of every self-constituted *tuchun*" in control of the region around
Shanghai. The Association, in addition, passed resolutions "to run a public-

[80] *Shanghai Municipal Gazette*, April 15, 1926, p. 125.
[81] See, for example, *China Weekly Review*, April 13, 1926, p. 107.
[82] *North China Herald*, July 24, 1926, p. 148.
[83] *Ibid.*
[84] Text of letter in *North China Herald*, July 17, 1926, pp. 108, 522.

ity campaign explaining the necessity of not returning the Court under the present conditions" and to appoint a committee "to go to Peking to lay before the Legations all details of the case against rendition."[85]

The activities of the American lawyers drew fire both from the *North China Herald* and the *China Weekly Review*. The former printed the letter of the American Bar Association but announced simultaneously that it would henceforth close its columns to any similar communications which it regarded as part of a "wild and unsubstantiated agitation worked up by interested parties" to create a scare in Shanghai that might do considerable harm.[86] The *China Weekly Review* declared that even if the interests of certain foreign attorneys were adversely affected — which it regarded as unlikely — these men should not permit personal interests to obstruct the solution of an international problem of the utmost importance to Chinese and foreigners.[87]

Both the *North China Herald* and the *China Weekly Review* greeted the terms of the rendition agreement when it was finally published with enthusiasm. The *China Weekly Review* wrote that:

"To consular and Chinese officials responsible for this diplomatic accomplishment are due the thanks of the entire community and save by the inevitable diehards and certain members of the legal profession they are being freely expressed."[88]

The *North China Herald* described the news of the rendition agreement as "welcome" and stated that it gave ample protection to the interests of foreigners and also guarded against the abuses which had become part of the Mixed Court practice. "There are already enough points of difference between Chinese and foreigners"; it added in a burst of frankness, "on some we are right; on others, the Chinese; and it is bad policy to obscure the issues in the former class by showing obstinacy where we have obviously 'no case.' "[89]

The rendition of the Shanghai Mixed Court took place on January 1, 1927, and the Provisional Court came into being. Thus the negotiations concerning the Court which had been carried on intermittently for so many years reached at least a temporary solution. From Mr. MacMurray's statements it is evident that the pressure exerted by the anti-foreign movement, after the spring of 1925, had its effect in bringing about a settlement of the Mixed Court issue. The approval with which the rendition agreement was

---

[85] Kotenev, *Shanghai: Its Municipality and the Chinese*, Shanghai, 1937, pp. 179-181.
[86] *North China Herald*, July 24, 1925, pp. 148, 158.
[87] *China Weekly Review*, July 24, 1926, p. 181.
[88] *Ibid.*
[89] *North China Herald*, January 8, 1927, p. 7.

greeted by a large part of the foreign community at Shanghai showed — in much the same way as the proposal for the reorganization of the Shanghai Municipal Council — the extent to which foreigners were willing to go in meeting the demands of the Chinese in 1926. In respect to the Mixed Court, as the *North China Herald* indicated, most foreigners felt that their "case" was far from sound; the right of the Consular Body to retain control of the Court since 1911 was regarded as decidedly dubious and some of the practices which had arisen, especially in connection with the trial of purely Chinese cases, were looked upon as unjust. Moreover, it is essential to recognize fully that the rendition of the Court in no way involved the relinquishment of any extraterritorial rights.

Unfortunately the widespread good will which greeted the establishment of the Provisional Court was to turn, in many quarters, into a feeling of acute disappointment, frequently expressed in the most severe criticism. The hope that a settlement of the Mixed Court issue would lead to a lessening of tension between Chinese and foreigners was in fact dissipated almost as soon as the Provisional Court began to exercise its judicial functions.[90]

[90] In articles and editorials too numerous to be cited, the *North China Herald* carried on an open war against the Provisional Court. For the less heated but very serious criticisms of Mr. MacMurray and his fellow-Ministers at Peking, see *Foreign Relations* (1929), pp. 562-566, 579. For an evaluation of the work of the Provisional Court, see Johnstone, *op. cit.*, pp. 160-162.

Despite these difficulties, however, an agreement was signed by representatives of the Powers concerned in February, 1930, which provided for the replacement of the Provisional Court by a District Court that was substantially the same as any of the regular District Courts of China and formed an integral part of the Chinese judicial system. (Pollard, *op. cit.*, p. 382.)

CHAPTER XI

STATEMENTS OF POLICY

From January, 1927, on, events in China moved forward with extraordinary and relentless speed as the National Revolution advanced toward its climax.

Although these developments will be discussed in this and the following chapters, an over-all picture should be kept in mind. Briefly stated, both Great Britain and the United States issued declarations of policy at the end of 1926 and the beginning of 1927 setting forth their views concerning a modification of the treaty system. While these documents were very liberal in their desire to meet some of the Chinese demands, the policies of both countries were complicated by the development of a highly critical military situation in China. In January, 1927, the fighting between the Northern and Southern forces was concentrated in the Yangtze Valley and was beginning to threaten seriously the centers where many foreigners resided. As a consequence the foreign Powers were faced with the immediate need of having to protect their nationals against the increasing danger which confronted them. In order to meet this situation, the British Government, late in January, began to dispatch a substantial body of troops to China, and the American Government, a few weeks later, ordered a contingent of marines to Shanghai. Thus, at the very time that the British and American Governments were making various suggestions concerning a revision of the treaties with the Chinese, they were also engaged in sending military forces to China.

In the United States, the picture was further complicated by the activities of Congress and the press. In January and February, 1927, the question of a modification of the treaties was discussed in the House of Representatives, where members showed that they were strongly in favor of the United States' adopting an independent policy in China if such independence was necessary to bring about a generous readjustment of China's treaty position. The action of Congress, coupled with the sensational stories that were filling the newspapers concerning the attacks on foreigners in China and the dispatch of American and British forces, naturally attracted the attention of the public and resulted in mobilizing editorial opinion in many parts of the United States. Much of the significance, however, of the debates in Congress and of the editorial activities of the press lay precisely in the fact that they occurred at a time when the security of our citizens in China was being placed in real jeopardy, a matter which would normally be expected to lead to a considerable rise in tension between the nations involved.

It was against this background that Secretary of State Kellogg issued one of his few public declarations of American policy toward China, on January 27, 1927. The Secretary's statement was intended as a response to the memorandum published by the British Government on Christmas Day in 1926. On receiving the British memorandum, Mr. Kellogg let it be known that he would send a reply but, for reasons which will be seen shortly, he continued to postpone taking further action until the 27th of the following month despite constant questioning by newspapermen in this country.[1]

Ostensibly, the reason for drafting the British memorandum, as already stated, was to settle the complications that had arisen over the tariff issue. Actually, however, the British went far beyond a discussion of the tariff problem and the memorandum consisted largely of a sweeping re-examination of the principles which had governed the relations of China and the Treaty Powers in the past. The reason which led the British to reconsider their policy was stated in the text of the memorandum,[2] namely, that the situation in China had altered entirely since the time of the Washington Conference and that it was therefore necessary to develop and adapt the policies that had been agreed upon at Washington to the changes that had since taken place. In the existing state of confusion, it was said, it had proved impossible to proceed with the larger program of treaty revision that had been foreshadowed at the Washington Conference. On the other hand, while the political situation in China had disintegrated and the authority of the Peking Government diminished almost to the vanishing point, this development had been accompanied by the growth of a "powerful nationalist movement" which aimed at obtaining for the Chinese nation an equal place among the countries of the world; "any failure to meet this movement with sympathy and understanding," the British said, "would not respond to the real intentions of the Powers towards China."

The British suggested that the foreign governments should issue a statement setting forth the essential facts of the situation and declaring their readiness to enter into a revision of the treaties and an adjustment of all other outstanding questions as soon as the Chinese had constituted a government with the authority to negotiate:

[1] See, for example, the *New York Times,* January 4, 1927, p. 27; January 5, p. 4; January 6, pp. 1-2.
[2] Text in *Foreign Relations* (1926), pp. 923-929.

His Majesty's Government propose that in this joint declaration the Powers should make it clear that ... they desire to go as far as possible towards meeting the legitimate aspirations of the Chinese nation. They should abandon the idea that the economic and political development of China can only be secured under foreign tutelage, and should declare their readiness to recognize her right to the enjoyment of tariff autonomy as soon as she herself has settled and promulgated a new national tariff. They should expressly disclaim any intention of forcing foreign control upon an unwilling China. While calling upon China to maintain that respect for the sanctity of treaties which is the primary obligation common to all civilized states, the Powers should yet recognize both the essential justice of the Chinese claim for treaty revision and the difficulty under the present conditions of negotiating new treaties in the place of old, and they should therefore modify their traditional attitude of rigid insistence on the strict letter of treaty rights. During this possibly very prolonged period of uncertainty the Powers can only, in the view of His Majesty's Government, adopt an expectant attitude and endeavor to shape developments so far as possible in conformity with the realities of the situation so that ultimately when treaty revision becomes possible, it will be found that part at least of the revision has already been effected on satisfactory lines. It would therefore be wise to abandon the policy of ineffective protest over minor matters, reserving protest — which should then be made effective by united action — only for cases where vital interests are at stake. Every case should be considered on its merits and the declaration should show that the Powers are prepared to consider in a sympathetic spirit any reasonable proposals that the Chinese authorities, wherever situated, may make, even if contrary to strict interpretation of treaty rights, in return for fair and considerate treatment of foreign interests by them. The declaration should show that it is the policy of the Powers to endeavor to maintain harmonious relations with China without waiting for or insisting on the prior establishment of a strong central Government.

These principles of policy, the memorandum stated, should be applied to the problems at hand. In respect to the question of extraterritoriality, it was suggested that the recommendations in the Report of the Commission on Extraterritoriality and other reforms not covered by the Report but "falling under the general heading of extraterritoriality" could be carried out with little delay. In regard to the tariff issue, the memorandum entered into a significant discussion of the work of the Special Tariff Conference which ran as follows:

The foreign Delegations at the Special Tariff Conference were not satisfied with the assurance given by the Chinese as to the purposes to which the Chinese Government would devote the proceeds of the Washington surtaxes; they were, in fact, only prepared to grant the surtaxes under conditions which would ensure that the proceeds would be placed under foreign control and applied in great part to the liquidation of the unsecured debt. The British Government had been opposed to dealing with the question of the unsecured debt from the outset, as they foresaw that it might defeat the intentions of the Washington Conference which were "to assist the economic and political development of China and to relax — not to tighten — foreign control." It had been said that debt consolidation would be of permanent benefit to China because it would restore her credit. But under the circumstances existing in China, debt consolidation could only enable the faction which happened to be in power in Peking to resort to fresh ruinous and unproductive borrowing. Moreover, a further objection to the inclusion of the unsecured debt in the negotiations of the Tariff Conference had been brought into relief by the grant, in principle, of tariff autonomy, which raised at once, in an acute form, the question of control over the customs revenue. His Majesty's Government viewed with grave misgivings the proposal that foreign control should be extended over additional revenues which might be increased by tariff autonomy. "In 1921 it was natural that the Powers should demand guarantees for the due fulfillment of the benevolent purposes which the Washington Conference aimed at achieving. But what might have been practicable in 1921 was no longer possible in 1926. It was obvious that China would not now submit to any extension of foreign control either for debt consolidation or for the abolition of *likin,* and it seemed to His Majesty's Government that for the Powers to unite in an attempt to impose control upon an unwilling China would be entirely opposed to the spirit of the Washington treaties and to the policy which His Majesty's Government had consistently advocated."

It was in this context that the British memorandum advocated the immediate and unconditional grant of the Washington surtaxes. The fundamental issue involved was obviously not the question of the levy of the surtaxes but the application of the principle that the Powers must "abandon the idea that the economic and political development of China can only be secured under foreign tutelage." The objection might be raised, the memorandum declared, that in view of the fact that the Washington surtaxes had already been imposed illegally in some parts of China, the proposal for the levy of the surtaxes throughout the country would, in strict logic, amount to a condoning of a breach of the treaties. This argument, it was said, did not sufficiently take into account the realities of the situation: the basic facts were that the treaties were in many respects out of date and that in an attempt to secure a revision of the treaties the Chinese were hampered, on the one hand, by their own internal disunity, and, on the other, by the necessity of obtaining the unanimous concurrence of the Powers. "His Majesty's Government," the memorandum asserted, "attach the greatest importance to the sanctity of treaties, but they believe that this principle may best be maintained by a sympathetic adjustment of treaty rights to the equitable claims of the Chinese. Protests should be reserved for cases where there is an attempt at wholesale repudiation of treaty obligations or an attack upon the legitimate and vital interests of foreigners in China and in these cases protests should be made by the united action of the Powers."

According to some of the press accounts of the times, the Christmas memorandum of the British Foreign Office was greeted with consternation by the governments of the other Treaty Powers. The New York *Herald Tribune* remarked, with a show of amusement, that Paris was "unhesitatingly skeptical," Tokyo "frankly unenthusiastic,"[3] and Washington "uncomfortably pleased."[4] The London *Times* correspondent in Washington reported to his paper that the United States Government regarded the British declaration as an "attempt to steal the American thunder."[5]

The British memorandum did in fact challenge the leadership which Secretary of State Kellogg had assumed in calling the Special Conference on the Chinese Customs Tariff and the Commission on Extraterritoriality. Moreover, it is clear from numerous assertions made in official and unofficial circles in the United States at this time that many Americans were especially sensitive to any action which threatened what they regarded as the leadership of their country in a progressive and sympathetic policy toward China. Some of this feeling may have been reflected in the rather grudging tone of the comments made by a State Department spokesman the day after the receipt of the Christmas memorandum, in which he described the British proposal as outlining a "more conciliatory attitude" and com-

[3] On December 31st, the Japanese Ambassador at Washington told Mr. Johnson that his Government was "somewhat surprised" at the action taken by the British in their memorandum. "He stated," Mr. Johnson records, "that the method which the British Government has used in this matter made it very difficult for co-operation among the Japanese, British, and American Governments on these matters, a thing which the Japanese Government had hoped very much could be brought about; his Government felt that the British memorandum had precipitated a very difficult situation in the Far East as regards China, and that it was almost impossible to know how to deal with it. He said that the Japanese Government desired very much to prevent any separation of China into several parts, a thing which he felt the British Memorandum rather encouraged than discouraged." (*Foreign Relations*, 1926, p. 936.)

[4] Quoted in the *Literary Digest*, January 15, 1927, p. 9.

[5] London *Times*, January 5, 1927.

The 1926 volume of the *Survey of International Affairs* states similarly: " . . . in the United States, the British memorandum caused an embarrassment almost indistinguishable in effect from disapproval, just because the British proposals advocated a fresh step forward on the very path in which the United States had long been accustomed to regard herself as the pioneer among foreign Powers concerned with China. . . . Even in American quarters which were not unfriendly to Great Britain, there were traces of a suspicion that the British Government had been moved by the pressure of Chinese strikes and boycotts to 'steal the thunder' of the State Department at Washington." (p. 330.)

ing "nearer to American policy toward China than any previous pronouncement from Great Britain on the situation."[6]

In Peking, the contents of the British memorandum had been made known in advance of publication, to the members of the Diplomatic Body. Mr. MacMurray cabled to Washington at once saying that the memorandum contained in essence only two new points: the willingness to accept immediately and unconditionally what was referred to as "tariff autonomy" and the proposal that the Powers adopt the policy of condoning all but the graver infractions of foreign treaty rights in China.

While it is justifiable and perhaps advisable for the Powers in their relations with China to adopt a mighty [less?] querulous and petty attitude in the matter of protests against insignificant infractions of the treaties, broad formula now proposed by the British with regard to condoning disregard of their obligations by the Chinese in all matters which the Powers may not unanimously consider vital, is in effect, an invitation to the Chinese to carry the principle of repudiation to whatever may prove to be the limit of tolerance on the part of the Powers.

It seems to me a matter of grave doubt whether these two fundamental points of the British program are well advised. With regard to obviously necessary modification of existing treaty rights there are in general three possible courses to pursue: First, renunciation by the Powers with a view to placating China's nationalistic feeling; second, acquiesence by the Powers (whether willingly or grudgingly) in a policy of repudiation by the Chinese; third, orderly negotiation with a view to readjustment of unsatisfactory or illiberal treaty provisions by mutual consent, simultaneously with insistence upon full respect for existing obligations until thus modified. The last-named seems to me to offer the only possibility of making the necessary readjustments reasonably and with fairness to the interests of both parties. The British program appears to ignore that possibility and to be directed towards placating Chinese feeling by concessions which I fear will scarcely at all appease nationalistic aspirations but will on the other hand encourage them to force other issues which are not contemplated by the British — such as the integrity of the Maritime Customs organization, the existence of Shanghai International Settlement, and of the various concessions, extra-territorial, special privileges of missionaries with regard to residence and ownership of land in the interior, and (what may prove of particular importance to us) the question of restrictions upon Chinese immigration into foreign countries.[7]

Irrespective of the opinions of other governments and their official members, the fact remained that the British had drafted and were about to make public the statement of policy incorporated in their memorandum. Therefore, in practical terms, the United States faced the question

[6] *United States Daily,* December 28, 1926.
[7] *Foreign Relations* (1926), pp. 920-921.

of the attitude it cared to take toward this unexpected move on the part of the British. Concerning this problem, Mr. MacMurray said in his dispatch to Washington:

The fact remains, however, that once the British program is made public . . . the mere fact that such radical concessions have been made by the nation which is still predominant in the trade of China will compel us whether we like it or not to offer the same concessions on our part. The British will have forced our hands in view of the impossibility of our maintaining consistently or with any hope of success an attitude ostensibly less liberal than theirs. And, if we are to be compelled to fall in with this policy, it seems to me advisable that we should do so with a good grace and in spirit of loyal co-operation toward making it a success in the interest of all foreign Powers, recognizing that though not ideal it offers possibility of uniting the Treaty Powers in what the statement itself terms "a constructive policy in harmony with the spirit of the Washington Conference but developed and adopted to meet the altered circumstances of the present time."[8]

As soon as the news of the British memorandum reached Washington, the Secretary of State wired to Mr. MacMurray: "It is my desire that you fully support the British program in the conferences of the Diplomatic Body."[9] The United States Government had been anxious, he said, to put into effect the Washington surtaxes and it was now willing to have them put into force unconditionally throughout China. "Our urging the Powers to broaden the scope of the Special Conference on the Chinese Tariff," he added, ". . . was done with a view to making certain that the Conference would take up . . . the question of granting tariff autonomy to China."[10]

He stated further:

There is no reason that I can see why you should not make known at Peking that the British recommendations have formed part of the United States Government's policy for a long time. And I wish you to know that I contemplate making an address soon on the subject of our relations with China. In this I expect to make a statement of the readiness of this Government to negotiate with a Government representing China for the purpose of revising the existing American treaties in the directions of relinquishing the extraterritorial privileges of Americans in China and of granting China the right to establish her own tariff rates on products of American origin.[11]

In reply to this message, Mr. MacMurray cabled advising the Secretary to reconsider his plan:

[8] *Ibid.*, p. 921.
[9] *Ibid.*, p. 922 (cable paraphrased).
[10] *Ibid.*
[11] *Ibid.*

My earnest advice is not to offer or to commit ourselves to make concessions, at present, beyond those in contemplation in the decisions of the Washington Conference as enlarged later in the Special Customs Conference. It would gain us no consideration or respect on the part of the [Chinese] to do so. Indeed it would give them courage to deprive us and other foreigners of all special privileges, and ordinary rights as well, and to open up again the issue of Chinese immigration. Furthermore, to do so would enable the charge to be made by the Japanese and the British that we had, to use the terms which would be used, betrayed the collective interests common to the Powers. . . .

Secretary Kellogg had, however, already completed the draft of the reply that he intended to make to the British memorandum and, on December 29, he forwarded the text to the Legation at Peking, requesting Mr. MacMurray to cable his criticisms in full. Mr. Kellogg explained the purposes he had had in mind in composing the draft: he had not wished completely to disregard or scrap the work of the Washington Conference and the treaties that resulted therefrom; but he had wanted to show that the United States was willing to make "ample concessions" to China and was prepared to enter into discussions concerning such concessions with any Chinese Government.[12]

The Secretary's reply to the British memorandum reviewed for the most part the efforts that had been made since June, 1925, to revise the Sino-foreign treaties placing particular emphasis upon the rôle which the United States had played in furthering these efforts.[13] It stated that the American Delegation to the Tariff Conference had been instructed not only to carry out the letter and the spirit of the Washington Customs Treaty but also to discuss any reasonable proposal that the Chinese Government might make for a general revision of the treaties on the subject of the tariff. The American Delegation had suggested that the Conference at once authorize the levy of the Washington surtaxes; it had affirmed the principle of respect for China's tariff autonomy; and it had announced its willingness to negotiate a new treaty that would bring that principle into effect. The American technical advisers at the Conference had co-operated with the other technical advisers in the working out of a new tariff schedule for China. While the Conference had continued its informal sessions into the summer of 1926, no agreement could be reached as the Central Government of China had ceased to exist. The Conference had, therefore, adjourned on July 3, 1926, the Delegates expressing their desire to proceed with its work at the earliest possible moment when the Delegates of the Chinese Government were in a position to resume negotiations. "The Gov-

[12] *Ibid.* (1925), p. 937 (cable paraphrased).
[13] Text in *ibid.* (1926), pp. 930-934.

ernment of the United States," the draft declared, "was ready then and is ready now to proceed with the program of the Special Conference"; further-more, it was said that "as a preliminary step and before the resumption of negotiations" the Government of the United States was prepared to consent to the immediate imposition of the Washington surtaxes.

The work of the Commission on Extraterritoriality and the official statements of the American Government in respect to the abolition of extra-territoriality were also briefly summarized in the draft reply. It was asserted that the United States had always regarded the extraterritorial system as a *modus vivendi,* necessary for harmonious relations with the Chinese until the laws and legal conceptions of China developed to a point that would make the existence of extraterritorial privileges unnecessary. In respect to the existing situation and the official attitude of the United States Gov-ernment, the draft reply stated that:

"As soon as a Government of China is established which demonstrates its ability to insure peace and security to its people in the legitimate pursuit of their affairs, the Government of the United States will be prepared im-mediately to enter into negotiations for the relinquishment of its extraterri-torial control over its citizens in China."

In its conclusion the draft dealt with a number of outstanding points:

The Government of the United States has watched with sympathetic interest the nationalistic awakening of China and welcomes every advance made by the Chinese people toward reorganizing their system of Government.

During the difficult years since the establishment of the new régime in 1912, the Government of the United States has endeavored in every way to maintain an attitude of the most careful and strict neutrality as among the several factions that have disputed with one another for control in China. Continuing its policy of non-interference in the internal affairs of the Chinese people, the Government of the United States awaits anxiously the day when a Government will appear in China which will be prepared to negotiate in China's behalf concerning the many questions outstanding. This Government wishes to deal with such a Government and the people of China in a most liberal spirit. It holds no concessions in China, enjoys no special privileges, and has never manifested any imperialistic attitude toward China. All that the United States desires is that its citizens be given equal opportunity with the citizens of the other Powers to reside in China and to pursue their legitimate occupations without special privileges, monopolies or spheres of special interest or influence.

From the above it will be seen that the concrete proposals concerning a further consideration of the tariff issue and the relinquishment of extra-territorial rights were based on the principle that the United States would only be prepared to negotiate with China when a Government was established which could maintain peace and security. This was of course the thesis to which the Secretary of State had adhered with persistence since the Chinese Revolution of 1925-1928 had got underway. In explaining this aspect of the draft reply to Mr. MacMurray, the Secretary stated: "In my opinion it seemed inadvisable to recognize at this time the different Chinese factions but instead to use at least our moral influence for a united China."[14]

When, on January 5, 1927, Mr. MacMurray sent his comments on the draft reply to Washington, it was to say that he thought the publication of the reply would be inadvisable as its purpose would be misconstrued by both foreigners in China and Chinese:

> I do not wholly like the substance of the British memorandum nor the time and manner of its presentation. But I feel nevertheless that we perforce must go as far as they; on the other hand, it would be dangerous for us to appear to outbid them, and if we ourselves were to present a program which was less adapted to the circumstances of the situation as they actually exist, it would react upon us unfavorably. Frankly, the impression is made upon my mind by a reading of the draft reply that it does not constitute a reply at all. Instead it is a declaration of which the interpretation would be made that it was a competitive protestation of American sympathy for China and that it offers actually less than the proposal of the British offers; everything in it, beyond granting the Washington surtaxes, is linked to the conditioning fact that we are awaiting the establishment in China of an effective government. Therefore, it would appear to the Chinese that the proposals embodied in the draft reply were completely illusory, if indeed, they did not appear to the Chinese to be, particularly in the last paragraph, unscrupulous. Apparently the intention of the draft reply is, by offering a program of negotiations that would be acceptable, to conciliate Chinese nationalist feeling. My conviction is that any question whether one or another program is acceptable to the Chinese must be discounted. No considerable element of the Chinese will accept any one of them....
>
> It seems to me, assuming, as granted, that we are sincere in our declarations of sympathy in regard to what is genuine in the aspirations of the Chinese people internationally, that it is not our immediate essential problem to declare in the face of Chinese importunities how much we will or must concede of our rights; it is to decide how we can arrange as a practical matter to grant what is necessary to the fulfillment of our own obligations and to avoid appearing to fail in carrying out the promises we made at the Washington and the Tariff Conferences....
>
> I assume your intention is to make the proposed draft reply public. If this were done, it would be considered by those few officials who read it as an academic recital of details not in themselves of any interest. It would seem to the very primitive native press, and to Chinese opinion in the large, merely to indicate that our Government felt lukewarm toward the proposal made by the British; that our Government was unable or unwilling to suggest of its own accord any alternative except generalities which are rendered

[14] *Ibid.*, p. 937 (cable parapharsed).

meaningless by the "joker" they contain; and that our Government, in disavowing imperialist motives and avowing readiness to accept for its nationals the same treatment which is acceptable to the other nations, is abandoning the leadership accruing to it out of the Conference at Washington and is reverting to the policy by which other nationalities are allowed to do the fighting for the United States. I admit regretfully that among the Chinese there is rather generally a disposition to believe that we may be expected always to make concessions up to the utmost limit and then to calculate upon profiting from what may be obtained by other Powers through individual action.

Most respectfully I say that I cannot but counsel you that without any question the publication of the draft reply would leave on Chinese minds the fundamental impression that in the new situation created by the fact that a central government in China has disappeared virtually completely and irretrievably, we have failed to confront the situation and adapt ourselves to it. Political thought in China is quite incapable of understanding the difficulties we find in meeting the problems which their own lack of national organization has created. If we Americans are to avoid giving the Chinese reason to be disappointed and disillusioned with our sincerity and ability we must find some way by which we can deal with the realities of China's condition of not having a real government and not likely to have one during an uncertain number of years in the future, except in the event, which is rather improbable, that the Kuomintang succeeds in extending its effective control over the whole country.[15]

It was approximately at the time that Mr. MacMurray sent the above dispatch that Secretary of State Kellogg decided to postpone the issuance of his reply to the British memorandum, in order to discuss matters with Mr. MacMurray when he arrived in Washington.[16] On January 4th, it was announced at the State Department that Mr. MacMurray had been asked to return home for consultation.[17] Some two weeks later the American Minister left Peking for the United States but was stopped shortly after his departure by the Department in Washington which requested him to return to his post at the Legation because of the increasing gravity of the military situation in China.[18]

In the meantime officials in Washington proceeded to redraft the American reply to the British memorandum. The final text was given to the press in the United States for publication on January 27, 1927, and instructions were sent to the Legation at Peking to release it at the same time in China.[19]

[15] *Ibid.,* pp. 937-940 (cable paraphrased).
[16] *New York Times,* January 6, 1927, p. 1.
[17] *United States Daily,* January 5, 1927, p. 3.
[18] *Ibid.,* January 22, 1927, p. 1.
[19] *Foreign Relations* (1927), pp. 350-353.

The final version of Secretary of State Kellogg's note to the British contained two extremely important amendments to the draft which had originally been sent to Mr. MacMurray. Both of these are to be found in the following paragraph:

The Government of the United States was ready then [in July, 1926, when the Special Tariff Conference adjourned] and is ready now to continue the negotiations on the entire subject of the tariff and extraterritoriality and to take up negotiations on behalf of the United States alone. The only question is with whom it shall negotiate. As I have said heretofore, if China can agree upon the appointment of delegates representing the authorities or the people of the country, we are prepared to negotiate such a treaty.

The first change is seen in Mr. Kellogg's announcement that the United States was prepared "to go it alone in China" — to quote the phrase that was popularly used — and would be willing to negotiate with the Chinese irrespective of the actions and the aims of the other Treaty Powers. The second significant change lay in the statement that the United States was ready to enter into negotiations with "delegates representing the authorities or the people" of China. This was clearly different from saying that the United States intended to wait until the time when there appeared a "government of China" capable of demonstrating "its ability to insure peace and security."

Exactly what the Secretary of State had in mind was specifically explained to the press at the Department of State, on the day following the publication of the reply to the British memorandum. The reply, an official spokesman said, was intended to convey the readiness of the United States Government to negotiate on the subjects of tariff autonomy and extraterritoriality with delegates from both the Cantonese and the Northern factions provided these factions could agree on entering into negotiations jointly.[20] In other words, Mr. Kellogg did not wish to deal separately with the Nationalist and the Peking régimes but was prepared to undertake formal discussions with one or more persons that had the authority to represent both groups.

Why Mr. Kellogg introduced these two changes into the original draft of his document must remain in the realm of speculation. Much had happened, however, since the first draft of his note was written, not the least important development being the action taken by Congress. Although this will be discussed in detail shortly, it is worth noting in connection with Mr. Kellogg's declaration of policy that the so-called Porter Resolution had been submitted to the House of Representatives on January 4th; that

[20] *United States Daily,* January 28, 1927, p. 1; *New York Times* of the same date, p. 1.

hearings on the Resolution had been held before the House Committee on Foreign Affairs in the week before Mr. Kellogg issued his statement; and that the Committee had passed a report in support of the Resolution. As it was specifically stated in the report that, in the view of the Committee, the United States Government should immediately enter into negotiations for a revision of the treaties with accredited agents of China "authorized to speak for the people of China" and should adopt a "distinctive American policy" operating independently, if necessary, of the other Treaty Powers, it is evident that Mr. Kellogg's policy was running parallel to the action taken in Congress.[21]

As far as Mr. Kellogg's intentions of pushing ahead with a program for a revision of the treaties is concerned, the public statements which he made at this time are supplemented by a series of memoranda, written by Mr. Nelson T. Johnson, Chief of the State Department's Division of Far Eastern Affairs, recording conversations which took place between the Secretary and Sao-ke Alfred Sze, the Chinese Minister at Washington, who was in touch with both the Northern and Southern régimes in China. According to one memorandum, Dr. Sze, on January 24th, urged Mr. Kellogg to make a statement of American policy; the Chinese, he said, were very much confused as to what policy the United States was in fact maintaining toward China.[22] The Secretary answered that he was planning to make a declaration shortly.[23] A few days later he told Dr. Sze that he was "very anxious to know what the Minister wanted him to say." Mr. Kellogg asked whether it would be satisfactory if he said that the United States was prepared to negotiate with anyone representing China for a revision of the tariff provisions of the treaty with a view to granting complete tariff autonomy to China. The Chinese Minister replied that this would be "very satisfactory." The Secretary then stated that, as regards extraterritoriality, the United

[21] It is probable that the Porter Resolution was introduced in order to test the opinion of Congress. Whether Mr. Porter took the initiative in introducing the Resolution or was prompted by the Department of State is not clear. In a memorandum written by Secretary of State Kellogg in November, 1928, there is, however, a strong suggestion that Mr. Kellogg was involved in the fate of the Bill in Congress. "I informed the Japanese Ambassador," the Secretary wrote in recording a conversation with the Japanese Ambassador, "that some time in December, 1926, as I recollect, Mr. Porter, . . . had passed [introduced?] a Joint Resolution calling on the United States to negotiate new treaties to take the place of the unequal treaties (as he called them) with China; that the Bill passed the House with very little objection and went to the Senate. I felt as though it would be better for the State Department to carry on the negotiations than to have the Bill pass and become a law." (*Foreign Relations*, 1927, p. 437.) On another occasion in the autumn of 1928, Secretary Kellogg again referred to the Porter Resolution and stated that it "would have passed the Senate if it had gone on there. . . ." (*Ibid.*, p. 428.)
[22] *Ibid.*, p. 52.
[23] *Ibid.*

States was ready to discuss the questions involved with the Chinese. The United States would, of course, expect that the Chinese would guarantee the protection of their courts for American citizens. He again asked whether this would be satisfactory to the Chinese and Dr. Sze answered that he could say without hesitation that it would. The Secretary added that he did not wish the conversation reported or in any way made public but was seeking to obtain information.[24]

On January 27th, after Mr. Kellogg's declaration of policy had been issued to the public, Dr. Sze called on the Secretary to discuss matters further. Speaking very frankly, he said, he felt that the Secretary's statement did not indicate clearly what the United States was prepared to do. The Minister declared that the Chinese were anxious to know the basis upon which the United States would be willing to negotiate, "whether on the old basis of the Tariff Conference and the Washington Conference or whether on a basis of equality and reciprocity." The Secretary replied that the State Department was willing to go into the whole question of the tariff and of extraterritoriality and was willing to do so at once. The Minister asserted that he thought the United States ought to name its delegation as the Chinese would be very much interested in the personnel of the delegation. The Secretary declared that he had not come to that question yet. Dr. Sze said that he understood the Secretary was not willing to negotiate with Wellington Koo (Foreign Minister at Peking) or with Eugene Chen. The Secretary answered that he did not understand that either Wellington Koo or Eugene Chen could claim to represent the whole of China. At this point in the conversation Mr. Johnson's memorandum records the following significant item: "The Secretary stated that he had understood the Minister to say that he felt sure he could obtain credentials from both sides for the conduct of negotiations with the Government of the United States or that both sides could agree upon representatives." The Minister said that this had been true early in December but that he did not believe it was still true.[25]

Whether because Peking and the Nationalists could not agree, or because of the mounting tension in the general relationship of China and the Powers, or for some other reason, negotiations between the United States and China were not begun at this time. On January 31st, a State Department representative made an oral statement to the press on behalf of Mr. Kellogg. The Chinese are at liberty, he said, to take advantage of Mr.

[24] *Ibid.*, p. 54.

[25] *Ibid.*, pp. 353-354. See also the comments on Mr. Kellogg's declaration which Dr. Sze issued publicly (the *New York Times*, January 29, 1927, p. 1). Dr. Sze did not mention in his public statement that he did not believe the Northern and Southern factions would be willing to conduct negotiations jointly.

Kellogg's offer of joint negotiations with both factions 'whenever they are prepared to do so. However, it was added, the Department "finds it difficult to take the initiative in a situation where Chang Tso-lin claims no negotiations may be carried on with Eugene Chen, and Eugene Chen, in turn, claims that no negotiations may be carried on with Chang Tso-lin."[26] A few days later, it was reported in the daily press that Mr. Kellogg had said that he had received no official indications that the Chinese wished to undertake joint negotiations.[27] On February 5th, President Coolidge reiterated that the United States was prepared to negotiate with both the Northern and Southern Governments of China and stated that there would be no change in the policy enunciated by the Secretary of State in his declaration of January 27th.[28]

In the following weeks news concerning any long-term policy such as that involved in a revision of the treaties was overshadowed by the more spectacular news of the fighting in China, the evacuation of foreign nationals from danger zones, and the dispatch of foreign troops either to China itself or to nearby points in the Pacific. Evidence that the State Department continued to think in terms of negotiating a treaty with the Chinese in the near future is, however, contained in the following cable sent to Mr. MacMurray by the Secretary of State on February 15th:

"Department desires that the Legation study the question of the provisions which should be written into a new treaty to take the place of existing treaties between the United States and China and that you report by mail your suggestions in this connection."[29]

[26] *United States Daily*, January 31, 1927, p. 1.
[27] New York *World*, February 3, 1927, p. 1.
[28] *Ibid.*, February 5, 1927, p. 4.
[29] *Foreign Relations* (1927), p. 383.

CHAPTER XII

CONGRESSIONAL ACTION AND EDITORIAL OPINION

THE PORTER RESOLUTION

The most important of the resolutions on China introduced into Congress in 1927 was the so-called Porter Resolution. This Resolution had been given the name of its author, Stephen G. Porter, Chairman of the House Committee on Foreign Affairs and Republican Representative from Pennsylvania, who submitted it to the House of Representatives on January 4, 1927.

The Resolution, when it was finally amended, read as follows:[1]

Whereas the United States in its relations with China has always endeavored to act in a spirit of mutual fairness and equity and with due regard for the conditions prevailing from time to time in the two countries, and since the development of conditions in China makes it desirable that the United States at the present time in accordance with its traditional policy should take the initiative in bringing about a readjustment of its treaty relations with China; therefore be it:

Resolved by the House of Representatives (the Senate concurring) that the President of the United States be, and hereby is, respectfully requested forthwith to enter into negotiations with the duly accredited agents of the Republic of China, authorized to speak for the people of China, with a view to the negotiation and the drafting of a treaty, or of treaties, between the United States of America and the Republic of China which shall take the place of the treaties now in force between the two countries which provide for the exercise in China of American extraterritorial or jurisdictional rights or limit her full autonomy with reference to the levying of customs dues or other taxes, or of such other treaty provisions as may be found to be unequal or nonreciprocal in character, to the end that henceforth the treaty relations between the two countries shall be upon an equal and reciprocal basis and will be such as will in no way offend the sovereign dignity of either of the parties, or place obstacles in the way of realization by either of them of their several national aspirations or of maintenance by them of their several legitimate domestic policies.

The Resolution in the form in which it was originally introduced into the House (before it was amended to read as quoted above) had a long preamble in which Mr. Porter presented various arguments in favor of the United States' entering independently into negotiations for new treaties

[1] House Concurrent Resolution 46, 69th Congress, 2nd Session.

with China that would be in accord with the principles outlined in the main body of the Resolution.[2] Among these arguments were: that the Chinese people were entitled to such aid and encouragement as the United States might properly give them in their efforts to place the republican form of government which they had adopted in 1912 upon a firm basis; that such efforts of the Chinese people were being rendered extraordinarily difficult because of the restraint upon China's exercise of sovereign powers imposed by the treaties; that it was highly unjust for a "great and civilized people" to be hindered by restraints put upon them in order to promote the interests of foreign Powers; that concerted action among the Powers had only resulted in the situation becoming progressively worse.

The Porter Resolution was referred to the House Committee on Foreign Affairs which proceeded to hold hearings on the subject. At the conclusion of the hearings, a Report,[3] written by Mr. Porter, was submitted to the Committee and accepted by a vote of 14 to 3.[4] The three who abstained from voting in favor of the Report were not opposed to its content, but objected on procedural grounds, maintaining that the hearings should have been continued for a longer period of time to make it possible for more witnesses to appear before the Committee.[5]

The Report, which was submitted to the House of Representatives, dealt at some length with the testimony that had been presented to the Committee. "Practically all the American cultural, financial, and missionary interests having relations with China," it said, "are united in support of this resolution as appears from the testimony."[6] Excerpts were given from the statements of those who testified — excerpts which read in part:[7]

Mr. Roger S. Greene (formerly Consul General of the United States in China and Director of the China Medical Board of the Rockefeller Foundation):

It is my impression that the articulate portion of the Chinese people is almost unanimous in the desire to terminate the conventional tariff and the extraterritorial jurisdiction of foreign Powers in China. . . .

It would appear from recent experience that any attempt to retain the special treaty rights referred to by application of force would result in failure unless force were applied on an inconceivably large scale. On the other hand, an undertaking by the United States Government to yield what the Chinese wish before it is compelled to do so, while it may have little immediate effect in arresting the present agitation against foreigners is likely

[2] *Ibid.*
[3] House of Representatives Report No. 1891, 69th Congress, 2nd Session.
[4] *United States Daily,* January 26, 1927, p. 2.
[5] *Ibid.*
[6] *Ibid.*   [7] The following are only partial quotations.

to gratify the more thoughtful minority of the people, may strengthen slightly the hands of their more reasonable leaders, and may lay the foundation for a friendlier relationship in the future.[8]

Mr. Grover Clark (Editor of the *Peking Leader*):

American action along the lines suggested and within the near future not only will restore Chinese good will toward the United States but it will also be of incalculably great effect in turning the whole trend of Chinese feeling . . . away from the conviction that force offers the one sure means of realizing even legitimate national aspirations.[9]

Mr. Joseph Washington Hall (University of Washington, Seattle):

There is something absolutely new in China today which has not existed before and that thing has grown up within the last ten months and it is just as strong and unusual and important as the Fascist movement in Italy. . . .
The feeling of the Chinese Nationalists is today that as far as the abrogation of the old treaties is concerned, that is a *fait accompli;* that from their standpoint the old treaties are gone already and there is no possible chance in the world of their ever coming back into execution except through the superior force imposed upon China from abroad; that is, if we go over there and conquer them.[10]

Dr. Paul Monroe (Teachers' College, Columbia University, member of the Board of Directors of the China Foundation for the Promotion of Education and Culture erected out of the remitted American Boxer indemnity):

One of the greatest defects in America's approach to China . . . has been that we have seldom if ever paid any attention to what the Chinese are thinking . . . and we have reached the stage when Chinese public opinion is of such significance and is of such determining character that if we wish to guide our own policy aright it seems to me highly important that we pay attention to what the Chinese really think. . . .[11]

Dr. Edward H. Hume (President of the College of Yale-in-China):

America has been losing ground, or, to put it in another way the Chinese Nationalist movement has been gaining ground, not within the last ten months but far longer. . . . We have got to recognize that the old treaties are on the verge of being wholly wiped out unless the western Powers will-

[8] House of Representatives Report No. 1891, p. 2.
[9] *Ibid.;* see also *United States Daily,* January 22, 1927, p. 2.
[10] *Ibid.*
[11] *Ibid.,* p. 3; see also *United States Daily,* January 22, 1927, p. 2.

ingly come forward and offer to revise them. . . . If we do not move, we shall throw China into the arms of eastern Europe which is waiting to be its counsellor and friend.[12]

Professor W. W. Willoughby (Johns Hopkins University):

Mr. Linthicum (member of the Committee): The result of the whole thing is just this, that nothing was accomplished at the Peking Conference [the Special Conference on the Customs Tariff] and it remains now as at the time of the Nanking Treaty?

Professor Willoughby: Yes; and I will say a word about that. China at the Washington Conference got very little specifically but she reserved the right to raise the question of complete tariff autonomy at an appropriate time and when the invitation finally went out for the Conference to convene China asked that the question of tariff autonomy be considered. The American Government wrote a very liberal answer to that in which it expressed its willingness to raise this general problem of tariff autonomy, not only in the conference at Peking, which was to meet, but at any other appropriate time.[13]

Further, it was stated in the Report that Mr. Henry K. Norton, Acting Secretary of the American Asiatic Association, had declared that the Executive Committee of the Association had, without exception, indorsed the Porter Resolution. In reply to a question as to whether the Association represented a large majority of the Americans with financial interests in China, Mr. Norton had said that the Association "either directly or indirectly" was very close to representing practically all of the American financial interests in China.[14]

The above witnesses were all that were heard by the Committee on Foreign Affairs. The hearings were closed because "of the urgency of the situation . . . and conclusive character of the evidence already presented."[15] Permission was, however, granted to other persons who had already been called as witnesses to file statements; all of these proved to be in favor of the Resolution.[16]

[12] *Ibid.*, see also *United States Daily*, January 22, 1927. Dr. Hume announced that the entire Board of the College of Yale-in-China had gone on record in favor of the Porter Resolution.

[13] *Ibid.*, p. 4; see also *United States Daily*, January 25, 1927, p. 2.

[14] *Ibid.*, p. 4.

[15] *Ibid.*, p. 4; see also *United States Daily*, January 25, 1927, p. 2.

[16] It is interesting to note, in relation to the interests which they represented (whether missionary, cultural, business, or of some other character) the people who were called as witnesses, in addition to those already cited. The list is as follows: Dr. A. L. Warnshuis, Secretary of the International Missionary Council; the Right Rev. Alfred A. Gilman, Protestant Episcopal Diocese of Hankow, President of the Central China University; Mr. Fletcher S. Brockman, Secretary of the Foreign Committee of the National

The account of the testimony presented to the Committee was followed in the Report by a discussion of the questions of extraterritoriality and of tariff autonomy as being the two major issues with which the United States was concerned in connection with a revision of China's treaties. "The controversy which centers around these two issues," it was said, "is disturbing the cordial relations which always have existed between China and the United States. . . . the settlement of these two issues would be incalculably far-reaching in its influence and effect." Both questions should be settled as promptly as possible through mutually fair and friendly negotiations.[17]

The problem was raised at the hearings of the Committee, the Report continued, as to whether, in view of the disturbed conditions in China, it would be possible for the Chinese to appoint representatives authorized to act for China as a whole for the sake of entering into negotiations with the United States. On this point the Committee concluded:

"Whether or not the Chinese Government is sufficiently well organized to appoint duly accredited agents with authority to bind by treaty the Republic of China can be determined only in one way and that is by the United States making the necessary proposal and thereby ascertaining the facts. We have no right to remain inactive for reasons which are based on assumption."[18]

Speaking for himself as the author of the Report, Mr. Porter asserted in the text that he was in entire accord with that part of the Secretary of State's declaration of January 27th in which Mr. Kellogg had affirmed that the United States was prepared to negotiate with China if the Chinese could agree upon the appointment of delegates representing the authorities or the people of the country. This statement, Mr. Porter wrote, cleared "the way for the opening of negotiations by transmission of a message to China through the Chinese Minister, Dr. Sao-ke Alfred Sze. . . ." The need

---

Y. M. C. A. of the United States and Canada; Miss Mary Elizabeth Wood, Boone University Library, Wuchang; Dr. John H. Latané, Johns Hopkins University; Mr. Felix Morley, Foreign Editor of the Baltimore *Sun;* the Right Reverend Charles H. Brent, formerly Bishop in the Philippines.

The Report in addition to quoting testimony from the above, stated that numerous resolutions and letters were received by the Committee and that among those who expressed themselves were: L. D. Froelick, editor of *Asia;* the Federation of Women's Boards of Foreign Missions of North America; the American Committee for Justice to China; James G. MacDonald, Chairman of the Foreign Policy Association; the American Committee for Fair Play in China, San Francisco; the Washington, D. C., Federation of Churches; the Women's Missionary Society of the District of Columbia.

As will appear from the above the only person representing business interests mentioned in the Report was Mr. Norton. (House of Representatives Report No. 1891, p. 5 and 6.)

[17] *Ibid.,* p. 7.
[18] *Ibid.,* p. 11.

for prompt action had been emphasized by all the witnesses who appeared before the House Committee; therefore "nothing was to be gained and much might be lost by inaction."[19] Mr. Porter concluded:

After considering these points in the light of the information secured by it at the hearings and from other sources, your committee voted to recommend that this resolution pass. In doing so it gave concrete expression to its belief that the United States should determine for itself a distinctive American policy in relation to China and should declare and pursue that policy independently, if necessary, of the other Powers. Such action by the American Government would insure the removal of the causes of misunderstanding between China and the United States without risk or delay arising out of controversies which China may have with other nations.[20]

Even before the Porter Resolution was introduced, however, there had been some consideration of the Chinese situation on the floor of the House of Representatives. In December, 1926, Representative Loring M. Black (Democrat, New York) had submitted a resolution the purpose of which was to urge the United States Government to "immediately accord recognition" to the "so-called Canton Government" as the Government of China.[21] Mr. Black had also delivered a speech in the House in favor of an immediate revision of our treaties with China.[22] The United States, he said, proclaimed friendship for China but often joined with other foreign Powers in stifling the Chinese nation. Good will could easily be lost and was hard to regain. Still, it was not too late for the United States to keep the good name it had earned in China. The American Government should take independent and immediate action to open negotiations with China in order to revise its treaties on a basis of equality. The Chinese were determined to obtain a modification of the treaties; therefore, to meet their demands was not only the magnanimous, it was also the practical, thing to do.

Something of the character and tone of Mr. Black's statements in respect to a revision of the treaties may be seen from the following excerpts:

"I wonder how we would relish extraterritoriality in the United States. Suppose our seaport towns were governed by foreign courts."

"I wonder how our business men would like foreign courts to fix our tariff duties. Yet, our business men insist that we fix the Chinese rates. Do you wonder that the celestials wonder at Christianity?"

"China to change its tariff rates must get the consent of 13 Powers. The United States which properly boasts of its freedom-loving 13 original colonies is one of these despots."

[19] *Ibid.*, p. 12.
[20] *Ibid.*, p. 12.
[21] House Resolution 328, 69th Congress, 1st Session.
[22] *Congressional Record*, 69th Congress, 2nd Session, Vol. 68, Part I, pp. 877-878.

Continuing, Mr. Black declared that the United States had a tendency to do nothing and leave its problems, whether domestic or foreign, unsolved. As an example of this he cited the Report of the Commission on Extraterritoriality. "The Report," he said, "is just a pettifogging effort to delay the consummation of the promises of the Nine Power Treaty to China. It is the sort of thing we do here when we do not want to do anything." The question with whom to negotiate in China did not, Mr. Black asserted, present insuperable difficulties; it would be possible, he thought, for North and South China to pick a representative agreeable to both factions. Some, he added, feared the Soviet influence in Canton; but Soviet influence was only possible because the foreign capitalists and the Western press alienated the Chinese people. Communism had only affected a few political leaders in China and "had barely touched the mass of the Chinese people"; the fact of the matter was that the Chinese people were traditionally religious and would never "assimilate the blasphemies of Bolshevism." Speaking of the Nationalist movement in general, Mr. Black compared recent developments in China with those which had taken place in the United States during the American Revolution; the May 30th Incident, he said, corresponded to the Boston massacre and had mobilized the nationalistic feelings of the people in the same way. In a final plea at the conclusion of his speech, he again asked that the United States should seek to earn the good will of the Chinese by ending "these unAmerican unilateral treaties."[23]

Several weeks intervened after Mr. Black's address before the Chinese situation again became the subject of discussion in the House of Representatives. On January 18th, J. Charles Linthicum (Democrat, Maryland) spoke in favor of the Porter Resolution which was then being considered by the Committee on Foreign Affairs of which he was a member.[24] Mr. Linthicum said that the purpose of the Porter Resolution was to denounce all former treaties with China and establish a new relationship with that country. As a result of the decisions reached at the Washington Conference, the State Department felt it must act concurrently with other Powers and, in consequence, nothing was done to alleviate the increasing hostility of the Chinese

[23] Mr. Black was especially severe in his condemnation of the Report of the Commission on Extraterritoriality. The Commission, he said, had been appointed to hear and report but it believed its function was to hear and determine. It had found some old prisons, conflicting laws, and inefficient courts in China, and so had reached the conclusion that the Chinese should not exercise jurisdiction over their own territory. Yet, any observers of our courts and jails could make the same report; if the word "United States" were substituted for the word "China" in many places in the Strawn Report, "you would," Mr. Black said, "get a fairly accurate idea of the administration of justice in America." Moreover, Mr. Black complained, Mr. Strawn, since his return, had repeatedly made public utterances the tenor of which created a wrong impression in China.

[24] *Congressional Record*, Vol. 68, Part II, p. 1863.

people. For this reason, the Porter Resolution requested the President to act independently, if necessary. China was quickly changing in every aspect but her people were united on one subject: a demand for the abrogation of the treaties. The House of Representatives should, therefore, act as speedily as possible. The great question at issue for the United States was: shall we wait until we are compelled to give up our treaty rights or shall we deal with China at this time as we deal with all other civilized nations?

China is knocking at the doors of the nations of this world and asking that she be treated as all other great civilized nations of the earth have been treated and I want to voice my sentiments in favor of denouncing the present treaties which we have, giving us rights which we do not enjoy with the other great nations of the world, and to say that, in my opinion, the time has come when, without compulsion, we should treat and deal with her with respect to treaties just as we deal with France and England and Japan as well as the other great nations of the world. I do not want to see our country wait until we are absolutely compelled by the forces of China, by the uprising of the people, to give up these rights.

Mr. Linthicum argued further that the United States had always been known as the friend of China and had always taken the lead in movements to secure justice for China. The United States should therefore take immediate steps toward effecting a revision of the treaties — "or it will be too late . . . as China will have obtained all she demands through her soldiers in the great revolution which is now taking place and which will eventually bring about a consolidated China under a single government."[25]

Several voices were raised in opposition to Mr. Linthicum's speech. Edward E. Denison (Republican, Illinois) declared that, as the question at hand was entirely related to the negotiation of treaties, it did not fall within the province of the House of Representatives but was solely a matter for the consideration of the Department of State. In reply to this argument, Mr. Linthicum asserted that if the State Department did not take the initiative, Congress ought to ask it to do so. For the sake of supporting this thesis, Mr. Linthicum read a letter from Dr. John H. Latané of Johns Hopkins University, in which the latter urged the House of Representatives to take action on the Porter Resolution. "Affairs in China are reaching a crisis very rapidly," Dr. Latané wrote, "and the present administration of this Government does not seem disposed to adopt any definite policy. I do not believe that President Coolidge will do anything unless his hand is forced."[26]

J. Mayhew Wainwright (Republican, New York), who proved to be one of the Representatives most interested in opposing the Porter Resolution,

[25] *Ibid.*
[26] *Ibid.*

answered Mr. Linthicum's speech by stressing the need for according protection to our nationals in China:

Now Mr. Speaker and gentlemen of the House, it seems to me that we
should pause before we put ourselves in a position from which we may have
to recede and which may prove very awkward for us in the solution of a
plan to protect American lives and property in China. It seems to me we
should be more concerned just now as to how our Government shall fulfill
its plain, its sacred, duty to its own citizens than as to whether we shall
change our general policy hitherto in dealing with China, and play a lone
hand, and keep away from any concert with the other Powers.[27]

On January 25th, Andrew L. Somers (New York)[28] introduced a resolution into the House of Representatives which stated that the United States
Government "desiring to withdraw all obstacles in the way of the Republic
of China's realization of her national aspirations" would take steps to abolish
American extraterritorial courts in China and further amend the treaties
so as to permit the citizens of China to enjoy the rights that the citizens
of the United States "hold sacred."[29] On the same day, there appeared in the
American press the spectacular announcement that the British Government
had determined to send some 12,000 additional British troops to China.
The following day, Tom Connally (Democrat, Texas), a well-known member
of the House Committee on Foreign Affairs, spoke in support of the Porter
Resolution.[30] Like Mr. Black, he denounced the rôle which the Treaty
Powers, including the United States, had played in China in the past:

As all of you know, for many years the Chinese have suffered in national
dignity by reason of a series of unequal treaties imposed on China by the
great Powers of the world, because of the fact that China as a nation has
not been able to resist the will of the Powers. . . .
   The treaties were extorted from China; she could not help herself; and
she had to accede to the treaties — it was by the authority of force and
influence.
   . . . This trouble in China goes back as far as the opium war in 1842. . . .
   From that day until this, in one form or another, the Powers of the world
have imposed their will on China. . . .

Turning to the current situation, Mr. Connally declared:

All I ask at this time is that the Secretary of State may make some sort
of pronouncement . . . in order that the Chinese people and the Chinese
Government, in this hour of tragedy, may know that the United States, which
has always been a friend of China and believes in international equality

---

[27] *Ibid.*, pp. 1864-1865.
[28] No party affiliation listed in Congressional Directory.
[29] House Concurrent Resolution 47, 69th Congress, 2nd Session.
[30] *Congressional Record*, Vol. 68, Part II, p. 2324.

and stands before the world as the champion of the rights of small nations and weak nations, is now ready and shall be ready in the future to enter into negotiations with the properly constituted authorities of China whereby America shall say to China that is now waking from her long sleep, that we propose to respect the rights of the Chinese, not because they are backed up by force and by navies and by armies, but we propose to respect them because they are founded on right and justice.

During the course of his argument, Mr. Connally was asked a number of questions by different members of the House which indicated a substantial ignorance of the subject under discussion. By what means — through treaties or otherwise — had such restrictions as tariff controls and the extraterritorial system become established in China? Did all the nations have extraterritorial courts similar to the United States? Were American offenders tried in Chinese courts or before their own Consuls? Was there in existence one treaty signed by various countries or were there treaties separately negotiated between China and the individual Powers? If there were general treaties signed by the various countries jointly at the Washington Conference, did they embrace all of the nations "in the way of controlling the tariff rates and all of her [China's] internal affairs"? What was meant by the reference to the existence of separate treaties with China?[31]

At the conclusion of the day's discussion the point was again raised as to how it was possible for the United States to negotiate with the different factions in China. Mr. Black asserted that it would be "very easy" for the State Department to announce the abrogation of the treaties to Dr. Sze and then go into conference with him.[32]

On the following day — January 27th — Secretary of State Kellogg's declaration of American policy toward China appeared in the morning papers. Mr. Connally referred to this matter at once:

I think the announcement by the State Department of American policy at this particular moment is to be commended. I regret that our State Department found it necessary to wait so long after other Powers had made announcements regarding their policy. It is probable that some of the turmoil that now exists in China might have been prevented; it is possible that some of the unrest that is now stirring within the breasts of the Chinese people might have been calmed if our State Department had formulated at an early period a definite policy and then had had the courage — if I may use that term — to boldly announce its policy.

Those of us who approve the action of the Department cannot, however, in all candor and frankness, fail to note a certain disappointment in our own minds at the lack of pointedness to some of the pronouncements of the State Department.

[31] *Ibid.*, Part II, p. 2326.
[32] *Ibid.*, p. 2324.

It seems to pulsate too much with the cryptic language of diplomacy rather than with the clear-cut announcements which our people prefer. It partakes too much of veneer rather than real substance. . . .[33]

Mr. Connally took pains to explain that he did not criticize the action of the Department of State but that he felt the United States should not be content at such a critical time, merely to follow other nations. "The trouble with the Chinese situation today," he said, "is that America has not announced in the past a definite American policy."[34]

At this point, Leonidas C. Dyer (Republican, Missouri) stated that he agreed with almost all that Mr. Connally had said. The Chinese people were much to be admired. A great national feeling had arisen in China in the last half-dozen years and had permeated the country; it would certainly result in a short time in the "establishment of a government of the people, by the people, and for the people." When that time came no one would be happier than the people of the United States who had always been "the true and great friend of the Chinese." But in the meantime it was the duty of the United States to protect its own nationals who had gone to China to reside, to establish industries, and to invest their capital extensively.[35]

A controversy ensued concerning the question of the protection of American nationals in China. While no direct reference was made to the news concerning the increasing danger confronting the foreign community in China or to the dispatch of British troops, Mr. Wainwright declared that the need to protect American citizens in China was the main point at issue; it would be time enough later, he said, to take up negotiations for a revision of the treaties with a Chinese Government — if a Chinese Government were established.[36] Mr. Connally replied to this that there could be no argument concerning the responsibility of the United States to protect its nationals in China; however, he added, the object he had in mind pointed in another direction, namely, that the United States should adopt a policy the very character of which made it unnecessary to send an armed soldier by the side of every American citizen to afford him protection.[37] Mr. Wainwright asked if Mr. Connally remembered the Boxer Rebellion.[38] Mr. Connally answered that he did indeed and that the Boxer disturbances had their origin in the same causes as were agitating the Chinese today and that if the gentleman

[33] Ibid., Part III, p. 2383.
[34] Ibid.
[35] Ibid.
[36] Ibid.
[37] Ibid.
[38] Ibid.

wanted to have a repetition of the Boxer situation, he should allow the same causes to exist.[39]

Henry Allen Cooper (Republican, Wisconsin), also a member of the House Committee on Foreign Affairs, took Mr. Wainwright to task for opposing the Porter Resolution. Many witnesses of long experience in China had appeared at the hearings of the Committee, he said, and all had urged the adoption of the Resolution. Moreover, all the witnesses had insisted that the Peking and Canton Governments would be willing to unite in sending representatives to the United States. It was his personal opinion, he added, that the State Department could at once open negotiations with Dr. Sze who would receive the active support of both North and South China.[40]

On a number of occasions throughout the debate, speakers were asked whether the Porter Resolution had been submitted to the State Department before its introduction into the House of Representatives.[41] The most nearly direct answer was given by Mr. Cooper who said that "the Committee on Foreign Affairs were given to understand that it met with the approval of the State Department."[42]

On February 2nd, Mr. Somers again introduced a resolution into the House. In the preamble he stated that it was the firm conviction of all those familiar with current conditions in China that the policy set forth by the State Department could be of greatest value only if effected immediately, and that it was "most desirable" that the United States' pledge of treaty equality should be fulfilled voluntarily rather than through compulsion. In the main body of the resolution, he requested the President to appoint a delegation (including a Senator and a Representative) which should be charged with the duty of negotiating new treaties with China; in the event that the Peking and Canton factions failed to agree on the personnel of a delegation, negotiations should be undertaken with each of the two groups separately.[43]

On February 4th and 18th, Mr. Black submitted further resolutions to the House the main purport of which was to ascertain whether there were in existence any "secret understandings" between officials of the United States Government and of the governments of other Treaty Powers as to

---

[39] *Ibid.*, p. 2387.
[40] *Ibid.*
[41] *Ibid.*, pp. 2388, 4386-4387.
[42] *Ibid.*, p. 2388.
[43] House Concurrent Resolution 50, 69th Congress, 2nd Session.

the joint use of military and naval forces in China in the event of the violation of any of the Sino-foreign treaties.[44]

Finally, on February 21, 1927, Mr. Porter moved to pass the Resolution which had adopted his name.[45] The time devoted to the debate on this matter was largely taken up by a small group of Republican members of the House who objected to the Resolution on the ground, already argued, that it involved the treaty-making functions of the Government and was at this stage primarily the concern of the State Department and the President.[46] A measure of this kind, it was declared, should not be passed by the House without the full support and full approval of that section of the United States Government which was charged with the responsibility for foreign affairs. "I do not believe," one speaker said, "we have ever requested the President to negotiate a treaty and set out the terms upon which the House believes the President should negotiate such a treaty." Moreover, it was asserted that the Resolution in no way altered the existing situation as it simply directed the State Department to do what, according to Mr. Kellogg's statement of January 27th, it was already doing.

A further argument against the Porter Resolution was offered by Carroll L. Beedy (Republican, Maine) who in a lengthy speech attacked the Chinese Minister, Dr. Sze. The interesting part of Mr. Beedy's address was that it showed his attitude toward the revolutionary movement in China:

"China today is attempting to write her declaration of independence. Her struggle ought to appeal, and it does appeal, to every liberty-loving American. I myself desire to express my sympathy for poor, struggling China in this hour of her great trial. I want my country to do her utmost to free China from the curse of unequal treaties and foreign misrule."[47]

The United States Government, Mr. Beedy declared, should not, however, enter into negotiations with Dr. Sze. In the Chinese Revolution of 1911, Dr. Sze, he insisted, had sided with Yuan Shih-kai and betrayed "the cause of the great Chinese patriot, Dr. Sun Yat-sen"; he was, for this reason, not to be trusted. Moreover as the republican armies of Canton were almost at the gates of Shanghai, the United States should for the time being await the outcome of the Revolution, expressing only its good will:

"Let us now bespeak our message of friendship, good will, and best wishes to the struggling masses of China; let us now express the hope that

[44] House Resolutions 408 and 431, 69th Congress, 2nd Session. For Secretary of State Kellogg's response to House Resolution 408 denying that there were any secret understandings, see *Foreign Relations* (1927), p. 73. For Mr. Grew's answer to House Resolution 431, see *United States Daily*, March 4, 1927, p. 2.

[45] *Congressional Record*, Vol. 68, Part III, p. 4386.

[46] *Ibid.*, pp. 4386-4389.

[47] *Ibid.*, p. 4388.

the Chinese people may succeed in their attempt to throw off the yoke of an unwelcome monarchy, to set up once more their own constitution and to administer their own government through the chosen representatives of four hundred million sovereign Chinese."[48]

At the end of the day's debate, a vote was taken on the Porter Resolution. The votes registered in favor of the Resolution were 262 and in opposition, 43.[49] The Resolution was then referred to the Senate where it was sent to the Committee on Foreign Relations which did not, however, act upon the matter.[50]

One further speech, made after the passage of the Porter Resolution by the House, is worth recording as furnishing additional evidence of the attitude of the House toward the relations of the United States with China. In the strongest terms of condemnation, David J. O'Connell (Democrat, New York), also a member of the Committee on Foreign Affairs, declared that the "deplorable conditions" existing in China were the result of the "unfair and unequal" treaties through which the Great Powers, including the United States, had oppressed the Chinese nation. After describing the extraterritorial system and the tariff controls exercised by the Powers in China, Mr. O'Connell said, "This is the essence of serfdom and has no parallel in American annals." The restrictions on sovereignty must, he added, be removed; China was fully capable of self-government and she should be permitted to work out her own destiny in her own way.[51]

In the middle of January, 1927, Carter Field, the Washington correspondent of the New York *Herald Tribune,* stated that it was well-known that President Coolidge and Secretary of State Kellogg were keenly interested in the development of public sentiment behind the Porter Resolution.[52] This was, no doubt, the case, and the President and the officials in the State Department in Washington must have felt encouraged by the support they received in the House of Representatives for the policy which they were pursuing in China. The Representatives who spoke in favor of the Porter Resolution could scarcely have denounced the Sino-foreign treaty system with greater vehemence or have been more insistent in urging the State Department to undertake, as soon as possible, a comprehensive revision of the treaties with or without the co-operation of the other interested nations. In addition, the Administration must have found encouragement in the tone of the debate in the House which revealed the attitude of the

[48] *Ibid.,* p. 4389.
[49] *Ibid.*
[50] *Ma, Wen Huan, American Policy Toward China,* Shanghai, 1934, p. 270.
[51] *Congressional Record,* Vol. 68, Part IV, p. 4672.
[52] New York *Herald-Tribune,* January 17, 1927, p. 1.

Representatives as much through the statements that were omitted as through those to which the speakers committed themselves. Only two arguments of any significance were advanced against the adoption of the Porter Resolution: one was that the United States Government should, for the moment, concentrate on the protection of its nationals in China; the other, that it was not the business of the House of Representatives to concern itself with the negotiation of treaties, a responsibility which belonged essentially to the President and the Department of State. Neither of these arguments suggested that any of the members were eager — or possibly even willing — to put themselves on record as approving a prolonged maintenance of the treaty system. On no occasion did any speaker advance views such as those which were being expounded by Mr. Strawn and many others, namely, that conditions in China were far too chaotic to allow the abandonment of the special privileges accorded to foreigners. Nor did any Congressman indicate that China's troubles were primarily internal and of her own making. On the contrary, it was generally taken for granted that China's problems were due to the restrictions imposed by the "unequal" — or, as Representative Black said, "unAmerican" — treaties. It was assumed that China was in the midst of a revolutionary process which was comparable to our own struggle for independence at the time of the American Revolution. No substantial anxiety was shown by the speakers, either by those who supported or those who opposed the Porter Resolution, concerning the Communist element in the Nationalist movement. This lack of anxiety was all the more conspicuous, first, because at the opening of 1927 it was still generally assumed by the American public that the Chinese Nationalist Party was subject to strong Communist influence (little then being known about the impending split in the Kuomintang); and, secondly, because there were many people in the United States at that time who feared the spread of Communism in any part of the world and were likely to oppose it on every occasion to the best of their ability.

EDITORIAL POLICIES IN THE UNITED STATES

One of the aims of Mr. Porter in introducing his Resolution into the House of Representatives may have been to sound out public opinion, not only in Congress but in the country at large. If this was his purpose, he was greatly assisted by the military developments along the Yangtze which created a situation that for many months placed all stories concerning China among the chief news items of the day. As far as that portion of public opinion which was represented by the press was concerned, January, 1927 may be regarded as the turning point when many editors in the United

States ceased to accord to China merely their casual and chance attention and began to formulate definite editorial policies.[53]

In an article published on February 5th, the *Literary Digest* stated that it was being "declared on every hand" that the United States must shape a new program for its dealings with the Far East.[54] There was widespread editorial agreement, it said, that the Chinese nation was finally awakening, that "ancient China" was dead, and that — in the words of the *Nation* magazine — there was taking place "another of those great uprisings of humanity which dot the endless struggle toward human freedom"; as a result, the Powers of the West, led by the United States, were inclined to concede that the day of forced treaties and spheres of influence was over.

During the past weeks of sensational happenings, the article continued, an insistent demand had been voiced by the American public for a restating of our Government's policy toward China.[55] This demand had been met in two ways: by the introduction of the Porter Resolution into the House of Representatives and by a formal statement of policy issued by the Secretary of State. Concerning the Porter Resolution, the *Digest* said that: "The idea of the Porter Resolution that the United States should go ahead on its own to cancel the old treaties and make a new deal with China on a basis of equality meets with emphatic press approval."[56] Supplementing this analysis it gave the following account of opinions expressed by various representative sections of the press:

To carry this [the Porter Resolution] into effect, says the Charleston *News and Courier*, 'will be an act of substantial justice, carrying out the policies and professions to which we have long been committed.' The policy is sound, declares the Brooklyn *Eagle*. It is a 'sane solution' in the opinion of the Troy *Record*. The Baltimore *Sun* feels quite certain that 'such a move would meet no opposition from the vast majority of Americans.' The Washington *Post* repeatedly calls for immediate action. So do the Scripps-Howard papers, and the New York *World* remarks:
'Passage of such a resolution two years ago would have gone far to force the hand of other Powers and to allay anti-foreign sentiment in China. It is too late now to lament what was not done at the right moment. But it is not too late to urge the passage of the Porter Resolution.'[57]

[53] In discussing the attitude of the press certain fundamental factors must be taken into consideration. There were no public opinion polls in the 1920's and the analyses of the press were probably done on an "impressionistic" rather than on a scientific basis. It is, therefore, impossible to measure public opinion, and judgments concerning the views of the press must be qualified.
[54] *Literary Digest*, February 5, 1927, p. 7.
[55] *Ibid.*, p. 8.
[56] *Ibid.*
[57] *Ibid.*, p. 9.

But the question being asked, the *Digest* said, was with whom could we enter into negotiations for the revision of our treaties with China? The Minneapolis *Tribune* urged the people of the United States to be sure that we would not have to act in concert with the other Powers for the sake of protecting our nationals before we undertook " 'to go it entirely alone in China.' " On the other hand, the *Digest* observed, Henry Kittredge Norton, in a special article in the New York *Herald Tribune*, urged the initiation of negotiations with agents duly accredited by both (Peking and Canton) and asserted that there were a number of Chinese leaders in a position to secure such credentials.[58]

In addition to this general analysis of press opinion made by the *Literary Digest*, it is interesting to note the editorial policy that was pursued by a few of our outstanding newspapers. In the forefront of those which developed an ardent Chinese policy was the Baltimore *Sun* which was generally regarded as belonging to the liberal press. In the four months starting with January, 1927, the *Sun* published over forty editorials on the Chinese situation, some of which attracted considerable attention.[59]

The *Sun* declared itself in favor of the Porter Resolution immediately after it was introduced into the House of Representatives and persistently urged its passage through Congress.[60] It also expressed its profound approval of the statement of policy issued by Secretary Kellogg on January 27th.[61] Fundamentally, the position of the *Sun* was that the United States Government should "wipe the slate clean in China" and back its promises to fulfill the demands of the Chinese with concrete action. The *Sun* believed that the diplomatic concert of the Powers in China was dead, and that, in any case, it had yielded nothing as far as the United States was concerned except a loss of prestige.[62] With a persuasive intensity of feeling, the editors argued that the Chinese had every right to demand a revision of the treaties and that the Chinese people had, in the past, allowed themselves "to be bullied and outraged by foreigners in a way no other great people ever tolerated;" the time for bullying was over however — according to the *Sun* — as China had increased her military strength to a degree that enabled her to challenge the West.[63] The Powers, the *Sun* maintained, would have to yield ground,

[58] *Ibid.*

[59] For editorial read on the floor of the House, see *Congressional Record*, Vol. 68, Part II, p. 1862. The *Literary Digest* relied a great deal on quotations from the Baltimore *Sun* in its articles on China. The *Sun's* articles were also frequently reprinted by American-edited newspapers in China.

[60] Baltimore *Sun*, January 8, 1927; January 23, 1927; January 24, 1927; January 29, 1927.

[61] *Ibid.*, January 29, 1927.

[62] *Ibid.*, January 8, 1927; January 9, 1927.

[63] *Ibid.*, January 10, 1927.

step by step, in the face of force.[64] Moreover, there was no use in the Powers adopting the attitude that the uprising in China was Russian-inspired and, therefore, furnished an adequate reason for refusing to revise the treaties.[65] The Chinese Nationalists represented "a perfectly normal patriotic movement";[66] their troops had a "spirit as fine as that which animated the revolutionary troops of General George Washington;"[67] and their campaigns were being "hailed as a crusade of redemption throughout the length and breadth of China."[68] The success of the Kuomintang was, in fact, necessary to restore civil order throughout the country.[69]

Following the announcement of the dispatch of British forces to Shanghai, the *Sun,* in editorial after editorial, virtually thundered against British policy. The British action, the *Sun* said, was "provocative and dangerous"; it was based on the fallacious theory that non-whites could be intimidated and that the Chinese in particular regarded temporization as a sign of weakness;[70] the sending of British troops to Shanghai was not a defensive but an aggressive measure;[71] the landing of a foreign army in the International Settlement could only be justified in "an emergency far more extreme" than that which existed.[72] The main moral which the *Sun* drew from these conclusions was that the United States must not imitate Great Britain. "As the troop ships sail from England," the *Sun* wrote in a picturesque manner that hardly concealed its bitterly critical attitude, "their bows will cut all tacit understandings which we have had with that nation for a united Chinese policy."[73] ". . . it is idle for Great Britain to talk of a united policy with us on China. She seems to be preparing for war and we are not."[74]

In many respects, the views of the Washington *Post* corresponded with those of the Baltimore *Sun* although the *Post* was in general a far more conservative newspaper. Like the *Sun,* the Washington *Post* supported the adoption of the Porter Resolution. In this connection it said that "President Coolidge, Secretary Kellogg, the United States Senate, the House of Representatives, and American public opinion" were " all solidly in back of the idea of unshackling China gracefully instead of waiting until China unshackles herself. . . ."[75] The *Post* urged the United States Government to

[64] *Ibid.,* January 24, 1927.
[65] *Ibid.,* January 18, 1927.
[66] *Ibid.,* January 10, 1927.
[67] *Ibid.,* March 22, 1927.
[68] *Ibid.,* February 12, 1927.
[69] *Ibid.*
[70] *Ibid.,* January 26, 1927.
[71] *Ibid.,* February 12, 1927.
[72] *Ibid.,* February 5, 1927.
[73] *Ibid.,* January 26, 1927.
[74] *Ibid.,* February 8, 1927.
[75] Quoted in *North China Star,* January 26, 1927, editorial page.

issue a declaration that it was "prepared to abandon its old treaties,"[76] and to take steps toward negotiating new treaties with any government that emerged,[77] or with the Peking and Canton factions if they could agree to act jointly.[78] The Chinese, it said, were fighting a civil war which promised to result in a "stable, republican Government" that would be willing to meet its international obligations. "The Republic of China is coming into being," the *Post* declared. "There is only one honorable course for the United States to pursue: that is to befriend the Chinese nation and deal with it as an equal."[79]

The *Post* placed as much emphasis as the Baltimore *Sun* on the importance of the United States' pursuing an independent policy in the Far East. It argued that there was no reason for the American Government's "joining a junta of the Powers for the purpose of imposing their will on China."[80] The European Powers had different interests from those of the United States and they attempted to take unfair advantage of the Chinese; there was no use in employing American influence for the furtherance of European schemes.[81] Mr. MacMurray, the *Post* declared, was commonly reported to be insisting that the United States should act in concert with the other Treaty Powers. If these Powers were willing to risk war with the Chinese rather than surrender their special privileges, Mr. MacMurray's advice would, in the *Post's* opinion, "lead straight to war between the United States and China."[82]

The New York *World,* as was to be expected from its militantly liberal character, also followed a "pro-Chinese policy." As shown in the article quoted from the *Literary Digest,* the *World* supported the Porter Resolution; on one occasion, in fact, it observed that the passage of the Porter Resolution would be the "most notable example of fair dealing by the West to the East" that had occurred in a generation.[83] Mr. Kellogg's proposal to enter into negotiations for a revision of the treaties, was termed a "handsome offer," though no more than a just one, and even though coming "late in the day."[84] Like the Baltimore *Sun,* the *World* believed that the development of military strength in China had fundamentally altered the relations be-

[76] Editorial of January 23, 1927, reprinted in *China Weekly Review,* February 26, 1927.
[77] *Ibid.*
[78] Washington *Post* editorial of January 9, 1927, reprinted in *China Weekly Review,* February 19, 1927.
[79] *Ibid.*
[80] Washington *Post,* editorial of January 5, 1927, reprinted in *China Weekly Review,* February 19, 1927.
[81] *Ibid.*
[82] *Ibid.,* January 23, 1927, reprinted in *China Weekly Review,* February 26, 1927.
[83] New York *World,* January 25, 1927.
[84] *Ibid.,* January 28, 1927.

tween the Chinese nation and the rest of the world. The West had no alternative, it said, but either to dare China to use force or to co-operate with the Chinese by making good the many pledges given by foreign statesmen in the past.[85] The *World* remarked wrily that when China was weak and demanded justice there had been no sign of a willingness on the part of the Powers to modify the treaties, but now that China had a threatening army — "at once generosity appears; sympathy exudes from every Foreign Office keyhole." With its customary editorial vigor, the *World* also derided those who feared the influence of Communism in China. Everything was tagged "Bolshevism," it said, whether in Mexico, Syria, India, or China; the Chinese movement was a Nationalist movement: "Chiang's army is as red as Washington's at Valley Forge."[86]

As the above newspapers were published on the Atlantic seaboard, it it interesting to observe that their fundamental point of view toward events in China was shared by some of the well-known papers of varying political complexion issued in other parts of the country. The Louisville *Courier-Journal*, for example, a liberal publication, was unsparing in its condemnation of the rôle which the Western Powers had played in the modern history of China. "The story of China's subjection to foreigners," it wrote, "and its struggle for deliverance from that subjection, must command the unreserved approval of every one hearing or reading it who has any proper appreciation of the rights of national sovereignty."[87] It was incredible, the *Courier-Journal* added, that in the twentieth century, one quarter of the world's population with a civilization older than that of any of the countries seeking to dominate it, should be "striving to rid itself of a foreign-imposed super-state;" but China would ultimately secure its rights, if not by peaceable, then by forcible means.[88] Like the New York *World*, the attitude of the *Courier-Journal* was that it was a fad to attribute signs of unrest wherever they occurred to Soviet influence. "Certainly," the editors said, "China's whole history warrants...a conviction that China will not turn Bolshevik;" moreover, in so far as China might yield to such a temptation it would be the result of the treatment she had been subjected to by the Powers rather than the consequence of any inspiration from Moscow.[89] The only way to cease provoking China to hostility, was to revise the treaties and to recognize China on the same footing as that of other independent nations:

[85] New York *World*, January 28, 1927.
[86] *Ibid.*, January 30, 1927.
[87] Louisville *Courier-Journal*, March 17, 1927.
[88] *Ibid.*
[89] *Ibid.*, March 28, 1927.

"Warships instead of removing provocation can only increase and intensify it."[90]

Although written in a more conservative and cautious fashion that was in line with its editorial attitude, the Kansas City *Star* nevertheless expressed many ideas that were similar to those already quoted. It recommended "a conciliatory and reasonable attitude" on the part of the United States Government, as being far more effective in ensuring the safety of our nationals in China than "all the gunboats and marines the United States could send to the treaty ports or up the Yangtze."[91] The *Star* regarded the Chinese Nationalist movement as "one of the most momentous events of the century" and predicted that it would continue to progress until the time when China had taken her place among the nations of the world.[92] Like so many other American observers of China, it compared the struggle of the Nationalists to the American Revolution: there was no evidence, it said, that "the Nationalist movement had gone 'red';" the Kuomintang officials welcomed Russian aid as we had welcomed French assistance during our Revolution, being interested only in obtaining financial and military support and caring little about the political concepts of the country that was prepared to grant them.[93]

On the west coast, the San Francisco *Chronicle,* whose manner of expressing itself was as sensational as that of the Kansas City *Star* was conservative, supported Mr. Kellogg's statement of January 27th on the assumption that it meant that the United States was "ready to relinquish all the restrictions upon China's full administrative control" as soon as possible.[94] The *Chronicle* was mainly concerned, however, with the protection of our nationals in China, and, more than that, with the prevention of war between China and the United States. An editorial published on February 5th sought to prove the thesis proclaimed in its title: "No One Wants War In China." On a later occasion, the *Chronicle* urged its readers not to pay too much attention to dispatches bearing a Shanghai and Peking dateline which indicated that there was a strong sentiment among foreigners, with large interests in China, in favor of intervention; the statesmen in the capitals of the foreign Powers were opposed to war and it was their opinions that mattered.[95]

It is evident that the purpose of the editorial policies developed in the newspapers which have been cited was, in the main, to denounce the Chinese

[90] *Ibid.*
[91] Kansas City *Star,* January 26, 1927.
[92] *Ibid.,* January 31, 1927.
[93] *Ibid.,* February 5, 1927.
[94] San Francisco *Chronicle,* February 5, 1927.
[95] *Ibid.,* February 24, 1927.

treaty system and urge the United States Government to undertake a fundamental revision of our treaties with China as soon as possible; to further the idea of independent action by the United States in China; to express sympathy with, and encouragement for, the Chinese Nationalist movement; and — possibly most of all — to register intense disapproval of any action on the part of our government that might lead to intervention in China.

On the other side of the balance these views were not shared by such influential newspapers as the Chicago *Tribune* and the *New York Times.* The *Tribune,* instead of denouncing the treaty system, took the position that "the outcry against foreign exploitation by the Chinese was largely a matter of domestic politics and a dangerous device."[96] The *Tribune* further condemned the Porter Resolution in no uncertain terms as either "indicating an abysmal ignorance of the notorious facts of Chinese conditions" or as "a play of cheap politics to conciliate a sentimentalism in this country which has no respect for the facts."[97] The latter point was one which the *Tribune* harped upon repeatedly. In numerous editorials,[98] it attacked the missionary movement in this country, and accused its members of deliberately spreading propaganda intended to give the impression that the United States was oppressing the Chinese and thwarting their efforts to achieve independence and prosperity.[99]

"It is high time," the *Tribune* proclaimed, "for this public to wake up to the fact that our foreign relations are being victimized by an organized opinion, which, except where its own special concerns are involved, has no intelligent conception of the international responsibilities of the United States and no proper regard for the right of American citizens abroad to proper protection from their government."[100]

The *Tribune* also blamed the missionaries for telling the American public that the Nationalist movement in China was nothing more than an "effort of patriots to rid China of greedy commercial and financial exexploitation."[101] Actually, the *Tribune* said, the Cantonese had the "closest relations with Moscow;" moreover, as the situation was developing, it was not the Chinese moderates who were gaining control, but the extremists, whose temper and opinions harmonized "most effectively" with the aims of the Soviet Union.[102] While the *Tribune* believed that the Kuomintang came

---

[96] Chicago *Tribune,* January 23, 1927; see also February 3, 1927 and February 9, 1927.
[97] *Ibid.,* January 28, 1927.
[98] *Ibid.,* January 8, 1927; January 30, 1927; February 5, 1927; March 27, 1927; March 30, 1927; April 5, 1927.
[99] *Ibid.,* January 28, 1927.
[100] *Ibid.*
[101] *Ibid.,* January 30, 1927.
[102] *Ibid,*

closer to representing a program than any of the northern warlords, and
that Sun Yat-sen had been a "patriot" who "bequeathed a real national
movement to his followers," it deplored the fact that Dr. Sun and the
Kuomintang had fallen under the influence of Moscow.[103] If it were not for
"Canton's entanglement with Moscow," the *Tribune* declared, the successes of the Nationalist troops might be welcomed.[104]

The *Tribune* supported and constantly emphasized those aspects of the
Administration's policy which were designed to insure the protection of
our citizens in China. It insisted that "substantial opinion" throughout the
United States wished to uphold the principle of the protection of nationals
despite the "clamor of sentimental minorities."[105] When the newspapers
carried accounts of foreign troops sailing to China, the *Tribune* centered
its objections on the fact that the American troops, unlike the British, had
not been provided with tanks.[106]

The *New York Times* shared some of the opinions of the Chicago
Tribune concerning developments in China. Like the *Tribune,* the *Times*
believed that China's problems were of her own making and had nothing
to do with external causes. "The question at issue," the *Times* declared,
"is not, as certain Chinese sympathizers pretend, whether or not 'foreign
domination' shall be thrown off. Foreign domination is a myth — except in
so far as the Cantonese are under the influence of Soviet Russia."[107] "It is
well to bear in mind," the editors observed on another occasion, "that even
if every treaty with the foreign Powers were abrogated to-morrow, the effect
on China's internal condition would be nil."[108] One of the main functions
of the anti-foreign movement in the view of the *Times* was that it served as
"the greatest single force in unifying China" and the editors stated frankly
that they suspected the Chinese would not enter into negotiations for a
revision of the treaties because a solution of this issue might cause "the
collapse of the so-called Nationalist movement,"[109] and threaten the as-
cendancy of the Nationalist leaders who were preaching anti-foreignism.[110]

The attitude of the *Times* toward the Kuomintang was also similar to
that of the Chicago *Tribune* in that it believed that if it were not "for the
powerful influence of Soviet Russia in stimulating anti-foreign sentiment
among the Cantonese, the sympathy of the American people would probably

[103] *Ibid.,* March 22, 1927.
[104] *Ibid.*
[105] *Ibid.,* February 3, 1927.
[106] *New York Times,* March 3, 1927.
[107] *Ibid.,* January 25, 1927.
[108] *Ibid.,* March 6, 1927.
[109] *Ibid.,* January 30, 1927.
[110] *Ibid.,* February 2, 1927.

be largely in their behalf."[111] The *Times* was, however, not concerned with the infiltration of communist doctrines into China, but with the effects of Russian imperialism:

> The Reds ... although nominally the friends of the new China are actually endeavoring not only to dominate that country but seriously to embarrass the foreign Powers in China. Their purpose is not the introduction of Communism. This fact cannot be sufficiently stressed. To speak, therefore, of 'Bolshevizing' China, or of the Cantonese as Reds, is misleading. But they do hope by their plots and their propaganda to further the cause of Russian imperialism. Their methods, not their aims, differ from those of their Czarist predecessors.[112]

In this period — from the beginning of January to the Nanking Incident — the *Times* favored neither a policy of intervention nor of conciliation in China.[113] In an editorial, published on January 23rd, it stated that there would be time enough to discuss a revision of the treaties when the current wave of anti-foreignism subsided: "Obviously this [a revision of the treaties] cannot be done at the moment. This is no time either for undignified efforts of propitiation or for the use of force."[114] The example of the British whose attempts to conciliate the Chinese had only been met by a fresh outburst of aggression suggested, the *Times* said, that "the Chinese were determined to be unreasonable whether faced by force or kindness."[115] On the other hand, the *Times* maintained that neither Great Britain, nor Japan, nor the United States wished to see force used in China except as a last resort to defend the lives of their nationals.[116] "Intervention in the internal affairs of China," the editors asserted, "is not at all the order of the day."[117]

The *Literary Digest,* as seen above, believed that there was emphatic press approval for the principles embodied in the Porter Resolution. The newspapers which it cited as endorsing with enthusiasm the idea of "a new deal for China," and as desiring independent action on the part of the United States Government, ranged from so-called liberal to conservative publications. If the *Digest's* views were correct, the Administration in Washington had good reason to feel that any official offer to enter into an immediate and extensive revision of the treaties with China would enlist staunch and widespread editorial support.

Currents of thought which were apparent in the Congressional debate

[111] *Ibid.,* March 6, 1927.
[112] *Ibid.,* March 19, 1927.
[113] *Ibid.,* January 23, 1927.
[114] *Ibid.*
[115] *Ibid.,* February 2, 1927; see also January 10, 1927.
[116] *Ibid.*
[117] *Ibid.*

on the Porter Resolution were also evident in the comments of the newspapers that favored a "pro-Chinese" policy. There was a marked tendency to look upon the history of the foreign Powers (including the United States) in China as one devoted largely to exploitation and other selfish purposes. China's ills were laid at the door of other nations and it was generally assumed that the Nationalist Revolution was — in the words of the Baltimore *Sun* — a "perfectly normal patriotic movement" whose success would solve many of China's problems. To brand the Kuomintang as "Communist" was regarded as inaccurate and unjust.

The sensational developments in the early months of 1927 served an important function as far as the American press was concerned. By placing China in the forefront of the news items of the day, they brought about the formation of editorial policies. As a consequence when the Nanking Incident occurred at the end of March, 1927, the press was well prepared to adopt the positive and aggressive rôle which it assumed in the crisis that followed. The cry against intervention which was raised after the Nanking Incident could in fact have been heard in varying forms by even a casual listener several months earlier.

Chapter XIII

THE PROTECTION OF NATIONALS

In the first week of January, 1927, a Chinese mob overran the British Concession at Hankow. There had, in fact, been many disturbances at Hankow since that city was captured by the Nationalist troops in September of 1926. A large number of labor unions had been organized and numerous strikes had taken place accompanied by large anti-foreign demonstrations.[1] As in the case of the riots and boycotts which followed the May 30th Incident at Shanghai, the Japanese were first called upon to bear the brunt of the attack, but the hostility of the Chinese soon shifted to the British. On December 21st, an attempt was made to enter the British Concession at Hankow but was repulsed by a cordon of British marines. Throughout Christmas week, the agitation among the Chinese increased in intensity and both anti-foreign and anti-Christian demonstrations were held at Hankow, Hanyang, and Wuchang.

On January 3rd, a mob of Chinese again tried to force its way into the British Concession at Hankow.[2] British troops were landed and took their place by the side of thirty-five British marines who were already on shore attempting to guard the Concession. The crowd subjected the troops to a hailstorm of bricks and stones for several hours, wounding three British marines and knocking down others. The British authorities commanded their men not to fire and, after receiving assurances that the Chinese would maintain order, withdrew their forces to warships lying at anchor in the Yangtze.

On the next day, a British naval party was again landed and again withdrawn. An agreement was made by which Chinese troops were to replace the British, but the arrangement did not prevent a Chinese mob from overrunning the Concession. On the 5th of January, the mob continued to roam over the Concession, and strike pickets took possession of all the public buildings with the exception of the British consulate. By January 6th, most of the British women and children at Hankow had been placed on board boats and sent to Shanghai, the men either departing with them

---

[1] The facts related in this paragraph are based on the account in the *Survey of International Affairs*, 1926, pp. 344-348.

[2] For a description of the attack on the British Concessions at Hankow and Kiukiang, see Sir Austen Chamberlain's speech in the House of Commons, February 10, 1927 (Parliamentary Debates Vol. 202, p. 321) and the *Survey of International Affairs*, 1926, pp. 348-350.

or concentrating at points along the river front from which they could be removed expeditiously.

On January 4th, a crisis similar to that which had arisen at Hankow occurred at Kiukiang. Here, the women and children were evacuated from the British Concession on the same day. On January 6th and 7th, the Concession at Kiukiang was also overrun by a Chinese mob which engaged in some looting and destruction of property. This was followed by the departure of all foreign nationals from the city.

The attacks on the British Concession at Hankow and Kiukiang emphasized sharply the danger with which foreigners were surrounded in China. These incidents were, in fact, to usher in a period of excessive tension for many foreigners, and a time of tragedy for some.

Abroad, the most concern was felt for the security of the foreign community at Shanghai, partly because of the large number of persons involved, and partly because it was generally assumed that the worst battle of the Revolution would take place over the possession of Shanghai. In January, 1927, Chiang Kai-shek renewed his military campaign against Sun Ch'uan-fang and heavy fighting occurred in Chekiang. With the increasing successes of the Nationalist troops in February, it became more and more evident that Shanghai would shortly be included in the area of conflict.

In the meantime, however, the position of foreigners in other sections of China constituted a very genuine cause of anxiety. On January 7th, the Department of the Navy at Washington announced that Admiral Clarence S. Williams, Commander-in-chief of the United States Asiatic Fleet, had been ordered to proceed to China to see that the proper precautions were taken to ensure the safety of American nationals.[3] On January 13th, the American Legation at Peking authorized all Consuls in Central and South China, at their discretion, to advise the withdrawal without delay of United States citizens to places where they might receive protection or from which they could be evacuated if an emergency arose.[4]

The need for the adoption of precautionary measures was unhappily illustrated on the day following the issuance of the Legation's order. There was serious rioting at Foochow which started with an attack on the Spanish Sisters and priests of the Dominican Holy Childhood Orphanage. The rioting spread rapidly and resulted in the looting of almost all the foreign mission property within the walled city of Foochow, including the American Methodist church and hospital and two residences of the American Board.[5]

The incident at Foochow was viewed with considerable apprehension

[3] *United States Daily,* January 12, 1927, p. 5.
[4] *Ibid.,* February 1, 1927, p. 1; *Foreign Relations* (1927), p. 254.
[5] *Foreign Relations* (1927), pp. 242-244.

in the United States as being the first to involve a serious attack on American citizens. Newspapers carried lurid headlines such as: "American Women Dragged in Street by Foochow Mob,"[6] "Foochow Mob Fury Burns Itself Out,"[7] "United States Warship Goes to Quell Foochow Riot."[8] Secretary Kellogg, on his part, expressed to the press his anxiety over the events at Foochow and indicated that this was the first of the incidents in China over which he had become deeply concerned.[9] Dr. A. L. Warnshuis, as Secretary of the International Missionary Council, was notified that, in the opinion of the Department of State, all American missionary organizations having representatives in the Yangtze Valley or in South China should make suitable preparations for the evacuation of their mission stations so that this might be accomplished in the least possible time in case of need.[10]

In China, Frank P. Lockhart, the American Consul General at Hankow, called on Eugene Chen to protest against the attack on American missionaries at Foochow. In the course of the conversation, Mr. Lockhart said that the Legation had reached the point of seriously contemplating the immediate withdrawal of all Americans from the territory under Nationalist control. Mr. Chen earnestly requested that the United States refrain from adopting such a measure and indicated that he was disturbed over the gradual withdrawal of American citizens that was already taking place; the wholesale departure of Americans he felt might be interpreted as having been undertaken to promote the interests of the British.[11] As a result of Mr. Chen's attitude Mr. MacMurray withheld the general warning he had considered issuing to American citizens to evacuate the provinces which were under Nationalist control.[12]

At the same time, the Legation felt that it was essential to withdraw Americans from certain regions and, on January 23rd, Mr. MacMurray ordered a number of Consuls to carry out the necessary measures as quickly and as quietly as possible. The Consuls at Chungking and Changsha were instructed to expedite the evacuation of all Americans in their districts, while the Consuls at Hankow and Nanking were told that Americans in the less accessible portions of their districts should concentrate in places from which they could be rapidly removed if essential.[13] These plans were put into effect immediately, with the result that on February 10th, the American

---

[6] *New York Times*, January 17, 1927, p. 1.

[7] *Ibid.*, January 18, 1927, p. 4.

[8] New York *Herald Tribune*, January 8, 1927, p. 1.

[9] *United States Daily*, January 26, 1927, p. 1.

[10] *Foreign Relations* (1927), p. 245.

[11] *Ibid.*, pp. 249-250.

[12] *Ibid.*, p. 250.

[13] *Ibid.*, p. 254; *United States Daily*, February 1, 1927.

Consul at Changsha reported that Americans were leaving as expeditiously as the transportation facilities would permit and that only ten missionaries and fourteen business men intended to remain;[14] and, on February 19th, the consul at Chungking stated that so far as Szechuan was concerned the field would "soon be largely cleared."[15] Similarly in South China, the evacuation of all Americans from Foochow was undertaken and American citizens residing in remote points in the Canton, Swatow, and Amoy districts were brought to centers where they could readily receive protection.[16]

Hand-in-hand with the news concerning the withdrawal of foreign nationals from certain sections of China, came the more startling news of the mobilization of troops to be sent to the Chinese scene. Early in January, by way of reassuring the American public, the Department of the Navy issued a list of the forty-one United States vessels of war stationed in Asiatic waters.[17] On January 22nd, it was officially stated that Mr. MacMurray, who was en route to the United States, had been ordered back to his post at Peking because of the gravity of the situation and that 250 marines had been instructed to go from Guam to Manila to be nearer the coast of China.[18] A few days later, January 24th, it was announced in London that the British Government intended to send a substantial body of troops to China to be known as the Shanghai Defense Force. The Force was to consist of three infantry brigades, two of which were to be dispatched from Great Britain and the Mediterranean, and one from India.[19]

The action of the British caused a wave of agitation in the United States. Banner headlines in the press proclaimed the news to the American public. A statement was immediately issued on behalf of President Coolidge at the White House, asserting that there were differences between the American and British policies in China and that while the United States sought to protect its nationals it did not need an extensive concentration of troops because — unlike the British — it maintained no Concessions on Chinese territory.[20] Senator Borah, on his part, made it plain at once that he was severely critical of the military measures undertaken by the British. In a statement given to the press on January 27th,[21] he declared that the most significant scene in the world was "to see a great people after years of turmoil and strife and oppression by outside Powers" come into their own

[14] Ibid., p. 259.
[15] Ibid., p. 261.
[16] Ibid., p. 254.
[17] United States Daily, January 8, 1927, p. 5; January 12, 1927, p. 5.
[18] Ibid., January 22, 1927, p. 1; New York Times, January 22, 1927, p. 1.
[19] Survey of Foreign Affairs, 1926, p. 374.
[20] United States Daily, January 26, 1927, p. 1.
[21] Ibid., January 28, 1927, p. 1.

and that such a scene was being enacted in China; he expressed himself as fully in sympathy with what the Chinese were doing. Referring to the protection of foreign nationals and the dispatch of troops to China, he continued:

It is inevitable of course that some wrongs may be committed and some injuries done to innocent people in the bringing about of the final results [of the Chinese fight for independence]. But I see every indication upon the part of the Chinese at the present time to protect the lives and property of foreigners to the utmost of their ability. The only thing which in my judgment may change that program will be just such things as the sending of fleets and armies to China with a view to crushing this [nationalistic] spirit through force. I am in favor of protecting our people but I am in favor of protecting them at the present time if necessary by bringing them out of danger until the danger is passed. I would not embarrass or impede China in her great struggle. I think, if I may say so, that the action of Great Britain in sending a large fleet and large forces to China may have a very disastrous result.[22]

President Coolidge was, however, not prepared to support Senator Borah's proposal that American citizens be brought out of danger zones in China until all danger had passed. In response to the Senator's remarks an authorized statement was given out at the White House in which the President said that, as far as the Americans in Shanghai were concerned, he did not believe that they should be forced to withdraw from China but rather that they should be given adequate protection. Americans, he pointed out, were living in Shanghai under the right of law and there was no reason for asking them to leave their property and their business; furthermore, if foreigners were to abandon their large and important interests at Shanghai, the Chinese themselves would be among the foremost to suffer.[23]

It is evident from the press releases issued by the President that the Administration in Washington was anxious to impress on the public its willingness, on the one hand, to protect its nationals in China, and its desire, on the other, to refrain from taking any action that might appear

---

[22] Senator Borah also took occasion to define again his attitude toward the question of the revision of China's treaties.

"China," he said, "is entitled to be rid of the old, antiquated, unjust and unilateral treaties. She is entitled to enjoy tariff autonomy. She is entitled in my judgment to be rid of extraterritorial rights. . . . If the nations do not assist, do not voluntarily aid, in bringing it about, we shall likely see the same thing accomplished through the decree of the Chinese people."

The Senator further pronounced himself in favor of the thesis advanced by the Porter Resolution, namely, that the United States should steer an independent course in China if circumstances made it necessary to do so. American interests as well as a sense of justice, he said, demanded a "free and disenthralled China."

[23] United States Daily, January 29, 1927, p. 1.

unnecessarily militant or aggressive. The latter aspect of American policy was, moreover, carried out in practice by the dispatch of a relatively small number of troops to China. The 250 marines which had been sent to Guam in January were instructed to go to Shanghai, where they arrived on the 10th of February.[24] Early in February, 1,228 additional marines sailed on board the *Chaumont* which reached Shanghai at the end of the month.[25] In addition, three cruisers were ordered to Honolulu in February, carrying approximately 160 men each.[26] These appear to have been the only American forces that were mobilized to reinforce the 800 United States troops that were already stationed on boats at Shanghai.[27]

The rôle which the United States played in the formulation and execution of the plan for the defense of Shanghai further illustrated the desire of the United States Government to avoid adopting any military measures that the Chinese — or the American public — might construe as going beyond the protection of our nationals and amounting to intervention. As early as December 19, 1926, Mr. MacMurray took up with the Department in Washington the question of plans for the defense of Shanghai. He reported that Clarence E. Gauss, temporarily United States Consul General at Shanghai (in the absence of Consul General Cunningham), had forwarded his views of the situation to the Legation after the holding of informal meetings by officials of the Shanghai Municipal Council, the Consular Body, and senior naval officers.

According to Mr. Gauss, the Shanghai Municipal Council maintained that if the Shanghai region were invaded by Cantonese armies, a landing force of from 4,000 to 5,000 foreign troops would be needed. While Mr. Gauss and Commander Armstrong, the senior American naval officer at Shanghai, believed that a larger body of troops would be required than on similar occasions which had occurred previously, they thought that — unless circumstances changed — the estimate of the Municipal Council was too high. Mr. Gauss and Commander Armstrong also agreed that in landing United States naval forces "it should be definitely understood" that they were to be employed *solely* for the protection of foreign life and property and would not, "except under orders of the higher American authorities, be used to oppose any organized occupation of the International Settlement by the armed forces of the Nationalist Government."[28]

It was the latter point which became a source of dispute among American

[24] *Ibid.*, February 12, 1927, p. 2.
[25] *Ibid.*, March 1, 1927, p. 1.
[26] *Foreign Relations* (1927), p. 66.
[27] *Ibid.*
[28] *Ibid.* (1926), p. 662.

officials. Commenting on this issue, Mr. MacMurray cabled to the Secretary of State:

> . . . I am of the firm opinion that the integrity of the International and French Settlements must be maintained under any circumstances even should it mean collision with organized Cantonese forces. Otherwise, occupation of other settlements, denunciation of extraterritoriality, and widespread and systematic disregard of foreign lives and interests would, in all probability, be only a matter of time. Should a landing force be required, I regard it as essential that its main objectives and the scope of its responsibility should be definitely understood in advance. Such a force should know what it is there for — the purpose of protecting both the integrity of the Settlements and foreign life and property, or only the latter.[29]

The Secretary of State responded to this message with decisive instructions that left no doubt of the Department's opinion:

> Should an emergency arise at Shanghai involving the necessity of landing force from American naval vessels present, it must be definitely understood that this force is present for the purpose of protecting American life and property at Shanghai. This Government is not prepared to use its naval force at Shanghai for the purpose of protecting integrity of the Settlement and should any question of this sort arise Department would desire to be consulted.[30]

At the time that these instructions were sent — December 23, 1926 — conditions along the Yangtze were, from the point of view of foreigners, still relatively quiet. After the incidents at Hankow and Kiukiang, however, tension increased in Shanghai, and, on January 11th, the Shanghai Municipal Council suggested to the Consular Body that it might be advisable to land approximately 1,000 troops in the International Settlement. The members of the Consular Body were in favor of the Council's proposal, with the exception of Mr. Gauss and the Italian representative.[31] Mr. Gauss believed that it was imperative to have sufficient forces on ships in the harbor but that no actual landing of troops should take place until disorder or violence was "unquestionably imminent;" he based his views on the conviction that a premature landing would only succeed in forming a pretext for further anti-foreign propaganda among the Chinese and in furnishing "the spark to kindle the fire."[32] Mr. Gauss' attitude was, furthermore, shared by Mr. MacMurray.[33]

---

[29] *Ibid.*, p. 663.

[30] *Ibid.*

[31] *Ibid.* (1927), p. 45. The British, French, and Japanese Consuls changed their minds later and decided against the landing of troops at this time. (*Ibid.*, p. 46.)

[32] *Ibid.*, p. 46.

[33] *Ibid.*

In regard to the general policy to be adopted by the United States for the defense of Shanghai, however, Mr. MacMurray again urged the Secretary of State, on January 15, 1927, to adopt a firm stand, acting in concert with the other foreign Powers:

Conditions are so inflammable in Shanghai that there is certain to be an explosion if the Nationalists extend control to that area unless the leaders of the Nationalists are convinced definitely that the limit of tolerance has been reached by the foreign Powers and that the Powers are prepared wholeheartedly to unite on a stand for the protection of their nationals and interests in Shanghai. The situation is one in which, it is my firm belief, the only possible escape from the necessity to employ force is an obvious readiness to employ it.[34]

Mr. MacMurray asserted, additionally, that he could not "recommend too urgently" that the Department endeavor without delay to obtain assurances concerning the attitude of the British and the Japanese.[35] On this occasion, he declared, moreover, that he did not believe a distinction could be made between the defense of the International Settlement and the defense of the lives and property of its residents; nor did he think it possible to differentiate between a concerted attack by organized forces and mob violence.[36]

On January 26th — two days after announcement had been made of the British decision to assemble the Shanghai Defense Force — Sir Esme Howard, the British Ambassador at Washington, handed a memorandum to Secretary of State Kellogg explaining the attitude of the Foreign Office toward the defense of the International Settlement.[37] As the Foreign Office saw the matter, the lesson of Hankow was that if a Chinese mob got out of control, either because the authorities could not or would not control it, the Nationalist army would act with, rather than against, the mob. Moreover the British believed that the Cantonese forces, under Bolshevik influence, would be encouraged by their success at Hankow to adopt similar methods with other Settlements unless it was made clear that the foreign troops available were not only amply sufficient to control a mob but also to deal with a mob if it was reinforced by individual soldiers or by armed contingents. If danger threatened it would be necessary to evacuate the smaller Settlements, but Shanghai and Shameen were, in the opinion of the British, on a different footing, "especially Shanghai." The evacuation of Shanghai they regarded as physically impossible and thought that, if attempted, it would both

[34] Ibid., p. 47 (cable paraphrased).
[35] Ibid., p. 49.
[36] Ibid., p. 47.
[37] Text of Note, ibid., pp. 56-58.

involve loss of life and affect the position and rights of the Treaty Powers in China to an extent that would be "disastrous." Bolshevik influence was, according to the reports of British official observers at Hankow, so strong in the Nationalist Government and army, that the Cantonese were "unlikely to be satisfied with anything short of complete and practically unconditional surrender, first by Great Britain and then by all the other Powers, of the whole treaty position."

In view of these circumstances, the British note stated, His Majesty's Government had determined that the duty to protect their nationals made it necessary to hold that part of the International Settlement within which British interests were concentrated "at all costs." The Foreign Office had, the memorandum explained, approached the Japanese with the idea of obtaining their co-operation in the formation of an international force for the defense of the Settlement. Nothing had come of the matter as the Japanese had replied that they neither considered such preparations necessary nor did they believe the time had come even to discuss them; they had, moreover, declined to give any assurance that in case of emergency they would be prepared to take any of the measures necessary for the defense of the Settlement, pending the arrival of military contingents from other countries, which, owing to the distance, could not be made available at once. His Majesty's Government had, therefore, decided to send reinforcements from India and Europe and had issued orders to that effect. In co-operation with the French, the British would, if possible, hold Shanghai. Any assistance the United States was prepared to give would be "warmly welcome." At the same time it was to be clearly understood that the military measures taken by His Majesty's Government were "purely precautionary."

The British memorandum was discussed in Washington, together with a cable from Admiral Williams and Mr. Gauss in which the latter stated that if Chiang Kai-shek's armies actually intended to take possession of the International Settlement any naval landing forces would be entirely inadequate to meet the situation; if the Powers really wished to insure the inviolability of the Settlement, he said, and the protection of life and property, it would be necessary to send about 20,000 troops.[38]

Plans for the defense of Shanghai were regarded as a very important issue in Washington. After the receipt of the British note, President Coolidge wrote a memorandum on the subject which was considered at a meeting of the Cabinet.[39] President Coolidge declared that, in his opinion, the United States' answer to the British note — and to Admiral Williams and Mr. Gauss — should be that Admiral Williams had "instructions to give

[38] *Ibid.*, p. 50.
[39] Text of memorandum, *ibid.*, p. 50.

Americans protection with his naval forces;" by this Mr. Coolidge meant, according to his own explanation, that he did not approve of sending "a large force of the Regular Army" to Shanghai. To show why he had reached this conclusion, he offered several different arguments:

(1) Only one country is reported to be landing a large force at Shanghai. Japan has declined to do so.

(2) If we sent to Shanghai a large force of the Regular Army it would mean arousing all of China and involve us probably in making war on Cantonese forces perhaps with opposing forces. It seems to us that while such action might succeed at Shanghai, if the Cantonese do not have too large a force, it inevitably would inflame all China against thousands of Americans not in Shanghai who probably cannot be evacuated or protected.

(3) Through our Minister we are immediately making efforts . . . to see whether it is possible to make an arrangement guaranteeing the neutrality of the International Settlement.

(4) I feel satisfied that for us at the present to send a large force of regular soldiers, outside of the Navy, would be very strongly condemned publicly here, in Congress and out, and would inflame China.

President Coolidge's statement that efforts were being made to see whether it was possible to make an arrangement guaranteeing the neutrality of the International Settlement referred to a plan that was being put into action by the State Department. On January 28, 1927, Secretary Kellogg wired to Mr. MacMurray the text of a note to be delivered to the leaders of the various warring factions in China. While the note spent some time in presenting facts concerning the importance of Shanghai as one of "the great ports of the world," the heart of the declaration lay in the following paragraphs:

The American Government in submitting these facts to some of the various parties powerful in China today is hopeful that their leaders will lend all possible support to the proposal now made that the International Settlement at Shanghai be excluded from the area of armed conflict and that the authorities in control of all the armed forces in China shall voluntarily undertake to abstain from all effort to enter the International Settlement by force and even to station military forces in its immediate vicinity.

Having solely in view the common good of foreign and Chinese citizens, the American Government invites all interested parties to maintain the neutrality of the foreign Settlement in order that American and other foreign lives may have adequate protection. The American Government will be ready, for its part, to become a party to a friendly and orderly negotiation regarding the changes in the protection and changes in the administration of the International Settlement and the reconsideration of the whole subject of its control.[40]

[40] *Ibid.,* p. 60.

The delivery of the Secretary of State's note was delayed for several days because Mr. MacMurray felt that the proposals involved were exceedingly ill-advised. "With all possible earnestness," he cabled to Mr. Kellogg, "I beg you to reconsider the proposed message . . . with regard to the neutralization of Shanghai. I am certain that such proposals would not accomplish their purpose and that any assurances given in reply would be merely illusory . . . and that the effect of such an appeal to the Chinese would be to encourage in them an aggressive mood which would measurably increase the danger to the lives and property of our citizens in Shanghai and elsewhere."[41]

Mr. MacMurray pointed out that the proposed message appealed to the Chinese to exclude the International Settlement from the area of conflict; to abstain from entering it by force; and to station no military forces in its immediate vicinity. As the first two points, he said, were matters of right, to submit them as new suggestions "prompted merely by motives of expediency" would amount to presenting the Nationalists with "a veritable challenge" to assert a right to do precisely that which the United States was supplicating them not to do. On the third point, Mr. MacMurray argued that to urge the Chinese not to station troops in the immediate vicinity of the Settlement meant either that the Northerners would have to evacuate the Shanghai area or that the Southerners would have to renounce taking any military action against them; either alternative would constitute an intervention in the factional war of the Chinese which would "hopelessly compromise" the position of the United States.[42]

Concerning the statement in the message, that the American Government was willing to enter into negotiations in respect to the International Settlement, Mr. MacMurray was equally emphatic in his objections:

". . . I feel strongly that for the United States to make an offer of fundamental changes in the status of the International Settlement without previous consultation and understanding with the other nationalists [nations?] jointly responsible with us would be not only an act of bad faith toward them but an incitement to the Cantonese faction to force the issue."[43]

The Secretary of State responded at once to Mr. MacMurray's criticisms with a dispatch that was especially interesting in that it re-emphasized the importance which President Coolidge had already attached to the state of public opinion in the United States in regard to the sending of troops to China:

"It is necessary for you to understand that American sentiment is very strongly opposed to military action in China by this Government except

[41] *Ibid.*, p. 64.
[42] *Ibid.*
[43] *Ibid.*, p. 65.

for protecting American life and property. No sentiment exists here that would support any military action on the part of this Government for the object of maintaining present status and integrity of the International Settlement at Shanghai."[44]

The United States Government did not, the Secretary stated further, intend to remove its naval forces from Chinese waters as long as their presence was required for the protection of American life; if landing forces became necessary for the protection of American citizens in the International Settlement there would be general approval of such action only if it could be "demonstrated that every effort to protect American citizens by peaceful measures had been exhausted beforehand."[45]

In regard to the question of opening negotiations concerning the International Settlement, Mr. Kellogg said that it was understood in Washington that in the negotiations being conducted between the Chinese and the British at Hankow, the British were making "considerable concessions . . . in the matter of administration of the residential Concessions held by the British in China. . . . As one of the Powers responsible," he added, "for the status possessed by the International Settlement at Shanghai, the United States cannot afford to be less ready in the matter of making concessions where responsibility for making them rests upon it."[46]

Relying in part upon the fact that the Cabinet had agreed that the State Department should undertake a plan such as that which had been outlined in his "neutralization message," the Secretary of State overruled Mr. MacMurray's objections and instructed him to deliver the memorandum to the Northern and Southern leaders in China.[47] In consideration of the American Minister's criticisms, however, the passage of the memorandum which has already been quoted was changed to read:

> In recalling these facts to the Chinese military commanders, the American Government is confident that they will lend their sincere support to the proposal now made — that the International Settlement at Shanghai be excluded from the area of armed conflict so that American citizens and other foreigners may receive adequate protection. The American Government will be ready for its part to become a party to friendly and orderly negotiations properly instituted and conducted regarding the future status of the Settlement.[48]

While the amended version still requested the Chinese to exclude the

[44] *Ibid.*, (cable paraphrased).
[45] *Ibid.*
[46] *Ibid.*
[47] *Ibid.*, p. 66.
[48] *Ibid.*

International Settlement from the area of conflict, it did not suggest — as had the earlier draft — that the Chinese refrain from stationing military forces within the vicinity of Shanghai. Apparently Mr. MacMurray's arguments had been convincing in this respect. The Secretary was, in fact, quite incensed when Eugene Chen denounced the American proposal as an attempt to "neutralize Shanghai" which would amount to intervention in favor of the Northern factions since it would make possible the release of Sun Ch'uan-fang's troops in the Shanghai area for use elsewhere.[49] The memorandum, Mr. Kellogg said, contained no recommendation for the neutralization of Shanghai, nor did it involve "in any way" a discussion of what troops might occupy or hold the area outside of the boundary of the International Settlement; the memorandum was, he insisted, "self-explanatory and should not be subjected to misinterpretation of this kind."[50]

The question of what Mr. Kellogg had in mind, in respect to negotiations regarding the future status of the Settlement, furnishes some interesting grounds for speculation. On the day after the message concerning the exclusion of the International Settlement from the area of conflict was made public — February 8, 1927 — Secretary Kellogg stated orally to the press at Washington that his proposal carried with it the willingness of the United States to enter into negotiations to provide the Chinese with partial control of the Settlement and contemplated giving China representation on the Shanghai Municipal Council.[51] While this was a clear enough statement of policy, there are indications that Mr. Kellogg would have been willing to go beyond any such plan as the Shanghai Ratepayers had adopted of offering three seats on the Municipal Council to the Chinese. In the original draft of his message, the Secretary had spoken of the American Government's readiness to discuss "changes in the protection and changes in the administration of the International Settlement" and to reconsider "the whole subject of its control." Mr. MacMurray, as we have seen, understood this to mean "fundamental changes in the status of the Settlement" which, indeed, the phraseology would seem to imply. Moreover, during conversations held at this time between the British Ambassador at Washington and American officials, references were made which suggest that the State Department was thinking in terms of a radical alteration of the status of the Settlement. In a memorandum of a conversation held on January 27th, the Secretary of State referred to some remarks of Sir Esme Howard's: "He repeated to me that they [the British] were perfectly willing to negotiate the giving up of the control of the foreign settlement but they did not propose to permit the

[49] Ibid., p. 72.
[50] Ibid., pp. 72-73.
[51] United States Daily, February 8, 1927, pp. 1-2.

Cantonese to take it by force or march into it."[52] On the following day
Mr. Nelson T. Johnson went, on the Secretary's request, to discuss the
Shanghai situation with the British Ambassador. He described his visit in
a note to the Secretary:

> I told him that, in a conversation with you, you had been led to under-
> stand that the British Government would not be averse to discussions for a
> change in the status of the International Settlement at Shanghai. I said to
> him that we were contemplating sending an instruction to our Minister at
> Peking, directing him to see what could be done toward taking the question
> of the neutrality of the area of the International Settlement . . . up with the
> contending factions concerned. . . . I said that I felt certain that to make
> such advances would bring a request for our attitude with regard to the
> future status of the Settlement and I wondered whether the British Govern-
> ment would be willing that we should say that we were prepared to nego-
> tiate for a change in the status of the Settlement. The Ambassador stated
> that he was not instructed on the matter and he did not think the British
> Government was prepared to go that far. He said, after all, the Settlement
> was not American. . . . He stated that he thought we could not go further
> than to express our willingness to consult the Powers with a view to discov-
> ering what their intentions would be in the matter.[53]

Whatever the desires of the United States Government may have been,
the proposal for entering into negotiations for the future status of the Settlement did not produce any more fruitful results than the similar proposal
advanced by the Secretary of State for a revision of the American treaties
with China. Nor did the State Department's memorandum to the Chinese
leaders, requesting the exclusion of the International Settlement from the
area of conflict, meet with a happy reception.[54] Eugene Chen made vigorous
protests to Mr. Lockhart at Hankow — partially on the grounds already
mentioned — but finally determined to make no public reply to the memorandum "as he did not wish to irritate what he described as an unpleasant
situation."[55]

As the month of February progressed, the time and the opportunity for
diplomatic discussion grew less and less. On February 15th, two battalions
of English troops landed at Shanghai.[56] A general strike was declared on
the 19th, involving the transportation services, the post office, the cotton mills
and many of the leading stores.[57] The strike while it lasted — which was
only over a period of five days — caused little disorder in the International

[52] *Foreign Relations* (1927), p. 59.
[53] *Ibid.*, p. 355.
[54] See *ibid.*, pp. 70, 72, 73, 74.
[55] *Ibid.*, p. 73.
[56] *Survey of International Affairs*, 1926, p. 376.
[57] *Ibid;* also, *United States Daily*, February 24, 1927, p. 2.

Settlement. In the Chinese city of Shanghai, however, the strike was suppressed by Sun Ch'uan-fang's men by means of what was termed "a veritable reign of terror."[58] The estimate of those who were killed on the side of the strikers varies considerably but it was said at the time that over one hundred were beheaded within a few days.[59]

On February 24th, the Diplomatic Body at Peking issued an announcement concerning the situation at Shanghai, the purpose of which was to declare that the authorities of the International Settlement were scrupulously maintaining a strict neutrality in the factional war in China and looked to the heads of the Chinese armies to avoid the occurrence of incidents that "would constrain the foreign authorities . . . to take the measures indispensable for insuring the safety of the persons and property of their nationals."[60] A day later, British troops were moved out to a defense line which had been planned to form a cordon around the International Settlement. Barbed-wire entanglements were erected, and patrols and pickets with machine guns were placed on duty along the line.[61]

At the same time that British troops were moved into position, Mr. Stirling Fessenden, as Chairman of the Shanghai Municipal Council, requested the other foreign Powers to lend military assistance for the defense of the Settlement boundaries in view of the large numbers of Chinese soldiers in the vicinity.[62] But Mr. Gauss was still opposed to the landing of American marines and stated that, in view of the absence of disorder or any threat of disorder in the International Settlement, he could see no justification for taking any such action.[63] The Japanese also took the attitude that there was no need to disembark forces at this time although they had actually already quartered a small body of a few hundred men at the Japanese naval club in Shanghai.[64]

The stand taken by Mr. Gauss was based, fundamentally, on the fact that the United States Government continued to insist that it would not fight to maintain the integrity of the International Settlement and was only willing to ensure the safety of the lives and property of its nationals. This matter came up again for discussion between American officials, late in February. According to a report sent to the State Department by Mr. Mac-Murray, Admiral Williams told the naval commanders of the other foreign Powers at Shanghai that his instructions were to protect Americans but that

[58] New York *World*, February 21, 1927, p. 1; February 22, 1927, p. 1.
[59] *Ibid.*, February 25, 1927, p. 1.
[60] *Foreign Relations* (1927), p. 78.
[61] *Ibid.*, p. 81.
[62] *Ibid.*, p. 82.
[63] *Ibid.*
[64] *Ibid.*

he was not ordered to assist in protecting the integrity of the Settlement against the Nationalist army; in carrying out this mission, he would co-operate and give protection to all foreigners up to such time when the Cantonese should demand the control of the city. If the Cantonese should demand the surrender of the Settlement, or should attack without a demand for its surrender, while the American landing party was ashore, the withdrawal of our men would be necessary and the only effective protection provided to United States citizens would be the evacuation of them.[65]

Mr. MacMurray believed that the instructions given to Admiral Williams would not furnish adequate protection to American nationals. From the standpoint of practical necessity, he reiterated in a cable to the Department, no distinction could be made between the defense of the Settlement and the defense of its residents, or between a concerted attack and mob violence. He, therefore, urged the Department to see that Admiral Williams be authorized to exercise his discretion in the employment of United States forces, so that he might use them in conjunction with other foreign troops, to protect American lives and property from attack whether by Chinese armies or by a mob. The American Minister's purpose was largely to prevent the withdrawal of American troops under fire (such as the instructions to Admiral Williams seemed to contemplate) in case foreign contingents came into conflict with organized Chinese forces — a withdrawal which would have meant, in his view, leaving the other foreign troops to meet the emergency and shoulder the responsibility for defending our nationals.[66]

In response to Mr. MacMurray's recommendations, the State Department made it clear that Admiral Williams was expected to take "all possible steps for the protection of American life and property."[67] The withdrawal of troops and the evacuation of American citizens was only to be effected as a possible last resort at such time as, in the judgment of the Admiral, military necessity dictated.[68] On the other hand, the Department declared that: "Admiral is aware that it is the earnest desire of this Government to avoid as far as possible any contingency whereby, through the use of its military forces, it may become involved in the political question of the status of the International Settlement."[69] Furthermore, the Department said, it wished to "avoid, firstly, interference with the military measures of the Chinese unless indispensably necessary to protect American life and property,

[65] *Ibid.*, p. 75.
[66] *Ibid.*, p. 76.
[67] *Ibid.*, p. 78; see also pp. 92, 93.
[68] *Ibid.*, p. 78.
[69] *Ibid.*

and, secondly, commitments to other foreign Powers as to protective measures."[70]

By the beginning of March, the organization of the defense line around the Settlement was virtually completed.[71] According to the plan agreed upon, the American troops were not to take part in the maintenance of the cordon but to limit themselves to the suppression of disorders within the Settlement boundaries.[72]

On March 21st, the Nationalist armies of Chiang Kai-shek arrived at a railroad junction four miles south of Shanghai.[73] General Pai Tsung-hsi, in command of the troops, announced that the Nationalists had no intention of recovering China's sovereign rights by military force or by any measures endangering foreign life and property but looked to the orderly negotiation of new treaties with the Powers.[74] Nevertheless, as the situation was obviously explosive, a state of emergency was declared in the International Settlement. The Municipal Council mobilized volunteers and police and requested the assistance of foreign naval forces. In response, American, Japanese, and Dutch troops were landed.[75] According to an official report of Admiral Williams, the number of troops on shore, after the landings, were 12,500: 9,000 British, 1,500 Americans, 1,500 Japanese, 400 French and 50 Italians. This did not include the Shanghai volunteers.[76]

From the point of view of the foreign community in the International Settlement and the French Concession,[77] the passing of Shanghai from the control of Sun Ch'uan-fang into the hands of the Nationalists took place without the creation of a major crisis such as had been anticipated. On the evening of March 21st, some Chinese troops, believed to be Shantungese, broke through the Settlement defense line and started looting. They were driven back by machine gun fire from two British armoured cars; four British soldiers were wounded; the casualties among the Chinese were unknown. On the following day, detachments of Northern soldiers, amounting to approximately 4,000, tried to rush the section of the Settlement held by

[70] *Ibid.*, p. 85.
[71] *Survey of International Affairs*, 1926, p. 376.
[72] *Ibid;* also *Foreign Relations* (1927), pp. 79, 82.
[73] *Ibid.*, p. 89.
[74] *United States Daily*, March 22, 1927, p. 2. A similar announcement had been made by Eugene Chen on January 22, 1927, and again in connection with the Hankow agreement; see below, pp. 287-288.
[75] *Foreign Relations* (1927), p. 89.
[76] *United States Daily*, March 22, 1927, p. 2.
[77] The French Government informed the State Department on March 17th, that their policy was to send "the minimum force possible to protect their concession" and that this force, including the police, did not number 2,000. They stated, furthermore, that they wished to remain "absolutely neutral and to wait for the settlement of Chinese affairs by the Chinese." (*Foreign Relations*, 1927, pp. 87-88.)

the British in order to save themselves from being disarmed by Nationalist "guerillas." The British, unable to stop them, fired, killing about sixty Chinese and wounding about one hundred. These conflicts constituted the most serious difficulties which arose between the Chinese troops and foreign forces at Shanghai.[78]

By March 23rd, the tension in the International Settlement began to decrease and from that time on the situation improved as far as the foreign community in Shanghai was concerned. This was in part due to the fact that the right wing of the Kuomintang — under Chiang Kai-shek's leadership — determined to restore order in the Chinese areas of Shanghai by the suppression of the radicals who had actually executed the insurrection against the Northerners which started on March 21st. It was the labor unions and the workers who on that day had called a general strike and had seized, among other important points, almost all the police stations in the Chinese territory of Shanghai and many military posts containing stocks of arms and ammunition. The strike had, however, been called off within three days by General Pai Tsung-hsi, and fighting had broken out between General Pai's armies and the local radical groups. In the first weeks in April, a bitter struggle developed, ending in the death of several hundred workers and the control of the situation in Shanghai by the right wing of the Kuomintang.[79]

Although the significance of these events was by no means clear to most foreigners at the time, they constituted one of the turning points of the Revolution. Since the beginning of 1927 — and even earlier — it had been evident that the friction within the Kuomintang was increasing and that the alliance between the various factions of the Nationalist movement might not be able to survive for long. In December, the Nationalist Government had moved from Canton to Hankow where it hoped to obtain the support of the peasant and labor unions of Central China.[80] To Chiang Kai-shek and the conservative members of the Kuomintang, this naturally meant a strengthening of the radical character of the Party. And, because their aims were very different from those of the Kuomintang group which established itself at Wuhan, they looked for assistance not to the organized labor of Hankow, but to the bankers, the merchants, and the industrialists of Shanghai.[81]

[78] *Survey of International Affairs*, 1927, p. 373; *Foreign Relations* (1927), p. 90.
[79] For these events, see Isaacs, *The Tragedy of the Chinese Revolution*, p. 157; *Survey of International Affairs*, 1927, p. 372; *Foreign Relations* (1927), p. 90; *Shanghai Municipal Council Gazette*, April 22, 1927, p. 151, and May 20, 1927, p. 187. Probably the best known and certainly the most colorful account of the Shanghai insurrections is that of André Malraux in *La Condition Humaine*.
[80] MacNair, *China in Revolution*, p. 110.
[81] *Ibid.*

In January, 1927, a dispute broke out over the coming meeting of the Central Executive Committee of the Kuomintang. General Chiang wished to have the Committee convene at Nanchang, rather than at Hankow, as his own headquarters were established at Nanchang which was therefore naturally more subject to his influence. The Wuhan group refused to concur in this proposal and the Committee — minus its conservative members — finally met at Hankow on March 10th. Resolutions were passed in which Chiang Kai-shek was demoted from the post of Commander-in-Chief of the Kuomintang armies and from the chairmanship of the Standing Committee of the Central Executive Committee.[82]

Eleven days later, as we have seen, General Chiang's troops arrived at Shanghai. On March 26th, the General himself reached Shanghai where he made contacts with, and received the support of, Chinese bankers and merchants and former members of the Kuomintang who had left the Party because of their opposition to Borodin and his followers.[83] According to reports, the Shanghai Chinese Bankers' Association arranged for an immediate loan.[84] It was at this time — April, 1927 — that Chiang Kai-shek undertook to "purge" the local Nationalist movement in Shanghai of its more radical and Communist influences.

The developments within the Kuomintang and the fall of Shanghai left the world abroad in a state of anxious confusion. Tremendous questions clamor for an answer, the *Literary Digest* said, as Shanghai, China's richest port, passes into the hands of the Cantonese. If the Southern army continues its triumphs and gains complete control of China, will it in turn be controlled by the strong Communist element in the Kuomintang and, under the direction of the Soviet Union, try to make China a center of world revolution, or will the moderates in the Nationalist movement be able to gain the upper hand? In any event, the *Literary Digest* declared, the world breathlessly awaits the answer to the question: what will be the fate of foreigners and foreign interests in China?[85]

This problem was indeed to take on a grave aspect elsewhere in China at the very time that the Northern forces were being ousted from Shanghai and the areas surrounding it. While the outside world was still riveting its attention on Shanghai and expressing fear for the safety of the foreign community in the International Settlement and the French Concession, the crisis which had been averted at Shanghai took place at Nanking.

[82] For these events, see Fischer, *The Soviets in World Affairs*, Vol. 2, p. 665; *Survey of International Affairs*, 1927, p. 339; MacNair, *op. cit.*, pp. 111-112.

[83] MacNair, *op. cit.*, p. 115.

[84] See George E. Sokolsky's statements in *China Year Book*, 1928, p. 1361, and in *The Tinder Box of Asia*, p. 45.

[85] *Literary Digest*, April 2, 1927, p. 9.

BRITISH POLICY

One of the most interesting features of the policies of both the United States and Great Britain, in the early months of 1927, was, as already indicated, that they were designed to fork out in two directions. On the one hand, both Governments emphasized strongly the need to accord their nationals the proper protection against the dangers that might arise in China while, on the other hand, they sought to advance the movement for treaty revision by effecting some constructive changes in China's treaty status.

The actions of the British, which were at this time the most spectacular of those undertaken by any of the Treaty Powers, became a center of controversy both inside and outside of Great Britain. The Chinese on numerous occasions objected bitterly to the dispatch of the Shanghai Defense Force.[86] In Washington, the Chinese Minister brought up the issue with the Secretary of State, asking him if he "would not be willing to use his influence to restrain the British at Shanghai." The Secretary gave the obvious answer that he could not be held responsible for the activities of the British and that doubtless they were taking "such steps as seemed to them necessary to protect their nationals."[87]

In the heated debates which took place in the House of Commons concerning the Shanghai Defense Force, leaders of the British Government explained that British troops were being sent to China because it was impossible to wait until an emergency arose that placed British lives in imminent and serious danger.[88] At the same time they emphasized that His Majesty's Government was willing to adhere to the policy set forth in the December memorandum and even to adopt measures that would implement that policy.[89]

In accordance with the latter statement, the British Government, on January 27, 1927, presented the Chinese authorities at Peking and at Hankow with a note which contained seven proposals for the modification of British privileges in China.[90] The British Government was prepared to recognize the modern Chinese law courts as competent courts for cases brought by British plaintiffs and was willing to waive the right of attendance of a British representative at the hearing of such cases. It was also ready to apply modern Chinese Civil Commercial Codes, together with certain duly enacted

[86] See, for example, New York *World*, February 1, 1927, p. 1; February 3, p. 4; February 10, p. 1; February 17, p. 1; February 19, p. 2.

[87] *Foreign Relations* (1927), p. 87.

[88] See Prime Minister Baldwin's statement (Parliamentary Debates, Vol. 202, p. 15); Sir Austen Chamberlain's statements (*ibid.*, pp. 323, 430).

[89] King's speech (*ibid.*, p. 10); Sir Austen Chamberlain's speech at Birmingham (London *Times*, January 31, 1927, p. 17).

[90] Text in *Treaties and Agreements With and Concerning China, 1919-1929*, pp. 197-198.

subordinate legislation, in the British courts in China. It was prepared to consider the application in British courts in China of a revised Chinese Penal Code as soon as such a code was promulgated and applied in Chinese courts. Further, the note stated that "His Majesty's Government" was "prepared to make British subjects in China liable to pay such regular and legal Chinese taxation, not involving discrimination against British subjects or British goods, as is in fact imposed on, and paid by, Chinese citizens throughout China." In respect to the Concessions held by Great Britain in China, it was said that the British Government was ready to enter into arrangements "for the modification of Municipal Administrations of British Concessions so as to bring them into line with the administrations of Special Chinese Administrations set up in former Concessions, or for their amalgamation with former Concessions now under Chinese control, or for the transfer of police control of Concession areas to the Chinese authorities." In its final proposal the note declared that the British Government was ready to accept the principle that British missionaries should no longer claim the right to purchase land in the interior, that Chinese converts should look to Chinese law and not to treaties for protection, and that missionary educational and medical institutions should conform to Chinese laws and regulations applying to similar Chinese institutions.

In handing the British note to Mr. Eugene Chen, Mr. O'Malley, speaking for his Government, stated that when a satisfactory settlement had been reached concerning the British Concessions at Hankow and Kiukiang, and when the Nationalist Government had given assurances that it would "not countenance any alteration, except by negotiation, of the status of the British Concessions and International Settlements," His Majesty's Government would be prepared to bring into effect the proposals which it had defined.[91]

The negotiations concerning the British Concessions at Hankow and Kiukiang to which Mr. O'Malley referred had been started on the 10th of January. The British had not attempted to take back the Concession at Hankow after it had been overrun by the Chinese mob on January 3rd to 6th; it had decided instead to make arrangements with the Nationalist Government for a complete change in the status of the Concession. The negotiations which were conducted by Mr. Eugene Chen and Mr. O'Malley had a long and bothersome career. A settlement was almost reached at the end of January but Mr. Chen suddenly broke off the discussions, saying that the concentration of British troops at Shanghai was virtually forcing his hand and that he wished to postpone any final decision until what he termed

[91] See *ibid.*

the "period of duress" was over. This deadlock was only temporary, however, and the negotiations were resumed to follow a stormy course once
more until the final papers were signed on February 19th. A similar agreement in relation to the British Concession at Kiukiang was concluded on
March 2nd.[92]

The so-called Chen-O'Malley agreement on Hankow provided that the
British municipality in that city should be dissolved on March 15th, after
which the administration of the concession area was to be handed over to
a new Chinese municipality to be set up by the Nationalist Government.[93]
A large portion of the agreement was devoted to the setting forth of regu-
lations which had been drafted for the Government of the new municipality.
There was to be a director, appointed by the Chinese Minister for Foreign
Affairs, to act as the chief executive officer of the Administration and a
Council of seven members consisting of the Director, three other Chinese
and three British. The Ratepayers at their annual meeting were to elect the
Council as well as perform many other duties such as the adoption of the
budget and the levy of rates and taxes.

As part of the agreement, Mr. Chen issued a declaration asserting that
it was the policy of the Nationalist Government to settle all outstanding
questions with the foreign Powers by negotiation and not by coercion. This
statement, he said, was specifically intended to apply to the foreign Concessions and Settlements: "This necessarily means that the policy of the
Nationalist Government is not to use force or to countenance the use of
force to effect changes in the status of any or all Concessions and International Settlements."

Like the British Government, the Government of the United States
declared persistently that its policy had two aspects: the protection of its
nationals and the furthering of the movement for the revision of China's
treaties. The way in which the Coolidge Administration developed both
strains of its policy has been indicated. While emphasis was laid upon the
need to protect our citizens in China, the Administration believed that an
aggressive policy was unnecessary; that it would result in further endangering the lives of American nationals; and that it would have no popular support in the United States. Not only were relatively few troops sent to China
but American officials took great pains to make it clear that American soldiers were expected to limit their action to insuring the safety of United

[92] For course of the negotiations at Hankow, see *Survey of International Affairs*, 1926,
p. 352. See also *Affairs of China*, by Sir Eric Teichman, who assisted Mr. O'Malley with
the negotiations.

[93] Text, China No. 3 (1927) Cmd. 2869, *Papers Respecting Agreements Relative to the
British Concessions at Hankow and Kiukiang.*

States citizens primarily from the attacks of uncontrolled mobs. One of the points at which American policy appears to have differed from that of the British was that the United States was not willing to fight to maintain the integrity of the International Settlement at Shanghai.

The United States did not offer any concrete proposals such as those set forth in the British note of January, 1927, or enter into any arrangements analogous to the Sino-British agreements on Hankow and Kiukiang but it sought to take steps toward a modification of our treaty relations with China by declaring its readiness to enter into comprehensive negotiations looking toward the conclusion of new treaties. It must always be remembered that Mr. Kellogg's statement of January 27th, and his later offer to negotiate a change in the status of the International Settlement, were made after the situation in China had become critical for foreigners. To those who objected to the Administration's views, Mr. Kellogg's policy seemed one of appeasement designed to soften the hostility of the Chinese. To those who approved the State Department's attitude, the Secretary's actions were merely a further indication of a genuine desire to improve China's international position.

Chapter XIV

THE NANKING INCIDENT

The Nanking Incident, which occurred on the 24th of March, 1927, marked the most critical phase of the Chinese Revolution from the point of view of China's relations with the major Treaty Powers. Questions of treaty revision, which had been such an important factor in the policies of the foreign governments since the May 30th Incident, were temporarily obscured by the more immediate and pressing issue of whether or not the Powers would undertake some form of intervention in China.

The contemporary accounts of the events which took place at Nanking on the 24th of March form a voluminous body of material in which certain highly controversial points are raised that have remained the subject of bitter dispute up to the present day. Among these accounts, there was one which was of particular importance to the authorities at Washington, namely, the official report of the American Consul at Nanking, Mr. John K. Davis.

Mr. Davis' report, which was written four days after the outbreak of the disorders at Nanking, relates in detail the story of his own experiences and those of the group of foreigners who were with him on March 24th. Because of the length of Mr. Davis' account, it is essential here to reduce it to its general outline.[1]

During the evening of the 23rd of March, Mr. Davis relates, a constant stream of defeated Northern soldiers moved through Nanking, retreating in front of the Nationalist troops who were advancing on the city.[2] The Northern soldiers were at first well disciplined, but on the evening of the 23rd, when owing to lack of transportation facilities some 10,000 troops were forced to remain in Nanking, disorders broke out which were accompanied by looting and indiscriminate firing that lasted throughout the night.

Early on the next morning, it was reported that Nationalist troops had entered the city and were rounding up the Northern soldiers who had not been able to escape. Mr. Davis spoke to a band of the Southern soldiers whose officer, "his face twisted with violent hate," pointed his pistol and said, " 'You are all alike. The British and Italians are killing our men at Shanghai and you Americans have drunk our blood for years and become rich. We are

[1] The text of Mr. Davis' report is in *Foreign Relations* (1927), pp. 151-163.
[2] As it had been evident for several days that Nanking would either be captured or laid under seige by the Kuomintang forces, several hundred American women and children were evacuated before March 24th.

busy now killing Fengtien soldiers but we will soon begin killing all foreigners in Nanking regardless of what country they are from.'" "I was surprised," Mr. Davis recounts, "but, thinking it a sporadic incident, did not give it any serious attention."

Reports of outrages soon began to pour into the consulate. A message from the University of Nanking related the death of Dr. John E. Williams, Vice-President of the University, who had "wantonly and with no provocation whatsoever" been shot "through the head and instantly killed" by Nationalist troops. The Japanese and the British Consuls were said to have been killed and crowds were rumored to be attacking the British consulate.

Seven American missionaries arrived at the United States consulate, stating that they had barely escaped with their lives. A group of some 24 Americans had by this time assembled at the consulate for protection. Mr. Davis got in touch with Mr. E. T. Hobart, Manager for the Standard Oil Company, who advised the party at the consulate to leave as soon as possible and try to escape through the open country to the Standard Oil residences. As a result Mr. Davis and those who had taken refuge with him started forth, only to find themselves under severe rifle fire. Before they reached the Standard Oil property known as Socony hill, they were fired at "no less than 300" times but none of the group was killed and only one person (an American bluejacket) was wounded. It was only the "unbelievably poor marksmanship of the Kuomintang soldiers," according to Mr. Davis, that saved their lives.

With the arrival of the party from the consulate, there were 52 foreigners altogether at Socony hill. For a time comparative quiet prevailed. A message from the United States consulate informed Mr. Davis that five minutes after his departure some 40 Nationalist soldiers had broken into the building, looted the entire house and fired at the Chinese office staff and servants, fortunately killing no one.

The quiet on Socony hill was broken, shortly after noon, when a small band of Chinese soldiers arrived. Most of the foreigners were sent upstairs in the Standard Oil house, while Mr. Davis and Mr. Hobart attempted to deal with the soldiers who sought entrance. The soldiers covered the American Consul and Mr. Hobart with loaded and cocked pistols and, on being informed that Mr. Davis was the American Consul, said they did not care, that all foreigners were alike, and that they intended to kill all of them. They were induced to leave only by being given the loot which they wanted.

With the departure of these men, a group of six other Chinese soldiers appeared and proceeded to ask Mr. Davis and those with him for money. When a substantial sum had been raised, they demanded more, stating that if they did not receive the amount required at once they would search the house and, if they found arms, kill everyone in it. Mr. Davis finally decided that the only way to avert disaster was to have the American bluejackets tie up the six Chinese soldiers. While an attempt was being made to do this, the Chinese escaped and, hiding behind various objects near the Standard Oil house where they obtained reinforcements, began a steady sniping fire.

At this point Mr. Davis decided that the group gathered at the Standard Oil house was being attacked in earnest. He signaled to an American and a British warship asking for a landing force. The men were landed but told to fire over the heads of the Chinese soldiers. The situation continued to grow worse and Mr. Davis and those around him became convinced that Standard Oil house was about to be rushed by overwhelming numbers of Chinese and that everyone inside would be killed. Mr. Davis, therefore, "reluctantly agreed" that the American bluejackets would have to "shoot to kill." It soon became evident that even this would not provide sufficient protection. The U.S.S. *Noa* and H.M.S. *Emerald* were therefore asked to lay down a barrage of gunfire behind which the group in the Standard Oil house could escape. The barrage was started at once and consisted of a "curtain of shells which were dropped with remarkable accuracy on both sides of and behind the Standard Oil residences in such a manner as to kill or drive off the attacking Nationalist soldiers."[3] The group on Socony hill escaped over the city wall and found their way to the riverbank from which they were taken on board a warship.

While this report of Mr. Davis' dealt almost entirely with the group of foreigners who had escaped with him from the consulate and from the Standard Oil house, there was another group of Americans — approximately 120 in number — assembled at the University of Nanking. It was here on the morning of March 24th, that Dr. Williams, who had commenced his missionary work at Nanking twenty-eight years earlier, was shot and killed by a soldier who appears to have had no purpose other than to rob him of a watch which he was a little slow in handing over.[4]

The experiences of the group at the University of Nanking were similar to those that Mr. Davis had witnessed and described.[5] Houses were looted from top to bottom. The soldiers, who were completely worn out from previous fighting, resorted to reckless and indiscriminate firing whenever they believed it would assist them in further robbing and plundering. The

[3] In addition to Mr. Davis' report, see the report of Captain England, Commander-in-Chief of H. M. S. *Emerald*, China No. 4. (1927) Cmd. 2953, *Papers Relating to the Nanking Incident of March 24 and 25, 1927*, pp. 12-22.

[4] W. Reginald Wheeler, *John E. Williams of Nanking*, New York, 1927. See Chapter 1, and Mrs. Williams' own account in Chapter XIV.

[5] *Ibid.* See also M. Searle Bates, "*The Ordeal of Nanking*" in *World Call*, Supplement, May, 1927, Vol. 9, p. 2.

situation grew worse as the day wore on, the soldiers who arrived late being bitterly resentful of the fact that all possible loot had already been taken. Dr. M. Searle Bates, describing the events that occurred at the University in an article written only a few weeks later, said that "scores of missionaries faced guns again and again, had shots fired over their shoulders or in their rooms, and were pressed about with bayonets and rifle muzzles. Death was on every hand."[6] Mrs. John E. Williams wrote similarly of the large group of Americans who had been assembled in a building of the University that there was one moment at least when ". . . we all expected to go together."[7]

Toward evening, after the barrage from the gunboats had subsided, the danger began to lessen and a guard of Chinese soldiers was stationed around the building.[8] During the night some fifty Americans that had been missing came, or were brought, to the University grounds; these included Miss Anna Moffet, an American missionary, who had been seriously wounded by Chinese soldiers.[9] On the following day, the entire group were allowed to go unmolested to the bank of the river, from which they were transported to the American boats awaiting them.[10]

While these events were taking place at Socony hill and at the University of Nanking, attacks were also being made on the Japanese and the British consulates. The Japanese Consul was shot at while ill in bed but not wounded; the consulate was raided for several hours.[11] The Japanese landed 50 men, who were covered by three destroyers, and proceeded to withdraw their nationals from the city.[12]

Developments at the British consulate proved more disastrous. According to an exceptionally vivid account written by the British Consul, Bertram Giles, Chinese soldiers filled the consulate early in the morning of March 24th.[13] Mr. Giles and a few Englishmen who were with him outside the house started toward the consulate on hearing of the presence of troops. The soldiers inside opened fire and killed one Englishman who died instantly; the Consul himself was wounded in the leg. On reaching the house, Mr. Giles attempted to hide, together with his wife and several other people,

[6] *Ibid.*
[7] Wheeler, *op. cit.,* p. 177.
[8] *Ibid.*
[9] *Ibid.,* p. 179; *Foreign Relations* (1927), p. 149.
[10] *Foreign Relations* (1927), pp. 149, 162.
[11] *Ibid.,* pp. 165, 168.
[12] *Ibid.,* pp. 149, 162. Japanese boats did not, however, take part in the naval barrage laid down by the British and American vessels in the harbor or at any time bombard the city of Nanking.
[13] China No. 4 (1927) Cmd. 2953, *Papers Relating to the Nanking Incident of March 24 and 25, 1927,* pp. 6-11.

behind barricaded doors, but they were discovered and stripped of all their valuables. At this point, the harbormaster, who was British also, entered the consulate, got into a conflict with a Chinese soldier, and was shot through the head and the body, dying at once. For many hours thereafter, bands of Chinese soldiers roamed through the consulate looting everything in sight, searching persons and property, and repeatedly threatening to kill the Consul and the small group about him. Finally, according to Mr. Giles' report, the "incessant round" of lootings, searchings, and threats were ended by the barrage of gunfire from the American and British destroyers which opened at 3:30 in the afternoon. "The effect of the firing was instantaneous," Mr. Giles wrote; "the street cleared as if by magic; no further parties of soldiers disturbed us for the rest of that evening and although they continued to stream in and out of the consulate on the following day we experienced but little trouble at their hands." Toward the evening of March 25th, the group from the British consulate was escorted to the bund by Chinese troops and placed on board the H.M.S. *Emerald*.

In the meanwhile, on the 24th and 25th of March, the American and British naval commanders and Mr. Davis, following his escape, had been trying to negotiate with representatives of the Nationalist forces for the safe-conduct of all foreigners who were still in Nanking.[14] They first demanded that all foreigners should be brought to the riverbank by reliable Nationalist soldiers before 10 o'clock on the 25th; failing this, they said, Nanking would be treated as a military area and the necessary steps would be taken. By noon on the 25th, however, the foreigners still remained in the city. The American and British naval officers thereupon wired their Commanders-in-chief informing them that, unless the situation changed radically, they proposed to shell the salient military points and the barracks at Nanking, late in the afternoon of the same day. They also told the Chinese of their intentions and declared that if the foreigners were not brought to the bund before the end of the afternoon they would take drastic action. For a time it seemed as though such action would be undertaken and a meeting was held between the British and American naval authorities to draw up a concerted plan of bombardment. Before the meeting was concluded however — around 6 p.m. — the party from the British consulate reached the bund and was followed only shortly afterwards by the American group from the University of Nanking. On March 26th, all foreigners, except a few who insisted upon remaining at Nanking, sailed without further casualties or serious damage, down-river for Shanghai.[15]

[14] The following account is based on the official British account in *ibid.*, p. 20. See also *Foreign Relations* (1927), pp. 147, 160-163.
[15] *Foreign Relations* (1927), pp. 150, 162.

The total number of foreigners killed during the Nanking Incident was six: one American, three Englishmen, one French priest and one Italian priest.[16] Two Americans, several Japanese, and two British were wounded.[17] Foreign business and missionary buildings were plundered and even hospital equipment taken and patients robbed;[18] ten mission buildings were burned and almost all the residences of missionaries were pillaged. The United States, British, and Japanese consulates were thoroughly gutted. Moreover, unrestrained looting of foreign houses continued for several days after foreigners had been withdrawn from Nanking.[19]

One of the first questions which arose after the Nanking Incident was whether the attacks on foreigners had been caused by the unorganized rioting of individual soldiers or bands of soldiers, or whether they were the result of a plan instigated and executed by higher authorities, representing either the Northern or the Southern factions in the Chinese civil war.[20] On these issues, Consul Davis notified the State Department on March 29th that "after careful investigation and consideration" he had reached the conclusion that the assaults on foreigners and their property were carried out by soldiers operating under orders from above:

From statements made to me and many other Americans by soldiers, from soldiers' conversations overheard by Americans in hiding, from the fact that soldiers proceeded in bands whose movements were under direction and were promptly assembled by bugle calls upon commencement of naval barrage, it is proved that outrages were planned and could not possibly have been an accidental getting out of hand of a few troops.[21]

In another dispatch to the State Department, Mr. Davis said that he was "convinced beyond the slightest possibility of doubt" that the soldiers involved in the disturbances at the American consulate and at Socony hill were "regular Kuomintang troops who were operating under orders." Moreover, he added that, "From all reports from all other Americans and other nationals I am certain that this condition was uniform and that not in a

[16] Survey of International Affairs, 1927, p. 387. Although rumors were circulated after the Nanking Incident that 2,000 Chinese had been killed by the bombardment from the American and British warships, the actual number of Chinese casualties appears to have been in the neighborhood of six killed and fifteen injured. (See Foreign Relations, 1927, p. 98; MacNair, China in Revolution, p. 114; and Isaacs, The Tragedy of the Chinese Revolution, p. 164.)
[17] Ibid.
[18] Bates, op. cit.
[19] Foreign Relations (1927), p. 169.
[20] This is one of the points concerning the Nanking Incident which has remained the subject of controversy. It should be understood that issues of this kind have been treated throughout this chapter solely in terms of American policy.
[21] Foreign Relations (1927), p. 168.

single instance was an American or other foreigner molested on March 24th by any defeated Northern soldiers."[22]

Mr. Davis' reports to the State Department were released to the press by the Government in Washington, together with statements issued by two separate groups of American missionaries who had lived through the events of March 24th at Nanking and who supported the American Consul's view that the attack on foreigners was premeditated and was carried out by Nationalist troops.[23]

In the meantime, however, another story was gaining ground, namely, that the disorders at Nanking had been instigated and directed by the so-called "radicals" in the Chinese Nationalist movement in order to discredit Chiang Kai-shek and bring about his destruction. The first appearance of this story in the *Foreign Relations of the United States* is in a cable sent by the American Ambassador at Tokyo to Secretary of State Kellogg on March 28th:

At interview with Minister for Foreign Affairs this afternoon he stated that the occurrences at Nanking had not caused the Japanese Government to change its Chinese policy and the Japanese Government did not at this time consider it necessary or advisable to send troops to China. The Minister for Foreign Affairs believed that Chiang Kai-shek was strongly opposed to these outrages upon foreigners and would exert his utmost efforts to suppress them and maintain order; that he believed the outrages at Nanking were caused by the radicals among the Cantonese who were trying to discredit Chiang Kai-shek; that the Japanese had advised Chiang Kai-shek that his future and the future of the Cantonese Government depended upon the maintenance of order and that [the?] suppression of these outrages and if order were [not?] maintained it would mean an end both of Chiang Kai-shek and of the Cantonese Government. The Minister for Foreign Affairs, believing that Chiang Kai-shek would be both willing and able to maintain order, thought it would be a mistake for any of the Powers to take oppressive

[22] *Ibid.*, p. 158.

[23] One of these statements was issued by a group of twelve missionaries who declared that the events which occurred at Nanking on March 24th "flatly contradicted" the convictions which they had previously held. This part of their statement said in paraphrase: We have been termed idealists in our attitude toward China and now we stand discredited. We protested against the gunboat policy. As recently as February 1st, 127 missionaries in Nanking sent a cablegram to the United States Government protesting the use of force and urging a policy of conciliation and prompt revision of the treaties. Little more than a month later we had to depend on foreign force to save our lives. We favored the return of the concessions, but today a foreign Settlement is our only place of refuge. We have assured people at home that the Nationalist movement is neither anti-Christian nor anti-foreign, but now we are driven from our home and dispossessed of our property. We who remained at Nanking on March 24th were not depending on extraterritorial rights but were putting our trust in the assurances of the Nationalists. "The events show that our faith was not justified." (State Department *Press Releases*, May 7, 1927.)

measures at the present time as this would merely assist the enemies of Chiang Kai-shek and enable the radicals amongst the Cantonese to get control of the Cantonese Government and army. The Minister for Foreign Affairs believed that the outrages at Nanking were committed partly by the Cantonese and partly by the Shantung defeated army but insofar as they were due to the Cantonese soldiers they were instigated by the radicals among the Cantonese who are aiming at the destruction of Chiang Kai-shek.[24]

The day following the above interview the British, American, and Japanese Ministers met at Peking to discuss the critical situation arising out of the Nanking Incident; at this meeting the Japanese Minister reiterated the views expressed by the Minister for Foreign Affairs at Tokyo. Mr. Mac-Murray's description of the conversation which took place — given in a cable to the State Department — read in part:

The British Minister suggested at first that in view of the conciliatory attitude of Eugene Chen, we should offer the Nationalist régime first an opportunity to show its good faith by proposing that representatives of the interested Powers and of the Hankow régime make a joint investigation.[25] The Japanese Minister thought, however, that all the essentials of the case had been established beyond doubt and that by endeavoring to negotiate with Chen, who has no authority of his own and is merely the spokesman of the radical elements in control, we would merely subject ourselves to dilatory action and evasions. The Japanese Minister believed that there was hope for far more satisfactory and prompt action regarding the punishment of the guilty from Chiang Kai-shek. The British Minister and I agreed with this view both because we know that due to an atmosphere of intimidation by Russian Communist agents Chen is not a free agent, and because the steps already taken by the Japanese with Chiang Kai-shek seem to give confirmation of a relationship between them, which makes it likely that he could be prevailed upon by Japanese influence.[26]

In addition to considering the question of whether to deal with Chiang Kai-shek or Eugene Chen in order to obtain satisfactory reparation for the Nanking Incident, the British, American, and Japanese Ministers discussed the general line of policy which they thought should be adopted by the various Powers involved. They apparently found themselves in thorough agreement on the main points at issue and consequently drafted a formula which all three men agreed to submit to their respective Governments for

[24] *Foreign Relations* (1927), p. 164.

[25] The British Ambassador, Sir Miles Lampson, had received a report from his representative at Hankow, Sir Eric Teichman, stating that Eugene Chen apparently had been genuinely dismayed and shocked when he heard of the Nanking Incident and that Mr. Chen said he was having an investigation made and would assume all responsibility if it developed that there was an appropriate case.

[26] *Foreign Relations* (1927), pp. 164-168 (cable paraphrased).

approval. The formula stated that the three Ministers had decided to recommend to their Governments:

A. To take the matter up at once with Chiang Kai-shek through our Consul-General at Shanghai and present to him the following terms: (1) Adequate punishment of the commander of the troops responsible for the murders, personal injuries, and indirect and material damage done; as also of all persons found to be implicated. (2) Apology in writing by the commander-in-chief of the Nationalist army including an express written undertaking to refrain from all forms of violence and agitation against foreign lives and property. (3) Complete reparation for personal injuries and material damage done.

B. Simultaneously to inform Chiang Kai-shek through our Consuls-General that unless he demonstrates to our satisfaction his intention to comply promptly with these terms the interested Powers will find themselves compelled to specify a time limit for compliance, failing which they reserve to themselves [the right?] to take such measures as they consider appropriate.[27]

The formula was also submitted to the French and Italian Ministers at Peking who agreed to take the matter up at once with their own Governments.[28]

In cabling the State Department concerning these matters, including the text of the formula, Mr. MacMurray added an exposition of his own views:

I do not see how we can ignore the affair at Nanking or request anything less than this studiously moderate degree of reassurance and amends if we are to avoid an unfortunate new Boxer movement, organized and encouraged with the audacity and adroitness which has been introduced into the Chinese anti-foreign movement by the Russians. We must frankly recognize, however, that most of all we are confronted by the possibility that Chiang Kai-shek will prove unable or unwilling to abandon the truculent attitude which, according to the press, he has assumed. His reported attitude is that the Incident is now over and is of no importance anyway. There is also the possibility that Chiang Kai-shek may prove to be fair-minded and reasonable, but that at the instigation of the Russian advisers who created the Incident, he may thereupon be removed from his position. We must be prepared in either case to take resolute action in collaboration with the other Powers chiefly interested to bring pressure upon the Nationalists. It is my understanding that the naval authorities have given favorable consideration to the possibility of destroying the forts at Kiangyin near Nanking. Apparently this can be done without unduly endangering non-combatants. Personally, however, I doubt the effectiveness of any purely local act of reprisal.

[27] Ibid., p. 166 (text of formula not paraphrased).
[28] Ibid., p. 169.

Should we indeed have to deal with a Nationalist China capable of instigating and condoning the Nanking Affair, it must be realized that the problem presented is greater and more serious than we have previously admitted to ourselves, and we must deal with it on broader lines than we have before conceived. It must be recognized that we have to deal with a vast number of people who are latently hostile to Americans no less than to other foreigners, and who are subject to incitement, to mob brutality.... With such a possibility in mind, I feel that we owe it to American citizens in Kuomintang territory to hasten their withdrawal completely from China or to Shanghai or to such other places, like Tientsin, where we can give reasonable assurance of their safety. With this evacuation completed, I see no effective way to bring pressure on China except to blockade all Chinese ports from Shanghai south....

Possibly there is some other constructive course of action in this situation which we have overlooked. Unless there is such a course open, I cannot urge too strongly that we face the facts as they are on the basis that we must obtain a satisfactory solution in order to avoid vastly greater evils in the future. There should be co-operation perhaps among the Powers chiefly interested, France and Italy not necessarily being included. I believe that action such as I have indicated could yet keep China from becoming a hostile agent of Soviet Russia against western Powers, including the United States. If this situation is not resolutely met, it will mean the downfall of western influences and interests in the Orient.[29]

On the day following the receipt of this message, Secretary of State Kellogg wired Mr. MacMurray that before reaching any final decisions he wanted to obtain the advice of Admiral Williams; at the same time he indicated that he questioned the advisability of presenting Chiang Kai-shek with a note embodying the terms proposed in the formula drafted by the Ministers at Peking:

To us in the Department, it seems that there may be danger of arousing further hostilities against Americans in the danger zones in the areas in China where Americans have not evacuated yet. There is also the question, as you say, whether Chiang Kai-shek would prove able to control the Nationalist army and to meet demands. Furthermore, consideration must be given to the question that in case this ultimatum is delivered to Chiang and nothing is done, the Governments concerned would be compelled to seek some kind of reprisal or take drastic action. We gravely doubt the advisability of delivering this ultimatum at the present time but suppose some formal demand for reparation and apology must be made by us either jointly or alone.[30]

While this exchange of communications was taking place between the Department of State and the Legation, the Japanese Government sent in-

[29] *Ibid.*, pp. 166-167 (cable paraphrased).
[30] *Ibid.*, p. 170 (cable paraphrased).

structions to its Minister at Peking which the latter presented to his foreign colleagues. The instructions stated primarily that "in the opinion of the Japanese Government it would be better to formulate terms without a time limit." The reason given for this was that, according to information in the possession of the government at Tokyo, the Communist element in the Kuomintang seemed to be contemplating Chiang Kai-shek's downfall by placing him in a difficult position in connection with the Incident at Nanking. "Our idea," it was said in the instructions, "is to induce Chiang Kai-shek to expedite a solution on his own initiative, leaving it to him and other healthy elements to settle the present affair thus preventing Chiang and the foreign Powers from being entrapped in this Communist intrigue. It is very necessary for us to avoid such steps as would result in rendering the downfall of Chiang Kai-shek and his associates more easy."[31]

On April 1st, the five Ministers concerned met at Peking to discuss the situation further. According to the report of the meeting sent by Mr. MacMurray to the Secretary of State, the British, Italian, and French Ministers announced that their governments were prepared to proceed immediately with the presentation of the terms incorporated in the formula excepting — in deference to the request of the Japanese Government — any reference to the specification of a time limit. But all decisions had to be postponed as Mr. MacMurray had not as yet received any indication of the views of the State Department. The five Ministers decided, nevertheless, to recommend to their governments that the terms be presented not only to Chiang Kai-shek but also to Eugene Chen. On this issue, the British Minister argued that his government felt that Mr. Chen should be given an opportunity of doing what he could to obtain compliance and that the Foreign Office believed, moreover, that it was inadvisable to single out Chiang Kai-shek for responsibility independently of the Nationalist régime — a view supported by the Japanese.

In concluding his account of this meeting, Mr. MacMurray added a sentence which left no doubt as to the attitude of the five Ministers at Peking towards the question of imposing sanctions on the Chinese in case the latter were not willing to meet the demands presented by the foreign Powers:

"The five interested Ministers," Mr. MacMurray said, "were in agreement that time is of the essence for the success of any demands but that it would be worse than useless, it would be calamitous, to make such demands if the interested Powers were not definitely resolved to follow them up by any necessary means to secure satisfaction."[32]

[31] *Ibid.*, p. 171 (cable paraphrased).
[32] *Ibid.*, pp. 172-173.

As Mr. MacMurray's report of the meetings of the Ministers crossed the Secretary of State's dispatch saying that he wished to postpone any final consideration of the formula submitted by the Ministers until he had received the advice of Admiral Williams, Mr. MacMurray cabled again, this time urgently appealing to the Secretary for instructions. Referring to his earlier message he said that action was being withheld by all the Powers involved in the Nanking Incident because of the fact that the United States Government had, as yet, reached no decision. "Thus," he declared, "full responsibility for the disastrous results which will follow delay or failure in exacting the minimum of satisfaction contemplated for the outrage at Nanking will fall on the American Government. In the situation confronting us in China, I beg you to realize that the personal danger to American citizens and other foreigners throughout the country is greatly and definitely increased by every day of delay in dealing effectively with the Nanking affair." In addition, the American Minister again expressed the opinion that the United States should adopt a policy that would provide for the enforcement, if necessary, of whatever demands were presented to the Nationalist authorities in China:

Obviously we must be prepared if necessary to enforce compliance if we make any demands for apology and reparation. Further outrages against Americans would be invited by a merely formal demand which we allow the Nationalists to ignore ... the only alternatives are to participate promptly and whole-heartedly in joint action with the other interested Powers or frankly to pursue an independent course. The latter alternative would result in either making us responsible for paralyzing the action now proposed by the other interested Governments or in allowing the common burden to be carried by those Powers which have become convinced of the fact that in reality there exists an unacknowledged state of war against us being waged by the element now in control of the political thought of China.

"With all respect," Mr. MacMurray stated at the end of his message, "the evidence of any hesitation on the part of our Government in meeting the necessities of the situation created by the Nanking affair fills me with consternation."[33]

In reply to Mr. MacMurray's communication, the Secretary of State wired specific instructions: the Department was prepared to have the demands proposed by the Ministers at Peking presented to Chiang Kai-shek and Eugene Chen; the demands should, however, not "contain anything of the nature of an ultimatum fixing a time limit"; the Department desired, moreover, to "reserve the right to ... take such action as it shall deem necessary in the light of Chiang's reply and the measures actually taken by him."[34]

[33] Ibid., pp. 173-174 (cable paraphrased).
[34] Ibid., pp. 175-176.

Concerning the latter point, it was said in a second set of instructions: "The American Government reserves its opinion with respect to what sanctions shall be employed if the use of sanctions becomes necessary."[35]

A few days after these instructions were sent to the Legation at Peking, the British Ambassador at Washington forwarded a memorandum to Mr. Kellogg informing him of the attitude of the British Government toward the developments which had taken place up to this point.[36] The British Government, the memorandum said, was willing to agree to the formula recommended by the Ministers, together with the Japanese proposal for the omission of a time limit from the note to be handed to the Nationalist authorities, on the understanding that their agreement was subject to two *provisos*. The *provisos*, of which the second was clearly the more important from the point of view of the United States, read as follows:

> 1. They [i.e. the British Government] fully appreciate the force of the view expressed by the Japanese Government that as there is reason for believing that Chiang is now endeavoring to form a nucleus of a moderate element directed against extremist faction of Nationalist Government which may constitute the one hope of China's future, it would be contrary to the interests of the Powers to humiliate him unduly at the present moment. His Majesty's Government strongly recommend, therefore, that the above demands be in the first place presented to Mr. Chen as representing the Nationalist Government, who must be held responsible for these outrages, and that a copy of the demands be communicated to Chiang....
> 2. In agreeing to the omission of a time limit in the formula ... His Majesty's Government do so on the understanding that the other Powers accept in principle the application of sanctions in the event of the Nationalist Government refusing to give satisfaction to their demands.

Concerning the practical difficulty of determining the kind of sanctions to be imposed if the situation reached the point where the imposition of sanctions was necessary, the British memorandum stated that:

> As regards the question of the sanctions to be applied, these should in the view of His Majesty's Government, form the subject of immediate discussion among the five Powers. They would suggest that this can best and most expeditiously be done by authorizing the naval authorities of the

---

[35] *Ibid.*, p. 177.

[36] An attempt has been made throughout this chapter to view the rôle which the British played in the negotiations for the settlement of the Nanking issue, through the eyes of officials in the American Department of State. The documents have with few exceptions been drawn from *Foreign Relations of the United States*. The facts presented should therefore not be regarded as forming in full detail the entire story of British policy but rather as constituting fragments of that story fitted into the history of American policy. The same is true of the treatment accorded the policies of the Japanese, French, and Italian Governments.

Powers in China to formulate an agreed plan for action, if necessary, by progressive steps, for the acceptance of their Governments.[37]

The British note was inadvertently an important factor in the development of American policy. It caused the State Department to take an immediate and definite stand concerning the question of the use of sanctions — a stand which it maintained with determination throughout the rest of the negotiations for the settlement of the Nanking Incident. The first expression of the Department's views was contained in a cable sent to the American Legation at Peking on April 5th:

> The Department completely dissents from the statement in the Ambassador's note that in agreeing to omit a time limit in formula ... the British Government does so with the understanding that in principle the other Powers accept the application of sanctions should the Nationalist Government refuse to give satisfaction to the demands made upon it. No implied agreement of any sort exists to this effect. The British Ambassador, in fact, presented to me a memorandum[38] in which it was stated that his Government reserved its opinion as to sanctions, and you will recall that in my instructions on the subject to you I also reserved, in behalf of the American Government, all opinion with respect to sanctions. That the American Government is under no obligation to use sanctions and is not ready as yet to confer on the subject with the other Powers should be made perfectly clear.[39]

On the day following the dispatch of this message, the Secretary sent for the British Chargé at Washington and read him the text of the cable forwarded to the American Legation at Peking. "I ... further informed him," Mr. Kellogg wrote in a memorandum recording his conversation with the British Chargé, "that as at present advised we were not in favor of applying drastic sanctions to the Nationalists."[40]

Something of the extent of the Department's determination to adhere to the policy thus defined may be seen in the number of occasions on which the authorities in Washington restated their attitude on the subject of sanctions to the governments of other countries. In an official note sent to the British Government on April 7th, Mr. Kellogg declared that "the United States Government regrets that it cannot accept in principle the application of sanctions in the event of the Nationalist authorities refusing to give satisfaction to its demands." Moreover, the Secretary said, "The United States is not prepared at the present time to confer with the other Powers on the question of sanctions."[41] Similar statements were again made to the British

[37] For text of British note, see *Foreign Relations* (1927), pp. 179-181.
[38] *Ibid.*, pp. 174-175.
[39] *Ibid.*, p. 181 (cable paraphrased).
[40] *Ibid.*, p. 182.
[41] *Ibid.*, pp. 184-185.

Ambassador orally and in formal communications on April 20th and 22nd;[42] to the Japanese Government on April 6th and 25th;[43] to the French Government on April 18th;[44] and, to the Italian Government on April 23rd.[45]

In the meantime, however, the question of sanctions was, in fact, being discussed in informal conversations held between the American, British, Japanese, and French naval Commanders in China. The problem under consideration was the nature of the measures to be adopted in case the demands of the Powers were rejected by the Nationalist authorities. As a result of these deliberations, Admiral Williams cabled the Department that in his opinion the following program should be carried out:

1. Capture of the Woosung forts and the destruction of the guns there; seizure of Cantonese naval vessels; withholding of the surtax which is now being paid to the Shanghai Cantonese authorities.
2. Progressive bombardment of the Yangtze River forts beginning at Kiangyin.
3. Arsenal at Hankow to be destroyed.
4. Military yamen, barracks, camps to be bombarded at selected points.
5. Blockade of portion of coast which is now under Cantonese control and this to be done as a last resort.[46]

Back in Washington the British Ambassador delivered a second memorandum to the Secretary of State informing him of the attitude of the British Government toward the identic notes which the five interested Powers were about to present to the Nationalist authorities in China:

... while His Majesty's Government are ready, in order to avoid unnecessary delay, and in the interests of solidarity, to waive their insistence on prior acceptance in principle of the application of sanctions, in case the demands of the Powers are not complied with by the Cantonese, and to authorize presentation of demands as these now stand, they still adhere to the suggestion originally made that the naval authorities of the Signatory Powers in China should examine the question of sanctions and should formulate an agreed plan of action for submission to the Governments.

His Majesty's Government hope, therefore, that the United States Government will authorize their naval authorities in China to join in making such an examination, so that a programme of sanctions may be in being in case it is found necessary at last to apply them.

Sir Austen Chamberlain declares that he entirely agrees with the objections Mr. Kellogg expressed ... to any plan for the further bombardment of Chinese cities or ports but he earnestly hopes that these objections would not be such as to exclude in advance the possibility of any collaboration by

[42] *Ibid.*, pp. 204, 206.
[43] *Ibid.*, pp. 182, 212.
[44] *Ibid.*, p. 200.
[45] *Ibid.*, p. 208.
[46] *Ibid.*, p. 178.

the United States in such sanctions as may be recommended, as practical and desirable, by the naval authorities of the five Powers in China.[47]

By April 9th, all five governments involved in the Nanking Incident were prepared to present the identic notes which incorporated their demands to Chiang Kai-shek and Eugene Chen immediately. The Ministers met at Peking to determine the date for the delivery of the notes. In cabling an account of the Ministers' meeting to the State Department, Mr. MacMurray expressed his personal views as follows:

I, and I believe my colleagues also, were convinced by conversations with Lampson that his Government is ready to assume the entire burden of action, if necessary, to obtain satisfaction for the affair at Nanking.[48] Being confident that our demands and the threat accompanying them would not be allowed to remain the same [sic], I [agreed?] with my colleagues that we should have the demands delivered with as little delay as possible in the manner and form upon which we have already agreed although the enforcement of the demands without the participation of the United States would be only less disastrous to American interests and position in the Far East than their remaining unenforced.[49]

As a result of the decisions reached at the meeting of the Ministers, the notes containing the demands of the Powers were handed to Chiang Kai-shek and to Eugene Chen on the 11th of April.[50] Three days later, Mr. Chen sent replies — which were however not identic — to each of the governments involved.[51] The most important points which Mr. Chen sought to

[47] *Ibid.*, p. 185.

[48] In a recent memorandum written to the author by Sir John T. Pratt, who was Adviser on Far Eastern Affairs in the British Foreign Office at this time, Sir John states specifically that even the idea that the four Governments of Great Britain, Japan, Italy and France would continue to threaten sanctions without the co-operation of the United States was "never given serious consideration by the Governments concerned."

[49] *Foreign Relations*, p. 186 (cable paraphrased).

[50] For statement given to the press together with this note, see *ibid.*, p. 187.

[51] On being asked by the Secretary of State for information concerning the differences in the notes delivered to the five Powers by Mr. Chen, the American Minister cabled: "Aside from minor changes of wording Chen's reply to the British note is in substance identical with the reply to our note except that there is included in it a suggestion that the proposed international commission also investigate the incidents at Shanghai and Shameen in 1925 and the affair at Wanhsien last fall.

"Chen's reply to the Italian note is very much like that to ours except that there is no occasion to refer to firing by warships or to the violation of consular privileges. As yet only half of the reply to the French note has been received. It seems to be practically the same as the reply to the Italian note. Only a résumé of the reply to the Japanese note has as yet been received by the Japanese Minister. From this summary it appears that the note has two paragraphs which are designed as 'bait,' as the Minister expresses it, for Japan; one of these paragraphs assumes that Japan will settle the matter by diplomatic negotiations and the other expresses confidence that it is not the wish of

make in his note to the United States Government were that: (a) the Nationalist Government was prepared to make good the damages suffered by Americans at Nanking, except in cases where it could definitely be proven that the damages had been caused by the British-American naval bombardment or by Northern troops and *agents provocateurs*;[52] (b) the issues of the punishment of specified individuals and of a written apology from the Commander-in-Chief should be set aside until the question of guilt concerning the Nanking Incident had been properly determined either by the government inquiry already underway, or by an international commission; (c) a commission of inquiry should investigate the circumstances of the bombardment of Nanking on March 24th by American and British warships; (d) in future, effective measures would be taken for the protection of foreign lives and property.

In addition, Mr. Chen declared that the best guarantee against the recurrence of incidents such as that which had taken place at Nanking would be to remove "the régime of the unequal treaties. . . . It is these inequitable treaties," Mr. Chen said, "that constitute the chief danger to foreign lives and property in China and this danger will persist as long as effective government is rendered difficult by foreign insistence on conditions which are at once a humiliation and a menace to a nation that has known greatness and is today conscious of renewed strength." Mr. Chen accordingly proposed that the United States Government and the Nationalist Government of China should enter into negotiations for a reconsideration of the existing treaties.[53]

On receipt of Mr. Chen's notes, the Ministers of the interested Powers conferred immediately at Peking and finding themselves again in agreement on the main issues involved, cabled identic recommendations to their respective governments. In these they declared that they were "in complete accord" in the conviction that the replies of Mr. Chen were "wholly unsatisfactory and unacceptable." After explaining their views on this subject further, they asked for authorization to present to Eugene Chen identic notes "of the following tenor":

On April 11th the representatives of the American, British, French, Italian and Japanese Governments presented in identic notes certain terms

---

Japan to obstruct the Chinese revolution." (Cable sent April 15, 1927; see *ibid.*, pp. 196-197; see also Pollard, *China's Foreign Relations, 1917-1931*, pp. 305-307, for a résumé of the various notes to the five Powers.)

[52] The Nationalists had claimed at the outset that the damage at Nanking was caused by Northern troops; see *Foreign Relations* (1927), p. 192; the *People's Tribune*, April 1, 1927, p. 1.

Mr. Chen also promised to make good all damage done to the American consulate at Nanking no matter who had caused the damage.

[53] For full text of Mr. Chen's note, see *Foreign Relations* (1927), pp. 192-194.

for the prompt settlement of the situation created by the outrages against their nationals committed by the Nationalist troops at Nanking on 24th March.

To these identic notes the Nationalist authorities have not returned . u identic reply but have answered such [each?] representative separately and in varying terms calculated rather to serve propagandist ends than to terminate the incident which has arisen. Not one of the demands made has been accepted unequivocally by the Nationalist authorities.[54] Reservations have been attached to the acceptance of each one.

The terms presented in identic notes of 11 April were not proposals open to discussion but the basic demands which the Powers concerned are determined shall be carried out. Only after the Nationalist authorities have signified with a plain and unqualified affirmative that they are prepared promptly and completely to comply with these terms can any discussion regarding details take place.

Unless, therefore, the Nationalist authorities state unequivocally and without delay that they intend to proceed to the integral fulfillment of the terms presented, the Governments concerned will be obliged to consider such measures as may be necessary to obtain compliance.[55]

While these matters were taking place in China, the policy of the five Powers was being developed further by their respective governments at home. On April 14th (before Mr. Chen had replied to the identic notes of the Powers) the British Government sent Secretary of State Kellogg a third memorandum in order to explain its views in regard to the situation resulting from the presentation of the identic notes of April 11th:

His Majesty's Government are of the opinion that in the event of failure to satisfy the demands put forward in the notes in question, the application of sanctions should devolve upon all five of the interested Powers. His Majesty's Government cannot but believe that, in the event of such failure to comply with their just demands, the Governments of the other interested Powers will insist upon that measure of redress which they have thought it necessary to claim, seeing that otherwise all violent elements in China would be encouraged to defy the Powers and to continue to outrage their nationals and representatives. In the face of this common peril, His Majesty's Government most earnestly hope that the union of the five Powers may be preserved for they see in this union the best hope of preserving the peace and protection of rights in which all the Powers are equally interested.

With the above object in view, the memorandum stated, the British Government was attempting to secure agreement among the five Ministers

---

[54] Mr. Kellogg pointed out in detail in a conversation with the Japanese Ambassador at Washington that he did not believe this statement to be accurate and that Mr. Chen had, in his opinion, met a number of the demands made by the five Powers "unequivocally." (*Ibid.*, pp. 212-213, 215.)

[55] *Ibid.*, p. 198.

at Peking concerning the following points: the acceptability or otherwise of the reply which the Nationalists would eventually make to the identic notes; the character of the sanctions to be applied in the event of the failure to satisfy the conditions of redress put forward in the identic notes; the time limit to be allowed for compliance with these conditions. In addition the British memorandum asserted that, if it was eventually necessary to apply sanctions, the British Government was prepared to act in concert with the American and Japanese Governments, even if the assent of the French and Italian Governments could not be obtained.[56]

It is interesting to observe that at this point the views of the British Government ran counter to the opinion of the American press and the American public — at least in terms of what the State Department conceived that opinion to be. On the very day that the British memorandum was delivered to Secretary of State Kellogg, the latter forwarded to the American Legation at Peking a summary of editorials which had appeared in leading newspapers throughout the United States, dealing with the demands which the five Powers had presented to the Chinese Nationalists on April 11th. Commenting on this résumé in his cable, Mr. Kellogg said:

"General tone of press approves action taken but indicates generally a feeling that in taking action this Government should act alone. It is believed here that any determination at this time to take drastic action against China would call forth from the press hostile criticism of the Government."[57]

Similarly, a few days later, Under-Secretary of State Joseph C. Grew in a conversation held with the French Ambassador in Washington spoke of public opinion throughout the United States as being opposed to the use of sanctions for an enforcement of the demands which had been made on the Chinese Nationalist authorities. "I said," Mr. Grew records, "that we were still in serious doubts as to the wisdom of applying sanctions. . . . There was also the question of American public opinion to be considered and we were convinced that the country at large would be wholly opposed to applying any sanctions whatever."[58]

It would seem from the record that the State Department believed that its policy of opposing the use of sanctions not only had the support of the American press and public but also of the United States Cabinet. On April 18th, by one of those accidents which occur from time to time in diplomatic circles, a memorandum based on instructions from the British Foreign Office was delivered through an error to the State Department, by the British Ambassador in Washington. In the memorandum, the British Ambassador

[56] *Ibid.*, p. 191-192.
[57] *Ibid.*, p. 194.
[58] *Ibid.*, p. 201.

— after quoting the text of the note which the five Ministers at Peking had drafted in response to Eugene Chen — stated that:

> His Majesty's Government point out to me that the last sentence of the proposed identic note . . . clearly supposed that the five Governments approving the dispatch of the reply in these terms to the communications addressed to them by Eugene Chen on the subject of the Nanking outrages are prepared in the last resort to concert active measures to enforce their demands for redress by the application of sanctions.
>
> On the understanding that this is the view and intention of the other Governments, and that they will all instruct their representatives at Peking to reply in these terms to the Cantonese Government . . . His Majesty's Government have notified His Majesty's Representative at Peking that he is authorized to join in the step contemplated.[59]

Secretary Kellogg took both the British notes of April 14th and April 18th to a meeting of the United States Cabinet. As the Secretary himself relates the story, he was explaining the content of the notes, together with his own ideas on the subject, to the members of the Cabinet when he was handed a memorandum stating that the British Ambassador had just received a telegram from the Foreign Office instructing him not to deliver the note of April 18th to the United States Government. As a result of this, the discussion at the Cabinet meeting was broken off but not before Mr. Kellogg had obtained the impression that the Cabinet was in general agreement with the views which he had presented.[60]

The views which Mr. Kellogg had put before the Cabinet are set forth in a memorandum in which the Secretary recorded a conversation which he had with the British Ambassador the day after the meeting of the Cabinet. Mr. Kellogg wrote at the outset of the memorandum that the statement which he made to the Cabinet was substantially the same as that which he made to the Ambassador and then went on to note:

> I told him that it was now evident that there was a split in the Nationalist organization between the Radicals and the Moderates, Chiang Kai-shek apparently being the leader of the Moderates; that it seemed to me that to send a further demand at this time might tend to drive Chiang Kai-shek and the Moderates into the arms of the Radicals and would really do no good and might do a great deal of harm to foreigners in various parts of China; that it seemed to me best under the circumstances for the present to let Eugene Chen's note remain unanswered and await developments. . . .
>
> I told him the same argument applied to sanctions. Against whom would we apply sanctions? If they could be applied against the really guilty

[59] *Ibid.*, pp. 201-202.
[60] *Ibid.*, pp. 203, 204-205. See also President Coolidge's speech delivered on April 25th (below, pp. 320-321) and President Coolidge's statement that Mr. Kellogg's policy had the support of the Cabinet (below, pp. 321-322).

parties that might make a difference; if there was a Government controlling China and its military forces which could be punished by punitive expeditions, that might make a difference; but neither condition existed; that it was probably impossible to lay hands and punish the guilty parties and why apply sanctions to the people of China by destroying property that simply was temporarily in the hands of certain military authorities.[61]

On the day this conversation took place, the United States Government made a final decision not to join in sending a second note to Eugene Chen such as that which had been drafted by the five Ministers at Peking. Secretary of State Kellogg cabled Mr. MacMurray accordingly that the State Department did not approve of his participating in the presentation of the reply which the Ministers had proposed and gave the following reasons:

In the final sentence of the note suggested in your telegram . . . there is a specific threat that sanctions will be applied if the Nationalist authorities fail to meet the demands. The Government of the United States is not now prepared to use sanctions nor to commit itself on the subject. It is the feeling of the Department not only that it might prove dangerous to our citizens to invoke sanctions in the present time and circumstances but also that sanctions would not prove effective as they would have to be used against a divided Kuomintang Party.

Moreover, Mr. Kellogg again advanced the argument that if pressure were brought at this time to enforce the demands of the Powers against the Chinese Nationalists it might weaken the moderate leaders in the Kuomintang who were seeking "to drive the radicals from control." He also referred once more to the attitude of the American public, saying in respect to the question of exerting pressure on the Chinese, "Certainly such action would lack support here."[62]

In the meantime the British, French, and Italian Governments had authorized their Ministers at Peking to present the draft reply to Eugene Chen, subject to the agreement of all the five Powers concerned. In a message forwarded to the State Department (presumably before the Foreign Office had been notified of the final decision of the American Government not to join in the reply to Mr. Chen) the British Ambassador informed Mr. Kellogg of the actions and attitude of his Government:

I now have the honour to inform you that His Majesty's Government have informed their Representative at Peking that they approve the proposed terms of the identic note and authorize him to concert with the Representatives of the other Powers concerned in the presentation of joint or identic notes and in making any minor modifications required to secure an agreement.

[61] *Ibid.,* p. 205.
[62] *Ibid.,* pp. 203-204 (cable paraphrased).

His Majesty's Government continue to assume that the Five Powers will insist on the fulfillment of the terms which all were agreed in presenting and consider that the character of sanctions to be applied in case of necessity can be separately discussed amongst them. At the same time, however, for the sake of maintaining united action amongst the Five Powers, His Majesty's Government, for their part, are prepared either to accept the identic note in question with the omission of the last sentence, or as it stands, leaving aside for the present the question of the eventual application of sanctions.[63]

To this Secretary of State Kellogg replied that he did not believe that there was anything to be gained by haste in the handling of the situation. He declared once more that in view of the fact that the Chinese Nationalist Government was disrupted by internal conflict he was not convinced that any good purpose would be served by making demands on Eugene Chen — especially when it seemed questionable as to whether Mr. Chen and the political organization which supported him had sufficient authority to enable them to comply with the demands. Mr. Kellogg also reaffirmed the position which he had hitherto maintained concerning the use of sanctions: "As regards the question of the application of sanctions . . . this Government is not prepared at this time to apply sanctions nor is it prepared to consider the question now."[64]

On April 23rd, Mr. MacMurray made a final attempt to dissuade the State Department in Washington from following the course upon which it had embarked with such firm determination. "I venture to place before you briefly," the Minister cabled to Mr. Kellogg, "certain eventualities which to me appear to be inevitable if our Government should discontinue actively co-operating with the Powers which are principally concerned in China, definitely giving up that leadership as to Chinese affairs which we assumed among the Powers at the Washington Conference."

Mr. MacMurray again advanced the thesis, pertaining to the so-called Washington formula, that the American Government at the Washington Conference of 1921 had persuaded the Powers to relinquish the "firmly individualistic policy" to which they had been adhering, in order to join together in the maintenance of a "co-operative policy of self-denial." The Anglo-Japanese alliance, Mr. MacMurray believed, had been abandoned on the part of Japan because she felt that her policy of aggression was rendering her position difficult in the concert of world Powers and, on the part of Great Britain because "in her post-war condition of exhaustion" she felt it desirable that the United States should continue the leadership assumed at

[63] *Ibid.*, p. 206.
[64] *Ibid.*, p. 207.

the Washington Conference; but both Great Britain and Japan had become "disappointed and disillusioned" over the failure of the United States to maintain the leadership in the co-operative policy which the American Government had, itself, inaugurated. Mr. MacMurray continued:

Having this in mind, it is my conviction that Japan and Great Britain must inevitably be thrown into intimate association in the Far East again, if not thrown into a formal alliance, by our refusal to proceed in regard to Nanking and other vital questions with firmness and to co-operate with the Powers which are concerned. This means scrapping what our Government succeeded in achieving over a long period of years and in embodying for the mutual advantage of China and the United States in the nine-power treaty on principles and policies. It seems certain to me that if the United States withdraws from co-operating actively with Great Britain and Japan they will find themselves impelled to join together in a policy on China which will necessarily exclude us and therefore will not be restrained by our leadership or even by our active participation. To state the fact bluntly, we have heretofore taken the leavings from the others' tables. Our opportunities for advantages in China, commercial and other, have been due to the forceful action by other Powers in China. If I judge rightly, this time there will not be any crumbs left for us.

Therefore, before it is definitely decided to do what public opinion in the United States has been clamoring for — to withdraw from international co-operation in China — I trust that most serious consideration will be given to the above-outlined ideas and to the far-reaching consequences, at present and in the future, of our refusing whole heartedly to join in common action in China for common purposes.[65]

Mr Kellogg responded to the American Minister's anxious request for a reconsideration of the essentials of American policy with an important definition of his own views. At no time, he said, had the United States Government "determined to withdraw entirely from co-operation with the other foreign Powers with regard to China." The American Government was continuing to abide by commitments made at the Washington Conference respecting co-operation with other nations in the revision of the tariff provisions of the treaties and the consideration of measures contingent upon "the abolition of extraterritoriality if possible." The United States Government was ready to protect the life and property of its citizens in China wherever such protection could be given and, to this end, had provided for a considerable naval force which was co-operating in joint plans with the other Governments involved, "although necessarily reserving to itself full control" of its own men.

To these assertions Mr. Kellogg added a paragraph which, possibly more than any other official statement of the period, caught the essence of

[65] *Ibid.*, pp. 209-210 (cable paraphrased).

the attitude shown by the State Department thoughout the negotiations for a settlement of the Nanking Incident:

At this time the question is not one of relinquishing our leadership in regard to Chinese matters. Leadership inheres in moderation as well as forceful action, and it is the feeling of the Department that at this time you should use your influence in behalf of moderate action. It is not the belief of the Department that the commercial advantage of the United States in China was obtained by reason of forceful action of the Powers or that trade and commerce in China is about to be parcelled out through military action to various countries. It believes that the time has passed when foreign countries can take over Chinese territory or maintain by force special spheres of influence in trade. At present the question is whether the United States will agree with other Powers to serve upon Eugene Chen another note which, in case he fails to comply, will further commit us to the use of force. To me it seems inadvisable for us to send to Eugene Chen a less drastic note than the first; and to make demands which would make it impossible for us not to apply sanctions seems more inadvisable.[66]

The above expression of Mr. Kellogg's views was sent to the Legation at Peking on April 25th, at a time when the negotiations between the five Powers over a settlement of the Nanking Incident were about to enter their final stage. The Japanese Government, in a final effort to secure agreement among the Powers, drafted an amended version of the reply to Eugene Chen which had been proposed by the five Ministers. When the revised draft was submitted to Secretary of State Kellogg by the Japanese Ambassador at Washington, the Secretary objected at once, primarily on the ground that it contained, in his opinion, as strong a threat of the use of sanctions as that which had been introduced into the original text. Nevertheless the Secretary did not reject the Japanese draft completely but stated that he was willing to postpone action in order to discuss the matter with President Coolidge.[67]

At Peking, the British, Japanese, French, and Italian Ministers met to talk over the Japanese draft. As they agreed in their outlook on the situation, they drew up a memorandum which was intended to provide the basis of joint recommendations to their governments concerning the action that should be taken (a) in order to bring the United States Government "back into line," and (b) in case the United States Government continued to refuse to come into line. The memorandum read as follows:

First. To inform our respective Governments of the Japanese proposal, of their modified draft note to be accompanied by a public declaration (to be agreed upon by the four Ministers later), to which we agree in the hope that it may bring America back into line. As regards the proposed declara-

[66] Ibid., (1927), pp. 210-211 (cable paraphrased).
[67] Ibid., p. 212.

tion, French, British, and Italian Ministers would prefer not to make it unless Japanese Government insist [s]; but will agree if they do so insist; the objection being that it merely opens the whole field for polemical discussion to Chen.

Second. Even if America does not come in in response to the present Japanese proposal, we four agree to go ahead with the draft note as now modified.

Third. The four Ministers being all authorized to agree to principle of sanctions, they will immediately after the despatch of the identic notes discuss again the question of entering on negotiations with Chiang Kai-shek, as also that of the application of sanctions at Hankow, in the event of an unsatisfactory answer.[68]

A report of the recommendations advanced by the four Ministers at Peking reached Washington on April 26th but appears to have had little effect on the Administration.[69] Two days later the Secretary of State cabled to Mr. MacMurray that he had informed the Japanese Ambassador that the draft even in its amended form was not acceptable to the United States Government. Mr. Kellogg explained his objections (which continued to be the same as he had stated to the Ambassador earlier) and said that it was his belief that it would be "much wiser" for the Powers to await developments and refrain from any further action for the time being. "I trust," Mr. Kellogg said at the end of his cable to the American Minister, "that your influence with the Ministers of the Powers will be used against drastic action. The American Government is very anxious to give the Powers the fullest co-operation possible but it cannot join them at this time in presenting identic notes to Chen on this subject."[70]

On May 3rd, the final curtain was lowered on the negotiations between the five Powers. The British Government addressed a note to Secretary of State Kellogg, declaring that they had decided against "either the bombardment of the Hanyang Arsenal as a sanction for the Nanking outrages or a reoccupation of the Hankow Concession" on the ground that "the disadvantages attending both of these operations" would "greatly outweigh any advantages which might possibly accrue from them." Having reached this decision and believing that the other interested Powers were "equally unprepared to

---

[68] There appears to have been considerable confusion in the minds of American officials as to whether the Japanese Government was or was not prepared to apply sanctions in China. Reporting his conversation with the Japanese Ambassador in Washington to Mr. MacMurray, Secretary Kellogg stated, "The Ambassador was very emphatic that his Government would not apply sanctions. . . ."

On the other hand, in the above formula of the four Ministers, the Japanese Minister joined in saying that he was authorized to agree to the principle of sanctions. (See *ibid.*, pp. 212-213, 214, 216.)

[69] *Ibid.*

[70] *Ibid.*, pp. 215-216 (cable paraphrased).

agree to a policy of sanctions in principle" and that, therefore, the question of applying any other particular sanctions would have to be relegated to an indefinite future, His Majesty's Government were of the opinion that no useful purpose would be served by addressing any further note on this subject to Eugene Chen. The British stated further that:

The mere issue of minatory notes and peremptory demands, which are unsupported by a unanimous determination to carry out joint concrete effective measures for ensuring their fulfillment in case of refusal cannot but lower the prestige of all Powers so acting. His Majesty's Government consider this argument is greatly strengthened by the fact that in the event of a further note being dispatched to Chen it would, in any case, be signed by only four out of the five Powers who presented the first note, and the presentation of such a note would therefore be a clear indication of fresh disunion among the Powers themselves.[71]

A few days later — on the 9th of May — Sir Austen Chamberlain delivered a speech in the House of Commons in which he declared that the British Government had decided "that the present application of sanctions for the outrages at Nanking . . . is inexpedient, however fully justified." Sir Austen argued primarily that the split between the "radicals" and "moderates" in the Chinese Nationalist movement had so altered the situation in China following the Nanking Incident as to render "inexpedient" the enforcement of demands against the Nationalist authorities.

The Nanking Affair . . . precipitated a long impending split within the Nationalist ranks. The looting of foreign property at Nanking and the shooting of foreigners were the culmination of a continued policy of agitation, rapine, terrorism and murder; the tools of this policy were the unpaid soldiery of the Nationalist armies and the mobs of great cities, but its organization and driving force were borrowed, directly or indirectly, from the Third International. This policy had failed to create an anti-British Incident at Hankow in January. It had been unable to seize Shanghai owing to the protective presence of the Defense Force. By March it was becoming directed against the Nationalist Generalissimo, Chiang Kai-shek, of whose power the Communists were jealous. The organized side of the Nanking outrages appears to have been an attempt to embroil Chiang Kai-shek with the foreign Powers.
The outrages at Nanking have already reacted in China in a dramatic and, to their authors, an unwelcome manner. Not two months ago it seemed as if the Southern Party and the Nationalist armies would sweep China from South to North. Nanking has already checked this victorious career if it has not wrecked it altogether. It has split the Communist wing from the Kuomintang Party and — most important of all — it has deeply discredited the Communists and their foreign advisers in the eyes of all China.

[71] *Ibid.*, pp. 216-217.

Under these conditions, Sir Austen maintained, the question of punish-
ment for the Nanking outrages had assumed an entirely new aspect. The
Nationalist Government at Hankow had lost its "dominating position" and
dwindled to a state where it consisted more of shadow than of substance;
Mr. Eugene Chen had become an isolated figure, "cut off by the tide of
events, in ruined and terror-stricken Hankow . . . the Minister for Foreign
Affairs of a Government which exists only in name." Consequently, Sir
Austen said, "so far as punishment is concerned those in high places responsible for the Nanking outrages have been punished with a promptitude
and completeness unusual in human affairs. . . ." It was in the light of these
circumstances, Sir Austen declared, that the British Government had decided
not to apply sanctions for the events which occurred at Nanking on March
24th, and not to address any further notes to Mr. Eugene Chen.[72]

At about the same time as the British Government in London was reaching these decisions, the British, French, and Italian Ministers at Peking had
come to the conclusion that it was "useless" for the Ministers of the five
Powers to make any further attempts to harmonize the policies of their
various Governments. They believed that in view of the refusal of the United
States Government to take further action, and in view of what they regarded
as the disposition of the authorities at Tokyo to fall in line with the policy
of the Administration at Washington, there was little chance of reaching an
agreement either on the question of a note to Eugene Chen or on the more
important issue of sanctions.

In submitting a joint report to this effect to their respective Governments, the three Ministers left little doubt as to their opinion of the consequences that would ensue from the pursuit of a so-called "conciliatory
policy" (such as they presumably felt the United States had been maintaining):

. . . the representatives of England, France, and Italy, cannot refrain
from regretting that the unity of action which was realized for one moment
cannot be maintained in face of a situation which nevertheless constitutes
a common danger whose seriousness has not been in the least diminished;
but they furthermore consider it their duty to put their respective Governments on guard against a policy of weakness which in encouraging by impunity anti-foreign feeling, and the activity of forces of disorder, will necessarily result shortly in placing in even greater danger the lives and property
of foreigners in China.[73]

After this time — the beginning of May, 1927 — the Powers no longer
sought to achieve joint action in bringing about a settlement of the Nanking

---

[72] Parliamentary Debates, House of Commons, Vol. 206, p. 19.
[73] Foreign Relations (1927), pp. 218-219.

Incident, and negotiations were undertaken separately between the Chinese and individual foreign Powers. No settlement was reached, however, until Mr. MacMurray succeeded in signing an agreement with the Chinese Nationalist Government — on March 30, 1928 — a little more than a year after the Nanking Incident had taken place.[74]

Certain factors which prolonged the negotiations between the representatives of the so-called Nanking Government and American officials will be discussed later. But it is interesting to see that the Nanking Government approached the American Consul at Shanghai as early as May, 1927, with an offer to effect a settlement of the Nanking issue.[75] On being informed of this matter Mr. Kellogg cabled to the American Minister at Peking that the Consul at Shanghai should accept any proposals which the Chinese wished to offer but should make no commitments. To this he added a statement which was so completely in line with his previous policy that it forms an appropriate ending to the history of the negotiations between the five Powers concerned with the Nanking Incident:

"Confidentially," the Secretary wrote to Mr. MacMurray, "I am not ready to say that our Government would not accept finally a settlement of the Nanking Incident modifying to some extent the terms originally demanded, but I do not see that it will serve any good purpose to write more notes on the subject until responsible authorities offer some definite proposition."[76]

[74] See Chapter XVII.
[75] *Foreign Relations* (1927), p. 219.
[76] *Ibid.*, p. 220 (cable paraphrased).

CHAPTER XV

REACTIONS IN THE AMERICAN PRESS

The first news of the Nanking Incident which reached the United States suggested a disaster worse than that which had actually taken place. The fate of the Americans who remained at the University of Nanking during the night of March 24th was unknown and it was generally thought that a large number of foreigners had been killed.[1] Within a few days, however, correct, though not detailed, reports were received and the newspapers printed accurate information both concerning the number of foreigners who had been killed and wounded at Nanking and concerning those who had, in the end, been able to depart in safety.[2]

In Washington, one of the first announcements made from the White House following the Nanking Incident was to the effect that President Coolidge believed that the United States had sufficient troops in China to secure the protection of American citizens and that no further purpose would be served by the dispatch of a larger force.[3] A few days later, this assertion was amended to the extent of saying that 1,500 additional marines and an aviation unit of twelve planes were being ordered to China but that this constituted the maximum number of men to be sent for the present.[4] Moreover, the President himself informed the press that he regarded the entire American armed force in China as a police force which had none of the character of an expeditionary army. He explained further that he believed the function of the troops was not so much to guard against organized assaults as to protect our nationals against disorganized attacks that

[1] New York *Herald Tribune*, March 25, 1927, p. 1; *Foreign Relations* (1927), p. 147.

[2] New York *Herald Tribune*, March 28, 1927, p. 1; *United States Daily*, March 28, 1927, p. 1.

[3] Mr. Coolidge explained that the only advantage to be gained from sending a larger force would be to send "a very much larger force"—a matter which he said was not being considered. (*United States Daily*, March 26, 1927, p. 1. See also New York *Herald Tribune*, March 26, p. 2.)

[4] New York *Herald Tribune*, March 30, p. 3; *United States Daily*, March 28, 1927, p. 1. It was subsequently announced that 1,500 additional marines would be held in readiness at San Diego in case of emergency (*United States Daily*, April 2, 1927, p. 7). The British also ordered more troops to be sent from Hongkong to Shanghai and by April 2nd had 13,000 men at Shanghai (*United States Daily*, April 4, 1927, p. 1). According to a memorandum furnished by the Royal Institute of International Affairs, 20,000 troops had been sent out in the Shanghai Defense Force by April 5, 1927. In addition, the Japanese Second Fleet was in Chinese waters in the first week of April (*United States Daily*, April 4, 1927, p. 1; April 5, 1927, p. 1).

were sometimes made by Chinese soldiers acting in accordance with a mob spirit in a manner which he assumed had nothing to do with the Chinese authorities.[5]

Throughout the next weeks, daily bulletins concerning the developments in China were given to newspaper correspondents by one or another of the Departments of the United States Government. Much emphasis was placed upon the question of the co-operation of the American troops in China with the forces of other nationalities.[6] It was stated that American soldiers would co-operate to the extent rendered necessary by particular circumstances (especially at Shanghai) to insure the safety of their own people, but that there was no intention of placing United States military units in China under a joint international command.[7] It was also explained that a policy was being adopted, not of evacuating American nationals from China, but of withdrawing them to central points of concentration where they could more readily receive assistance.[8]

Official press releases were also given out concerning the diplomatic negotiations being conducted for a settlement of the Nanking Incident. Following the publication of the identic note delivered by the five Powers to Chiang Kai-shek and Eugene Chen on April 11th, it was stated at the White House that the President would take no further action until replies had been received, as he had every expectation that the Cantonese authorities would give a satisfactory answer.[9] After the receipt of Mr. Chen's response, President Coolidge announced that he had nothing to say for the present but indicated that the Administration had no intention of deviating from the policy toward China maintained before the Nanking Incident.[10] A few days later, Secretary of State Kellogg denied a report from Paris that the five interested Powers were in agreement on joint action to enforce demands against the Chinese Nationalists.[11] On April 25th, the Secretary told the press that no decision had been reached concerning an answer to Eugene Chen and explained that while the five Ministers at Peking had forwarded the draft of a reply to their respective governments, the United States Government, as well as some of the other Powers, had not been willing to accept the draft.[12] On the 4th of May (the day after the British Govern-

[5] *United States Daily*, March 30, 1927, p. 1.

[6] *Ibid.*, March 30, 1927, p. 1; April 1, 1927, pp. 1-2; April 2, 1927, pp. 1-2; April 6, 1927, pp. 1-2.

[7] *Ibid.*, March 30. 1927, p. 1.

[8] *Ibid.*, April 6, 1927, pp. 1-2; April 22, 1927, p. 2; New York *Herald Tribune*, April 2, 1927, p. 2.

[9] *United States Daily*, April 13, 1927, pp. 2, 6.

[10] *Ibid.*, April 16, 1927, pp. 1-2; New York *Herald Tribune*, April 17, 1927, p. 3.

[11] *United States Daily*, April 19, 1927, p. 2.

[12] *Ibid.*, April 26, 1927, p. 2.

ment had informed Washington that they had decided to drop all plans for sending a reply to Eugene Chen) a statement was issued at the White House declaring that President Coolidge "was unable to see where the United States" would "gain by acting in concert with other Powers in the immediate presentation of a note to the Cantonese Government in China."[13] It was also said that the President did not believe that the British, Japanese, French, and Italian Governments had agreed on a note to be sent to Eugene Chen although their representatives at Peking might have reached such an agreement.[14] Mr. Coolidge was furthermore represented as being willing to co-operate with the other Powers in so far as possible, but as recognizing that "different Powers" had "different interests in China."[15]

As the foregoing constituted in general terms the official American version of the events following the Nanking Incident, it is evident that the Administration wished to stress that it was sending a minimum number of troops to China; that these troops were regarded only as a police force intended primarily as a protection against mob attack; and that the United States harbored no aggressive intention against the Chinese. On the question of the negotiations for a settlement of the Nanking Incident, the Administration appears to have wished to steer a middle course in the eyes of the public, indicating, on the one hand, that it was opposed to the enforcement through sanctions of the demands against the Nationalists and avoiding, on the other, giving the impression that the United States was taking an entirely independent stand.

This general line of policy was reinforced by a speech delivered by President Coolidge at a dinner of the United Press Association on April 25th, in which he dealt with American foreign policy as applied to Mexico, Nicaragua, and China.[16] Possibly the most significant feature of the President's remarks concerning China was that, after reviewing the Nanking Incident, he spoke of the attacks on foreigners in China as though he regarded them as an inevitable part of the lawlessness which accompanies every major civil war:

> In the turmoil and strife of the present time we realize fully that forces may be let loose temporarily beyond their power to control which may do injury to American nationals. It is to guard against that eventuality that our forces are in Chinese waters and to do what China itself would do if peace prevailed.
>
> We do not wish to pursue any course of aggression against the Chinese people. We are there to prevent aggression to our people by any of their disorderly elements.

[13] *Ibid.*, May 4, 1927, p. 1.
[14] *Ibid.*; New York *Herald Tribune*, May 4, 1927, p. 1.
[15] *United States Daily*, May 4, 1927, p. 1; New York *Herald Tribune*, May 6, 1927, p. 9.
[16] Text in *United States Daily*, April 26, 1927, pp. 1-2.

Ultimately the turmoil will quiet down and some form of authority will emerge which will no doubt be prepared to make adequate settlement for any wrongs we have suffered. We shall of course maintain the dignity of our Government and insist upon proper respect being extended to our authority. But our actions will at all times be those of a friend, solicitous of the well-being of the Chinese people.

Mr. Coolidge also took the occasion to go beyond the immediate events in China and to assure the Chinese that the United States Government was still prepared to undertake a revision of the existing treaties:

In a public statement issued by the Secretary of State on the 27th of January, we indicated that we were ready to negotiate a treaty giving China complete tariff autonomy and to negotiate the release of extraterritorial rights as soon as China is prepared to give protection to American citizens and their property.

The friendship of America for China has become proverbial. We feel for her the deepest sympathy in these times of her distress. We have no disposition to do otherwise than to assist and encourage every legitimate aspiration for freedom, for unity, for the cultivation of a national spirit and the realization of a republican form of government.

While the Government in Washington was thus willing to trace the broad outlines of its policy, it is evident that officials exhibited considerable reticence in their relationship with the press in discussing the developments that grew out of the riots at Nanking. Mr. Coolidge himself explained this matter at a press conference held in the middle of April, saying that some of his earlier statements had been misconstrued so as to suggest that the United States was changing its Chinese policy and that cables to this effect had exercised a harmful influence in China.[17] According to Carter Field of the New York *Herald Tribune,* the President said "again and again" in the weeks following the 24th of March that he wished the press would stop printing rumors about a change in the policy of the United States in respect to China.[18] Mr. Coolidge felt so strongly on this point that when stories were circulated that Mr. Kellogg might retire because of "ill health" and be replaced by Herbert C. Hoover, then Secretary of Commerce (who was thought to be in favor of a more vigorous policy for the protection of American business in China), the President took the unusual step of announcing that even if Mr. Kellogg retired he would not appoint Mr. Hoover as Secretary of State; he added that in any case there would be no change in the Government's policy toward China and that Mr. Hoover — as well as the

[17] New York *Herald Tribune,* April 17, 1927; also April 2, 1927, p. 2.
[18] *Ibid.,* April 18, 1927, p. 2.

entire United States Cabinet — were in sympathy with the attitude and the actions of the State Department in regard to China.[19]

Despite all efforts on the part of Government officials, rumors concerning the events in China literally flooded the columns of the metropolitan newspapers. As early as the first days in April, banner headlines proclaimed: "British Cabinet Drafts An Ultimatum to Canton,"[20] "Britain Favors Bombs For Chinese If Nanking Reparation Is Refused,"[21] "Britain To Coerce China,"[22] "British To Back Rights In China."[23] The British were said to be contemplating the recovery of their Concession at Hankow and a naval blockade of the Yangtze.[24] After Mr. Chen's reply to the Note of the five Powers, it was reported that Great Britain was urging the delivery of an ultimatum — with a time limit and threat of sanctions — to the Chinese, and, finally, that the United States Government had agreed to co-operate in such action.[25] Toward the end of April these stories were changed to indicate that the United States would not join in a threat of punitive measures, but that the British were prepared to act alone.[26] At the same time newspaper correspondents wrote that it was an "open secret" in Washington that Mr. MacMurray was opposed to the conciliatory policy of the United States Government,[27] and there was a stream of stories (mostly from European sources) to the effect that Mr. MacMurray intended to resign — a matter which finally reached sufficient proportions to elicit public denials from both President Coolidge and Secretary of State Kellogg.[28]

Based upon this large pool of information, which frequently filled several pages in the big metropolitan dailies, many editors made up their minds concerning the significance of the Nanking Incident to the United States, in record time. This was no doubt in part owing to the fact, discussed in a previous chapter, that ever since January, 1927, the press had been devoting a great deal of attention to China, and editors were, therefore, prepared to state their views with alacrity and vehemence.

We have already seen that the Administration in Washington was following various indications of the attitude of the American public toward developments in China with keen interest. President Coolidge, as noted

[19] *Ibid.*

[20] New York *World*, April 1, 1927, p. 1.

[21] *Ibid.*, April 2, 1927, p. 1.

[22] New York *Herald Tribune*, April 1, 1927, p. 1.

[23] *Ibid.*, April 2, 1927, p. 1.

[24] *Ibid.*, April 17, 1927, p. 1.

[25] *Ibid.*, April 2, 1927, p. 2; New York *World*, April 14, 1927, p. 1.

[26] New York *Herald Tribune*, April 28, 1927, p. 2.

[27] New York *World*, May 3, 1927, p. 14.

[28] New York *Herald Tribune*, May 4, 1927, p. 1; *United States Daily*, May 4, 1927, pp. 1-2.

earlier, opposing the dispatch of a large force of regular soldiers to Shanghai at a Cabinet meeting held at the end of January, 1927, had given as one of the primary reasons for his objections the fact that in his opinion any such action "would be very strongly condemned" by the American public "in Congress and out." Secretary of State Kellogg had, on several occasions, when making decisions of outstanding importance concerning the situation in China, referred to the state of American public opinion as though he sincerely accepted it as one of the factors which should determine American policy. Mr. Kellogg appears to have been especially impressed by two aspects of the public's thinking: that "American sentiment" — in his own words — was "very strongly opposed to military action in China . . . except for protecting American life and property;" and, that the American people in general (as well as the members of Congress) were in favor of the United States Government's acting in accordance with its own independent judgment disregarding, if necessary, the so-called co-operative policy of the Powers in China.

The cable referred to previously, which the Secretary of State sent to Mr. MacMurray summarizing what he regarded as "the more important part of the American press comment" on the identic note of the five Powers delivered to Chinese Nationalist authorities on April 11th, not only furnishes an interesting bird's-eye view of editorial opinion at this time but also throws further light on the government's impression of editorial opinion in the United States:

New York *World,* April 13th, deplores united front on the Nanking Incident and advocates reiteration of our willingness to negotiate new treaties; Philadelphia *Public Ledger,* 12th, approves absence of time limit in demands and states especially advantageous for United States to avoid definite commitments in China today; Baltimore *Sun,* 12th, states fortunately note was not ultimatum and questions whether we are not surrendering traditional independence of attitude in China adding it is not American destiny to side with either Russia or Great Britain against China; Washington *Post,* 12th, asserts American people will not be pleased with joint demands which constituted commitment by the American Government to join action against the Chinese if further violence occurs; St. Paul *Pioneer Express* [Press?], 12th, regrets the United States did not play lone hand but glad present co-operation does not mean joint action later since the United States has kept free hand in matter of sanctions. This journal voices the rather widely held opinion that the Nanking Incident was really trivial. Cleveland *Plain Dealer,* 12th, considers that now joint demands have been presented separate action is advisable for the United States which should do its own thinking [a commonly voiced opinion]; Des Moines *Register,* 12th, warns that Nanking Incident must not result in our being drawn into conflict for maintenance of British power in China; Boston *Herald,* 13th, insists demands not inconsistent with traditional American policy in China and points out our freedom of action preserved; Richmond *Times Despatch*, 13th, condemns demands which link the United States with questions of unity and sanctions; Buffalo *Evening News*, 12th, comments on fact that demands constitute recognition by the United States of two governments in China; Boston *Transcript*, 12th, points out that the United States is not necessarily committed to specific intervention because of the fact that this country suffered similarly to other Powers and presented similar demands.[29]

As the Secretary himself indicated, the general tone of these editorials was hostile to the idea of the United States Government's undertaking any drastic action in China and was in favor of the United States pursuing an independent course. These impressions of press opinion were supported in another informal survey of American editorials which was made at this time by one of the wire editors of the Associated Press, Mr. Robert S. Pickens.[30] According to Mr. Pickens' analysis, both the urban and the rural press were consistently opposed to any armed intervention after the Nanking Incident. Here and there, a paper objected to a lack of definiteness on the part of the government, but nowhere were objections raised to a policy of non-intervention in China. Moreover, the final decision of the President to act independently of other foreign Powers brought forth "chants of praise all over the country" — even in the southern part of the United States where acts of a Republican official were likely to be "wholeheartedly condemned." "Hundreds of editorials," Mr. Pickens said, could be quoted to substantiate these generalizations. The main conclusion which the author himself drew from this study was that: "Had the Government of the United States contemplated military action in China following the Nanking Affair, the attitude of the American people would have made such a course thoroughly unpopular, if not impossible."

A similar picture of the press, during the aftermath of the Nanking Incident, was presented by the *Literary Digest* in its issue of April 16th:

. . . the advocates of intervention in China are few and far between. Seldom are American newspapers so unanimous as they are in indorsing President Coolidge's policy of protecting our people and interests in China, without committing ourselves to joint action with the other Powers. The London *Morning Post*.is glad to see that the United States Government has 'rallied to our side in the common cause' and the British Chancellor of the Exchequer has acknowledged 'a strong feeling of sentiment' in reading of the 'Coldstream Guards and the United States Marines standing side by side'. . . . But the average editor on this side of the water is seemingly more impressed by what we do not have in common with the other Powers, as far

---

[29] *Foreign Relations* (1927), p. 194.
[30] *China Weekly Review*, June 11, 1927, pp. 28-29.

as China is concerned — Britain in particular. President Coolidge's states-
manship wins emphatic praise from representative papers all over the country like the New York *World,* Brooklyn *Eagle,* Raleigh *News and Observer,*
Louisville *Courier-Journal,* St. Louis *Star,* and Duluth *News Tribune. . . .*
These editors seem to be willing to 'keep cool with Coolidge' as far as China
is concerned.[31]

In commenting on President Coolidge's speech dealing with American
foreign policy as applied to Mexico, Nicaragua, and China, the press, according to the *Literary Digest,* indicated widespread approval of the President's
remarks concerning China.[32] ". . . the general tone and tenor of the President's speech evoked almost universal approbation on the part of the press,"
the *Digest* declared; ". . . the sympathetic remarks about China pleased even
the most insistent critics of the Administration."[33] A few weeks later, after
Sir Austen Chamberlain announced in the House of Commons that the
British would take no further action for the time being in relation to a
settlement of the Nanking Incident, the *Literary Digest* wrote that the attitude of editors throughout the United States was that America's Chinese
policy had prevailed among the Powers. Although, the *Literary Digest*
observed, according to a story in the New York *World,* " 'Sir Austen did not
reveal that the British change of mind was due primarily to the refusal of
the United States and Japan to join in punitive measures' . . . American
newspapers in their cable dispatches and editorials, have amply made up
for that omission."[34] Quoting from various newspapers, the *Digest* gave a
résumé of the events that had taken place since March 24th, which pictured
the American Government as holding out for a peaceful settlement of the
Nanking Incident against extreme pressure exercised by other governments,
by foreign experts in China, and by the foreign community at Shanghai.[35]

Supplementing these more extensive surveys, it is interesting to consider some of the specific arguments set forth in a few leading newspapers
representing different political convictions. Immediately after the Nanking
Incident, both the New York *World* and the Baltimore *Sun* tended to minimize the responsibility of the Chinese for the events which had taken place.
The *World* asked the Administration angrily why American nationals had
not been withdrawn from Nanking "weeks ago" when it was plain that there
would be fighting in the Nanking area.[36] The *Sun* accused Americans and
Englishmen of seeking to capitalize on a "nerve-wracking situation" by

[31] *Literary Digest,* April 16, 1927, pp. 8-9.
[32] *Ibid.,* May 7, 1927, p. 9.
[33] *Ibid.,* p. 8.
[34] *Ibid.,* May 21, 1927, p. 9.
[35] *Ibid.*
[36] New York *World,* March 25, 1927.

painting such a lurid picture of conditions in China that it amounted to a "triumph in exaggeration."[37] The *World* went even further than the *Sun* in this respect and declared repeatedly that many American correspondents in China were cabling sensational stories by way of urging the United States to use military force to uphold a "political and economic *status quo*" in China which the United States had not established and did "not like."[38]

Within a few days after the Nanking Incident, both the *Sun* and the *World* had made it clear that they would use whatever influence they possessed to oppose any aggressive action by the United States against the Chinese. Both papers consequently maintained a verbal barrage against anyone whom they suspected of attempting to drag the United States into a conflict in the Far East. The attitude of the New York *World* (which in the six weeks following the Nanking Incident published editorials on the situation in China at the rate of one every other day) may be gathered from the following very typical expression of its views printed on March 31st, under the title, "Well Done, Mr. Coolidge":

Mr. Coolidge shows himself aware that an effort is being made to push this country into the front rank of a new adventure in the Far East. He has taken occasion to state that our troops are in China solely to protect American lives and for no other purpose. They are not there to make war on Chinese nationalism. . . . They will co-operate with other foreign troops for the specifically limited purpose of protecting American lives when co-operation promotes this end but there will be no "unified command." There will especially be no unified command for the purpose of upholding a one-sided treaty system forced upon China by the European Powers on the fine theory that by so doing we are protecting our own interests. We shall, in other words, pull nobody's chestnuts from the fire.

Efforts to induce this country to do just that have been tireless and unrelenting since the Nanking riots. Despatches from both Shanghai and London have whooped up the theory that a community of "Anglo-Saxon" interest exists in China by virtue of which it becomes our duty (presumably in exchange for the fact that we have some missionaries) to uphold Great Britain's special privileges in the Yangtze Valley. We have been told that Britain's and our own interests in the Yangtze Valley are identical: this despite the fact that 29 years ago Britain formally declared the Yangtze Valley to be her special sphere of influence. . . . To this day the Yangtze Valley formally remains Britain's "sphere of influence" upheld by treaties conferring upon Britain exclusive railway construction and mining rights. The Nationalist movement now challenges these treaties. This is the background for pleas for "Anglo-Saxon" unity, a joint effort to "protect foreign interests" and an expeditionary force under "unified command." This is the

[37] Baltimore *Sun*, March 27, 1927.

[38] New York *World*, March 29, 1927; see also March 30, 1927; March 31, 1927; April 5, 1927; May 2, 1927.

background of eager efforts to din into everybody's ears the news that all China has gone "Bolshevist" and "murderously anti-foreign."

Well, Mr. Coolidge declines to fall for it. He declines to agree that the protection of a treaty system forced on China thirty years ago is now indissolubly a part of protecting our own interests. He declines to believe that despite Nanking and despite the danger of more murder and more looting, the whole Nationalist movement has as yet gone mad; he prefers to believe that the Nanking riots were the work of "disorganized mobs" rather than of authoritative Nationalist leaders. In any case he says that our troops are in China solely for one purpose, but that they will be diverted from it to no other.

This is a statesman talking. Mr. Coolidge has made a timely effort to put a stop to a mischievous propaganda. The effort shows understanding of our own responsibilities, gumption as to where they end and tolerance toward a young and chaotic nationalism struggling to assert itself in China.[39]

The Baltimore *Sun*, in the early stages of developments after the Nanking Incident, showed less confidence in the Administration's policy than the New York *World*. It was alarmed at the dispatch of 1,500 additional marines to China and afraid that the Government might place our forces under a unified international command. "Now it is virtually certain," the *Sun* said on the 29th of March, "that neither Congress, were it in session, nor the American people, were they articulate, would sanction war with China.... But toward such an eventuality we are perhaps drifting...."[40] Following the delivery of the Powers' note of April 11th to Nationalist officials, the *Sun* expressed extreme concern over America's participation in the co-operative action of the Powers and warned the government that "the great majority of American people ... would regard military opposition to Chinese nationalism as a betrayal of our own traditions."[41]

The *Sun* was, if anything, more bitter than the *World* in its denunciation of the rôle the British were reported to be playing in the negotiations for the settlement of the Nanking Incident. On one occasion, it spoke of the action of the Austrian Government in 1914 in "sending an ultimatum to Serbia so couched that compliance was impossible," and asserted that if Great Britain followed this example she would be "equally defamed;"[42] on another occasion, it urged the United States Government to issue "an official pronouncement ... making it plain to the humblest English intelligence that there is no desire whatsoever over here for a joint Anglo-American war."[43]

[39] *Ibid.*, March 31, 1927.
[40] Baltimore *Sun*, March 29, 1927.
[41] *Ibid.*, April 12, 1927.
[42] *Ibid.*, April 18, 1927.
[43] *Ibid.*, April 3, 1927.

Moreover, both the *Sun* and the *World* attacked influences other than the British for attempting to draw the United States into a war with China. One of the main targets for their criticism was the American Chamber of Commerce at Shanghai which, early in April, passed a resolution urging the United States Government to take a strong stand in China "in immediate concerted action" with the other Powers.[44] The *World,* commenting on the Chamber's action, declared that it was "necessary to pronounce as utterly fantastic" the Chamber's proposal that American troops "be used in a unified effort 'to suppress disorder and restore conditions favorable to the formation of responsible government' " in China; ". . . to just how many years of warfare in a nation of four hundred million people would the Chamber pledge us?" the *World* asked.[45] The *Sun* compared the members of the Chamber (and the foreign "Treaty Porters" in general) to a Humpty Dumpty who, having fallen off the wall, should recognize that it could not be reinstated in its privileged position because the time had passed when privileged positions could be maintained — even by American warships and marines.[46] When, early in May, there were reports from Shanghai that Mr. Mac-Murray disapproved of American policy and was "urging the State Department to act with Britain for 'strong positive measures,' " the *World* criticized Mr. MacMurray in several editorials and in a cartoon portraying him as a small figure bending all his strength to push the giant form of Uncle Sam into flames that were marked, "Intervention in China."[47]

As the situation eased gradually and rumors began to spread that the United States had refused to join in the presentation of a second identic note to Eugene Chen with threats of sanctions, the *World* predicted that the action of the American Government would not lead to a "break" among the Powers, but rather "to the other Powers adopting the policy of the Administration." "American policy in China," the editors declared, "has been thwarted time after time not because it has been too bold but because it has been compressed away to nothing."[48] When, in the end, it became known that the plan for sending a reply to Eugene Chen had in fact been abandoned by all the nations involved, the *World* wrote that this final outcome of the negotiations should be instructive "in at least three quarters. . . . It should serve notice on the interventionists in Shanghai and in London that to date they have made small headway. It should encourage the moderates in China to believe that we do not wish deliberately to make their

---

[44] See below, pp. 342-344.
[45] New York *World*, April 5, 1927. See also the *World*'s editorial attacking the *North China Daily News*, April 30, 1927.
[46] Baltimore *Sun*, April 5, 1927.
[47] New York *World*, May 2, 1927; May 3, 1927; May 3, 1927, cartoon.
[48] *Ibid.*, April 27, 1927.

problem harder for them. It should convince the American Government that it does not have to be in a majority to carry a point in China."[49]

The Louisville *Courier-Journal,* while it was just as staunch a supporter of the policy of non-intervention in China as the New York *World* and the Baltimore *Sun,* followed a somewhat different line of reasoning. From the outset it tended to minimize the seriousness of the attack on foreigners which had been made at Nanking.[50] The bombardment of Nanking by American and British warships, it said, was "unnecessary and high-handed"; troops should have been sent ashore, instead of shelling a town and killing innocent people.[51] Moreover, it declared, with unvarnished hostility, that the real cause of the outrages against foreigners in China was the fact that the foreigners themselves were "supercilious," "contemptuously condescending," and "arrogantly assumed white superiority."[52]

When the question of the use of sanctions for the enforcement of the demands against the Nationalists loomed uppermost in the American press, the *Courier-Journal* argued that any such action would require an armed force of half a million men to occupy China for ten years, and ". . . all it would achieve," it said, "would be satisfaction for half a dozen lives at the cost of hundreds, perhaps thousands, more."[53] It regarded the demands of the Powers as expressed in their note of April 11th as "brusque" and "imperious" and applauded Mr. Chen for "refusing to comply cringingly."[54] In general the *Courier-Journal* believed that the United States should maintain its policy of supporting the integrity of the Chinese nation and not lend itself to the promotion of the "ulterior motives of other Powers." Like the New York *World,* it maintained that if the United States Government adhered firmly and consistently to its convictions, it would determine the policies of the other nations in respect to China.[55] Moreover, it did not believe that the British Government would in any way oppose the conciliatory policy of the United States in the Far East, arguing that it was the British commercial community in China and not the Government at home which wanted intervention.[56] After Sir Austen Chamberlain announced that the British would take no drastic action to enforce a settlement of the Nanking Incident, the *Courier-Journal* declared that this decision "was to be ex-

[49] *Ibid.,* May 5, 1927.
[50] Louisville *Courier-Journal,* March 29, 1927; April 1, 1927.
[51] *Ibid.,* April 1, 1927.
[52] *Ibid.,* March 28, 1927.
[53] *Ibid.,* April 4, 1927.
[54] *Ibid.,* April 16, 1927.
[55] *Ibid.,* April 14, 1927.
[56] *Ibid.,* May 14, 1927.

pected" and that "what looks like patriotism to a British trader in China looks like pure foolhardiness in London."[57]

Despite the more conservative character of the Washington *Post,* its editorial policy in dealing with the Nanking Incident followed along lines similar to those of the New York *World,* the Baltimore *Sun,* and the Louisville *Courier-Journal.* As early as March 28th, the *Post* asserted that the United States would be "guilty of unspeakable folly" if it allowed itself to be drawn into a conflict in China. "At this hour," it said, "the friendship of the American people toward the Chinese should be made clear beyond question."[58] Two days later, the *Post* fulminated against the American community in Shanghai which was reported to be in favor of "vigorous military and naval action along the Chinese coast." "It is well," the *Post* declared, "in this crisis that the policy of the United States in dealing with China is determined in Washington instead of in Shanghai"; ". . . the rights of the American people as well as the rights of Americans in China are involved in this situation"; ". . . American citizens have been repeatedly warned to get out of foreign countries where their lives were endangered. . . . It would be an act of insanity on the part of the United States Government to involve itself in war with China on account of individual citizens who persist in remaining in the path of destruction."[59] The Government in Washington, the *Post* argued, in another editorial printed on April 3rd, had a right to demand indemnity for the damages sustained at Nanking, but "there should be no threat of a punitive expedition and no undertaking of a retaliatory nature in common with other Powers."[60]

Throughout the next weeks the *Post* constantly and emphatically reasserted its objections both to a policy of intervention in China and to a policy of co-operation with other foreign Powers. Following the participation of the American Government in the delivery of the identic note of April 11th, the *Post* declared that Secretary Kellogg had made a "serious mistake" in associating the United States with the action of the other Governments: "The United States in dealing with China has nothing in common with other Powers. Its interests are not their interests and its purposes are not their purposes. They may resort to force if they wish. The United States cannot resort to force without arousing a furore of protest from the American people."[61] What was the intention of the Powers, the *Post* asked, "mili-

[57] Louisville *Courier-Journal,* May 14, 1927.
[58] Washington *Post,* March 28, 1927; reprinted in *North China Star,* April 28, 1927.
[59] *Ibid.,* April 1, 1927; reprinted in *North China Star,* April 29, 1927.
[60] *Ibid.,* April 3, 1927; reprinted in *North China Star,* April 30, 1927.
[61] Washington *Post,* April 12, 1927; reprinted in *North China Star,* May 24, 1927.

tary action against the Cantonese? The suggestion is abhorrent to the American people."[62]

Unlike the New York *World*, the Baltimore *Sun*, and the Louisville *Courier-Journal*, the *Post* paid considerable attention to the conflict between the "radical" and the "moderate" factions in the Kuomintang.[63] The *Post* believed that the Russian-influenced elements in the Nationalist movement were exerting "every effort to embroil the foreign Powers in the Chinese war in order to enflame anti-foreign feeling and thus promote the cause of 'world revolution.' "[64] This was given as one of the reasons for urging the United States Government, as well as the other Powers, to refrain from making any threat of forcible reprisals in connection with the settlement of the Nanking Incident.[65]

The Kansas City *Star*, although far less concerned with the situation in China than any of the above newspapers, was also clearly opposed to the use of military force against the Chinese. While it published a number of scathing editorials making fun of the "pinks" and "idealists" who desired the complete withdrawal of American troops from China[66] and was emphatic in its insistence that it was the Government's duty to accord the proper protection to its nationals, it advocated in general a policy of patience and watchful waiting. During the period when the negotiations for a settlement of the Nanking issue were being conducted between the five Powers, the *Star* consistently maintained that there was nothing the United States could do in China except to protect its citizens and await the day when there would appear a national Chinese Government capable of concluding new treaties with the Government of the United States.[67] As one of the arguments in support of this point it asserted that a policy of non-aggression would help the cause of Chiang Kai-shek who had "now broken with the Communists" in the Kuomintang and was the "greatest hope" of China.[68]

The story of the editorial policy of the Chicago *Tribune* is somewhat different from that of other newspapers at this time, partly because of cer-

[62] *Ibid.*, April 16, 1927; reprinted in *North China Star*, May 27, 1927.
[63] *Ibid.*, April 3, 1927, reprinted in *North China Star*, April 30, 1927; April 13, 1927, reprinted in *North China Star*, May 25, 1927; April 15, 1927, reprinted in *North China Star*, May 1, 1927; April 16, 1927, reprinted in *North China Star*, May 27, 1927; April 17, 1927, reprinted in *North China Star*, May 28, 1927.
[64] *Ibid.*, April 3, 1927; reprinted in *North China Star*, April 30, 1927.
[65] *Ibid.*, April 15, 1927; reprinted in *North China Star*, May 1, 1927. It is interesting to note that the *Post* classed Eugene Chen among the "moderate" leaders of the Kuomintang (see April 16, 1927; reprinted in *North China Star*, May 28, 1927, p. 6). The same was true of the Chicago *Tribune* (see editorial of March 25, 1927).
[66] Kansas City *Star*, April 12, 1927; April 22, 1927.
[67] *Ibid.*, April 2, 1927; April 11, 1927; May 10, 1927.
[68] *Ibid.*, May 10, 1927.

tain peculiar circumstances which developed. Following the events of March 24th, the *Tribune* took the position that the revolution in China was passing from a phase of moderation to a phase of excess which might result in the expulsion of all foreign interests from China and in the creation of a Russian-dominated Asia.[69] While the *Tribune* recognized that there were leaders in the Chinese Nationalist movement who were opposed to the "philosophy of Moscow," its general attitude was that the trend toward a "radical extreme" was so powerful in China that it would submerge all "moderate" elements.[70] In the face of these eventualities, the *Tribune* believed that the United States should adopt a "firm policy" and act in conjunction with the other Powers to combat the influence of the Soviet Union in China.[71] If the foreign Governments exhibited "weakness, confusion, or a division of policy," they would assist "Bolshevik machinations" in China and "thrust the country into the arms of Moscow;"[72] an impression that the Powers were afraid to act with the necessary force would only harm both foreign interests and the eventual interests of the Chinese.[73]

Editorials setting forth these views appeared in the *Tribune* up until the middle of April. In the third week in April, news reached this country that Mr. J. B. Powell, the editor of the *China Weekly Review,* who was also the Shanghai correspondent of the Chicago *Tribune,* had been asked to resign from the American Chamber of Commerce at Shanghai partly — according to reports — because of a disagreement over American policy in China in which Mr. Powell supported the principle of non-intervention.[74] The *Tribune* at once came to the defense of Mr. Powell in an editorial which placed that newspaper on the side of those who were opposed to aggressive action against the Chinese:

... we heartily endorse Mr. Powell's statement of policy in his spirited reply to the Shanghai Chamber. It is the right and the interest of the United States to keep clear of any interference with the domestic affairs of the Chinese people save as they involve the rights of our nationals under international law. We have a sound general policy toward China which civil war and chaotic conditions do not countermand or alter in principle. . . .

When Mr. Powell says he is unqualifiedly opposed to any effort to involve America in complications of far-reaching extent, even to the extreme of another world war, he may or may not be right in his apprehensions but he will certainly have the endorsement of his fellow countrymen at home in his opposition to any such involvement as may threaten.[75]

[69] Chicago *Tribune,* March 25, 1927; March 31, 1927.
[70] *Ibid.,* April 5, 1927; see also March 30, 1927 and April 13, 1927.
[71] *Ibid.,* March 31, 1927.
[72] *Ibid.,* April 5, 1927.
[73] *Ibid.,* April 2, 1927.
[74] See below, p. 345 *et seq.*
[75] Chicago *Tribune,* April 28, 1927.

The *Tribune* not only supported Mr. Powell but attacked the forces in Shanghai with which he had come into conflict: "In Shanghai we more than suspect Mr. Powell is encountering an especially stubborn and short-sighted policy which has had much to do with anti-foreignism in that region. ... Neither our Government nor our people intend to be drawn into the support of such a policy. ..."[76]

The *New York Times*, which had previously been opposed both to a policy of intervention and to a policy "of propriation" in China, as soon as the news of the Nanking Incident reached this country, expressed the earnest hope that the crisis would not "lead to active fighting between the Powers and the various Chinese factions."[77] Like the Kansas City *Star*, it emphasized the need to accord proper protection to foreign nationals but believed that the first essential of American policy was "patience and cool judgment."[78] Early in April, when there were rumors that pressure was being brought from several directions to urge the United States to maintain a forceful policy in China together with the other Powers, the *Times* said:

Reports from Shanghai, London and Tokyo, deal more and more with a possible joint action by Great Britain, Japan and the United States in China. Great Britain's desire for American co-operation — a desire loudly echoed by the American Chamber of Commerce in Shanghai — is doubtless based on the conviction that if there must be intervention, it will be less difficult and costly if undertaken in common. But Americans would view such concurrent action with grave apprehension. . . .

In the present crisis America is unwilling to join in any action which may seem like intervention against the Cantonese or any other Chinese party. Fortunately the foreign Governments realize that despite the protests of the American Chamber of Commerce at Shanghai, the United States has shown no indication of departing from its traditional policy of using military and naval forces in China conjointly with those of other Powers, only for the protection of American lives and interests. Whatever demands may be made on the Cantonese for the Nanking affray, there can be no thought of active interference in the civil war in China.[79]

Throughout the remainder of the spring of 1927, the *Times* continued to adhere to an editorial policy based on the concept of "benevolent inaction" in China.[80] It welcomed the "friendly and unselfish" feeling toward China expressed in President Coolidge's speech of April 25th and declared:

[76] *Ibid.* For an earlier attack on the Shanghai Municipal Council, see the *Tribune* editorial of April 11, 1927; for an attack on the *North China Daily News*, see editorial of April 30, 1927.

[77] *New York Times*, March 25, 1927.

[78] *Ibid.*, March 27, 1927; see also March 28, 1927; April 19, 1927.

[79] *Ibid.*, April 5, 1927.

[80] *Ibid.*, April 19, 1927.

Our government is most anxious to see a strong and unified government set up in that country. With it, Mr. Coolidge said, the Washington Administration would be more than willing to enter into cordial relations and to negotiate new treaties recognizing to the full Chinese sovereignty and helping in every way within our power to establish a modern and republican system of government. To all these benevolent purposes . . . it is certain that the great majority of Americans are ready to give warm approval.[81]

On May 4th, the *Times* again asserted that while it was natural for Americans whose lives and property were being threatened in China to want their government to "do something vigorously and instantaneously," a "longer and cooler view" was "properly" being held and acted upon in Washington.[82]

Besides discussing the issues involved in America's rôle in the settlement of the Nanking Incident, the *Times* devoted a great deal of attention to the news reaching the United States concerning the struggle for power between the so-called "right" and "left" wings of the Kuomintang. Its general line of argument was somewhat different from any of those which have been described thus far. On numerous occasions the editors discussed at length the relationship between the "Hankow group" of the Kuomintang and the internal politics of the Soviet Union. Their main contention was that Stalin was "much more concerned with the ultimate effect of China on domestic Russian problems than with the progress of the world revolution."[83] Translated into practical terms, this was regarded as meaning that Stalin did not wish China to "go proletarian," as any such outcome might invite a conflict with the Western Powers and Japan, a situation which the Soviet Union would regard as "exceedingly unwelcome." "Stalin knows," the *Times* said, "that his régime needs peace."[84] The *Times* was, moreover, persuaded that as a result of this situation Moscow was urging the Nationalist officials at Hankow to beat a "strategic retreat" and to "placate" the "imperialist" Powers which they had, up until this time, been opposing.[85] In contrast to the Chicago *Tribune*, which was convinced that the radical tide in China was rising, the *Times* believed that in the month following the Nanking Incident the internal situation in China had altered materially because of the slackening of the current of radicalism "with its anti-imperialist and anti-capitalist war cries."[86] Although the *Times* in speaking of Chiang

[81] *Ibid.*, April 26, 1927.
[82] *Ibid.*, May 4, 1927.
[83] *Ibid.*, April 16, 1927.
[84] *Ibid.*
[85] *Ibid.*, May 3, 1927.
[86] *Ibid.*, April 29, 1927.

Kai-shek observed that there was "no special reason" to suppose that he differed much from any of the other Chinese warlords,[87] it nevertheless disapproved of the Powers taking any aggressive action which might hamper Chiang or any other supporters of the movement that aimed at moderation in China.[88]

While in general it was the opinion of the press concerning the crisis in China which evoked the most comment after the Nanking Incident, the collective voice of American editors had one challenging rival in the attention of the public, namely, Senator Borah, who spoke his mind in respect to developments in China in the spring of 1927, with compelling forcefulness and sincerity.

As we have already seen, Senator Borah became interested in the situation in China following the May 30th Incident of 1925, and from that time on made it clear to the American public that he was in sympathy with the struggle of the Chinese people for full independence from foreign control.

In May of 1927, Senator Borah delivered two important speeches on the critical international situation which had developed out of the Nanking Incident.[89] In these he took the position that American policy toward China as enunciated by President Coolidge was solely concerned with protecting our nationals and removing them from zones of danger wherever necessary, and was otherwise directed toward leaving the Chinese to manage their own affairs. With deep conviction, Senator Borah endorsed the policy of the Administration at Washington and warned that "powerful influences" were attempting to dissuade the Government from pursuing its course. There were people, he said, who insisted that force should be used against the Chinese because force was the only argument the Chinese were capable of respecting and understanding. "If force is to be used," the Senator declared, "it will not be because it is the only thing which China respects but it will be because it is the only thing those using it understand." He further attacked those "desirous of intervention" for carrying on a highly-organized propaganda campaign in which they exaggerated every possible incident in order to play on the feelings of the American people, and in which they criticized the Secretary of State for not using information — which they claimed he had in his possession — for the sake of arousing public opinion in the

[87] *Ibid.*, April 22, 1927.
[88] *Ibid.*, April 29, 1927.
[89] According to a cable dispatch from New York to the *Peking Leader*, Senator Borah asserted in an address in New York on March 24, 1927, that the United States Government should open negotiations for a revision of the treaties, not with both the Peking and Canton Governments, but exclusively with the Nationalist Government. For texts of the speeches delivered in Cleveland and in New York in May, 1927, see the *Peking Leader*, May 28, 1927 and June 10, 1927.

United States.[90] The Senator's own attitude toward incidents involving attacks on foreigners in China was that President Coolidge was right in asserting that the Chinese nation was in the midst of a stupendous political, social, and economic upheaval in which some forces would almost inevitably be "unleashed" that might inflict injury on American citizens.

Rather than intervene in China, the Senator argued, the United States should seek to be of assistance to the Chinese. It was to the interest not only of China but of the whole world, he said, to establish a strong, united, and independent Chinese nation. The United States could further this end by maintaining a "policy of sympathy and co-operation." "I am perfectly aware of course," he declared, "that under present conditions it is difficult to find a responsible authority with which to co-operate but if there is a government sufficiently responsible to which to send an ultimatum, then there is a government sufficiently responsible to which to send a message of co-operation."

Views which were in many respects similar to those held by Senator Borah were expressed by William Green as spokesman for the American Federation of Labor. Like Senator Borah, Mr. Green went on record as supporting whole-heartedly the declared purpose of the United States Government to limit its activities in China solely to the protection of American nationals:

> The laboring people of the United States would be opposed to our Government doing anything more in China than to extend the protection of American lives and property which the Government of the United States is under obligation to give to its citizens in danger.
> The American labor movement believes that the Chinese people should be given the widest and fullest opportunity to establish a government of their own choosing and to exercise its sovereignty without interference from other nations. The Great Powers which have admittedly been encroaching upon Chinese territory should immediately declare their purpose to withdraw from Chinese soil, to give up every concession which they have gained through force or otherwise, and thus leave China free to work out her own destiny.

There is no doubt that the American press as a whole opposed the use of sanctions following the Nanking Incident. It would, in all probability, be difficult to find a single instance in which a newspaper advocated the use of force to settle the Nanking crisis; even the Chicago *Tribune*, which came close to adopting this attitude early in April when it supported a "firm policy" on the part of the United States Government, changed its mind within a few weeks.

Leading sections of the press felt so strongly on the question of inter-

[90] This was a reference to an attack on the Secretary of State made by the *North China Daily News and Herald*, see below, p. 345.

vention in China that they attempted to counteract any influence which might possibly lead toward drawing the United States into a conflict in the Far East. The co-operative policy of the Powers, which had been almost continuously criticized since the introduction of the Porter Resolution into Congress, was denounced with a vehemence that left a strong impression on observers.[91] Certain influential newspapers, especially those belonging to the liberal wing of the press, were equally relentless in their condemnation of the British; the idea that Great Britain should fight her own wars for her own purposes, and that British interests in China were very different from those of the United States, was frequently expressed. Possibly even more widespread was the criticism of the "Shanghai interests" as represented by the American Chamber of Commerce of Shanghai, the Shanghai Municipal Council, and the *North China Daily News and Herald,* which were thought to be urging their governments at home to use military force in China. Even an outstandingly liberal newspaper like the New York *World* was no more determined in its attacks on the "Shanghai diehards" than papers of such varied political complexion as the Chicago *Tribune,* the *New York Times* and the Washington *Post.*

President Coolidge's speech of April 25th found a responsive audience in the American press. The idea that the conflict in China was a great, national revolution which made it impossible to maintain conditions of security for foreigners was accepted with approval by editors in many parts of the country. In respect to the struggle between the "right" and "left" wings of the Nationalist movement, the American press was, according to all indications, in favor of supporting the conservative elements in the Kuomintang. But newspapers varied greatly in the extent to which they emphasized this issue; moreover, they showed a substantial ignorance concerning the developments that were taking place within the Chinese Nationalist Party.

One of the most important consequences of the activities of the American press during the Nanking crisis was the amount of attention which they attracted. In considering the reactions of the Shanghai community it will be seen, for example, that many people in China felt that editorial opinion in the United States was exercising a determining influence on American policy.

[91] It is interesting to note that Secretary Stimson in July, 1929, opposed certain important measures recommended by the American Legation at Peking partly on the ground that they would involve substituting a policy of international co-operation for the independent policy which the United States had been pursuing in China; this, he said, would be a matter of great moment, as "such a reversal of policy would mean losing the country's support which the Coolidge Administration had for its independent policy." (*Foreign Relations,* 1929, p. 582.)

Chapter XVI

CHAPTER XVI

REACTIONS AT SHANGHAI

If, during the critical period of 1927, officials in Washington hoped that they could rely on public opinion to support a conciliatory and independent American policy in China, they must have had their misgivings as they looked toward Shanghai.

The first problem in connection with Shanghai arose over the making of plans for the defense of the International Settlement. As we have already seen, the United States Government sent a relatively small force of 1,500 marines to Shanghai and laid down the principle that American troops should not be used to defend the integrity of the International Settlement but solely for the protection of American lives. In accordance with this policy, it was decided not to station United States marines in the cordon placed around the Settlement, but to reserve them for the suppression of any disorder which might occur within the Settlement boundaries. Consequently when, on February 24th, the British soldiers were moved into position in certain sectors of the cordon, the American Consul General, Mr. Gauss, refused to recommend the landing of the American troops quartered on boats anchored in the harbor, on the ground that there was as yet no threat of disorder within the Settlement itself.

Mr. Fessenden, the Chairman of the Shanghai Municipal Council, who it will be remembered was an American, expressed his disapproval of the policy adopted by the United States at this time in numerous public addresses and press interviews. On January 27th, according to a story printed in the New York *Sun*, Mr. Fessenden informed the *Sun's* correspondent that he was very grateful indeed to the British Government for the dispatch of the Shanghai Defense Force and hoped that the American Government would follow suit. He was openly critical of American policy and said that it had not always been one of which Americans in China could be proud, explaining that he believed that at important moments throughout history the United States had "let the British down" by following an independent course in China. He placed himself on record as objecting to the Bills pending in Congress "to recognize Canton and abolish extraterritoriality," and said that to recognize the Nationalist Government would be "equivalent to recognizing Red Russia" and that the extraterritorial provisions of the treaties guaranteed "certain things which should not be destroyed."[1]

[1] Interview reprinted in the *North China Herald*, March 5, 1927, p. 373.

As the Nationalist armies approached Shanghai, and the situation in respect to the Settlement grew more acute, Mr. Fessenden spoke his mind with even greater candor. Early in March, he told an audience at Shanghai that he regretted that the United States and Great Britain were not working hand-in-glove in China (referring to the defense plans for Shanghai) and that he believed the fault lay with the large number of Americans in the United States who did not understand the gravity of the situation.[2] A few days later, according to press reports, he told a United Press correspondent that in his opinion America was "leaning over backward in her policy of 'hands off China' " and added that he regarded the attitude of the United States as hypocritical. He appears to have based the latter view on the theory that the State Department was being influenced by some business groups in the United States who were not genuinely friendly toward the Chinese but wished to maintain a conciliatory policy for the sake of expanding their commercial interests. "I believe," Mr. Fessenden is reported to have said, "ninety-eight per cent of the Americans in Shanghai would like to see the Government at Washington take a more firm stand. As it is, all the assurance we have now is that we will be able to drive up to the wharf in safety and board a ship . . . leaving all our goods, the fruits of many years of labor, behind."[3]

Mr. Fessenden appears to have retained these views even after conditions in Shanghai had settled down to a state of relative quiet. Several weeks after the Northern troops had been driven out of Shanghai and the city had been taken over by the Nationalists, Mr. Fessenden — according to Thomas Steep in the New York *Herald Tribune* — declared that if it had not been for the British Defense Force "we would all have been butchered." He explained further that the policies of the United States and Great Britain differed "radically" in that Great Britain was prepared to defend the Settlement and the United States was merely willing to defend the lives of its own citizens; in his opinion, he added, "the United States should have taken a policy identical with that of Great Britain" and American forces should have shouldered the responsibility equally with the British by assuming a position in the first line of defense instead of remaining "on the defensive behind the British lines."[4] While expressing himself less pointedly on these issues at the Annual Ratepayers' Meeting held at Shanghai in April, 1927, Mr. Fessenden nevertheless appeared to criticize United States policy indirectly: he explained at length that the Municipal Council felt that it had every right to attempt to preserve the political and territorial integrity of the

[2] *Ibid.*, March 5, 1927, p. 372.
[3] *North China Star*, March 11, 1927, p. 1.
[4] New York *Herald Tribune*, April 11, 1927, pp. 1-2.

Settlement "in *statu quo*" until such time as changed by orderly and peaceful negotiations, and declared that he believed this to be the opinion of an overwhelming majority of the responsible public in Shanghai; he then stated that the Powers had not all agreed on a policy for defending the integrity of the Settlement but that the Municipal Council had derived "intense satisfaction" from the fact that the policy of the British and Italian Governments was "identical" with its own.[5]

According to Mr. Fessenden's own description of the matter, the Shanghai Municipal Council had become alarmed at the dangers that confronted the International Settlement long before either the general public or the foreign Powers were aware of the situation. Apparently the members of the Council were convinced that an effort would be made by the contending factions in China's civil war to occupy the Shanghai area and they believed that, to quote Mr. Fessenden, "one faction at least" would attempt to take possession of the International Settlement. In line with these ideas they approached various people in a position to influence their home governments, in order to impress upon them the need for adopting measures which would insure the International Settlement against attacks made either from without or from within its borders. It was, however, only after the invasion of the British concession at Hankow, that the Council was satisfied that it was making headway and that "the governments of some of the foreign Powers were aroused to a full consciousness of the danger threatening Shanghai."[6]

It was at this time, early in January, 1927, that the Shanghai Municipal Council itself issued a proclamation which expressed its views of the gravity of the situation.[7] The proclamation declared that political meetings, demonstrations, and propaganda "of any description" were prohibited within the Settlement and that the Council was directing its energies and resources to the maintenance of order and would rigorously suppress every form of disorder and violence "with all means at its disposal." It warned the residents of the Settlement "against the activities of professional agitators who, taking advantage of the disturbed conditions" in China, were preaching "doctrines of force and class hatred" at a time when toleration and moderation were more than ever necessary.

The American Chamber of Commerce at Shanghai appears to have shared the anxiety of the Municipal Council concerning the dangers that lay ahead. On January 18th, it called a meeting of its members — which proved to be the largest meeting in the history of the Chamber up to that time — for the express purpose of urging the United States Government to recognize

[5] The Shanghai Municipal Council *Gazette*, April 14, 1927, p. 137.
[6] *Ibid.*, April 14, 1927, p. 136.
[7] *Ibid.*, January 14, 1927, p. 9.

the seriousness of the situation. A resolution was passed and cabled to Washington asking the American Government to co-operate to the fullest extent with the authorities in the Settlement in any efforts they might be called upon to make to safeguard the life and property of American nationals. After the issuance of Secretary of State Kellogg's declaration of policy on January 27th, the Chamber again cabled the State Department endorsing Mr. Kellogg's statement in general terms but singling out for special approval the assurances given in respect to the protection of American life and property.[8]

On February 7th, Mr. Kellogg issued his proposal for the so-called neutralization of the Settlement area with its offer to enter into negotiations with the Chinese regarding the future status of the International Settlement. No official comment was made on this subject by the Shanghai Municipal Council at the time, but late in March the Council issued a Manifesto which it specifically declared was "a public announcement of its considered views as regards the local situation" and which dealt in part with the question of effecting any drastic change in the Settlement's status under existing conditions. The Manifesto was sent to the members of the Consular Body, the local press, and the press in Europe, America, and Japan. Loosely paraphrased it read as follows:

The Shanghai Municipal Council is vested with full authority as regards all matters for the maintenance of order and good government in the International Settlement. Under its administration Shanghai has developed into one of the principal ports of China. At the present time, however, agents in the service of revolutionary interests are actively engaged in spreading subversive doctrines among the less responsible elements of the Chinese community; if these nefarious schemes are successful they will inevitably lead to civil commotion and mob violence and result in crippling all forms of industrial enterprise and destroying the trade of Shanghai. The Council realizes the possible repercussions that this situation may have throughout the civilized world and will use all the resources at its disposal to control the situation. Concurrently with these sinister activities a national spirit is gradually taking form throughout China with many aspects of which the Council finds itself in sympathy. Unfortunately an influential section of this movement is at present dominated by persons holding extreme and revolutionary views who are seeking to cloud and distort the legitimate aims of the Chinese in order to serve an evil purpose of their own.

The Council is fully alive to the fact that the rapid growth of the Chinese population at Shanghai has rendered an alteration in its constitution

---

[8] See extracts from *Annual Report of the American Chamber of Commerce,* reprinted in the *North China Herald,* April 30, 1927, p. 209.

desirable so as to allow for the inclusion of Chinese members on the Municipal Council. At the Ratepayers' Meeting of 1926, a proposal for the addition of three Chinese Councilors was approved and the Council is now awaiting their appointment by the Chinese community.

It is the Council's opinion, however, that the present is not a suitable time for the Powers concerned to consider any drastic change in the Shanghai Administration. Influences have been released in China with the express and avowed purpose of stirring up discontent, class hatred, and racial prejudice, and until these influences have been eliminated it would be a fruitless task to attempt to reconcile Sino-foreign viewpoints. In making this statement the Council does not wish it to be inferred that it is in any sense opposed to increasing Chinese representation in the affairs of the Municipality but rather that further changes shall be effected by evolutionary as opposed to revolutionary methods and that they will be considered in an atmosphere created by mutual good will, respect, and conciliation.

Pending the outcome of the struggle that is now being waged throughout China between the forces of temperance and intemperance, of evolution and revolution, the Council appeals to moderate-minded Chinese and foreigners alike to support the measures being undertaken for the protection of the Settlement. The Council also urges the Powers concerned to insist upon due respect being accorded to treaty obligations until the time arrives when these obligations can be reviewed in proper perspective.[9]

While the Shanghai Municipal Council was thus expressing its views, events in China were developing rapidly. No sooner did it become apparent that Shanghai would pass under Nationalist control without any serious consequences to the residents in the International Settlement than news reached Shanghai of the attack made by Chinese soldiers on the foreign population at Nanking. While, therefore, foreigners at Shanghai came at this time to fear less for their own safety, there was an inevitable heightening of tension in the relationship between Chinese and foreigners in general.

These pressures appear to have finally induced the American business community at Shanghai to make known its views in an official expression of opinion. As indicated earlier, few groups of American business men had attempted to take a hand in the situation since the development of the anti-foreign movement in 1925 and the silence and "timidity" of the commercial community had at times been a subject of criticism even among its friends and supporters.[10]

On April 2nd, the American Chamber of Commerce at Shanghai issued

[9] Text in Shanghai Municipal Council *Gazette*, April 1, 1927, p. 109.
[10] See Chapter V.

a statement which attracted a good deal of attention.[11] The statement was one in which the Chamber sought to express itself, to use its own words, "in favor of armed intervention," and it amounted to an appeal to the United States Government to co-operate with the other interested Powers in a joint plan for intervention in China.[12]

The Chamber's declaration opened with the forceful statement that: "Militarism, brigandage, and Bolshevism have destroyed all semblance of law and order throughout the greater part of China and have brought about a condition where life and property of both Chinese and foreigners are in constant danger from mob violence, military terrorism and unrestrained activities of individual criminals." The great mass of conservative and law-abiding Chinese, it was said, had been reduced to a state of helpless intimidation and could neither protect themselves nor the foreigners who resided among them. The adoption of a conciliatory policy by the foreign governments had "merely strengthened the position of the lawless elements and encouraged outrages like that of Nanking."

The American Chamber, the statement continued, endorsed the decision of the United States Government to take adequate measures for the protection of American lives and properties at Shanghai. Through "unscrupulous propaganda designed to inflame the Chinese masses against foreigners," a degree of hostility had been created which was causing the withdrawal of hundreds of Americans throughout China and the desertion to mobs of millions of dollars of American property. Although Shanghai was comparatively safe — due "entirely to the presence of foreign warships and military forces" — this was not sufficient under the circumstances; a protective policy applied to Shanghai alone would not enable China to put its house in order nor prevent enormous losses resulting from the evacuation of the interior districts. The Chamber concluded:

We are convinced that the future welfare of the Chinese people and the ultimate safety of American and other foreign residents throughout China can be attained only through unified action by the Powers to suppress disorder and to restore conditions favorable to the formation of a responsible Government.

We believe that immediate concerted action by the Powers to restore a condition of security for foreign lives and property in all treaty ports and to recover all foreign properties which have been destroyed or confiscated will have a far-reaching influence throughout China to the ultimate benefit of

[11] In connection with the amount of publicity given to developments in Shanghai at this time, it should be remembered that during the crisis of the spring of 1927 a far larger number of American newspapermen were in Shanghai than were there under normal circumstances.

[12] See statement of the American Chamber of Commerce at Shanghai, reprinted in British Chamber of Commerce *Journal*, September, 1927, p. 251.

the Chinese people. This result should not be difficult to attain with the naval forces now in Chinese waters.

In our opinion the future peace of the world and the general welfare of the Chinese people will be best served by the maintenance of the alignment of the Powers established under the Washington treaties and their co-operation in the service pledged to China during the Washington Conference.[13]

As the Chamber intended this statement primarily as a message to be cabled to the United States, it was released to all the representatives of the American press services and American newspapers who were in Shanghai at the time.[14] While official Washington gave no indication of its reaction to the Chamber's appeal, or to any other expressions of opinion that had emanated from Shanghai up to this point, it did respond with alacrity to the attacks on its policy made by the British-owned *North China Daily News and Herald*.

One of the difficulties in respect to achieving any degree of understanding between the United States and the foreign community at Shanghai was that none of the newspapers at Shanghai received news directly through an American news service but depended entirely on Reuter's Service, which reported happenings in the United States by means of a roundabout route via London, Calcutta, Singapore, and Hongkong.[15] As a consequence during most of April, 1927, relatively little was known in China concerning the attitude of either the United States Government or the American public toward the crisis that had developed over the Nanking Incident. In the third week in April, however, hitherto unconfirmed rumors that the United States Government would not co-operate with the other Powers in any action that depended upon a threat of sanctions against the Chinese began to gain credence. On April 26th, Rodney Gilbert, then at Peking, wrote an article which was published in the *North China Herald* under the title "Washington Leaves Her Allies." "It is no secret," Mr. Gilbert said, "that Mr. Kellogg's statement that America will participate in no punitive measures, as cabled, understates the American policy of withdrawal. This whole community, official as well as commercial, is disgusted and discouraged beyond expression."

Mr. Gilbert declared further that "a responsible authority speaking for the Legation says that American officialdom in China has been abominably treated by the Washington Administration." Consular and diplomatic

[13] Text in *ibid.*, May, 1927, p. 134.
[14] Extracts from the *Annual Report* of the Chamber, published in the *North China Herald*, April 30, 1927, p. 209.
[15] John B. Powell, *My Twenty-Five Years in China*, New York, 1945, p. 162.

reports, it was said, had furnished more than enough material to shape public opinion if the Government had "cared to face conditions honestly by giving out information at its disposal." Instead, Mr. Gilbert charged, the Administration "wafted hither and thither by petty politics" had suppressed facts, denied a knowledge of them in public statements, and "smugly" pretended to follow public opinion in its policy. The American press, "unguided by Washington despite the plethora of the latter's information," had assumed a tone of making light of insults to the American flag, assaults upon the Consuls, and the murder of American citizens, and continued "to see a hopeful uplift movement in 'Nationalist' enterprise."[16]

Commenting on Mr. Gilbert's article, the editors of the *North China Daily News and Herald* fully endorsed his stand and accused the Administration in Washington of playing politics with an eye on the next presidential election. They reiterated Mr. Gilbert's charge that the State Department was well-informed in respect to conditions in China but refused to share its information with the public because it did not wish to "involve itself in a major foreign issue" at this time. Americans in China, especially in Shanghai, the editors declared, were as "chagrined and mortified" at the attitude of the United States Government as the rest of the foreign community.[17]

In response to these accusations, Secretary of State Kellogg at a press conference in Washington told newspaper correspondents that he had from the beginning "given out every particle of news not only on the Nanking affair but on all subjects affecting American citizens" in China. By way of emphasizing this point, he repeated it several times and later in the day had a formal written statement to the same effect issued by the State Department.[18]

A few weeks later the American Chamber of Commerce at Shanghai appeared again in the columns of the American press owing to a dispute that developed between the Chamber and Mr. J. B. Powell, editor of the *China Weekly Review,* who was an old and, admittedly, a prominent member of the Chamber. At the annual meeting of the Chamber, held on April 26th, the President, Mr. F. F. Fairman, introduced a resolution drafted by the Board which requested Mr. Powell's resignation from the organization. In submitting the resolution, Mr. Fairman declared that members of the Chamber had "viewed with grave concern the trend of editorials in the

[16] *North China Herald*, April 30, 1927, p. 187.
[17] *Ibid.*, April 30, 1927, p. 192.
[18] *United States Daily*, April 29, 1927, p. 2. This episode was frequently commented upon in the United States and the *North China Daily News and Herald* was severely criticized. See, for example, Senator Borah's speech above, pp. 335-336.

China Weekly Review." "The great majority of us," he said, "cannot sub-scribe to the line of thought which has been advanced in those editorials, and, as it is so opposed to the opinions we hold, and as it may be taken to a certain extent as expressing American opinion, we thought it advisable to make known that those opinions as expressed in the *China Weekly Review* do not coincide with ours." The Board of Directors, he explained, not wish-ing to act merely on its own responsibility, was presenting a resolution for adoption or veto by the entire membership.[19]

In order to understand the significance of this episode it is necessary to consider for a moment the policy which the *China Weekly Review* had been pursuing. As stated earlier, Mr. Powell had maintained over a period of years that military intervention in China was impossible as it would require a large force of men which the peoples of the foreign countries involved, and especially the United States, would never be willing to supply. More-over, Mr. Powell had repeatedly contended that from the point of view of American interests — whether business, missionary, or otherwise — the only constructive solution to the Chinese situation was the development of a strong and independent China. In line with this idea he had advocated a revision of the treaties at a moderate pace and a "realistic" recognition of the fundamental changes taking place in China as represented by the Nation-alist movement. He had with increasing vigor attacked the so-called foreign "diehards," especially in Shanghai, on the ground that they refused to make any concessions to the demands of the Chinese despite the fact that China was in the throes of a profound struggle, seeking to adjust her national life to more modern concepts.

Following the attack on the British Concession at Hankow and the general development of critical conditions in China, the *China Weekly Review* consistently interpreted the policy of the United States Government as being opposed both to intervention and to the continuance of a co-opera-tive policy among the Powers in China.[20] The *Review* believed that the debate on the Porter Resolution in Congress and Mr. Kellogg's statement of January 27th, as well as other matters, indicated that the United States would "not participate in a military adventure on the coast of Asia."[21] "America's case," it said, "is simply that America has no interest in, or reason for, sending armed forces to China except for the protection of American lives. . . . America has no interest whatsoever in the protection of so-called

---

[19] Based on an account of the meeting in the *North China Herald*, April 30, 1927, p. 209.

[20] In addition to the articles cited hereafter, see *China Weekly Review*, January 22, 1927, p. 198; January 29, 1927, p. 222; February 12, 1927, p. 274; February 19, 1927, p. 297; February 26, 1927, p. 331.

[21] *Ibid.*, February 5, 1927, p. 251.

'foreign interests' in China. . . . America's first and primary interest in respect to the present situation is to keep her hands free from entanglements which might drag America into a maelstrom of international complications in the Far East."[22] In another editorial the *Review* observed that by "no stretch of the imagination" could the dispatch of United States troops to Shanghai for the protection of American citizens be regarded as an act of aggression: "America wants no Chinese territory and American policy since earliest times has been predicated upon the hypothesis that American interests in the Far East would be best served by a strong and independent China, capable of protecting itself against foreign aggression. . . ."[23] After the Nanking Incident the *Review* maintained that American policy had not altered despite the fact that reports had at first been circulated that the Administration's policy "was changing in the direction of greater firmness, if not in the direction of intervention." It based this view on statements given out by President Coolidge to the press in Washington — statements which the *Review* declared "proved definitely" that there was no shift in American policy and that the American forces in China were to be used only for policing purposes and "not for purposes of intervention."[24]

Hand-in-hand with these comments on the Administration's policy went caustic criticisms of the defense plans executed by the authorities of the International Settlement. The *Review* referred to the elaborate preparations for the protection of the Settlement — which included such matters as the erection of barbed-wire fences, sandbag barricades, machine-gun fortifications, etc. — as "barbed wire hysteria" and declared that soon the "diligent and energetic" Municipal Council might object to the rays of the sun penetrating the International Settlement, suspecting it of "spreading 'red' propaganda."[25] Underneath this bit of satire, lay a serious and far-reaching criticism, namely that, while the defense of the Settlement was proving effective from a military point of view, it was being maintained at the price of attempting to reach any compromise with the Chinese, a matter which might in the end prove disastrous. There was no object, the *Review* argued, in holding on to the physical territory embraced in the Settlement, if so much hostility was created against the foreign community at Shanghai that the Chinese took their trade and business away from that port, leaving it "an empty shell . . . not worth holding."[26] By "foreigners," the *Review* explained, clearly and carefully, it did not mean all the foreigners in Shang-

---

[22] *Ibid.*, p. 252.
[23] *Ibid.*, March 19, 1927, p. 58.
[24] *Ibid.*, April 2, 1927, p. 119.
[25] *Ibid.*, April 9, 1927, p. 143.
[26] *Ibid.;* and April 16, 1927, p. 170. See also Mr. Powell's letter in the *North China Herald,* April 30, 1927, p. 213, and the attack on him in an editorial in the same issue.

hai as these by no means shared one and the same opinion, but "the small group of willful men" dominating the situation through the governmental administration of the city."[27] "The Shanghai Municipal Council," the *Review* said, "is the real 'nigger in the woodpile' and the cause of most of the past trouble from the standpoint of Sino-foreign relations owing to the Council's past policy of opposition to a compromise or conciliatory policy...."

It was presumably these trends in the *Review's* policy which caused the Board of the American Chamber of Commerce at Shanghai to draft a resolution requesting the *China Weekly Review's* resignation from the Chamber.[28] As already indicated, this resolution was proposed at the annual meeting of the Chamber by Mr. Fairman, who read aloud the text in full:

Whereas it is the opinion of the American Chamber of Commerce in annual meeting assembled that having regard to the adverse criticism published in recent issues of the *China Weekly Review* concerning measures of local defense, together with the general welfare of American citizens in Shanghai, this Chamber emphatically declares that the present policy of the *China Weekly Review* appears to be in direct opposition to the opinions and views as held by members of this Chamber on these matters of such serious and supreme importance, thereby lending aid to disruptive instead of constructive elements. Therefore be it resolved that the *China Weekly Review* is hereby requested to resign its membership in this Chamber.

After Mr. Fairman's presentation of the resolution, Mr. J. B. Powell arose to say that while he realized that many people in Shanghai did not approve of his editorial comments he had been trying not so much to present his own ideas as to describe what he believed to be the policy of the United States Government in respect to China. He told the meeting that he had just received a message that afternoon stating that the Powers had decided not to take strong action in connection with the Nanking Incident, owing primarily to the refusal of the United States to participate in any plan involving the use of sanctions. This meant, Mr. Powell said, that "the stories about a blockade of the Yangtze and the occupation of Chinese territory now fall through"; that was, he added, what he had tried "honestly and seriously" to express in his paper. "If I should adopt a different policy," Mr. Powell asserted, "and urge occupation and the bringing out of a vast American army, I know it would be contrary to my Government's idea."

In response to Mr. Powell's statement, one of the members of the Chamber declared that if the message which Mr. Powell said he had just

---

[27] *Ibid.*, April 16, 1927, p. 170.
[28] *Ibid.*, April 9, 1927, p. 143. The account of the meeting is based on the reports in the *North China Herald*, April 30, 1927, p. 209; the *China Weekly Review*, April 30, 1927, p. 220; the *Far Eastern Review*, August, 1927, p. 344.

received proved to be correct, it was the duty of the meeting to vote for the proposed resolution and declare itself against the "half-hearted policy" of the Administration in Washington.

An oral vote was thereupon taken on the resolution in which only one dissenting voice was heard. Following the meeting Mr. Powell handed a statement for publication to the American, British, and local press correspondents in Shanghai which asserted in part that he had no intention whatever of changing his views, which were that the American people had no business or interest in intervening in the political affairs of the Chinese although the American Chamber of Commerce at Shanghai apparently believed 'in involving America in complications . . . which, in my opinion, may be far reaching even to the extent of another world war."

One of the most significant aspects of this dispute was that it attracted the attention of many editors in the United States and was commented upon not only in the large dailies but also in many smaller newspapers throughout the country.[29] The American Chamber of Commerce of Shanghai itself came to feel that it was receiving a "bad press" in the United States and that a distorted version of its views was being presented to the American people.[30] As the entire question of the failure of the business community in China to present its case to the American public was under discussion in Shanghai at this time, the American Chamber proceeded to take action. One of the measures which it adopted was to authorize Mr. George Bronson Rea, the editor of the *Far Eastern Review,* to serve as its representative in Washington; in accordance with this assignment Mr. Rea published articles and delivered speeches in the United States in which he sought to explain the views of the American Chamber of Commerce of Shanghai.

On May 27, 1927, Mr. Rea, specifically stating that he was a representative of the American Chamber of Shanghai, delivered an address before a convention of the National Foreign Trade Council in Detroit.[31] He charged that the "Uplift element" in the United States was monopolizing the channels of propaganda and flooding Washington "with resolutions recommending acceptance of the Chinese viewpoint." For the past six

[29] See editorials from newspapers published in the United States, quoted in *China Weekly Review* throughout June and July. In his recent book, *My Twenty-Five Years in China,* Mr. Powell states concerning the publicity which his dispute with the American Chamber received in the United States: "The correspondents for American and British newspapers who were covering the Shanghai crisis sent to their papers stories of the actions of the American Chamber and as a result I was deluged by telegrams and cables congratulating me on my stand and urging me to stand my ground in opposition to armed intervention. Among those who approved my stand were representatives of most of the mission boards." (p. 167.)

[30] See previous chapter for some editorial comments on the American Chamber.

[31] Text in *Far Eastern Review,* July 1927, pp. 285-289.

months, he said, in every instance where China had been the subject of discussion on a public platform in the United States, the speaker had been "either a missionary, an educator, a Y.M.C.A. secretary or a propagandist in the pay of the Nationalist Government"; not once had the papers recorded an occasion where a banker, a merchant, or a Chamber of Commerce member had spoken in defense of their trading rights. He indicated that the silence of the foreign business men in China might be due to intimidation by Chinese Nationalist agents, whom he accused of sending "confidential statements" to individual foreign firms threatening their continued existence if they did not support the Nationalist movement.

"The resolution of the American Chamber of Commerce of China," Mr. Rea declared, "calling upon our Government for international armed intervention for the preservation of foreign lives and properties, is the only instance where our business men have gone on record in defense of their own interests." Perhaps, he added:

The American Chamber of Commerce of China worded its resolution too strongly but there were good reasons for it. If it came out fairly and squarely for armed international intervention it is because it had reached the limit of human endurance and felt compelled to make some effort to counteract the campaign of scuttle advocated in this country by sentimentalists and Chinese propagandists.

Mr. Rea praised President Coolidge emphatically for resisting "the campaign of scuttle" and sending troops to China for the protection of American nationals. He declared that the danger in China was not yet over and that before the end of the chapter was reached the United States would again be called upon to defend its citizens. In the light of these circumstances he urged his audience to support a policy of American co-operation with the other Powers in China:

We are committed to play the game with them but the other members of this Far Eastern League of Nations now learn that when our co-operation becomes essential . . . we decide to play a lone hand. As many American newspapers put it 'America will not rake the chestnuts out of the fire in China for Europe'. . . . There may be excellent reasons why America should pursue a lone hand in China at this time, but there are equally good reasons why we should stand shoulder to shoulder with Great Britain and Japan. Whether we like it or not we are committed by every conception of honor, of loyalty, of good faith, and common decency to co-operate fully with these nations in the preservation of foreign lives and properties in China.

At the conclusion of his speech Mr. Rea asked the members of the convention to write the President of the United States individually in order to accomplish two purposes: to indicate their approval of the measures which the United States Government had taken for the protection of American interests in China — measures adopted in the face of the "most powerful campaign" directed toward the surrender of American treaty rights and the abandonment of American citizens; and to urge the United States Government to maintain unity of action in China in concert with the other foreign Powers. "The American commercial community in China expects you to stand by them in their appeal for international co-operation," Mr. Rea declared. "There is no other honorable way out."

Five months after the delivery of this speech, in October, 1927, Mr. Rea appeared before the annual convention of the Chamber of Commerce of the United States in order to request the support of its members for a resolution which had been passed by the American Chamber of Shanghai.[32] The resolution in effect asked the United States Government to grant adequate protection to its citizens in China and to insure "as far as possible" the maintenance of American treaties until the treaties were revised by means of negotiations conducted with a "recognized, representative government" in China "capable of discharging its obligations and assuring to foreigners some measure of justice and security."

Mr. Rea declared that there was every indication that when Congress convened "another campaign" would be started to influence the Administration at Washington to enter into immediate negotiations with one or another of the political factions in China for a revision of the treaties and for the abandonment of American rights. Mr. Rea argued that a revision of the treaties which recognized the full sovereignty of the Chinese Government in all matters would "automatically kill" the doctrine of the Open Door, and would result in the relinquishment of the right of the United States to intervene in the domestic concerns of the Chinese nation. "If we admit," Mr. Rea said, "that Soviet Russia has a right to intervene in the internal affairs of China and use the Chinese armies as a screen behind which to carry forward its warfare against the interests of other Powers, then the Powers whose interests are menaced have the same right to intervene in the internal affairs of China for the protection of their interests." In accordance with this idea, Mr. Rea advocated that the United States should undertake a policy "based on a friendly or benevolent intervention" in China — acting either alone or in conjunction with other foreign Powers — and warned that unless such a policy was adopted China would come under the "Red influence of Moscow" and American traders would be driven out of the country.

At the close of his speech, Mr. Rea again asked for the assistance of

[32] Text of speech in the *Bulletin* of the American Chamber of Commerce of Shanghai, November, 1927.

the Chamber of Commerce of the United States; the members of the American Chamber of Shanghai, he said, looked to the Chamber of Commerce of the United States for such "aid and support" as would strengthen their position and would guide the Administration and Congress in formulating a program in respect to China. Following this appeal the meeting adopted a resolution urging the United States Government to "continue the Washington Conference policy of co-operation with other treaty Powers" and to "ensure as far as possible to American citizens in China not only the protection of the law but the impartial enforcement of obligations and equal enjoyment of rights" pending a revision of the treaties undertaken by negotiations "with a recognized government representing the people of China."[33]

In editorials and articles published in its *Bulletin*, the American Chamber of Commerce of Shanghai expressed many of the same views as those which Mr. Rea set forth in the speeches that he delivered in the United States. In July, 1927, the Chamber assured its members in an editorial entitled "The Truth Must Win"[34] that they need have no concern over the adverse criticisms of the Chamber's policy appearing in the American press since it was evident that editors in the United States were being "misled." "The executive officers of the Chamber," it was said, "feel that the truth in regard to the entire situation in China must eventually win out as neither the American public or official opinion can long continue to be misled by the propaganda and distortion which has been carried on in the United States for subversive ends."

Some of the "propaganda and distortion" was, the Chamber felt, directed toward keeping the United States Government from making any attempts to counteract the influence of the Soviet Union in China.[35] The Chamber was particularly emphatic in its view that Russia was the real factor to be reckoned with in China and that the Chinese Nationalist movement was "neither spontaneous nor native but ready-made in the U. S. S. R." and "Soviet-managed and engineered."[36] In other instances, the Chamber believed, the motive behind the propaganda consisted of the desire to influence the American Government and public opinion to support a "premature" and "voluntary" surrender of the rights accorded to American citizens under the existing treaties.[37]

[33] *Ibid.*, p. 9.
[34] Reprinted in *Far Eastern Review*, August, 1927, p. 344. Almost every issue of the *Bulletin* in 1927 carried articles on the extent to which American public opinion was "misinformed concerning China."
[35] *Bulletin* of American Chamber of Commerce of Shanghai, August, 1927, p. 4.
[36] *Ibid.*; see also pamphlet entitled *Soviet in China Unmasked*, published by the *North China Daily News and Herald* and distributed by the American Chamber of Commerce.
[37] *Far Eastern Review*, August, 1927, p. 344.

The Chamber objected to the fact that it was, according to its own statement, being accused of conducting a "long and expensive" propaganda campaign of its own in favor of intervention in China, and being criticized for opposing the policy of the United States Government in respect to China, and for attempting to stand in the way of a "square deal" for the Chinese.[38] It declared that none of these charges were justified and, in order to keep the record clear, made repeated attempts to explain its position. In respect to American policy it maintained that the aim of the Administration in Washington was to protect and defend its nationals in China and that the attitude of the American Government was, therefore, the same as that of the Chamber at Shanghai. In regard to the question of granting a "square deal" to the Chinese, the Chamber took the position that it was "entirely in sympathy with" the "legitimate" national aspirations of the Chinese people but that the "self-appointed" political factions in China were largely operating under Soviet influence and could not be regarded as representative of the people of the country. "We believe," the Chamber stated in its September *Bulletin,* "that if the Chinese people were articulate today their cry would be for peace and the unmolested opportunity to earn food. These are the vital problems of the masses of the Chinese people and the slogans and hullabaloo are the manufactured products of the professional agitators and opportunists who find that their activities pay handsome returns in cash and power at the expense of, rather than to the benefit of, the deluded Chinese people."[39]

Not only did the American Chamber of Commerce at Shanghai object to the so-called "radicals" in the Hankow group of the Nationalist movement, it also came into conflict with the Nanking Administration which was established under the leadership of Chiang Kai-shek in April, 1927.[40] Toward the end of July, the authorities at Nanking announced that they intended to levy surtaxes ranging from $7\frac{1}{2}\%$ to 57% on all foreign goods imported into China, beginning September 1, 1927. As a consequence the American Chamber passed a resolution, which was forwarded to the Secretary of State in Washington, calling on the United States Government for determined action. The resolution declared that various political and military factions in China were "usurping" functions of government in certain areas over which they exercised temporary control and were seeking to levy taxes in "flagrant violation" of the existing international treaties and trade agreements. Under these circumstances, the resolution "petitioned" the United States Government "to take such action as may be necessary" to

---

[38] *Ibid.*
[39] *Bulletin* of the American Chamber of Commerce of Shanghai, September, 1927, p. 6.
[40] See also attack on Chiang Kai-shek in *ibid.*

protect American exports to China against illegal taxes and to "immediately issue a public declaration of its intention so to do." The resolution further recommended the adoption of certain measures to prevent American goods from being subjected to higher taxes and closed with the following appeal:

"That the United States Government be and is hereby requested to authorize the employment of the American forces now in China to guard American goods against unlawful seizure or restraint while in process of importation into China."[41]

In connection with the latter point, the President of the American Chamber of Shanghai declared, in a letter written to accompany the resolution, that in the opinion of the Chamber "the desired end" could be accomplished "without augmenting the American forces already in China" and through the adoption of "a firm stand" at those Treaty Ports which were readily accessible.[42]

As the State Department at Washington took no notice of the appeal from the American Chamber at Shanghai, either by issuing an official reply or by taking action, the President of the Chamber dispatched a second letter which read in part:

This Chamber has repeatedly emphasized the fact that America requires a future outlet for the rapidly increasing surplus products of her industries and that the welfare of the people of the United States demands that our Government do everything possible to retain and develop this great potential market in Asia. The disorderly and lawless elements in China have been and are now pursuing a course of aggression against the United States calculated to destroy America's present and prospective foreign trade with China and to ruin American nationals who are engaged in promoting such trade. In this crisis we call upon our Government for the protection to which we, as loyal American citizens, are entitled under the existing treaties; we call upon our Government to protect American foreign trade against the lawless activities of those who seek to destroy it; we call upon our Government to maintain the dignity of the United States of America . . . and to insist upon proper respect for and observance of the present treaties until they shall have been abrogated or revised in accordance with recognized international procedure.[43]

The resolution of the American Chamber of Commerce and the letters of its President were attacked by a spokesman "of the Ministry of Foreign Affairs of the Nanking Government" in an article issued by the Kuo Min News Agency on August 29th. The spokesman accused the American Chamber of departing from the "usual policy of a trade chamber and . . . devoting

[41] *Ibid.,* August, 1927, pp. 1-2.
[42] *Ibid.*
[43] *Ibid.,* p. 2.

itself to propaganda calculated to induce the American Government to intervene in a military way in China." Particular attention was directed to "resolutions and cables sent to Washington . . . demanding that American marines be used to prevent China from increasing her customs duties." The spokesman also asserted that the American Chamber at Shanghai had "been circulating newspapers and trade bodies in America with 'literature' compiled by notorious tools of local 'diehard' interests," the general purpose of which was to embroil the American Government in military intervention in China. In conclusion the spokesman said, "In view of the fact that the American Chamber has its headquarters on Chinese soil, the Nationalist Government is forced . . . to issue a warning that, unless the American Chamber ceases its under-handed activities, the Nationalist Government will be forced to . . . ask that action may be taken by the American authorities to curb the Chamber. . . ."[44]

Although the Administration in Washington gave no official indication of its reactions to the views of the American Chamber of Commerce of Shanghai, there can be little doubt that the State Department was not only aware of the attitude of the Chamber but also of other highly articulate groups in Shanghai, outstanding among which were the editors of the British *North China Daily News and Herald*. It was, in fact, impossible to exclude the opinions of the *North China Daily News and Herald* from any appraisal of the attitude of the foreign community in the International Settlement toward the crisis existing in China at this time.

Like the American Chamber of Commerce, the editors of the *North China Herald* were concerned over the state of public opinion abroad even before the Nanking Incident. In conjunction with the representatives of other organizations, including the Board of Directors of the American Chamber, the editors of the *North China Herald* had decided early in 1927 to publish a special Supplement for circulation in the United States and great Britain.[45] The Supplement, which was largely prepared before the Nanking Incident, was issued in April, 1927. The text stated specifically that the purpose of the publication was to acquaint the people at home with the "truth" about conditions in China and bring "intelligent public opinion" abroad in line with "sober opinion" in China.[46] The editors declared that they were motivated by the same idea as Mr. Silas Strawn had expressed on many occasions since he left China, namely, that the only

---

[44] *Ibid.*, September, 1927, p. 4. In the United States, Mr. Rea asserted that he was evidently the "notorious tool of the Shanghai diehards" to which the Nanking Government referred. (See *ibid.*, December, 1927, p. 1.)

[45] *Ibid.*, February, 1927, p. 4.

[46] *China in Chaos*, p. 2.

way of helping the Chinese people was to tell the truth about conditions in their country.[47]

The special Supplement was called *China In Chaos* and contained a brief preface entitled "Our Message."[48] In this, the editors explained that the Supplement attempted to show that Chinese nationalism was not a spontaneous movement but Russian-inspired and that the efforts of the Powers to conciliate the Chinese Nationalists had produced nothing but the most destructive results.

> Any such publication as this Supplement must have a moral to convey to the world and the foreigners in the Orient do have a very definite appeal to the Occident. The Chinese people . . . must be saved from themselves, rescued from their frenzied and unscrupulous military tyrants, Red agitators, and professional exploiters. . . . Upon the cost of the trifling military effort needed to police China, the Chinese people would, through their tireless industry, immediately yield an enormous return. . . . Our appeal, then, is for such an international effort as will give the Chinese people relief from persecution and a chance to work.
>
> Incidental to this appeal is our vigorous assertion that a settlement of China's troubles by negotiation is impossible. Whoever calls for negotiations calls forward self-appointed representatives who are the notorious wreckers and looters of this wretched land, while immediately behind them stand the Bolshevist agitators. . . . The principal self-appointed leaders of the present day include a British subject, a native of Trinidad . . .; a commander-in-chief who has standing against him, in the police records of Shanghai, charges for murder and armed robbery; a dictator who is an ex-bandit; and a warlord who is notorious for his immoral and profligate conduct and who is still wanted for a murder perpetrated many years ago. . . . It would be next to impossible to bring forward a Chinese negotiator now against whom there is not some criminal charge. Evil times are bringing the vilest elements to the surface in China and whoever would 'negotiate' must deal with exalted rogues, the worst enemies of the Chinese people.

While the articles in *China In Chaos* dealt with many aspects of the current situation, one of the primary themes running through the entire issue was that the conciliatory policy of the foreign Powers had proved an unqualified failure. " 'Patient conciliation' in China," it was asserted, "the much advertised policy of Great Britain, America, Japan, and other major Powers has meant for some years past the surrender to China in chaos . . . no 'graceful gesture' made by any Power in China during the last five years has yielded any fruit but a series of insults, treaty violations, debt repudiations, anti-foreign demonstrations and declarations of

[47] *Ibid.*, Part I, section: "Mr. Strawn Seeks the Truth." The back cover of *China in Chaos* carried quotations from Mr. Strawn's speeches.
[48] *Ibid.*, p. 2.

'rights'."[49] The people of the Occident, it was argued, supported the demands of the Chinese because they were dressed up in the appealing name of Nationalism"; but the very word was misleading as Chinese Nationalism was not synonymous with patriotism as conceived in the West.[50] "Whatever 'Nationalism' is," the editor said, "the foreigner in China . . . has found it spleenful, vicious, cruel, a force with which there is no possible compromise and upon which 'conciliation' has the effect of an intoxicant."[51]

In line with its attacks on the "conciliatory" policy of the Powers, *China In Chaos* condemned with particular vehemence the various attempts that had been made by the British Government during the winter of 1926-27 to meet some of the nationalistic demands of the Chinese. The text of the so-called December or Christmas memorandum was published under the denunciatory title of "Showing the White Feather."[52] The Chen-O'Malley Agreement concerning the British concession at Hankow was referred to as "The Great Betrayal" and described as an exhibition of "weak deference" on the part of the British Government to the "mad passion" of the Chinese Nationalists for economic destruction.[53]

China In Chaos was an expression of the point of view of the *North China Daily News and Herald* immediately prior to the Nanking Incident. After the Nanking Incident, the *North China Daily News and Herald* took the position that the attack on the foreign community at Nanking was a natural consequence of the patience which foreign governments had been demonstrating toward the Chinese since the development of the anti-foreign movement in 1925, and that it was more than time for the Powers to change their attitude. In an editorial published in the *North China Herald* on April 2nd the editors wrote in part:

Far too long have the Nationalists . . . been permitted with impunity to trample on treaties, to steal, to preach anti-foreignism and stir up the vilest mob passions against innocent men and women. . . . It is time the Powers acted swiftly and severely to punish the wrong done at Nanking and to teach Mr. Eugene Chen and his fellows that if we cannot prevent them

[49] *Ibid.*, p. 3.
[50] *Ibid.*, pp. 2-3.
[51] *Ibid.*, p. 15.
[52] *Ibid.*, p. 22.
[53] *Ibid.*, p. 9. The rendition of the British Concession at Hankow had been greeted with consternation by sections of the British community in China. The Shanghai British Chamber of Commerce and the China Association issued a statement saying that the Hankow Agreement filled them "with dismay" and was a "capitulation" that could only be regarded as a further proof of weakness. (See *China Year Book*, 1928, p. 749.) For discussions of this form two different points of view, see Eric Teichman, *Affairs of China*, London, 1938, p. 146, and O. M. Green, *The Story of China's Revolution*, New York, 1945, p. 101.

ruining their own countrymen, we can at least avenge the crime committed against ours.[54]

In another editorial published on the same day, the editors expressed the belief that the Chinese Nationalists had finally "gone too far" and that the British Government had reached the turning point and was beginning to recognize that its generous gestures towards the Chinese would not produce any constructive results.[55] Specifically, the *North China Herald* advocated the occupation of Hankow and the Wuhan area; to take such a step, it said, would not be difficult and it would be supremely effective in bringing about the restoration of order throughout China.[56]

As time went by and the Powers took no action other than to deliver the identic note of April 11th to the Nationalist authorities, the *North China Herald* began to show an angry impatience. "If not already too late," the editors declared on April 23rd, "we would protest most strongly against any further parley with the Reds at Hankow." It could not be too emphatically insisted, they said, that "Nanking was a test case in every sense"; the Nationalists should be taught "once and for all that their iniquities will no longer be endured." For the Powers to "shilly-shally," argue, and send more notes was only a dangerous waste of time. If Great Britain could not obtain the co-operation of the Powers, she should act alone.[57]

The *North China Herald* not only urged the British Goverment to act alone but, even after it was generally understood at Shanghai that the United States would not join in any program that might necessitate the use of sanctions, the *North China Herald* appears to have believed that the British and Japanese Governments would proceed without American assistance.[58] Only when Sir Austen Chamberlain's speech announcing to the House of Commons that none of the Powers intended to enforce their demands in respect to the Nanking Incident was reported at Shanghai did the *North China Herald* give up hope that sanctions would, in the end, be imposed on the Chinese. At the same time the editors bitterly attacked the policy of the British Government, declaring that they could not pretend to be "stupid enough to take seriously and solemnly such grotesque distortions" of the facts as were embodied in Sir Austen's review of the situation.[59]

The *North China Herald* apparently felt that the failure of the Powers to exact reparations for the Nanking Incident was, in large measure, due

[54] *North China Herald*, April 2, 1927, p. 13.
[55] *Ibid.*, p. 14.
[56] *Ibid.*, May 7, 1927, p. 233; see also April 23, 1927, p. 147, and April 30, 1927, p. 191.
[57] *Ibid.*, April 23, 1927, p. 147.
[58] *Ibid.*, April 30, 1927, p. 192.
[59] *Ibid.*, May 14, 1927, pp. 279-280.

to the state of public opinion in Great Britain and in the United States. In the same issue in which it published the attack on Sir Austen's statement quoted above, the *North China Herald* printed an editorial entitled "Our Most Urgent Need." According to this, the most urgent need of the foreign community at Shanghai was to embark on a campaign of "highly-organized and intensive publicity" abroad; the editors argued that even if all the silver in Shanghai were spent on bombarding the British, American, and Japanese Governments with informative material, nothing would come of the matter as long as the public — to which the Governments were essentially responsive — continued to be "saturated with misinformation."[60]

Like the American Chamber of Commerce of Shanghai, the British *North China Herald* had gradually become more and more determined to offset what it regarded as one-sided propaganda being fed to peoples in other countries, especially in the United States. Editorials, articles, and letters on this subject were carried in increasing and impressive quantity throughout the spring of 1927. As part and parcel of this problem, the *North China Herald* redoubled its attacks on the American and British missionaries who it believed were influencing the communities at home by means of a deluge of Chinese Nationalist propaganda.

As we have already seen, the *North China Herald* had consistently objected to the activities of the National Christian Council in China — in so far as they related to political matters — ever since the May 30th Incident at Shanghai.[61] As events developed the editors became even more convinced that the N.C.C. did not represent the large body of missionary opinion in China but spoke only for a small minority group. They charged that the N.C.C. had secured control of the political machinery of the missionary movement in China, and through this medium was forcing men in the field to abide by decisions that were "against their principles and consciences."[62] In an article written on March 23rd, it was suggested that the foreign Chambers of Commerce in Shanghai should denounce the N.C.C. as a "subversive" organization in the United States and Great Britain, thereby giving "sane" missionaries a chance to express themselves under the protection of powerful business groups; if, it was said, foreign business men in China did not have the vitality to "exterminate such pests as the N.C.C.," they were "not fit, under natural law, to survive."[63]

It is important to note one further aspect of the views which were main-

[60] *Ibid.*, p. 280.
[61] See above, p. 84 *et seq.*
[62] *North China Herald*, April 23, 1927, p. 148; see also two editorials of April 16, 1927, p. 105. Additional ammunition was furnished the *North China Herald* by the manifesto of 32 missionaries quoted below, pp. 362 *et seq.*
[63] *Ibid.*, March 26, 1927, p. 516.

tained by the editors of the *North China Daily News and Herald* at this time, namely their attitude toward the régime established at Nanking by Chiang Kai-shek in April, 1927. Like the American Chamber of Commerce at Shanghai, the *North China Herald* showed little enthusiasm for the Nationalist Administration at Nanking and during the whole of 1927, it published editorials which, with few exceptions, demonstrated an uncompromising hostility to the new government and its supporters. Chiang Kai-shek was described as being opposed to Michael Borodin and other Russian advisers of the Kuomintang merely for the sake of eliminating his political rivals and as being in all other respects under Russian influence.[64] in June, for example, the *North China Herald* declared in one editorial[65] that General Chiang had no intention of severing his relations with the "Reds," while in another it stated bluntly:

> Those foreigners who see in the revolt against Soviet dictation or in the ruthless suppression of communist labor groups, evidence of a sincere change of heart or of the rise of power among the 'Nationalists' of a better element, are blind to the fundamental motives behind these changes. Neither in the forwarding of the Bolshevist program nor in the revolt against it, have we ever been able to see anything but cold, calculating hypocrisy, utterly reckless of the miseries imposed upon the Chinese people.[66]

A few weeks later the editors predicted that a new Soviet-Kuomintang entente would be concluded, this time on the basis of terms imposed by the Nationalist régime at Nanking.[67]

Together with its objections to the new Administration at Nanking, the *North China Herald* continued to voice the need for the foreign Powers to change their policies toward China. It frequently expressed the opinion that as the members of the foreign community at Shanghai could no longer depend on their home governments for protection they should learn to defend themselves.[68] In line with this view, it supported the formation of a group of *Fascisti*, which was organized in Shanghai in the summer of 1927. There had been many similar manifestations throughout history, the *North China Herald* said — referring for one example to "the general principle known as 'Judge Lynch' in the old Wild West" — in which "substantial, law-loving, enthusiastic and determined men" had taken the law into their own hands when the properly constituted authorities could no longer enforce order.[69] The *North China Herald* praised the Shanghai *Fascisti* espe-

[64] See, for example, *ibid.,* June 4, 1927, p. 411.
[65] *Ibid.*
[66] *Ibid.,* June 18, 1927, p. 499.
[67] *Ibid.,* July 9, 1927, p. 51.
[68] See, for example, *ibid.,* August 13, 1927, p. 268.
[69] *Ibid.,* August 20, 1927, p. 58.

cially for their "courage and initiative . . . designed to demonstrate to our several Home Governments that Shanghai is worth saving" and should not be abandoned like the British Concession at Hankow.[70]

In December, 1927, the *North China Herald* was still inveighing against the Chinese Nationalists and their inability to establish and maintain law and order throughout China. "They have no hope," it said, "of being able to do constructive and useful work that will wipe out the memory of their criminally insane activities nor can they hope to evolve a government that will elicit such respect that the Powers can afford to let the dead past bury the dead."[71] In a review of the events which had taken place during the year 1927, it was further stated that "the Kuomintang has dragged the word of 'Nationalism' through such a mire that nothing will ever wash it clean of its aroma of false pretense, savagery, and blind and bitter anti-foreignism."[72]

The views expressed in 1927 by the *North China Daily News and Herald*, the American Chamber of Commerce, and the Shanghai Municipal Council might under ordinary circumstances have been challenged, at least indirectly, by mission groups or individual missionary leaders. The circumstances were by no means ordinary, however, and compared to the marked activity of missionaries in 1925 and 1926, American missionaries appear to have issued relatively few statements of opinion in the period following the Nanking Incident.[73]

Many reasons have been suggested for the comparative silence of the mission body at this time. The missionary movement in China had been disrupted; well over half of its members had left China by June of 1927, and those who remained were for the most part in the Treaty Ports, many hundreds of them away from their stations in the interior.[74] Under these

[70] *Ibid.*, October 8, 1927, p. 49.

[71] *Ibid.*, December 3, 1927, p. 394.

[72] *Ibid.*, p. 395.

[73] It should be clearly understood that, owing to the confusion that followed the Nanking Incident, data for this period are difficult to obtain and by no means as reliable as the material for missionary activity in 1925 and 1926. The author has, however, looked through many of the Annual Reports of the Mission Boards as well as a large number of the reports from the field which are part of the invaluable collection of the Missionary Research Library in New York City; in addition, a questionnaire was sent to a group of missionary organizations.

[74] A little over 8,000 foreign missionaries were stationed in China before the withdrawal in the spring of 1927. Out of the 3,000 who remained at that time, 2,500 were at Shanghai or other treaty ports. (*Chinese Recorder*, May-June 1927, p. 359.) Report after report of the Mission Boards for 1927 emphasizes that the missionaries would have preferred to remain at their posts but left at the insistence of the United States Consuls. There were, obviously, many reasons for leaving, among which were the fear of international complications if missionaries remained at their stations and were subject to further attack, and the possibility that their presence, by increasing anti-Christian hostility, would further endanger the lives of Chinese Christians.

circumstances, it was impossible for any mission organization to express the views of its constituency as there was no way of knowing what those views were. Moreover, it is evident that the practical problems involved in so general an exodus were immense and, together with other issues directly related to mission work, left little room for the consideration of political matters.

In addition, there was clearly friction within the ranks of the American missionaries in China. In April, 1927, a sharp controversy arose between the N.C.C. and a group of thirty-two missionaries, which included such outstanding figures in the American mission movement as President A. J. Bowen of Nanking University, President F. L. Hawks Pott of St. John's University, and Bishop Graves of Shanghai.[75] The thirty-two missionaries accused the N.C.C. of having departed from the provisions of its constitution and caused a division in the ranks of missionaries in China by engaging in political activities. The N.C.C., they asserted, had repeatedly put forth pronouncements concerning political matters without consulting the wishes of its constituency and had, thereby, lost the confidence of a large part of the mission body. "We are making this protest," the signatories declared, "against it [the N.C.C.] being considered as representing our views and opinions."

As this statement raised very different issues (one, for example, being the question of whether the N.C.C. had a right to take political action; another being the broader problem of whether many missionaries disagreed with the stand allegedly taken by the N.C.C. in opposition to the "unequal treaties"), it was possible that the signatories signed it with different aims in view. However, many of the signatories belonged to the so-called "conservatives" among the mission body. In any case, the Manifesto of the thirty-two missionaries indicated a conflict of opinion and was answered at length by the N.C.C. In part, the N.C.C. declared that it had not made official statements without ascertaining the wishes of co-operating organizations and declared that, in its own belief, it retained "the confidence of a very large number of missionaries." The critics, it said, who originally objected to the formation of an organization of the character of the N.C.C., were largely the same people as those who were still opposing it; others had been added to "this body of critics," but this was largely due to the misrepresentations in regard to the Council which had appeared in the press and which made it "practically impossible to secure a fair hearing of the Council's case."[76]

---

[75] *The National Christian Council: A Five Years' Review, 1922-1927*, contains the statement of the thirty-two missionaries with the names of all the signatories; it also has a summary of the reply of the N.C.C. (See Appendix E; this pamphlet was, in fact, written as a response to the manifesto of the thirty-two missionaries.)

[76] The N.C.C. also pointed out that more than a third of the thirty-two signatories belonged to organizations which did not co-operate with the N.C.C. and that only three were members of the Council.

Besides being barred from united action on political questions by these differences of opinion, the energies of many missionaries after the Nanking Incident were absorbed by problems directly connected with their own immediate responsibilities. A large number of missionaries who had been stationed in the interior of China had gone through difficult, if not tragic, experiences, accompanied in many instances by a serious loss of property. Missionaries, despite the fact that many were known to be sympathetic to the Nationalist movement, had been attacked and driven out of Kuomintang territory. Under these circumstances, it was inevitable that disillusionment should be widespread and that, with disillusionment, should come the feeling that the work which the missions had built up in China was being torn down and rejected by the Chinese people. One of the large American Mission Boards, in a statement typical of those made at the time, reported that: "The year 1927 will be remembered as an outstanding one in the history of Christian Missions in China. The words tragedy, disillusionment, disappointment, discouragement, doubt, uncertainty, perplexity have been constantly heard in speaking of the events of the year. . . ."[77] Nevertheless it was usually pointed out that the Christian movement in China might, in the end, find that it had been strengthened by the crisis of 1927.

One of the reasons given by many who held the latter view was that the Chinese Christians had themselves taken over much of the mission work in the interior of China when their foreign colleagues had been forced to withdraw, thus hastening the movement for a "chinafication" of the Church. This point was conspicuously emphasized by many mission organizations and leaders. Foreign Secretary James H. Franklin of the American Baptist Foreign Mission Society, for example, cabled from Shanghai in April, 1927: "Mission work in China is not ended. While the situation gives great cause for concern and is exceedingly serious, yet eventually it may give opportunity for desirable reconstruction of the work with larger Chinese direction."[78] Based on a report written by Dr. Diffendorfer, after a trip to China following the Nanking Incident, the Board of Foreign Missions of the Methodist Episcopal Church adopted a statement which said, in part, that "we rejoice in the notable way in which the Chinese have taken places of leadership in schools, hospitals, evangelistic work throughout China. . . ." "As to the return of missionaries who have been called out of China in recent times," it added, "we recommend that only those missionaries should return to China who are acceptable to the Chinese . . . and who, above all, are prepared in the

[77] *Annual Report,* 1927-1928, Board of Foreign Missions, Presbyterian Church in U.S.A., p. 11.
[78] *Annual Report,* Board of Foreign Missions of the Methodist Episcopal Church, Exhibit E.

light of the new situation in China to identify themselves with the Chinese churches and people to the limit of their ability. . . ." While these pronouncements are important indications of opinion, it should be remembered that here as elsewhere the views of missionaries differed and that there were missionaries who felt that the work of the missions in China was being transferred to the Chinese at too rapid a pace.[79]

The shouldering of responsibility by the Chinese Christians was, however, only one aspect of the tremendous challenge presented to the missionary movement. The withdrawal of so many missionaries was forming the closing of an era for the mission movement in China. Missionaries were asking themselves whether they would ever return to China in large numbers. Would they be able to work effectively among the Chinese people after the events of 1927? In view of the sudden strengthening of the "indigenous" Church, the problem of the relation of missionaries to such a Church was, more than ever, a matter of concern. The fact that it was impossible to look into the future and see the outcome of the political situation in China, meant that no one could foretell the relationship that might develop between the Chinese Government and the mission organizations. Reviewing these problems, which essentially formed the heart of the situation confronting the missionaries, the *China Christian Advocate* (the official organ of the East Asia Conference of the Methodist Episcopal Church) stated in an editorial that was characteristic of those appearing in many mission publications: "Some missionaries are utterly discouraged and see no hope for further work by foreigners. Others feel that a period of years must elapse before missionaries dare return to the interior. Others are more optimistic and have hopes that by early autumn work can be resumed"; ". . . missionary work must be entirely recast. . . . It is a safe prediction that it cannot begin where it left off. A re-valuation, a new planning, and new methods are pre-requisites for any further missionary work."[80]

While the preoccupation of missionaries with issues that concerned their own profession was certainly an important factor in their failure, as a body, to take an aggressive and determined stand in respect to political matters after the Nanking Incident, nevertheless such vigorous commentators as the editors of the *Christian Century* were highly critical of the attitude adopted by the Mission Boards. On April 28th, the *Christian Century* published a fiery editorial in which it blamed the Church for its silence as the governments of the Powers "flouted" the precepts of religion that were opposed to

[79] See Kenneth S. Latourette, *A History of Christian Missions in China*, p. 802. The first General Assembly of the United Church of Christ in China met in Shanghai in October, 1927.
[80] April, 1927, editorial.

the use of force.[81] A few months later, in an article written by Stanley High, the Mission Boards were accused of "six months of unexampled sidestepping and evasion."[82]

Nevertheless some of the mission organizations did express their views. Outstanding among these was the North China Mission of the American Board at Peking which in April, 1927, cabled home that "Mission strongly urges Prudential Committee advocate a new treaty immediately. Oppose all you can U. S. participation military force against China. Mission strongly urges missionaries now on furlough establish bureau counteract sensational news. Publish friendly China attitude. Try to encourage as much as you can optimism regarding Chinese nationalism."[83]

A month later, the National Council of Congregational Churches adopted a resolution reaffirming "its confidence in the traditional American policy in China — viz., independent action, non-intervention, and constructive friendliness; and that we hereby express our strong approval of the patience and sympathy shown in the private as well as the official attitude of the President and the Department of State. . . . We publicly and definitely," the resolution added, "affirm our unalterable opposition to military intervention in China . . . America should immediately take the initiative in moving toward new treaties. . . ."[84] Similarly, in early April, 1927, the Board of Managers of the American Baptist Foreign Mission Society passed a resolution to "re-emphasize its stand for the unity and sovereignty of the Chinese people and against foreign aggression and exploitation in China."[85]

While the above steps were taken shortly after the Nanking Incident and were, therefore, clearly related to the crisis that developed in April of 1927, further measures were adopted later which indicated that important sections of missionary opinion continued, despite the events of 1927, to favor a revision of the Sino-American treaties. At its annual meeting in January, 1928, the Foreign Missions Conference of North America expressed this point of view in a resolution that urged the United States Government to begin negotiations with China "at the earliest opportunity."[86]

[81] April 28, 1927. This editorial provoked an unusual amount of criticism in missionary circles.

[82] Stanley High, "Only A Miracle Can Save in China!", in the *Christian Century*, July 21, 1927, p. 872.

[83] Annual Meeting, North China Mission of the American Board, Minutes, p. 6.

[84] *The Congregationalist*, June 16, 1946, p. 788.

[85] Annual Report, 1927, p. 20.

[86] *Foreign Missions Conference of North America*, 1928, pp. 10, 103.

CHAPTER XVII

AFTER THE NANKING INCIDENT

AMERICANS IN NORTH CHINA

The withdrawal of American nationals from the interior of China, which had started before the Nanking Incident, was carried on at an accelerated pace after the 24th of March. The United States Legation continued to hold to the policy that American citizens should be evacuated from potential zones of danger and concentrated at a few large seacoast ports from which they could be withdrawn if an emergency should arise.[1]

As a result American nationals left the interior of China in large numbers after the Nanking Incident. By the end of May, four United States consulates had been closed, namely those at Chungking, Changsha, Nanking, and Kalgan. Moreover, Americans had either entirely or largely withdrawn from sixteen of the more important cities in the interior (including Hankow) and from a number of smaller cities in the provinces of Kwangtung and Kwangsi.[2]

While these developments were taking place the question arose as to what would happen if the Nationalist armies continued their successful advance north of the Yangtze Valley and conquered Peking and the general North China area. Mr. MacMurray and his colleagues in the Diplomatic Body at Peking were greatly concerned over this issue as they feared the emergence of a crisis that might seriously endanger the lives and the properties of foreign nationals throughout North China. After the Nanking Incident it was naturally felt that some very grave disaster might occur to foreigners in China and the responsibility of adopting all possible precautions fell to a large extent upon the already heavily burdened shoulders of the Ministers and Consuls of the nations involved. Moreover, if Peking were taken over by the Nationalist forces and there should be an outbreak directed against foreigners, the Ministers might be faced with the need for protecting the Legation Quarter from an attack, a situation which raised the specter of the siege experienced in 1900 during the days of the Boxer Rebellion.

Mr. MacMurray apparently felt that almost any of the situations likely to develop would threaten the security of foreigners in North China. By

[1] *Foreign Relations* (1927), pp. 302-303.
[2] *Ibid.*

366

the end of March there were rumors that Chiang Kai-shek and Chang Tso-lin might reach some understanding in order to pool their strength in opposition to the Nationalist group at Hankow. In that case Mr. MacMurray feared Chang Tso-lin might be sufficiently influenced by the "anti-foreignism of the moderate element in the Kuomintang" to prevent his continued control "of Soviet agents and of Chinese Communist factions in the North." If no understanding was arrived at between Chiang and the Administration at Peking, Mr. MacMurray believed that Chang Tso-lin might withdraw to Manchuria — either through his own volition or as a consequence of military defeat — leaving the territory of North China in a state of anarchy accompanied by "a tyrannic reign of terror" which would make the position of foreigners throughout the region unsafe, if not entirely untenable.[3]

In view of these considerations two alternative decisions appeared to be practicable: either to plan to withdraw foreigners from North China and move the United States Legation to some readily accessible location such as Tientsin, where it would not be "trapped" as in the siege of 1900, or, dispatch a body of troops, comparable to the Shanghai Defense Force, to the Peking-Tientsin area.[4]

Immediately after the Nanking Incident, Mr. MacMurray presented his views on these matters to the Secretary of State in Washington. While most foreigners in North China, he said, agreed that very serious trouble lay ahead, there was no way of predicting whether the situation would take a turn for the worse within the immediate future or only after a lapse of several months. This uncertainty increased the difficulties involved as, although it might seem prudent to evacuate all women and children from the North China area as soon as possible, any such action ran the danger of creating needless panic and, also, of antagonizing Chang Tso-lin by indicating a lack of confidence in his ability to maintain control of the situation.[5]

Under these circumstances, both Mr. MacMurray and Admiral Williams (who agreed with the American Minister's estimate of the situation) informed Washington that, in their opinion, steps should be taken immediately to afford the proper protection to American nationals in North China through the dispatch of additional troops to Tientsin.[6] Mr. MacMurray

---

[3] *Ibid.,* p. 95 (cable paraphrased).
[4] *Ibid.,* p. 94 (cable paraphrased).
[5] *Ibid.,* p. 99.
[6] *Ibid.,* p. 104. Admiral Williams suggested that a contingent of 1,500 marines which was en route to Shanghai should be diverted to Tientsin; that a brigade be made ready to sail to Tientsin on short notice; and that enough troops be sent and held in readiness in the Philippines "to form an expeditionary force of about one division." He wanted these troops to supplement the 1,380 American soldiers and marines who were already in North China. (*Foreign Relations,* 1927, p. 100; see also Mr. MacMurray's cables, *ibid.,* pp. 95, 99, 104-105.)

believed that if Chang Tso-lin were given sufficient advance notice of the arrival of American reinforcements to enable him to "save face" by announcing that he had known and approved of these measures in advance — as constituting a precaution against the possible activities of Chinese extremists — he would not be hostile to any such enterprise.[7]

The Department of State in Washington took a different view of the matter, however. Concerning the political considerations involved, Secretary Kellogg objected to Mr. MacMurray's recommendations on the ground that the actions which he proposed would be interpreted as indicating a desire on the part of the United States Government to side with Chang Tso-lin against other Chinese factions.[8] In respect to the military issues raised in the suggestions advanced by Mr. MacMurray and Admiral Williams, the Secretary decided to follow the advice of the United States War Department which was furnished him on the 5th of April in an unusually interesting memorandum that stated in part:

It is believed that nothing has as yet happened to justify reinforcing by the Army our garrison either in North China or Shanghai. It is not believed that the Chinese will attack Americans unprovoked by us. Moreover, it is deemed very unwise for this country to appear to lead in the matter of increasing the foreign forces now present in China. . . .

The foreign forces now in Tientsin and Peking are able to protect themselves and the foreign nationals from mob violence. No small reinforcement would be of value for this purpose nor would the present troops with small reinforcements be able to withstand any attack from a Chinese Army. Such an attack is believed to be most improbable. The Chinese leaders know that the foreign nations would probably send an army to overcome them and this would defeat their own ambition.

However, if one or more of the foreign nations should commit an act of war on China, such as bombarding the forts on the Pei Ho River or attacking Chinese troops, the leaders would undoubtedly assume the offensive. It is believed that by refraining from interfering with Chinese leaders and their forces no serious menace will exist to our nationals.

If foreign Governments believe protection in China is necessary and the United States concurs in such views, then a combined expedition should be sent whose strength and respective proportions should be established by mutual arrangements.

It is believed that a minimum force of 50,000 men would be required to prevent any serious harm by Chinese troops to officials and nationals of the foreign Powers in Tientsin and Peking.

Our proportion, if such an international force should be sent, should be one division of approximately 15,000 men. . . .[9]

[7] *Ibid.*, p. 104.
[8] *Ibid.*, p. 107.
[9] *Ibid.*, pp. 102-103.

The part of this memorandum which especially interested the Department of State was that as many as 50,000 men would be needed merely for the defense of Peking and Tientsin, and that an even larger force would be required to keep open the communications between Peking and the sea if any Chinese armies decided to make an organized attack on foreigners in North China. To the Department of State an estimate as high as 50,000 men suggested a military undertaking too costly for the Powers to enter into and indicated a need for adopting some solution to the problem other than the dispatch of a military contingent.[10]

While the Administration in Washington was thinking over these matters, word came from Peking that the foreign Commandants had met at a conference in Tientsin and unanimously decided that the more troops there were on the spot the less likely the necessity for military action; in line with this opinion they had agreed to recommend the increase of the foreign garrisons in North China to 25,000 men.[11]

The suggestion of the Commandants was reinforced by the Ministers of the United States, England, Japan, France, and Italy, who forwarded a joint recommendation to their respective governments requesting them to adopt measures that would guarantee the safety of the foreign community at Peking and at Tientsin which, they said, could not be guaranteed by the existing force of 4,000 men. By way of emphasizing the urgency of their plea, the Ministers underscored the fact that they regarded the situation in North China as extremely precarious:

> The state of anarchy which exists at present at Hankow, where the Government is entirely under Communist and Bolshevik influence, the repeated incidents in the Yangtze Valley which resulted in the Nanking massacre organized by the local Communist cell, the fact that at Shanghai the moderate Kuomintang element represented by Chiang Kai-shek is overborne by the unions, the campaign of anti-foreign propaganda which is being carried out methodically not only in the provinces occupied by the Southerners, but in Tientsin, in Peking, and even in Manchuria, as is shown by the documents seized at the time of the search of the Dal Bank, demonstrate clearly that the least weakening on the part of Chang Tso-lin might result in the North in disorders even more grave than those at Nanking deliberately organized by the Communists with the assistance of Soviet agents.[12]

On receiving the above statement of the Ministers, together with the Commandants' estimate that an international force of 25,000 men was needed for the defense of Peking and Tientsin, the British Government

[10] *Ibid.*

[11] *Ibid.*, p. 106.

[12] *Ibid.* For raid on the Dal Bank and other Russian institutions in Peking and Tientsin, see below, p. 374.

communicated its views to the Department of State at Washington. The Foreign Office stated that in view of the fact that the British Government had undertaken the main burden of the defense of the International Settlement at Shanghai, they did not feel it was reasonable to expect them to assume an equal burden in North China. They had therefore decided that unless Japan and the United States were prepared to accept "their share" in the defense of the common interests of the Powers in the North China area they would prefer, in case of necessity, to withdraw British citizens from both Peking and Tientsin. To this, the Foreign Office added that, in its opinion, the Commandants' figure of 25,000 men needed for the protection of the Peking-Tientsin region was too low but that, in any case, the British Government would at most be able to supply one brigade and that even that brigade would not be available for some time.[13]

In a formal reply to the note of the British Foreign Office, Secretary of State Kellogg declared that, on the advice of the War Department, he also believed that the Commandants' estimate of 25,000 men was insufficient and that a minimum force of 50,000 would be required for the defense of Peking and Tientsin. Under these circumstances, the Secretary stated, the cost in life and in monetary expense needed for the protection of the Legations and of the foreign communities in North China was, in the view of the United States Government, too high to be undertaken. "The Government of the United States is frankly of the opinion," the Secretary said, "that if there is any likelihood that the incidents of the summer of 1900 are to be repeated at Peking and Tientsin, it would be better to evacuate the American Legation and American citizens from Peking and, if necessary, from Tientsin rather than go to the great expense and the almost certain loss of life necessary to maintain our nationals and Legation by force at Peking and Tientsin."[14]

In accordance with these views, the Secretary of State cabled the American Legation at Peking that the Administration in Washington was not prepared to make a large number of troops available for the defense of the North China area. In addition to the 1,300 American marines and soldiers already at Peking, Mr. Kellogg said, 1,500 marines could be transported from Shanghai to North China in case of an emergency and 1,500 more from the Philippines; if it were "absolutely necessary," he added, an additional regiment of 2,000 marines might be made available from the Philippines.[15]

As a further precautionary step in line with the determination not to attempt to defend the Peking-Tientsin area with a large military force, both

---

[13] *Ibid.*, p. 108.
[14] *Ibid.*, pp. 113-115; see also p. 109.
[15] *Ibid.*, p. 116; see also p. 114.

the United States and British Governments advised their nationals residing outside of the Legation Quarter at Peking to arrange for the immediate departure of their women and children from the city and stated that men wishing to remain for business reasons did so on their own responsibility.[16] While the British felt that in an emergency the men who remained could withdraw rapidly to the Legation Quarter for protection, this was complicated in the case of the United States by the fact that the Administration at Washington tended to favor the immediate removal of the United States Legation from Peking.

The possibility that the Legations might be isolated in Peking under circumstances similar to those which had arisen during the Boxer Rebellion was naturally a matter of concern. Soon after the Nanking Incident, the Secretary of State cabled to Mr. MacMurray that he believed that "in the event of serious danger the Legation and staff should remove to Tientsin in order to avoid a repetition of the situation in 1900."[17] Mr. MacMurray on his part felt that he was caught in the predicament of, on the one hand, not wishing to withdraw the Legation before the danger of the situation had become apparent (as such action might result in a needless sacrifice of American interests and prestige) and, on the other, of believing that when the danger had actually developed to a point where it was fully recognized by the public in general it might well be too late to make evacuation possible.[18] Toward the end of May, a new factor, resulting from the action of the Japanese Government, entered the situation which led the American Minister to urge the Department in Washington to leave the Legation at Peking at least for the time being.

On the 28th of May, the Japanese Government informed the other Powers concerned that it was sending additional troops to China. In a formal statement the Japanese declared that they intended, if possible, to avoid injuries being inflicted on their nationals in North China similar to those which had been committed at Nanking and elsewhere throughout the Yangtze Valley and southern China, and were sending some 2,000 additional troops to Tsingtao. The Japanese stated that this step was being undertaken especially for the protection, in case of need, of the substantial Japanese community living at Tsinan, which could only be reached by land forces because of its location in the interior. "In adopting this measure of dispatching troops in self-defense," the Japanese said, "the Japanese Government has no intention whatever of keeping them there long. Immediately the fear of menace against the safety of the Japanese people in the locality is

[16] *Ibid.*, pp. 128, 129.
[17] *Ibid.*, p. 101.
[18] *Ibid.*, p. 129.

removed, the whole contingent of these troops will be withdrawn without delay."[19]

The Japanese Minister at Peking informed his British, American, French, and Italian colleagues that the Japanese Government was prepared to dispatch a body of 2,000 soldiers to the Peking-Tientsin area if the situation seemed to require it. While the total number of troops involved was relatively small, Mr. MacMurray felt that the action of the Japanese was none the less significant. ". . . it seems to me," he cabled the State Department, "that the Japanese Government's long delayed avowal of its determination to take military measures of a precautionary character to protect Japanese interests in North China puts a wholly new light upon the various questions which relate to the situation of Legations and foreign interests in this area. The decision has the effect of serving notice on all the Chinese factions concerned that the Government of Japan is prepared to take measures against any menacing condition of affairs in North China." Under these circumstances, Mr. MacMurray believed that the Chinese would not dare to plan an organized military operation against the Legation Quarter and that the United States Government could dismiss from further consideration the question of the removal of the Legation in order to avoid a repetition of the Boxer siege.[20]

The Department at Washington was apparently not totally convinced by Mr. MacMurray's argument. Mr. Kellogg wired to Mr. MacMurray that the question of the temporary removal of the Legation from Peking had been considered carefully at Washington and the embarrassment such a measure was likely to cause was fully recognized. However, he added: "We are all very anxious that there shall be avoided any conflict in Peking between the mob of outgoing and incoming soldiers which might cause bloodshed and cause further agitation in China. Our desire is to remove any inducements to such conflicts as far as possible." In line with these views, Mr. Kellogg again suggested that the American Legation staff should at least prepare for an early departure from Peking.[21]

[19] *Ibid.*, p. 124. The 2,000 Japanese troops at Tsingtao were moved inland in July, 1927, and occupied several points on the railroad including Tsinanfu, where they almost came into conflict with Chiang Kai-shek's troops which were advancing northward. A clash was averted but took place at Tsinanfu a year later. (See MacNair, *China in Revolution*, p. 124.)

[20] *Ibid.*, p. 125 (cable paraphrased). Mr. MacMurray's belief, that the policy of the Japanese Government had changed, may well have been influenced further by the fact that the Cabinet of Baron Shidehara had been replaced in Tokyo, in the middle of April, by a new Cabinet in which Baron Tanaka was serving both as Prime Minister and Foreign Minister. Baron Shidehara had been well known for his conciliatory policy in respect to China and it was assumed that his resignation and replacement by Baron Tanaka foreshadowed the termination of that policy.

[21] *Ibid.*, p. 129 (cable paraphrased).

To this, Mr. MacMurray responded with a statement of his estimate of the situation in which he indicated that he thought the Administration in Washington was, through necessity, manoeuvring between the demands of the American public for a conciliatory policy in China and the need to grant adequate protection to the lives and property of its nationals:

I have sought to keep in mind in dealing with question of possibly withdrawing Legation from Peking not only the responsibility . . . charged me in respect to determination of a state of facts, but in addition the peculiar difficulties confronting you because of the trend of opinion at home regarding China. As I understand it your problem is to give American lives and property in China the fullest protection without laying open our Government to the charge of taking aggressive action in general against the Chinese people or perhaps in particular against the so-called Nationalist movement.

Mr. MacMurray argued that the Legation need not be evacuated from Peking because the danger surrounding it was relatively slight at the moment. Further, he believed that any such action would have a "stunning effect" upon the Chinese people in general who would regard it as a "calamity" that in the face of a negligible amount of danger the United States Government should withdraw its diplomatic representation at the most crucial moment in the modern history of China. The gesture would, he felt, be regarded as an abandonment of the field to Great Britain and Japan and would negative the influence of the United States in any new situation that might be created through the conquest of Peking by the Nationalist forces and the ousting of Chang Tso-lin.[22]

Mr. Kellogg appears to have been particularly impressed by the American Minister's belief that the danger to the Legation Quarter was slight under the existing circumstances. No further action was taken by the United States Government to remove the Legation from Peking.[23] No doubt if the situation had suddenly become more threatening the entire issue would have been reconsidered. As it was, the northern advance of the various Nationalist armies was halted in the summer of 1927 and, by the time the Southern troops reached Peking a year later, they represented a new and conservative government established after the Nationalist movement had undergone a profound change.

THE EMERGENCE OF A NEW NATIONALIST GOVERNMENT

Since the Ministers at Peking felt that the safety of foreigners in China depended to a large extent on the maintenance of Chang Tso-lin in power

---

[22] *Ibid.*, p. 132 (cable paraphrased).
[23] *Ibid.*, p. 137.

and on the latter's desire and ability to control the more radical elements among the Chinese, their sense of security inevitably fluctuated with the changes in China's domestic politics that were being effected with kaleidoscopic speed.

On the 6th of April, the metropolitan police at Peking together with a small body of troops searched a number of Russian buildings within the Legation Quarter. Authorization for the search had been properly secured from the Senior Minister of the Diplomatic Corps, but the raiding party went beyond its authorization and invaded not only certain private properties but also the compound of the former Russian Legation Guard which contained the offices of the Soviet military attaché. A number of Chinese and Russians were arrested and the police subsequently announced that they had found many documents, a vast amount of Communist propaganda material of all kinds (including posters, flags, leaflets, etc., such as were being dispersed throughout China), an assortment of firearms, and a list of 4,000 members of the Communist Party in the Peking area. The police published a series of pamphlets which they claimed contained photostat copies of a number of the papers that had been seized together with English translations of the texts.[24] The most important feature of these documents was that they were regarded as showing that the Russian Embassy had an extensive secret service organization operating in all parts of China; that the so-called Soviet Advisers to the Nationalist Government were the paid agents of the Russian Government at Moscow; and that the Soviet Union was furnishing supplies of war to the various enemies of Chang Tso-lin and his Northern allies.[25]

The raid on the Russian buildings at Peking was followed by a similar search of certain Russian-administered institutions in Tientsin on the following day. The Soviet Government formally objected to these actions on the part of the Peking Government and presented various demands which Chang Tso-lin was, however, not willing to meet. As a result the Soviet diplomatic representative withdrew from China, although the Soviet consulates remained open in Manchuria and North China.[26]

While these events were operating in North China to the disadvantage of the more radical elements in the Chinese Nationalist movement, developments were taking place in the Yangtze Valley which widened the breach between the Hankow régime and Chiang Kai-shek. On the 18th of April,

[24] These documents were denounced as forgeries in Moscow. (See *Survey of International Affairs*, 1927, p. 346.)

[25] See foreword written by the Metropolitan Police in Peking in *Soviet Plot in China*, which contains the photostat copies mentioned above. (Published in five installments.)

[26] *Survey of International Affairs*, 1927, p. 346; Pollard, *China's Foreign Relations, 1917-1931*, p. 391.

after Chiang had succeeded in gaining control over the left-wing forces in Shanghai, he established his own government at Nanking which was intended as a rallying point for the more conservative elements among the Chinese and as a challenge to the group supporting the Hankow Administration. In response the latter formally excommunicated Chiang Kai-shek from the Kuomintang.[27]

The establishment of what amounted to two Nationalist Governments in China had the effect of making the outside world more conscious of the deep cleavage in the interests and the ideology of the different factions which had for several years remained united within the Kuomintang. Coming at the time when the negotiations for a settlement of the Nanking Incident were being conducted between China and the foreign Powers, this naturally had its effect abroad. However, it should be remembered that the foreign governments — with the possible exception of the Japanese — had a very imperfect knowledge of the developments within the Chinese Nationalist movement even as late as April, 1927.

Actually the political currents and cross-currents that were battling against each other within the Kuomintang formed the most highly complicated pattern. The Nationalist group which was administering affairs at Hankow did not, for one thing, consist merely of "radicals" — as was often stated — but contained Communists, liberals many of whom belonged to the so-called "petit bourgeoisie," and military leaders sometimes referred to as the "Hankow Generals." Part of the problem, which was accentuated by the disaffection of the right wing of the Kuomintang, was whether the groups remaining at Hankow would continue to work as a coalition or whether some faction would gain control which would seek to oust those who did not share its views. While the militarists were likely to be largely interested in the fulfillment of their own ambitions, and many moderates were becoming increasingly hostile to the Communists, further confusion was presented by the fact that the Communists differed among themselves. Both in China and in Russia, the Communists were involved in a fundamental controversy over the vital issue of whether the peasant and labor organizations in China had attained sufficient strength to allow the left wing of the Kuomintang to break away from the groups with which it had been co-operating and turn the Chinese Nationalist Revolution into a genuinely radical movement, or whether conditions in China necessitated the maintenance of a coalition and ruled out the possibility of a revolution which was other than nationalist and democratic in character.

[27] *Ibid.*, p. 340.

From the time of the establishment of the Nanking Government in April, 1927, these conflicts within the Kuomintang moved rapidly toward an abrupt conclusion. In May, severe fighting took place between the Hankow armies and the forces of Chang Tso-lin. Although the Northern troops were forced to retreat from Honan, the Nationalist victory was won at the bitter cost of 13,000 casualties, which greatly weakened the military strength of the Government at Hankow. The result was that Feng Yu-hsiang who, acting in co-operation with the Nationalist troops, had attacked the Northern forces from the west and moved into Honan, became more or less the arbiter between the Hankow and the Nanking Governments, both of which were in need of his assistance.[28]

In June, 1927, Marshal Feng held two conferences, first with representatives of the Nationalist Administration at Hankow, and secondly with Chiang Kai-shek. Marshal Feng appears to have become convinced that the Hankow group had nothing to offer him and he determined to ally himself with General Chiang partly for the sake of continuing the Northern Expedition, the ultimate object of which was to capture Peking.[29] Both Feng and Chiang took the position that Borodin and his Russian colleagues who were acting as advisers to the Hankow régime would have to be dismissed and that the Chinese Communists — together with their program for social and agrarian reform — would have to be suppressed.[30]

In the meanwhile, a drive against the Russian advisers and the radicals in the Kuomintang had been launched within the Hankow Administration itself by a group of prominent leaders, outstanding among whom was Wang Ching-wei. After about six weeks of deliberation behind the scenes, it was decided to expel the Communist members from the Kuomintang and to insist on the return of Michael Borodin and his Russian colleagues to the Soviet Union. Three days later martial law was proclaimed at Hankow and there were wholesale arrests of Communist and labor leaders, of whom as many as 4,000 were reported to have been put to death.[31] On the 27th of July, Borodin left Hankow to travel back to Russia. He was followed shortly afterwards by others, both Russian and Chinese, who had long been in the vanguard of the Chinese Nationalist Revolution; notable among these were Madame Sun Yat-sen and Eugene Chen.

Following these developments an attempt was made to unite the groups which remained in the Kuomintang under one government. In order to expedite this matter Chiang Kai-shek, who believed he was a source of fric-

[28] Fischer, *The Soviets in World Affairs*, p. 669.
[29] *Ibid.*, pp. 670-671.
[30] MacNair, *op. cit.*, p. 119.
[31] *Survey of International Affairs*, 1927, p. 355.

tion, resigned as head of the Government at Nanking, on August 12th, and conferences were held between representatives of the Hankow and Nanking groups which culminated in the establishment of a united Kuomintang Government in September, 1927.

Unfortunately for its own longevity the so-called "September Government," which was inaugurated at Nanking, was not born under encouraging circumstances. Among the numerous difficulties involved was the fact that Wang Ching-wei and T. V. Soong had decided not to support the new administration but to set up an independent régime at Canton which was organized by the beginning of November, 1927. After a series of complicated events, a Communist *coup* took place in Canton, on December 11th, which was accompanied by what has been termed a "red terror." Communist control of the city did not, however, last for more than three days, when an anti-Communist drive was executed, resulting in a "white terror" in which 2,000 Communists were said to have been killed.[32]

In the international sphere the counter-*coup* against the Communists in Canton precipitated a break of consular relations between the new Nationalist Government at Nanking and the Soviet Union. During the so-called "white terror" at Canton, the Russian consulate was attacked and several members of the staff were put to death. The consulate was closed and the Consul-General was deported. Similar action was taken against the Russian consulates at Shanghai and Hankow and was followed by a general order from Nanking closing all the Russian consulates throughout South and Central China.[33]

The Government at Nanking was, in the meanwhile, eking out a precarious existence unsupported by Wang Ching-wei, Chiang Kai-shek, Feng Yu-hsiang and many others whose assistance was needed, and faced with innumerable problems that essentially arose out of the confused conditions in China. In November, Chiang Kai-shek returned to China from Japan, where he had been in retirement, and re-entered the political and military scene. Early in January, 1928, he was restored to his former post of Commander-in-Chief of the Nationalist armies and was made Chairman both of the Central Executive Committee of the Kuomintang and of the Military Council, positions which granted him extensive power.[34] All connections between the Chinese Communists and the Kuomintang were severed and the peasant and labor movements were further suppressed. An attempt was made to reorganize the Kuomintang along lines that would include a large number of its former leaders, including many who, like

[32] For description of these events, see *ibid.*, p. 266.
[33] MacNair, *op. cit.*, p. 130; *Survey of International Affairs*, 1927, p. 362.
[34] MacNair, *op. cit.*, p. 132.

Wang Ching-wei, were rapidly withdrawing into a self-imposed exile in Europe. The object was to obtain as high a degree of unity as possible within the Nationalist Government in order to renew the Northern Expedition in a final effort to unseat Chang Tso-lin and his allies, and bring Peking and North China under the control of the Nationalist forces. Military preparations were made throughout the early part of 1928 and, on April 7th, the Nationalist armies began to advance on Peking from three separate directions in what proved to be the closing stage of the Northern Expedition.[35]

In the year after the Nanking Incident the situation within China had therefore altered materially. Whereas in the opening months of 1927, the foreign Powers were confronted by a Nationalist movement that was a patchwork of political convictions, in the spring of 1928 they faced a new Kuomintang Government "purged" of its left-wing elements and relying for its support on the conservative Chinese capitalist and middle classes. Both the Governments at Nanking and at Peking had broken off their relations with the Soviet Government at Moscow. Whether for better or for worse, many of the innumerable circles-within-circles in the Nationalist movement had been obliterated — at least for the time being — and the primary issue which remained was whether the Nationalist Government at Nanking would eliminate its rival in the North and establish itself as *the* Government of China. Under these circumstances it would be in a better position to request *de jure* recognition from the foreign Powers and to seek the revision of the Sino-foreign treaties which had for so long been under discussion.

SETTLEMENT OF THE NANKING INCIDENT

One of the first acts in the sphere of international politics undertaken by the new Government established at Nanking in January, 1928, was to conclude a settlement of the Nanking Incident with the Government of the United States.

It will be recalled that almost as soon as Chiang Kai-shek had openly broken with the Hankow Administration and set up a rival régime at Nanking in April, 1927, a representative of that régime had approached officials of the United States Government with a view to effecting a settlement of the Nanking Incident. The attitude of Secretary of State Kellogg had been that, as he wished to dispose of the complications which had arisen over the Incident as soon as possible, he would be willing to accept a settlement based on more moderate terms than those which had originally been demanded by the five Powers.

[35] *Ibid.*, pp. 131-134.

Throughout the following months informal negotiations were conducted intermittently between American officials in China and representatives of the Administration at Nanking. Definite proposals were made by the Chinese both in May and in July of 1927. For the most part these dealt with the same issues as those which had been raised in the original demands of the Powers, including such matters as the punishment of the persons mainly responsible for the events of March 24th; the granting of an assurance that "all forms of violence and agitation" against American nationals would be prohibited in the future; the payment of reparations for damages suffered by the United States Government and by American nationals during the Nanking Incident; and the rendering of some form of apology for the "outrages" which had taken place. In deference to the sentiment of the Chinese people who were likely to be extremely hostile to the acceptance of stringent terms by any régime representing the Chinese side of the case, the proposals also asked for an expression of regret on the part of the United States for the bombardment of Nanking by American warships on the afternoon of March 24th. Moreover, an additional provision was incorporated which had nothing to do with the Nanking Incident itself but constituted a request that the United States should immediately conclude a new treaty with the "Nationalist Government of the Republic of China" that would replace the treaties then in existence between the two countries.[36]

Mr. MacMurray felt that the proposals submitted by the Chinese did not form what he termed "an adequate basis of amends for the outrages" which had been committed on the 24th of March. While he believed that the United States Government might do well to make substantial concessions to the wishes of the Chinese, he thought the proposals of the Nanking Government, taken as a whole, asked more than the State Department could reasonably be expected to grant.[37] In particular he objected to some of the individual terms suggested by the Chinese, pointing out that in his opinion the Nanking Government had not given adequate assurances against the recurrence of violent, anti-foreign activities or made any definite promises concerning the punishment of persons implicated in the Nanking Incident.

While the objections Mr. MacMurray raised[38] might have been smoothed out under ordinary circumstances, the situation was complicated by the political upheaval in the Kuomintang which made it impossible to foresee even the immediate future of any government, faction, or leader.

[36] For both sets of proposals, see *Foreign Relations* (1927), pp. 222, 225.
[37] For both sets of proposals, see *ibid.*, p. 226-227.
[38] Mr. MacMurray's objections were in general supported by the Department in Washington (*ibid.*, p. 232).

Under these circumstances, the American Minister felt that there was no need to rush into negotiations for the conclusion of an agreement.

After the retirement of Chiang Kai-shek in July and the setting-up of a refurbished Government at Nanking in September, representatives of the Nanking régime sought to open negotiations with the United States for a settlement of the Nanking Incident.[39] As Mr. MacMurray was in Washington in the autumn of 1927, the matter was taken up by Ferdinand L. Mayer who had been left in charge of the Legation at Peking. Mr. Mayer, after careful consideration, came to the conclusion that the existing conditions did not offer a good opportunity for the United States to seek a solution of the Nanking Incident and that the issue should, temporarily, be set aside.[40] The continued existence of the Nanking régime was hanging in the balance, and Mr. Mayer felt that the authorities at Nanking were mainly anxious to negotiate with the Powers in order to gain "face" for their administration at a critical moment in its history. Whatever faith the Powers might have in the sincerity of the officials at Nanking had, he thought, been dispelled by the fact that General Cheng Chien, who had been in charge of the Nationalist troops at Nanking on March 24th, had not only not been held to account for his rôle in the Incident but had actually been elevated to the chairmanship of the Military Council in the Nanking régime. Mr. Mayer's views were fully shared by the other interested Ministers at Peking who regarded the appointment of General Cheng Chien to the Military Council as nothing short of an insult to the Powers and, therefore, recommended to their Governments that any overtures made by Nanking officials for the opening of negotiations in respect to the Incident should be turned down.[41]

Matters were left to rest at this point until some time after Mr. MacMurray had returned to China from his trip to the United States. In February, 1928, the American Minister decided to make a tour of the Yangtze Valley area and while in Shanghai encountered General Huang Fu who had just been made Minister for Foreign Affairs of the new Nationalist Government established at Nanking under the leadership of Chiang Kai-shek. General Huang extended an invitation to the American Minister to be the guest of the Nanking authorities during his trip up the Yangtze; but Mr. MacMurray declined (an action which was approved by the Government in Washington)[42] and on being pressed by General Huang gave his reasons. "I reminded him," Mr. MacMurray wrote in reporting the conversation to the Department in Washington, "that the Nanking outrages remain un-

[39] Ibid., pp. 229-230.
[40] Ibid., pp. 230-231.
[41] Ibid., pp. 231, 234-235.
[42] Ibid. (1928), p. 327.

settled; that nothing has been done as yet by the Nationalist authorities to change the underlying conditions brought about by the Nanking outrages . . . and that the properties of our citizens are subjected constantly to depredations, and those of our citizens who have returned are not free to live their normal lives in safety or to do their normal work."[43]

Mr. MacMurray found, however, that the attitude of General Huang seemed genuinely friendly and constructive, and agreed that preliminary conversations might take place between representatives of the Nanking régime and the American Consul General at Shanghai with a view to determining the basis for an agreement. The American Minister apparently maintained only a qualified optimism concerning the outcome of the negotiations because of the possibility that both General Huang and the Nanking Administration, as a whole, were quite likely to fall from power at any moment.[44]

Nevertheless discussions were started and a new set of proposals was presented by the Chinese. These were submitted to Mr. MacMurray in the second week in March; but he found them so disappointing that he was unwilling even to consider them as a basis for further negotiation. The chief stumbling block appears to have been that the proposals incorporated, to quote Mr. MacMurray, "a wholly unwarranted attempt to charge us with a share of the blame for the outrages at Nanking in such terms as would make it appear that we had more to regret and be ashamed of than the Nationalist régime...."[45]

When Mr. MacMurray reported his views on the Chinese proposals to the State Department in Washington, the latter responded by asking whether there was no acceptable feature of the suggestions made by the Chinese which might be used as a starting point for profitable discussions. The Department wished, it explained, to settle the problem of the Nanking Incident as soon as possible and hoped that negotiations might be carried on as rapidly as the circumstances would permit.[46]

In the meantime the Nanking Government had made conciliatory gestures through the publication of mandates which in themselves fulfilled some of the demands the Powers had made in respect to the Nanking Incident. One mandate, issued on March 16th, announced that a group of nineteen soldiers and thirty-two "local diehards" implicated in the Nanking Incident had been executed and that orders had been given for the arrest of the Director of the Political Department of the Army who had been prin-

[43] *Ibid.*, p. 324 (cable paraphrased).
[44] *Ibid.*, pp. 325-326.
[45] *Ibid.*, p. 326.
[46] *Ibid.*, p. 329.

cipally responsible for the Incident; a second mandate, issued simultaneously, demanded that full protection be given to foreigners and to foreign property.[47]

The British, who had been conducting negotiations for a settlement of the Nanking Incident at the same time as the United States, were prepared to regard the mandates of the Nationalist authorities as constituting a settlement of the controversy. According to Sir John T. Pratt, then Adviser on Far Eastern Affairs in the Foreign Office, the British proposed to drop all idea of a written settlement, to accept the mandates already promulgated, to leave the question of the amount of the reparation to subsequent negotiations, and to have the British Consul General return to Nanking. But these suggestions were refused by officials of the Nationalist Government who insisted on a final settlement which would include apologies for the firing on Nanking by British warships on March 24th and which promised that a revision of the treaties would be undertaken.[48]

Only five days after negotiations had been broken off between the British and the Chinese, Mr. MacMurray and General Huang Fu met at Shanghai to launch into a whirlwind attempt to bring the Nanking issue to a close. At a conference which opened on the morning of the 29th of March, they threshed out the matter until after midnight, at which time they reached a final agreement. Notes were signed and exchanged on the following day and Mr. MacMurray immediately cabled the texts to Washington.[49] Secretary of State Kellogg answered within a few hours with an enthusiastic endorsement of Mr. MacMurray's accomplishment, stating that the Department of State was "very much gratified" and wished to extend its congratulations upon the successful outcome of the Minister's efforts.[50]

The settlement which had been effected between Mr. MacMurray and General Huang consisted of three notes addressed to the American Minister and Mr. MacMurray's replies to these notes.[51] In the first note General Huang, speaking as "Minister for Foreign Affairs of the Nationalist Government," dealt with the points which had formed the original basis of the demands of the five Powers in April of 1927. Referring to the Nanking Incident he stated that this Government profoundly regretted the indignities to the American flag and to official representatives of the United States Government; the loss of property sustained by the American consulate; and the personal injuries and material damages done to the American residents at

---

[47] Pollard, op. cit., p. 339.
[48] Memorandum to the author.
[49] Foreign Relations (1928), p. 335.
[50] Ibid., p. 333.
[51] Text of the notes will be found in ibid., pp. 332-333, 337.

Nanking. Although it had been found after investigation of the Incident that it was "entirely instigated by the Communists prior to the establishment of the Nationalist Government at Nanking," the latter was prepared to accept responsibility for the Incident. "With the extermination of the Communists and their evil influences," it was said, the Nationalist Government felt confident that the task of protecting foreigners would hence-forth be easier and that it would undertake specifically to see that there would be "no similar violence or agitation against American lives or legiti-mate interests." Effective steps, it was asserted, had been taken for the pun-ishment of the soldiers and other persons implicated in the Nanking Inci-dent. The Nationalist Government was, moreover, willing to compensate in full for all personal injuries and material damages done to the American consulate and its officials and to American residents and their property at Nanking.

In response to General Huang's note, Mr. MacMurray gave the follow-ing answer:

In the full realization of the inherent justice and honor of the Chinese people when not affected by the incitations of subversive influences, and with a deep appreciation of the sorrow and humiliation caused to all elements of that people by the Nanking Incident, and believing that the earnest given as to the punishment of those guilty of the Incident will be completely ful-filled at the earliest opportunity ... the American Minister accepts in be-half of his Government the terms set forth in the note from the Minister for Foreign Affairs in definite settlement of the questions arising out of that Incident.

Confident of the spirit of sincerity in which the present settlement has been made, the American Government looks to the loyal fulfillment of the said terms of settlement, as affording a measure of the good faith and good will with which it may anticipate being met, by the Nanking authorities, in other phases of the relationship between the American and the Chinese peoples.

The second note of General Huang's referred to the fact that American warships had opened fire on Socony hill at Nanking on the afternoon of March 24th: "In view of this fact," it was said, "the Nationalist Government earnestly hope that the American Government will express regret at this action." To this, the American Minister replied that he wished to point out that the act in question had constituted a "protective barrage," strictly con-fined to the immediate neighborhood of the house in which the American Consul, together with many others, was seeking refuge and had provided the "only conceivable means" by which the lives of this party and other Ameri-cans in Nanking had been saved. "The American Government, therefore," the reply stated, "feels that its naval vessels had no alternative to the action taken, however deeply it deplores that circumstances beyond its control should have necessitated the adoption of such measures for the protection of the lives of its citizens at Nanking."

In his third and final note General Huang proposed that further steps be taken for the revision of the treaties then in existence between the United States and China. In reply to this suggestion, the American Minister said in part:

It is unnecessary to recall the traditional friendship existing between the United States and China. As is manifest alike from the course of action consistently pursued by the American Government and from the statement of policy made by the Secretary of State on January 27, 1927, the Government and the people of the United States are in full sympathy with the desire of the Chinese people to develop a sound national life of their own and to realize their aspirations for a sovereignty so far as possible unrestricted by obligations of an exceptional character. With that in view, the American Government entertains the hope that the remedying of the conditions which necessitated the incorporation of such provisions in the earlier treaties may, from time to time, afford opportunities for the revision, in due form and by mutual consent, of such treaty stipulations as may have become unnecessary or inappropriate.

To that end, the American Government looks forward to the hope that there may be developed an administration so far representative of the Chinese people, and so far exercising real authority, as to be capable of assuring the actual fulfillment in good faith of any obligations such as China would of necessity have for its part to undertake incidentally to the desired readjustment of treaty relations.

As far as the United States was concerned, the exchange of notes between General Huang and Mr. MacMurray brought to a close the diplomatic difficulties which had arisen over a settlement of the Nanking Incident. An agreement was concluded between the Chinese Nationalist Government and the British Government in August, 1928, which was similar in substance to the agreement made with the United States but was different in wording and more business-like in tone.[52] Unlike the Americans and the British, the Japanese were not able to reach a solution of the Nanking issue and the matter dragged on until May of 1929, the delay being due in large part to the acute friction which developed between the Chinese and the Japanese over the so-called Tsinan Incident in the spring of 1928.[53]

Although the adjustment of the controversy over the Nanking Incident seemed to pave the way for the immediate reoccupation of the American consulate at Nanking — which might have been the start of closer and more

[52] China No. 1 (1928), Cmd. 3188, *Papers Relating to the Settlement of the Nanking Incident of March 24, 1927, H.M.S.O.*, London.
[53] Pollard, *op. cit.*, p. 360.

friendly relations between the Nationalist Government and the Government of the United States — hopes of this nature were to be disappointed. Mr. MacMurray, when he signed the Nanking agreement with General Huang on the 29th of March, planned to go to Nanking at once and reopen the consulate with ceremonies conducted jointly with the Chinese authorities.[54] But this proved impossible as General Chiang Kai-shek was pre-occupied with the renewal of the Northern Expedition and had already departed for the military front.[55] Mr. MacMurray believed that without the holding of ceremonies, which would constitute a gesture of good will and reconciliation that might furnish at least some guarantee of improved relations, it might be dangerous to re-establish the consulate and permit the return of American citizens to Nanking.[56] The subject was set aside for the time being, but, as the Administration in Washington was extremely anxious to reopen the consulate,[57] the issue was again raised with Nationalist officials in September, 1928, and arrangements were made to reoccupy the consulate in the third week of September with certain agreed-upon ceremonies that included a salute by the Chinese to the American flag.[58] After making these arrangements, however, the Chinese changed their minds and decided that they did not wish to take part in a program that required honors of this character to the flag of the United States.[59] Under these circumstances, Mr. MacMurray and the American consular representatives concerned felt that the United States should take no further action and that the terms proposed by the Chinese were, in fact, "humiliating."[60] The Department in Washington, on its part, took the position that if the Chinese did not desire to take part in the exchange of ceremonies, which had been agreed upon, the consulate should be reopened without any ceremonies whatever.[61] In accordance with this idea, the American Consuls were instructed to resume their work at Nanking in a purely routine manner. The consulate was reopened on December 15th, 1928, almost a year and nine months after the American Consul and his staff had been forced to withdraw from Nanking.[62]

[54] *Foreign Relations* (1928), p. 335.
[55] *Ibid.*, pp. 335-336.
[56] *Ibid.*, p. 338.
[57] *Ibid.*, pp. 339, 349, 362.
[58] *Ibid.*, p. 355.
[59] *Ibid.*, pp. 360, 363.
[60] *Ibid.*, pp. 363, 364.
[61] *Ibid.*, p. 365.
[62] *Ibid.*

CHAPTER XVIII

TREATY REVISION

The final phase of the Northern Expedition opened in the first week of April. The object of the campaign was to reach Peking and oust Chang Tso-lin, thereby giving the Nationalists at least nominal control over China south of Manchuria. According to the concerted plan of the various armies marching under the Nationalist banner, Chiang Kai-shek's troops were to advance north up the Pukow-Tientsin Railway. This was accomplished with success until the end of April when General Chiang found himself confronted by Japanese military contingents at Tsinanfu.[1] Severe fighting took place intermittently for ten days, the Japanese acting in what they termed the defense of the lives and interests of their nationals in the Shantung area. The Chinese were defeated with casualties which, according to unofficial reports, amounted to over 2,000, and were forced to retreat. General Chiang's road to Peking was effectively barred and the General himself returned to Nanking.

Despite the reverses of Chiang Kai-shek's troops, other Nationalist armies, operating on different parts of the military front, advanced toward Peking. The first Kuomintang troops, under the command of Yen Hsi-shan, the "peace lord" of Shansi, entered the capital and were immediately followed by General Yen. Chang Tso-lin, realizing that he was in a precarious position, partly because of the victories of the Southern forces and partly because he had been informed by the Japanese that he had better retire to Mukden at once, had left Peking on the night of June 2nd. A day later his train was bombed and General Chang was killed. The defeat and death of the Manchurian warlord and the capture of Peking marked the end of the Northern Expedition and of the military phase of the Nationalist Revolution.

The conquest of Peking — which was renamed Peiping by the Nationalists — raised two questions of fundamental importance in the minds of officials in Washington: should the United States accord recognition, either on a *de facto* or a *de jure* basis, to the Nationalist Government;[2] and should an attempt be made to effect some form of treaty revision?

[1] For a detailed account of the Tsinan Incident, see the *Survey of Foreign Affairs,* 1928, pp. 403-414. The reports of the Chinese casualties quoted above are based on unofficial Japanese sources.

[2] As will be seen later there seems to have been some confusion in the minds of authorities in Washington as to whether the United States was or was not already in *de facto* relationship with the Nanking régime.

The interesting point in respect to a modification of the treaties was that Mr. Kellogg had apparently become increasingly determined throughout his stay in office to bring about some basic readjustment of the treaty relations between the United States and China. He himself regarded his statement of January 27, 1927, as a definite commitment to enter into negotiations as soon as the Chinese were able to agree on an individual representative, or a delegation, that could speak for the Chinese people as a whole. While the conquest of Peking by the Nationalists made it seem more likely that there would be a governmental entity in China that could represent the Chinese nation, Secretary Kellogg had in actual fact been attempting for many months to find some method of procedure by which he could negotiate even if China remained under the divided control of different factions.

In the autumn of 1927, Mr. MacMurray had gone to Washington to discuss the Chinese situation with the Secretary of State and other officials in the State Department. One of the main subjects which was thrashed out in detail was the question of a revision of the Chinese treaties. Mr. MacMurray was asked to set forth his views on this matter in a memorandum and did so, in a document dated October 21, 1927, that was to be referred to on numerous occasions throughout the next nine months until a tariff treaty with China was finally concluded by the United States.

In his memorandum,[3] Mr. MacMurray indicated that while the United States Government had adopted the "logical" position that it was prepared to negotiate "with any group fairly representative of China," the Chinese, on their part, had a tendency to look upon the attitude of the State Department as a tactical manoeuvre to delay the issue indefinitely by laying down conditions that were not likely to be fulfilled within the foreseeable future. Mr. MacMurray suggested, therefore, that the American Government might "go rather more than half way" and demonstrate its good faith by initiating a plan for at least a partial revision of the treaties. To further this end, he thought the Department of State might authorize him to make an attempt to persuade the various political factions in China to co-operate for the sake of negotiating with the United States. Mr. MacMurray stated frankly that he approached the entire enterprise with little optimism, but that if there were any chances of success they could only be achieved by proceeding in a very private manner through informal conversations with Chinese leaders; any publicity would, he believed, "virtually compel the various factions to treat the proposal as a matter of rivalry among themselves."

In respect to the subject matter of a treaty to be entered into with the Chinese, Mr. MacMurray observed that there were only two genuinely important points at issue, namely, the questions of extraterritoriality and of

[3] Text of memorandum in *Foreign Relations* (1928), pp. 363-365.

restrictions on the Chinese tariff. Any negotiations concerning the abolition of extraterritoriality, Mr. MacMurray "ruled out" on the basis that the Chinese did not as yet have "such laws or judicial organization as would enable them to assume the function of dispensing justice" in cases in which foreigners were defendants; more than that, he felt that even to broach the subject of extraterritoriality would be dangerous in view of the importance which it had "artificially been made to assume as a political slogan among the Chinese."

On the question of tariff autonomy, Mr. MacMurray believed, however, that it might be well to attempt to negotiate a treaty with the Chinese. He thought that the actions of the foreign Powers at the Special Conference on the Chinese Customs Tariff amounted to something of a moral commitment to grant the Chinese tariff autonomy on January 1, 1929, and were, in any case, so interpreted by the Chinese themselves. "If within the next fifteen months," Mr. MacMurray wrote, "we are to confront such a claim [i.e. a claim to tariff autonomy] on the part of the Chinese which we are not for our part prepared to resist, there would be everything to gain and nothing to lose if we were able to assure ourselves in advance that the tariff increases made by the Chinese would not come into effect with such abruptness as to dislocate trade and that above all there should be an assurance that American trade would be protected from discriminatory treatment."

Mr. MacMurray suggested that the Department consider negotiating with the Chinese a simple treaty, similar to that concluded between the United States and Siam in 1920, which would recognize tariff autonomy on condition that American trade would not be subjected to any discriminatory treatment as compared with the treatment accorded to other countries. The matter was discussed in detail between the officers of the Department in Washington and the text of a treaty was drafted and put into legal form by the Solicitor. While the draft does not appear among the documents published by the State Department, it formed the basis of — and apparently closely resembled — the treaty which was finally concluded in July of 1928.

On his return to China, Mr. MacMurray's feeling of uncertainty in respect to the possibility of getting the Chinese to set aside their political rivalries and enter into joint negotiations for a treaty with the United States was heightened by the action of the Government at Peking. It will be remembered that in the autumn of 1926 the Peking Government had adopted what amounted to the first steps in a policy of unilateral denunciation of the agreements between China and the various foreign Powers.[4] Because of the strength of the anti-foreign sentiment among the Chinese people, it was recognized that any government desiring to maintain even a limited degree

[4] See above, p. 135 et seq.

of popular support and to compete with the leaders of the Nationalist movement would have to make at the least an attempt to secure a substantial
alteration in the treaty system.

The Peking Government had, therefore, taken action concerning the
Sino-Japanese Treaty of 1896 and the Sino-Belgian Treaty of 1865, both of
which contained clauses that made them subject to revision in 1926. In the
case of the Japanese the authorities at Peking had demanded an extensive revision of the existing agreements and threatened to denounce the old treaty
in its entirety if a new treaty had not been concluded within six months.
Despite the fact that the Chinese in taking this position were standing on
questionable legal ground, the Japanese showed a conciliatory attitude and
opened negotiations for a new agreement in January, 1927. Although the
1896 treaty was due to expire in April, 1927, an adjustment was made whereby the life of the treaty was extended several times for periods of three
months, in order to give the Japanese and Chinese Governments the fullest
opportunity to find some solution through negotiation.[5]

As has already been seen, a similar difficulty arose over the Sino-Belgian
Treaty of 1865. In this instance, however, the Peking Government abrogated the treaty first and only after considerable confusion and discussion
was the controversy resolved by the opening of negotiations, in January,
1927, between representatives of the Peking Government and of the Belgian
Government for the conclusion of a new agreement.

The determined policy which the Peking Government had adopted
in relation to the Japanese and Belgian treaties was next applied to the
Spanish treaty of 1864. In November, 1926, the Spanish Minister was told
that the Chinese Government wished to revise the old agreement. Negotiations were started in August, 1927, but appear at no time to have shown any
signs of progress. On November 10, 1927, the Peking Government issued a
mandate announcing the abrogation of the 1864 treaty.[6]

The termination of the Spanish treaty furnished a source of considerable anxiety to the Ministers of the Powers at Peking who anticipated that
the Chinese Government would similarly denounce the Portuguese, Danish,
and Italian treaties which were due to expire within the next few months.
Mr. MacMurray wrote to the Secretary of State on December 31, 1927, that
there had been "much discussion among the diplomatic representatives in
regard to the practicability of the Powers manifesting a concerted attitude
toward the increasing propensity of the Chinese to repudiate international
obligations."[7] An informal meeting was consequently held with the Dutch,

[5] Pollard, *China's Foreign Relations, 1917-1931*, p. 324.
[6] *Ibid.*, pp. 325-326; *China Year Book*, 1929-30, p. 854.
[7] For text of this telegram, see *Foreign Relations* (1928), pp. 398-400 (cable paraphrased).

British, French, American, Italian, and Japanese Ministers attending. As Mr. MacMurray explained in his account of the meeting forwarded to Secretary Kellogg, the Ministers felt that if the Chinese continued to set aside the treaty rights of one country after another without any "demonstration of concern" on the part of all the other interested Powers, the Chinese would soon "be emboldened to force the issue of voluntary repudiation." Commenting on this, Mr. MacMurray said, "I am in entire agreement with the view that the course of action by which the Chinese not only are contravening foreign rights but also are creating very serious perils for the future international relations of China would be very soon halted by the manifestation of disapproval on the part of the Powers."

The scheme worked out by the Ministers and submitted to their respective governments proposed that the Powers should arrive at an understanding by which each of them when faced with the denunciation of their own country's treaty in the future would reply along the lines of a formula which had been agreed upon in advance. The formula drafted by the Ministers was in the form of a note addressed to the Chinese Government by the Minister of the nation whose treaty had been abrogated:

> Even if it be assumed that you are to be regarded as the other government party to my treaty, I entirely contest any right on your part to denounce the treaty in the way you have done.
> I have no intention, however, of discussing with you the question as to whether you are legally entitled to denounce the treaty. Nothing in the treaty gives to you the right to take any such action. . . .
> There is entire willingness on my part that the matter of your right to denounce the treaty should be decided by the Permanent Court. Unless, however, the matter is submitted to arbitration, and, pending a decision in your favor, I shall continue to consider that my treaty is in force.
> There is no implication in this that my Government is not willing to negotiate a revision of the treaty, but it must continue to be understood that if, in the meantime, you take any action inconsistent with the treaty, I reserve the right to take such steps as I may deem appropriate for the protection of my interests and those of my countrymen.[8]

The Ministers proposed in addition that if the treaty of one country should be denounced by the Chinese and the above note sent, the representatives of the other Powers — or as many of them as felt in a position to do so — should forward a communication to the Chinese Foreign Office in the following terms:

> The action taken by the Peking Government in regard to the (blank) treaty has been learned by my Government with concern, such action being

[8] *Ibid.*, 398-399 (cable paraphrased).

in their opinion an additional exhibition of a spirit of disregard of international obligations. The communication of (date) by the (blank) Minister is, therefore, endorsed by my Government.[9]

The scheme suggested by Mr. MacMurray and his colleagues at Peking did not, however, receive the endorsement of the Secretary of State or the Department in Washington. "It is not considered advisable by the Department," Mr. Kellogg wired to the American Minister, "that any commitment be entered into which purports to bind the Government of the United States in advance in regard to the action which will be taken by it or the phraseology it will use in the event that it is confronted with the action of any Chinese régime in denouncing a treaty between the United States and China."[10]

While these matters were under consideration, an attempt was being made by Chinese officials in Washington to form a joint delegation for the sake of conducting negotiations for a revision of the treaties with the United States. Conversations were held between Secretary Kellogg, Mr. Johnson, Frank W. Lee, a representative of the Nanking Government, and Dr. Sze, who was still Chinese Minister in Washington but appears to have spoken in this instance in a purely personal capacity. In communicating the content of some of these conversations by wire to Mr. MacMurray, Secretary Kellogg stated that "Sze and Lee both emphasized the difficulties confronting the Nationalist authorities in consequence of the break with the Communists and Soviet Russia and the urgent desirability that the Nationalist Government have the incidental support to be derived from an open approbation by the American Government of the proposal for establishing a joint Peking-Nanking Commission to commence treaty revision negotiations." The Secretary said that he had informed Dr. Sze that he had "no desire to become entangled in China's domestic politics," but that in case China had a specific proposal to make he would be glad to present it for the consideration of the Government of the United States. Mr. Kellogg observed further:

If the Peking Government and the Nationalists should come together to the extent of creating a Delegation or joint commission . . . which substantially is the suggestion made by you to me during our conversations and which I approved, then, of course, we should in good faith show our willingness to fulfill the promises contained in my statement of January 27, 1927. We would have to know of course whether such delegates had sufficient authority for negotiating. If a joint commission is formed spontaneously, I am inclined to think that an announcement of our willingness to conduct negotiations with it might conceivably lead to a further rapprochement be-

[9] *Ibid.*, p. 399 (cable paraphrased).
[10] *Ibid.*, p. 400 (cable paraphrased).

tween Peking and Nanking, and afford a basis for terminating the civil war, and serve toward mitigating anti-foreign feeling in China, as well as give satisfaction to that portion of the American public which insists that every opportunity possible be given the Chinese for achieving their national aspirations. Initiation of the negotiations would also afford an opportunity to insist that until replaced the present treaties must stand.[11]

In response to Mr. Kellogg's observation that the plan being proposed by the Chinese for negotiating through a joint Peking-Nanking commission was the same as that which Mr. MacMurray had recommended in his conversations with the Secretary and in his memorandum of October, 1927, the American Minister pointed out that there was in fact a "radical difference" between the two suggestions. His own scheme, the Minister said, had been limited to the question of tariff restrictions while the Chinese program contemplated negotiations in conformity with Mr. Kellogg's declaration of January, 1927, which involved the idea of a general revision of the treaties, including both tariff and extraterritorial issues.[12]

Mr. MacMurray's point was that a relinquishment of the tariff privileges of the United States in China did not necessitate constructive action on the part of the Chinese; on the other hand, Mr. Kellogg's January statement had presupposed "the establishment of safeguards corresponding with the development of Chinese law and judicial institutions." For the latter purpose China would have to assume and carry out certain obligations and responsibilities. "Obviously," Mr. MacMurray said, "no group of Chinese representatives is in a position effectively to bind China or any portion of China to such obligations. Therefore, no negotiations in regard to extraterritoriality would be anything but a delusion at this time." Moreover, Mr. MacMurray felt that if the United States undertook to initiate negotiations and then "stopped short of a complete and unconditional surrender" of extraterritorial privileges, it might direct much of the anti-foreign hostility in China against the American Government.[13]

In addition, the American Minister argued that the negotiations should be carried on in China rather than in the United States. To conclude a treaty in Washington would, he felt, emphasize the "assumptions" on the part of the Chinese that treaty questions were "abstractions" that bore no relation to the actual conditions in China as they affected foreigners and their interests and would, thereby, serve to obscure "the necessity of even an effort on the part of the Chinese to set their own house in order. . . ."[14]

[11] Ibid. (1927), p. 368 (cable paraphrased).
[12] Ibid., p. 369 (cable paraphrased).
[13] Ibid., p. 370 (cable paraphrased).
[14] Ibid., p. 370 (cable paraphrased).

From this point on — January, 1928 — the situation altered little until Mr. MacMurray and General Huang Fu discussed various aspects of Chinese-American relations in the conversations which led to the conclusion of a settlement of the Nanking Incident. During the course of the discussions, General Huang inquired as to whether the United States Government would not be willing to take the lead in securing an alteration of the tariff provisions of the Chinese treaties. According to a memorandum of this conversation, Mr. MacMurray answered:

that the difficulty lay in the fact that there was no one group in China with which such a new treaty could be negotiated; that in the event that the Nationalists should unify China he would be ready at once to discuss such an agreement with them; or that he would be equally ready to discuss such a new treaty with the Northern Government in the event that they should be able to bring the country under one unified Government; or that in the event that both failed to unify the country, he would be prepared to discuss the matter with any such joint commission of both Governments as the American Government might be convinced . . . was not a purely formal body, but one representing an actual agreement between the Chinese factions on the subject-matter and competent to bind the entire country to any provisions agreed to. He said that in any such negotiations the American Government was prepared to be as helpful as possible, and would make for its part no demands beyond such obvious conditions as the assurance of non-discriminatory treatment for our nationals, and that meanwhile it was not a question of unwillingness on the part of his Government to negotiate, but of actual impossibility of finding actually representative and responsible parties with whom such negotiations could be carried out.[15]

Apparently General Huang's answers to Mr. MacMurray served, among other things, to convince the American Minister that the Nationalist régime was not willing to set aside its conflict with the Peking Government to the extent of permitting joint negotiations with the United States. "General Huang," Mr. MacMurray cabled to the Secretary, "while speaking in general terms of appreciation of the friendly disposition of the American Government made no concrete response with regard to any of the alternatives suggested; . . . it was quite clear that under existing circumstances he was not prepared to carry on negotiations with the Nanking and Peking régimes, either jointly or concurrently."[16]

Not long after this conversation was held between Mr. MacMurray and General Huang, the last phase of the Northern Expedition was started and within a brief time the Nationalist troops had occupied Peking. With the retreat of the Northern forces and the sudden death of Chang Tso-lin, it

[15] *Ibid.* (1928), p. 412.
[16] *Ibid.*, p. 409.

was evident that the political situation in China had undergone a decisive change and that the Nationalist Government, despite the fact that its control throughout China was still limited, was likely to claim that it was now in a position to represent the Chinese nation as a whole.

In the face of this denouement, Secretary of State Kellogg lost little time in adjusting himself to the new conditions which confronted the Powers in China. On the 15th of June, he cabled Mr. MacMurray that as the internal warfare in China appeared to be at an end, it would be necessary for the United States soon to deal with the Nationalist Government "as the *de facto* Government of China at least" and to be prepared to fulfill the promises set forth in the Secretary's statement of January 27th. "An indication of the readiness of the United States to enter into negotiations on the basis of that statement," he said, "with or without recognition of the existing Government, would, I now believe, have considerable influence toward making the situation more stable." To this, Mr. Kellogg added a significant remark which indicated the extent of the negotiations he had in mind: "I should like to be prepared," he asserted, "also to negotiate at the same time in regard to extraterritoriality, not necessarily with a view to the immediate abandonment of rights of an extraterritorial nature, but with the idea of their relinquishment gradually, with certain provisions for protection, in the *interim,* of American citizens and their interests."[17]

Only a week later Secretary Kellogg sent specific instructions to the American Minister to enter into conversations with the Nationalist authorities "at an appropriate time (and an early date is suggested)." He restated the terms upon which he was willing to negotiate a tariff treaty which were, in all essentials, the same as those the Department had had in mind since October, 1927. In respect to the question of negotiating an agreement that would lead to the abolition of extraterritorial privileges, Mr. Kellogg gave the following instructions:

It may be stated by you that upon the conclusion, in the manner suggested, of an agreement regarding the tariff provisions, the United States Government will be willing to proceed with discussions on the subject of extraterritorial rights. . . . Of course it will be necessary, whenever discussions in regard to possible relinquishment are begun, to take into account the condition of laws of China and the administration of such laws, the independence of the Chinese courts and the quality and effectiveness of the protection to be afforded the citizens of the United States. Considering that the entire subject of commerce and treatment of the citizens of the two countries is covered in various aspects by the treaties entered into between 1844 and 1920 between the United States and China, it is the view of this Government that negotiations bearing upon the question of releasing extra-

[17] *Ibid.,* p. 182 (cable paraphrased).

territorial rights would involve necessarily a modification or revision of virtually all the treaties between the United States and China. It is my opinion that, with a view to expedition, it would not be advisable to embark at this time upon a project so large, but that in all probability this will have to be done in the not distant future.[18]

To this, the Secretary added:

> For the information of the Minister: In the event that there is established by the Chinese a government that is fairly stable and gives substantial evidence of a capacity to fulfill obligations entered into, this Government is prepared to proceed with negotiations in relation to extraterritorial rights.[19]

The Secretary stated further that he did not wish to have Mr. MacMurray raise the question of recognition of the Nationalist Government. "We are at present," he said, "undoubtedly, in *de facto* relationship with the Nanking Government and negotiations for a treaty with that Government would be at least a recognition of that status. Although the making of a treaty with them would certainly have the effect of *de jure* recognition, the question of such recognition need not be raised at this time."[20]

In China, Mr. MacMurray found that there were barriers which made it difficult to carry out the instructions cabled by the Secretary of State. While he hoped for the opportunity to enter into discussions with representatives of the Nationalist Government in respect to a customs treaty, he felt that the situation was fundamentally complicated by the fact that the Nationalist authorities were maintaining a "diplomatic vacuum" in which their attitude was one of such "complete aloofness" that it was impossible to gain any conception of the purposes which they had in mind.[21] He also believed that there were indications that the Nanking Government would prefer to take an independent initiative in fixing the Chinese tariffs regardless of the treaties, rather than seek an understanding with the foreign Powers.[22] Mr. MacMurray based this view in part on the fact that while he had informed General Huang Fu of the readiness of the United States to negotiate a tariff treaty — and had repeated this statement later to the personal representative of Dr. C. T. Wang who succeeded General Huang as Chinese Minister for Foreign Affairs — the Nationalist Government had given no signs of response.[23] Under these circumstances, Mr. MacMurray felt that it

[18] *Ibid.*, pp. 450-451 (cable paraphrased).
[19] *Ibid.*
[20] *Ibid.*, p. 450 (cable paraphrased).
[21] *Ibid.*, p. 452 (cable paraphrased).
[22] *Ibid.*, p. 457 (cable paraphrased).
[23] *Ibid.*, p. 457 (cable paraphrased); see also *ibid.*, p. 452.

would be "a tactical mistake" for the United States "to show any inclination toward haste or to take any positive initiative . . . and that such action . . . would result almost certainly in a rebuff. . . ."[24]

Concerning the questions involved in the relinquishment of extraterritorial rights, Mr. MacMurray held the same opinions in the summer of 1928 that he had expressed in October and in December of 1927. He was no doubt partially influenced by the fact that while it was evident that the conquest of Peking by the Nationalists had altered the political and military situation in China materially, he was by no means convinced that the new conditions offered any substantial promise of stability. On June 20th, he wrote to Mr. Kellogg that he regarded as "extremely problematical" the ability of the Nationalists to establish "within any predictable future," a government genuinely capable of fulfilling its domestic and international obligations. "I am unable," he said in this connection, "to avoid the feeling that it is premature to rest any further plans on the supposition that internal warfare is actually at an end. The situation as affecting the present conflict of forces among the military leaders who actually comprise the Nationalist movement is entirely precarious. Unity and peace in China are not actualities as yet, but are still a very doubtful hope, however much we may desire to believe the contrary."[25]

In view of the uncertainties surrounding the Nationalist Government, Mr. MacMurray continued to maintain the view that as the United States was "not prepared to make a full and unconditional relinquishment of extraterritorial rights" for the present, it would have to insist on provisions for the establishment of an *interim* system of jurisdiction that would require a whole new set of obligations which the Chinese were not in a position to meet. As a result he thought the State Department would either have to yield more than it was prepared to yield or withdraw its offer to negotiate on extraterritorial matters under circumstances that would lay the American Government open to the criticism that, although it had recognized the equity of China's position, it had been unwilling to abide by its convictions. Mr. MacMurray believed, furthermore, that the "thoughtful and intellectually honest" leaders among the Chinese recognized for the most part that the legal and judicial institutions in China had not yet been established upon a basis that warranted raising the issue of the abolition of the extraterritorial system, for, if once raised, they felt it would "lead to circumstances that could not be coped with by either side without further needless bitterness."

In a cable sent to the Secretary of State on July 11th, Mr. MacMurray summarized the above views and recommended that the State Department

[24] *Ibid.*, p. 457.
[25] *Ibid.*, p. 185 (cable paraphrased).

set aside for the time being any further program for a revision of the extra-territorial terms of the treaties: "It is my earnest recommendation," he said, ". . . that until there emerges a stable Government capable of meeting its responsibilities in such matters the question of negotiations for revision of the treaty provisions on extraterritoriality be postponed."[26]

In the meantime the Nationalist Government was itself adopting meas-ures for a revision of the treaty system. On April 12, 1928, General Huang Fu, taking a leaf out of the record of the Peking Government, had informed the Portuguese Minister of the termination of the treaty of 1887.[27] On the first of July, Dr. C. T. Wang similarly announced that the Nationalist Gov-ernment considered the Italian treaty of 1866 and the Danish treaty of 1863 "terminated as from June 30, 1928."[28] In addition, the Nationalist authori-ties began shortly after the conclusion of the Northern Expedition and the capture of Peking to issue a series of pronouncements concerning their foreign policy. In a manifesto addressed to the foreign Powers, they stated that as the unification of China had been accomplished and as the military period of the Chinese Revolution was coming to a close, the work of rehabili-tation and reconstruction would commence forthwith; the moment was, therefore, ripe for taking immediate steps "to negotiate — in accordance with diplomatic procedure — new treaties on a basis of equality. . . ."[29] On July 7th, the Chinese Foreign Office made public a declaration involving three main points: all the unequal treaties between China and other coun-tries which had already expired should be *ipso facto* abrogated and new treaties should be concluded; the Nationalist Government would immedi-ately take steps to terminate, in accordance with proper procedure, the un-equal treaties which had not expired, and to conclude new agreements; in the case of the old treaties which had already expired, but which had not as yet been replaced by new treaties, the Nationalist Government would promul-gate appropriate *interim* regulations.[30] By way of implementing the latter point, provisional rules were published at the same time as the declaration itself.[31]

While the Nationalist Government was thus launching an active cam-paign to secure a basic readjustment of China's treaty position, Secretary of State Kellogg was becoming even more determined to achieve immediate action on the part of the United States. On July 11th, he cabled to Mr. MacMurray that while he was aware of the fact that the apparent unwilling-

[26] *Ibid.*, p. 458.
[27] Pollard, *op. cit.*, p. 341; *China Year Book*, 1929-30, p. 858.
[28] Pollard, *op. cit.*, p. 342; *China Year Book*, 1929-30, pp. 864-869.
[29] *Foreign Relations* (1928), p. 414.
[30] *Ibid.*, p. 416.
[31] *Ibid.*, pp. 416-417.

ness of the Nationalist authorities to make the requisite overtures made it difficult to take any steps toward the negotiation of a tariff treaty, he was, nevertheless, convinced that the United States should "go forward," and believed that the American Minister should seize the first opportunity to open discussions along the lines of the Department's previous instructions. Mr. Kellogg also declared that he wished to make a public statement of the intention of the United States to negotiate a tariff treaty with the Chinese, and of the nature of the treaty which he had in mind.[32]

On the same day — July 11th — Secretary Kellogg addressed a formal request to President Coolidge asking for his endorsement of the program which he planned to adopt for a revision of the Sino-American treaties. After informing the President in general terms of the content of the tariff agreement which had been drafted in the Department in October, 1927, Mr. Kellogg gave the following explanation of the existing situation:

It seemed to me, since the consolidation of the Nationalist authorities in China, that the time had come when we should be prepared to make good our promise and take up negotiations if the Nationalist authorities were willing. With that in view, I telegraphed instructions to Mr. MacMurray on June 23, 1928. . . .

Mr. MacMurray has had some conversations with the Nationalist authorities but nothing definite has occurred. In the meantime the press, to a considerable extent in this country, has been calling on the United States to take action for the recognition of the present Chinese Government and that we enter into negotiations for the revision of the treaty. I am of the opinion that the time has come when we should make some statement of our position, and then if the Chinese authorities are prepared, we will first go ahead with the tariff negotiations, which are comparatively simple, and afterwards take up the revision of the other treaties which will be more difficult and require much time and also a consideration of the facts in relation to extraterritoriality which I will not stop to discuss at this time.

. . . I do not see that we can be in any way prejudiced. We stand pledged to the release of tariff control and if China guarantees us equal treatment under a treaty I do not think we can suffer. One thing is sure, tariff control of China is doomed. Whether the present government is going to evolve into a stable civil government of course I can not say, but I think any encouragement which can be given it by the world Powers will strengthen their hands in dealing with the enormously difficult domestic problems.

I should be glad to have your views as to whether this program is approved. I wish this at present to be strictly confidential as the press are constantly questioning me about what we are going to do in China and I have refrained from making statements.

Mr. Coolidge responded at once to the Secretary's request for an opinion

[32] Ibid., p. 454 (cable paraphrased); contains draft of statement also.

by stating, with the economy of words for which he was famous, that he approved of the Department's program regarding the matter of treaty negotiations with China.[33]

No sooner had these arrangements been made, than the Secretary of State received, on July 13th, a formal request from C. C. Wu, who was acting as Special Representative of the Chinese Nationalist Government in Washington, to open negotiations for a new treaty between China and the United States "on a footing of equality and reciprocity." The Nationalist Government, Dr. Wu said, had decided to appoint delegates for the purpose of such negotiations and hoped that the United States Government would, on its part, appoint delegates with the same aim in view.[34]

The message of the Nationalist Government reached the Department of State on the same day as there arrived, from the American Legation at Peking, the cable which has already been referred to, in which Mr. Mac-Murray suggested that the United States Government should not, for the present, take the initiative in urging the Chinese to open negotiations, and, recommended that the question of altering the extraterritorial provisions of the treaties be postponed until the emergence of a stable and fully responsible government in China. To the first point, raised by Mr. MacMurray, Secretary Kellogg replied that the Chinese were already requesting the commencement of negotiations and that there was a rising demand in the press of the United States for action; concerning the problem of relinquishing extraterritorial rights, he wrote, "I quite agree with you about the negotiations for the present being confined to the tariff. . . . I think it would be better in the first instance to confine your offer to negotiate on the tariff."[35]

On July 20th, Mr. Kellogg forwarded to the Legation at Peking the text of a note which he desired to have delivered in his name to the Nationalist Government on July 25th, and which he proposed to give to representatives of the other foreign Powers and — twenty-four hours later — to the press. The note declared in part:

The good will of the United States toward China is proverbial and the American Government and people welcome every advance by the Chinese in the direction of unity, peace and progress. We do not believe in interference in their internal affairs. We ask of them only that which we look for from every nation with which we maintain friendly intercourse, specifically, proper and adequate protection of American citizens, their property and their lawful rights, and, in general, treatment in no way discriminatory as compared with the treatment accorded to the interests or nationals of any other country.

[33] *Ibid.*, p. 456.
[34] *Ibid.*, p. 415.
[35] *Ibid.*, p. 461.

With a deep realization of the nature of the tremendous difficulties confronting the Chinese nation I am impelled to affirm my belief that a new and unified China is in process of emerging from the chaos of civil war and turmoil which has distressed that country for many years. Certainly this is the hope of the people of the United States.

As an earnest of the belief and the conviction that the welfare of all the peoples concerned will be promoted by the creation in China of a responsible authority which will undertake to speak to and for the nation, I am happy now to state that the American Government is ready to begin at once, through the American Minister in China, negotiations with properly accredited representatives whom the Nationalist Government may appoint, in reference to the tariff provisions of the treaties between the United States and China, with a view to concluding a new treaty in which it may be expected that full expression will be given reciprocally to the principle of national tariff autonomy and to the principle that the commerce of each of the contracting parties shall enjoy in the ports and the territories of the other treatment in no way discriminatory as compared with the treatment accorded to the commerce of any other country. Further, I am happy to state that when the question of the tariff, which is of primary importance to China, shall have been disposed of, I shall hope to discuss with the Government of China other aspects of the treaty relationships between the two countries, with a view to concluding, if the conditions warrant, a new treaty in regulation thereof.[36]

In commenting on the content of this note to Mr. MacMurray, the Secretary pointed out that there was no express reference in any part of the text to the problem of extraterritoriality. "In answering questions," he informed the Minister, "I shall say that I desire the tariff question to be disposed of before anything is done about extraterritoriality."[37] As matters actually turned out, the only alteration that was effected in the note before its delivery to the Nationalist Government was the omission of the final sentence in the excerpt quoted above, in which Mr. Kellogg offered to discuss "other aspects of the treaty relationships" between China and the United States. This omission was made by the Secretary of State in response to a last minute plea from Mr. MacMurray, who again expressed the conviction that to invite negotiations that extended beyond the tariff issue "would threaten us with the dangerous dilemma of having either to surrender our entire position or suffer the odium of having failed to satisfy expectations which had been encouraged by us."[38]

While, at the time, the decision to present a note of this kind to the Chinese Government seemed a large step in advance, events took such a sudden and unexpected turn that in the end the publication of the note resulted mainly in the creation of considerable confusion. On July 21st,

[36] *Ibid.*, p. 466.
[37] *Ibid.*
[38] *Ibid.*, pp. 471-473 (cable paraphrased).

during a visit to Peking, T. V. Soong, then Minister of Finance of the Nationalist Government, inquired in a conversation with Mr. MacMurray concerning the general attitude of the United States Government toward treaty revision. "When I indicated to him," Mr. MacMurray related in an account of the conversation to the Department, "that we were ready to proceed to a revision of the tariff provisions, in the manner indicated, Soong surprised me by inquiring whether I would be prepared to negotiate with him a treaty of such a nature prior to his return to Nanking, not later than July 26. . . . I informed Soong that I was prepared to do as he suggested. . . ."[39]

On the following day, Mr. MacMurray and Dr. Soong agreed on the text of a treaty that incorporated the ideas which the Department of State had had in mind for many months. The draft was immediately endorsed by the Secretary of State in Washington and apparently received the enthusiastic approval of General Chiang Kai-shek.[40] One of the few problems which presented itself was the question whether or not to include a clause in the body of the treaty making tariff autonomy conditional upon a substantial abolition of *likin*. Mr. Kellogg cabled his disapproval of inserting such a provision, stating that in the view of the Department there was "nothing practicable to be gained by fixing as a condition something which, at best, could be fulfilled in part only and which, if not fulfilled, will in all likelihood be ignored." Instead, the Secretary proposed that the tariff agreement might contain an annex consisting of an exchange of notes in which the Chinese Government might make "an unequivocal and forceful declaration" of its intention to abolish *likin*.[41] Such an exchange of notes was drawn up by Dr. Soong and Mr. MacMurray, but as the Nationalist Government stated subsequently that it did not desire to make a declaration of this nature in connection with the tariff treaty, the notes did not become effective.[42]

The new tariff treaty between the United States and China was signed at Peking on July 25th by Mr. MacMurray and Dr. Soong. It consisted of two brief articles which asserted, in the main, that:

All provisions which appear in treaties hitherto concluded and in force between the United States of America and China relating to rates of duty on imports and exports of merchandise, drawbacks, transit dues and tonnage dues in China shall be annulled and become inoperative, and the principle of complete national tariff autonomy shall apply subject, however, to the condition that each of the High Contracting Parties shall enjoy in the territories of the other with respect to the above specified and any related

[39] *Ibid.*, pp. 467-468 (cable paraphrased).
[40] *Ibid.*, pp. 470, 472.
[41] *Ibid.*, p. 472.
[42] *Ibid.*, p. 481.

matters treatment in no way discriminatory as compared with the treatment accorded to any other country.

The nationals of neither of the High Contracting Parties shall be compelled under any pretext whatever to pay within the territories of the other Party any duties, internal charges or taxes upon their importations and exportations other or higher than those paid by nationals of the country or by nationals of any other country.

The above provisions shall become effective on January 1, 1929, provided that the exchange of ratifications hereinafter provided shall have taken place by that date; otherwise, at a date four months subsequent to such exchange of ratifications.[43]

The exceptional speed with which the tariff treaty had been negotiated and concluded made it difficult to carry out Secretary Kellogg's original plan of making a public announcement of the fact that the United States was prepared to enter into negotiations leading to a tariff agreement. Mr. Kellogg, however, persisted in the execution of his program with the result that the declaration that the American Government was ready to open negotiations was issued to the Chinese Government and to representatives of other interested Powers on July 24th, and published in the press on July 25th, only to be followed two days later by the news that the treaty had already been concluded and signed.[44] This sequence of events, which was so rapid as scarcely to seem plausible, naturally caused considerable bewilderment in the minds of observers and has given rise at times to the charge that the United States kept the facts concerning the negotiation of the tariff treaty secret in order to "steal a march" on the other foreign Powers. Actually, American officials had repeatedly intimated to representatives of Great Britain, Japan, France, and other nations that they were hoping to effect a revision of the Sino-American tariff agreements and that they might well do so even before according recognition to the Nationalist Government as the Government of China.[45]

Immediately after the signing of the tariff treaty, an incident arose which demonstrated that Secretary of State Kellogg, while not intending to negotiate on extraterritoriality and other outstanding issues at once, continued to maintain the expectation of doing so within the near future. In a note (of which the original Chinese version bore the date of July 28th) the Chinese Foreign Office responded to Mr. Kellogg's declaration, received on July 24th, asserting that the United States was prepared at once to conclude a new tariff treaty. Ignoring the fact that Secretary Kellogg had limited his offer to negotiate a new agreement to the subject of the tariff,

[43] *Treaties and Agreements With and Concerning China, 1919-1929,* pp. 230-231.
[44] *Ibid.,* pp. 473, 485.
[45] *Foreign Relations* (1928) , pp. 182, 184, 188, 190, 484.

the Chinese note stated that it was the hope of the Nationalist Government that negotiations between the United States and China would "result in a proper settlement of all questions which are in need of immediate solution." Moreover, the note made no mention of the tariff treaty which had been signed three days earlier by Mr. MacMurray and Dr. Soong. Proceeding instead on the unlikely basis that the Nationalist Government was not yet aware of the conclusion of the tariff treaty, the note declared that the Nationalist Government had appointed C. C. Wu as the delegate to negotiate with representatives of the United States and "deemed it advisable to have the negotiations commenced at an early date," so that a new treaty could be concluded within the shortest possible time.[46]

As the Chinese Foreign Office informed Mr. MacMurray on delivery of the note that it might be released to the press almost at once, and as Mr. MacMurray believed that the note would confuse the public, minimize the importance of the tariff treaty, and place the United States on the defensive in respect to a further revision of the treaties, he felt compelled to send Dr. Wang an immediate reply without delaying to exchange views with the Department in Washington. He, therefore, on July 30th, dispatched a message to Dr. Wang which said in part:

> Since the time at which it may be presumed your note was written, you have no doubt learned of the signature ... of the treaty regulating tariff relations between the United States and China. In the conclusion of that treaty, the Government of the United States very promptly and completely fulfilled what had been offered in Mr. Kellogg's note of the 24th. In order, therefore, to avoid any possibility of misconception as to the purposes of my Government under present circumstances, I must point out that, whereas your note to me refers to "negotiations soon to commence," it is now the fact that such negotiations as the American Government had in contemplation have already been satisfactorily concluded.[47]

On receipt of a cable from Mr. MacMurray informing him of the content of the note which he had sent to Dr. Wang, Secretary Kellogg replied

[46] *Ibid.*, p. 482. As the tariff treaty was publicly announced in China on July 27th, it is difficult to reach any conclusion other than the one which Mr. MacMurray cabled to the Department at the time: "As a matter of fact there can be no reasonable doubt that when Wang wrote his note of July 28th he had full knowledge of the conclusion of the treaty three days before." (*Foreign Relations,* 1928, p. 485, cable paraphrased.) Why Dr. Wang made such a gesture has not been explained and no interpretation is given in the published papers of the State Department. One answer may, however, lie in the rivalry among Kuomintang leaders which at times resulted in their detracting from, or actually interfering with, each other's accomplishments. Although this is a point not often referred to in the written material of the period, there is ample testimony in the oral statements of a wide variety of people. (Also see below, pp. 411-412.)

[47] *Ibid.*, p. 483.

that he "regretted" that the American Minister had found it necessary to send such a communication to the Nationalist Government "without consulting me." The Secretary added:

Although of course I had no intention of beginning negotiations immediately on other subjects, it is inevitable that we will have to do so in the near future and it was preferred by me if the Chinese insisted on such negotiations, to discuss the reasons why it is not possible for us to sign such a treaty immediately. Serving upon them notice that we do not intend to go further is likely, I feel very strongly, to result in controversy and counterbalance much of the good which may have been achieved by us in the original negotiations and will be quite embarrassing to us. It is not my plan to give your note to the press here.[48]

If the Nationalist authorities did gain the idea from Mr. MacMurray's note that the American Government was unwilling to consider a further revision of its treaties with China, this misconception was no doubt dispelled some two weeks later by a conversation between Secretary Kellogg and the Chinese Minister in Washington. In an account of the conversation, written by Mr. Johnson, it is said:

The Chinese Minister called on the Secretary . . . and reminded the Secretary that he had mentioned the question of new treaties to him and that the Secretary had asked him to come back this morning. Sze went on to say that the American Minister's note to C. T. Wang, subsequent to the negotiation of the tariff treaty, left them in some doubt as to our attitude on the whole question of treaties. The Secretary stated that he did not wish them to be of the opinion that the door was closed to further discussions of this matter; that if the Chinese Minister cared to make inquiry of the Nationalist Government as to any suggestions which they might have with regard to the question of treaty revision, the Secretary had an open mind on the subject and would be very glad to hear what suggestions they had.[49]

As will be seen shortly, Mr. Kellogg and Mr. Johnson entered into conversations concerning a revision of the extraterritorial provisions of the treaties with Chinese officials in the autumn of 1928. In the meantime, the question arose as to whether the tariff treaty constituted *de jure* recognition of the Nationalist Government on the part of the United States.[50]

The problem of whether or not to accord recognition to the Nanking régime had, as noted earlier, been under discussion in Washington since the middle of June, when Secretary Kellogg had cabled the American Minister at Peking asking whether he believed that the United States should

[48] *Ibid.*, pp. 484-485.
[49] *Ibid.*, p. 195.
[50] For discussion of this point, see Charles Cheney Hyde, *International Law Chiefly as Interpreted and Applied by the United States*, 2nd revised edition, Boston, 1945, Vol. 1, p. 190.

take steps toward granting recognition to the Nationalist Government "on a *de facto* basis at least." Mr. MacMurray responded that, in his opinion, the American Government was already in a *de facto* relationship with the Administration at Nanking and that he assumed the question of *de jure* recognition "did not arise under present circumstances."[51] From conversations which both Secretary Kellogg and Mr. Johnson had with representatives of other countries in Washington it is clear, however, that while they were somewhat vague as to whether *de facto* recognition had already been accorded to the Nationalist Government in China, they were definitely considering not only *de facto* but also *de jure* recognition. The main point which they were seeking to determine, as they explained on a number of occasions, was whether or not the Nanking régime could be regarded as sufficiently stable.[52]

Approximately two weeks after the conclusion of the tariff treaty, Secretary Kellogg again took up the question of recognition, this time in a letter to the President of the United States. There was no doubt in his mind, he informed Mr. Coolidge, that the signing of the treaty constituted technically a recognition of the Nationalist Government, and that ratification by the Senate was not necessary to give effect to recognition. "In other words," Mr. Kellogg wrote, "you have the exclusive right to recognize a foreign government. It is true the provisions of the treaty are not binding until they are ratified by the Senate but the ratification is not necessary to give effect to your act of recognition. This we have understood all the time."

Mr. Kellogg explained further that since many people did not seem to be clear on the subject of whether or not the signing of the tariff treaty constituted recognition he would like to make an announcement to this effect. "The more influence we can give to the Nationalist Government," he said, "the better just now." In conclusion he asked the President's approval of his position and obtained it immediately.[53]

The matter was finally settled in the second week in August when Mr. Kellogg informed the Chinese Minister in Washington that it was the opinion of the Department that the signing of the tariff treaty constituted a recognition of the Nationalist Government and declared that, if the Chinese so desired, he was willing to make an announcement of this fact.[54] After

---

[51] *Foreign Relations* (1928), p. 184.

[52] *Ibid.*, pp. 182, 188, 190-191.

[53] *Ibid.*, p. 193; see also p. 192 and, especially, p. 194 for further statements on this subject.

[54] *Ibid.*, p. 196. It is interesting to note that in the meantime, on August 1st, the Vatican addressed a message to the Chinese people which was generally regarded as a gesture of recognition of the Nationalist Government. See Archbishop Marius Zanin, Bishop Haouissée, S. J. and Bishop Yu-Pin, *The Voice of the Church in China*, London, 1938, p. xi.

communicating with his own Foreign Office, Dr. Sze responded that in the view of the Nationalist Government no further attention need be paid to the matter as "it had been taken care of by the treaty" and recognition was regarded as having been accomplished.

The Senate of the United States ratified the tariff treaty with China on February 13, 1929, and ratifications were exchanged in Washington a week later.[55] Before these events took place, however, a strange situation arose which caused the Secretary to delay consideration of the treaty by the Senate and illustrated the unexpected turns that Chinese foreign policy was likely to take during this period.[56]

Early in January, 1929, the Netherlands Minister informed the American Legation at Peking that the Chinese Government's construction of the Sino-American Tariff Treaty of July, 1928, assured "the United States of non-discriminatory treatment only for goods imported into China by American nationals — and not for the produce and manufactures of the United States irrespective of the nationality of the importer."[57] Any such limited interpretation of the most-favored-nation clause could scarcely fail to be an unwelcome surprise, as well as a matter of grave concern, to American officials. Secretary Kellogg sought at once to get Dr. C. T. Wang to agree to a formula that would give "reciprocal, unequivocal, and complete assurance" of the "all-inclusiveness of the nondiscriminatory clause in the American treaty."[58] But it was not until the 6th of February, after weeks of negotiation, that a solution was reached consisting of an exchange of notes between Dr. Wang and Mahlon F. Perkins, Counselor of the American Legation, in which the former agreed in essence to a formula proposed by the Department of State.[59]

[55] *Ibid.*, p. 475, footnote.

[56] *Ibid.* (1929), p. 776.

[57] *Ibid.*, p. 774; quoted from a paraphrased cable of Mr. MacMurray's.

Apparently as a result of this incident, a number of the tariff treaties signed between China and other countries in December, 1928, were supplemented by exchanges of notes which contained an explicit interpretation of the most-favored-nation clause. (See the agreements made with the Dutch, British, and Swedish Governments in *Treaties and Agreements With and Concerning China, 1919-1929*, pp. 249, 257, and 265, respectively. Also see *Foreign Relations*, 1929, pp. 773-775.)

For a good discussion of the most-favored-nation clause used in Chinese treaties since the middle of the nineteenth century, see Willoughby, *Foreign Rights and Interests in China*, Vol. 1, Chapter II.

[58] *Foreign Relations* (1929), pp. 775, 778.

[59] Mr. Perkins' note agreed to by Dr. Wang declared that "it is the understanding of my Government that it was, and is, the intention of the High Contracting Parties to agree to the abrogation of certain provisions of existing treaties, namely, provisions relating expressly and specifically to rates of duty on imports and exports of merchandise, drawbacks, transit dues and tonnage dues in China, and to provide that in relation to these matters neither of the High Contracting Parties shall in any way discriminate

In the week after the settlement of this issue, the tariff treaty was considered and passed by the Senate. In a formal request, written in December, asking President Coolidge to submit the treaty to the Senate, Mr. Kellogg had said that it was "believed that by the signing of this treaty a benefit has been conferred upon all concerned, in that, while safeguarding American interests and doing no injury to the interests of any other country, the way has been pointed and a model has been provided for a procedure whereby the Powers may relinquish their so-called 'control' over China's tariff."[60]

In making this statement Secretary of State Kellogg emphasized what was in fact the most important aspect of the tariff treaty. By concluding such an agreement with the United States, the Chinese had a far better chance of obtaining similar treaties with other Powers. And the restoration of tariff autonomy might well mean the beginning of the end of the treaty system.

In order to understand subsequent developments, it is necessary to turn back to July 19, 1928, just before the opening of the negotiations for the Sino-American tariff treaty. As already noted, the Chinese authorities, by a series of measures which were first adopted in 1926, had abrogated the treaties with Belgium, Spain, Portugal, Italy and Denmark. The one treaty which had reached a terminal period but had not as yet been denounced by the Chinese was the Japanese treaty of 1896. In this instance, the course pursued by the Chinese had led to repeated extensions of the life of the treaty while negotiations were being conducted for a new agreement. This plan of action had apparently been chosen by the Peking Government because of fear of the results that might accrue from an outright denunciation of a treaty with Japan. On July 19, 1928, however, Dr. C. T. Wang altered the situation and, with courage in hand, notified the Japanese Minister at Peking that both the treaty of 1896 and the supplementary treaty of 1903 had expired, and that no new lease of life would be granted after July 20th, 1928, when the period extending the treaty would come to an end. Dr. Wang stated further that it was the intention of the Nanking Government to negotiate new agreements with the Japanese but that, in the meantime, the provisional regulations published by the Nanking authorities on July 7th would be applied to Japanese subjects.[61]

---

against the other or its nationals, or articles grown, produced or manufactured in its territories or imported or exported by its nationals as compared with treatment accorded to any other country or its nationals, or to articles the growth, produce, or manufacture of any other country, it being the intention of the Contracting Parties that in relation to these matters there shall be complete, reciprocal and unequivocal most-favored-nation treatment." (*Foreign Relations*, 1929, p. 786.)

[60] *Ibid.*, p. 492.
[61] Pollard, *op. cit.*, pp. 343-344.

The reaction of the Japanese to Dr. Wang's announcement was one of surprise and of strong disapproval.[62] On July 31st, the Japanese Minister informed the Chinese Foreign Office, in frank and unvarnished terms, concerning the attitude of his Government: on legal grounds, the Japanese refused to accept the view that the treaty of 1896 had expired; moreover, they regarded the Chinese assertion that the provisional rules of July 7th would be applied to Japanese citizens as "an outrageous act" disregarding the good faith between the two nations; further, the Japanese were prepared to negotiate a revision of the treaties if the Nationalist Government would withdraw its declaration to enforce the provisional regulations, but if, on the other hand, the Chinese continued to insist on an enforcement of the regulations and on the unilateral termination of the Sino-Japanese treaty, the Japanese would be "obliged to take such measures as they deemed suitable for safeguarding their rights and interests."[63]

The acrimonious feeling between the Chinese and Japanese Governments over the question of the abrogation of the treaties was naturally increased by the hostility that had already resulted over the Tsinan Incident and other issues — such as the settlement of the Nanking Incident — that were still outstanding between the two countries. From the point of view of the Chinese, the Japanese were therefore a decided obstacle to the improvement of China's treaty position. Despite this fact the Chinese proceeded to effect arrangements with other Powers.

In November of 1928, announcements of the conclusion of new treaties began to issue from the Chinese Foreign Office in quick succession. The nations whose agreements had been unilaterally denounced by the Chinese all fell in line, and between November 22nd and December 28th new treaties were signed with Belgium, Italy, Denmark, Portugal, and Spain. All five of these treaties extended beyond the scope of the Sino-American Treaty of July 25th. As far as the tariff provisions were concerned the agreements were similar to the American treaty and granted China tariff autonomy subject only to most-favored-nation treatment. There were, however, additional clauses which dealt with the question of the abolition of extraterritoriality. With minor deviations in the Belgian treaty, the general pattern followed was to declare that extraterritorial jurisdiction would no longer apply to the citizens of the two contracting parties, after an agreement regarding the surrender of extraterritorial rights had been reached "with all the Powers signatory to the Washington treaties."[64]

[62] *Foreign Relations* (1928), p. 418.
[63] Pollard, *op. cit.*, p. 344; *Foreign Relations* (1928), pp. 423-424.
[64] *Treaties and Agreement With and Concerning China, 1919-1929*, contains the Belgian treaty, p. 240; the Italian treaty, p. 243; the Danish treaty, p. 246; the Portuguese treaty, p. 252; the Spanish treaty, p. 270.

Besides effecting these arrangements with the nations whose treaties had already been declared at an end, the Chinese Government concluded treaties with five other countries which, like the United States, possessed commercial agreements with China that were admittedly still in force. These treaties dealt entirely with the question of the tariff and were signed — also in November and December of 1928 — with the British Empire, France, the Netherlands, Norway, and Sweden.[65] The Norwegian, Dutch, and Swedish agreements were similar in substance and to a large extent identical in wording to the Sino-American Treaty of July 25th. The British and French treaties were both accompanied by an exchange of notes which dealt with various supplementary issues, among them being the question of the abolition of *likin*. The Chinese Government announced that it was the intention of the Nationalist Government to take steps "as soon as possible" to abolish *likin* and similar taxes on imported goods, whether levied in transit or on arrival at destination. In the British exchange of notes, the Chinese also affirmed that the tariff schedules to be incorporated in the new National Customs Law (which the Nanking Government was about to adopt) would be the same as the rates that had been "discussed and provisionally agreed upon at the Tariff Conference in 1926," and that these would constitute the maximum rates to be imposed on British goods for at least one year from the date of the enforcement of the new tariff.

By the beginning of 1929, eleven of the Treaty Powers had agreed to abandon all restrictions on the Chinese customs duties, subject primarily to the condition that there would be no discrimination in tariff matters. But even under these circumstances tariff autonomy was still, legally speaking, out of reach of the Chinese as Japan had not consented to enter into any arrangements on the tariff or other outstanding issues with the Nationalist Government.[66] Nevertheless the authorities at Nanking proceeded to draft a new tariff law which included moderate rates that varied for the most part from $7\frac{1}{2}\%$ to $27\frac{1}{2}\%$.[67] Early in December, 1928, the Chinese Foreign Office forwarded copies of the new tariff schedules to the Treaty Powers and declared that it intended to put the new tariff law into operation on February 1, 1929.[68]

The manoeuvres of the Nanking Government met with success. Although up until the eleventh hour it seemed as though the Japanese would

[65] *Ibid.*, Dutch treaty, p. 249; British treaty, p. 257; Swedish treaty, p. 263; French treaty, p. 265; Norwegian treaty, p. 273.
[66] For abortive negotiations between Chinese and Japanese, see Pollard, *op. cit.*, pp. 356-358.
[67] Harold S. Quigley and George H. Blakeselee, *The Far East*, p. 130.
[68] Pollard, *op. cit.*, pp. 362-363.

refuse to consent to the enforcement of the new tariff provisions, on January 30th they agreed to the proposed schedules for a period of one year.

While in general terms it may be said that February 1, 1929, marked the end of China's long and arduous struggle for tariff autonomy, complete tariff autonomy was not in fact obtained for some time. In the first place, China had promised in her treaty with Great Britain not to increase her tariff rates above a certain level for one year; secondly, Japan did not enter into a formal adjustment of tariff matters with the Chinese Government until May of 1930 and, even then, it was stipulated that the Chinese must maintain the rates contained in the tariff law of 1929 on certain specified classes of goods for another three years. As this agreement was not renewed, the Chinese finally did attain tariff autonomy in May, 1933, without any qualifications or restrictions.

Although the Chinese-American tariff treaty concluded in the summer of 1928 did, as Mr. Kellogg said, form the model for the tariff treaties that followed within a few months, neither the American Government nor any other major Power with extensive interests in the Far East made corresponding changes in the extraterritorial provisions of the treaties.

When in August, 1928, Secretary Kellogg informed Dr. Sze that the door was still open for further discussion of a complete revision of the treaties between China and the United States, and declared that he would be "very glad" to consider any proposals which the Nanking Government cared to make, he was obviously hoping that the Chinese would take the initiative in achieving some action. Whether rightly or not, the Department received the impression, however, that the Nationalist Government did not care to discuss the issue of extraterritoriality and other related subjects, at this time. This is made clear in a memorandum of Mr. Nelson Johnson's recording a conversation which he held with Dr. C. C. Wu on September 1st — a memorandum which also suggests indirectly that there was a certain amount of friction among the officials of the Nanking Government that prevented their exchanging information and may well have made it difficult for them to work together for the achievement of any common goal:

Dr. Wu . . . stated that he understood that we had asked Sze to find out from Nanking whether it had any suggestions to offer as to treaties. I asked Dr. Wu whether Mr. Sze had told him about the conversation which he had with the Secretary, and Dr. Wu said that he had not talked with Mr. Sze but that he had heard through a friend of this conversation. I told Dr. Wu that we had had a conversation with Mr. Sze during which the Secretary had said to Mr. Sze that he had an open mind on the subject of treaty revision and would be prepared to consider any suggestions which the Nationalist Government might care to offer. I said that Mr. Sze had come to me on August 20 and had reported that he had telegraphed this to the Nationalist Government and had received a reply which he had some difficulty in understanding but which was generally to the effect that in view of the fact that C. C. Wu was authorized to discuss treaties, he did not need to bother about the situation. Dr. Wu said he hoped we had not interpreted this as meaning that the Nanking Government was not interested in the treaties. . . . I said to him that I had certainly interpreted this as meaning that it was not immediately interested.[69]

Nevertheless the Secretary and Mr. Johnson continued to make an effort to find some basis upon which it would be possible to carry on negotiations, or at the least informal conversations, with the Chinese. Late in September, in answer to an inquiry from a representative of the Japanese Government, Secretary Kellogg declared that although the American treaty of 1903 would not be subject to revision until 1934, the State Department had determined not to wait until that time before considering a readjustment of treaty relations. The only question, he said, which confronted the Department was the question of what to do. The Chinese had not enacted any codes of law such as those called for by the Report of the Commission on Extraterritoriality and, until they did so, it was "very difficult to do anything about extraterritoriality"; however, the whole subject was being studied, and if the Department could find an acceptable formula, the matter would be taken up with the Chinese. Questioned further by the Japanese representative as to whether he was in favor of an exchange of ideas and of co-operative action among the Powers in regard to a more extensive revision of the Chinese treaties, Mr. Kellogg said he felt that one of the greatest dangers confronting the Powers in China at this time was that of "Communist activities inspired from Russia" and that he believed the Powers should co-operate to strengthen the efforts of the Nationalist Government to create a stable administration in China. It was the feeling of the Department, he added, that this might be done "by going as far as each country could go, considering its own interests, towards solving these questions of the treaties. . . ."[70]

Early in October, 1928, the Nationalist Government, through Minister Sze and Dr. Wu, made a proposal to the United States for the conclusion of a new treaty which proved too drastic to be acceptable to the Secretary of State and Mr. Johnson, despite the very sympathetic and flexible attitude which both these officials had adopted toward the question of treaty revision. The Chinese suggested that the American Government should enter into a treaty under whose terms American interests and nationals would cease to enjoy extraterritorial rights in China, even though the nationals of other Powers — whose treaties remained in operation — retained their extrater-

[69] *Foreign Relations* (1928), p. 197.
[70] Based on a memorandum of Mr. Johnson's, *ibid.* (1929), pp. 429-430.

ritorial status. The Chinese requested the United States Government to open negotiations immediately for a new treaty of this character and urged that the Secretary of State should, after the conclusion of such an agreement, use his influence "in an effort to induce other Powers to take steps at once to meet the 'policy for treaty revision' of the Nationalist Government."[71]

Mr. Kellogg replied to these proposals that the United States could not first negotiate independently of other Powers and then advise other nations to follow its example. He asserted that he was willing to canvass the governments concerned for an expression of opinion, but warned that this did not signify that any concrete program would be put forward. On being pressed again to commence negotiations, he declared emphatically that the situation did not warrant such action and that it was impossible to accept the formula offered by the Chinese as a basis for negotiation. However, he expressed his willingness to authorize the conduct of informal conversations with officials of the Department of State.[72]

Despite the definite invitation extended by Mr. Kellogg to undertake informal discussions, the Chinese made no move to accept his suggestion for some weeks. Finally arrangements were made and conversations were started at the beginning of November, 1928.[73]

At the same time Mr. Kellogg began to canvass other Treaty Powers for the sake of obtaining their views concerning a revision of the Chinese treaties. In an *aide-mémoire* despatched to seven of the interested countries, he explained that the American Government had been approached by the Nationalist régime with a view to a general revision of the treaties, especially in respect to extraterritorial jurisdiction, and that officers of the State Department were engaged in informal conversations with the Chinese in the hope of discovering a basis for negotiation. The American Government, he said, "feels that the Nationalist Government gives promise of greater stability and national unity than has prevailed heretofore; it believes that all possible encouragement should be given to the Nationalist Government; it is willing to discuss the subject of the revision of the treaties. . . ." In conclusion, he asked the various governments concerned for a statement of their opinions.[74]

Answers to the Secretary's *aide-mémoire* were received at the Department of State during the closing weeks of 1928. The British took the position that the tariff issue was still the most immediate and pressing problem in respect to China's international relations and that the issue to be disposed of first was the negotiation of a Sino-British tariff treaty. In respect to the abolition

[71] *Ibid.* (1928), p. 433; (1929), p. 544.
[72] *Ibid.* (1928), p. 433; (1929), pp. 547-548.
[73] *Ibid.* (1928), p. 434.
[74] *Ibid.*, pp. 436, 439, 444.

of extraterritoriality, the British pointed out that they had made an offer in January of 1927 of the waiver of certain treaty rights, and that this offer had been the subject of considerable discussion with the Chinese Government. They were prepared to continue these discussions and take such practical steps as conditions would allow but doubted whether it was possible to proceed beyond the point reached in the memorandum of January, 1927.[75]

While the general attitude of the Belgian and Italian Governments had been indicated in the treaties that both countries signed with the Nanking régime in November, 1928, the Italian Government informed Secretary Kellogg privately, that, in their opinion, the abolition of extraterritorial jurisdiction would have to be accompanied by certain guarantees in order to avoid the effects of the sudden transition from the old system to the new.[76] The Dutch, on their part, advised "extreme caution" in effecting the cancellation of extraterritorial rights, asserting that conditions in China did not warrant any such action and that the Powers had best proceed on the basis of the recommendations submitted by the Commission on Extraterritoriality.[77] The discouraging views of the Dutch Government were fully shared by the French who wrote to Mr. Kellogg that they believed the relinquishment of extraterritorial privileges would "disorganize" the economic life of the Chinese nation and would "be more detrimental than favourable" to the gradual development of a normal administration. "The suppression of extraterritorial privileges," they said, "can only be considered without danger in the measure as, in the practice of their policy, the Chinese people will be inspired by modern principles and when experience shall have demonstrated that the actual modernization of Chinese administration and justice render valueless the dispositions of the present treaties."[78]

The Japanese, who were the last to answer Mr. Kellogg's *aide-mémoire*, presented the State Department with a memorandum which was supplemented by a conversation between the Japanese Ambassador at Washington and Mr. Johnson. The Ambassador stated that the Japanese could never assent to the unilateral denunciation of their treaty with China but that if the Nanking régime would retreat from this "unreasonable attitude" the Japanese Government was prepared to enter into discussions for a revision of the extraterritorial terms of the treaties on the basis of the Report of the Commission on Extraterritoriality.[79]

The Ambassador emphasized throughout the conversation that his Government "placed great importance upon the hope that the nations

[75] *Ibid.*
[76] *Ibid.*, p. 442.
[77] *Ibid.*, p. 443.
[78] *Ibid.*, pp. 443-444.
[79] *Ibid.*, pp. 445-449.

should concert themselves while lending assistance to China for the realization of her aspirations," insisting at the same time upon China's not entirely
disregarding the actual conditions within her own territories or the commitments she had made to other Powers. Mr. Johnson replied to these remarks
with the interesting observation that the Powers seemed in the past to consider it necessary to concert themselves only "when one or more of them were
in the position of the defensive," and that that fact had reduced action to
one of mutual interest in the Powers' defense but individual interest in all
other matters; as a future policy, he suggested, they might take "concerted
action in constructive measures, or in the line of moderation."[80]

The net result of the exchange of views between the Powers concerning
a revision of the treaties that would lead to the abolition of the extraterritorial system was clearly not one of boundless encouragement. The Department of State in Washington continued, however, to conduct unofficial
conversations with representatives of the Chinese Government in the hope of
finding a common ground for negotiation.

The conversations which were for the most part held between Dr. C. C.
Wu and Mr. Stanley K. Hornbeck, Chief of the State Department's Division
of Far Eastern Affairs,[81] made little headway despite the fact that they
involved a detailed and prolonged exchange of opinion. Dr. Wu continued
to maintain the position that the American Government should conclude a
treaty in which the "United States would simply give up its extraterritorial
rights"; what the Chinese wanted, he said, was a treaty "which would abolish
extraterritoriality, definitely, conclusively, and promptly."[82] In line with this
conception, Dr. Wu submitted proposals recommending: (1) that the United
States enter into an agreement declaring that its extraterritorial rights
would terminate on July 1, 1930; (2) that an annex be appended to the agreement in which China promised to put into force two new codes of law,
before January 1, 1930; (3) that the Chinese Government affirm that it would
take into its service for a period of three years a number of foreign legal
counselors as employees of the Chinese Government who would act as observers in the Chinese courts, without any power of interference, and report to
the Chinese Judicial Council.[83]

From the point of view of the American Government, the demand of the
Chinese for a treaty that would require American citizens to relinquish their
extraterritorial status, while the nationals of other Powers continued to

[80] *Ibid.*, p. 448.
[81] Mr. Hornbeck became Chief of the Division of Far Eastern Affairs in 1928; Mr. Johnson
had been made Assistant Secretary of State in August, 1927.
[82] *Foreign Relations* (1929), p. 544.
[83] *Ibid.*, pp. 544-546.

enjoy that status, remained at all times unacceptable. On one occasion during the course of their conversations, Mr. Hornbeck stated definitely to Dr. Wu that it could not be expected that the United States Government, or any other Government responsible for a large number of persons and for substantial interests in China, would agree to place its citizens and its interests in a special position which they would regard as one of disadvantage.[84] Similarly Mr. Johnson in a conversation held toward the middle of January, 1929, declared that the State Department would not "consider a proposal which would provide for placing Americans in a position less favored than that of nationals of 'most-favored' nations."[85]

On the 10th of January, Mr. Hornbeck indicated to Dr. Wu that the only way out of the impasse, which had clearly been reached in their discussions, was to concentrate on the major problem confronting them, namely, the problem of devising a "working scheme" for the transition period during which there would be a gradual relinquishment of extraterritorial rights by the United States, paralleled by a gradual taking over of jurisdiction by the Chinese. Mr. Hornbeck, on being questioned by Dr. Wu, said he was not prepared to state what the provisions of such a scheme should be, but that they ought to be designed to meet the situation described by the Commission on Extraterritoriality and should take the Commission's recommendations into account. Dr. Wu inquired whether the Department of State would be willing to conclude a treaty similar to that which had recently been signed by the Italian Government. Mr. Hornbeck answered that he could not commit the Department but that, if a proposal of this general character were reduced to writing, he would present the matter for consideration to higher officers in the Department.[86]

The conversations between Dr. Wu and members of the State Department did not proceed beyond this point before March, 1929. In March, the Coolidge Administration came to an end and Secretary of State Kellogg was succeeded in office by Mr. Stimson. In April, the Chinese Government sent a note to the United States Government and five other Treaty Powers, stating that China desired "to have the restrictions on her jurisdictional sovereignty removed at the earliest possible date."[87] The Chinese note was carefully considered by the State Department for a period of several months and the views of Mr. Stimson and Mr. MacMurray were recorded in a series of remarkable documents which appear in the 1929 volume of the *Foreign Relations of the United States*.[88] Although these fall outside the province of this

[84] *Ibid.*, p. 544.
[85] *Ibid.*, p. 547.
[86] *Ibid.*, pp. 548-549.
[87] *Ibid.*, p. 561.
[88] *Ibid.*, p. 543 *et seq.*

study, it is interesting to observe that, according to a memorandum of Mr. Johnson, Secretary Stimson informed the British Ambassador in June, 1929, that "his opinion was that China was not in a position to permit the relinquishment of extraterritorial rights."[89] It is also of significance that Mr. MacMurray's dispatches showed clearly that the American Minister had not changed his mind since the beginning of his term in office on the subject of negotiating a new treaty on extraterritoriality. In May of 1929 he cabled the Department:

> ... The means or capacity to administer justice, as this is understood in civilization of the western type, has not yet been developed by the Chinese; so that if they were put in a position again to exercise jurisdiction over aliens, prior to preparedness for satisfactory exercise of this responsibility, it is my own earnest belief that the result would be once more a progressive intensifying of ill feeling and misunderstanding between foreign nations and China. This, then, would lead to constantly growing tension, and sooner or later a trivial incident even would precipitate a clash and intervention quite probably by one or more foreign Powers.[90]

A few months later Mr. MacMurray stated that unless the principal Powers concerned were prepared to agree on common action to resist the increasing demands of the Chinese, American and other foreign interests would be "subjected" to a kind of treatment that would tend to "drive them out" of China.

> This is sensed in the temper and attitude among the Chinese, even of one's personal friends, and is also apparent in incidents, in themselves trivial, which constantly recur and convey in their total the inevitable impression that a desire is widespread and easily aroused to humiliate and be rid of foreigners as such. . . .
> In the absence of extraterritoriality, it seems to me that the expected intensified harassment of foreigners and their interests would lead inevitably to a year-after-year embitterment of relations. The contention that a premature concession on the part of the United States would ease the situation is, in my opinion, entirely without foundation. No one who is familiar with Chinese temperament and traditions can suppose that any yielding on an issue will dissuade the Chinese from raising further issues.[91]

Nevertheless, as is well known, formal negotiations on extraterritoriality were carried on between China and Great Britain, and China and the United States, in 1930 and 1931. Through seemingly interminable discussion (in which Great Britain frequently took the lead) the drafts of treaties were gradually hammered into shape. By the summer of 1931 agreement had been

[89] *Ibid.*, p. 573.
[90] *Ibid.*, p. 563.
[91] *Ibid.*, p. 589.

reached on a wide variety of questions although a few important issues remained unresolved.[92] At this point the Manchurian crisis interfered and negotiations were suspended. As a consequence the American Government did not conclude a treaty relinquishing its extraterritorial rights in China until 1943 — fifteen years after the Coolidge Administration had opened discussions that were intended to lead to the abolition of the extraterritorial system.

[92] The recently published *Foreign Relations of the United States* for 1930 and 1931 include a wealth of detail on the negotiations for a treaty concerning extraterritoriality and follow the draft of the American treaty through all its varying stages.

CHAPTER XIX

CONCLUSION

The end of the Coolidge Administration marked the close of an important period in the history of Chinese-American relations. In 1925, the Chinese showed, with an extraordinary intensity of feeling, that they objected to the privileged position of foreigners in their country and that they would no longer adjust themselves with patience to existing conditions. Moreover, as the Chinese Nationalist movement developed, it became evident that not only the treaty rights but the interests and even the lives of foreigners in China were in jeopardy. This raised the crucial question of what policy the Powers would adopt under these circumstances.

As far as the issue of treaty revision was concerned, the Powers had expressed their opinions as recently as 1922. As indicated at the outset of this study, they had taken the position at the Washington Conference that they did not desire to alter the treaty system to any substantial degree. They were willing, they said, to convene a Tariff Conference which would effect moderate changes in the tariff rates and to appoint a Commission on Extraterritoriality that would investigate the situation in China and suggest certain measures of reform. Further than this they were not prepared to go and, owing to various difficulties, even the Tariff Conference and the Commission on Extraterritoriality had not met by 1925.

Moreover, as we have seen, the attitude of the Powers which determined the decisions made at Washington was that China should put her own house in order before any serious consideration was given to the question of treaty revision. In the years following the Washington Conference, the Chinese were unable to stabilize conditions within their country and throughout most of China the rule of the warlords offered little hope for the future. Although the Kuomintang, largely confined to Kwangtung, was initiating a concrete program of political, social, and economic reform, the fact that the Kuomintang itself was under Soviet influence was not likely to strengthen the confidence of governments abroad.

Matters might have drifted along without any marked change for some time, if the crowd at the Louza Police Station on May 30, 1925, had not provoked the Shanghai police to fire upon and kill a number of Chinese. The demonstrations after the May 30th Incident showed clearly that the Chinese people believed, whether rightly or not, that their national development was seriously handicapped by the treaty system and that the treaty system must, therefore, be abolished. Moreover, to them the treaties were "unequal" and unjust and they saw no reason why foreigners should be permitted to maintain a position of superiority over the people among whom they lived.

The attitude of the Chinese raised the question of whether it was wise for the foreign Powers to attempt to defend the treaty system. It had been one thing to dictate terms in the past to a people that showed a readiness to accept them, but it might be quite another to enforce them in the future against intense resistance. The issue was largely a matter of judgment, first, as to whether the Powers were either politically or morally justified in upholding their treaty rights in China and, secondly, as to what the price would be and whether it was worth paying.

Possibly the main factor that determined the way in which the United States answered these problems lay in the personalities of the officials who shaped American Far Eastern policy during the Coolidge Administration. There appears to be little doubt that Secretary of State Kellogg and Mr. Nelson Johnson approached the Chinese situation from the same point of view and that President Coolidge was in sympathy with their aims and ready to endorse their decisions.

The attitude of Secretary Kellogg became evident almost as soon as the outbreak of the anti-foreign movement in 1925 showed that the Chinese were definitely prepared to challenge the position of the Treaty Powers. The only part of the Washington Conference that the Secretary adhered to with real enthusiasm was the idea that the United States should maintain a leadership among the Powers in a progressive policy toward China. When Mr. Kellogg took the initiative in calling the Tariff Conference and the Commission on Extraterritoriality, he was acting in accordance with his conception of the rôle the United States ought to play. As far as the Washington program itself was concerned, he felt that the Powers should fulfill the commitments they had made, but that the Washington program was not sufficient to satisfy the nationalistic demands of the Chinese after 1925, or even to meet the dictates of common sense. It was evident from the outset that the Secretary hoped to devise a plan that would lead directly to granting full national independence to China within the shortest possible time.

One of the interesting aspects of the negotiations conducted in the summer of 1925 was that they suggested that Mr. Kellogg's views were not the result of any involved or profound thinking but were, rather, the outcome of a simple almost instinctive reaction to the situation in China. Mr. Kellogg believed, according to his own statements, that a nation of four hundred million people could not be expected to submit to foreign control and that such matters as extraterritoriality were awkward and old-fashioned pieces of machinery which no one could reasonably hope to maintain in a modern world. The sympathy which he expressed for the Chinese in his statements in the summer of 1925 appears to have been entirely genuine, and if any further proof of this was needed it was given in the emphasis which he placed on approaching the negotiations on tariff and extraterritorial issues in a spirit of co-operating with, rather than of dictating to, the Chinese.

While Mr. Kellogg's desire to advance the movement for treaty revision was a fundamental element in American policy, he did not attempt to formulate any definite plan at the outset of his administration, although he was fully aware of his objective. The sudden and unexpected development of the anti-foreign movement in China caught all the Powers by surprise so that they found themselves carried along by the tide of events rather than in a position to steer a settled course. Moreover, the situation in China was far too explosive and contained too many imponderable factors to make it possible to see far ahead.

But as time went by, the anti-foreign movement merged into the Chinese Nationalist Revolution and it became apparent that the Powers would have to deal with something more compelling than demands for treaty revision, even though these were supported by riots, demonstrations and boycotts. With the start of the Northern Expedition, the strength of the Kuomintang began to make itself felt, and it was clearly only a matter of time until the Nationalists would begin to break the provisions of the treaties without waiting for any legal and orderly adjustments. Moreover, if the Kuomintang adopted such tactics they would virtually force the hand of the Administration at Peking which could not afford to disregard the anti-foreign sentiment throughout the country if the Nationalists succeeded in wresting concessions from the Powers. In addition, if large-scale fighting developed between the Nationalists and the Northern warlords there was every chance that some of the terms of the treaties would be broken during the ordinary course of the conflict.

As we have seen, all these things happened during the year 1926. The governments in both North and South China imposed measures in defiance of the treaty system, and the Administration at Peking actually launched into a systematic denunciation of the treaties. Furthermore, the privileges, the interests, and at times the lives of foreigners were endangered by the conduct of the civil war.

Secretary of State Kellogg's attitude toward the developments of 1926 was in accord with his earlier views. He did not believe that the United States should attempt to enforce American rights in China either by military or naval pressure or by a "firm policy" that was designed to threaten the Chinese. He wished, at this point at least, to maintain a strict neutrality between the various factions in China and apparently was genuinely convinced that China's internal struggle was her own affair. In the meantime he thought the United States should avoid being drawn into difficulties with either the Canton or the Peking Government and should remain free to discuss the possibility of revising the treaties when the opportunity presented itself.

Mr. Kellogg's willingness to enter into negotiations with the Chinese was unlikely, however, to produce any fruitful results as long as he insisted that he would only deal with a government in China that had effective control over the country as a whole. Long after the Nationalist troops had reached the Yangtze, people were still speculating on whether they could conquer North China, and the outcome of the Revolution was in doubt until the spring of 1928. While there were many who shared Mr. Kellogg's view that to establish relations with the governments at Peking and at Canton separately might lead to dividing China permanently into two parts, nevertheless a policy based on the condition that China must be a united nation with a responsible government seemed far removed from the realities of the situation.

As we have seen, this aspect of the State Department's policy changed early in 1927. There were several causes which may have helped to bring about such a result. The Christmas memorandum of the British was the first imaginative and courageous public statement made by any foreign government since the beginning of the Nationalist Revolution. As far as fundamental principles of policy were concerned, the heart of the British statement lay in the assertion that the situation in China had changed and that the Powers should, on their part, "abandon the idea that the economic and political development of China can be secured under foreign tutelage" and "disclaim any intention of forcing foreign control upon an unwilling China." The British memorandum came as a surprise and probably not as a very welcome "Christmas present" (the name popularly given it in the State Department) to officials in the American Government. There are many indications that Mr. Kellogg was anxious to keep the initiative in shaping a "pro-Chinese" policy in the hands of the United States and was not likely to be pleased at finding his rôle stolen from him by the British. Nevertheless, he was entirely justified in his assertion that the essence of the British statement was no more liberal than the ideas which he had himself maintained in respect to the situation in China from the beginning of his administration. In any case, the net result was that the action of the British led the Secretary to issue a response in the form of his declaration of January 27, 1927.

Another event which may have influenced Mr. Kellogg to effect a change in policy was the debate in Congress on the Porter Resolution. If the Porter Resolution was intended as a trial balloon to test public opinion in the

United States, it proved a very successful experiment. The reaction of members of the House of Representatives as well as of important sections of the American press indicated that, as far as a revision of the Sino-American treaties was concerned, a significant portion of the public was willing to endorse a blank check for the Administration. Moreover, Congress showed that it was also convinced that the United States should play a leading rôle in making concessions to the Chinese and that it was likely to view any signs of hesitation or timidity on the part of the State Department with considerable impatience.

While these matters could scarcely have failed to affect Mr. Kellogg, it is impossible to gauge the extent of their influence. In any event the change in policy which he brought about in January, 1927, was in keeping with his fundamental objectives. As will be remembered, he announced in his statement of January 27th that he would be willing to negotiate a new treaty "on the entire subject of the tariff and extraterritoriality" with any representative or delegation capable of speaking for both the Cantonese and the Northern factions in China. At the same time he declared — for the first time in any public statement — that he was prepared to act "on behalf of the United States alone" if it was impossible to secure co-operation from the other Powers. In making this assertion, Mr. Kellogg was only reiterating a principle which he had long maintained and had, in fact, emphasized in his instructions to the American Delegation at the opening of the Special Tariff Conference. There can be no doubt, however, that this aspect of the Secretary's policy had the overwhelming support of the American public.

The crisis which arose in 1927 and came to a climax after the Nanking Incident presented an issue as far-reaching in its implications as that of the maintenance of the treaty system. As the reaction of the British Foreign Office showed, it was one thing to accept an assault on the treaty position of foreigners in China but another to acquiesce in a direct attack on the lives and property of foreign nationals. The Nanking Incident raised the question whether the critics of the so-called conciliatory policy, embodied in the Christmas memorandum of the British and pursued by the State Department in Washington, were not amply justified in their comments. If the Chinese were allowed to go "unpunished" for the Nanking Incident, there was a chance that similar events would take place in other parts of China and that the Chinese would make a successful attempt to drive all foreigners out of the country. These possibilities were so serious that while people in the United States frequently described the attitude of Americans in China as "hysterical" there was very genuine cause for alarm.

Mr. Kellogg's refusal to use sanctions after the Nanking Incident flowed, at least in the opinion of this writer, from the same kind of thinking that characterized his approach to the entire situation in China. Mr. Kellogg had no elaborate ideas concerning the crisis in China but proceeded on the basis of a few simple convictions which he maintained with astonishing tenacity. It was only on rare occasions that he expressed his views forcefully, but as far as his actions were concerned he seldom deviated from his course. In regard to the Nanking Incident he was determined not to apply sanctions or to exert any military or naval pressure against the Chinese. In defense of this position he advanced many arguments which were sound from his point of view. He undoubtedly desired to give what support he could to the "conservatives" in the Kuomintang in their struggle against the "radicals." The clamor of the American press and of thundering voices such as that of Senator Borah indicated that the dispatch of a large Expeditionary Force to China would have serious repercussions in Washington. The idea that sanctions would serve no constructive purpose but might in the end bring a general assault on foreigners in China was a reasonable criticism. Nevertheless, for anyone familiar with the workings of the State Department at this time, it is impossible to escape the impression that all these factors were of secondary importance, and that Mr. Kellogg was largely motivated by a deep feeling that the foreign Powers should not engage in punitive action against the Chinese through the use of military force. That Mr. Johnson was an outspoken and staunch advocate of a policy of non-intervention undoubtedly strengthened the Secretary's determination to hold to his own convictions.

One argument which was used by the United States Government against the application of sanctions revealed an important aspect of the attitude of the interested officials in Washington. This argument was most clearly expressed by President Coolidge in his speech of April, 1927, which, it will be remembered, was delivered before the settlement of the Nanking crisis. Instead of launching into a denunciation of the Chinese for the attack on the foreign community at Nanking, Mr. Coolidge took the position that there were times in the midst of a revolutionary conflict when it was impossible fully to protect the lives and the property of foreigners. "Ultimately," he said, "the turmoil will quiet down and some form of authority will emerge which will no doubt be prepared to make adequate settlement for any wrongs we have suffered." In this remarkable statement, Mr. Coolidge suggested what was, in fact, the case, that officials in Washington had a very different picture of conditions in China from that which was held by many other observers. In contrast, for example, with the views of the authors of the Report of the Commission on Extraterritoriality, they did not believe that the disorder in China was merely a state of meaningless confusion, but regarded it as a natural outgrowth of the profound revolution through which

China was passing. Moreover, unlike many foreigners, they tended to accept the revolution as an inevitable part of China's modern development, an internal problem of the Chinese, rather than as primarily an issue in the power politics of the nations in which the major concern of the United States should be the defeat of Soviet influence in the East. These attitudes, which no doubt had their source in the Far Eastern Division of the State Department, were of fundamental significance because they led to the conclusion that foreigners should not interfere in China's struggle but should await the outcome with patience and understanding.

In the final year of the Coolidge Administration, after the Kuomintang under Chiang Kai-shek had succeeded in overthrowing the Northern régime, Mr. Kellogg again took up the question of treaty revision. Although his main purpose was to fulfill part of his program of relieving China from foreign control, he also wished at this time to strengthen the new Nationalist Government, partly because it represented the conservative element in the Kuomintang and partly because he believed it had a chance of stabilizing conditions within the country. As a result he managed, through the effective work of Mr. MacMurray, who acted with lightning speed, to conclude a tariff treaty less than two months after the Nationalist troops had reached Peking and had, in theory at least, established control over a united China. Mr. Kellogg had never relinquished his intention of going as far as the United States could go in helping China to achieve tariff autonomy and the negotiation of a tariff treaty had been delayed largely because the Chinese themselves had not been prepared to act earlier.

Following the conclusion of the tariff treaty, Secretary Kellogg stated on a number of occasions that he wished to leave the door open for a reconsideration of the extraterritorial issue. He attempted to produce concrete results by canvassing the other foreign Governments for an expression of their views and by authorizing discussions between officials of the State Department and representatives of the Chinese Nationalist Government. If he had in mind the definite draft of an agreement which he would have been willing to conclude, he did not lay all his cards on the conference table. He did, however, indicate that he was prepared to accept some scheme whereby the United States would promise to relinquish its extraterritorial rights on a most-favored-nation basis (following the pattern of the Sino-American tariff treaty) if a plan could be devised for the adequate protection of American interests during an *interim* period. There is, moreover, considerable evidence, though no positive proof, that Mr. Kellogg would have been willing to set the date for the abolition of extraterritorial privileges, not at some discouragingly distant time, but within the near future. That the conversations between officials of the State Department and the Chinese

Nationalist Government, conducted during the last months of the Coolidge Administration, did not make any substantial progress appears to have been primarily because of the attitude of the Chinese. It is difficult to imagine that the Nanking Government seriously expected the State Department to accept their proposal for the immediate and unconditional termination of extraterritorial rights, to be undertaken irrespective of the action of other Treaty Powers.

[It may be appropriate at this point to quote the following comment from Mr. Nelson T. Johnson on the above paragraph:

I think you would be justified in saying that Mr. Kellogg at the time when he announced his attitude toward the treaty revision movement in China would have negotiated a treaty in regard to extraterritoriality with very few conditions attached. I can at the moment remember no document to which you could go to prove this. My recollection is that at the time no precise outline or prospectus for a treaty had been prepared. Mr. Kellogg was concerned with the broad matter of policy and hoped that he could bring the whole question into the field of negotiation and let the details be handled then. Mr. Kellogg talked to me on several occasions about his hope that he might bring about the elimination of extraterritoriality from the category of questions between the United States and China, and I think that it was a matter of great regret with him that he found this impossible to realize. He had a deep sympathy for the Chinese point of view on this question.

Now what would have happened once negotiations began and the pressure of public opinion began to be felt by the President and Mr. Kellogg no one can say. . . . Mr. Kellogg might well have considered concluding a treaty similar to the broad outlines of the Sino-American treaty of 1943. Certainly Mr. Kellogg would not have accepted a treaty without a most-favored-nation clause because he would not have placed American citizens in China on a basis less favorable than that of the most favored national there.]

While the official policy of the United States was shaped in Washington, it is evident that Mr. MacMurray frequently disagreed with the decisions made by the Secretary of State. This was a significant matter because the American Minister's views represented the opinions of many people at the time and especially of many of the leading foreign officials in China. It is a striking fact that on the most critical occasions during the period of the Nationalist Revolution, the members of the Diplomatic Body reached an agreement on fundamental questions of policy with apparent ease.

The reason for the great difference between the point of view of the Secretary of State and the American Minister was that they proceeded from basic assumptions that were diametrically opposed. Mr. Kellogg was not interested in maintaining the treaty system but believed, on the contrary, that

China should, as far as possible, be freed from foreign control. Mr. Mac-Murray, on the other hand, was convinced that conditions in China did not warrant a relinquishment of the safeguards of the treaties, and he wished, therefore, to adhere to the so-called Washington formula which demanded the maintenance of the treaty system until the Chinese proved their capacity to govern their own land.

Starting off from what might be termed the Washington platform, Mr. MacMurray believed that the provisions of the treaties should be defended against encroachments by the Chinese. Like most foreigners who were in China in 1925, he was deeply impressed by the intensity of the anti-foreign feeling throughout the country. He thought that the Chinese were in an aggressive mood which, if given the slightest encouragement, would lead them to oust all foreigners from China. From his point of view the policy of the Administration in Washington was a policy of appeasement designed to placate the anti-foreign sentiment of the Chinese, and he was convinced that it would not achieve its purpose. He felt that any concessions made to the Chinese would merely serve to "intoxicate" them further until they had destroyed the treaty system and all foreign rights in China. He was, moreover, afraid that, unrestrained by the foreign Governments, the Chinese would engage in more and more provocative actions, thereby constantly increasing the tension between China and the Powers until the situation reached a point where it would bring on a new war in the Far East.

Given this line of reasoning, the only practicable solution was for the Powers to adopt a firm policy that would prove to the Chinese that the foreign Governments were prepared to defend their rights in China by the use of military force if necessary. Mr. MacMurray was convinced that this was the course which the United States should pursue and, like the Administration in Washington, he clung to his ideas with persistence. From the very outset — in the summer of 1925 — he urged the Secretary of State to fulfill the obligations which the United States had undertaken in the Washington agreements. When, in 1926, the Chinese began to take matters into their own hands and break the provisions of the treaties by imposing illegal taxes at Canton, Mr. MacMurray advised the Secretary to take "resolute action" even to the extent of using military pressure to keep the Chinese from adopting a policy of indirect repudiation of the treaties. As the Administration in Washington did not follow his recommendations, and made little effort to stop the levy of the illegal duties at Canton, Mr. MacMurray felt that the United States had been manoeuvred into a defensive position. Subsequent events seemed to confirm his worst fears, and he believed that the failure of the Powers to take a determined stand in regard to the Cantonese taxes encouraged the Peking Government to embark on a course of denouncing the Sino-foreign treaties and stimulated the Nationalists to take further illegal action. As Mr. MacMurray saw the matter, the Powers were constantly retreating, and every time they yielded ground found themselves in a greatly weakened position from which, in the end, they would be unable to stage a comeback.

The most serious difference of opinion between the Administration in Washington and the American Minister occurred after the Nanking Incident. Mr. MacMurray believed that the United States should engage in a co-operative policy with the other interested Powers and enforce sanctions against the Chinese. He thought that if the foreign governments overlooked the gravity of the Nanking Incident, or sought to condone the actions of the Chinese, they would further endanger the lives and property of the foreign community in China. He was convinced that any refusal to face squarely the magnitude of the problems involved meant storing up for the future even "greater evils" than those which existed in the present. Any attempt to ignore the Nanking Incident would, he believed, strengthen the hand of Soviet Russia in the Far East and lead to the "downfall of western influences and interests in the Orient." That Mr. MacMurray's views were shared by many experienced observers of conditions in China is evident from the fact that the Ministers of the other interested Powers went out of their way to warn their governments against adopting a "policy of weakness" which would encourage "by impunity anti-foreign feeling and the activity of forces of disorder" in China. Even among the foreign Governments in other capitals, the voices that were raised in support of the State Department's policy were few and feeble.

When the Nanking Incident was finally settled and the question of treaty revision once again raised, Mr. MacMurray agreed that it would be wise for the United States to attempt to conclude a tariff treaty with the Chinese. He regarded it as probable that the Chinese would themselves bring up the tariff issue, claiming that the Powers were under a moral obligation as a result of their actions at the Special Tariff Conference to grant tariff autonomy to China by January 1, 1929. Unless the American Government was prepared to resist such a claim, he thought there was everything to gain and nothing to lose by entering into an arrangement that would protect American trade from discriminatory treatment and insure a gradual increase in tariff rates.

The American Minister did not, however, change his mind concerning the inadvisability of negotiating a treaty on the subject of extraterritoriality. He believed that the ability of the Chiang Kai-shek régime to establish an effective and responsible government was decidedly open to question and that the state of China's laws and judicial institutions did not justify the United States Government in surrendering the safeguards of the extraterritorial system. He felt that it would be a mistake even to start negotiations on extraterritoriality as he was afraid that they would end in bitter disappointment for the Chinese who would consequently direct much of the hostility that they were exhibiting toward foreigners in general against the American Government. As the discussions on extraterritoriality were subsequently conducted in Washington, the issue was taken out of Mr. MacMurray's hands, but the conflict of opinion between the American Legation at Peking and the State Department at home was clearly not resolved by the end of the Coolidge Administration.

While the American people entertained a wide variety of views they also were, in a very general sense, divided into two camps. As indicated throughout this study there were certain groups in particular — such as missionaries and business men with important interests in the Far East — who were naturally anxious to influence American policy as far as possible. As the situation in China grew more critical, Congress and important sections of the American press became highly vocal, and individual leaders such as Mr. Strawn and Senator Borah added their voices to the chorus of public opinion.

Since these matters have already been discussed in detail, it is only necessary to summarize them briefly here. The most important factor in the activities of the missionaries was that almost all the large Boards in the United States informed the Administration at Washington, during the early stages of the Chinese Revolution, that they were in favor of the abolition of extraterritoriality. The same attitude was adopted by the Federal Council of Churches of Christ in America, which called upon "all Christian people to join in creating a public opinion which will stand unequivocally for the abolition of extraterritoriality" and requested the American Government to act independently of the other Treaty Powers, if necessary, in negotiating new agreements. The editors of the *Christian Century* and many mission leaders in the United States spoke out in denunciation of the treaty system and urged the State Department to take some quick and imaginative action that would meet the Chinese demand for national independence. Various missionary statements also condemned the so-called "gunboat policy" of the Powers and asked the American Government not to use force in its dealings with the Chinese.

While there was nothing to indicate a breach in the ranks of the missionary movement in this country, there was obviously a division of opinion among American missionaries in China, although it is difficult to estimate the situation with any degree of accuracy. The National Christian Council asserted, in 1926, that it was impossible to judge what proportion of the missionary body in China was in sympathy with the position taken by their Home Boards; but, they added, there were apparently some missionaries who wished to maintain the *status quo,* and others who felt that it was not their function to "meddle" in political affairs. Although important groups of missionaries, both official and unofficial, adopted resolutions that were in line with the policy of their Boards, a considerable number did not express their opinions. Behind this silence there may well have been a substantial amount of criticism of the active rôle which American (and also British) missionaries were playing in demanding an extensive revision of the treaty system.

According to the information that is available, it would seem that few missionary organizations took a definite stand on political issues after the Nanking Incident. Little appears to have been said officially by the Boards (with a few exceptions) concerning the question of the use of force by the United States and other governments in the spring of 1927; nor did many of the mission groups seize the occasion to reiterate their convictions that the "unequal" treaties should be revised. While the inactivity of the Boards called forth some sharp criticism, many reasons were also given in defense of their policy. Among these were the immensity of the practical problems involved in the withdrawal of so many missionaries from China; the insecurity that was felt in regard to the future of the missionary movement in China; the uncertainty surrounding political developments inside the Kuomintang; the conflict of views among the missionaries themselves; and the preoccupation of missionaries with fundamental issues directly connected with their own calling.

About the time that American missionaries ceased to play an active rôle in political affairs, American business men became most excited over questions involved in United States policy. The declaration issued by the American Chamber of Commerce of Shanghai, in April, 1927, calling on the United States Government to undertake armed intervention in China in co-operation with other foreign Powers, was the most important measure adopted by any American business group during the period of the Revolution. Placed side by side with other statements of the Chamber's, it indicated clearly the views entertained by that organization.

The Chamber was convinced that the Chinese Nationalist Revolution was not a genuine revolution. It believed, in its own words, that the Nationalist movement was "neither spontaneous nor native" but was "Soviet-managed and engineered," and that the basic conflict in China was, therefore, that of the Western Powers and Japan against the Soviet Union. The Chamber regarded the Chinese people as helpless victims of Communist propaganda and of the avarice of their own warlords and, like Mr. Strawn, thought that China's misery was owing to internal factors that had nothing to do with the "unequal" treaties or other matters pertaining to the action of the Powers. As China's disorder had, in the Chamber's view, reached a state where the Chinese people were unable to protect either themselves or foreigners from the "militarism, brigandage and Bolshevism" with which the country was saddled, it thought that the only solution was intervention by the foreign Powers. The conciliatory policy of the foreign Governments, the Chamber stated in its declaration of April, 1927, had "merely strengthened the position of the lawless elements and encouraged outrages like that of Nanking." Firm and concerted action by the foreign Powers was, therefore, necessary not only for the protection of foreign interests but also for the ultimate good of the Chinese people.

It is interesting that the Chamber in its statements consistently emphasized that it was in sympathy with the views of the Administration in Washington. American policy, it said, was designed to protect American nationals in China, and with this aim it was fully in accord. The Chamber's chief concern was over what it regarded as the misrepresentation of its attitude in the United States, and it developed something of a mania on the subject of missionary influence on American public opinion. Whether the missionaries who advocated a policy of treaty revision — or what Mr. Rea termed "a policy of scuttle" — really possessed the influence for which their opponents gave them credit is open to question. Nevertheless the fact remained that the policy of the Coolidge Administration toward China was far more in line with the thinking of the articulate groups among missionaries than with similar groups among business men.

The contrast between the views of the American Chamber at Shanghai and of the House of Representatives in Washington was very striking indeed. Far from believing that the Nationalist movement was Russian-manufactured, the House regarded the Chinese Revolution as comparable to the Revolution which the American people had fought to gain their own independence, and as equally worthy of support. China's troubles were laid at the doors of the Powers, and the Administration was urged to take the lead in a progressive policy that would free China from foreign control, and to act alone if necessary. No Congressman appeared as a defender of the treaty system and the Powers, including the United States, were severely condemned for the part they had played in China's development in the past. While there were Congressmen who took the position that, in view of the crisis in China, the main concern of the United States should be the protection of its nationals, their comments had little effect. The final vote on the Porter Resolution showed that the House was prepared to applaud any action the Administration might take toward a revision of the treaty system, no matter how quick or how liberal. The debate on the Porter Resolution and its passage by the House was an extraordinary example of American sympathy for China at a critical time in the relationship of the two countries.

In so far as it is possible to draw any conclusions concerning the attitude of the American press from accounts such as those published in the *Literary Digest*, and from a small sampling of selected newspapers, it would seem that press opinion was divided before the Nanking Incident. There appears, however, to have been widespread approval of the Porter Resolution, which suggests that most of the leading newspapers favored a conciliatory policy toward China. After the Nanking Incident, the press as a whole was undoubtedly opposed to the use of sanctions and expressed its views on this subject with astonishing vehemence. The basic feeling seemed to be that the American people did not want war in China and that the Government would be severely condemned if it allowed itself to be drawn into any such conflict. Like the action of the House on the Porter Resolution, the attitude of the press after the Nanking Incident was a measure of the pro-Chinese feeling in the United States.

Finally, it may be said that the Coolidge Administration moved through the tides of opinion that swirled around it by making as few public statements as possible. When announcements were issued by the State Department or the White House, they were usually carefully prepared in order to give the impression that the Administration was acting in accordance with everyone's wishes. The result was that many people thought that the United States had no policy toward China but was feeling its way slowly and uncertainly. As the situation in China became clearer, those close to the Administration recognized that it had very definite objectives and was steering a consistent course. Secretary of State Kellogg undoubtedly felt that his policy was primarily a policy of moderation and that his desire to help China achieve national independence was no more than natural and reasonable. In this he was wrong; his policy was both bold and imaginative in intent and his ideas were considerably in advance of his time.

BIBLIOGRAPHY

BOOKS

Amann, Gustav, *Legacy of Sun Yat-sen* (translated from the German by Frederick Philip Grove), L. Carrier & Co., New York, 1929.

Baker, Ray Stannard, and Dodd, William E., eds., *The Public Papers of Woodrow Wilson,* Harper & Bros., New York, 1927.

Baker, Ray Stannard, *Woodrow Wilson and World Settlement,* Doubleday, Page & Co., Garden City, New York, 1922.

Bau, Mingchien Joshua, *China and World Peace,* Fleming H. Revell Co., New York, 1928.

Beach, Harlan P., and Fahs, Charles H., eds., *World Missionary Atlas,* Institute of Social and Religious Research, New York, 1925.

Buell, Raymond L., *The Washington Conference,* D. Appleton & Co., New York, 1922.

Bryn-Jones, David, *Frank B. Kellogg,* G. P. Putnam Sons, New York, 1937.

Chapman, H. Owen, *The Chinese Revolution, 1926-1927: A Record of the Period Under Communist Control as Seen from the Nationalist Capital, Hankow,* Constable & Co., Ltd., London, 1928.

Fischer, Louis, *The Soviets in World Affairs,* Jonathan Cape, London, 1930.

Gallagher, Patrick, *America's Aims and Asia's Aspirations,* Century Co., New York, 1920.

Green, Owen Mortimer, *The Story of China's Revolution,* Hutchinson & Co., Ltd., London, 1945.

Griswold, A. Whitney, *The Far Eastern Policy of the United States,* Harcourt, Brace & Co., New York, 1938.

High, Stanley, *China's Place in the Sun,* Macmillan Co., New York, 1922.

Hobart, Alice Tisdale, *Within the Walls of Nanking,* Jonathan Cape, London, 1928.

Holcombe, Arthur N., *The Chinese Revolution,* Harvard University Press, Cambridge, Mass., 1930.

Hornbeck, Stanley, K., *The United States and the Far East: Certain Fundamentals of Policy,* World Peace Foundation, Boston, 1942.

Hudson, Geoffrey F., *The Far East in World Politics,* Clarendon Press, Oxford, 1937.

Hyde, Charles Cheney, *International Law As Interpreted and Applied by the United States,* 2nd rev. ed., Little, Brown & Co., Boston, 1945.

Institute of Pacific Relations, *Problems of the Pacific,* New York, 1929.

Isaacs, Harold R., *The Tragedy of the Chinese Revolution,* Secker & Warburg, London, 1938.

Johnstone, William C., Jr., *The Shanghai Problem,* Stanford University Press, Stanford University, Calif.; H. Milford, Oxford University, London, 1937.

Johnstone, William C., Jr., *The United States and Japan's New Order,* Oxford University Press, London, New York, 1941.

Jones, Francis C., *China,* J. W. Arrowsmith, Ltd., London, 1937.

Keeton, G. W., *The Development of Extraterritoriality in China,* Longmans, Green & Co., London and New York, 1928.

Kotenev, Anatol M., *Shanghai: Its Mixed Court and Council: Material Relating to the History of the Shanghai Mixed Court and the History, Practice and Statistics of the International Mixed Court,* North China Daily News and Herald, Ltd., Shanghai, 1925.

Kotenev, Anatol M., *Shanghai: Its Municipality and the Chinese: Being the History of the Shanghai Municipal Council and Its Relations With the Chinese, the Practice of the International Mixed Court and the Inauguration and Constitution of the Shanghai Provisional Court,* North China Daily News and Herald, Ltd., Shanghai, 1937.

Lansing, Robert, *War Memoirs of Robert Lansing, Secretary of State*, Bobbs Merrill Co., New York, 1935.

Latourette, Kenneth S., *A History of Christian Missions in China*, Macmillan Co., New York, 1929.

Ma, Wen Huan, *American Policy Toward China, As Revealed in the Debates of Congress*, Kelly & Walsh, Ltd., Shanghai, 1934.

MacNair, Harley Farnsworth, *China in Revolution*, University of Chicago Press, Chicago, 1931.

Malraux, André, *La Condition Humaine*, (*Man's Fate*, translated from the French by Haakon M. Chevalier), Random House, New York, 1934.

Millard, Thomas F., *The End of Extraterritoriality in China*, A. B. C. Press, Shanghai, 1931.

Millard, Thomas, F., *China, Where It Is Today and Why*, Harcourt, Brace & Co., New York, 1928.

Miller, David Hunter, *My Diary at the Conference of Paris, With Documents*, printed for the author by the Appeal Printing Co., New York, 1924.

Morse, Hosea Ballou, and MacNair, Harley Farnsworth, *Far Eastern International Relations*, Commercial Press, Ltd., Shanghai, 1928.

Pollard, Robert T., *China's Foreign Relations, 1917-1931*, Macmillan Co., New York, 1933.

Powell, John B., *My Twenty-five Years in China*, Macmillan Co., New York, 1945.

Pratt, Sir John T., *War and Politics in China*, Jonathan Cape, London, 1943.

Quigley, Harold S., and Blakeslee, George H., *The Far East: An International Survey*, World Peace Foundation, Boston, 1938.

Reinsch, Paul S., *An American Diplomat in China*, Doubleday, Page & Co., New York, 1922.

Remer, Charles F., *Foreign Investments in China*, Macmillan Co., New York, 1933.

Remer, Charles F., *A Study of Chinese Boycotts*, Johns Hopkins Press, Baltimore, Md., 1933.

Seymour, Charles, *The Intimate Papers of Colonel House*, Houghton, Mifflin & Co., New York, 1928.

Sharman, Lyon, *Sun Yat-sen, His Life and Meaning*, John Day Co., New York, 1934.

Sheean, Vincent, *Personal History*, Doubleday, Doran & Co., Inc., Garden City, New York, 1935.

Sokolsky, George E., *The Tinder Box of Asia*, Doubleday, Doran & Co., Inc., Garden City, New York, 1932.

Steiger, George Nye, *A History of the Far East*, Ginn & Co., Boston, New York, 1944.

Sun Yat-sen, *San Min Chu I*, ed. by L. T. Chen, (translated by Frank W. Price), China Committee, Institute of Pacific Relations, Shanghai, 1927.

T'ang, Leang-li, *The Inner History of the Chinese Revolution*, E. P. Dutton & Co., New York, 1930.

Teichman, Sir Eric, *Affairs of China, A Survey of Recent History and Present Circumstances of the Republic of China*, Methuen & Co., London, 1938.

Tyau, M. T. Z., *China Awakened*, Macmillan Co., New York, 1922.

Vinacke, Harold M., *A History of the Far East in Modern Times*, rev. ed., F. S. Crofts & Co., New York, 1933.

Wheeler, W. Reginald, *John E. Williams of Nanking*, Fleming H. Revell Co., New York, 1937.

Whyte, Sir Fredrick, *China and the Foreign Powers*, Royal Institute of International Affairs, Oxford University Press, London, 1927.

Willoughby, Westel Woodbury, *Foreign Rights and Interests in China*, revised and enlarged edition, Johns Hopkins Press, Baltimore, Md., 1927.

Willoughby, Westel Woodbury, *China at the Conference: A Report*, Johns Hopkins Press, Baltimore, Md., 1922.

Wilson, Woodrow, *The Hope of the World*, Harper & Bros., New York, 1920.

Woo, T. C., *The Kuomintang and the Future of the Chinese Revolution*, Allen & Unwin, Ltd., London, 1928.

Wright, Stanley F., *China's Struggle for Tariff Autonomy, 1843-1938*, Kelly & Walsh, Ltd., Shanghai, 1938.

Zanin, Archbishop Marius, Bishop Haouissée, S. J., and Bishop Yu-Pin, *The Voice of the Church in China, 1931-1932, 1937-1938*, Longmans, Green & Co., London, 1938.

OFFICIAL PUBLICATIONS AND TREATY TEXTS

Conference on the Limitation of Armaments, 1921-1922: Treaty Between the U. S., Belgium, the British Empire, China, France, Italy, Japan, the Netherlands and Portugal regarding Principles and Policies to be Followed in Matters Concerning China, Signed at Washington, February 6, 1922, U. S. Government Printing Office., Washington, 1925.

Congressional Record, Vol. 68, Part I, U. S. Government Printing Office, Washington, D. C.

Feetham, Richard, *Report of the Honourable Richard Feetham to the Shanghai Municipal Council*, North China Daily News and Herald, Ltd., Shanghai, 1931.

Great Britain, Foreign Office, China No. 1 (1926), *Papers Respecting the First Firing in the Shameen Affair of June 23, 1925*, H. M. Stationery Office, London, 1926, Cmd. 2636.

Great Britain, Foreign Office, China No. 3 (1927), *Papers Respecting Agreements Relative to the British Concessions at Hankow and Kiukiang*, H. M. Stationery Office, London, 1927, Cmd. 2869.

Great Britain, Foreign Office, China No. 4 (1927), *Papers Relating to the Nanking Incident of March 24 and 25, 1927*, H. M. Stationery Office, London, 1927, Cmd. 2953.

Great Britain, Foreign Office, China No. 1 (1928), *Papers Relating to the Settlement of the Nanking Incident of March 24, 1927*, H. M. Stationery Office, London, 1928, Cmd. 3188.

Great Britain, House of Commons, *Parliamentary Debates*.

International Commission of Judges, 1925, *Report of the Proceedings of the International Commission of Judges*, reprinted from *Shanghai Mercury*, Shanghai, October, 1925.

MacMurray, John Van Antwerp, ed., *Treaties and Agreements With and Concerning China, 1894-1919. A Collection of State Papers, Private Agreements, and Other Documents, in Reference to the Rights and Obligations of the Chinese Government in Relation to Foreign Powers, and in Reference to the Interrelation of Those Powers in Respect to China, During the Period From the Sino-Japanese War to the Conclusion of the World War of 1914-1919*. Oxford University Press, New York, 1921.

Report of the Commission on Extraterritoriality in China, U. S. Government Printing Office, Washington, D. C., 1926.

Report of the Trial of the Chinese Arrested During the Riots of May 30, 1925. A verbatim report of the trial of the Chinese arrested during the riot of May 30, 1925, at the International Mixed Court, Shanghai, on June 2, 3, 9, 10, and 11, from the Mixed Court Register, North China Daily News and Herald, Ltd., 1925.

Shanghai Municipal Council, Annual Report of, Shanghai.

Treaties and Agreements With and Concerning China, 1919-1929, Carnegie Endowment for International Peace, Division of International Law, Washington, D. C., 1929.

Tyau, Dr. M. T. Z., *The Special Conference on the Chinese Customs Tariff (October 1925-April 1926)*, Wai Chiao Pu, Peking, 1928.

United States Congress (69:1), *House Resolution 328*.

United States Congress (69:2), *House Resolution 408, 431*.

United States Congress (69:2), *House Concurrent Resolution 45, 47, 50*.

United States Congress (69:2), *House of Representatives Report #1891*.

United States, State Department, *Bulletin*.

United States, State Department, *Papers Relating to the Foreign Relations of the United States, With the Annual Message of the President*, U. S. Government Printing Office, Washington, D. C., 1925, 1926, 1927, 1928, 1929.

United States, State Department, *Press Releases*.

NEWSPAPERS

Baltimore *Sun*, Baltimore, Md.
China Press, Shanghai.
Chicago *Tribune*, Chicago, Ill.
Kansas City *Star*, Kansas City, Mo.
London *Times*, London.
Louisville *Courier-Journal*, Louisville, Ky.
New York *Herald-Tribune*, New York.
New York *Times*, New York.
New York *World*, New York.
North China Daily News and Herald, Shanghai.
North China Herald, Shanghai.
North China Star, Tientsin.
Peking Leader, Peking.
People's Tribune, Hankow.
San Francisco *Chronicle*, San Francisco.
United States Daily, Washington, D. C.
Washington *Post*, Washington, D. C.

REPORTS, MAGAZINES, JOURNALS, PAMPHLETS, AND BULLETINS

American Chamber of Commerce of Shanghai, *Bulletin*.
American Chamber of Commerce of Shanghai, *Annual Report*.
American Chamber of Commerce of Tientsin,
  Memorandum No. 7: *China's Civil War and Militaristic Factions, May, 1926.*
  Memorandum No. 8: *Chinese Confirmation of Foreign Views, May, 1926.*
  Memorandum No. 11: *The Tariff Conference, June, 1926.*
  Memorandum Relative to Extraterritoriality in China, 1925.
American Journal of International Law, Washington, D. C.
American Relations With China: A Report of the Conference Held at Johns Hopkins University, September 17-20, 1925, Johns Hopkins Press, Baltimore, 1925.
Blakeslee, George Hubbard, *The Pacific Area*, World Peace Foundation pamphlet, Boston, 1929.
British Chamber of Commerce Journal, Shanghai.
China Weekly Review, Shanghai.
Chinese Recorder, Shanghai.
Chinese Social and Political Science Review, Peking.
Chinese Students' Monthly, The, Boston.
Christian Century, The, Chicago.
Far Eastern Review, Shanghai.
Foreign Affairs, New York.
Foreign Missions Conference of North America, *The Present Situation in China and Its Significance for Christian Missions*, Committee of Reference and Counsel, New York, 1925.
Foreign Missions Conference of North America, *Report of Conference of Officers and Representatives: Includes Report of Activities of the Year 1924-1925*, New York.
Hornbeck, Stanley K., *The Situation in China*, China Society of America, Inc., New York, 1927.
Hodgkin, Henry T., *Recent Events in China*, Friends' Bookshop, London, 1925.
Hodgkin, Henry T., *The Missionary Situation in China: An Address Delivered at the Foreign Missions Conference of North America in Atlantic City, New Jersey — January 10-13, 1928*, Foreign Missions Conference of North America, New York, 1928.
Literary Digest, The, New York.

Millard, Thomas F., *The Shantung Case at the Conference*, in *Millard's Review of the Far East*, Shanghai, 1921.
Nation, The, New York.
National Christian Council, *Annual Report*, Shanghai.
National Christian Council, *Bulletin*, Shanghai.
National Christian Council, *A Five Years' Review, 1922-1927*, Shanghai, 1927.
National Christian Council, *Report of the Conference on the Church in China Today: The Report of a Conference of Christian Workers with Dr. John R. Mott, Chairman of the International Missionary Council, January 5-7, 1926, Under the Auspices of the National Christian Council of China*, The China Press, Shanghai, 1926.
North China Daily News and Herald, April 1, 1927, special issue, *China in Chaos*.
North China Daily News and Herald, "The Soviets in China Unmasked: Documents Revealing Bolshevistic Plans and Methods, Seized in the U.S.S.R. Embassy," April 6, 1937.
Shanghai Municipal Council Gazette, Shanghai.
World Call, The, St. Louis, Mo.

YEAR BOOKS

China Christian Year Book, (now *China Mission Year Book*), Shanghai.
China Year Book, Shanghai.
Survey of International Affairs, London.
Year Book of the Churches, 1924-1925, Baltimore.

PERIODICAL ARTICLES OF SPECIAL INTEREST

Arnold, Julean, "The Missionaries' Opportunities in China," *Chinese Recorder*, October, 1925.
Bates, M. Searle, "The Ordeal of Nanking," *The World Call*, supplement, May, 1927.
Hudson, Manley O., "The Rendition of the International Mixed Court at Shanghai," *American Journal of International Law*, Vol. 21, 1927.
Orchard, Dorothy, "China's Use of the Boÿcott as a Political Weapon," *Annals of the American Academy of Political and Social Science*, November, 1930.
Wang, Dr. C. T., "What China Expects to Get from Tariff Autonomy," in Special Tariff Conference issue supplement, *China Weekly Review*, November 1, 1925, p. 9.
"Critical Hours in China," *The Literary Digest*, January 9, 1926, p. 8.
"The Missionary Debacle in China," *The Christian Century*, April 28, 1927.

INDEX